Ancient Civilizations

HARCOURT BRACE SOCIAL STUDIES

Series Authors

Dr. Richard G. Boehm

Claudia Hoone

Dr. Thomas M. McGowan

Dr. Mabel C. McKinney-Browning

Dr. Ofelia B. Miramontes

Dr. Priscilla H. Porter

Series Consultants

Dr. Alma Flor Ada

Dr. Phillip Bacon

Dr. W. Dorsey Hammond

Dr. Asa Grant Hilliard, III

HARCOURT BRACE & COMPANY

Orlando Atlanta Austin Boston San Francisco Chicago Dallas

New York Toronto London

 Visit The Learning Site at http://www.hbschool.com

Series Authors

Dr. Richard G. Boehm
Professor and Jesse H. Jones Distinguished Chair in Geographic Education
Department of Geography and Planning
Southwest Texas State University
San Marcos, Texas

Claudia Hoone
Teacher
Ralph Waldo Emerson School #58
Indianapolis, Indiana

Dr. Thomas M. McGowan
Associate Professor
Division of Curriculum and Instruction
Arizona State University
Tempe, Arizona

Dr. Mabel C. McKinney-Browning
Director
Division for Public Education
American Bar Association
Chicago, Illinois

Dr. Ofelia B. Miramontes
Associate Professor of Education and Associate Vice Chancellor for Diversity
School of Education
University of Colorado
Boulder, Colorado

Dr. Priscilla H. Porter
Co-Director
Center for History–Social Science Education
School of Education
California State University, Dominguez Hills
Carson, California

Series Consultants

Dr. Alma Flor Ada
Professor
School of Education
University of San Francisco
San Francisco, California

Dr. Phillip Bacon
Professor Emeritus of Geography and Anthropology
University of Houston
Houston, Texas

Dr. W. Dorsey Hammond
Professor of Education
Oakland University
Rochester, Michigan

Dr. Asa Grant Hilliard, III
Fuller E. Callaway Professor of Urban Education
Georgia State University
Atlanta, Georgia

Media, Literature, and Language Specialists

Dr. Joseph A. Braun, Jr.
Professor of Elementary Social Studies
Department of Curriculum and Instruction
Illinois State University
Normal, Illinois

Meredith McGowan
Youth Services Librarian
Tempe Public Library
Tempe, Arizona

Rebecca Valbuena
Language Development Specialist
Stanton Elementary School
Glendora, California

Grade-Level Consultants and Reviewers

Dr. Sandra Alfonsi
Assistant Professor
Fordham University
Bronx, New York
Member, Academic Advisory Board
Hadassah Curriculum Watch (History Specialist)

Penny S. Arnold, Ph.D, NBCT
Assistant Professor
Ashland University
Ashland, Ohio

Dr. Philip P. Arnold
Professor
Department of Religion
Syracuse University
Syracuse, New York

Dr. Adelaida Del Castillo
Associate Professor
Chicana and Chicano Studies Department
San Diego State University
San Diego, California

Dr. Brian Fagan
Department of Anthropology
University of California, Santa Barbara
Santa Barbara, California

David Grant
Teacher
DeAnza Middle School
Ontario, California

Dr. Charles Hamilton
Department of History
San Diego State University
San Diego, California

Joyce Haynes
Consultant
Department of Ancient Egyptian, Nubian, and Near Eastern Art
Museum of Fine Arts
Boston, Massachusetts

Peter Lew
Teacher
David Reese Elementary School
Sacramento, California

Dr. Randolph H. Lytton
Associate Professor
Department of History and Art History
George Mason University
Fairfax, Virginia

Shabbir Mansuri
Founding Director

Susan L. Douglass
Affiliated Scholar
Council on Islamic Education
Fountain Valley, California

Lawrence W. McBride
Professor
Department of History
Illinois State University
Normal, Illinois

Edward A. McCord
Associate Professor of History and International Affairs
George Washington University
Washington, D.C.

Dr. Alden Mosshammer
Professor
Department of History
University of California, San Diego
La Jolla, California

Dr. Mary Pickering
Associate Professor
Department of History
San Jose State University
San Jose, California

Ann B. Powell
Teacher
Baker Elementary
Mobile, Alabama

Dr. Jeffrey Riegel
Professor
Department of East Asian Languages
University of California, Berkeley
Berkeley, California

Dr. David R. Smith
Professor
Department of History
California State Polytechnic University
Pomona, California

Dr. Stuart Tyson Smith
Assistant to the Director
Institute of Archaeology
University of California, Los Angeles
Los Angeles, California

Debra Sparks
Teacher
Walker Elementary School
Northport, Alabama

Dr. Cynthia Talbot
Assistant Professor
University of Texas at Austin
Austin, Texas

Rev. Dwayne J. Thoman
Pastor
Holy Rosary and St. John Parishes
LaMotte, Iowa

Kim Uebelhardt
Teacher
Westlake Hills Elementary School
Westlake Village, California

Glenn Walker
Coordinator of Social Studies
Fayette County Board of Education
Fayetteville, Georgia

Dr. Gordon D. Young
Associate Professor
Department of History
Purdue University
West Lafayette, Indiana

Contents

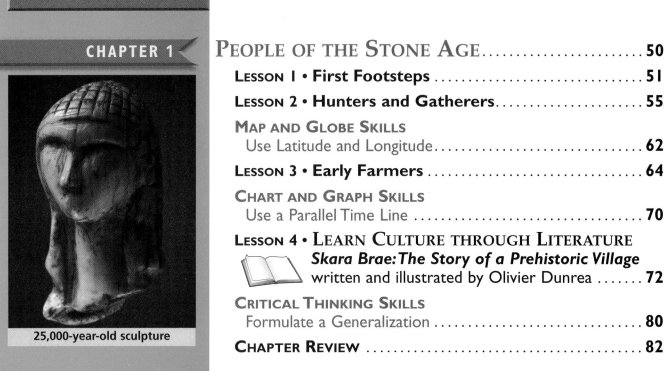

25,000-year-old sculpture

Hammurabi

Girl from India

Qin Chinese Soldier

4

Greek charioteer

Julius Caesar

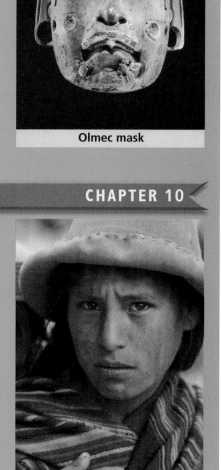

Girl from Senegal

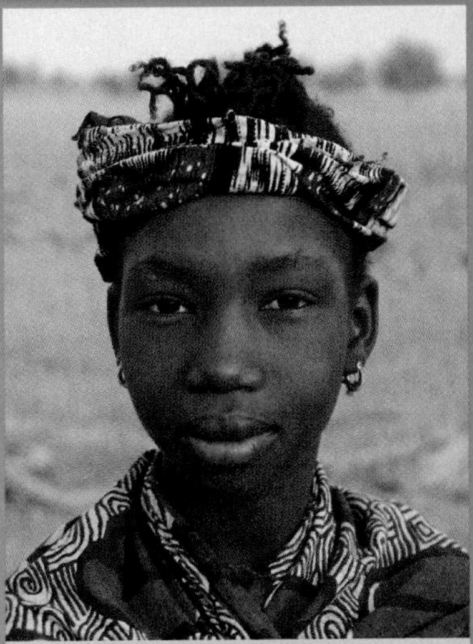

Boy from Bosnia

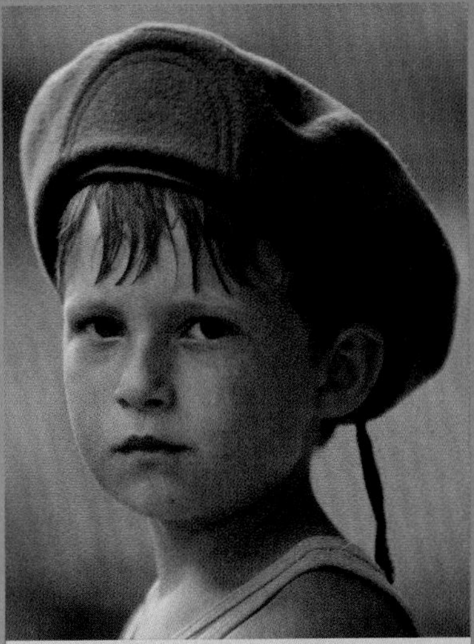

ix

Library of Congress, Washington, D.C.

F.Y.I.

Building Basic Study Skills

Building Citizenship

F.Y.I.

Features

Maps

Time Lines

F.Y.I.

Charts, Graphs, Diagrams, and Tables

Atlas

Contents

Atlas

The World: Political

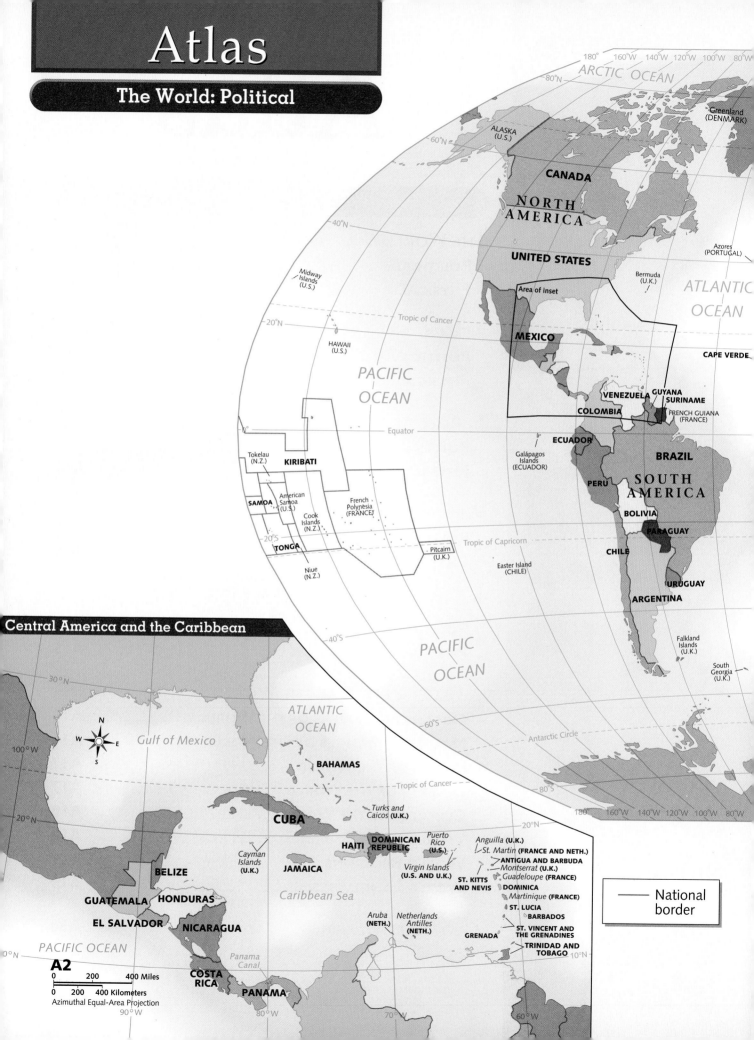

ARCTIC OCEAN

180° 160°W 140°W 120°W 100°W 80°W
80°N

Greenland (DENMARK)

ALASKA (U.S.)
60°N

CANADA

NORTH AMERICA

40°N

UNITED STATES

Azores (PORTUGAL)

Midway Islands (U.S.)

Bermuda (U.K.)

ATLANTIC OCEAN

20°N Tropic of Cancer

Area of inset

MEXICO

HAWAII (U.S.)

CAPE VERDE

PACIFIC OCEAN

VENEZUELA GUYANA SURINAME
COLOMBIA FRENCH GUIANA (FRANCE)

Equator 0°

Galápagos Islands (ECUADOR)

ECUADOR

BRAZIL

Tokelau (N.Z.)

KIRIBATI

PERU

SOUTH AMERICA

SAMOA

American Samoa (U.S.)

Cook Islands (N.Z.)

French Polynesia (FRANCE)

BOLIVIA

PARAGUAY

20°S

TONGA

Niue (N.Z.)

Pitcairn (U.K.)

Tropic of Capricorn

Easter Island (CHILE)

CHILE

URUGUAY

ARGENTINA

40°S PACIFIC OCEAN

Falkland Islands (U.K.)

South Georgia (U.K.)

60°S

Antarctic Circle

80°S

180 160°W 140°W 120°W 100°W 80°W

Central America and the Caribbean

30°N

100°W

Gulf of Mexico

ATLANTIC OCEAN

N
W E
S

20°N

BAHAMAS

Tropic of Cancer

CUBA

Turks and Caicos (U.K.)

20°N

BELIZE

Cayman Islands (U.K.)

DOMINICAN REPUBLIC

Puerto Rico (U.S.)

Anguilla (U.K.)
St. Martin (FRANCE AND NETH.)
ANTIGUA AND BARBUDA

HAITI

GUATEMALA HONDURAS

JAMAICA

Virgin Islands (U.S. AND U.K.)

Montserrat (U.K.)
Guadeloupe (FRANCE)

ST. KITTS AND NEVIS DOMINICA

EL SALVADOR NICARAGUA

Caribbean Sea

Martinique (FRANCE)

ST. LUCIA

PACIFIC OCEAN

Aruba (NETH.)

Netherlands Antilles (NETH.)

BARBADOS

ST. VINCENT AND THE GRENADINES

National border

GRENADA

10°N

A2

Panama Canal

TRINIDAD AND TOBAGO

COSTA RICA

PANAMA

0   200   400 Miles
0 200 400 Kilometers
Azimuthal Equal-Area Projection

90°W 80°W 70°W 60°W

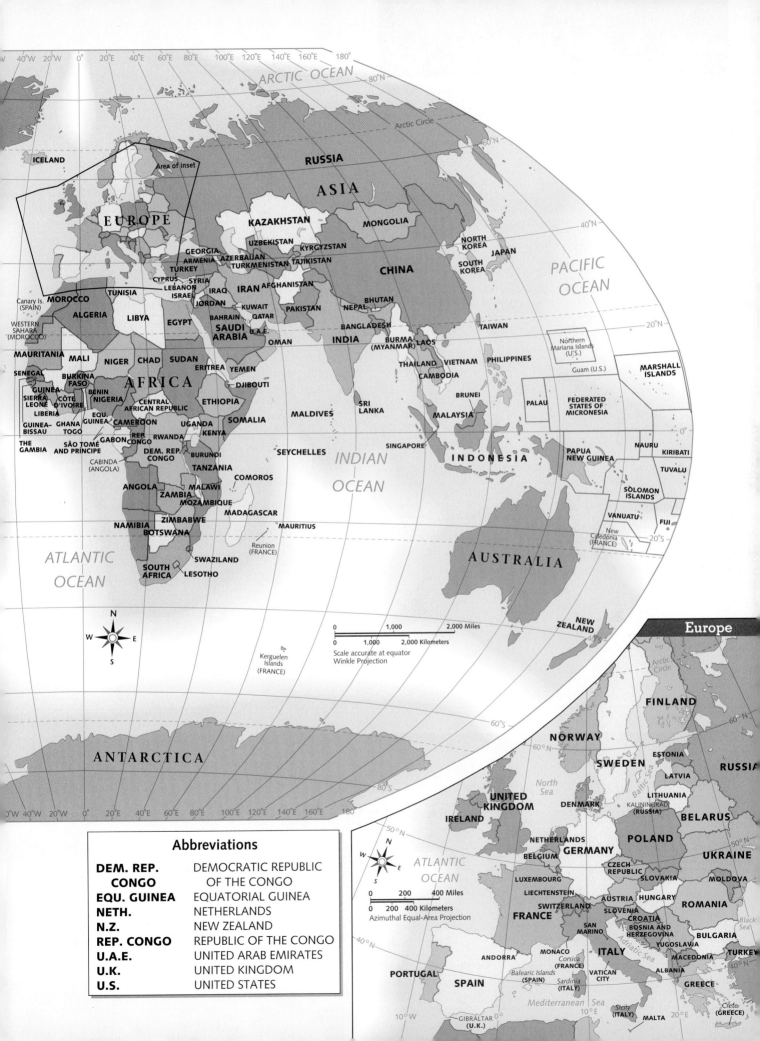

40°W   20°W   0°   20°E   40°E   60°E   80°E   100°E   120°E   140°E   160°E   180°

ARCTIC OCEAN

80°N

Arctic Circle

ICELAND

Area of inset

RUSSIA

60°N

ASIA

EUROPE

KAZAKHSTAN

MONGOLIA

40°N

NORTH
KOREA

JAPAN

PACIFIC
OCEAN

UZBEKISTAN   KYRGYZSTAN

GEORGIA
ARMENIA   AZERBAIJAN
TURKEY   TURKMENISTAN   TAJIKISTAN

SOUTH
KOREA

CHINA

CYPRUS   SYRIA
LEBANON   IRAQ   IRAN   AFGHANISTAN
ISRAEL
JORDAN   KUWAIT

BHUTAN

NEPAL

TAIWAN

20°N

TUNISIA

Canary Is.
(SPAIN)

MOROCCO

PAKISTAN

ALGERIA   LIBYA   EGYPT

BAHRAIN
QATAR
SAUDI
ARABIA   U.A.E.

BANGLADESH

BURMA   LAOS
(MYANMAR)

WESTERN
SAHARA
(MOROCCO)

OMAN

INDIA

MAURITANIA   MALI   NIGER   CHAD   SUDAN

ERITREA   YEMEN

THAILAND   VIETNAM

PHILIPPINES

Northern
Mariana Islands
(U.S.)

Guam (U.S.)

MARSHALL
ISLANDS

SENEGAL

AFRICA

DJIBOUTI

CAMBODIA

GUINEA
SIERRA   BURKINA
FASO
LEONE   CÔTE   BENIN
D'IVOIRE   NIGERIA
LIBERIA

CENTRAL
AFRICAN REPUBLIC   ETHIOPIA

BRUNEI

PALAU

FEDERATED
STATES OF
MICRONESIA

GUINEA-
BISSAU   GHANA
TOGO   EQU.
GUINEA   CAMEROON

UGANDA   KENYA
RWANDA
REP.
CONGO

SOMALIA

SRI
LANKA

MALDIVES

MALAYSIA

0°

THE
GAMBIA   SÃO TOMÉ
AND PRÍNCIPE   GABON

SINGAPORE

INDONESIA

PAPUA
NEW GUINEA

NAURU

KIRIBATI

CABINDA
(ANGOLA)

DEM. REP.
CONGO   BURUNDI

SEYCHELLES

INDIAN

TUVALU

TANZANIA

ANGOLA   MALAWI
ZAMBIA
MOZAMBIQUE

COMOROS

MADAGASCAR

OCEAN

SOLOMON
ISLANDS

VANUATU

NAMIBIA   ZIMBABWE
BOTSWANA

MAURITIUS

New
Caledonia
(FRANCE)

FIJI

20°S

Reunion
(FRANCE)

AUSTRALIA

ATLANTIC

SWAZILAND

SOUTH
AFRICA   LESOTHO

OCEAN

N
W   E
S

0   1,000   2,000 Miles

0   1,000   2,000 Kilometers

Scale accurate at equator
Winkle Projection

NEW
ZEALAND

40°S

Kerguelen
Islands
(FRANCE)

Europe

60°S

FINLAND

Arctic
Circle

NORWAY

60°N

ESTONIA

ANTARCTICA

SWEDEN

LATVIA

RUSSIA

80°S

North
Sea

Baltic Sea

LITHUANIA

UNITED
KINGDOM

DENMARK

KALININGRAD
(RUSSIA)

BELARUS

IRELAND

POLAND

50°N

NETHERLANDS

GERMANY

UKRAINE

BELGIUM

CZECH
REPUBLIC

SLOVAKIA

MOLDOVA

LUXEMBOURG

ATLANTIC

N
W   E
S

AUSTRIA   HUNGARY

ROMANIA

LIECHTENSTEIN

OCEAN

SWITZERLAND

SLOVENIA

CROATIA

Black
Sea

0   200   400 Miles

FRANCE

SAN
MARINO

BOSNIA AND
HERZEGOVINA

YUGOSLAVIA

BULGARIA

0   200   400 Kilometers

Azimuthal Equal-Area Projection

40°N

MONACO

Corsica
(FRANCE)

ITALY

Adriatic Sea

MACEDONIA

TURKEY

ANDORRA

VATICAN
CITY

ALBANIA

PORTUGAL

SPAIN

Balearic Islands
(SPAIN)

Sardinia
(ITALY)

GREECE

10°W   0°   Mediterranean   Sea

GIBRALTAR
(U.K.)   10°E

Crete
(GREECE)

Sicily
(ITALY)   MALTA   20°E

40°W   20°W   0°   20°E   40°E   60°E   80°E   100°E   120°E   140°E   160°E   180°

Abbreviations

**DEM. REP.
CONGO**   DEMOCRATIC REPUBLIC
OF THE CONGO
EQU. GUINEA   EQUATORIAL GUINEA
NETH.   NETHERLANDS
N.Z.   NEW ZEALAND
REP. CONGO   REPUBLIC OF THE CONGO
U.A.E.   UNITED ARAB EMIRATES
U.K.   UNITED KINGDOM
U.S.   UNITED STATES

Atlas

The World: Physical

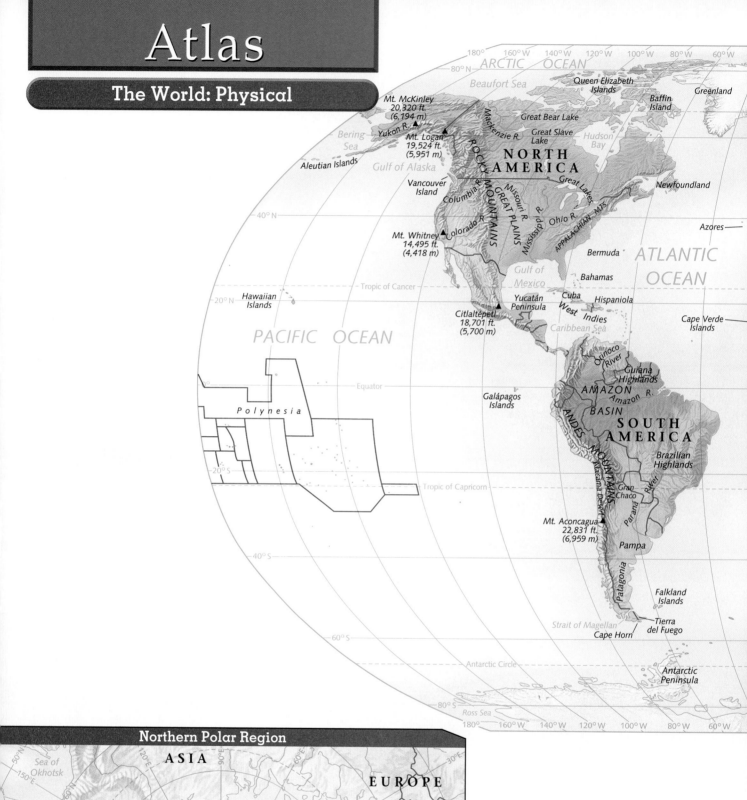

Mt. McKinley
20,320 ft.
(6,194 m)

ARCTIC OCEAN

Beaufort Sea

Queen Elizabeth Islands

Greenland

Baffin Island

Great Bear Lake

Mackenzie R.

Great Slave Lake

Hudson Bay

NORTH AMERICA

Bering Sea

Yukon R.

Mt. Logan
19,524 ft.
(5,951 m)

Aleutian Islands

Gulf of Alaska

Vancouver Island

Columbia R.

ROCKY MOUNTAINS

GREAT PLAINS

Missouri R.

Mississippi R.

Great Lakes

Ohio R.

APPALACHIAN MTS.

Newfoundland

Azores

Mt. Whitney
14,495 ft.
(4,418 m)

Colorado R.

Bermuda

ATLANTIC OCEAN

Gulf of Mexico

Bahamas

Hawaiian Islands

Tropic of Cancer

Yucatán Peninsula

Cuba

Hispaniola

Cape Verde Islands

Citlaltépetl
18,701 ft.
(5,700 m)

West Indies

Caribbean Sea

PACIFIC OCEAN

Polynesia

Equator

Galápagos Islands

Orinoco River

Guiana Highlands

AMAZON

Amazon R.

BASIN

SOUTH AMERICA

ANDES MOUNTAINS

Atacama Desert

Brazilian Highlands

Gran Chaco

Paraná River

Mt. Aconcagua
22,831 ft.
(6,959 m)

Pampa

Patagonia

Falkland Islands

Strait of Magellan

Tierra del Fuego

Cape Horn

Antarctic Circle

Antarctic Peninsula

Ross Sea

Northern Polar Region

ASIA

EUROPE

Sea of Okhotsk

Kamchatka Peninsula

Novaya Zemlya

Severnaya Zemlya

New Siberian Is.

Barents Sea

Baltic Sea

| 0 | 400 | 800 Miles |
| 0 | 400 | 800 Kilometers |

Azimuthal Equidistant Projection

Svalbard

Norwegian Sea

North Sea

ARCTIC OCEAN

North Pole

Wrangel Island

Bering Sea

Bering Strait

Greenland Sea

British Isles

BROOKS RANGE

Beaufort Sea

North Magnetic Pole

Queen Elizabeth Islands

Greenland

Iceland

ATLANTIC OCEAN

Baffin Bay

Arctic Circle

A4

PACIFIC OCEAN

NORTH AMERICA

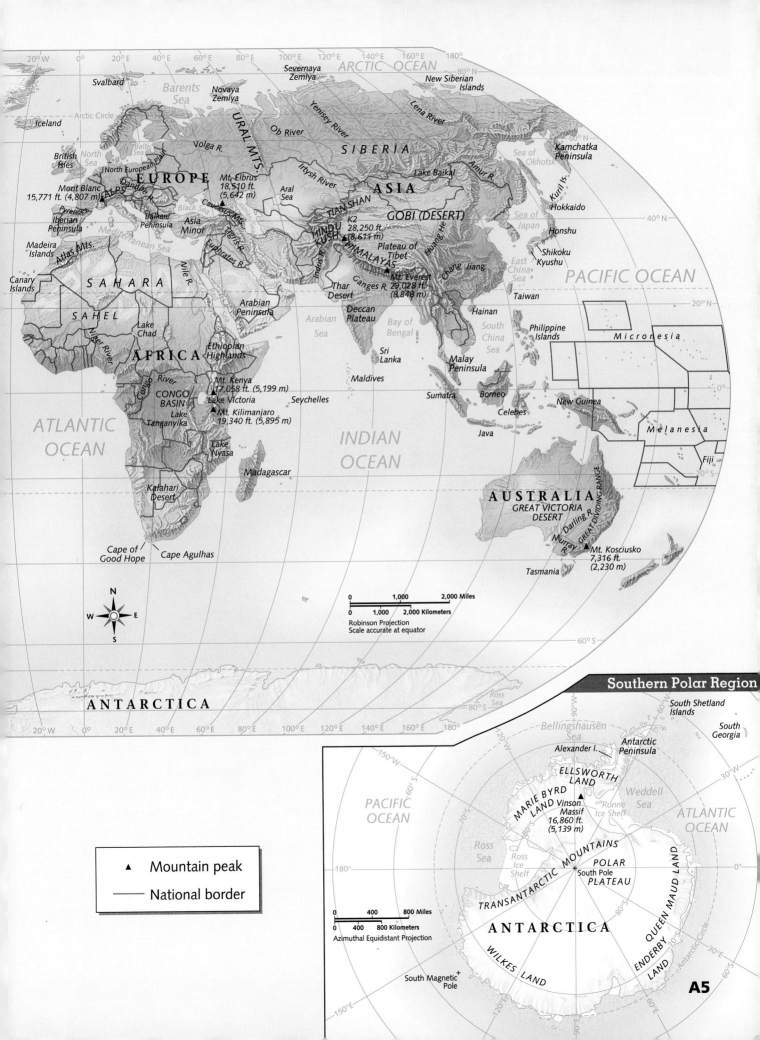

ARCTIC OCEAN

20° W | 0° | 20° E | 40° E | 60° E | 80° E | 100° E | 120° E | 140° E | 160° E | 180°

Svalbard
Barents Sea
Novaya Zemlya
Severnaya Zemlya
New Siberian Islands
80° N

Iceland
Arctic Circle

British Isles
North Sea
Baltic Sea
Volga R.
URAL MTS.
Ob River
Yenisey River
Irtysh River
SIBERIA
Lena River
60° N
Kamchatka Peninsula
Sea of Okhotsk

EUROPE
ALPS
Danube R.
Mont Blanc
15,771 ft. (4,807 m)
Pyrenees
Iberian Peninsula
North European Plain
Balkan Peninsula
Black Sea
Asia Minor
Caucasus Mts.
Mt. Elbrus
18,510 ft. (5,642 m)
Aral Sea
TIAN SHAN
ASIA
K2
28,250 ft. (8,611 m)
HINDU KUSH
GOBI (DESERT)
Lake Baikal
Amur R.
Kuril Is.
Hokkaido
Honshu
Shikoku
Kyushu
Sea of Japan
40° N

Madeira Islands
Atlas Mts.
Mediterranean Sea
Tigris R.
Euphrates R.
Nile R.
Persian Gulf
HIMALAYAS
Plateau of Tibet
Mt. Everest 29,028 ft. (8,848 m)
Indus R.
Ganges R.
Huang He
Chang Jiang
East China Sea
Taiwan
PACIFIC OCEAN

Canary Islands
SAHARA
SAHEL
Arabian Peninsula
Thar Desert
Deccan Plateau
Arabian Sea
Bay of Bengal
Hainan
South China Sea
Philippine Islands
Micronesia
20° N

Lake Chad
Niger River
AFRICA
Ethiopian Highlands
Mt. Kenya 17,058 ft. (5,199 m)
Sri Lanka
Maldives
Malay Peninsula
Sumatra
Borneo
Celebes
New Guinea
Melanesia
0°

Congo River
CONGO BASIN
Lake Victoria
Mt. Kilimanjaro 19,340 ft. (5,895 m)
Lake Tanganyika
Seychelles
INDIAN OCEAN
Java
Fiji

ATLANTIC OCEAN
Lake Nyasa
Madagascar
AUSTRALIA
GREAT VICTORIA DESERT
GREAT DIVIDING RANGE
Darling R.
20° S

Kalahari Desert
Murray R.
Mt. Kosciusko 7,316 ft. (2,230 m)

Cape of Good Hope
Cape Agulhas
Tasmania

N
W E
S
0 1,000 2,000 Miles
0 1,000 2,000 Kilometers
Robinson Projection
Scale accurate at equator
60° S

ANTARCTICA
Ross Sea

20° W | 0° | 20° E | 40° E | 60° E | 80° E | 100° E | 120° E | 140° E | 160° E | 180°

▲ Mountain peak
— National border

Southern Polar Region

80° S
South Shetland Islands
South Georgia
Bellingshausen Sea
Antarctic Peninsula
Alexander I.
ELLSWORTH LAND
Weddell Sea
PACIFIC OCEAN
MARIE BYRD LAND
Vinson Massif 16,860 ft. (5,139 m)
Ronne Ice Shelf
ATLANTIC OCEAN
Ross Sea
Ross Ice Shelf
TRANSANTARCTIC MOUNTAINS
POLAR PLATEAU
South Pole
QUEEN MAUD LAND
ANTARCTICA
WILKES LAND
ENDERBY LAND
Antarctic Circle
South Magnetic Pole

0 400 800 Miles
0 400 800 Kilometers
Azimuthal Equidistant Projection

A5

Atlas

Africa: Political

EUROPE

ASIA

ATLANTIC
OCEAN

Mediterranean Sea

Madeira Islands
(PORTUGAL)

Ceuta **(SPAIN)** · Algiers ⊛ · Tunis ⊛
Tangier · Constantine
Rabat · Oran · **TUNISIA**
Melilla **(SPAIN)**
Casablanca ⊛ Fès · Sfax · Tripoli ⊛
Marrakech · Banghazi
MOROCCO

Canary Islands
(SPAIN)

Alexandria · Port Said
Tanta ⊛ Suez Canal
Al Jizah ⊛ Suez
Cairo

WESTERN
SAHARA
(Occupied by Morocco) · El Aaiún

ALGERIA

LIBYA

EGYPT

Tropic of Cancer

Aswan · · *Tropic of Cancer*

MAURITANIA
· Nouakchott ⊛

Port Sudan

ERITREA
⊛ Asmara

Dakar ⊛
SENEGAL
GAMBIA · Banjul ⊛
GUINEA-
BISSAU · Bissau

Timbuktu · ·
MALI · Gao

Niamey ⊛
NIGER

CHAD

Omdurman
Khartoum ⊛

DJIBOUTI
⊛ Djibouti

Lake Chad

N'Djamena ⊛

SUDAN

Addis Ababa ⊛
· Dire Dawa

Bamako ⊛ **BURKINA**
FASO · Ouagadougou ⊛
GUINEA · Kano
Conakry ⊛ · **BENIN**
SIERRA · **TOGO**
LEONE · **CÔTE** **GHANA**
Freetown ⊛ **D'IVOIRE** Abuja ⊛
Monrovia ⊛ Yamoussoukro ⊛ Lomé · Ogbomosho
LIBERIA Abidjan · Accra · Ibadan
Porto-Novo
Lagos · Malabo ⊛
NIGERIA

ETHIOPIA

CENTRAL AFRICAN
REPUBLIC
· Bangui

SOMALIA
· Mogadishu

CAMEROON
· Douala
· Yaoundé ⊛

UGANDA
Kisangani · Kampala ⊛
KENYA
Kisumu · · Nairobi
Kismaayo ·

EQUATORIAL
GUINEA

Gulf of Guinea

SÃO TOMÉ AND
PRÍNCIPE
São Tomé · Libreville ⊛
REPUBLIC
OF THE
CONGO
GABON

Annobón
(EQUATORIAL GUINEA)

Kigali ⊛ *Lake Victoria*
RWANDA · Mwanza
BURUNDI
Bujumbura · **TANZANIA** · Mombasa

Brazzaville ⊛
· Kinshasa ⊛
DEMOCRATIC
REPUBLIC
OF THE CONGO
· Kananga

Lake Tanganyika · Dodoma ⊛
Dar es Salaam ·

CABINDA
(ANGOLA)

· Mbuji-Mayi

Ascension
(UNITED KINGDOM)

Equator

· Luanda

· Kolwezi

Lake Malawi

COMOROS
· Moroni

ATLANTIC

OCEAN

Lobito ·
ANGOLA
· Huambo

· Lubumbashi
· Kitwe · **MALAWI**
ZAMBIA Lilongwe ⊛
· Lusaka ⊛ · Blantyre

St. Helena
(UNITED KINGDOM)

Harare ⊛ **MOZAMBIQUE**
ZIMBABWE · Beira
· Bulawayo

· Antananarivo ⊛

NAMIBIA

BOTSWANA

MADAGASCAR

Tropic of Capricorn

Windhoek ⊛

Gaborone ⊛
Johannesburg · · Pretoria ⊛
· Mbabane ⊛ Maputo ⊛
SWAZILAND
Kimberley ·
· Bloemfontein
Maseru ⊛ **LESOTHO** · Durban
SOUTH
AFRICA
Cape Town · · Port Elizabeth

Mozambique Channel

Tropic of Capricorn

N
W · E
S

—— National border

⊛ National capital

· Major city

0 — 500 — 1,000 Miles
0 — 500 — 1,000 Kilometers

Azimuthal Equal Area Projection

A6

Red Sea

Gulf of Aden

INDIAN
OCEAN

Atlas

Africa: Physical

EUROPE

ASIA

ATLANTIC OCEAN

Strait of Gibraltar

Madeira Islands

Canary Islands

Atlas Mountains

Mediterranean Sea

Nile Delta

Qattara Depression

Suez Canal

Sinai Peninsula

Gulf of Suez

S A H A R A

Ahaggar Mountains

Tibesti Mountains

Aïr Massif

Libyan Desert

Nile River

Lake Nasser

Nubian Desert

Tropic of Cancer

Red Sea

Cape Verde

Senegal River

Niger River

S A H E L

Black Volta R.

White Volta

Lake Chad

Chari River

Athara River

Blue Nile

Lake Tana

Gulf of Aden

Bab el Mandeb

Fouta Djallon

Cape Palmas

Niger River

Benue River

Lake Volta

Gulf of Guinea

Bioko

Mt. Cameroon 13,353 ft. (4,070 m)

Mt. Cameroon

Bomu River

Uele River

White Nile

Bahr el Jabal

Ethiopian Highlands

Lake Assal -509 ft. (-155 m)

Great Rift Valley

Príncipe

São Tomé

Annobón

Equator

Sangha River

Ubangi River

Congo River

Congo Basin

Margherita Peak 16,762 ft. (5,109 m)

Lake Albert

Mitumba Mts.

Lake Turkana

Mt. Kenya 17,058 ft. (5,199 m)

Equator

INDIAN OCEAN

Ascencion

Kasai River

Lualaba River

Lake Victoria

Serengeti Plain

Mt. Kilimanjaro 19,340 ft. (5,895 m)

Pemba Island

Zanzibar Island

ATLANTIC OCEAN

Katanga Plateau

Lake Tanganyika

Comoro Islands

St. Helena

Bié Plateau

Lake Malawi

Mozambique Channel

Madagascar

Namib Desert

Zambezi River

Victoria Falls

Kariba Lake

Tropic of Capricorn

Kalahari Desert

Limpopo River

Tropic of Capricorn

Vaal River

Orange River

Drakensberg Escarpment

N

W E

S

Cape of Good Hope

Cape Agulhas

— National border

▲ Mountain peak

▼ Below sea level

⊔⊔⊔ Canal

∥ Falls

500

1,000 Miles

0

500

1,000 Kilometers

Azimuthal Equal Area Projection

A7

Atlas

Europe and Asia: Political

Legend

- National border
- ----- Disputed border
- ⊛ National capital
- • Major city

Abbreviations

AUST.	AUSTRIA
BELG.	BELGIUM
BOS. & HERZ.	BOSNIA AND HERZEGOVINA
CZECH REP.	CZECH REPUBLIC
CRO.	CROATIA
LIECHT.	LIECHTENSTEIN
LUX.	LUXEMBOURG
MAC.	MACEDONIA
NETH.	NETHERLANDS
SLOV.	SLOVENIA
SWITZ.	SWITZERLAND
U.K.	UNITED KINGDOM
U.S.	UNITED STATES
YUGO.	YUGOSLAVIA

A8

Robinson Projection

Atlas

Europe and Asia: Physical

Kara Sea

Arctic Circle

Iceland

Norwegian Sea

Lapland

Kölen Mountains

Scandinavian Peninsula

Galdhøpiggen 8,100 ft (2,469 m) ▲

Kola Peninsula

White Sea

Mt. Narodnaya 6,214 ft. (1,894 m) ▲

Novaya Zemlya

Gulf of Ob

West Siberian Plain

URAL MOUNTAINS

Ob River

Irtysh River

ATLANTIC OCEAN

Faeroe Islands

Highlands

Gulf of Bothnia

Lake Onega

Lake Ladoga

NORTHERN

EUROPEAN

PLAIN

Volga River

Kama River

British Isles

North Sea

Jutland

Baltic Sea

Gulf of Finland

Central Russian Upland

Ireland

Great Britain

Celtic Sea

Rhine R.

Oka-Don Lowland

Volga Upland

Ural River

Kazakh Upland

English Channel

Carpathian Mountains

Donets Basin

The Steppes

Lake Balkhash

Bay of Biscay

Mt. Blanc 15,771 ft. (4,807 m) ▲

ALPS

Danube River

Sea of Azov

Don River

Don

El'brus 18,510 ft. (5,642 m) ▲

Caspian Lowland

Aral Sea

Lowland

Kyzyl Kum (Desert)

Syr Darya

TIAN SHAN

Massif Central (Plateau)

Pyrenees

Apennines

Dinaric Alps

Adriatic Sea

Balkan Peninsula

Balkan Mts.

Crimea

Black Sea

Caucasus Mts.

Pontic Mountains

Caspian Sea

92 ft 28 m ▽

Turan

Kara Kum (Desert)

Amu Darya

Pamirs

Takla Makar (Desert)

Kunlui

Iberian Peninsula

Corsica

Sardinia

Balearic Islands

Tyrrhenian Sea

Pindus Mts.

Aegean Sea

Dardanelles

Bosporus

Plateau of Anatolia

Mt. Ararat 16,946 ft. (5,165 m) ▲

Tigris River

Elburz Mts.

Mt. Damavand 18,934 ft. (5,771 m) ▲

Dasht-e Kavir (Desert)

HINDU KUSH

K2 28,250 ft. (8,611 m) ▲

HIMALAYAS

Strait of Gibraltar

Sicily

Crete

Ionian Sea

Taurus Mts.

Cyprus

Mesopotamia

Euphrates R.

Zagros Mountains

Plateau of Iran

Indus River

Thar Desert

Ganges River

Mediterranean Sea

Syrian Desert

Dead Sea 1,319 ft. (-402 m) ▽

Sinai Peninsula

Plateau of Iran

Strait of Hormuz

Narmada River

Deccan

Godavari River

Western Ghats

Eastern Ghats

Tropic of Cancer

Red Sea

Arabian Peninsula

Persian Gulf

Gulf of Oman

Plateau

AFRICA

Rub' al Khali

Arabian Sea

Palk Strait

15° N

Gulf of Aden

Socotra

Sri Lanka

INDIAN OCEAN

0°

—— National border

- - - Disputed border

▲ Mountain peak

▽ Point below sea level

N
W   E
S

15° S

A10

0   500   1,000 Miles

0   500   1,000 Kilometers

Robinson Projection

ARCTIC OCEAN

75°N

Laptev Sea

New Siberian Islands

East Siberian Sea

Wrangel Island

165°W

Chukchi Sea

Bering Strait

Taimyr Peninsula

North Siberian Lowland

Central Siberian Plateau

Kolyma Lowland

Arctic Circle

Chukchi Peninsula

Yenisey River

S I B E R I A

Verkhoyansk Range

Lena River

Kolyma R.

Kolyma Mountains

Korya Range

60°N

Bering Sea

Ob River

Angara River

Stanovoy Range

Dzhugdzhur Range

Central Range

Kamchatka Peninsula

Arctic Circle

Sayan Mountains

Yenisey R.

Yablonovyy Range

Lake Baikal

Greater Khingan Range

Amur River

Sikhote-Alin Range

Sea of Okhotsk

Sakhalin

Altai Mountains

Plateau of Mongolia

Manchurian Plain

Kuril Islands

45°N

Junggar Basin

▼ Turpan Depression -505 ft. (-154 m)

Gobi (Desert)

Hokkaido

Tarim Basin

Qilian Shan

Sea of Japan

Shan

North China

Yellow Sea

Honshu

▲ Mt. Fuji 12,388 ft. (3,776 m)

NORTH PACIFIC OCEAN

Plateau of Tibet

Huang He

Plain

Korean Peninsula

Kyushu

Shikoku

▲ Mt. Everest 29,028 ft. (8,848 m)

Sichuan Basin

Chang Jiang

East China Sea

30°N

▲ Kanchenjunga 28,208 ft. (8,598 m)

Ganges R.

Irrawaddy River

Ryukyu Islands

Tropic of Cancer

Bay of Bengal

Mekong R.

Gulf of Tonkin

Taiwan

Philippine Sea

Khorat Plateau

Hainan

Indochina Peninsula

South China Sea

Luzon

15°N

Andaman Islands

Gulf of Thailand

Philippine Islands

Andaman Sea

Palawan

Sulu Sea

Nicobar Islands

Mindanao

Malay Peninsula

Celebes Sea

Strait of Malacca

Halmahera

0° Equator

Sumatra

Borneo

Moluccas

SOUTH PACIFIC OCEAN

G r e a t e r   S u n d a

Celebes

▲ Rantekombola 11,335 ft. (3,455 m)

Ceram

Banda Sea

New Guinea

I s l a n d s

Java Sea

Java

Bali

Sumbawa

Flores

Lombok

Sumba

Lesser Sunda Islands

Timor

Timor Sea

Arafura Sea

15°S

A11

90°E

105°E

120°E

135°E

150°E

165°E

AUSTRALIA

Atlas

Western Hemisphere: Political

A12

——	National border	
✹	National capital	
•	City	

0   1,000   2,000 Miles
0   1,000   2,000 Kilometers
Miller Cylindrical Projection

Atlas

Western Hemisphere: Physical

North Magnetic Pole +

Queen Elizabeth Islands

Ellesmere Island

Melville Island

Devon Island

Baffin Bay

Greenland

Viscount Melville Sound

Banks Island

Beaufort Sea

Point Barrow

Brooks Range

Victoria Island

Great Bear Lake

Baffin Island

Foxe Basin

Arctic Circle

Mt. McKinley 20,320 ft. (6,194 m)

Yukon River

Mackenzie Mts.

Mackenzie River

Great Slave Lake

Hudson Strait

Davis Strait

Cape Farewell

60° N

Yukon Plateau

Liard River

Peace River

Labrador Sea

Alaska Range

Mt. Logan 19,524 ft. (5,951 m)

Coast Mountains

ROCKY

Athabasca R.

Lake Athabasca

Saskatchewan River

Lake Winnipeg

Hudson Bay

James Bay

Labrador

SHIELD

Gulf of Alaska

Kodiak Island

CANADIAN

Alaska Peninsula

Aleutian Islands

Queen Charlotte Islands

Vancouver Island

Puget Sound

Coast Ranges

Cascade Range

GREAT

MOUNTAINS

NORTH AMERICA

Great Lakes

St. Lawrence R.

Newfoundland

Gulf of St. Lawrence

Nova Scotia

Bay of Fundy

Snake R.

Black Hills

Missouri R.

Mississippi

APPALACHIAN MTS.

Cape Cod

Long Island

Sierra Nevada

Great Salt Lake

GREAT BASIN

PLAINS

Platte R.

INTERIOR PLAINS

Ohio R.

Sierra Madre Occidental

Mt. Whitney 14,495 ft. (4,418 m)

Colorado R.

Arkansas R.

Ozark Plateau

River

Cape Hatteras

ATLANTIC OCEAN

Death Valley (lowest point in N.A.) -282 ft. (-86 m)

Sonoran Desert

Rio Grande

COASTAL PLAIN

30° N

Baja California

Gulf of California

Sierra Madre Oriental

Gulf of Mexico

Bahamas

Hawaiian Islands

Tropic of Cancer

Citlaltépetl 18,701 ft. (5,700 m)

Yucatán Peninsula

Cuba

Greater Antilles

Hispaniola

Puerto Rico

Lesser Antilles

Caribbean Sea

PACIFIC OCEAN

Lake Nicaragua

Isthmus of Panama

Lake Maracaibo

Orinoco R.

Llanos

Guiana Highlands

Line Islands

Equator

Galápagos Islands

Chimborazo 20,561 ft. (6,267 m)

Rio Negro

Amazon R.

Cape São Roque

Marquesas Islands

ANDES

AMAZON BASIN

Tapajós River

Xingu River

Tocantins R.

São Francisco River

Huascarán 22,205 ft. (6,768 m)

Mato Grosso Plateau

Brazilian Highlands

Cook Islands

Tuamotu Archipelago

Society Islands

Lake Titicaca

Altiplano

Atacama Desert

Paraguay R.

SOUTH AMERICA

Tropic of Capricorn

MOUNTAINS

Gran Chaco

Paraná R.

Iguazú Falls

Uruguay R.

Mt. Aconcagua 22,831 ft. (6,959 m)

Rio de la Plata

30° S

Pampa

Patagonia

Valdés Peninsula (lowest point in S.A.) -131 ft. (-40 m)

| 0 | 1,000 | 2,000 Miles |
| 0 | 1,000 | 2,000 Kilometers |

Miller Cylindrical Projection

▲ Mountain peak

▼ Point below sea level

— National border

≈ Waterfall

N W E S

Falkland Islands

Strait of Magellan

Tierra del Fuego

Cape Horn

South Georgia

150° W   120° W   90° W   60° W   30° W

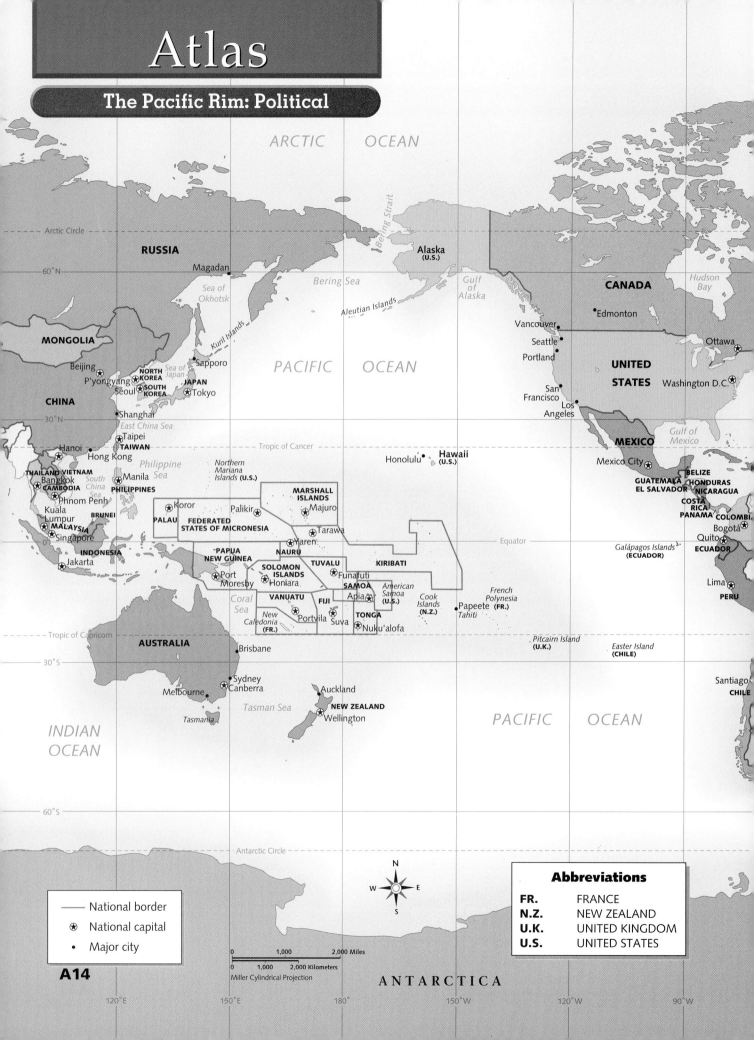

Atlas

The Pacific Rim: Physical

Severnaya Zemlya

Laptev Sea

Taymyr Peninsula

New Siberian Islands

East Siberian Sea

ARCTIC OCEAN

Chukchi Sea

Wrangel Island

Chukchi Peninsula

Bering Strait

Beaufort Sea

Amundsen Gulf

Ellesmere Island

Melville Island

Banks Island

Victoria Island

Baffin Island

Melville Peninsula

SIBERIA

Kolyma Lowland

Kolyma R.

Chukchi Range

Brooks Range

Mackenzie River

Great Bear Lake

Great Slave Lake

Ungava Peninsula

Arctic Circle

Kolyma Range

Central Range

Korya Range

60°N

Bering Sea

Yukon River

Mt. McKinley 20,320 ft. (6,194 m) ▲

Mt. Logan 19,524 ft. (5,951 m) ▼

Peace R.

Hudson Bay

Lena River

ASIA

Lake Baikal

Amur R.

Sea of Okhotsk

Kamchatka Peninsula

Aleutian Islands

Alaska Peninsula

Gulf of Alaska

Coast Range

Saskatchewan R.

ROCKY MOUNTAINS

NORTH AMERICA

Great Lakes

Gobi (Desert)

Greater Khingan Range

Manchurian Plain

Sakhalin

Sikhote Alin Range

Kuril Islands

PACIFIC OCEAN

Vancouver Island

Columbia R.

GREAT PLAINS

Missouri R.

Huang He

Sea of Japan

Hokkaido

Mt. Whitney 14,495 ft. (4,418 m) ▲

Colorado R.

Sierra Madre

APPALACHIAN MTS.

North China Plain

Yellow Sea

Honshu

Mt. Fuji 12,388 ft. (3,776 m) ▲

30°N

Chiang Jiang

Shikoku

Kyushu

East China Sea

Tropic of Cancer

Baja California

Gulf of Mexico

Yucatán Peninsula

Cuba

Greater Antilles

Taiwan

South China Sea

Philippine Sea

Northern Mariana Islands

Hawaiian Islands

Caribbean Sea

Indochina Peninsula

PHILLIPPINE IS.

MARSHALL ISLANDS

Gulf of Panama

SOUTH AMERICA

Malay Peninsula

Mt. Kinabalu 13,455 ft. (4,101 m) ▲

Celebes Sea

CAROLINE ISLANDS

MICRONESIA

Equator

Galápagos Islands

ANDES

Sumatra

INDONESIA

0°

MELANESIA

POLYNESIA

Huascarán 22,206 ft. (6,768 m) ▲

Greater Sunda Islands

Java

New Guinea

American Samoa

TUAMOTU ARCHIPELAGO

French Polynesia

Timor

Great Barrier Reef

Coral Sea

Cook Islands

Tahiti

Great Sandy Desert

New Caledonia

Tropic of Capricorn

Pitcairn Island

Easter Island

Aconcagua 22,831 ft. (6,959 m) ▲

AUSTRALIA

GREAT VICTORIA DESERT

Great Dividing Range

Darling R.

30°S

Mt. Kosciusko 7,310 ft. (2,228 m) ▲

Tasman Sea

PACIFIC OCEAN

Tasmania

Mt. Cook 12,349 ft. (3,764 m) ▲

New Zealand

INDIAN OCEAN

60°S

Cape Horn

Antarctic Circle

Thurston Island

Alexander Island

Amundsen Sea

Bellingshausen Sea

N
W — E
S

Ross Sea

Legend

— National border

▲ Mountain Peak

▼ Point below Sea Level

0 — 1,000 — 2,000 Miles

0 — 1,000 — 2,000 Kilometers

Miller Cylindrical Projection

ANTARCTICA

A15

120°E   150°E   180°   150°W   120°W   90°W

Atlas

Oceans and Rivers of the World

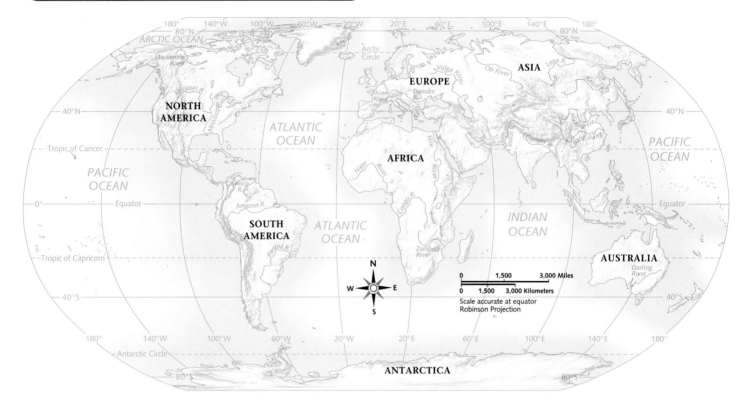

Mountain Ranges of the World

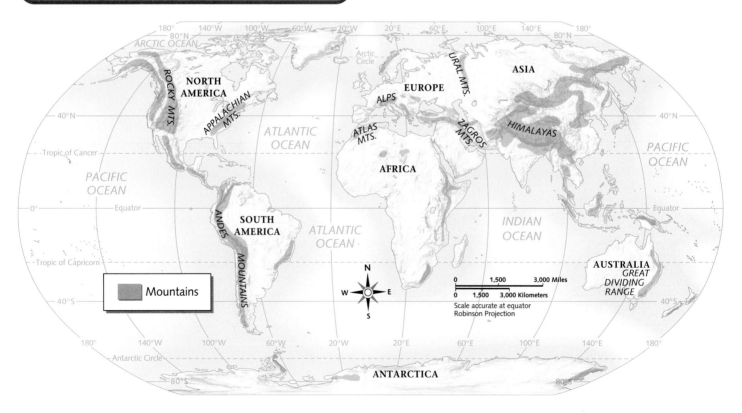

Atlas

Plains of the World

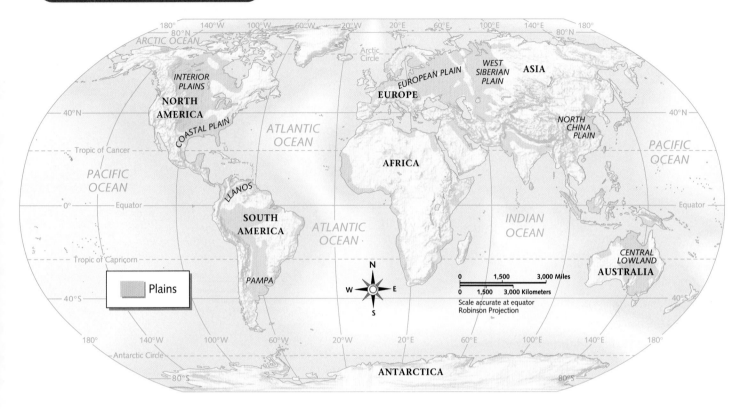

Deserts of the World

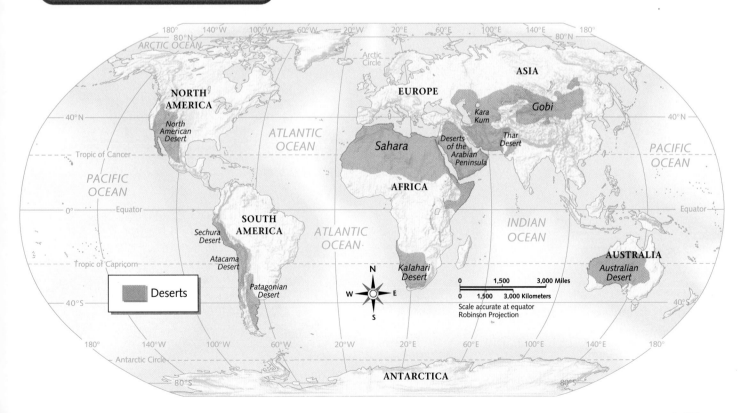

Atlas

Climates of the World

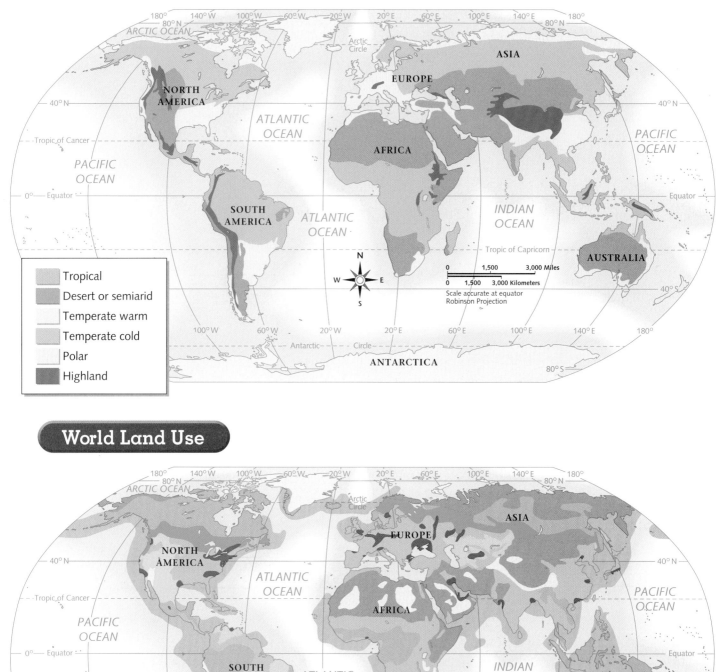

Tropical
Desert or semiarid
Temperate warm
Temperate cold
Polar
Highland

0   1,500   3,000 Miles
0   1,500   3,000 Kilometers
Scale accurate at equator
Robinson Projection

World Land Use

Manufacturing
Farming
Grazing
Nomadic herding
Hunting and gathering
Forests
Little used land
Fishing

0   1,500   3,000 Miles
0   1,500   3,000 Kilometers
Scale accurate at equator
Robinson Projection

Atlas

World Religions

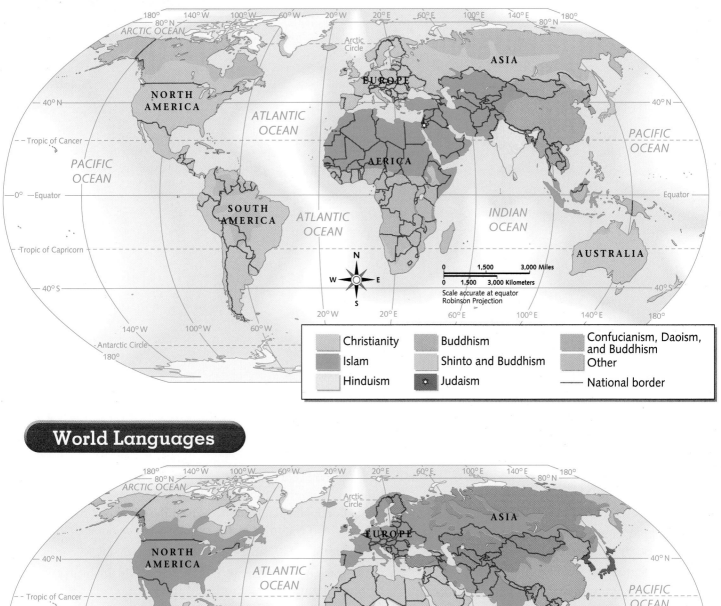

Legend:
- Christianity
- Islam
- Hinduism
- Buddhism
- Shinto and Buddhism
- Judaism
- Confucianism, Daoism, and Buddhism
- Other
- National border

Scale accurate at equator
Robinson Projection

0   1,500   3,000 Miles
0   1,500   3,000 Kilometers

World Languages

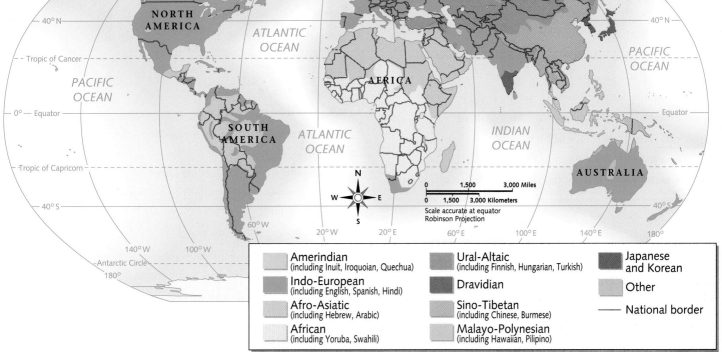

Legend:
- Amerindian (including Inuit, Iroquoian, Quechua)
- Indo-European (including English, Spanish, Hindi)
- Afro-Asiatic (including Hebrew, Arabic)
- African (including Yoruba, Swahili)
- Ural-Altaic (including Finnish, Hungarian, Turkish)
- Dravidian
- Sino-Tibetan (including Chinese, Burmese)
- Malayo-Polynesian (including Hawaiian, Pilipino)
- Japanese and Korean
- Other
- National border

Scale accurate at equator
Robinson Projection

0   1,500   3,000 Miles
0   1,500   3,000 Kilometers

Atlas
Geography Terms

Timberline

Sea level

Glacier

Slope

MOUNTAIN RANGE

VALLEY

PLATEAU

Inlet

Canyon

Mesa

COASTAL PLAIN

PLAIN

Coast

Sea level

Mouth of river

Channel

Lake

Lagoon

Isthmus

Peninsula

Cape

OCEAN

basin bowl-shaped area of land

bay body of water that is part of a sea or ocean and is partly enclosed by land

bluff high, steep face of rock or earth

canyon deep, narrow valley with steep sides

cape point of land that extends into water

cataract large waterfall

channel deepest part of a body of water

cliff high, steep face of rock or earth

coast land along a sea or ocean

coastal plain area of flat land along a sea or ocean

delta triangle-shaped area of land at the mouth of a river

desert dry land with few plants

dune hill of sand piled up by the wind

fall line area along which rivers form waterfalls or rapids as the rivers drop to lower land

floodplain flat land that is near the edges of a river and is formed by the silt deposited by floods

foothills hilly area at the base of a mountain

glacier large ice mass that moves slowly down a mountain or across land

gulf body of water that is partly enclosed by land but is larger than a bay

hill land that rises above the land around it

inlet a narrow strip of water leading into the land from a larger body of water

island land that has water on all sides

isthmus narrow strip of land connecting two larger areas of land

lagoon body of shallow water

lake body of water with land on all sides

marsh lowland with moist soil and tall grasses

mesa flat-topped mountain with steep sides

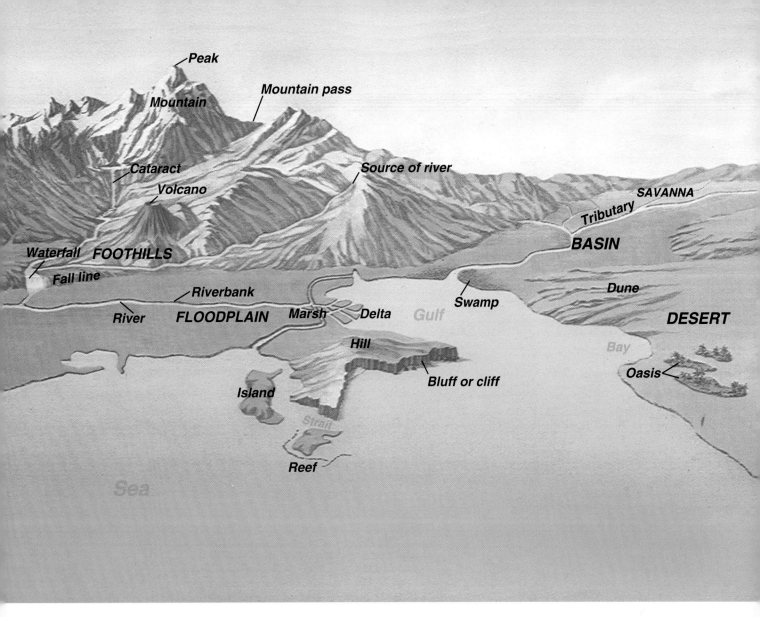

Peak

Mountain pass

Mountain

Source of river

Cataract

SAVANNA

Volcano

Tributary

Waterfall FOOTHILLS

BASIN

Fall line

Riverbank

Dune

Swamp

River FLOODPLAIN Marsh Delta Gulf DESERT

Hill

Bay

Oasis

Bluff or cliff

Island

Strait

Reef

Sea

mountain highest kind of land

mountain pass gap between mountains

mountain range row of mountains

mouth of river place where a river empties into another body of water

oasis area of water and fertile land in a desert

ocean body of salt water larger than a sea

peak top of a mountain

peninsula land that is almost completely surrounded by water

plain flat land

plateau area of high, flat land with steep sides

reef ridge of sand, rock, or coral that lies at or near the surface of a sea or ocean

river large stream of water that flows across the land

riverbank land along a river

savanna area of grassland and scattered trees

sea body of salt water smaller than an ocean

sea level the level that is even with the surface of an ocean or sea

slope side of a hill or mountain

source of river place where a river begins

strait narrow channel of water connecting two larger bodies of water

swamp area of low, wet land with trees

timberline line on a mountain above which it is too cold for trees to grow

tributary stream or river that empties into a larger river

valley low land between hills or mountains

volcano opening in the Earth, often raised, through which lava, rock, ashes, and gases are forced out

waterfall steep drop from a high place to a lower place in a stream or river

WHY STUDY
SOCIAL
STUDIES?

"Every one of you already holds the important office of citizen. Over time you will become more and more involved in your community. You will need to know more about what being a citizen means. Social studies will help you learn about citizenship. That is why social studies is important in your life."

The authors of
Harcourt Brace
Social Studies

The Themes of Social Studies

Think about the many groups of which you are a part. Your family, your class, and your community are different kinds of groups, and you are a member of each one. You are also a member—or **citizen**—of your town or city, your state, and your country. Citizens work to improve the many groups they belong to and to make their world a better place.

To help you think, feel, and act as a citizen, *Harcourt Brace Social Studies* begins every lesson with a question. That question connects the lesson to one or more of five themes, or key topics, of social studies. Citizens need to understand these themes in order to make decisions. Each question also links you to the lesson's story, helping you see how the story relates to your own life. The lesson helps you learn about being a citizen by letting you see how people from many places and times have thought, felt, and acted. Each lesson will help you organize your thinking around one or more of the following five themes of social studies.

In this painting the Roman orator Cicero delivers a speech in the Roman senate. By taking part in government, Cicero and the Roman senators were carrying out the office of citizen.

Commonality and Diversity

In some ways people everywhere are alike. We all have the same basic needs for things such as food, clothing, and shelter. We all laugh, get angry, and have our feelings hurt. These are a few examples of our commonality (kah•muh•NAL•uh•tee), or what we all share. At the same time, we need to understand that each person is different from everyone else. We each have our own ways of thinking, feeling, and acting. That is our diversity (duh•VER•suh•tee). Learning about commonality and diversity can help you see that every person is unique and deserves understanding and respect.

All people are alike in some ways, but each person has different ways of thinking, feeling, and acting.

Conflict and Cooperation

Because people are different from one another, they sometimes have conflicts, or disagreements. People can often settle their conflicts by cooperating, or working together. In social studies you will learn about the disagreements people have had in the past and about many of the ways people have found to settle their disagreements. You will also learn ways to cooperate and to settle conflicts in your own life.

Continuity and Change

While some things change over time, other things stay the same. Many things have stayed the same for years and will probably stay the same in the future. This means that they have continuity (kahn•tuhn•OO•uh•tee). Understanding continuity and change can help you see how things in the world came to be as they are. You will learn how a past event, or something that has happened, may have helped shape your life. You will also learn how present events can help you make better decisions about the future.

Individualism and Interdependence

Citizens can act by themselves to make a difference in the world. Their actions as individuals (in•duh•VIJ•wuhlz) may be helpful or harmful to other citizens. Much of the time, however, people do not act alone. They depend on others for help, and others depend on them. People depend on one another in families, schools, religious groups, government groups, and other groups and organizations. Such interdependence (in•ter•dih•PEN•duhns) connects citizens with one another.

When you take part in a student government meeting (above), vote for class officers (below), or campaign in a school election (bottom), you are carrying out the office of citizen. Understanding each of the powerful ideas will help you make decisions as a citizen.

Interaction Within Different Environments

People's actions affect other people. People's actions also affect their environment (in•VY•ruhn•muhnt), or surroundings. This is true of their physical environment, their home environment, their school environment, and any other environments of which they may be a part. Their environments affect them, too.

Understanding such interactions is important to understanding why things happened in the past and why things happen today. Understanding interaction is important for understanding social studies. The subjects that make up social studies are all related. You will learn, for example, that history—the study of people's past—is related to geography—the study of the Earth's surface and the way people use it. Civics and government, or the study of how people live together in a community, is related to economics, or the study of how people use resources. And all of these subjects are related to the study of culture. Culture is a people's way of life, including customs, ideas, and practices. These subjects interact with one another to tell a story. Together they tell how people have lived over time and how they have made contributions as citizens. Understanding this story will help you learn how to hold the office of citizen.

REVIEW *What are the five themes of social studies?*

Read Social Studies

1. Why Learn This Skill?

Social studies is made up of stories about people, places, and events. Sometimes you read these stories in library books. At other times you read them in textbooks like this one. Knowing how to read social studies can make it easier to study and do your homework. It can help you find important ideas and learn about people, places, and events.

2. Getting Started

Your book is divided into six units. At the beginning of each unit, you will find several pages that will help you preview the unit and predict what it will be about.

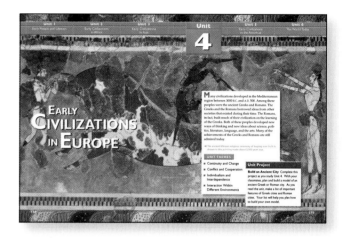

▲ Each unit begins with a short overview of the unit and a list of the social studies themes it teaches. You will also read about a project you can complete as you study the unit.

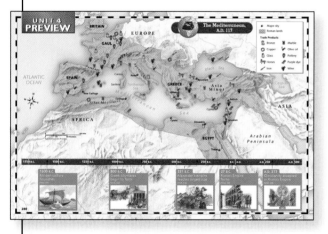

▲ The Unit Preview has a map that shows where some of the important events you will read about took place. It also has a time line that shows the order in which the events happened. There may be a story line that shows some of the people, places, or events.

▲ Each unit has at least one literature selection that helps you understand the time and place you are studying.

3. The Parts of a Lesson

Each unit has two chapters, and each chapter is divided into lessons. The beginning and the end of a lesson are shown below.

The time line shows the period of time in which the events in the lesson took place.

This question helps you see how the lesson relates to life today.

This statement gives you the lesson's main idea. It tells you what to look for as you read the lesson.

These are the new terms you will learn in the lesson.

The first time a vocabulary term appears in the lesson, it is highlighted in yellow.

Each lesson, like each chapter and each unit, ends with a review. A time line may show the order of some of the events in the lesson. The review questions and activities help you check your understanding and show what you know.

4. Understand the Process

You can follow these steps to read any lesson in this book.

1 Preview the whole lesson.

- Look at the title and the headings to find out what the lesson is about.

- Look at the pictures, the captions, and the questions to get an idea of what is most important in the lesson.

- Read the Focus question at the beginning of the lesson to see how the lesson relates to life today.

- Read the Main Idea statement to find out the main idea of the lesson.

- Look at the Vocabulary list to see what new terms you will learn.

2 Read the lesson to learn more about the main idea. As you read, you will come to a number of questions with the label **REVIEW**. Be sure to answer these questions before you continue reading the lesson.

3 When you finish reading the lesson, say in your own words what you have learned.

4 Look back over the lesson. Then answer the Lesson Review questions from memory. These questions will help you check your understanding of the lesson. The activity at the end of the review will help you show what you know.

5. Some Other Parts of Your Book

Your textbook has many other features to help you learn. Some of them are shown below.

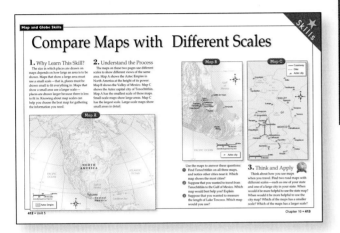

▲

Skill lessons help you build basic study skills. They also help you build citizenship skills as you work with others.

▲

The Counterpoints pages help you understand the different points of view people may have about certain issues.

▲

The feature called Making Social Studies Relevant helps you see how social studies is connected to your life and the lives of other people.

At the back of your book is a section called *For Your Reference*. It includes the following reference tools.

- How to Gather and Report Information
- Almanac
- Biographical Dictionary
- Gazetteer
- Glossary
- Index

6. Think and Apply

Use the four steps in Understand the Process each time you read a lesson in *Harcourt Brace Social Studies*.

History

History helps you see the links between the past and the present. It also helps you understand how things that happen today can affect the future. History is about what happened last month and last year as well as in the ancient past.

As you read about the people, places, and events of the past, ask yourself the four questions below. They will help you think more like a historian, a person who studies the past.

- What happened?
- Who took part in it?
- When did it happen?
- How and why did it happen?

What Happened?

To find out what really happened in the past, you need proof. You can find proof by studying two kinds of sources—primary sources and secondary sources. Historians use these kinds of sources in writing history.

Primary sources are the records made by people who saw or took part in an event. They may have written down their thoughts in a journal. They may have told their story in a letter or a poem. They may have taken a photograph, made a film, or painted a picture. Each of these records is a primary source, giving the people of today a direct link to a past event.

Hourglass (top), ancient writing from southwestern Asia (center), Egyptian wall painting (bottom)

A **secondary source** is not a direct link to an event. It is a record of the event written by someone who was not there at the time. A magazine article, newspaper story, or book written at a later time by someone who only heard or read about an event is a secondary source. A newspaper may include both primary sources and secondary sources.

When there are no written records of an event, historians gather proof with the help of archaeologists. Archaeologists study buildings, tools, and other objects people make or use. Based on their studies of these things, archaeologists form opinions about people and places in the past.

In this book, you will read many kinds of primary and secondary sources. The stories told in each lesson contain primary sources—the words and photographs of people in the past—as well as secondary sources written by historians. Maps, graphs, literature, pictures, and diagrams also help tell the stories you will read.

Archaeologists study items made or used by peoples of the past. This archaeologist is looking at a tomb of the ancient Mayas in what is today Mexico.

People of the past often depended on the spoken word rather than the written word to tell of their past. Below left is a nineteenth-century painting of a Native American storyteller. Below right a present-day storyteller holds students' interest with a tale about the past.

Who Took Part in It?

To understand the stories of the past, you need to know something about the people who took part in them and about the times and places in which they lived. This will help you understand their actions and feelings. Understanding of how people acted and felt long ago is called **historical empathy**. Historical empathy helps make the past seem alive.

By reading the words of people of the past, you can come to understand their **perspective**, or point of view. A person's perspective will depend on whether that person is old or young, a man or a woman, and rich or poor. Perspective is also shaped by a person's culture and race. Your understanding of history will grow as you study the many perspectives of the people who took part in a story. You will see that all people, even those living in other places and times, are a lot like you.

History puts scenes of the past at your fingertips.

When Did It Happen?

One way to tell or write a story of the past is to put the events in the order in which they happened. This presents the story's **chronology**, or time order. As you read this book, you will notice that it is organized by chronology. The events described at the beginning of the book happened before the events described at the end of the book.

You will see many time lines in this book. They will help you understand each story's chronology. A time line is a diagram that shows the events that took place during a certain period of time in the order in which they happened. Time lines may show a period of a month or a year. They may show a period of 10 years, 100 years, or 1,000 years. Time lines can help you understand how one event may have led to another.

How and Why Did It Happen?

Many events in history are linked to other events. To find the links between events, you will need to identify causes and effects. A **cause** is any action that makes something happen. What happens because of that action is an **effect**. Historians have found that most events have many causes and many effects.

To understand an event, you need to analyze its causes and effects. When you **analyze** something, you break it into its parts and look closely at how those parts connect with one another. Once you have analyzed an event, you can summarize it or draw a conclusion about how or why it happened.

REVIEW *What questions should you ask yourself when you read about the past?*

Three Hundred Years Ago

Two Hundred Years Ago

One Hundred Years Ago

The Present

Time lines help you understand *when* in the past something happened.

33

Participation Skills

Work Together in Groups

1. Why Learn This Skill?

Many of the projects you do in social studies will be easier if you work with a partner or in a group. Each of you can work on part of the project. For a group project to succeed, each member needs to cooperate with the others. Knowing how to work together is an important skill for students and for all citizens.

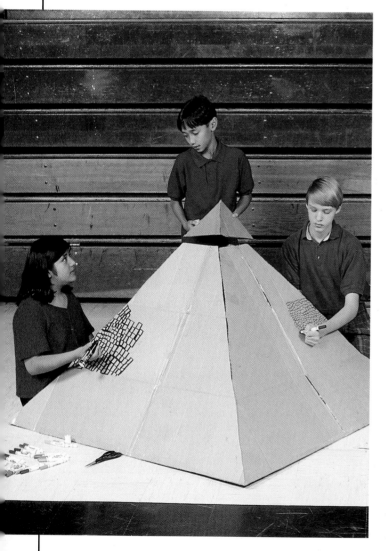

2. Understand the Process

Suppose your group were asked to do a project, such as presenting a short play about everyday life long ago. You might find it helpful to follow a set of steps.

1 Organize and plan together.
  • Set your goal as a group.
  • Share your ideas.
  • Cooperate with others to plan your work.
  • Make sure everyone has a job.

2 Act on your plan together.
  • Take responsibility for your work.
  • Help one another.
  • If there are conflicts, talk about them until they are settled.
  • Show your group's finished work to the class.

3 Talk about your work.
  • Discuss what you learned by working together.
  • Discuss what could have been done differently to improve how your group worked together.

3. Think and Apply

Follow the steps above for working together as you take part in the activities in *Harcourt Brace Social Studies*.

These students are preparing for a class play about life in ancient Egypt.

Geography

The stories you will read in this book all have a setting. The setting of a story includes the place where it happened. Knowing about places is an important part of **geography**—the study of the Earth's surface and the way people use it. **Geographers**, people whose work is to study geography, think about the following five topics and questions when they study a place.

- **Location**
  Where is it?

- **Place**
  What is it like there?

- **Human-environment interactions**
  How does this place affect the lives of people living there?
  How do people living there affect this place?

- **Movement**
  How and why do people, ideas, and goods move to and from this place?

- **Regions**
  How is this place like other places? How is it different?

Thinking about these topics and questions will help you understand the setting of a story. These five topics are so important that people call them the five themes of geography.

Location

Everything on the Earth has its own location. Knowing your location helps you tell other people where you are. It also helps you know more about the world around you.

To tell exactly where you live in your town or city, you can use the names and numbers of your home address. To find your **absolute location**, or exact location, on the Earth, you can use the numbers of your "global address." These numbers appear on a pattern of imaginary lines drawn around the Earth.

The location of a place can also be described in relation to the location of other places. You describe the **relative location** of a place when you say what it is near. You might say that the city of Rome is south of the city of Amsterdam.

Place

Every location on the Earth has a place identity made up of unique features that make it different from all other locations. A place can be described by its **physical features**—landforms, bodies of water, climate, soil, plant and animal life, and other natural resources. Many places also have **human features**—buildings, bridges, farms, roads, and the people themselves. People's culture, or way of life, also helps form a place's identity.

The physical and human features of a place can be seen in this photograph of Bergen, Norway.

Human-Environment Interactions

Humans and the environment interact, or behave in ways that affect each other. People interact with their environment in different ways. Sometimes they change it. They clear land to grow crops. They build cities and towns. Sometimes people pollute the environment. The environment can also cause people to change the way they act. People who live in cold places wear warm clothing. Sometimes things that happen in nature, such as hurricanes, tornadoes, and earthquakes, cause great changes in people's lives.

Humans and the environment they live in affect one another in many ways. In this photograph people cope with the effects of the flooding of the Red River in Vietnam.

Movement

Each day, people in different parts of the country and different parts of the world interact with one another. People, products, and ideas move from place to place by transportation and communication. Geography helps you understand the causes and effects of this movement. It also helps you understand how people came to live where they do.

Emigrants from other countries celebrate becoming citizens of the United States.

Regions

Areas on the Earth with features that make them different from other areas are called **regions**. A region can be described by the physical features, such as mountains or a dry climate, that exist there. A region can also be described by its human features, such as the language spoken there or the kind of government. Sometimes a region is described by its political, cultural, or economic features.

Regions are sometimes divided into smaller regions that are easier to compare. Some geographers who study the Earth's surface and its people divide large areas of land into regions named for their relative locations. The huge continent of Asia is often divided into these regions—northern Asia, central Asia, southern Asia, southwestern Asia, southeastern Asia, and eastern Asia. The countries in each region are alike in many ways. They are all in the same part of Asia. They may have the same kind of landforms, climate, and natural resources.

REVIEW *What are the five themes of geography?*

LEARNING FROM DIAGRAMS

The continent of Asia can be separated into six geographic regions.

■ *Which country is a part of two regions?*

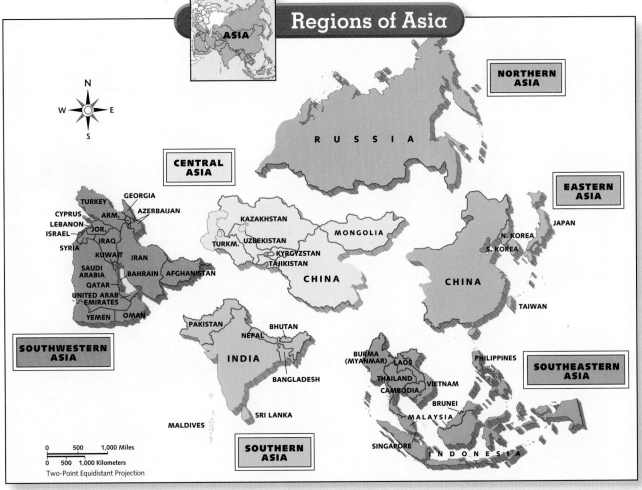

Regions of Asia

Read a Map

1. Why Learn This Skill?

To answer questions about the world around you, you need information. One way you can get this information is by studying maps. Maps tell you about the world by using one or more of the five themes of geography. Knowing how to read and understand maps is an important skill both for learning social studies and for taking action as a citizen.

2. The Parts of a Map

Maps are drawings that show the Earth or part of the Earth on a flat surface. To help you read maps, mapmakers add certain features to most maps they draw. These are a title, a map key, a compass rose, a locator, a map scale, and an inset map. Mapmakers may also show a grid of numbered lines on maps to help people locate places more easily.

The United States

✪	National capital
★	State capital
—	National border
—	State border

The **map title** tells the subject of the map. What is the title of the map shown on page 38? A map title may also help you understand what kind of map it is. Physical maps show landforms and bodies of water. Sometimes, shading is used to help you see where the hills and mountains are located. Political maps show cities and national boundaries, or borders. Many of the maps in this book are historical maps that show parts of the world as they were in the past. Historical maps often have dates in their titles. When you look at any map, look for information in the title to find out what the map is about.

The **map key**, sometimes called a map legend, explains what the symbols on the map stand for. Symbols may be colors, patterns, lines, or other special marks, such as circles, triangles, or squares. According to the map key for the map on page 38, stars are used to show state capitals. What symbol is used to show the national capital?

The **compass rose**, or direction marker, shows the **cardinal directions**, or main directions—north, south, east, and west. A compass rose also helps you find the **intermediate directions**, which are between the cardinal directions. Intermediate directions are northeast, northwest, southeast, and southwest.

The **locator** is a small map or picture of a globe. It shows where the area shown on the main map is located in a state, in a country, on a continent, or in the world. The locator on the map of the United States on page 38 is a globe that shows the continent of North America. The United States is shown in red.

The **map scale** compares a distance on a map to a distance in the real world. A map scale helps you find the real distance between places on a map. Each map in this book has a scale that shows both miles and kilometers.

0	200	400 Miles
0	200	400 Kilometers

Map scales are different, depending on the size of the area the map shows. Look at the map of the United States on page 38. On that map are two smaller maps—one of Alaska and one of Hawaii. A small map within a larger map is called an **inset map**. The boxes around Alaska and Hawaii show that they are inset maps. Inset maps have their own scales. Inset maps make it possible to show places in greater detail or to show places that are beyond the area shown on the main map.

The north-south and east-west lines on a map cross each other to form a pattern of squares called a **grid**. The east-west lines are **lines of latitude**. The north-south lines are **lines of longitude**. This grid helps you find the absolute location, or global address, of a place.

3. Understand the Process

Use the map of Venezuela on this page to answer the following questions.

❶ What is the title of the map?

❷ What three countries share a border with Venezuela?

❸ In which direction would you travel if you went from Valencia to Canaima?

❹ Find the map key. What symbol is used to show a national capital?

❺ What line of latitude is closest to Barcelona?

❻ Find the locator map. How is the location of Venezuela shown?

❼ Find the map scale. How long is the line that stands for 200 miles?

❽ Find the inset map. What area is shown in the inset map?

4. Think and Apply

Look again at the map of Venezuela. Find the different parts of the map, and discuss with a partner what information the map gives you about Venezuela.

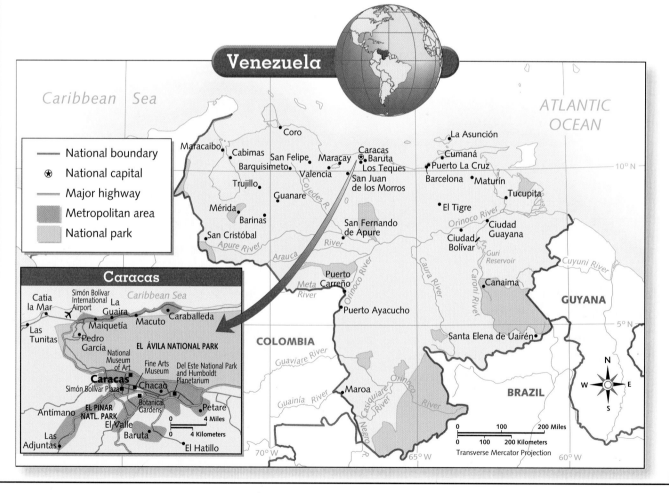

Civics and Government

Civics and government is the study of citizenship and the ways in which citizens govern themselves. A government is a system of leaders and laws that helps people live together in their community, state, or country.

In *Ancient Civilizations* you will find out how the government worked in the past. You will also learn about the different systems of governing that exist in the present.

Economics

The **economy** of a country is the ways its people use its resources to meet their needs. The study of how people do this is called economics. In this book you will read about how people in the past made, bought, sold, and traded goods to get what they needed or wanted. You will learn about different kinds of economies—from the simple ones of the ancient past to the more complex ones of today—and how they came to be.

Culture

In this book you will learn about the people of the past who shaped the present. You will learn who these people were, what they looked like, and how they spoke and acted. You will explore their customs and beliefs and their ways of thinking and expressing ideas. You will look at their families and communities. All these things make up their culture. Each human group, or **society**, has a culture. This book will help you discover the many cultures that are part of our world's story, both past and present.

REVIEW *What kinds of things do you learn when you study civics and government, economics, and culture?*

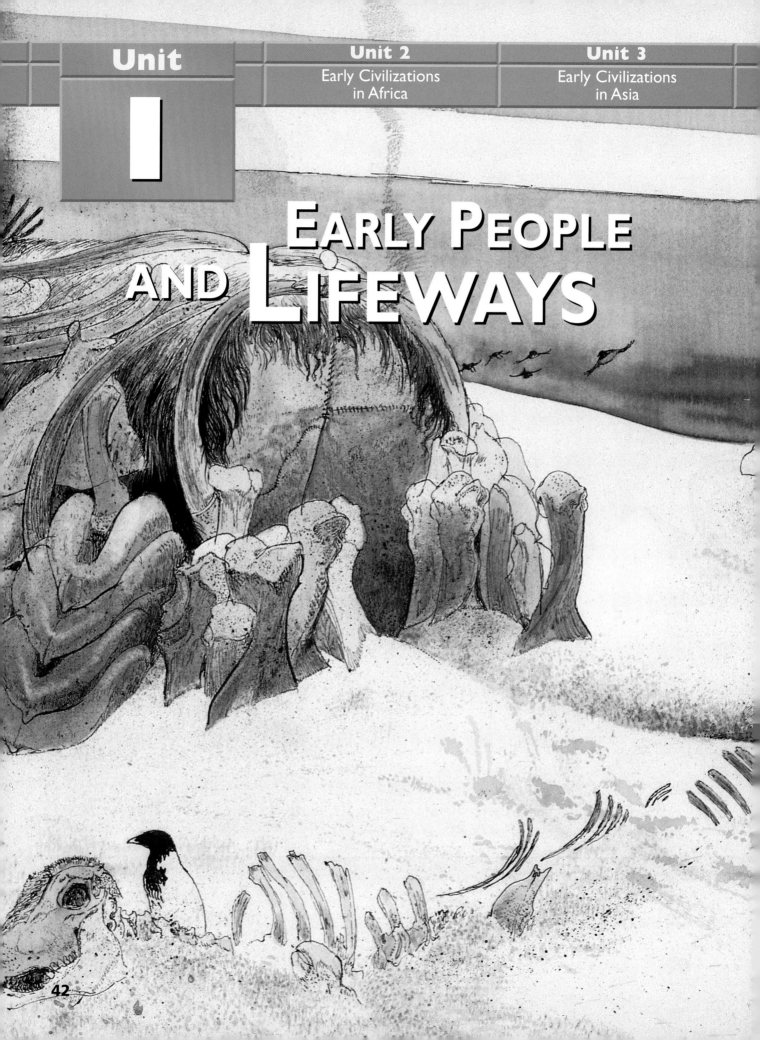

EARLY PEOPLE AND LIFEWAYS

Humans much like ourselves appeared on the Earth about 200,000 years ago. For a long time, all early humans wandered the world in small groups, hunting animals and gathering plants for food. Then some of these people started producing their own food and living in settlements. This development was one of the most important in world history. From a simple way of life, groups of early people created their own customs, ideas, languages, and tools.

◄ This scene shows what life may have been like for early people about 15,000 years ago.

UNIT THEMES

- Interaction Within Different Environments
- Conflict and Cooperation
- Commonality and Diversity
- Continuity and Change

Unit Project

Make a Map of Early Times
Complete this project as you study Unit 1. Draw an outline map of the world on a large sheet of paper. Label each continent. As you read about a place, add it to the map. If an important event happened at a place, list it alongside its location.

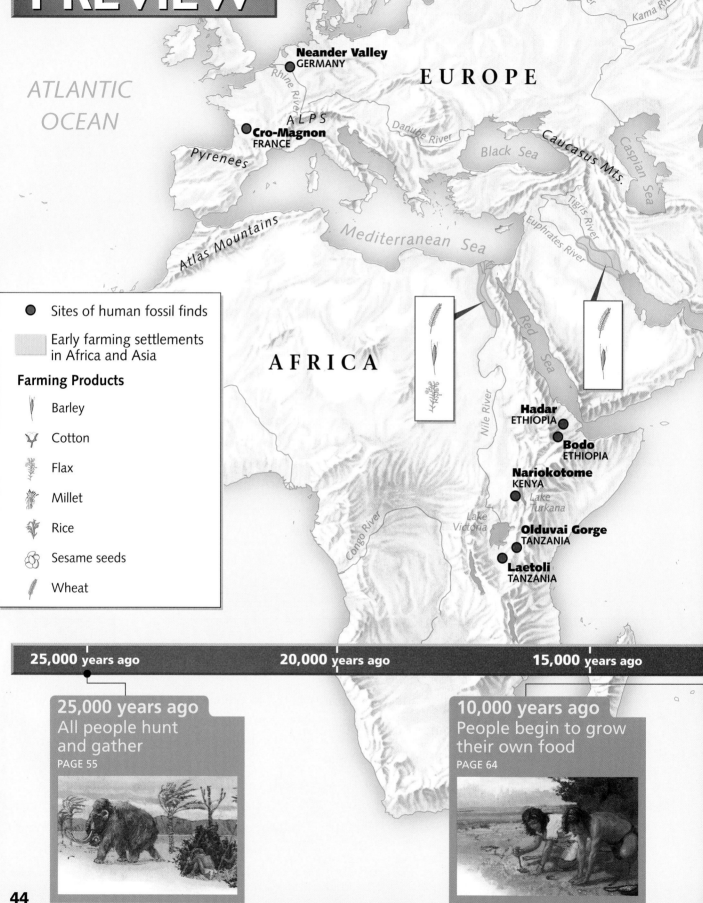

ATLANTIC
OCEAN

Neander Valley
GERMANY

EUROPE

Rhine River

A L P S

Cro-Magnon
FRANCE

Pyrenees

Volga River

Kama River

Danube River

Black Sea

Caucasus Mts.

Caspian Sea

Tigris River

Euphrates River

Atlas Mountains

Mediterranean Sea

AFRICA

Nile River

Red Sea

● Sites of human fossil finds

▨ Early farming settlements
in Africa and Asia

Farming Products

⚘ Barley

⚘ Cotton

⚘ Flax

⚘ Millet

⚘ Rice

⚘ Sesame seeds

⚘ Wheat

Hadar
ETHIOPIA

Bodo
ETHIOPIA

Nariokotome
KENYA

Lake Turkana

Olduvai Gorge
TANZANIA

Lake Victoria

Laetoli
TANZANIA

Congo River

25,000 years ago   **20,000** years ago   **15,000** years ago

25,000 years ago
All people hunt
and gather
PAGE 55

10,000 years ago
People begin to grow
their own food
PAGE 64

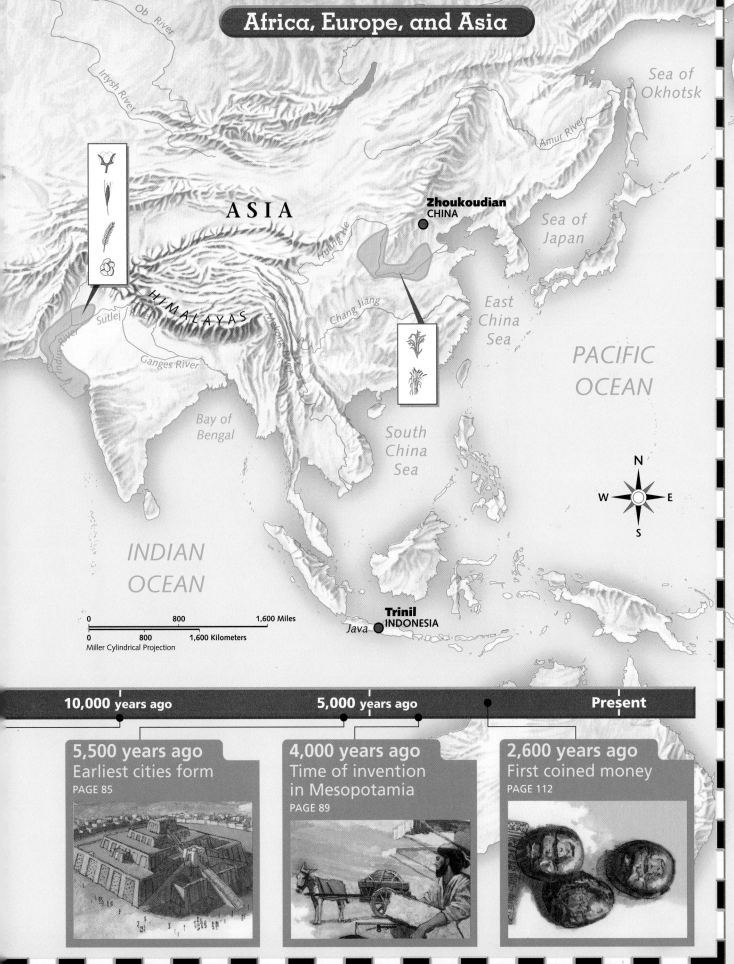

Africa, Europe, and Asia

Ob River

Irtysh River

Sea of Okhotsk

ASIA

Amur River

Zhoukoudian
CHINA

Sea of Japan

Huang He

HIMALAYAS

Chang Jiang

Mekong River

Sutlej River

Indus River

Ganges River

East China Sea

PACIFIC OCEAN

Bay of Bengal

South China Sea

N
W   E
S

INDIAN OCEAN

| 0 | 800 | 1,600 Miles |
| 0 | 800 | 1,600 Kilometers |

Miller Cylindrical Projection

Trinil
INDONESIA

Java

| 10,000 years ago | 5,000 years ago | Present |

5,500 years ago
Earliest cities form
PAGE 85

4,000 years ago
Time of invention in Mesopotamia
PAGE 89

2,600 years ago
First coined money
PAGE 112

Boy of the Painted Cave

by Justin Denzel

From rocky cliffs in Africa to caves in Europe, Australia, and the Americas, early people left behind clear images of life thousands of years ago. The world's earliest artists covered the cave walls and rocks with beautiful paintings. Some of the earliest paintings are patterns of handprints. Other paintings show magnificent scenes of the animals the early people hunted for food.

No one knows for sure why the early people of the world began painting. Perhaps they painted as part of their religious beliefs. Perhaps they wanted to tell about how they lived and what they did.

The following story is set more than 30,000 years ago in the Stone Age, a time when people made tools and weapons from stone. The main characters are Tao and Graybeard. Tao is a young boy who is fascinated by the wild animals that his people depend on to meet their needs. Young Tao dreams of becoming a cave painter like Graybeard. Read now about Stone Age people who counted on the natural resources around them for all their needs.

Ancient artists used their own handprints to create this cave painting found in the South American country of Argentina.

Tao winced as he saw the worn face, the pinched cheekbones. He was worried, but he knew the old man would not want him to show concern. "The cave is ready," Tao said. "But first you must rest and eat." He took some dried meat and fish from his leather pouch and they sat with their backs against an old red oak and ate their meal. Tao wondered if Graybeard remembered his promise.

When they were finished, they started across the valley. Graybeard stopped many times, poking around the streambeds and gravel banks with the shaft of his spear, searching. Then he found what he was looking for. He picked up a stick and dug out a handful of bright red earth.

"Here," he said, as he poured it into an empty leather sack. "This will make good red paint. Now we must find yellows and whites."

Ancient artists used tools similar to these. On a grindstone rest two rocks used for sculpting, pieces of manganese and ocher for painting, and a paint scraper.

"I have yellow clay," said Tao. The old man did remember.

"Good. We can dig up some limestone powder near the foot of the cliffs. That will mix well for the lighter colors."

When they had all the red, white and yellow earth they needed, they went up to the top of the cliff, using the easy path that Graybeard had found. They reached the tunnel to the Hidden Cave and removed the cover of branches to let in the sunlight.

In the cave Graybeard sat on the ground and Tao squatted beside him. The old man poured some of the red earth into one of the saucer-shaped rocks that Tao had collected. Then, using a smooth, round stone, he began grinding it into a fine powder. When it was to his liking, he added some of Tao's fish oil, mixing it into a dark red paint. He poured a small amount of this into three other shallow stone dishes. In the first one he added a lump of yellow clay, in the second he sprinkled limestone powder and in the third he added charcoal dust. Using a small, clean stick for each, he mixed them well, ending with three different colors: a bright orange, a salmon pink and a dark brown.

Tao was amazed. He sat quietly, watching. This too was magic, he thought. Graybeard spread out more saucers and began blending shades of yellows, browns, grays and blacks. Some he mixed with honey, and some with the boiled fat and clotted blood from the boar.

"Next we must make our brushes," he said. He took a handful of twigs from his pouch and began mashing the ends with a stone until they were soft and ragged. He held one up in the shaft of sunlight beaming through the cave entrance. He turned it around for Tao to see. "These are small," he said, "for painting eyes and fine lines of hair and fur."

He made larger brushes by tying feathers and boar bristles around the ends of long sticks with strings of vegetable fiber.

Cave painting from South America, near Perito Moreno, Argentina

When all the paints and brushes were made, the old man got to his feet. "Now," he said, "we are ready to paint."

Tao held out the shoulder blade of the horse, while Graybeard poured spots of the colored paints onto its broad white surface. He handed the boy one of the large brushes and pointed to Tao's pictures of the rhinos, bison and mammoths.

The boy held his breath. He had never had a brush in his hand before. "Which one will I paint?"

Horses seem to come alive in this ancient cave painting from Lascaux, France.

Graybeard smiled. "You are the image maker. Paint the one you like the best."

"The mountain-that-walks," said Tao.

Graybeard nodded. "Then begin."

Tao hesitated, glancing at the paints on the shoulder blade, uncertain.

"You saw the mammoths," said Graybeard. "What color were they?"

"Reddish-brown."

"Good," said the old man. "Then mix a little black with the red until you have the color you wish."

Tao dipped his brush into the spot of black, then mixed it with the red. He lifted his hand and touched it to the drawing. It was still too light, so he dipped in another dab of black. Again his brush touched the drawing. He smiled. It was a deep reddish-brown, the color he wanted. He continued to dip and touch.

Graybeard watched as Tao repeated the motion again and again. He reached out and stopped the boy's hand. "You are not painting on an antler or a seashell," he said. "You are painting on a wall. Do not dab. Swing the brush with your whole arm."

Graybeard took the brush and began sweeping it across the drawing, following the lines of the mammoth's body.

Tao saw the old man's face brighten as he worked, laying on great swaths of color. He felt the excitement as the picture came alive.

"Do not be afraid," said Graybeard, his eyes glowing. "You can always go over what you do not like."

He gave the brush back to Tao and the boy tried again. This time he let his arm go free, swinging the brush across the wall. He mixed gray with yellow to fill in the light

North American rock carving, found in Monument Valley, Utah

areas around the chest and stomach. He painted dark shadows on the shoulders and back to add shading. He saw his mammoth begin to breathe as he filled in the eye and the waving trunk.

When the painting was finished, Graybeard cracked open the duck eggs. He separated the yolks and set them aside. He poured the whites into a clean cockleshell, stirred them with a stick and handed the shell to Tao.

The boy was puzzled. "What is this for?"

"Spread it over your painting and you will see."

With a feather brush Tao washed the egg white over the picture. This time the mammoth came alive with bright new colors. He stared at it in surprise. This had been done by his own hand. He smiled. Never had he felt so happy.

As you read more about early people in this unit, you will discover how people on different continents met their needs and developed unique ways of life.

PEOPLE OF THE STONE AGE

"The sudden emergence of full human creativity among the advanced hunters of this period . . . is surely one of the most astonishing chapters in all our history."

Jacquetta Hawkes,
The Atlas of Early Man

Found in France, this 25,000-year-old sculpture of a woman is one of the earliest images of a human face.

First Footsteps

I magine digging through layers of rocks and sand to find out about people and places of the past. That is what scientists do to help us learn about the world's prehistory. **Prehistory** is history that happened before the invention of writing. To find out about prehistory, experts must look at **evidence**, or proof, rather than written words. They must search for clues to piece together the puzzle of the distant past.

Fossil Finds

Many different kinds of scientists work to uncover facts about the past. Together, they find out how, where, and when early people lived. Among these detectives of the past are archaeologists and paleoanthropologists. **Archaeologists** (ar•kee•AH•luh•jists) locate and study the things left behind by people. **Paleoanthropologists** (pay•lee•oh•an•thruh•PAH•luh•jists) study the ancestors of modern people. They carefully look at **fossils** (FAH•suhlz), or remains of once-living things.

For more than 100 years, people have been searching for the fossils of early human ancestors, or hominids. In 1896 Eugene Dubois (dyoo•BWAH), a Dutch surgeon, dug beneath a river in Indonesia in southeastern Asia. He uncovered what he believed to be the remains of a human ancestor. He named his find *Homo erectus,* meaning "human who stands upright." Other scientists laughed at Dubois's claims. However, in 1927 another hominid was found near Beijing, China.

At about the same time, a South African scientist named Raymond Dart found a still earlier human ancestor in his home country. He had unearthed fossils of an australopithecine (aw•stray•loh•PIH•thuh•syn). Later,

FOCUS
Why do people today want to find out more about the past?

Main Idea   Read to find out how present-day experts have learned about human ancestors.

Vocabulary
prehistory
evidence
archaeologist
paleoanthropologist
fossil
excavate
band

Paleoanthropologist Don Johanson

51

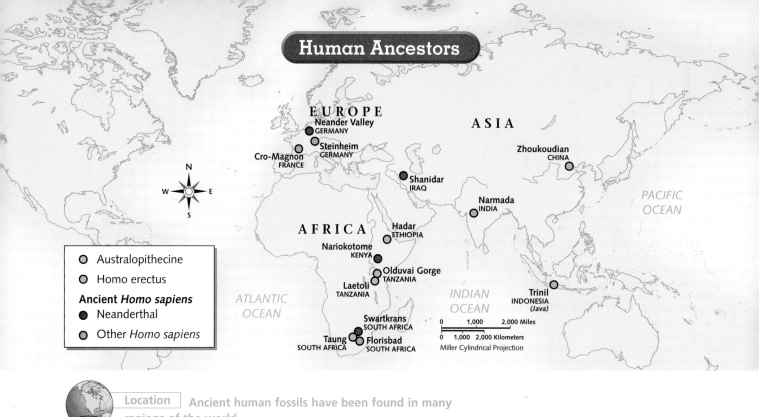

EUROPE
Neander Valley
GERMANY
Steinheim
GERMANY
Cro-Magnon
FRANCE

ASIA

Zhoukoudian
CHINA

Shanidar
IRAQ

PACIFIC
OCEAN

Narmada
INDIA

AFRICA
Hadar
ETHIOPIA
Nariokotome
KENYA
Olduvai Gorge
TANZANIA
Laetoli
TANZANIA

INDIAN
OCEAN

Trinil
INDONESIA
(Java)

ATLANTIC
OCEAN

Swartkrans
SOUTH AFRICA
Taung
SOUTH AFRICA
Florisbad
SOUTH AFRICA

0   1,000   2,000 Miles
0 1,000 2,000 Kilometers
Miller Cylindrical Projection

○ Australopithecine
○ Homo erectus
Ancient *Homo sapiens*
● Neanderthal
○ Other *Homo sapiens*

Location Ancient human fossils have been found in many regions of the world.

■ *Which continent has the most fossil sites?*

MAP THEME

more australopithecine fossils were found in southern Africa. Then, in 1959 Louis and Mary Leakey found australopithecine fossils at Olduvai (OHL•duh•vy) Gorge in Tanzania (tan•zuh•NEE•uh), eastern Africa.

Soon after these discoveries, the Leakeys found other early hominid fossils. One of these hominids appeared to have been round-headed and small-boned. Louis Leakey believed this hominid to be a direct ancestor of modern humans. He named it *Homo habilis* (HAH•buh•lis), a Latin term meaning "handy person." He gave it this name because he also found stone tools nearby.

Louis and Mary Leakey's son Richard continued his parents'

In this photograph Mary Leakey examines ancient footprints.

work. He has found dozens of hominid fossils while searching at Lake Turkana in northern Kenya. Among these are remains of *Homo habilis* from about 2.5 million years ago, the time when toolmaking began.

Other scientists have also made astonishing finds. Near the Awash (AH•wahsh) River in Ethiopia, paleoanthropologist Don Johanson unearthed a 3-million-year-old australopithecine. Johanson and his team nick-named their find "Lucy."

"I just can't believe it!" Johanson cried out upon making his 1974 discovery of Lucy. He was surprised to find almost half of an ancient skeleton. Usually paleoanthropologists are not that fortunate. Often they find just a small piece of ancient life, such as a jawbone or part of an arm bone, as they excavate a site. **Excavate** means to uncover by digging.

In 1994 University of California scientist Tim White revealed that, while excavating in Ethiopia, he had found an even earlier australopithecine than Johanson's. This African hominid may have walked the Earth as much as 4.5 million years ago.

REVIEW *How have Don Johanson and the Leakeys contributed to the search for early hominids?*

Early Ancestors

From the discoveries of archaeologists, paleoanthropologists, and other scientists, we can begin to know what the distant past was like. Many experts agree that the first hominids appeared south of the Sahara in Africa more than 3 million years ago.

By Lucy's time, several kinds of australopithecines lived in eastern Africa. All were mainly plant-eaters. Most may also have eaten meat left over from lion kills.

By 2.5 million years ago, at least one larger-brained group of hominids lived in eastern Africa. These belonged to *Homo habilis*. Within 500,000 years they had spread throughout eastern Africa and into southern Africa. They usually traveled across open grasslands in search of food. As they traveled, they gathered and ate many different kinds of plants. In addition, they scavenged meat from lion and leopard

Don Johanson's camp at Hadar, Ethiopia, where the paleoanthropologist unearthed Lucy

"Lucy"

The name *Lucy* might seem unusual for an ancient hominid. Don Johanson tells how Lucy got her name. At the time of the discovery, a tape recorder in Johanson's camp was playing the Beatles' song "Lucy in the Sky with Diamonds." As Johanson explains,

"At some point during that unforgettable evening . . . the new fossil picked up the name of Lucy, and has been so known ever since."

Back in the United States, Don Johanson and Tim White rebuilt Lucy's skeleton from tiny bone fragments. When she was alive, Lucy stood just about 4 feet high. She was 19 to 21 years old when she died. Lucy walked on two feet and probably spent much of her time in open country rather than in forests.

Lucy (above) is the most complete australopithecine skeleton ever found.

An archaeologist's work includes carefully removing artifacts from a site and recording their exact location. This site is in Israel.

kills. To cut the meat, they used stone choppers and knives, which they made by hitting two stones against each other.

About 1.9 million years ago *Homo erectus* also could be found in Africa. *Homo erectus* had greater brainpower than *Homo habilis*. Even so, *Homo erectus* probably could not make more than a few different sounds.

These early Africans were the first to tame fire. This action gave them a way to protect themselves against lions and other wild animals. It also allowed them to live in colder climates because they could use fire to keep themselves warm.

Like earlier hominids, *Homo erectus* survived by hunting and gathering. In time, hunting and gathering led **bands**, or small groups, of these hominids across Africa's Sahara and into Asia. Later, bands appeared throughout much of Asia and in Europe as well.

For more than 1.5 million years, *Homo erectus* flourished in Africa, Asia, and Europe. Life changed little for *Homo erectus*—except in Africa. On this continent the first modern humans began to appear by 200,000 years ago. These newcomers, *Homo sapiens*, would greatly affect the ways of life of Africa's *Homo erectus*.

REVIEW *How did controlling fire help Homo erectus?*

LESSON 1 REVIEW

Check Understanding

1 **Remember the Facts** According to experts, which came first, *Homo sapiens*, *Homo habilis*, or *Homo erectus*?

2 **Recall the Main Idea** How have experts learned what they know about human ancestors?

Think Critically

3 **Think More About It** Many people debate about the ways in which early people lived. Why do you think this is so?

4 **Past to Present** Fire was important to early humans for protection and warmth. Why is fire important today?

Show What You Know

Diary Activity Imagine that you are a member of Don Johanson's excavation team on the day of Lucy's discovery. Write a diary entry describing the event. Be sure to explain why everyone is so excited about the discovery. Exchange diary entries with a classmate and compare what the two of you have written.

Hunters and Gatherers

FOCUS
Why do people join groups today?

Main Idea As you read, look for reasons early people lived and worked in groups.

Vocabulary
artifact
radiocarbon dating
consequence
extinct
migration
Ice Age
glacier
tundra
culture
society

40,000 years ago	25,000 years ago	10,000 years ago

Most experts believe that Africa was not only the cradle of human ancestors but also the home of the world's first modern people—people like us. According to these experts, the earliest *Homo sapiens* lived in tropical Africa at least 200,000 years ago. By about 150,000 years ago, some *Homo sapiens* had migrated to the eastern and southern parts of Africa.

Homo erectus and *Homo sapiens* probably lived side by side for some time. Then *Homo erectus* died out while *Homo sapiens* continued to exist. Today all people on Earth are *Homo sapiens*. The name *Homo sapiens* means "wise human," and this tells us why *Homo sapiens* lived on. The early *Homo sapiens* had larger brains than the early hominids did. They were able to make better tools and communicate more easily using language.

Survival Skills

Most of what we know about ancient *Homo sapiens* comes from the work of archaeologists and other scientists. To do their work, archaeologists choose a place where they believe humans once lived. This place is called a site. When excavations are underway, a site is often referred to as a dig. At their site, archaeologists begin by tying string in a pattern of squares called a grid. Then they dig through the soil layer by layer. As they dig, they carefully sift through the dirt, looking for fossils and **artifacts**, or human-made objects.

Archaeologists record the square and the layer each fossil or artifact was found in. This important information will help them later as they examine their findings. A careful examination might reveal such information as a fossil's age

These blades from southwestern Asia (bottom) and this carved rock from northern Africa (top) are examples of early tools used to hunt and kill wild animals.

or the purpose of a piece of pottery or other artifact.

One way that experts judge the age of fossils is through radiocarbon dating. **Radiocarbon dating** tells how much carbon remains in a once-living person, animal, or plant. All living things contain radioactive carbon. After death, however, the radioactive carbon begins to decay. By measuring the amount of carbon left in a fossil, experts can identify its age. Radiocarbon dating can only be used for fossils 50,000 years old or younger.

Archaeologists and other scientists have uncovered many important facts about *Homo sapiens*. Like the early people before them, the first *Homo sapiens* lived together in bands. Usually the bands were made up of related families. About 20 people lived in each band. Band members worked together to meet their basic needs for food, clothing, and shelter. Without such cooperation, individuals probably would not have survived.

The small bands spent many hours of their days searching for the food they needed to survive. Much of their diet consisted of wild fruits, nuts, roots, and seeds. They also caught and ate fish, turtles, birds, and small rodents. Experience taught them which plants and animals could be eaten without an unwanted **consequence**, or effect, such as illness.

These early people also hunted large animals. Many of these animals, such as giant oxen, woolly rhinoceroses, and the elephant-like mammoths, are now **extinct**, or no longer living. Other common prey, such as reindeer and bison, still exist. All these animals provided meat for food, bones for tools, and skins for clothing and shelter.

To kill large animals, early hunters needed special tools. Unlike *Homo erectus*, *Homo sapiens* made different kinds of tools for different needs. These people sharpened stones, animal bones, antlers, or tusks to make spears and knives for hunting. They also made needles for sewing animal skins together and hooks for fishing.

Because early bands were always on the move, they had no permanent

HISTORY

Neanderthals

In 1856, workers digging for stone made an unusual discovery in a buried cave in Germany's Neander Valley. They found an odd-looking human skull along with leg and arm bones. Later, British biologist Thomas Huxley identified the discovery as an early *Homo sapiens* fossil, the first ever found. The fossil soon gained the name *Neanderthal*, after the valley in which it was found. Scientists now know that while *Neanderthals* are *Homo sapiens*, they are not our direct ancestors.

LEARNING FROM DIAGRAMS
Hunters and gatherers in different regions used the resources in their environment to make clothes, tools, weapons, and shelters. They hunted large animals, such as mammoths and deer, and gathered any fruits, nuts, and roots they could find.
■ *Look at the three scenes. What kinds of resources are shown in each scene?*

AFRICA

year-round settlements. Instead, they set up seasonal camps in caves or rock shelters near places where plants and animals were plentiful. When food was no longer available in one place, bands moved on to the next place. Usually, bands traveled around a particular area as they searched for food. By following a regular seasonal pattern of **migration**, or movement from one place to another, bands of hunters and gatherers found enough to eat.

REVIEW *Why was cooperation important for early hunters and gatherers?*

Spreading Through the World

As some bands grew in number, they had to roam farther from their usual hunting-and-gathering grounds to find enough food. Each new generation expanded the band's migration pattern. Some experts believe that just two or three miles (3.2 to 4.8 km) were added every 20 years—the average length of an early person's life. By this slow process, humans began to spread throughout the world. It probably

A World of Hunters and Gatherers

EUROPE

ASIA

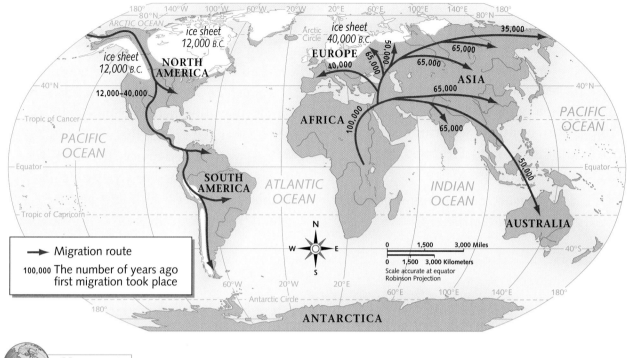

Migrations of Early People

Map labels:

- ice sheet 12,000 B.C. (North America)
- ice sheet 12,000 B.C.
- NORTH AMERICA
- ARCTIC OCEAN
- ice sheet 40,000 B.C.
- Arctic Circle
- EUROPE
- AFRICA
- ASIA
- PACIFIC OCEAN
- ATLANTIC OCEAN
- INDIAN OCEAN
- SOUTH AMERICA
- AUSTRALIA
- ANTARCTICA
- Tropic of Cancer
- Equator
- Tropic of Capricorn
- Antarctic Circle

Migration dates shown on map: 12,000–40,000; 100,000; 40,000; 50,000; 65,000; 35,000; 50,000

Legend:

→ Migration route

100,000 The number of years ago first migration took place

Scale:
0   1,500   3,000 Miles
0   1,500   3,000 Kilometers
Scale accurate at equator
Robinson Projection

Movement Early people probably began to migrate from Africa about 100,000 years ago.

■ *On what continents had people arrived by about 65,000 years ago?*

took hundreds of generations thousands of years to do this!

For a long time, *Homo sapiens* lived only in Africa. Gradually, some bands began moving farther north as they hunted and gathered. In time, bands had traveled across the dry grasslands of the Sahara, into the Nile Valley, and then into southwestern Asia. This movement of people set the stage for the settlement of the entire world. Between 12,000 and 100,000 years ago, the descendants of the earliest African bands spread to Asia, Europe, Australia, and finally to the Americas.

Much of this settlement was made possible by the last Ice Age. An **Ice Age** is a long period of bitter cold. In the distant

past, the Earth had several Ice Ages. The last Ice Age began about 115,000 years ago and ended about 10,000 years ago.

During each Ice Age, huge sheets of ice called **glaciers** covered parts of the Earth's surface. Because much of the ocean was ice, sea level was nearly 300 feet (90 m) lower than it is today. This meant that there was more dry land than there is now. Land bridges connected some islands and continents. Early people were able to use the land bridges to travel between places that are now divided by water.

Some archaeologists believe that early hunters and gatherers first set foot in southwestern Asia about 100,000 years ago. There they found herds of gazelle and deer. Following these herds, generation after generation of early people spread out in many directions.

By about 65,000 years ago, hunters and gatherers had traveled all the way east in Asia to the land now known as China. Later generations followed land bridges to what is now Indonesia. From there, men, women, and children paddled log rafts across the open ocean to Australia. People probably reached this continent by 50,000 years ago.

Early people also moved in other directions. About 40,000 years ago some groups of people spread from southwestern Asia

into Europe. Others migrated to the northeast, following herds of wild animals. They reached what is now Siberia in Russia about 35,000 years ago. There they faced a harsh environment as they adapted to life in the **tundra**, or large treeless plains found in Arctic regions. Archaeologist Göran Burenhult describes early life in Siberia's tundra this way:

66 The hunters who inhabited these immense, frozen, and treeless expanses had to cover vast territories in pursuit of game and other food. There were few caves and rock shelters for protection, so they had to build huts that could withstand the severe cold. 99

The bitter cold of the tundra made life difficult for the early people of Siberia. They needed to keep fires burning almost all the time to stay warm. Also, their clothes had to fit snugly to prevent them from

Treeless tundra regions, such as this one in what is now Canada, provided a harsh climate for early hunters and gatherers.

Making Tools
with Natural Resources

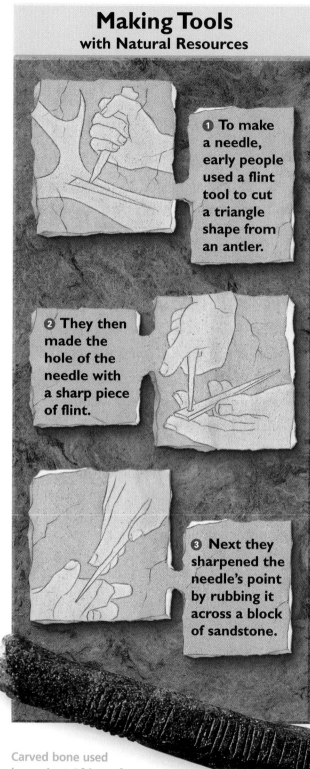

1 To make a needle, early people used a flint tool to cut a triangle shape from an antler.

2 They then made the hole of the needle with a sharp piece of flint.

3 Next they sharpened the needle's point by rubbing it across a block of sandstone.

Carved bone used by ancient Africans for counting (back); mammoth-tusk sculpture (front). Why do you think early people made such items?

freezing. The huts they built were made of sod—a layer of soil with grass growing from it—and mammoth bones. Mammoths were large, hairy elephants with long tusks. Early people used mammoth bones not only for building but also for fuel and tools. Other parts of the mammoth gave the early Siberians food to eat and hides for clothing.

The migration of early people did not stop in Siberia. Bands moved east from Siberia over a land bridge that crossed the Bering Strait, a shallow sea between Asia and North America. Between 12,000 and 40,000 years ago, early people moved into North America. Eventually some hunter-gatherers reached South America.

REVIEW *What effect did the movement of early people have on the world?*

Early Cultures and Societies

All early people hunted animals and gathered wild plants. However, each group had its own unique culture. A **culture** is a way of life. A group's culture is made up of its beliefs, customs, language, and arts.

LEARNING FROM DIAGRAMS Early people made needles by following the three steps shown at left.
■ *Why do you think early people decided to make needles?*

In part, early cultures varied because of each group's location and available resources. Each culture lived in a unique place. This led each culture to make different kinds of clothing, live in different kinds of shelters, and make different kinds of artifacts, including tools. For example, in the far north of Europe, individuals may have carved tools from reindeer antlers. People in the ancient Americas may have used caribou or elk antlers and bones. Ancient people living in rocky areas may have made great use of stones for tools.

Early cultures also varied because each was made up of unique individuals, all with their own ideas. Different cultures, therefore, came up with different solutions to problems and different ways to meet their needs.

Over time, all cultures change. New ideas and new ways of doing things cause some changes. Shifts in climate or changes in the land may affect a culture as well. Contact with other cultures also may lead people to change their way of life.

The increased use of language helped early people further develop their own cultures. Older band members passed on customs and knowledge to younger members. The spoken word also helped people share new ideas, warn of dangers, and work together as a team. Language helped early people join together to become a society. A **society** is an organized group of people living and working under a set of rules and traditions.

In some ways people today are very different from those who lived long ago. In other ways they are still much the same. Modern people look much like early *Homo sapiens*. It is the differences in society and culture that set them apart.

REVIEW *How is a culture different from a society?*

LESSON 2 REVIEW

40,000 years ago	25,000 years ago	10,000 years ago

35,000 years ago
• Groups of early people have migrated from Africa to Asia and Europe

12,000 years ago
• People have reached the Americas

Check Understanding

1 Remember the Facts How did early people get the food they needed to survive?

2 Recall the Main Idea Why did early people work together?

Think Critically

3 Think More About It Why do you think early people formed small groups rather than large ones?

4 Past to Present How do people in our society cooperate today?

Show What You Know
Story-Writing Activity
Imagine that you are a hunter-gatherer in a band in southwestern Asia. Tell about a day in your life. Describe what you did, what you ate, and what you saw that day. Once you have completed your story, share it with a classmate.

Use Latitude

1. Why Learn This Skill?

When you study world history, it is important to know exactly where places in the world are located. To show location, mapmakers use imaginary lines called lines of latitude and lines of longitude. These lines are drawn as a grid on maps and globes. This grid is much like the grids that archaeologists use to divide their dig sites. Archaeologists' grids help people know where artifacts were found. Similarly, grids of lines of latitude and longitude help you know where places are on Earth.

2. Lines of Latitude

The lines that run east and west on a map or globe are **lines of latitude**. Lines of latitude are also called **parallels** (PAIR•uh•lelz) because they are parallel, or always the same distance from each other. Parallel lines never meet.

Lines of latitude are measured in degrees north and south from the equator, which is labeled 0°, or zero degrees. Parallels north of the equator are marked *N* for *north latitude*. This means they are in the Northern Hemisphere. Parallels south of the equator are marked *S* for *south latitude*. This means they are in the Southern Hemisphere. The greater the number of degrees a parallel is, the farther north or south of the equator it is.

3. Lines of Longitude

The lines that run north and south on a map or globe are **lines of longitude**. Lines of longitude are also called **meridians**. Each meridian runs from the North Pole to the South Pole. Unlike parallels, which never meet, meridians meet at the poles. Meridians are farthest apart at the equator.

Meridians are numbered in much the same way as parallels. The meridian marked 0° is called the **prime meridian**. It runs north and south through Greenwich near London in Britain. Lines of longitude west of the prime meridian are marked *W* for *west longitude*. They are in the Western Hemisphere. The meridians to the east of the prime meridian are marked *E* for *east longitude*. They are in the Eastern Hemisphere. The Eastern and Western hemispheres meet at the 180° meridian. The 180° meridian runs exactly opposite to the prime meridian.

4. Understand the Process

The map on page 63 shows some sites throughout the world where prehistoric art has been found. The map has both lines of latitude and lines of longitude drawn over it. These lines overlap each other to form a grid. The crossing lines of latitude and longitude make it possible to describe absolute, or exact, location.

and Longitude

Look at the map of Ancient Art Sites carefully. It shows every twentieth line of latitude and every twentieth line of longitude. At either side of the map, find the line of latitude marked 40°S. Near the bottom of the map, find the line of longitude marked 60°W. Trace these lines with your fingers to the point where they meet and cross. Notice that the site of Perito Moreno is not far from this point. Perito Moreno lies halfway between 20°S and 40°S and just east of 60°W. Using this information, you could say that the absolute location of Perito Moreno is 30°S, 58°W.

5. Think and Apply

Use the map and what you already know about latitude and longitude to answer these questions:

A. Which sites shown on the map lie between 0° and 40°E?

B. Which line of latitude is closest to Monument Valley?

C. Which site lies between 40°N and 60°N?

D. Which line of longitude is closest to Lake Mungo?

E. Which site is closest to the prime meridian? Which sites are closest to the equator?

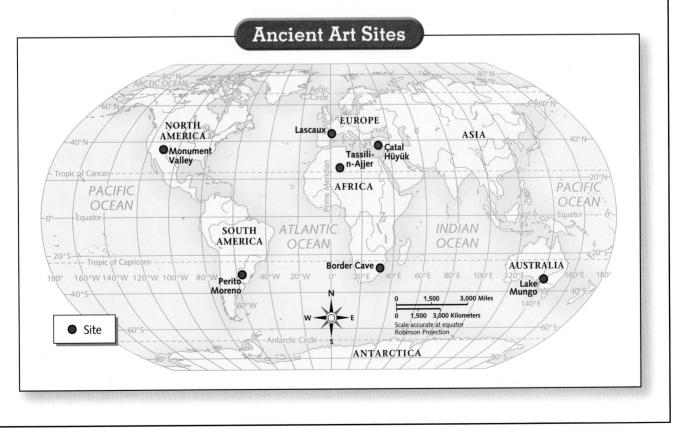

Ancient Art Sites

FOCUS

How does change affect your life today?

Main Idea Consider the effects of change on the early people who became food producers instead of food collectors.

Vocabulary

domesticate
economy
livestock
nomad
agriculture
division of labor
environment
maize
subsist

Early Farmers

| 10,000 years ago | 8,000 years ago | 6,000 years ago |

As early societies grew, many bands of early people found that they could no longer depend on hunting and gathering for their needs. This method did not always bring in enough food. For a more steady supply of food, some early societies began to change from food collecting to food producing—growing crops and raising animals.

Producing Food

About 10,000 years ago some hunter-gatherer societies began to produce some of their food. This change meant that people no longer depended just on what they could find or hunt. Instead, people learned to domesticate plants and animals. To **domesticate** living things means to tame them for people's use.

Women probably did most of the food gathering in early societies and may have been the first to domesticate plants. They probably began this process as they cared for wild plants. They learned that seeds from fully grown plants produced new plants. As time passed, they most likely began planting seeds from carefully selected wild plants. They chose seeds from plants that were plentiful, grew fast, and tasted good. Over time some societies came to depend less on wild plants and more on crops grown in small gardens by early farmers. Wheat and barley were among the first crops to be domesticated. Growing crops also meant staying in

As people began to raise their own crops, they needed new types of tools. Early people used this tool, called a quern, to grind grain. How do you think early people made this tool?

Early Farming Areas

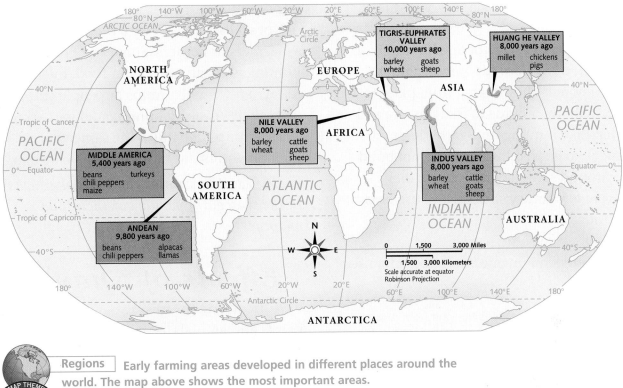

MIDDLE AMERICA
5,400 years ago
beans · turkeys
chili peppers
maize

ANDEAN
9,800 years ago
beans · alpacas
chili peppers · llamas

NILE VALLEY
8,000 years ago
barley · cattle
wheat · goats
· sheep

TIGRIS-EUPHRATES
VALLEY
10,000 years ago
barley · goats
wheat · sheep

HUANG HE VALLEY
8,000 years ago
millet · chickens
· pigs

INDUS VALLEY
8,000 years ago
barley · cattle
wheat · goats
· sheep

Regions Early farming areas developed in different places around the world. The map above shows the most important areas.
■ *What does this map tell you about where early farming areas developed?*

one place, however. Planting, caring for, and harvesting crops took many months. Once the crops were harvested, they needed to be stored. Early farming societies built year-round shelters and grew crops on the land around their small villages. Their **economy**—the way people use resources to meet their needs—became based mainly on their crops.

No one place can claim to be the birthplace of farming. Farming started independently at different times in different parts of the world. Early people in southwestern Asia, southeastern Asia, northern Africa, and South America all made the shift to farming without learning about it from elsewhere in the

world. In each part of the world, word of farming passed from one person to another.

The shift to farming did not happen suddenly either. The change from a hunting-and-gathering society to a farming society took place over a long period of time.

Animals remained an important resource. Some societies that farmed also continued to hunt. At the same time, people began to domesticate some animals. Dogs had long been tamed and used for hunting. Now people began to domesticate wild sheep and goats as well. These newly domesticated animals provided a ready supply of meat, milk, and wool. Some early people came to

Wheat was one of the main food crops of early people.

depend less on raising crops and more on raising livestock. The term **livestock** refers to domesticated animals such as cattle, sheep, and pigs.

Some of the early people who cared for livestock were **nomads**, people with no settled home. They moved from place to place with their herds to find pasture and water. Like hunting-and-gathering nomads, those who herded livestock did not build year-round settlements. Instead, they lived in temporary shelters and traveled in bands.

In settled societies herders and farmers grew to depend on one another. Each raised something that the other did not. Together they worked to supply their society with important resources.

Not all people took up a new way of life as farmers or herders. Some went on hunting and gathering their food. Even today, a few small groups of people still meet their needs by hunting and gathering. These groups live much the same way as their ancestors did thousands of years ago.

REVIEW *What major change took place in the way early people got their food supply?*

Some cave paintings, such as this one from Algeria, Africa, reflect everyday life thousands of years ago. In this painting men, women, and children work alongside herds of cattle.

Effects of Change

Agriculture, the raising of domesticated plants and animals, changed human societies forever. Agriculture provided a reliable food source. In fact, agriculture allowed farmers to grow more food than they needed. This extra amount could be traded for other resources the farmers needed or wanted.

As early people turned to agriculture, the size of their communities began to grow. With more food available, more people could live in one place.

Some people today still live as nomads, traveling from place to place with their herds. The country of Sudan in Africa is the setting for this scene.

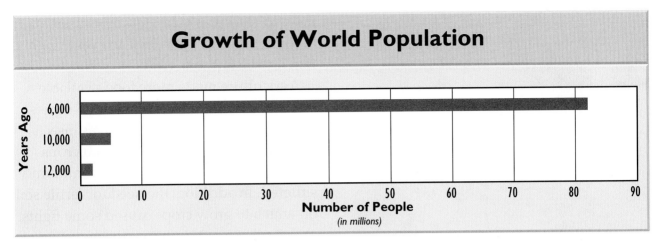

Growth of World Population

Years Ago (vertical axis)

- 6,000
- 10,000
- 12,000

Number of People (horizontal axis)
(in millions)

0   10   20   30   40   50   60   70   80   90

LEARNING FROM GRAPHS The population of the world grew dramatically as a result of the introduction of agriculture.

■ *What was the world's population 12,000 years ago? How many more people were there by 6,000 years ago?*

As the size of societies increased, not everyone needed to spend the day farming. Because of this, a **division of labor** began. Different members of a society were able to do different tasks based on their abilities and the group's needs. Some people still farmed, but others made tools, sewed hides for clothing, or built shelters. Still others served as leaders.

The leaders of farming societies made important decisions for the community. Duties may have included deciding what crops to plant, where to plant them, and who would care for them. Leaders may have also been responsible for deciding how much food would be used at certain times. Leaders might have also come up with ways to protect their community against the dangers of nature or other people.

One common means of protection was the building of walls. Some societies built walls around their villages to prevent attacks from other societies. Others built walls to keep floodwaters from reaching their settlements. One of the oldest known walled villages was built at a site in southwestern Asia known today as Jericho. The people lived in mud-brick huts grouped inside stone walls. The village walls were 20 feet (6.1 m) high and 6 feet (1.8 m) thick.

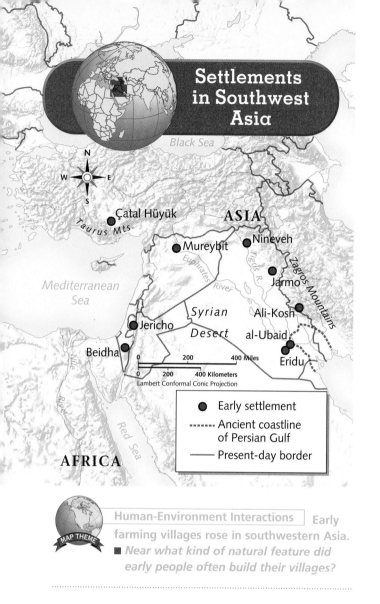

Settlements in Southwest Asia

Black Sea

ASIA

Taurus Mts.

Çatal Hüyük

Mureybit

Nineveh

Euphrates River

Tigris R.

Jarmo

Zagros Mountains

Mediterranean Sea

Syrian Desert

Ali-Kosh

al-Ubaid

Jericho

Beidha

Eridu

Nile River

Red Sea

AFRICA

0   200   400 Miles
0   200   400 Kilometers
Lambert Conformal Conic Projection

● Early settlement
------- Ancient coastline of Persian Gulf
——— Present-day border

MAP THEME | Human-Environment Interactions | Early farming villages rose in southwestern Asia.
■ *Near what kind of natural feature did early people often build their villages?*

The ruins of another early farming community can be found in present-day Turkey. This community is known today as Çatal Hüyük (chat•AHL hoo•YOOK). As many as 6,000 people lived side by side in ancient Çatal Hüyük. The community of Çatal Hüyük looked more like a sprawling apartment complex than a village. Its people built mud houses right next to each other. They came into and left their homes through holes in the

This tower (far right) is part of the ruins of Jericho, a village once surrounded by stone walls. This small statue (near right), found at the ancient village of Çatal Hüyük, is more than 9,000 years old.

roof. To reach the holes, residents used ladders. Outside the village in every direction lay the farmers' fields.

Agriculture made more food available, but it also brought new concerns. Farmers faced threats to their crops such as insects, plant disease, and flooding. When crops failed for any reason, the whole community suffered. In addition, the need for fertile soil on which to grow crops caused some fights over land.

Sometimes the ways in which early people farmed had consequences for their **environment**, or surroundings. For example, many farmers cleared land for crops by cutting and burning the wild plants that grew there. Although new crops could be grown, wild plants that supported herds of wild animals were lost. Also, after years of growing the same crops, the land was no longer fertile. It could not be used for a period of time. Many early societies were often unaware of such consequences. It took farming communities a long time to learn the best ways to farm and to raise livestock.

REVIEW *What were some advantages and disadvantages of agriculture?*

Diversity in Early Agriculture

Around the world early people domesticated a wide variety of plants and animals. Agriculture in southwestern Asia was based on growing wheat and barley and on raising sheep, goats, and cattle. In the Nile Valley in northern Africa, farmers raised wheat, barley, sheep, goats, cattle, and pigs. Far to the east, people settling the river valleys of present-day Pakistan and China raised grains such as rice and millet and kept pigs, chickens, and water buffaloes.

In the Americas early farmers also began growing crops. Farmers in what is now southern Mexico grew chili peppers, squash, and other vegetables. In the mountain valleys of what is now Peru, farmers raised beans and chili peppers. Potatoes were a major crop in what is now Bolivia. Later, Native Americans would also grow **maize**, or corn. Maize would be important throughout American history.

At its beginning, agriculture simply offered another way besides hunting and gathering for people to **subsist**, or survive. Once people began to depend on farming for their subsistence, they were less likely to move. They needed to stay near their fields so that they could care for the crops. In many places, agriculture gradually led to year-round villages and more complex societies.

REVIEW *What were the main food crops raised in northern Africa? in the Americas? in southwestern Asia?*

LESSON 3 REVIEW

10,000 years ago	8,000 years ago	6,000 years ago

About 10,000 years ago
• Early domestication of plants and animals

About 8,000 years ago
• Farming communities form in southwestern Asia

Check Understanding

1 **Remember the Facts**   What new way of getting food changed societies?

2 **Recall the Main Idea**   How did early people become food producers? What effect did this change have?

Think Critically

3 **Think More About It**   Why did farming societies feel a need to control land while hunter-gatherers did not?

4 **Past to Present**   Clearing forest land today affects the environment just as clearing wild plants did long ago. What were the effects then? What are they now?

Show What You Know

Debate Activity   Form a group of six students. As a group, think about how domesticating plants and animals changed societies. Now divide your group in two and have a debate about the consequences of the change from hunting and gathering to agriculture among early people. Three students should take the side of an early farmer. The other students should take the side of a hunter-gatherer. Be sure to narrow your debate to a specific topic. Present your debate to another group of classmates. Then, be part of the audience for that group's debate.

Use a Parallel

1. Why Learn This Skill?

Just as maps help you understand *where* something happened, time lines help you understand *when* something happened. Time lines let you put events in sequence.

Some time lines are simple to read and understand. Others, such as the one below, are more difficult. It is important to look at complex time lines carefully to be sure you understand them fully.

2. Think About Time Lines

The time line you see on this page is a **parallel time line**. It is really several time lines in one. Parallel time lines are useful if you want to show related events. You could show when the same kind of events happened in different areas. Or you could also show events that happened in different places at the same time.

Parallel Time Line: Early Agriculture

AFRICA

8000 B.C.   6000 B.C.   4000 B.C.   2000 B.C.   B.C. A.D.   A.D. 2000

6000 B.C.
• Northern
  Africa

2500 B.C.
• Western
  Africa

A.D. 100
• Southern
  Africa

AMERICAS

8000 B.C.   6000 B.C.   4000 B.C.   2000 B.C.   B.C. A.D.   A.D. 2000

7800 B.C.
• South
  America

3400 B.C.
• Middle
  America

2000 B.C.
• North
  America

ASIA

8000 B.C.   6000 B.C.   4000 B.C.   2000 B.C.   B.C. A.D.   A.D. 2000

8000 B.C.
• Southwestern
  Asia

6000 B.C.
• Western
  Asia

3000 B.C.
• South-
  eastern
  Asia

2500 B.C.
• Southern
  Asia

EUROPE

8000 B.C.   6000 B.C.   4000 B.C.   2000 B.C.   B.C. A.D.   A.D. 2000

6000 B.C.
• Southeastern
  Europe

5300 B.C.
• Central
  Europe

4000 B.C.
• Northern
  Europe

Time Line

Each section of this parallel time line is divided into spans of 2,000 years, beginning at 8000 B.C. and ending at A.D. 2000. The abbreviation **B.C.** stands for "before Christ." **A.D.** stands for *anno Domini*, a Latin phrase meaning "in the year of the Lord." This abbreviation tells how many years have passed since the birth of Jesus Christ. Some time lines are labeled B.C.E. and C.E. rather than B.C. and A.D. The abbreviation **B.C.E.** stands for "before the Common Era" and **C.E.** stands for "Common Era." The terms B.C.E. and C.E. refer to the same years as B.C. and A.D.

No one knows exactly when some events happened long ago. Therefore, a date on a time line sometimes is approximate, or not exact. This usually means that the earliest **evidence**, or proof, is from about that time. Approximate times are often shown after the Latin term *circa*, or *c.*, its abbreviation. The term *circa* means "about."

The time line on page 70 shows when agriculture developed during the Stone Age in different geographic regions. The Stone Age is divided into two parts. The Paleolithic period, or Old Stone Age, is the time before 8000 B.C. The Neolithic period, or New Stone Age, is the time from 8000 B.C. to as late as the present day. During the Paleolithic period, all people were hunters and gatherers. During the Neolithic period, people began to domesticate plants and animals.

3. Understand the Process

Look down the left-hand side of the time line. Find the top bar labeled *Africa*. What is the first date that is highlighted on the top bar? If you said 6000 B.C., you are right. Under that date are the words *Northern Africa*. This means that agriculture began in northern Africa about 6000 B.C. Now look at the other bars on the time line. In which regions of the world did people develop agriculture at about the same time?

4. Think and Apply

Make a parallel time line comparing important events in your life with events in the lives of family members or friends. Make sure that your time line has a bar for each person and a title. Write three questions for a classmate to answer using your time line.

The following suggestions will help you make your time line:

- Identify the events you want to show.
- Determine the length of time over which the events took place.
- Make the time line, divide it into equal parts, and mark the years on it.
- Add the events you want to display. It is always a good idea to double-check the dates of events to be sure your information is accurate.
- Give your time line a title that explains its contents.

Skara Brae

THE STORY OF
A PREHISTORIC
VILLAGE

written and illustrated
by Olivier Dunrea

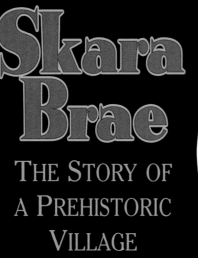

Skara Brae was an early farming village on an island off northern Scotland. Shortly before 2400 B.C. a sudden storm covered the village in sand. It remained covered for more than 4,200 years. Then, in A.D. 1850, a powerful windstorm stripped the sand from the dunes and uncovered the stone walls of the village. What archaeologists know about life in Skara Brae comes from studying the stone huts and the objects the early people left behind. Through careful study of this evidence, archaeologists were able to piece together the story of this village of long ago.

Read now about what life may have been like in Skara Brae and in other farming villages long ago. Think about how life in these early settlements compared with life in hunter-gatherer societies and with our lives today.

Writer/illustrator Olivier Dunrea pictures what life may have been like in Skara Brae.

Pins made of bone in Skara Brae around 2500 B.C.

Orkney Islands

0   5   10 Miles
0   5   10 Kilometers
Lambert Conformal Conic Projection

3°W

2°30′W

North Ronaldsay

N
W   E
S

Westray

ATLANTIC OCEAN

Sanday

North Sea

Rousay   Eday

Stronsay

SKARA BRAE

Shapinsay

59°N   59°N

Mainland
• Stromness   • Kirkwall

2°30′W

Hoy

South Ronaldsay

UNITED KINGDOM

3°W

FRANCE

Place | Study the map.
■ *What do you think were some advantages and disadvantages of living in Skara Brae?*

By 3500 B.C. farmers and herders had reached a group of islands to the north of Scotland—the Orkneys.

They found the Orkneys an ideal place to live. There were gently rolling hills, open grasslands for their sheep and cattle, and wide, sand-fringed bays. The islands had no predatory animals that would attack their livestock. It was a good area to settle.

Orkney was a strange place to these early settlers. They were accustomed to trees and forests. In Orkney there were far fewer trees.

But though there was very little wood, there was plenty of fuel. Mosses and other plants had decayed in bogs to form peat. The peat could be burned like coal. The settlers could keep warm and cook their meat around a peat fire.

Most of all, there was a great abundance of stone on the islands. Stones were everywhere—on the beaches, on the grasslands, and on the hills. The herders and farmers chose these stones to build their permanent homes and monuments.

In time the Orkneys became more populated. New masses of migrating people reached their shores. Several generations of settlers came and went, and some ventured off to the smaller and less populated islands.

One band of settlers, seeking better grazing land for their animals, moved farther out on the main island. Making their way to the farthest west coast, they explored the land for a suitable place to live.

As they marched northward along the rugged cliffs and inlets, they came to a beautiful wide bay—the Bay of Skaill. There were sand dunes, open grassland, and no other settlers to compete for the land's resources. It was here the band decided to make their new home.

There were twenty people in the group: four small families. Together they owned a flock of sheep, a small herd of cattle, and a few pigs.

After surveying the land around the bay, they chose the southwest corner in which to erect their temporary shelters. The women and older children put up the tents, using wooden poles they had brought with them. These tents made of skins would protect them from rain and wind.

It was the task of the older children to tend the livestock, even though the animals mostly fended for themselves and found food wherever they could.

During this period, settlers lived off their animals. To their diet of meat and milk they added wild foods foraged[1] from the land and sea—birds and eggs, fish, shellfish such as limpets,[2] and wild grains. The men sometimes brought in the meat of deer and other wild animals as well.

Through the summer, autumn, and winter the band continued to live in their tents. During the winter months they started construction of a new village that would have proper houses for all the families.

While they built the permanent stone houses, everyone worked. The men gathered the larger stones needed for the foundations and walls. The women and children also gathered stones to be used in the construction of the huts.

[1] **foraged:** searched for food
[2] **limpets:** small shellfish

Example of building method used in Skara Brae home

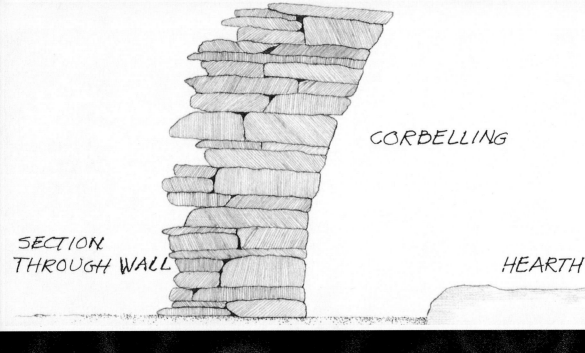

SECTION THROUGH WALL

CORBELLING

HEARTH

Layout of a typical Skara Brae home

Everyone worked together on all the houses. One partly completed house was used as a shelter for the cattle, sheep, and pigs. The band continued to live off their animals as well as the land and sea.

There were plenty of stones on the beach around the bay, and collecting them went quickly. The stones could be easily split to make straight, uniform surfaces for building.

The stones were laid one on top of another without the use of mortar.[3] We now call this method of building drywall construction. The settlers might have used curved whalebones washed up on the beach to help support the roofs.

---

[3]**mortar:** mixture of lime, sand, and water for holding stones or bricks together

The houses were small when completed, measuring only twelve feet long by six to nine feet wide in the interior. The plan of each house was basically square, with rounded corners. In one of the corners, there was a small, beehive-shaped cell, used either for storage or as a latrine.[4]

The walls were built by piling stone upon stone. A few feet above the floor the stones began to project a little toward the inside of the hut. This overlapping construction is called corbelling.[5]

Each hut was big enough to allow room for a central hearth,[6] a stone bed set into the wall on either side of the hearth, and a stone dresser built into the rear wall. The mother and small children slept in the bed to the left of the hearth; the father slept in the bed to the right.

The stone beds were filled with heather[7] and skins, making them comfortable and warm for sleeping.

There were one or two small recesses for keeping personal possessions in the wall above each bed.

Within a few weeks the little huts were completed.

---

[4]**latrine:** toilet
[5]**corbelling:** way of building a wall so that it curves as it goes up
[6]**hearth:** fireplace
[7]**heather:** low evergreen shrub

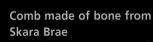

Comb made of bone from Skara Brae

And so began the occupation of the village. It was around 3100 B.C.

As they went about the routine of their daily life, the villagers allowed their refuse to pile up against the outside walls of their huts. Shells, broken bones, fragments of pottery, sand, and everything no longer used was heaped around the structures.

This refuse, called midden, helped to insulate the huts. It kept the cold winds from blowing through the chinks in the stones. Over the years these midden heaps mixed with sand and became a claylike covering from which grass grew.

Now the huts looked like the surrounding dunes of the Bay of Skaill. And thus came into existence the village we now call Skara Brae—the village of the hilly dunes.

As the generations came and went, so did the huts. The older huts were sometimes taken down stone by stone to build new huts.

The wind-blown sands constantly shifted around the dunes and the dwellings of Skara Brae. Sometimes one of the huts was overcome by the drifts and disappeared. Another hut was often built on top of it, and life continued as before.

The shifting sands and the ever-increasing midden heaps continually changed the appearance of the village. Other changes also took place. The new huts were built to be larger and more comfortable.

The beds had stone pillars at each corner supporting a canopy made of skins. The stone dresser was now built against the rear wall and was no longer set into it.

Inside, the hearth remained the focal point of the room. The stone beds, however, were no longer built into the walls but projected out into the room. Sometimes a third bed was added for the children.

Necklace of bone and teeth made in Skara Brae around 2500 B.C.

The collecting of limpets, a kind of shellfish, had become increasingly important to the villagers. Limpet shells were heaped in great quantities around the huts along with the other refuse.

In the floor of the huts the villagers built stone boxes carefully sealed with clay to make them watertight. In these holding tanks they kept their limpets in the water for later use as bait or perhaps as food. Several tanks were built so that there could always be a ready supply of limpets.

At some point in their history the inhabitants of Skara Brae most likely began to cultivate small plots of grain. They remained an isolated group, living a quiet life off the land and sea and their stock of animals.

As the village grew, so did its population. The villagers were bound together by common need, common activity, and the beliefs and ceremonies that characterize all Stone Age peoples.

Evidence of one of these beliefs was found underneath a wall of one of the later huts. Two aged women of the village had died. Their bodies were buried beneath the wall in the hope and belief that their spirits would support the wall and help sustain the life of the village. This was the only time the villagers performed this rite. Henceforth the dead would be buried in communal burial mounds.

When the settlers were first building their permanent homes, there was little time for anything else. Several generations later, the village was well established and had settled into an ordered pattern of life. The villagers now attended to other matters. They were able to focus on the social and ceremonial life that keeps a community together.

For the Neolithic villagers of Skara Brae, one such activity might have been the construction of a communal burial mound, or cairn.

The construction of the cairn took longer than that of the huts because it was much larger. Once it was completed, it served generation after generation.

The exterior of the cairn was covered with earth, and in time grass grew over it. It looked like a hill in the landscape.

There was also time for the villagers to practice their various crafts. The women made pottery. Sometimes they made engraved or raised designs on their pots. But the people of Skara Brae, unlike many Neolithic peoples, were not especially skilled at this craft.

The men spent hours carving strange, intricate patterns on stone balls.

The teeth and bones from sheep, cattle, and whales were used to make beautiful beads and necklaces.

For a long time the life of Skara Brae continued uninterrupted. Then, around 2400 B.C., when the village had settled into its way of life, a terrible catastrophe occurred that caused it to be abandoned forever.

As the villagers went about their daily tasks of collecting food and tending their herds or practicing their crafts, a sudden and violent storm arose. The storm came so unexpectedly and with such severity that the inhabitants fled without being able to collect all their belongings.

In her haste to escape, one woman broke her string of beads as she squeezed through the narrow doorway of her hut. The necklace fell to the floor of the passageway, and there it remained.

In another hut an old man was gnawing a choice bit of mutton when the storm took him by surprise. He dropped the bone by his bed and fled the hut in panic.

Then the wind-driven sands quickly filled all the stone huts, burying the necklace and the half-eaten bone for the ages.

The storm raged with a fury the villagers had never experienced before. They fled the village in blind terror.

The sea pounded in the bay, and to the prehistoric people of Skara Brae it must have seemed that the world was coming to an end.

The villagers abandoned their village in the hilly dunes. Several times a small number of them returned and camped under the remaining exposed walls of the huts. And then they never returned again. Over the centuries the sand continued to drift in, until nothing was visible.

Although the name Skara Brae remained, memory of the village itself vanished.

LITERATURE REVIEW

1. In your own words, describe what life was like in Skara Brae.
2. In what ways was village life different from life in hunter-gatherer societies and from life today?
3. Make a diagram or model of what you think Skara Brae may have looked like. Use labels to identify and explain various features of your project.

Formulate a

1. Why Learn This Skill?

Sometimes the same kind of event happens to you over and over again. When this occurs, you can make a general statement about the cause or the effect of the event. For example, suppose you usually had a good breakfast in the morning. Three times, though, you skipped breakfast. On those days you did not seem to have enough energy. Based on your experiences, you could make this general statement: *Whenever you don't have a good breakfast, you feel tired all day.*

This kind of statement is called a generalization. A **generalization** is a summary statement made about a group of related ideas. By making generalizations you can describe events or relationships and tell how they are alike.

Generalizations can be true, but they can also be false. A true generalization is based on a list of facts. False generalizations are based on an incomplete list of facts.

Generalizations are useful because they can treat many ideas as one simple idea. They may also find similarities in ideas that at first seem different. Suppose that you stayed up late and were too tired the next day to do your best on a science test. Your friend, kept awake by noise, did poorly in math that same day.

On the surface these examples seem different because they are about different problems. Both have something in common, though. In each case a student didn't get enough sleep and didn't do his or her best work at school. You could make a generalization and say, *People don't do their best work when they haven't had enough sleep.*

2. Remember What You Have Read

Soon you will have a chance to write a generalization based on what you read about in *Skara Brae: The Story of a Prehistoric Village*. To prepare for writing a generalization about what you have read, answer these questions:

- What materials did the people of Skara Brae use to build houses? Where did they get those materials?
- What did they eat at first? Where did they get that food?
- What did they use as fuel? Where did they get that fuel?

3. Understand the Process

To formulate a generalization, use the following steps:

1. List the facts or events.
2. Think about how the facts or events are alike.
3. Write a sentence that makes a general statement linking the facts or events.
4. Test your generalization. Make sure it is true for most things that might happen.

Generalization

Now look at your answers from *Remember What You Have Read*. Think about ways in which all your answers are related. Then following the steps on page 80, think of a generalization that explains how the people of Skara Brae met their basic needs. Your generalization might be: *People in simple societies met their basic needs by using materials from the environment around them.*

4. Think and Apply

How do people today meet their basic needs? How do they get housing materials, food, and fuel? Develop a generalization based on these questions. Test your generalization to make sure it is true. Discuss your generalization with those developed by other students.

Gathering fuel in Skara Brae

40,000 B.C. • 30,000 B.C.

About 35,000 B.C.
• Groups of early people
  have migrated from Africa
  to Asia and Europe

CONNECT MAIN IDEAS

Use this organizer to describe the ways of life of people who lived during the Stone Age. Write two examples for each box. A copy of the organizer appears on page 9 of the Activity Book.

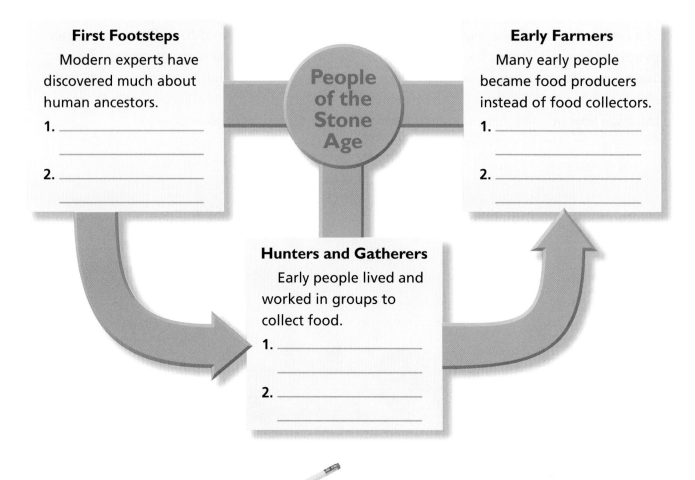

First Footsteps

Modern experts have discovered much about human ancestors.

1. _____

   _____

2. _____

   _____

People of the Stone Age

Early Farmers

Many early people became food producers instead of food collectors.

1. _____

   _____

2. _____

   _____

Hunters and Gatherers

Early people lived and worked in groups to collect food.

1. _____

   _____

2. _____

   _____

WRITE MORE ABOUT IT

Write a Diary Entry Imagine that you are a young person who is part of a band of early people. Your band survives by hunting and gathering. Write a diary entry about going on a hunt. Describe the animals you are hunting and the tools you are using. Your entry should also describe what the land and the climate are like where your band hunts.

Write a Magazine Article Describe a home in Skara Brae as if you were writing an article for a magazine about homes. Write as though you are giving a tour from one part of the home to another. Be sure to tell how the home fits into the environment. Your final article should look as if it is part of a magazine. You may include your own illustrations.

About 10,000 B.C.
• People have reached the Americas

About 8000 B.C.
• Early domestication of plants and animals

USE VOCABULARY

Write a term from this list to complete each of the sentences that follow.

agriculture   culture   migration

artifact   excavate

1. Archaeologists _____ sites to find signs of life long ago.

2. Movement from one place to another is called _____.

3. A _____ is a unique way of life.

4. An _____ is an object made and used by people.

5. The raising of plants and animals for the use of people is called _____.

CHECK UNDERSTANDING

6. What is prehistory?

7. What plants and animals did early people domesticate?

8. What is a society?

9. Which provided a more steady food supply, hunting and gathering or agriculture?

10. Why did the people of Skara Brae build stone houses?

THINK CRITICALLY

11. **Personally Speaking** What do you think it would be like to take part in an excavation?

12. **Past to Present** What are some of the objects, customs, and clothing that identify your culture?

13. **Think More About It** How do you think controlling the food supply might have helped a leader of early people keep order?

APPLY SKILLS

Use a Parallel Time Line After the development of agriculture, societies with governments and social classes formed. Look at the time line on page 70. After which date would you expect to find such a society in South America? in North America? in southeastern Asia?

Formulate a Generalization Make a generalization about the development of agriculture and the daily work of early people.

READ MORE ABOUT IT

Digging Up the Past: The Story of an Archaeological Adventure by Carollyn James. Franklin Watts. Damien, his mother, and his friend Joe, complete an archaeological dig to find out where treasures and junk they have found in their neighborhood came from. Soon they discover the history of their town and the people that lived there. As you read, you will find out how to do an archaeological dig from start to finish.

Visit the Internet at **http://www.hbschool.com** for additional resources.

Chapter 1 • **83**

SOUTHWEST ASIA

"I am Hammurabi, noble king. I have not been careless or negligent toward humankind. . . . I have sought for them peaceful places. I removed serious difficulties."

Hammurabi,
King of Babylon
about 1750 B.C.

Bronze statue of Hammurabi

Geography of Ancient Mesopotamia

Not far from the sites of the ancient farming settlements of Jericho and Çatal Hüyük rose some of the world's first cities. Fertile soil and twin waterways combined to provide the setting for early **urban**, or city, growth in southwestern Asia. For centuries historians have referred to the area of southwestern Asia's first cities as the Fertile Crescent.

The Land Between Two Rivers

The name Fertile Crescent describes the land found there. On a map the Fertile Crescent appears to be shaped somewhat like a crescent moon. *Fertile* refers to the rich soil found in parts of the region.

The Fertile Crescent of ancient days included parts of what are now the countries of Iraq, Iran, Turkey, Syria, Lebanon, Jordan, and Israel. Bordering this region on the west is the Mediterranean Sea. On its southeastern edge lies the Persian Gulf. To the northwest are the Taurus Mountains. The Zagros (ZAH•gruhs) Mountains tower over the Fertile Crescent in the east.

Cutting through the region are two rivers, the Euphrates (yoo•FRAY•teez) and the Tigris. Between these rivers lies the region's richest soil. This fertile land area has long been known as Mesopotamia, "the land between the rivers."

The northern part of Mesopotamia is a **plateau**, or high, flat area of land. The southern part is an **alluvial plain**, or low, flat land formed from fine soils deposited by rivers.

The soil of ancient Mesopotamia was dry, the climate was hot, and the rivers were unpredictable. The region also

FOCUS
How does the geography of an area affect where people live today?

Main Idea As you read, discover how the geography of Mesopotamia made it possible for people to settle there and build cities.

Vocabulary
urban
plateau
alluvial plain
tributary
silt
drought
irrigation

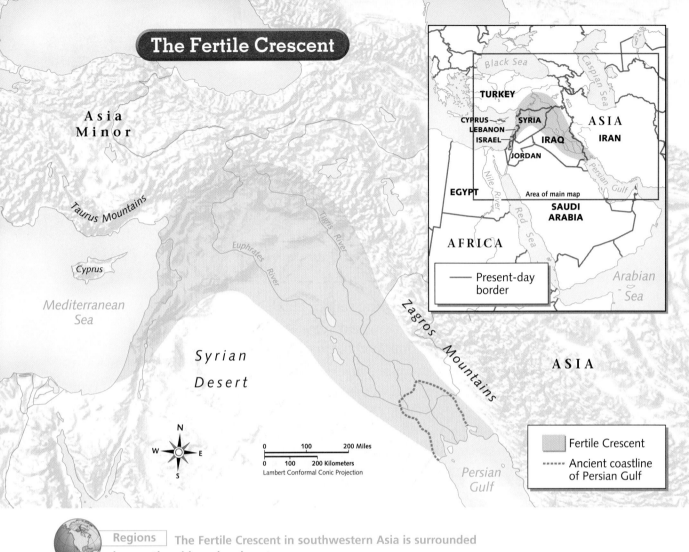

The Fertile Crescent

Asia Minor

Taurus Mountains

Cyprus

Mediterranean Sea

Euphrates River

Tigris River

Syrian Desert

Zagros Mountains

ASIA

Persian Gulf

N
W E
S

0 100 200 Miles
0 100 200 Kilometers
Lambert Conformal Conic Projection

Fertile Crescent
Ancient coastline of Persian Gulf

Black Sea
TURKEY
CYPRUS
LEBANON
ISRAEL
SYRIA
IRAQ
JORDAN
ASIA
IRAN
Caspian Sea
Nile River
Red Sea
Persian Gulf
EGYPT
Area of main map
SAUDI ARABIA
AFRICA
Arabian Sea

Present-day border

Regions The Fertile Crescent in southwestern Asia is surrounded by mostly arid, or dry, desert.

■ *What two large bodies of water also touch the Fertile Crescent?*

provided few different kinds of natural resources. The earliest people of the area found life there a challenge. Living as hunter-gatherers was a constant fight for survival.

Perhaps it was these challenges that led early people to turn to farming and to build settlements. Early people had to find a better way to get food in the hot, dry region. Caring for wild plants and growing their own plants seemed to be their best chance for survival. Although harsh, the region had what settlers needed to survive: water, and land on which food can grow.

REVIEW *What made settlement possible in Mesopotamia?*

Working with Water

Flowing through the Fertile Crescent, the Tigris and Euphrates rivers played an important role in shaping the lives of the people who lived nearby. The Euphrates is a slow, winding river with few **tributaries**, or branches. With its many curves, it stretches out for 1,250 miles (2,012 km). Unlike the Euphrates, the Tigris River moves rapidly along its 1,720-mile (2,768 km) course and has many tributaries.

The source of both rivers is high in the Taurus Mountains. The rivers flow downward through Mesopotamia's plateau to its area of plains. Finally the rivers join together and flow into the Persian Gulf.

The two rivers helped make it possible for early settlers to survive on the land alongside them. The two rivers often overflowed their banks, flooding the land. When the floodwaters drained back into the river, a layer of **silt**, a rich mixture of bits of rock and soil, remained. The silt made the land suitable for growing crops.

The Tigris and Euphrates rivers enriched the soil, but they could not be counted on to water the farmers' crops. Unfortunately, the rivers seldom flooded at the time farmers really needed water—when crops were first planted. In addition, it hardly ever rained over the land between the rivers, particularly in the south. **Droughts**, or long times with little or no rain, were common. During these times, the sun baked and hardened the clay soil.

The Tigris and Euphrates rivers provided a likely source for water. Farmers needed some way to get water to the land.

To get river water to their fields at just the right time, farmers had to learn to tame the Tigris and the Euphrates. To do this, they developed a system of irrigation. **Irrigation** is the use of connected ditches, canals, dams, and dikes to move water to dry areas. Irrigation allowed water from the Tigris and Euphrates rivers to be stored and used when needed. Farmers could now water their crops during dry months.

Irrigation also helped farmers prevent and control flooding. Exactly when the rivers would flood had always been impossible to predict. Often, the floods caught the early settlers completely by surprise. When the rivers did flood, the rush of water

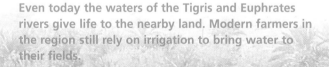

Even today the waters of the Tigris and Euphrates rivers give life to the nearby land. Modern farmers in the region still rely on irrigation to bring water to their fields.

The writing on this ancient clay tablet from Sumer lists crops of long ago.

Besides the main crops planted in fields, farmers grew vegetables such as onions and cucumbers in gardens. Their orchards produced fruits such as figs and apples.

Fields not suited for crops were used for grazing animals. On these fields shepherds herded goats, sheep, and cattle. These domesticated animals provided meat, milk products, and wool. Eventually the early people of Mesopotamia also used horses, camels, donkeys, and other animals to help them in their work.

REVIEW *What important crops were grown in ancient Mesopotamia?*

destroyed not only crops but shelters as well. Entire villages could be swept away. Sometimes many lives were lost. Irrigation allowed settlers to protect their villages. The canals and ditches carried away flood-waters that would have otherwise brought destruction.

REVIEW *What is irrigation and how did it affect the people of Mesopotamia?*

Farming in Mesopotamia

At the ruins of the city of Nippur in Mesopotamia, archaeologists found ancient clay tablets that tell about farming long ago. The tablets explain how farmers raised such crops as barley, wheat, and a wheat-like grain called emmer. Each spring farmers harvested their crops. After harvesting they threshed, or separated, the grain from the husk, or outer shell, of the plant. Threshing continued throughout the summer.

Civilization in Mesopotamia

| 4000 B.C. | 3000 B.C. | 2000 B.C. |

Main Idea As you read, think about the new ideas developed by the ancient societies of Mesopotamia.

Vocabulary

civilization
technology
ziggurat
government
city-state
monarchy
authority
surplus
merchant
social class
scribe
innovation

The world's earliest cities formed in Mesopotamia. As people began to live and work together in these cities, they formed a complex society, or civilization. A **civilization** is a centralized society with developed forms of religion, ways of governing, and learning. A civilization also depends on a stable food supply and on division of labor. Along with its many advances, city life also brought new problems. The need arose to find creative ways to solve them.

New Inventions

Farmers in the southern part of Mesopotamia, which was called Sumer (SOO•mer), used the Tigris and Euphrates rivers to water their crops. But when these rivers flooded the land without warning, the results could be disastrous. For people who depended on agriculture, the loss of crops meant starvation.

Using their knowledge of irrigation, farmers in Sumer built dikes and dug canals. Dikes, or walls made of earth, held the flooding rivers within their banks. Canals carried some of the extra water back to the rivers after floods. Reservoirs stored the remaining floodwater. Building dikes, canals, and reservoirs took special knowledge of making and using tools. The skills and knowledge to make products or meet goals is called **technology**. By about 3500 B.C. the early settlers of Sumer developed the technology to carry out successful agriculture and to build cities.

These gypsum statues show how one early artist pictured the Sumerians.

89

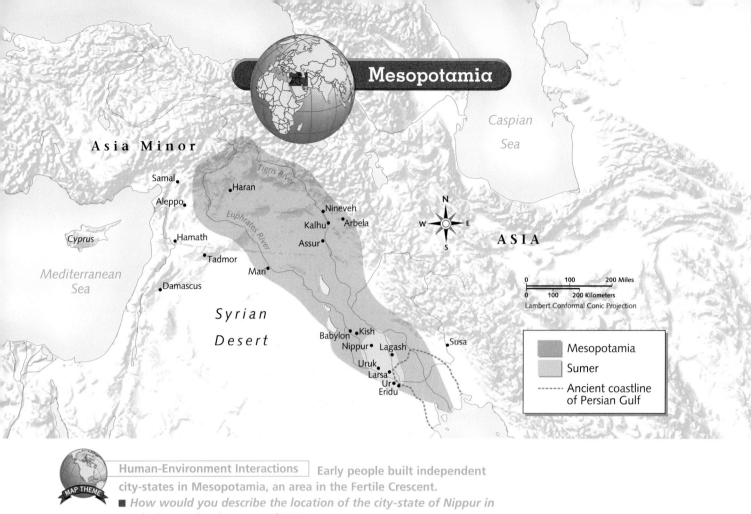

Mesopotamia

Asia Minor

Samal
Haran
Aleppo
Tigris River
Nineveh
Kalhu · Arbela
Assur
Hamath
Tadmor
Mari
Euphrates River

Cyprus

Mediterranean Sea

Damascus

Syrian Desert

Babylon · Kish
Nippur · Lagash
Uruk
Larsa
Ur
Eridu

Susa

Caspian Sea

ASIA

N
W · E
S

| 0 | 100 | 200 Miles |
| 0 | 100 | 200 Kilometers |

Lambert Conformal Conic Projection

Mesopotamia
Sumer
Ancient coastline of Persian Gulf

Human-Environment Interactions   Early people built independent city-states in Mesopotamia, an area in the Fertile Crescent.
■ *How would you describe the location of the city-state of Nippur in relation to the city-state of Ur?*

The technology of Sumer was greatly advanced by the use of the wheel, which may have been invented by an earlier people. Farmers in Sumer made their wheels by attaching boards together and rounding them off. To make the wheels last longer, the Sumerians covered the rims with pieces of copper.

Wheel technology made possible other inventions, including the wheeled cart.

With a wheeled cart, a domesticated animal such as an ox or a donkey could pull a heavy load. Wheeled carts were needed to move construction materials for houses and other buildings in Sumer's growing cities. To help them move goods and travel, the Sumerians also built some of the world's first sailboats.

REVIEW *What were two inventions that helped Sumerian people move things?*

Architecture and Religious Beliefs

The largest building in most Sumerian cities was a huge mud-brick temple called a **ziggurat** (ZIH•guh•rat). Some ziggurats stood as tall as a seven-story building. They towered above the houses like skyscrapers. To build such a large building required both planning and teamwork skills.

Builders constructed a ziggurat in layers, each one smaller than the one below. On the top of each ziggurat stood a shrine for the city's special god. Like other ancient people, the Sumerians believed in many gods.

The religious beliefs of the Sumerian people showed the importance of agriculture in their lives. They believed that if they pleased their gods, they would get large harvests in return. Floods and other natural disasters, they thought, were signs that the gods were angry with them. Chief among the gods of Sumer were Enlil, the god of wind, storm, and rain, and Ea, the god of the waters and of wisdom.

In time a ziggurat became more than a shrine for a god. The people in Sumer built smaller buildings around the base of the ziggurat. Some of these buildings had workshops for craftworkers. Other buildings were temples. The ziggurat was the center of activity in each city.

REVIEW *How did religion in Sumer reflect the importance of agriculture?*

A Ziggurat

LEARNING FROM DIAGRAMS
Ancient ziggurats towered above the landscape in Mesopotamia about 5,000 years ago. Even after many years of erosion, the Ziggurat Assur (left) still stands in what is now Iraq.

The Role of Government

Constructing dikes, canals, ziggurats, and other city buildings took large numbers of people. When large numbers of people live and work together, laws are needed to keep order. In large societies, such as the one in Sumer, the making of laws could be done only with a government. A **government** is an organized system that groups use to make laws and decisions.

Sumer was made up of several independent city-states. A **city-state** included a city and the farmlands around it. Each city-state had its own leaders and its own government. In early days each government was run by a small group of leaders and a chief leader chosen by that group. Together they made laws and decided what work had to be done.

The city-states of Sumer often waged war on outsiders and on each other to enlarge their farmland or to protect it. Wars were also fought over the right to use water supplies. In times of danger the group of leaders could not always agree on what to do. To provide stronger leadership, each Sumerian city-state formed a new kind of government. The new government of each city-state was a **monarchy**, in which one person had complete **authority**, or right, to rule in peacetime and to lead soldiers in wartime.

Sumerians called the rulers of their city-states "big men," or kings, because the rulers were always men. The Sumerian kings ruled over every part of Sumerian life, including religion, agriculture, and building plans.

The Sumerians believed that their gods selected the rulers. Because of this belief, Sumerian leaders were thought to have great strength and power. Many stories and legends tell about Sumerian leaders.

One of the oldest stories in the world is a story-poem from Sumerian times. It tells the adventures of a Sumerian king, Gilgamesh. The story praises Gilgamesh as "he who knew everything."

REVIEW *What kind of government did Sumerian city-states form to provide stronger leadership?*

BIOGRAPHY

Gilgamesh

Gilgamesh was probably a real king who ruled over the ancient Sumerian city-state of Uruk sometime between 2700 B.C. and 2500 B.C. As the years passed, he became a figure of legend. People described Gilgamesh as one-third man and two-thirds god. Stories of Gilgamesh and his adventures were passed on as oral tradition for centuries before being written down in about 2500 B.C. Today people still read about this hero.

Statue of Gilgamesh, made of terra-cotta

Changing Economies

Sumerian pitcher

By about 3000 B.C. some of the Sumerian city-states had grown to great size. For example, more than 60,000 people may have lived in the city-state of Uruk. This large population growth was made possible by the success of agriculture. Sumerian farms produced enough food to create a **surplus**, or extra supply, to feed the people who came to settle in Sumer.

Having a surplus led to a division of labor. Some people became craftworkers in stone, clay, cloth made of wool, and leather. Others became metalworkers, using copper and tin and later combining those metals to make bronze. With the addition of new products, some Sumerians became managers, people who were skilled at directing the work of others. Others became merchants. **Merchants** are people who buy and sell goods to make a living.

Sumerian merchants traded with merchants throughout the Fertile Crescent, even as far away as the Mediterranean Sea. The Sumerians traded what they had in surplus—wheat, barley, and copper tools such as axheads and plowheads. In return they got resources that they needed, including wood, salt, precious stones, and raw copper and tin.

REVIEW *What effect did a surplus of food have on life in Sumer?*

Divisions in Society

Over time, ancient Sumerian society became divided into **social classes**, or groups with different levels of importance. The highest social class in Sumer was made up of the king, priests, and other important leaders and their families.

Only a few of Sumer's people were leaders and priests. Most were members of the middle class. The social ranking of a person within this class was probably based on the amount of property owned or a family's standing in the community.

A division of labor meant that Sumerians held a variety of jobs. Some earned a living as merchants or managers. Others worked as carpenters, potters, bricklayers, doctors, or scribes. A **scribe** was a person who wrote things for others. Writing was a valuable skill in Sumer at a time when most people—including kings—could

This ancient model of a house shows what Sumerian living quarters may have looked like.

Development of Cuneiform

MEANING	PICTOGRAPH (About 3100 B.C.)	EARLY CUNEIFORM (About 1800 B.C.)	LATER CUNEIFORM (About 700 B.C.)
Sun			
Star			
Mountain			
Head			
Bird			
Grain			

LEARNING FROM TABLES Sumerian writing began with scribes (left) using picture symbols (above).
■ *In what columns do the symbols most resemble what they stand for?*

neither read nor write. Sumerian scribes kept records, wrote letters for other people, and copied down stories and songs. Scribes and other working people exchanged their services or the goods they made for the services and goods they needed.

Slaves made up the lowest class in Sumerian society. Most slaves were prisoners of war. Others were enslaved as punishment for crimes or to pay off debts. Slaves within Sumerian society were not enslaved for life. For example, those who owed a debt could gain their freedom when the debt was paid.

In all classes of Sumerian society, men had more authority and more rights than women. Men controlled their households and could divorce their wives for any reason. Men also held most of the leadership roles in Sumer.

However, women could serve as leaders and many did. Sumerian women often held high office as religious leaders. In fact, the female high priest at the ancient city-state of Ur was second in power only to the king. In addition, some Sumerian women were trained to be scribes.

For the most part women in ancient Sumer had more rights and freedoms than women in other ancient civilizations. Unlike in many early civilizations, the women of ancient Sumer were allowed to own property, divorce cruel husbands, and own businesses.

REVIEW *What kind of leadership role did women often fill?*

Innovations

The needs of a large, complex society led to further **innovations**, or new ways of doing things. The need to mark boundaries for farming in Sumer led to a unit of land measurement the Sumerians called the *iku*. Today we call it the *acre*.

The need to measure wheat and barley harvests established the quart as a basic unit of measurement. The need to carry trade goods up the river led people to build cargo boats with sails. The need to keep a record of ownership, taxes owed, and trade led to one of the Sumerians' greatest innovations—writing.

At first the scribes of Sumer marked picture symbols in pieces of wet clay and let the clay dry. They then attached these pieces to baskets as tags to identify the contents and the owner. By about 2000 B.C. the Sumerians had developed their symbols into a complete writing system. This system was based on *cuneiform* (kyoo•NEE•uh•fawrm), or wedge-shaped symbols. Each symbol stood for a different syllable and was based on a spoken sound.

To make the cuneiform marks in the soft clay, Sumerian scribes used a stylus, which they made by sharpening the end of a piece of reed. The clay was then baked or left in the sun until it was hard. Cuneiform writings that have been found give a record of Sumer's growing economic activity and way of life.

REVIEW *What innovations did the Sumerians develop?*

LESSON 2 REVIEW

4000 B.C.	3000 B.C.	2000 B.C.
	About 3500 B.C. • Sumerian city-states begin	**About 2000 B.C.** • Development of cuneiform

Check Understanding

1 **Remember the Facts**   What new type of government was formed in Mesopotamia?

2 **Recall the Main Idea**   How did the need for organization affect the development of city-states in Sumer?

Think Critically

3 **Cause and Effect**   What effect did a food surplus have on early Sumerian civilization?

4 **Think More About It**   How might our understanding of the Sumerians be different if they had never developed writing?

5 **Past to Present**   Which of the problems faced by people in Sumer are similar to problems people face in the United States today?

Show What You Know
News-Writing Activity
Prepare a news story that describes what might have happened in Sumer when an innovation was introduced. For example, you might tell about the invention of the wheel. Set up your news story as it might look if it appeared in a real newspaper. You may include illustrations. Display your completed news story in your classroom.

FOCUS

Why are laws important today?

Main Idea   As you read, look for ways in which early civilizations protected themselves and kept order within their societies.

Vocabulary

conquer
empire
emperor
taxation
Code of Hammurabi
equal justice

Conquests and Empires

2500 B.C.	1500 B.C.	500 B.C.

As city-states all over Mesopotamia kept growing in area and population, conflict among them increased. City-states competed with one another to control fertile land and water sources. Soon people were fighting wars to **conquer**, or take over, the lands of others.

Causes and Effects of Conflict

Most wars among early agricultural societies such as those in Mesopotamia were fought to protect farmland and water rights. A Sumerian saying warned of how unstable ownership was: "You can go and carry off the enemy's land; the enemy comes and carries off your land."

The land between the Tigris and Euphrates rivers was flat. No natural boundaries such as mountains separated one city-state from another. Without natural boundaries, city-states put up pillars to mark their borders. When one city-state moved or destroyed another city-state's pillars, it "violated both the decree [orders] of the gods and the word given by man to man." Such acts often led to war.

As more disagreements about land and water arose, more wars were fought. The need for weapons resulted in new technology. Craftworkers created new inventions such as war chariots. A war chariot was a light, two-wheeled cart pulled by horses. From a fast-moving war chariot, a soldier could speed by and throw

This Sumerian helmet was hammered from a single sheet of gold. About 4,500 years old, the helmet was uncovered in the royal cemetery of the ancient city of Ur.

This scene from the *Standard of Ur* shows ancient Mesopotamians in battle.

spears or shoot arrows at an enemy who was on foot. The new war technologies meant that more people died in battle.

REVIEW *What was the major cause of wars among the people of Mesopotamia?*

Sargon the Conqueror

The first known conqueror in Mesopotamia was a warrior named Sargon. He was born to a nomadic people who lived in northern Mesopotamia. As a young man he served as an official in the Sumerian city-state of Kish. Sargon later killed the king of Kish and took control of the city-state. Sargon gathered an army and marched through Mesopotamia, establishing an empire. An **empire** is a conquered land of many peoples and places governed by one ruler. Sargon

Mesopotamian ruler, possibly Sargon

became the region's first **emperor**, or ruler of the empire.

In the middle of his empire, Sargon built a capital city called Akkad (AH•kahd). His empire and its people came to be known as Akkadian. Though the Akkadians were not

Chapter 2 • **97**

2500 B.C.	2000 B.C.	1500 B.C.	1000 B.C.	500 B.C.
About 2350 B.C. • Sargon establishes the Akkadian Empire	**About 1790 B.C.** • Hammurabi becomes king of Babylon	**By 1750 B.C.** • Hammurabi conquers and reunites most of Mesopotamia	**721 B.C.** • Assyria conquers the kingdom of Israel	

LEARNING FROM TIME LINES Many rulers fought for control of ancient Mesopotamia between 2500 B.C. and 500 B.C.
■ *Which of these rulers reigned longest ago?*

Sumerians, they adopted the Sumerian culture as their own. As a sign of his conquest over the huge area, Sargon ordered every boundary pillar and city wall torn down.

For the next 55 years Sargon ruled over his empire. He maintained his rule both by force and by organization. Sargon was probably one of the first kings in Mesopotamia to set up a standing army made up of paid soldiers who served for a long period of time. Before that time, people became soldiers only in time of war. Sargon also appointed loyal nobles as governors to control conquered cities.

Sargon was an effective ruler and his empire was well organized. By about 2300 B.C. the Akkadian Empire stretched from what is now Iran westward to the Mediterranean Sea. When the empire finally weakened, the Mesopotamian city-states found themselves caught between two strong centers of power—Assyria (uh•SIR•ee•uh) and Babylonia (ba•buh•LOH•nyuh).

REVIEW *Why did Sargon tear down boundary pillars and city walls?*

Hammurabi the Lawgiver

Between 1790 and 1750 B.C. Hammurabi (hah•muh•RAH•bee), king of the city-state of Babylon, conquered and reunited most of Mesopotamia and the upper valley of the Tigris and Euphrates rivers. In doing this, he created a large empire. This empire became known as the Babylonian Empire.

Like Sargon, Hammurabi was more than a military leader. He improved each city-state under his rule by promoting trade, building projects, and keeping up dikes and canals. Under his rule, Babylon thrived as a center for trade.

One of Hammurabi's most important achievements was his reorganization of Mesopotamia's system of **taxation**. Under a system of taxation, people are required to pay taxes to support the government. Hammurabi made changes to the tax system to ensure that all the people of Mesopotamia paid their share. Tax collectors traveled throughout the region, collecting tax money. The money collected paid for all of Hammurabi's improvements.

Perhaps Hammurabi is best remembered for the work he did with the laws of his land. Each city-state had long had its own set of laws, or rules. Hammurabi collected all these laws, sorted through them, and came up with one complete listing of laws. The collection of laws compiled by the Babylonian leader is known as the **Code of Hammurabi**.

Hammurabi's collection consisted of 282 laws that dealt with almost every part of daily life. The laws covered such topics as marriage, divorce, adoption, slaves, murder, stealing, military service, land, business, loans, prices, and wages. Almost no area was overlooked.

The old laws were complicated and often unfair. The Code of Hammurabi explained the laws in clear statements and set standard punishments.

Some of the laws within the Code of Hammurabi followed the idea of "an eye for an eye." These laws explained that whoever caused an injury should be punished with that same injury. This means that a person who broke someone's arm in a fight would be punished by having his or her arm broken.

From the Code of Hammurabi

In this part of the Code of Hammurabi, the ruler describes his role as king and gives some reasons for creating the code.

I am Hammurabi, noble king. . . . I put an end to wars, I enhanced the well-being of the land. . . . I held the people of the lands of Sumer and Akkad safely. . . . They prospered under my protective spirit, I maintained them in peace, with my skillful wisdom I sheltered them.

In order that the mighty not wrong the weak. . . . I have inscribed my precious pronouncements [laws] upon my stela and set it up . . . in the city of Babylon . . . in order to render the judgments of the land, to give the verdicts of the land, and to provide just ways for the wronged.

On this stela, or stone marker, Hammurabi stands before the Babylonian sun god. Hammurabi's laws are carved into the base of the stela.

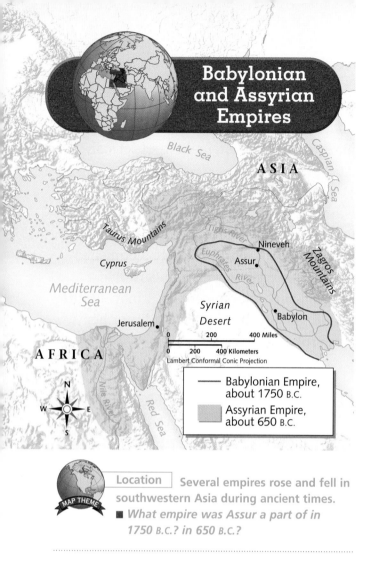

Babylonian and Assyrian Empires

Black Sea

ASIA

Taurus Mountains

Tigris River

Euphrates River

Cyprus

Nineveh

Assur

Zagros Mountains

Mediterranean Sea

Syrian Desert

Jerusalem

Babylon

AFRICA

Nile River

Red Sea

0   200   400 Miles

0   200   400 Kilometers
Lambert Conformal Conic Projection

N   W   E   S

— Babylonian Empire, about 1750 B.C.

▨ Assyrian Empire, about 650 B.C.

Location Several empires rose and fell in southwestern Asia during ancient times.

■ *What empire was Assur a part of in 1750 B.C.? in 650 B.C.?*

Not all Hammurabi's laws offered "an eye for an eye" punishment. Some laws outlined specific fines for crimes. Others imposed a penalty of death.

In describing the purpose of his code, Hammurabi explained that he wrote it

66 To cause justice to prevail . . .
To destroy the wicked . . .
To enlighten the land and to further the welfare of the people. 99

In addition to putting together a code of laws, Hammurabi introduced the idea of **equal justice**, or fair treatment under the law. His equal justice, however, was limited to equality within each social class. Under the Code of Hammurabi, leaders, priests,

and the wealthy were often favored over other people.

Hammurabi's code lasted over the years, but the leader's empire did not. By 1600 B.C. the Babylonians, too, had been conquered by another people.

REVIEW *What is an "eye for an eye" law?*

The Assyrians in Mesopotamia

After the collapse of Hammurabi's Babylonian Empire, Mesopotamia was ruled by several different groups of people. Around 1600 B.C. the Kassites, from what is now the country of Iran, claimed the region. The Kassites ruled Mesopotamia for more than 400 years. Eventually the Assyrian Empire gained control of the region. This empire included lands that lay outside of Mesopotamia, such as parts of present-day Turkey, Egypt, and the Persian Gulf.

Assyria was a region of rolling hills between the Tigris River and the Zagros Mountains in northern Mesopotamia. Some Assyrians lived in cities, of which the most important were Assur, Kalhu, and Nineveh. Around each city were many small farming villages.

The Assyrians had a great desire to control trade routes in southwestern Asia. By conquering neighboring lands, they could better meet this goal. Advancing in war chariots, the Assyrians conquered their neighbors one by one. They continued to claim land until their empire covered much of southwestern Asia.

After completing their conquest, the Assyrians worked to bring the people of their many lands together. They began building a system of roads throughout their empire.

During this time, the Assyrians made many improvements to their city of Nineveh. Throughout the city many new buildings rose, including a magnificent palace. Nineveh's new buildings dazzled with stone carvings.

In time the mighty Assyrian Empire was brought down. In 612 B.C. the Medes attacked Nineveh and killed its king. The Medes came from Media, a land

This stela shows Assyrian warriors riding a chariot into battle.

that was located in what is now north-western Iran. A writer who may have lived near Nineveh described the fall of the city. The description offers evidence of how violent this age of conquest was.

66 Woe to the bloody city! . . .
The noise of a whip and the
noise of rattling wheels,
And of the prancing horses,
and of leaping chariots.
The horseman lifts up the
bright sword and glittering
spear,
And there is a multitude
slain. . . . 99

REVIEW *Why did the Assyrians seek more land?*

LESSON 3 REVIEW

2500 B.C.		1500 B.C.		500 B.C.

About 2350 B.C.
• Sargon establishes Akkadian Empire

1750 B.C.
• Hammurabi builds an empire

Check Understanding

1 **Remember the Facts**   What collection of "an eye for an eye" laws was developed in Babylon?

2 **Recall the Main Idea**   How did the people of Mesopotamia maintain order and protect themselves from outsiders?

Think Critically

3 **Think More About It**   Most people living today would consider some of Hammurabi's punishments to be cruel. Why do you think that the Code of

Hammurabi was so well accepted by people living long ago?

4 **Past to Present**   What kinds of laws in your community do you consider the most important? Why?

Show What You Know
Brainstorming Activity
Hammurabi wrote a code of laws that seemed fair for his time. In a group, write a short code of rules for the students in your school. Include consequences that seem fair for your time. Discuss your rules with other groups.

Compare Maps with

1. Why Learn This Skill?

Throughout this book you will see many different kinds of maps. Some maps show the sizes and shapes of countries differently. You may wonder why this is so.

Over the centuries Arab, Chinese, and European mapmakers have developed different ways to show the round Earth in the form of a flat map. These different representations of the Earth are called **projections**. Each projection has its own name, such as Robinson Projection or Mollweide Projection.

Every map projection has **distortions**, or parts that are not accurate. This is because the shape of the round Earth needs to be split or stretched to make it flat. Identifying these distortions will help you understand how map projections can best be used.

2. Map Projections and Their Uses

Different kinds of map projections have different kinds of distortions. Some map projections distort the shape or the size of the area shown. Some show distances to be greater or less than they actually are. One way that mapmakers classify map projections is by the properties that are distorted the least.

Map A is an equal-area projection. Notice that there is equal area on either side of the equator and on either side of the prime meridian. An **equal-area projection** shows the sizes of regions in correct relation to one another, but it distorts shapes. Because an equal-area projection shows correct size relations of regions, it is useful for

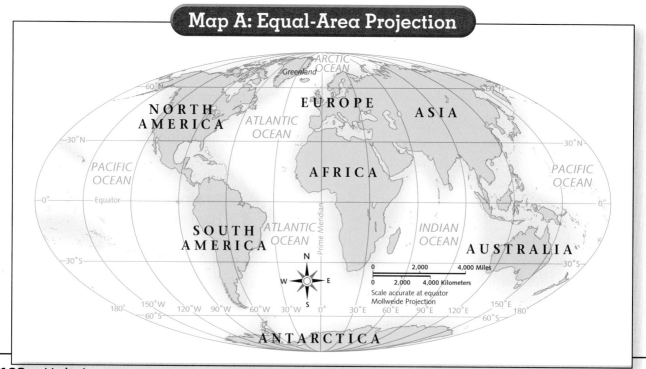

Map A: Equal-Area Projection

Different Projections

comparing information about different parts of the world.

Map B is a conformal projection. A **conformal projection** shows directions correctly, but it distorts sizes, especially of places near the poles. On Map B the lines of longitude are all an equal distance apart. On a globe the lines of longitude get closer together as they near the poles, where they meet. Also notice on Map B that the lines of latitude closer to the poles are farther apart. On a globe the lines of latitude are an equal distance apart. The Mercator projection, shown on Map B, is just one example of a conformal projection. Map C on page 104 is an example of a Robinson projection, a

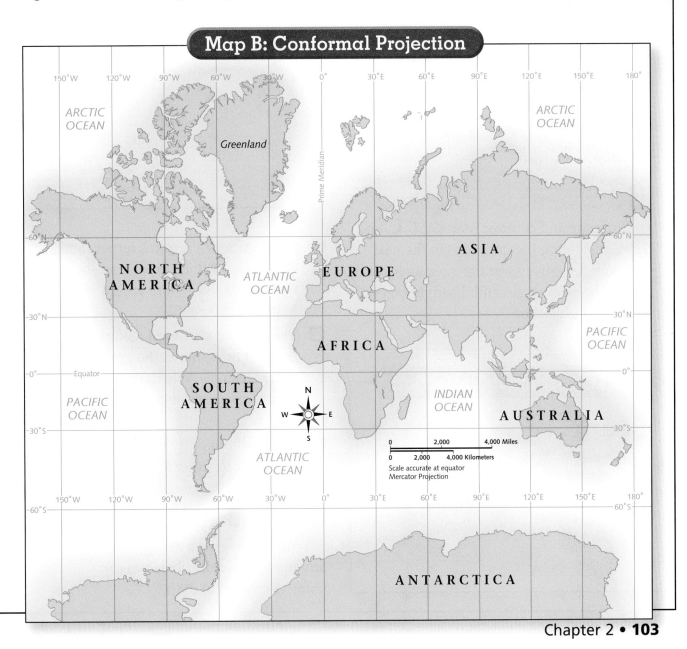

Map B: Conformal Projection

0   2,000   4,000 Miles
0   2,000   4,000 Kilometers
Scale accurate at equator
Mercator Projection

combination of equal-area and conformal projections.

Map D, which appears on this page, is an **equidistant projection**. It shows accurate distances from a central point. Any place on Earth can be chosen as the central point. When one of the poles is the chosen central point, the map is called a **polar projection**. Either the North Pole or the South Pole can be the center of a polar projection. Notice on Map D that the North Pole is at the center. Map D is both a polar projection and an equidistant projection. The lines of latitude appear as circles, and the circles farther from the center are larger. Lines of longitude on Map D appear as straight lines that extend from the center in all directions like the spokes of a wheel.

3. Understand the Process

Compare and contrast Maps A, B, C, and D by answering the questions in the next column. As you answer the questions, think about the advantages and disadvantages of each map projection.

Map C: Robinson Projection

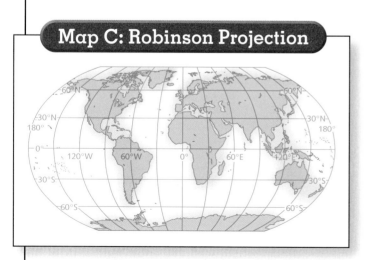

Map D: Equidistant Projection

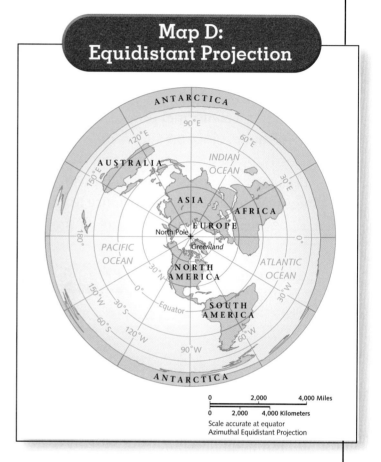

0   2,000   4,000 Miles
0   2,000   4,000 Kilometers
Scale accurate at equator
Azimuthal Equidistant Projection

❶ South America is much larger than Greenland. Which projection shows Greenland's *size* more accurately, Map A or Map B?

❷ The greatest east-west distance in Africa is about the same as the greatest north-south distance. Which projection shows Africa's *shape* more accurately, Map A or Map B?

❸ On which maps do the lines of longitude get closer together toward both poles?

4. Think and Apply

Write a paragraph about the advantages and disadvantages of using each kind of map.

The Ancient Israelites

2000 B.C.　　1500 B.C.　　1000 B.C.　　500 B.C.

FOCUS
What changes have individuals and groups brought about in your community?

Main Idea　As you read, look for the ways in which the Israelites contributed to change.

Vocabulary
monotheism
covenant
Exodus
Ten Commandments
Judaism
Torah
Sabbath
exile
Diaspora
synagogue

Between 2000 B.C. and 500 B.C., small kingdoms arose in southwestern Asia. Among them was the kingdom of the Israelites, the ancestors of the Jewish people. The Israelites contributed greatly to the religious and cultural ideas of ancient peoples of southwestern Asia. Many people look to the Hebrew Bible, or the Old Testament, as the source for information about the Israelites. Modern scholars, using the Bible, other ancient writings, and archaeological findings, have added to our understanding of these people.

Abraham

Many people all over the world trace their identity as a people to a man named Abram. Scholars believe that Abram may have lived at about the time of Hammurabi. According to the Bible, Abram was born in the Sumerian city of Ur.

The Mesopotamians, like most early people, worshipped many gods. They prayed to one god for water, another god for good harvests, and still another for both love and war. The Mesopotamians also thought of the sun, the moon, and the winds as gods.

Unlike their neighbors Abram and his family worshipped one God. Belief in one God is called **monotheism**. According to the Bible, God spoke to Abram, saying, "Leave your country, your people, and your father's house and go to the land I will show you."

Abram left southern Mesopotamia and traveled north to Haran along with his family. After living for a while in

Jewish people today read from the Torah, just as their ancestors, the ancient Israelites, did.

Chapter 2 • 105

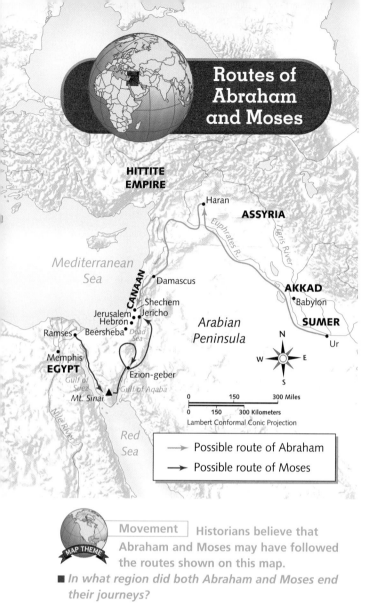

Routes of Abraham and Moses

HITTITE EMPIRE

Haran

ASSYRIA

Euphrates R.

Tigris River

Mediterranean Sea

CANAAN

Damascus

Shechem

Jerusalem • Jericho

Hebron

Beersheba • Dead Sea

Ramses

Arabian Peninsula

AKKAD

Babylon

SUMER

Ur

Memphis

EGYPT

Gulf of Suez

Ezion-geber

Gulf of Aqaba

Mt. Sinai

N W E S

0   150   300 Miles
0   150   300 Kilometers
Lambert Conformal Conic Projection

Red Sea

Nile River

→ Possible route of Abraham
→ Possible route of Moses

Movement Historians believe that Abraham and Moses may have followed the routes shown on this map.

■ *In what region did both Abraham and Moses end their journeys?*

Haran, Abram and his family continued their journey. This time they traveled first west and then south into the land of Canaan until they reached a place called Shechem (SHEH•kuhm). It was there, according to the Bible, that Abram heard God say, "I will give this land to your children." The Bible tells that Abram made a **covenant**, or special agreement, with God. In the covenant, Abram promised to be faithful to God and God promised to give Abram's descendants the land of Canaan. As a sign of his promise, Abram changed his name to Abraham. The name means "father of many nations." Abraham became known

as the father of the Jewish people through his son Isaac and the father of the Arab people through his son Ishmael.

REVIEW *How did Abraham's religious beliefs differ from the beliefs of other people of Mesopotamia?*

Moses and the Ten Commandments

Abraham's son Isaac had a son called Jacob. Jacob, who also became known as Israel, had 12 sons. All of Jacob's descendants, including his sons, became known as Israelites. Each son led a separate Israelite tribe.

When famine came to their land, many Israelites left there for Egypt, where food was available. The Israelites found not only food but also work during their early years in Egypt. Later, however, Egyptian rulers enslaved the Israelites.

In about 1225 B.C. Moses, a leader of the Israelites, led a revolt against the Egyptians. Many enslaved Israelites followed Moses from Egypt, across the Red Sea, through the desert, and back toward Canaan. This journey is known as the **Exodus**. The word *exodus* is sometimes used today to describe any large movement or migration of people. The story of the Exodus is retold by Jews around the world during the Jewish holiday of Passover.

The Exodus was filled with hardships and took many years. Moses and the Israelites often faced lack of water and food during the journey. The Israelites also had disagreements with each other.

The Bible says that during the Exodus God instructed Moses to climb a mountain in the Sinai desert. There God gave Moses the **Ten Commandments**, a set of laws for responsible behavior.

THE TEN COMMANDMENTS

According to the Bible, God spoke to Moses, and these were his words:

1 I am the Lord your God, who brought you out of Egypt, out of the land of slavery. You shall have no other gods before me.

2 You shall not make for yourself an idol in the form of anything in heaven above or on the earth beneath or in the waters below. . . .

3 You shall not misuse the name of the Lord your God, for the Lord will not hold anyone guiltless who misuses his name.

4 Remember the Sabbath day by keeping it holy. Six days you shall labor and do all your work, but the seventh day is a Sabbath to the Lord your God. On that day you shall not do any work. . . .

5 Honor your father and your mother. . . .

6 You shall not murder.

7 You shall not commit adultery.

8 You shall not steal.

9 You shall not give false testimony against your neighbor.

10 You shall not covet your neighbor's house . . . or anything that belongs to your neighbor.

Exodus 20:2-17
(Source: The New International Version of the Bible)

The Ten Commandments became an important part of **Judaism**—the religion of the Jewish people—and later of Christianity and Islam. Judaism teaches that God is just and that God's qualities must be imitated. In Judaism, a person's service to God is measured by how many good things he or she has done for other people.

The stories of Abraham, Moses, the Exodus, and the return to Canaan are in the first five books of the Hebrew Bible. The first five books are also sometimes called the Five Books of Moses. Jewish people refer to these five books as the **Torah**. Genesis, the first book of the Torah, tells of many of the important ideas introduced by the Israelites. For example, the **Sabbath**, a day of rest after a week of work, appears for the first time in the story of creation at the beginning of the book of Genesis.

REVIEW *What set of rules became an important part of three major religions?*

Israel and Judah

After the Israelites returned to Canaan, they set up their own country and named it the Land of Israel. Saul became Israel's first king in about 1020 B.C. King Saul was followed by King David, who built up the capital city at Jerusalem. After David's death in 961 B.C., his son Solomon became king.

The Ten Commandments are just one part of the Torah, writings holy to the Jewish religion. The Torah cover at left was made during the eighteenth century.

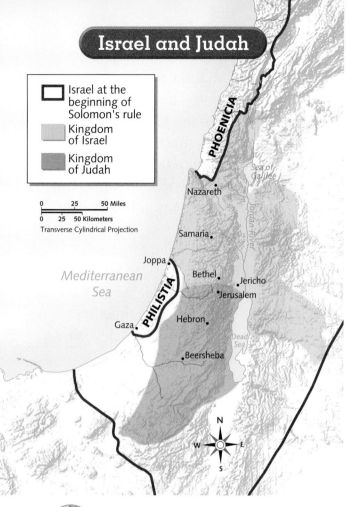

Israel and Judah

Israel at the beginning of Solomon's rule

Kingdom of Israel

Kingdom of Judah

0 25 50 Miles
0 25 50 Kilometers
Transverse Cylindrical Projection

PHOENICIA

Mediterranean Sea

Sea of Galilee

Jordan River

Dead Sea

PHILISTIA

Nazareth

Samaria

Joppa

Bethel

Jericho

Jerusalem

Gaza

Hebron

Beersheba

N W E S

Place The land of Israel divided into two parts, the kingdom of Israel and the kingdom of Judah.

■ Which kingdom would have been more likely to transport goods by water?

King Solomon became known for his great wisdom.

"Solomon's wisdom excelled the wisdom of all the children of the east country," says the Bible. Under King Solomon the Israelites built a large temple in Jerusalem to worship God.

After Solomon's time Israel was divided into two parts, north and south. The northern kingdom, made up of ten of the twelve tribes, kept the name Israel. The southern kingdom, with little more than two tribes, was called Judah. Its people were known as Judaeans. The kingdom of Israel lasted until 721 B.C., when it was conquered by the Assyrians. Judah lasted until 586 B.C., when it was defeated by the Babylonians. The Babylonians destroyed the temple in Jerusalem and broke down the walls of the city. They enslaved the Judaeans and forced them to go to Babylonia and live in **exile**. A person in exile may not return to his or her home country. In 539 B.C., Babylonia was conquered by Persia. The Persians allowed the Judaeans to return to Judah and to rebuild the city walls and the temple in Jerusalem.

BIOGRAPHY

David
About 1025 B.C.–960 B.C.

King David is admired by Jews, Christians, and Muslims alike. David was born in Bethlehem. While growing up, he cared for his father's sheep. In the fields David learned to worship God through music. He played a stringed instrument and sang praises to God. David wrote many religious songs called psalms, which are recorded in the Bible's Book of Psalms. The Bible also describes events in David's life. One well-known Bible story tells how David killed Goliath, a fearsome enemy, using a sling. Later, King David expanded his kingdom by victories and treaties.

Ancient stone carving of a man using a sling

When the Judaeans returned they found no trace of the Israelites. The ten tribes had vanished completely. Scholars believe the Israelites may have been sold into slavery.

Later the Judaeans were conquered by the Romans. Judah became known as Judaea. While under Roman rule, the Judaeans completed their second temple. In A.D. 70, however, the Romans destroyed it. Later, around A.D. 130, the Romans ordered the Judaeans to leave Jerusalem. Judaea and the land around it became the Roman province of Palestine.

REVIEW *In which city did King David build his capital?*

Movement Through the World

Ever since the Babylonian exile, Jews have settled in places outside Israel. Through the centuries they moved to nearly every country in the world. The settling of Jews outside of Israel is called the **Diaspora**. The word *diaspora* comes from the Greek word for "sowing," as in the spreading of seeds.

Strabo, a Greek geographer who lived at the end of the first century B.C., wrote this about the world's early Jews:

66 [They] are scattered in all the towns, and it is difficult to find a place in all the inhabited world which has not received them. . . . 99

During the Babylonian exile, the Judaeans realized that they did not need to be near the temple in Jerusalem to worship God. Wherever groups of Jews settled, they built houses of worship. Today Jewish houses of worship, or **synagogues** (SIH•nuh•gahgz), can be found in many different parts of the world.

REVIEW *What is the Diaspora?*

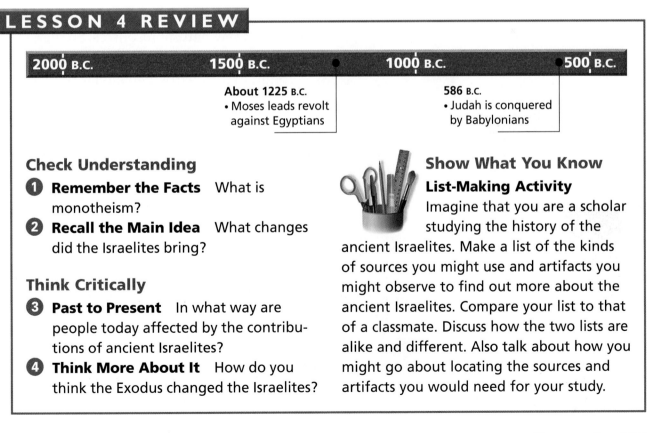

LESSON 4 REVIEW

2000 B.C.   1500 B.C.   1000 B.C.   500 B.C.

About 1225 B.C.
• Moses leads revolt against Egyptians

586 B.C.
• Judah is conquered by Babylonians

Check Understanding

1 **Remember the Facts** What is monotheism?

2 **Recall the Main Idea** What changes did the Israelites bring?

Think Critically

3 **Past to Present** In what way are people today affected by the contributions of ancient Israelites?

4 **Think More About It** How do you think the Exodus changed the Israelites?

Show What You Know

List-Making Activity
Imagine that you are a scholar studying the history of the ancient Israelites. Make a list of the kinds of sources you might use and artifacts you might observe to find out more about the ancient Israelites. Compare your list to that of a classmate. Discuss how the two lists are alike and different. Also talk about how you might go about locating the sources and artifacts you would need for your study.

The Phoenicians and the Lydians

1500 B.C.	1000 B.C.	500 B.C.

FOCUS

What new technology or innovations have changed the lives of people you know?

Main Idea As you read, think about the ways Phoenician and Lydian innovations changed the lives of people living in southwestern Asia.

Vocabulary

colony
cultural diffusion
barter
money economy

Gold and bronze statue of the Phoenician god Baal. Here he is pictured as a young warrior, raising his arm to throw a lightning spear.

Ancient cultures all over southwestern Asia developed many new ways to improve their lives. Between 2000 B.C. and 500 B.C., the Phoenician (fih•NEE•shuhn) and Lydian (LIH•dee•uhn) cultures contributed important innovations that related to trade. Although their cultures never became large empires, their contributions to history continue to live on today.

The Alphabet

In the northwestern part of the Fertile Crescent lay Phoenicia. Phoenicia consisted of a loose union of city-states, each governed by a king. Phoenicia had little land to farm and few natural resources. So the people of Phoenicia traded cedar wood found in the nearby Lebanon Mountains to get the food and other supplies they needed. To reach trade ports, they built ships and sailed the Mediterranean Sea. The Phoenicians were skilled shipbuilders and masters of navigation. They even learned to use the North Star to guide their ships at night.

For hundreds of years the Phoenicians sailed the waters of the Mediterranean Sea and beyond. They traveled through the Strait of Gibraltar to Morocco and possibly north to Britain, in search of metals, ivory, and other goods they could not find at home.

Between 1000 B.C. and 700 B.C., the ancient Phoenicians began to establish colonies all over the Mediterranean region. A **colony** is a settlement separate from, but under the control of, a home country. Phoenician colonies around the Mediterranean served as rest stops for sailors traveling on long sea voyages. The colonies also provided trade links between civilizations in Africa and Europe.

One such colony was Carthage in northern Africa. The Phoenicians settled Carthage in about 814 B.C. The colony of Carthage quickly grew into a successful trading port, linking Africa with the Mediterranean. Carthage eventually grew so independent that it split away from Phoenician control. However, the Phoenician influence in Carthage continued to spread through trade.

Phoenicia's location between the Mediterranean and the Fertile Crescent brought it into contact with many other cultures. The Phoenicians modeled their civilization after those of the many different peoples with whom they traded. They borrowed ideas from the Egyptians, the Babylonians, and other trading partners.

One idea that the Phoenicians borrowed was the alphabet. However, the Phoenicians changed the writing systems they borrowed from. They trimmed the alphabet to just 22 letters. Each letter stood for a single consonant sound. By simplifying the alphabet, the Phoenicians made it easier to learn to write. More and more people began to master the art of writing. No longer was writing limited to scribes. Later the ancient Greeks borrowed the Phoenician alphabet to shape their own. The Greek alphabet is the base of many modern alphabets, including the English alphabet.

Development of the Alphabet

EGYPTIAN (About 3000 B.C.)	PHOENICIAN (About 1000 B.C.)	GREEK (About 600 B.C.)	PRESENT-DAY
𓃾	K	A	A
⊓	𐤁	B	B
◻	△	△	D
⌁	𐤆	I	I, J
⌐	𐤋	∧	L
∿∿∿	𐤌	M	M
⬭	𐤍	Γ	P
X	+	T	T
Υ	Υ	Υ	Y
⊳•⊲	I	Z	Z

LEARNING FROM TABLES The Phoenician alphabet was an important step in the development of many present-day alphabets.
■ *Which Phoenician letters look most like letters in our alphabet today?*

The Phoenicians used their improved alphabet in their businesses to record trade agreements and to write bills. Knowledge of the alphabet spread quickly among the Phoenician colonies and to other Mediterranean cultures. The spreading of new ideas to other places is called **cultural diffusion**.

REVIEW *How did the use of the Phoenician alphabet spread?*

Phoenician Purple

The Phoenicians are remembered not only for their alphabet but also for a color. In the coastal waters of Phoenicia lived a certain kind of mollusk, a sea animal with a hard shell. Phoenicians in the city-state of Tyre used this mollusk to make a purple dye called Tyrian purple. Kings often wore clothes dyed this beautiful color. Soon purple came to be thought of as a royal color. Some leaders even ordered that only they could wear it. The Phoenicians' sea trade grew as more and more rulers demanded Tyrian purple. Over time the dye became very closely connected with the land where it was made. In fact, the name *Phoenician* comes from a Greek word for a reddish purple.

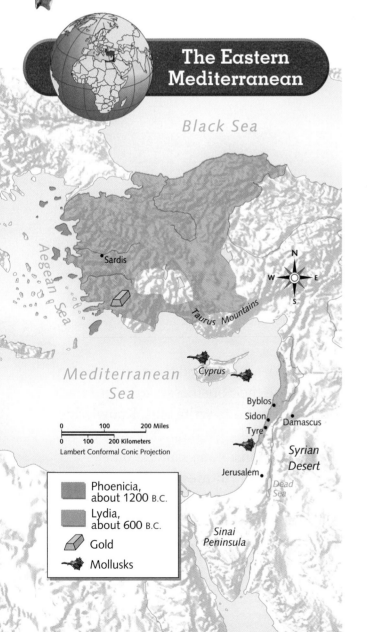

The Eastern Mediterranean

Black Sea

Aegean Sea

•Sardis

Taurus Mountains

N W E S

Mediterranean Sea

Cyprus

Byblos•
Sidon• •Damascus
Tyre•
Syrian Desert

Jerusalem•

Dead Sea

Sinai Peninsula

0   100   200 Miles
0   100   200 Kilometers
Lambert Conformal Conic Projection

■ Phoenicia, about 1200 B.C.
■ Lydia, about 600 B.C.
▱ Gold
🐚 Mollusks

Coined Money

The Lydians lived in an area northwest of Phoenicia in what is today the country of Turkey. Like the Phoenicians, the Lydians made a major contribution to the people of the Fertile Crescent. Theirs, too, was related to trade. Around 600 B.C. the Lydians became the first people to use coined money put out by their government.

As people around the Mediterranean began to trade with one another, they needed a kind of money. Its value had to be agreed on, and it had to be light enough to be carried on ships without sinking them. The first Lydian coins were the size of beans. They were made of a naturally occurring mixture of gold and silver called electrum. All the coins were the same weight and, therefore, had the same value.

Long before coined money, traders had relied on **barter**, the exchange of one good

Movement The ideas of the Lydians and Phoenicians influenced the peoples around them.

■ *Why do you think ideas traveled freely among peoples of the eastern Mediterranean?*

or service for another. The problem with barter was that two people could make a deal only if each had a good or a service that the other wanted. After a while, traders worked out a system of trading based on weighing silver. This system also proved difficult to use. Coined money meant that people no longer had to weigh silver each time they made a trade. The purity of the silver in coined money was also certain.

The use of money allowed traders to set prices for various goods and services. Societies could then develop a **money economy**, an economic system based on the use of money.

REVIEW *How did the use of coined money change trade?*

ECONOMICS

Money

After the Lydians, other cultures began to make coins for use in trading. However, some people began to shave off bits of gold and silver from the coins. These shaved coins were still used at their original value. Yet they were really worth less because they weighed less. To stop this, governments began to require that coins be milled, or cut several times along their edges. People were then able to identify the less valuable shaved coins as ones with smooth edges. They now knew whether they were getting their money's worth.

Lydian coins, made around 600 B.C.

LESSON 5 REVIEW

1500 B.C.	1000 B.C.	500 B.C.

About 1000 B.C.
• Phoenician alphabet

About 600 B.C.
• Lydian government issues coined money

Check Understanding

1 Remember the Facts What did the Phoenicians and the Lydians each contribute to the civilization of southwestern Asia?

2 Recall the Main Idea How did the innovations of the Phoenicians and Lydians change the lives of people in southwestern Asia?

Think Critically

3 Think More About It What were some of the advantages of a written alphabet and coined money?

4 Past to Present How do the contributions made by the Phoenicians and the Lydians affect our lives today?

Show What You Know

Speech Activity Imagine that you are a trader in 600 B.C. Choose either the Phoenician alphabet or Lydian coined money. With a partner, prepare a speech to persuade people who have never heard of the innovation to adopt it. Practice your speech out loud. Then, with your partner, present it to your class.

Compare Information

1. Why Learn This Skill?

The Phoenicians sailed the waters of the Mediterranean to trade cedar and purple dye for goods they did not have. They were among the most successful traders of their day. Imagine that you want to prepare a report on world trade today. You need to show a lot of information in a brief and clear way. One way you might do this is by making graphs. A **graph** is a diagram that shows relations between numbers. Knowing how to read and make graphs will help you see and compare large amounts of information.

2. Bar, Circle, and Line Graphs

Different kinds of graphs show information in different ways. A **bar graph**, which is made up of different-sized bars, is especially useful for quick comparisons. Notice that the bars on the graph titled Selected U.S. Exports are horizontal, or go from left to right. Bar graphs can be vertical, too, with the bars going from bottom to top.

A **circle graph**, often called a pie chart, divides information into parts. The circle graph below shows the total amounts of the United States' exports. The parts of the

Selected U.S. Exports*

Item: Machinery, Chemicals, Food, Vehicles, Mineral Fuels

Dollar Amount *(in billions)*
0 20 40 60 80 100 120 140 160 180

Top Five Trading Partners of the U.S.:
Exports

5% Germany
5% United Kingdom
9% Mexico
11% Japan
20% Canada
50% 22 other countries

*Exports: goods sent out for sale to other places

with Graphs

graph represent the amounts of trade between the United States and certain other countries. Like other graphs, circle graphs can help you make comparisons. You can compare the parts to each other or to the whole.

A **line graph** shows change over time. The line graph below shows how the amount of goods exported from the United States changed between the years 1970 and 1995. Each dot shows how much trade took place in one year, and a line connects all the dots. Depending on the information, the line may go up or down or stay at the same level. Line graphs are most useful in showing a **trend**, or the way something changes over time.

3. Understand the Process

Compare and contrast the information in the bar, circle, and line graphs by answering the following questions. As you answer, think about the advantages and disadvantages of each kind of graph.

1 Which graph or graphs would you use to find how much machinery the United States exports? Explain your choice.

2 Which graph or graphs would you use to find the percent of goods the United States exports to Japan? Explain your choice.

3 Which graph or graphs would you use to find how much change there was in the United States' exports between the years 1970 and 1980? Explain your choice.

4 Do you think the information on the line graph can be shown on the circle graph? Explain your answer.

4. Think and Apply

Using the graphs on these pages, write a paragraph summarizing information about the United States' international trade in recent years. Share your paragraph with a partner, and compare your summaries.

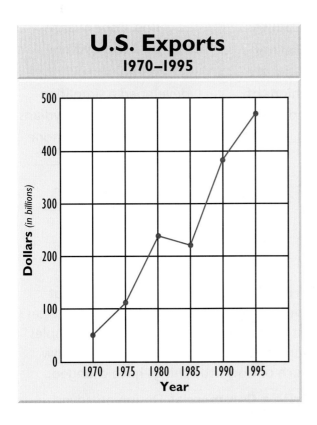

U.S. Exports
1970–1995

CONNECT MAIN IDEAS

Use this organizer to tell about the achievements of the early people of southwestern Asia. List two examples for each box. A copy of the organizer appears on page 22 of the Activity Book.

Geography of Ancient Mesopotamia

The geography of the Fertile Crescent affected the people there in both positive and negative ways.

1. _____
2. _____

Southwest Asia

Civilization in Mesopotamia

The people of ancient Sumer developed new ways of doing things.

1. _____
2. _____

Conquests and Empires

Early civilizations protected themselves and kept order within their societies.

1. _____
2. _____

The Ancient Israelites

The ancient Israelites believed in one God and lived by the teachings of the Ten Commandments.

1. _____
2. _____

The Phoenicians and the Lydians

The Phoenicians developed a simplified alphabet, and the Lydians introduced coined money.

1. _____
2. _____

WRITE MORE ABOUT IT

Write a Short Story To understand the importance of writing, imagine that you are a scribe in Sumer. Write a short story telling how and why writing developed.

Write a Report Explain the importance of agriculture by telling how a surplus of food affected life in Sumer.

Write Your Opinion Do you think that inventions always change life for the better? List reasons for your opinion. Use examples from the past and from today to see how much or how little things have changed.

Write a Commercial Design an advertisement for a new invention—the wheel.

About 2350 B.C.
• Sargon establishes Akkadian Empire

About 2000 B.C.
• Development of cuneiform

About 1225 B.C.
• Moses leads revolt against Egyptians

586 B.C.
• Judah is conquered by Babylonians

USE VOCABULARY

Use each term in a sentence that will help explain its meaning.

1. city-state
2. empire
3. equal justice
4. innovation
5. scribe
6. technology

CHECK UNDERSTANDING

7. What were some needs that led to innovations in Sumer? What were the innovations?

8. What were some of the causes of war in Mesopotamia?

9. Why was Hammurabi's Code so important?

10. How was the worship of one God different from the beliefs of other religions in the area of southwestern Asia?

11. Why was the development of a written alphabet important?

THINK CRITICALLY

12. **Think More About It** What do you think was the most important achievement of the Sumerians?

13. **Cause and Effect** How did the waging of wars affect the government of Sumer?

14. **Personally Speaking** Do you think that Hammurabi's idea of equal justice within classes was fair or unfair for its time? Explain your answer.

15. **Past to Present** How many things can you think of in today's world that would not work without the wheel? What would

life be like without it? Can you think of an innovation of our time that seems as important as the invention of the wheel?

APPLY SKILLS

Compare Information with Graphs Use the graphs on pages 114 and 115 to answer these questions.

16. Which graph would you use to find the year in which United States exports totaled about $394 billion?

17. Which graph would you use to find out what rank Mexico holds as an export partner to the United States?

Compare Maps with Different Projections In your library, locate an atlas or another book containing many maps. Look through the maps to identify different projections. Make a list of the kinds of projections that you find. Beside each projection name, describe the features of that projection.

READ MORE ABOUT IT

Gilgamesh the King by Ludmila Zeman. Tundra Books. This ancient tale, retold from clay tablets more than 5,000 years old, is about the stern ruler Gilgamesh, who is taught to be kind to his people by the wild man Enkidu.

Visit the Internet at
http://www.hbschool.com
for additional resources.

Will There Be Enough Food?

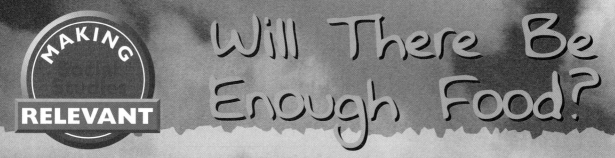

From the distant past to the present day, agriculture has made it possible for civilizations to feed their many people. Today, however, people wonder whether agriculture can produce enough food for a world population that grows by 90 million people each year.

Already, more than 700 million people are at risk of starving to death every day. Right here in the United States, 30 million people—12 million of them children—do not get enough food to stay in good health.

New technology is helping farmers grow more food. On large commercial farms, machines plant, care for, and harvest crops faster and better than people can. New ways of breeding produce larger and healthier plants and animals. Modern chemicals improve the soil, fight plant diseases, and kill pests. New methods also protect the soil for future crops.

Yet even with these new and better ways of farming, many people in the world go to bed hungry every night. In some cases political disorder and poor leadership prevent food from getting to hungry people. Technology alone will not solve the problem of hunger.

Hydroponic farming, or raising plants without soil, in Japan

Carrot harvesting in the United States

Think and Apply

BUILDING CITIZENSHIP

Think about ways you might help people who do not get enough to eat each day. One way might be to collect food in your school for a community food bank. Make a list of ideas, and share your list with the class.

HARCOURT BRACE

Visit the Internet at **http://www.hbschool.com** for additional resources.

CNN
Turner
Le@rning

Check your media center or classroom video library for the Making Social Studies Relevant videotape of this feature.

A young child in India

Soybean harvesting in Zambia

UNIT 1 REVIEW

Summarize the Main Ideas
Study the pictures and captions to help you review the events you read about in Unit 1.

Interpreting Pictures
Look closely at the scenes in the visual summary. In a group, discuss how people's lives differed during the time periods illustrated.

1 Early people lived in groups and cooperated to hunt animals and gather plants.

3 The domestication of plants and animals let people settle and caused great changes in their ways of life.

4 As populations increased, some farming villages grew into cities.

6 Unlike many other early cultures, the ancient Israelites believed in one God. They lived by the teachings of the Ten Commandments.

2 Early people learned to domesticate plants and animals.

5 The ancient Sumerians developed creative ways to solve the problems of city life.

7 The Phoenician alphabet and the Lydians' use of coined money brought about great changes.

USE VOCABULARY

To show that you know what these words mean, use each pair in a sentence.

1 band, migration

2 agriculture, domesticate

3 civilization, government

4 technology, innovation

5 city-state, monarchy

CHECK UNDERSTANDING

6 What were some advantages of living in bands?

7 How did migration change the population of the world?

8 How did agriculture change early societies?

9 How did food surpluses lead to a division of labor in Sumer?

10 Why did early societies need governments?

THINK CRITICALLY

11 **Cause and Effect** Agriculture changed society forever. In what ways were the effects of agriculture positive? In what ways were the effects negative?

12 **Explore Viewpoints** Why might some people dislike using new technology or inventions?

13 **Personally Speaking** A story about King Gilgamesh calls him "he who knew everything." Do you think it is wise to feel that a leader knows everything? Explain.

14 **Past to Present** How did the Israelites, the Phoenicians, and the Lydians change society?

15 **Think More About It** How would life be different today if we bartered instead of using money? What would a trip to a store be like?

APPLY SKILLS

Compare Maps with Different Projections Identify the projections of these maps as polar, conformal, or equal-area.

Map A

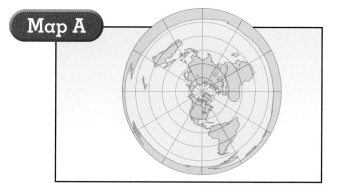

Map B

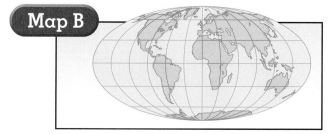

Map C

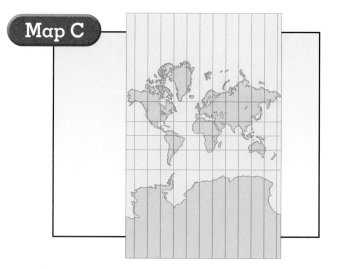

REMEMBER

- Share your ideas.
- Cooperate with others to plan your work.
- Take responsibility for your work.
- Help one another.
- Show your group's work to the class.
- Discuss what you learned by working together.

 *Make a*
Classroom Midden

One way in which archaeologists learned about Skara Brae was by studying its middens, or garbage piles. To see how people can learn from garbage, make a classroom "midden." At home, choose some items that you will probably throw away or recycle. Make sure that what you choose is clean and safe. At school, work with a group to make a "midden" by placing everything collected in a pile. Change places with another group and examine that group's midden. What do the things found in the midden tell about the group that made it?

 *Present a*
Play

Work with a group to write and act out a brief play about the advances of early people. The first scene should show life as hunters and gatherers. The second scene should show the settled life of farmers. The third scene should show early city life.

ACTIVITY *Draw Plans*
for a Model Home

Work with several classmates to draw a picture of the outside of a home at Skara Brae. Then draw the inside of the home. Show your drawings to the class, and explain how the environment helped determine the way the home looked.

Unit Project Wrap-Up

Make a Map of Early Times Work in a group to finish the Unit Project on page 43. First, double-check that you have added all places correctly. Next, review the unit to find out where important events happened long ago. Use symbols on your map to show the locations of ancient cultures. Identify your symbols and explain any other important information on a map key. If you wish, add illustrations to the map.

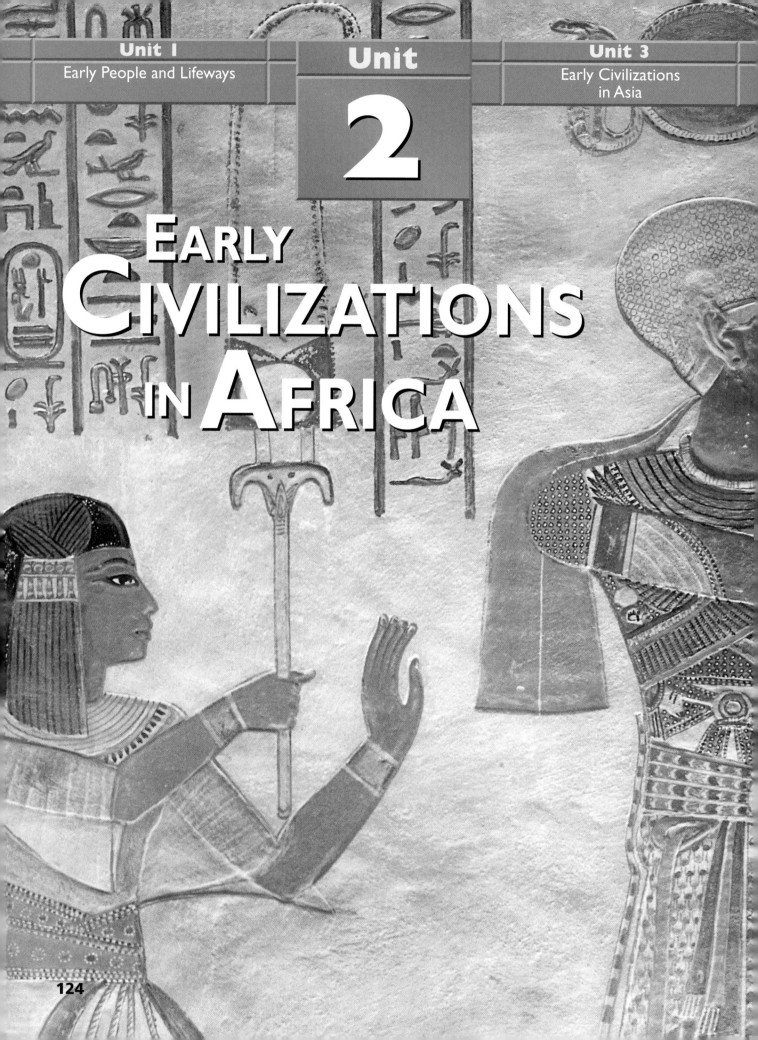

Unit 1
Early People and Lifeways

Unit

2

Unit 3
Early Civilizations
in Asia

EARLY CIVILIZATIONS IN AFRICA

In the same centuries in which civilizations were developing in Asia, other civilizations were forming in Africa. African civilizations rose up in areas where conditions were right for growing crops and raising livestock. Northern Africa provided the setting for one of the continent's earliest civilizations.

◀ **Wall painting from a tomb at the Valley of the Queens, Egypt**

UNIT THEMES

- Continuity and Change
- Interaction Within Different Environments
- Conflict and Cooperation

Unit Project

Make a Scroll Complete this project as you study Unit 2. Make a scroll that describes ancient Egyptian and Nubian life. As you read this unit, jot down important information about the Egyptians and the Nubians. You can then use this information as you create your scroll.

UNIT 2 PREVIEW

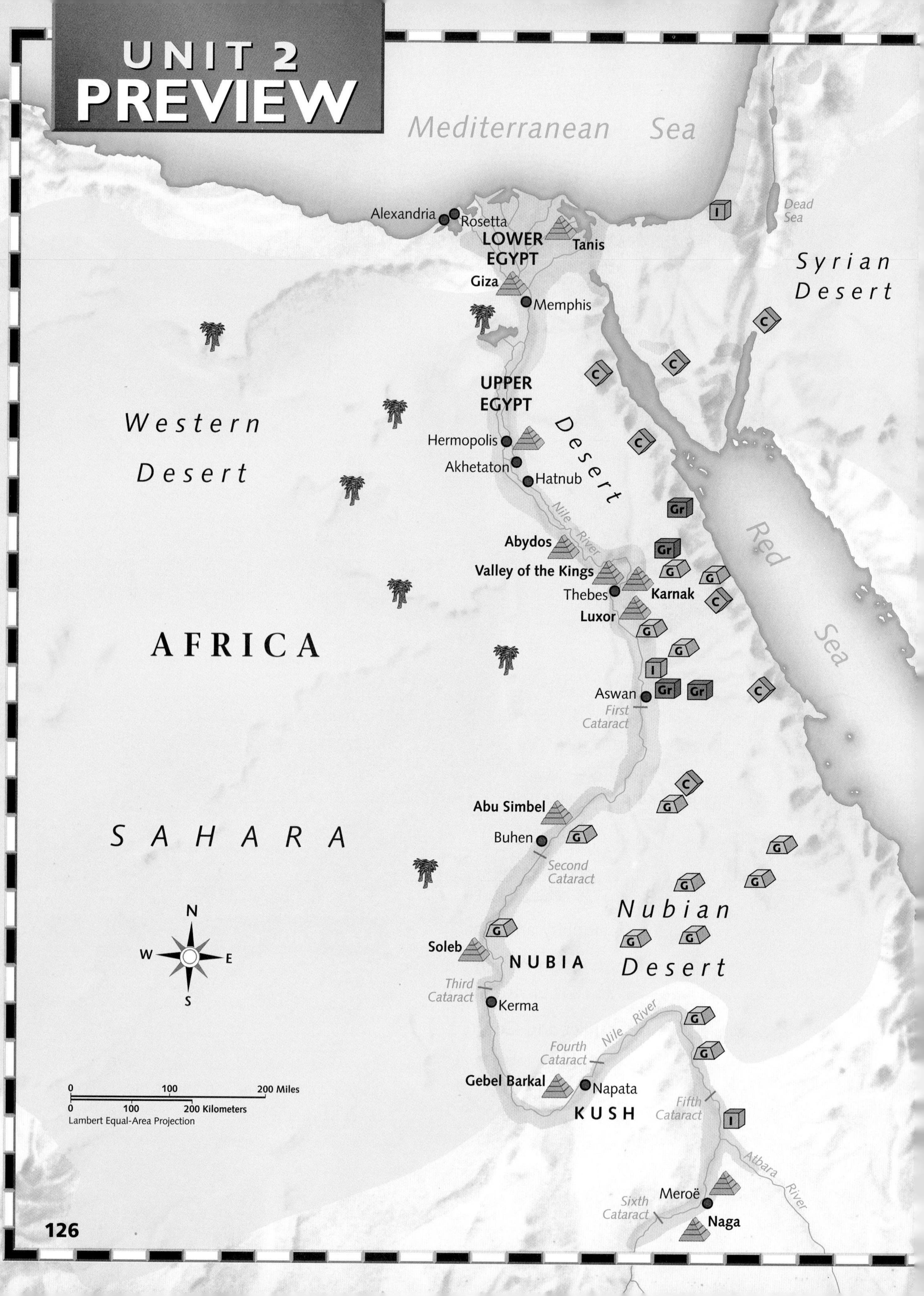

Mediterranean Sea
Dead Sea
Alexandria
Rosetta
LOWER EGYPT
Tanis
Syrian Desert
Giza
Memphis
UPPER EGYPT
Western Desert
Hermopolis
Akhetaton
Hatnub
Desert
Nile River
Red Sea
Abydos
Valley of the Kings
Thebes
Karnak
Luxor
AFRICA
Aswan
First Cataract
Abu Simbel
Buhen
SAHARA
Second Cataract
Nubian Desert
N
W
E
S
Soleb
NUBIA
Third Cataract
Kerma
Fourth Cataract
Nile River
Gebel Barkal
Napata
KUSH
Fifth Cataract
Atbara River
Meroë
Sixth Cataract
Naga
C
G
Gr
I
0 100 200 Miles
0 100 200 Kilometers
Lambert Equal-Area Projection

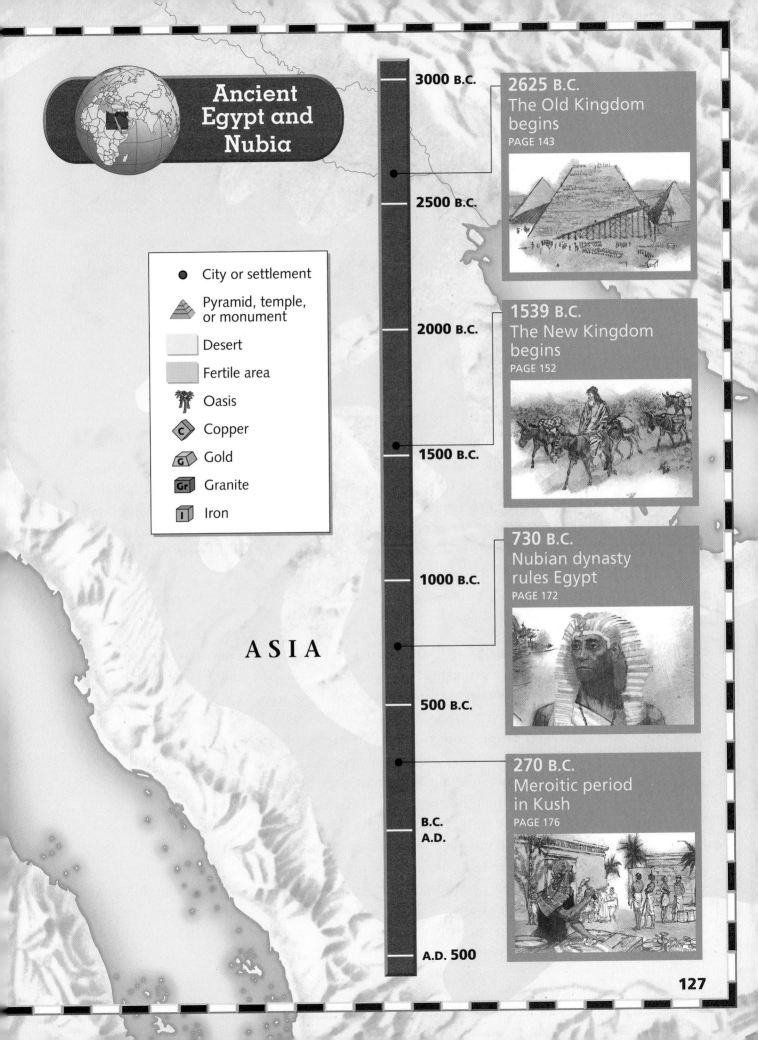

Ancient Egypt and Nubia

ASIA

Legend:
- ● City or settlement
- ◭ Pyramid, temple, or monument
- ▢ Desert
- ▢ Fertile area
- 🌴 Oasis
- **C** Copper
- **G** Gold
- **Gr** Granite
- **I** Iron

3000 B.C.

2500 B.C.

2625 B.C.
The Old Kingdom
begins
PAGE 143

2000 B.C.

1539 B.C.
The New Kingdom
begins
PAGE 152

1500 B.C.

1000 B.C.

730 B.C.
Nubian dynasty
rules Egypt
PAGE 172

500 B.C.

B.C.
A.D.

270 B.C.
Meroitic period
in Kush
PAGE 176

A.D. 500

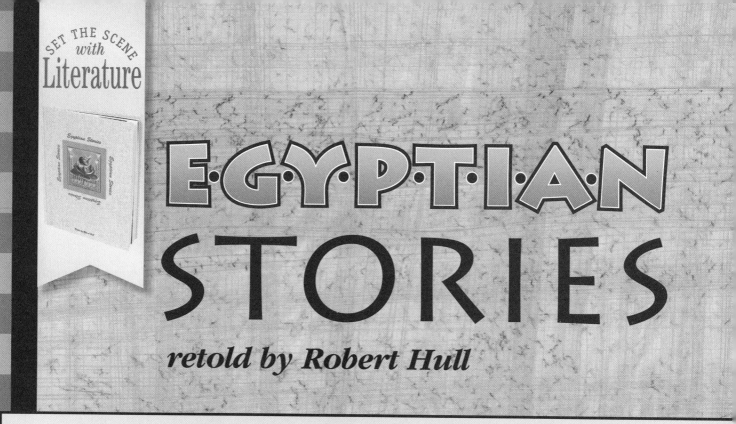

E·G·Y·P·T·I·A·N STORIES

retold by Robert Hull

People in ancient civilizations looked for ways to explain the world and their place in it. For many people religion was a way to do this. The ancient Egyptians worshipped many gods. The Egyptians thought that one of these gods, Osiris, gave life to the Earth. Ancient Egyptian stories told of the adventures of Osiris and other gods. This retelling of one ancient story describes how Osiris helped the ancient Egyptians survive on Earth.

Osiris taught the people of the world when to expect the gentle wind from the north. He taught them how to make buildings and raise them up toward the stars, how to make words, how to write down memories with marks on stone, how to make laws. Osiris spoke a law to keep people from killing and eating each other.

Osiris wondered what else he could give to the people. One day, he was walking near the Nile, among the high barley grasses. A breeze swept through the grass, and Osiris watched the ripe grains being blown through the air and rolling along the earth. Then his sharp eyes noticed that though most of the ripe grains blew away in the wind, some of the heavier ones fell alongside the plant, and stayed there, undisturbed. "Next year," he thought, "those seeds will grow again here, in the same place. Most grains will be scattered and lost, but if a few fall where they have grown, men can gather the grains and keep them. In that way men can make barley grow always in the same place."

Agriculture was an important part of the lives of the ancient Egyptians. This painting from ancient times shows farmers planting seeds.

Osiris kept the grain that hadn't blown away and buried it in the earth. Next year, in the same place, the barley grass grew. He had found the way to make barley stay in one place. He told men to scrape at the earth with sticks and make a safe place to put the heavy barley grain, the grain that fell where it had grown.

Osiris had given the people fields.

Then Osiris saw something else. When the Nile came, and the soft wind blew from the north and the world shone with water, the barley grew more thickly. He told men and women to dig small channels to the fields and guide the waters out along these channels. So, with the guidance of the great god-king Osiris, the people learned to lead the waters to the barley and spread the waters there.

Gradually the people had learned to till and sow the earth and guide water to it from the Nile, and to gather the crops that grew from the fields. Osiris had taught them to be farmers. He had given them the harvest.

As you read this unit, you will learn more about the ancient Egyptians and their lifeways. You will also learn about other civilizations around the world.

ANCIENT EGYPT

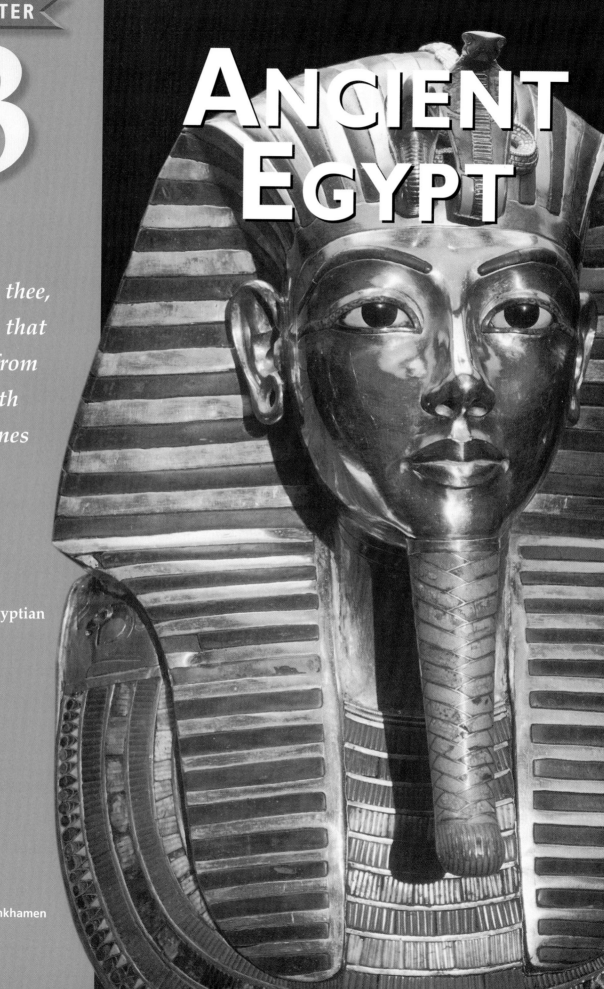

"Hail to thee, O Nile, that issues from the Earth and comes to keep Egypt alive!"

from the ancient Egyptian "Hymn to the Nile"

Gold mask of Pharaoh Tutankhamen

Geography of Northern Africa

The Nile River runs like a thin ribbon through the vast northern African desert known as the Sahara. All along its course, the river brings life to a dry land. Long ago the Nile's annual flood was a central part of life in ancient Egypt. The flooding of the Nile brought both water and rich soil to the land along its banks. This gift of the Nile made possible the great ancient Egyptian civilization.

The Nile Valley

During the Paleolithic period, or Old Stone Age, the Sahara was a vast **savanna**, or grassy plain, with many trees and animals. The early people living there were hunter-gatherers. Then, about 5000 B.C., the climate began to change and the Sahara slowly dried up. As the land dried, plants died and animals left to search for water. Over time, the rich savanna turned into a harsh desert.

Without plants and animals, people could no longer survive in the Sahara. They began to move into the Nile Valley. The Nile Valley is made up of fertile land along both sides of the Nile River. The winding Nile is the world's longest river. It flows northward more than 4,000 miles (6,437 km) from its main source at Lake Victoria in central Africa, to

FOCUS

How do people depend on water and other natural resources today?

Main Idea Read to find out how the Nile River affected the land around it.

Vocabulary

savanna

delta

cataract

Sailboats called *feluccas* (fuh•LEW•kahs) have been a common sight on the Nile River for centuries. Above is a satellite image of the Nile Delta.

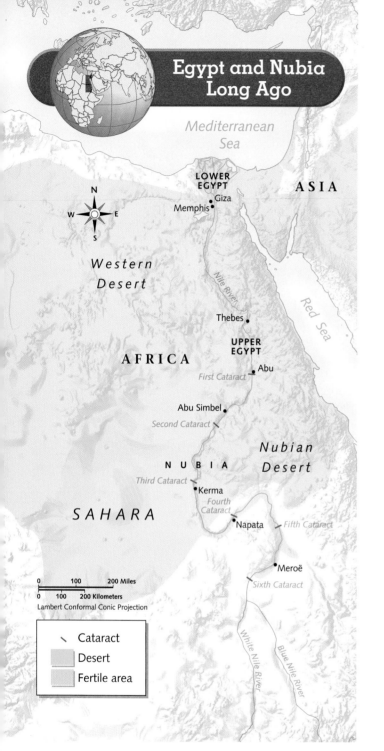

Egypt and Nubia Long Ago

Mediterranean Sea

ASIA

LOWER EGYPT
Giza
Memphis

N
W E
S

Western Desert

Nile River

Red Sea

Thebes

UPPER EGYPT

AFRICA

First Cataract
Abu

Abu Simbel
Second Cataract

Nubian Desert

N U B I A
Third Cataract
Kerma
Fourth Cataract
Napata
Fifth Cataract

SAHARA

Meroë
Sixth Cataract

White Nile River
Blue Nile River

0   100   200 Miles
0   100   200 Kilometers
Lambert Conformal Conic Projection

\ Cataract
Desert
Fertile area

the Mediterranean Sea. The Nile also has sources in the mountains of eastern Africa.

As with all rivers, the land is higher at the beginning of the Nile and lower near its mouth. This led the ancient people of the region to call the lower land in the north Lower Egypt. The higher land in the south they called Upper Egypt.

Lower Egypt is made up mainly of the Nile Delta. A **delta** is low land formed at the mouth of some rivers by the silt the river drops there. The Nile Delta fans out in a huge triangle where the Nile enters the Mediterranean Sea. Long ago the Nile River broke into many branches as it passed through the delta. Today only two of these branches remain.

In Upper Egypt high cliffs surround the Nile. In some places a narrow strip of flat fertile land lies between the river and the cliffs. In other places the cliffs reach all the way to the river's edge. The cliffs are mostly made up of limestone and sandstone. Over thousands of years, the Nile River has cut a deep channel, or path, through these soft stones. Farther south, in the land that was known as Nubia, the cliffs also include very

MAP THEME

Place   This map shows the fertile areas and deserts of ancient Egypt and Nubia.
■ *Why do you think the land to the north was called Lower Egypt and the land farther south was called Upper Egypt?*

hard granite. The Nile has been unable to cut a clear path through these cliffs. Instead, the river runs through **cataracts**, a series of rapids and waterfalls.

Lower Egypt and Upper Egypt have one important thing in common—both have rich soil. The early people who settled in the Nile Valley found the land perfect for growing crops. Instead of continuing to hunt and gather, they settled as farmers on the Nile Delta and in the narrow river valley to the south.

REVIEW *How would you describe the Nile River?*

Black Land, Red Land

Every year heavy rains fall in eastern Africa at the sources of the Nile River. For many centuries this rainfall caused the river to rise and overflow its banks. When the floodwaters drained away, the silt they carried was left behind on the land. The rich silt acted as a natural fertilizer. The deep black color of the rich soil inspired the ancient Egyptians to call their home Kemet, or the Black Land.

The ancient Egyptians believed that their god Hapi caused the important yearly flooding. To Hapi, the Egyptian farmers offered this prayer:

> **66** Hail to you, Hapi!
> Sprung from the Earth,
> Come to nourish Egypt! **99**

For thousands of years farmers depended on the flooding of the Nile to make their farmland new again. The completion of the Aswan High Dam in 1972 changed the Egyptian way of life and Egyptian agriculture forever. The dam brought an end to the yearly flooding of the Nile River. Today Egyptians must use pumps, canals, and chemical fertilizers to keep the land suitable for farming.

In contrast to the Black Land, the dry and barren lands of the Sahara were known as Deshuret (deh•SHOO•ret), or the Red Land. The Nile River slices the eastern part of the Sahara in two. Today the land on the east side of the river is known as the Eastern Desert, or the Arabian Desert. The land on the west side is called the Western Desert.

REVIEW *Why was the annual flooding of the Nile River important to the Egyptians?*

For centuries people have settled on the fertile land near the Nile. The modern Egyptian capital, Cairo (inset), lies near the site of the ancient Egyptian capital of Memphis.

Agriculture is still a way of life for many people in the Nile Delta and Nile Valley.

Farming in the Nile Valley

In ancient Egypt, wealthy landowners controlled almost all the farmland. Most Egyptian farmers rented land from these landowners. In return, the landowners got a part of the crops as rent. During harvest time, farmers gathered huge amounts of wheat and barley and some vegetables, such as onions, lettuce, and beans.

Egyptian farmers also raised cattle, goats, sheep, and pigs for food. From these animals the Egyptians got meat and milk products, including cheese. Beef from cattle was mainly for the wealthy. Most Egyptians could afford it only for special days. More often, birds and fish were their main sources of protein. Using small boats, fishers caught huge Nile perch and catfish with nets or with hooks and fishing lines. Hunters used throwing sticks and large nets to catch geese and ducks.

Some plants and animals were important to the Egyptians for uses other than as food. Egyptians used the fibers of the flax plant to spin linen thread. Sheep's wool was spun and woven, too. Both of these materials were used to make clothing. Craftworkers also sewed together pieces of leather to make containers, sacks, and shoes. From plants they made products such as sandals, boxes, and tabletops.

REVIEW *What were some of the crops ancient Egyptians depended on?*

LESSON 1 REVIEW

Check Understanding

1 Remember the Facts What is the difference between the Black Land and the Red Land?

2 Recall the Main Idea How did the Nile River affect the land of ancient Egypt?

Think Critically

3 Past to Present The construction of the Aswan High Dam stopped the yearly flooding of the Nile River. How has this changed life in modern Egypt?

4 Think More About It How might Egypt have developed differently if the Sahara had not dried up?

Show What You Know

Map Activity Make a three-dimensional map that shows the geography of ancient Egypt. Use a variety of materials, such as blue and brown cloth, clay, and sand, to show the important physical features of the region. Display your finished map in your classroom.

Importance of the Nile River

| 5000 B.C. | 4000 B.C. | 3000 B.C. |

Just as Mesopotamia is remembered for having the first cities, ancient Egypt is remembered for being the first united nation-state. A **nation-state** is a region with a single government and a united group of people. Their common experience of living in the Nile Valley and their shared religion brought the Egyptians together to form a single society.

Giver and Taker of Life

The Nile River was thought to be the "giver of life" for the ancient Egyptians. It affected all Egyptian activities, including farming, religious beliefs, and ways of governing. The Nile also helped bring together the peoples who lived along its banks.

For the early Egyptians the Nile served as a river highway. To use this highway, the Egyptians became expert shipbuilders. The first Egyptian ships were made of bundles of reeds. By the time Egypt was united, some Egyptian boats were made of wooden planks and were as long as 60 feet (18 m). All year round, reed or wooden

FOCUS

How might people today be affected by their physical environment?

Main Idea As you read, think about how the Nile River affected the development of Egyptian society and religion.

Vocabulary

nation-state
predict
inundation
afterlife
nome

Ancient water clock (above); the Nile River near the second cataract (below)

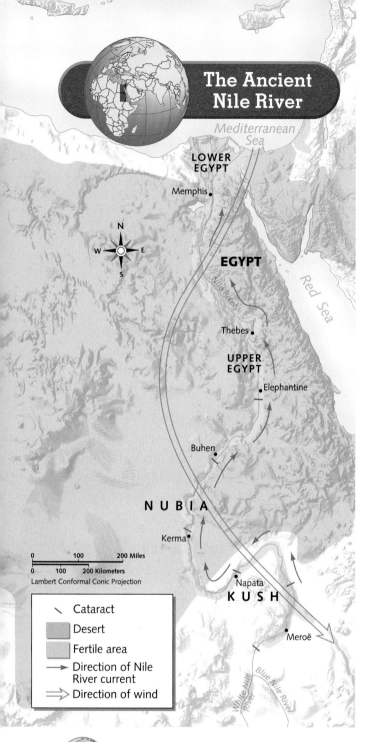

The Ancient Nile River

LOWER EGYPT

Mediterranean Sea

Memphis

EGYPT

Red Sea

Nile River

Thebes

UPPER EGYPT

Elephantine

Buhen

N U B I A

Kerma

0   100   200 Miles
0   100   200 Kilometers
Lambert Conformal Conic Projection

Napata
K U S H

Meroë

White Nile River   Blue Nile River

Legend:
- Cataract
- Desert
- Fertile area
- → Direction of Nile River current
- ⇒ Direction of wind

MAP THEME

Human-Environment Interactions This map of ancient Egypt and Nubia shows the direction of the flow of the Nile River and the direction of wind.
■ *Why do you think the use of the sail was so important in ancient Egypt?*

The Egyptians understood how important the Nile was to their survival. Because of this, the Nile played a role in their religion, their writing, and their art. This painting (right) shows a ruler and his wife traveling to a life after death.

sailboats traveled on the Nile. Boats going downriver could use the river's fast currents to travel north. Boats sailing upriver relied on Egypt's steady north wind to go against the current. This two-way travel made visiting and trading easier.

No matter where they lived along the Nile River, the Egyptians had many of the same concerns. Some years the Nile, the giver of life, took life away. When rains fell too lightly upriver, the Nile did not overflow. The land lay baked by the sun, and the crops dried up. Without a harvest, people starved. But when too much rain fell at the Nile's source, the river flooded wildly. It washed away the crops and drowned people and animals. These common problems helped unite the Egyptian people. Together, the ancient Egyptians tried to understand their changing environment and developed innovations to solve their problems.

REVIEW *How did the Nile bring the Egyptian people together?*

Source of Innovation

Like the Mesopotamians, the Egyptians depended on floodwaters for their agriculture. Unlike the Mesopotamians, however, Egyptian farmers were able to **predict**, or tell ahead of time, when floods would come. The yearly flood, or **inundation**, took place at about the same time each year. The need to keep track of this important event led the Egyptians to develop a calendar. The Egyptian calendar is the oldest known calendar based on the sun. Like our calendar, it had 365 days.

The Egyptians divided their year into three seasons based on the action of the Nile River. These three seasons were Inundation, Emergence, and Harvest.

Because the time of flooding was so important to the Egyptians, they considered it to be the start of their new year. During Inundation the land was made new again with silt from the floodwaters that covered the farmland.

Inundation was followed by Emergence, the time when the land emerged once more from beneath the waters. As this season began, farmers planted their crops. To plant crops, Egyptian farmers used plows or hoes to create furrows, or long grooves. They dropped seeds along each furrow and then led cows or other farm animals through the fields. As the animals walked over the furrows, they pushed the seeds into the ground.

The growing season was only long enough to produce one crop of grains such as wheat. However, as many as three or four crops of some vegetables could be produced in the fertile soil.

The final season was Harvest, the time when the crops were ready. In most years Egyptian farmers could be certain of having large harvests. "It is to be a beautiful year, free from want and rich in all herbs," an Egyptian farmer said in a year of plentiful crops.

The Nile was "the giver of life," but life was not easy for the ancient Egyptians. Their environment created many hardships for farmers. Because of this, the Egyptians developed innovations both to bring water to their fields and to take it away.

Rain hardly ever fell in Egypt itself. To keep their land watered during the growing season, the Egyptians developed ways to irrigate it. During Emergence, people trapped water in ponds to use in case of drought.

The season of Emergence was a time of great activity for Egyptian farmers. In this wooden model from 2000 B.C., an Egyptian farmer plows the land after it is no longer flooded.

Source of Religion

The Egyptians believed that their religion was important to their survival in the Nile Valley. The people of ancient Egypt used stories about their gods to explain events in nature. The ancient Egyptians believed the sun was a god who was born each day and died each night. This explained why the sun seemed to go away at night and return each morning. The sun became a symbol of the life cycle.

The ancient Egyptians believed in many gods, each with a different responsibility. For example, Thoth was the god of wisdom. Hathor was the goddess of love. Osiris ruled over the dead. Hapi was the god of the Nile River.

Hapi is often shown in Egyptian art as a man with a papyrus plant sprouting from the top of his head. The ancient Egyptians believed that the Nile floods were controlled by their gods. Many celebrations in honor of Hapi usually took place during Inundation.

The sun god, Re, was among the most important of the Egyptian gods. In Egyptian wall paintings, Re is often pictured as a falcon, soaring in the sky. At other times he is shown as the sun, riding in a special kind of boat called a solar bark. The ancient Egyptians believed that Re sailed through the sky just as they sailed on the Nile.

Re is the subject of many ancient Egyptian stories. One of these stories says that long ago a small island appeared out of

The Egyptians painted scenes like the one above to show the positions of stars. The Egyptians were also excellent metalworkers, as shown by this bronze statue of the Egyptian sun god, Re (right). The Egyptians often thought of their gods as part animal and part human.

When too much rain caused flooding, the Egyptians, like the people of Mesopotamia, built dams and dikes to hold back the river. They also dug canals to carry excess water back to the river.

Most Egyptians were farmers and many of their inventions had to do with agriculture. Inventions such as the shaduf (shah•DOOF) are still used in rural parts of Egypt. A shaduf is a long pole with a basket for holding water on one end and a weight on the other. The shaduf allows farmers to draw water from the Nile and use it in their canals or fields.

REVIEW *What did the Egyptians do to control the Nile River?*

nothingness. On that island grew a lotus blossom. From this blossom came the sun god, Re. Re then created the other gods and the world as the Egyptians knew it. Re was later combined with another Egyptian god, Amon. Amon-Re became the Egyptians' most powerful god.

The Egyptians prayed to their gods and believed in a life after death, or **afterlife**. Some Egyptian prayers were collected in what is now known as the *Book of the Dead*. Egyptians placed a copy of the *Book of the Dead* in their tombs and believed it would serve as a guide in their afterlife.

REVIEW *How did the Egyptians explain events in nature?*

Unified Egypt

About 5000 B.C., small farming villages of ancient Egypt grew up along the Nile River between the delta and the first cataract. As population increased, villages became towns with more buildings and land. Some towns became capitals of city-states called **nomes**. Often the leaders of the different nomes competed for control of power and wealth.

Over time, nomes joined together until by about 3500 B.C., there were two large kingdoms—one in Upper Egypt and the other in Lower Egypt. These kingdoms were known as the "Two Lands." The rulers of each kingdom wanted to control all of Egypt.

This tomb painting shows the Egyptian pharaoh Seti I with the goddess Hathor. Such paintings were thought to ensure the success of a person in the afterlife.

From the *Book of the Dead*
The Negative Confession

1. Hail, Usekh-nemmt, who comes forth from Anu, I have not committed sin.

2. Hail, Hept-khet, who comes forth from Kher-aha, I have not committed robbery with violence.

3. Hail, Fenti, who comes forth from Khemenu, I have not stolen.

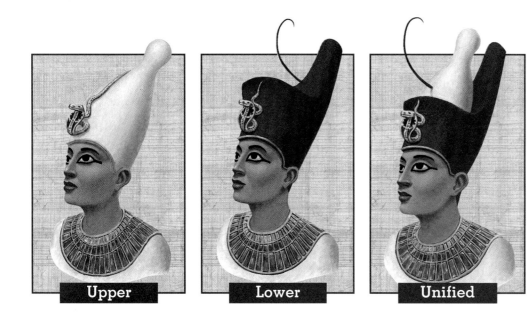

| Upper | Lower | Unified |

LEARNING FROM DIAGRAMS The double crown of unified Egypt was formed by placing the crown of Upper Egypt inside the crown of Lower Egypt.
■ *Why do you think the crowns of Upper and Lower Egypt were combined?*

By about 3000 B.C. Upper Egyptian kings had gained control of Lower Egypt. The Two Lands united as one. Ancient Egyptian legend says that Menes (MEE•neez) was the king who united Egypt.

Who really united the two kingdoms is not known. Some experts think that a king named Narmer may have brought the Two Lands together. In ancient artwork Narmer is shown wearing a double crown that combines the white crown of Upper Egypt and the red crown of Lower Egypt.

The uniting of Egypt had an important result. It marked the beginning of the world's first nation-state, which lasted for 3,000 years.

REVIEW *Why was the uniting of Egypt important?*

LESSON 2 REVIEW

| 5000 B.C. | 4000 B.C. | 3000 B.C. |

About 5000 B.C.
• Small farming villages begin in Egypt

About 3000 B.C.
• Egypt is united

Check Understanding

1 Remember the Facts How was the Nile River like a highway for the ancient Egyptians?

2 Recall the Main Idea How did the Nile River affect the development of Egyptian society and religion?

Think Critically

3 Past to Present How do natural features such as rivers, lakes, and mountains help unite people or keep them isolated from each other?

4 Think More About It Why did the Egyptians unite to become the world's first nation-state, while the Sumerians remained divided into warring city-states?

Show What You Know
Writing Activity The ancient Egyptians told stories to explain events in nature. Think of such an event, and create a story to explain it. Write down your story, illustrate it, and share it with a classmate.

Early Egyptian Rule

| 3000 B.C. | 2500 B.C. | 2000 B.C. |

Modern experts trace the beginning of the ancient Egyptians to the rule of King Narmer. When Narmer died, rule of Egypt passed on to a family member. This continued for several generations, creating Egypt's first **dynasty**, or series of rulers from the same family. Over the next 3,000 years, about 33 dynasties ruled Egypt.

The Early Period

The kings of Dynasties 1 and 2 had names that showed a relationship with the gods. Later, Egyptians began to call their king **pharaoh**. The word means "great house" and referred to the ruler's magnificent palace.

Egyptians believed that their pharaoh was the son of Re, their sun god. As a god in human form, the pharaoh had total authority over Egypt. The pharaoh was also a link between the Egyptian people and their gods.

The strong rule of the pharaoh helped the Egyptian civilization survive for thousands of years. Because the pharaoh was usually obeyed without question, the structure of Egyptian government changed little.

The most important government official was the **vizier** (vuh•ZIR), or adviser. The vizier carried out the pharaoh's **decrees**, or commands, and took care of the day-to-day running of the government. Many other officials helped the pharaoh govern Egypt. These people collected taxes, planned building projects, and made sure the laws were obeyed.

FOCUS

How do people create strong governments today?

Main Idea Think about how Egyptian kings used their political and religious authority to create a strong government.

Vocabulary

dynasty	hieroglyphics
pharaoh	papyrus
vizier	pyramid
decree	mummy

The Great Sphinx was built during the Old Kingdom in Egypt.

141

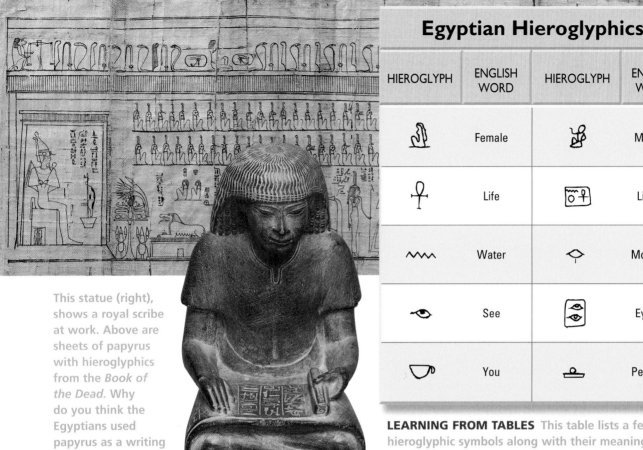

This statue (right), shows a royal scribe at work. Above are sheets of papyrus with hieroglyphics from the *Book of the Dead*. Why do you think the Egyptians used papyrus as a writing material?

Egyptian Hieroglyphics

HIEROGLYPH	ENGLISH WORD	HIEROGLYPH	ENGLISH WORD
	Female		Male
	Life		Live
	Water		Mouth
	See		Eyes
	You		Peace

LEARNING FROM TABLES This table lists a few hieroglyphic symbols along with their meanings.
■ *Which symbols most clearly show their meaning?*

We know about Egypt's earliest kings and their governments because the Egyptians left written records. They developed a system of writing known as **hieroglyphics** (hy•ruh•GLIH•fiks). Egyptian hieroglyphic writing used more than 700 different symbols. Most of these symbols stood for sounds, though some stood for whole words or ideas.

Egyptian scribes were educated for many years to learn hieroglyphics. Beginning scribes practiced writing on broken pieces of pottery. Scribes also learned mathematics, since their job often involved tax collecting and record keeping.

Egyptian scribes wrote in stone and on a paperlike material called **papyrus** (puh•PY•ruhs). Our word *paper* comes from *papyrus*. The invention of papyrus helped make the Egyptians' central government

possible. They used papyrus for keeping all the important written records of their society.

To make papyrus, the Egyptians cut strips from the stalk of the papyrus plant, a reed that grows in marshy areas. The strips were laid close together, with their edges touching. Another layer of strips was laid across the first. Then the layers were pressed together with heavy stones until a single sheet was formed.

For the Egyptians a "book" was a scroll— a roll made of papyrus sheets joined end to end. Some rolls were more than 100 feet (30 m) long. Scribes recorded the history of ancient Egypt on these scrolls. Ancient Egyptian history can be divided into three main parts: the Old Kingdom, the Middle Kingdom, and the New Kingdom. During each of these three kingdoms, one ruler at a time controlled Egypt. In the times between these kingdoms, competing dynasties ruled parts of Egypt and sometimes fought with each other. These periods are called intermediate periods.

REVIEW *Who controlled the land and people of ancient Egypt?*

The Old Kingdom

The Old Kingdom lasted from about 2625 B.C. to 2130 B.C. During this 500-year period, the Egyptian kings of Dynasties 4 through 8 began to look outside of Egypt for resources. They started a colony in Lower Nubia to make use of resources found there. Traders were sent farther south into Africa in search of incense, oils, ebony, ivory, and other items. Traders also traveled into southwestern Asia and returned with goods such as cedar wood and silver.

The Old Kingdom is perhaps best remembered for its achievements in building. During this period the Egyptians developed the technology to construct the biggest stone buildings in the world—the pyramids. A **pyramid** is a burial place for the dead. The Egyptians built many pyramids for their rulers and other important people. It is no wonder that

the time of the Old Kingdom is often called the Age of Pyramids. Pyramids were much larger and more magnificent than earlier Egyptian tombs. Before this time the kings of Egypt had been buried beneath flat-topped, mud-brick tombs called mastabas (MAS•tuh•buhz).

The Egyptians built strong tombs because they believed that they would need their bodies in the afterlife. For the same reason the Egyptians also developed ways to preserve the dead body.

The process of preserving a body began by removing all the internal organs except for the heart. The removed organs were placed in special jars. The heart remained in the body because the ancient Egyptians believed it was the home of the soul.

After the organs were removed, the body was covered with natron, a kind of salt. The natron absorbed water and caused the body to dry out. Next, the body was rubbed with special oils and wrapped in linen cloth. The entire process took 70 days. Only then was the preserved body, or **mummy**, ready to be placed in its tomb.

This mummy case was made for Paankhenamun, an Egyptian who lived sometime between 900 B.C. and 700 B.C. Mummy cases were usually made to look like the person they held.

All the things a person might need in the afterlife were also placed in the tomb. Clothing, jewelry, furniture, and even games were included. Tomb walls were covered with painted scenes of the person's life. Prayers from the *Book of the Dead* were also carved in tomb walls. The Egyptians thought that these practices would help the soul in the afterlife.

The Egyptians believed that the soul of a dead person appeared before the god Osiris and a group of judges. The judges placed the dead person's heart on one side of a scale. They placed a feather, the symbol of truth, on the other side. If the two balanced, the soul earned life forever. The judges would say,

66 I have judged the heart of the deceased, and his soul stands as a witness for him. His deeds are righteous in the great balance, and no sin has been found in him. 99

An unbalanced scale meant that a soul was heavy with sin. This soul, the Egyptians believed, would be eaten by an animal that was part crocodile, part lion, and part hippopotamus.

REVIEW *Why did the Egyptians preserve bodies as mummies?*

LEARNING FROM DIAGRAMS
This diagram shows the Great Pyramid at Giza:
1 Air vent
2 King's burial chamber
3 Queen's burial chamber
4 Entrance
5 Exit
6 Underground burial chamber
7 Smaller pyramids
8 Wall
■ *What do you think the function of the air vent was?*

Building the Pyramids

About 2650 B.C., King Zoser's architect, Imhotep, began a new style in royal tombs. He decided to build his king's tomb of stone instead of mud brick. While building the stone mastaba, Imhotep had another idea. He built a second layer on top of the first, and then another and another. Each new layer was smaller than the one below. The layers formed a pyramid that looked like a set of steps. Today we call this early pyramid a step pyramid.

The ancient Egyptians believed that after death the pharaoh went to live with their most powerful god, Amon-Re. One of their religious writings said, "A staircase to heaven is laid for him [the pharaoh] so that he may climb to heaven." Imhotep may have built the step pyramid to help the pharaoh reach Amon-Re.

About 2600 B.C. pyramid builders tried still another idea. They made pyramids with slanting sides

The Great Pyramid

Giza

The city of Giza (GEE•zuh) is located on the Nile River across from Cairo, the present-day capital of Egypt. The two most famous monuments of ancient Egypt—the Great Pyramid and the Great Sphinx—are near Giza.

Mediterranean Sea

N
W E
S

GIZA ⬚ ⊛Cairo

Great Pyramid
and Great Sphinx

EGYPT

Nile River

Red Sea

0   100   200 Miles
0   100   200 Kilometers

1
2
3
4
5
6
8

The pyramids at Giza are still one of the world's most amazing building feats.

and a pointed peak instead of steps. The slanting sides of the pyramids may have stood for the rays of the sun.

The best known of Egypt's pyramids is the Great Pyramid built at Giza. This pyramid was built for the Pharaoh Khufu. He wanted his tomb to be the largest pyramid ever built. Workers may have spent 20 years building the Great Pyramid, completing it in about 2566 B.C.

A labor tax supplied the Egyptian government with the workers it needed to build the Great Pyramid. Just as a money tax requires people to pay money, a labor tax required the ancient Egyptians to work. During the time of Inundation, when no farming could be done, the Egyptian farmers had to work for the pharaoh. As many as 10,000 farmers worked on the Great Pyramid at any one time.

The workers cut and moved more than 2 million blocks of stone. Each block weighed about 5,000 pounds (about 2,300 kg). The blocks were probably brought to the Great Pyramid on strong sleds. Egyptian workers may have used temporary ramps to move the blocks up into place.

Today the Great Pyramid of Khufu still stands in Giza. It is about 480 feet (about 146 m) high and covers 13 acres!

REVIEW *How did the Egyptian government get workers for the pyramids?*

This Dynasty 18 pectoral, or chest plate, is in the form of a scarab, or Egyptian beetle.

Egyptian Way of Life

Craftworkers held an important position in ancient Egypt. These workers—artists, builders, carpenters, and stonecutters—were responsible for building and decorating the tombs, temples, and pyramids. They often lived in villages at the construction site since many temples and pyramids were located far from cities or towns. Workdays were sunrise to sunset, and generally work was done 10 days at a time, followed by one day of rest. There were also several religious holidays in ancient Egypt on which people did not work.

Egyptians enjoyed their time off. Most listened to music and sang and danced at religious festivals and parties. Scenes painted on the walls of tombs show party-goers dressed in their finest clothes. As everyday clothes, women wore long, sleeveless dresses made from linen. Men wore knee-length linen skirts, with or without short-sleeved shirts. Men and women of all classes and ages wore jewelry and makeup. Wealthy Egyptians also often wore fancy wigs.

Egyptian houses were made of mud brick. In each house was a small shrine for the worship of household gods. Furniture included chests, stools, chairs, and beds.

Egyptian women were in charge of most household matters. Though they usually did not hold positions in government, several were priestesses at Egyptian temples. Some women were craftworkers. Most weavers were women. Since the linen they wove was in high demand, weavers could earn a good living. Unlike women in some societies, Egyptian women were allowed to own property and had full legal rights.

In ancient Egypt, children were often seen as gifts from the gods. In Egyptian art, children are usually shown with their parents or playing games. Some of the games Egyptian children played are still enjoyed today, including leapfrog, wrestling, and tug-of-war.

Education started at an early age in Egypt. Most boys learned their father's trade. Most girls learned weaving and

Egyptian craftworkers are shown making weapons in this limestone tablet.

household skills from their mother. Children of the upper class were usually the only ones to learn writing, mathematics, and literature.

REVIEW *What did women do in ancient Egypt?*

LESSON 3 REVIEW

3000 B.C.		2500 B.C.		2000 B.C.
2625 B.C. • Old Kingdom begins		About 2566 B.C. • Great Pyramid is completed		2130 B.C. • Old Kingdom ends

Check Understanding

1 **Remember the Facts** Into what three main periods is the history of ancient Egypt divided? What are times between these periods usually called?

2 **Recall the Main Idea** How did the Egyptian pharaohs use their political and religious authority to create a strong government?

Think Critically

3 **Past to Present** How were ancient Egyptian government and society like our government and society today? How were they different?

4 **Personally Speaking** Most Egyptian pharaohs became rulers because their father had been the pharaoh before them. In the United States, the people choose their President in an election. Which do you think is the better way of gaining a leader? Explain.

Show What You Know
Oral Report Activity Imagine that you live in Egypt during the Old Kingdom. Prepare an oral report telling what your life is like. Present your oral report to a classmate.

Solve a Problem

1. Why Learn This Skill?

You have to solve problems almost every day. Some problems are bigger than others, but most problems are easier to solve if you follow a set of steps. Knowing the steps to use can help you solve problems your whole life.

2. Remember What You Have Read

The builders of the Great Pyramid at Giza had a *big* problem. The pharaoh Khufu had ordered a pyramid built that was to be larger than any ever made. It was to cover 13 acres and rise as high as a modern 36-story building. Mud bricks would not be strong enough, so the Great Pyramid was to be built of limestone blocks. The builders of the Great Pyramid had to move the huge blocks without pulleys or wheels. Wheel technology was still unknown to the ancient Egyptians during this time.

3. Understand the Process

No one knows exactly what steps the Egyptian builders followed to solve their problem. The fact that the Great Pyramid was built, however, proves that they did find a solution. Listed below are some steps you can follow to solve problems, whether large or small. Under each step is a brief description of how it would have related to the Egyptian builders' problem.

1 **Identify the problem.** The builders had to be able to raise huge blocks of stone to the top of the pyramid. Remember that pulleys and wheels were unknown to the Egyptians during this time.

2 **Think of possible solutions.**
   a. Workers could lift the stone blocks up each step of the pyramid.
   b. Workers could use rollers to move the blocks up ramps built on the side of the pyramid.

3 **Compare the solutions, and choose the best one.**

   a. Many workers would be needed to lift each block up one step at a time. This would be hard to do and would take much time.

   b. Fewer workers would be needed to move the blocks up ramps. By placing blocks on rollers, the job could be done more easily and in less time.

4 **Plan a way to carry out the solution.** Temporary ramps could be built on each side of the pyramid. With four ramps, workers could move stones into place faster.

5 **Try your solution, and think about how well it solves the problem.** The solution the Egyptian builders chose solved the problem, because the Great Pyramid at Giza was built. It is still standing after 4,500 years.

Pyramids show the Egyptians' understanding of mathematics, engineering, and architecture.

4. Think and Apply

What if the Great Pyramid had to be built today? How might the problem the Egyptian builders faced be solved now? With a partner, brainstorm ways builders of today might solve the problem. Use the steps you just learned, and share your solution with your class.

Egyptian workers pull a block up a ramp (left). The Egyptians may have used several ramps at once (above).

FOCUS

What causes some societies to change over time and others to stay the same?

Main Idea Think about how the Egyptians kept their civilization as it was for thousands of years while changing some things to meet new conditions.

Vocabulary

intermediary
civil war
bureaucracy

Later Egyptian Rule

| 2000 B.C. | 1000 B.C. | B.C. | A.D. |

The Middle Kingdom and the New Kingdom were times of growth and prosperity for Egypt. At the same time, however, the Egyptians stopped believing in the pharaoh as an **intermediary**, or go-between, for humans and gods. This weakening of the pharaoh's power eventually led to a breakdown of the Egyptian government.

The Middle Kingdom

At the end of the Old Kingdom, ancient Egypt went through troubled times. About 2080 B.C. the country was divided as rival kings fought for power. Egypt was torn by a civil war. In a **civil war** groups of people from the same place or country fight one another. A scribe named Neferti described this troubled time in Egypt:

66 Dry is the river of Egypt, one crosses the water
on foot. . . .
I show you the land in turmoil. . . .
Men will seize weapons of warfare. . . .
I show you the son as enemy, the brother
as foe. . . . 99

The ancient Egyptians left behind many examples of fine artwork and jewelry. This ring made from solid gold was worn by Pharaoh Ramses II.

Egypt reunited in about 1980 B.C. That year also marks the beginning of the Middle Kingdom, which lasted until about 1630 B.C. The rule of Dynasty 12 is considered the high point of the Middle Kingdom. Dynasty 12 started about 1938 B.C. when a vizier in Lower Egypt named Amenemhet (AHM•uhn•em•HET) took over as pharaoh. He and those who ruled after him conquered all of Lower Nubia. Then

Egypt's Social Pyramid

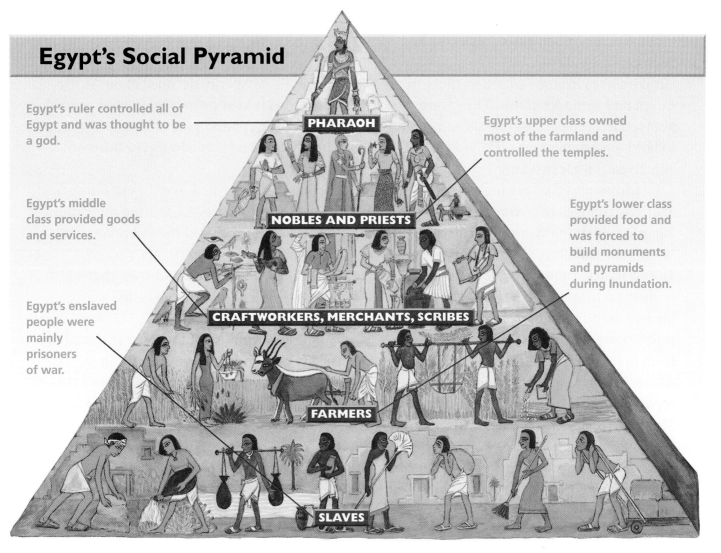

Egypt's ruler controlled all of Egypt and was thought to be a god.

Egypt's upper class owned most of the farmland and controlled the temples.

Egypt's middle class provided goods and services.

Egypt's lower class provided food and was forced to build monuments and pyramids during Inundation.

Egypt's enslaved people were mainly prisoners of war.

PHARAOH

NOBLES AND PRIESTS

CRAFTWORKERS, MERCHANTS, SCRIBES

FARMERS

SLAVES

LEARNING FROM CHARTS This pyramid-shaped chart shows the different classes of Egyptian society.
■ *What people owned most of the farmland?*

they set up a chain of forts to protect this land and to advance against Upper Nubia.

Egyptian trade also expanded during the Middle Kingdom. Boats and furniture were built of cedar and pine wood from Lebanon. Important metals such as gold from Nubia, silver from Syria, and copper from the Sinai peninsula were brought to Egypt by traders. Egyptians received products such as gold, ebony, ivory, and incense from the African savanna through trade with Upper Nubia.

During the Middle Kingdom, Egyptian society changed. Some of the rights that had once been for pharaohs alone were now available to all Egyptians. For example, the burial prayers that had once been used only for kings could now be used by everyone. Despite this change, Egyptian society remained strongly divided by social class.

Historians have compared Egyptian society to a pyramid. At the top of the social pyramid stood the pharaoh. Just below the pharaoh were the royal family and the priests and nobles. Below them were the scribes, craftworkers, and merchants. Egypt's farmers followed. At the very bottom of the pyramid were the slaves.

Most of Egypt's enslaved workers had been captured during military campaigns. Unlike slaves in some societies, those in Egypt had some freedoms. They were allowed to own personal items and even to hold government jobs. They were also able to earn their freedom.

In addition to changes in society, Egypt also saw changes in government. A Middle Kingdom pharaoh named Sesostris III (suh•SAHS•truhs) reorganized Egypt's **bureaucracy**, or network of appointed government officials. Under the old system the leaders of individual nomes had gained much power. Sesostris III removed these leaders from office and replaced them with a system of governors. The new governors were controlled by the pharaoh's vizier. This gave the pharaoh greater control over the government.

REVIEW *How did Egyptian government change during the Middle Kingdom?*

The New Kingdom

Egypt's prosperity declined about 1630 B.C. when the Hyksos (HIK•sahs) gained control of Lower Egypt and part of Upper Egypt. The Hyksos had come to Egypt from western Asia.

Hyksos kings ruled over Egypt for about 100 years as Dynasty 15. During their rule the Hyksos introduced the Egyptians to many important military innovations. These included the horse-drawn chariot and a stronger kind of bow called a composite bow.

Pharaoh Ahmose of Dynasty 18 defeated the Hyksos and reclaimed Egypt in 1520 B.C. The beginning of Dynasty 18 in 1539 B.C. marks the beginning of the New Kingdom.

Egypt's first full-time army began during the New Kingdom. Army troops protected Egypt and conquered lands beyond the Nile Valley. Pharaoh Thutmose I sent troops as

Scenes of Pharaoh Hatshepsut's expedition to Punt (left) are shown inside her temple at Deir al-Bahari (below).

far north as the Euphrates River. He also conquered parts of Nubia, pushing Egypt's border past the fourth cataract. His son, Thutmose II, continued to expand Egypt.

After Thutmose II died, his wife Hatshepsut (hat•SHEP•soot) became pharaoh. Hatshepsut was the only woman in ancient Egypt's history to take on all the titles of a pharaoh. Queen Hatshepsut sent armies into Nubia and southwestern Asia. She also sent a trading expedition south on the Red Sea to the land of Punt. Punt may have been located in what is today Ethiopia or Somalia.

Hatshepsut's stepson, Thutmose III, followed her as pharaoh. Under his rule, the Egyptian empire reached its largest size. By 1450 B.C. Egypt controlled lands from Syria to Nubia.

The early years of the New Kingdom were a time of splendor. The Egyptians of this period built huge temples to the gods, larger than any before them. The temple of Amon-Re at Karnak was the largest in the Two Lands.

Although the Egyptians of this time constructed many buildings, they no longer built pyramids. The mummies of Egyptian kings were instead placed in hidden tombs in the Valley of the Kings. This was done so that tomb robbers would not find the tombs and their buried treasures.

At the height of Egypt's prosperity, the Egyptian people faced change. In 1353 B.C. Amenhotep IV came to the throne. He and his wife Nefertiti (nef•er•TEE•tee) focused worship on a single god, the Aton. Some scholars think of this as the first example of monotheism in ancient Egypt.

Amenhotep was so devoted to the god known as the Aton that he changed his own name to Akhenaton (ahk•NAHT•uhn),

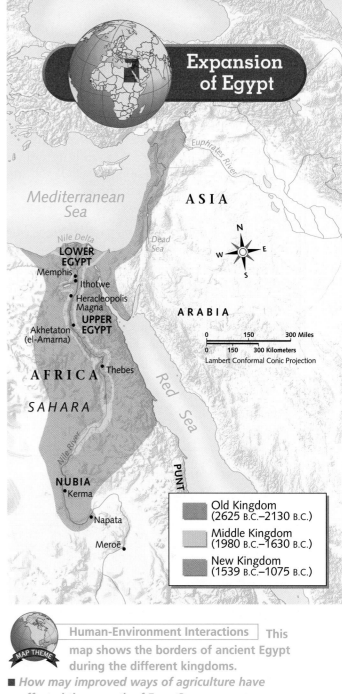

Expansion of Egypt

Old Kingdom (2625 B.C.–2130 B.C.)

Middle Kingdom (1980 B.C.–1630 B.C.)

New Kingdom (1539 B.C.–1075 B.C.)

Human-Environment Interactions This map shows the borders of ancient Egypt during the different kingdoms.

■ *How may improved ways of agriculture have affected the growth of Egypt?*

meaning "servant of the Aton." Akhenaton ordered that the names of many other gods be removed from temples and tombs. Most Egyptians, however, continued to worship the old Egyptian gods along with the Aton.

To help strengthen belief in the Aton, Akhenaton moved Egypt's capital to Akhetaton, also called el-Amarna, in the central part of the country. There he built

The Rosetta Stone

After the Egyptians were conquered, the written languages of their conquerors were used rather than hieroglyphics. For thousands of years, no one could read ancient Egyptian writing. Then, in A.D. 1798, French armies led by Napoleon Bonaparte invaded northern Africa. A year later a French army officer found a large black stone near the city of Rosetta in the Nile Delta. On the stone's shiny surface, a royal decree appears in three kinds of writing—two Egyptian and one Greek. The Greek gave scholars the key to one of the Egyptian scripts. The other script, Egyptian hieroglyphics, remained a mystery. Then, in 1822, Jean-François Champollion decoded the hieroglyphics, using the other forms of writing as a guide. The ability to read hieroglyphics unlocked all the recorded history of the ancient Egyptians for today's world.

The Rosetta Stone was made about 196 B.C. It praises the Egyptian ruler at the time, Ptolemy V.

Akhenaton and the royal family offer gifts to the Egyptian god the Aton, shown here as a sun disk.

large open-air temples to the Aton. Because of this move, present-day historians call this time the Amarna period.

After Akhenaton's death, a nine-year-old boy named Tutankhaton became pharaoh of Egypt. Under pressure from his ministers, the new pharaoh restored the old Egyptian gods and changed his name to Tutankhamen (too•tahng•KAHM•uhn), or "Living Image of Amon." Tutankhamen died at age 18 and was buried in a solid-gold coffin in a tomb packed with gold and jewels.

About 1215 B.C., the Egyptians began to lose parts of their empire to invaders known as the Sea Peoples. The Sea Peoples came from Asia Minor and lands in the Mediterranean and Aegean seas. Egypt itself remained united through Dynasty 20, which ended in 1075 B.C.

REVIEW *Where did Akhenaton move Egypt's capital?*

Egypt Under the Rule of Others

Rival dynasties arose in the Delta. By 730 B.C. Dynasty 25, a Nubian dynasty, had taken control of Egypt. For almost 50 years they fought with the Assyrian Empire for control of southwestern Asia. The Assyrians finally defeated the Nubians.

By about 664 B.C., the Assyrians had reunited all of Egypt. Egypt continued under Assyrian rule for more than 100 years. Egypt remained at peace until a Persian king named Cambyses II (kam•BY•seez) made Egypt a part of his empire in 525 B.C. Egypt regained its independence from 404 B.C. to 343 B.C., only to be conquered a second time by Persia.

In 332 B.C. Alexander the Great conquered the Persian Empire. In doing so, he gained control of Egypt and made it part of his Greek Empire. His general, Ptolemy (TAHL•uh•mee), took control of Egypt in 305 B.C. Egypt remained in Greek hands until the Greeks were defeated by the Romans. Egypt was made a part of the Roman Empire in 30 B.C. Egyptian civilization continued under Roman rule. By A.D. 395 the Egyptians had begun to replace many of their original religious beliefs with Christian beliefs.

REVIEW *Which different peoples controlled Egypt after the New Kingdom?*

LESSON 4 REVIEW

2000 B.C.	1500 B.C.	1000 B.C.	500 B.C.	B.C.	A.D.
1980 B.C. • Middle Kingdom begins	**1539 B.C.** • New Kingdom begins		**730 B.C.** • Nubians conquer Egypt	**30 B.C.** • Egyptian dynasties end	

Check Understanding

1 **Remember the Facts**   What areas did the Egyptians conquer during the Middle Kingdom and the New Kingdom?

2 **Recall the Main Idea**   What changes did Egyptians make in their government, religion, and way of life over time?

Think Critically

3 **Past to Present**   In what ways has the United States stayed the same over the years? How has it changed?

4 **Think More About It**   How did the pharaohs keep ancient Egyptian civilization the same while changing some things?

Show What You Know

Map Activity   Egypt built a huge empire during the Middle Kingdom and the New Kingdom. Make a map of Egypt's empire at its greatest size. Include Egypt's trading partners. Then add pictures of the products the Egyptians got from each place.

His Majesty
Queen Hatshepsut

by Dorothy Sharp Carter

Women in ancient Egyptian society shared with men the right to own property and businesses. Some women in ancient Egypt became government officials and trusted advisers to pharaohs. Historians believe that Queen Tiye, wife of Pharaoh Amenhotep III, ruled along with her husband, making many important decisions. Few women, however, became pharaohs.

Queen Hatshepsut also ruled with her husband, Thutmose II. Hatshepsut had married her half-brother, a common custom among Egyptian royalty. After the death of her husband, Hatshepsut refused to give up her rule to young Thutmose III, the son of Thutmose II and another of his wives. Because he was male, Thutmose III stood next in line to the throne. However, Hatshepsut believed she deserved to rule because she was the daughter of Thutmose I.

Hatshepsut did become pharaoh. In doing so, she became the first important woman ruler in world history. Advised by her vizier Hatshepsut ruled Egypt during the period of the New Kingdom. As pharaoh, she helped bring strength and wealth to Egypt. Hatshepsut is remembered for her expansion of trade routes, and for sending expeditions to the land of Punt.

Read now a story about Queen Hatshepsut's coronation, or crowning, as pharaoh. As you read, think about what it might be like for a person to take on a new role in a society.

And so arrangements for my coronation go forward. The sooner it takes place, the better. For plots of defiance to hatch, time is essential. We will dispense with time.

Throughout the Two Lands and abroad, the edict of my ascension to the throne is sent, only a few weeks before the ceremony. By tradition the event takes place on a major religious holiday, in this case the Feast of Opet. Hapusoneb insists this is a bit hurried but perfectly proper. But then anything Pharaoh-to-be decides is proper.

The edict reads:

A letter of the King to cause thee to know that My Majesty is risen as King on the throne of Horus, without equal forever. My titles are: for my Horus name, Usert-Kau, mighty in kas; for Vulture-Cobra, Uadjit-Renpet, fresh in years; for Golden Horus, Netert-khau, divine in apparitions;[1] my royal and birth names, Makare Hatshepsut.

Cause thou that worship of the gods be made at the desire of the King of Upper and Lower Egypt,

---

[1]**apparitions:** religious spirits

....

This painted sandstone sculpture captures the beauty of Queen Hatshepsut. Hatshepsut ruled Egypt as pharaoh from 1479 B.C. to 1458 B.C.

Hatshepsut. Cause thou that all oaths be taken in the name of My Majesty, born of the royal mother Ahmose. This is written that thou mayest bow thy head in obedience and knowest that the royal house is firm and strong.

The third year, third month of Inundation, day 7. Day of Coronation.

I worry over my dress. As ceremony demands that the king wear the royal braided beard strapped to his chin (no matter whether he has a beard of his own or not), I shall certainly do so. Ought I, then, to wear the long dress of a queen or the short kilt of a king? With a question Hapusoneb supplies the answer.

He is preoccupied, poor man, at having to oversee so many elaborate arrangements in such a short period of time. At each succeeding audience with me he appears more harried, more bent with care, until his back curves like a strung bow.

"One of the problems, Majesty, is that the titles and coronation ceremonies are designed for men. How are we to change them?"

The solution strikes me, clear as Hapusoneb's harassed face.

"There is no need to change anything, Vizier. I mean to rule as a king, with the full powers of a king. And I shall dress as a king. The rituals, the titles, will remain the same as those initiated by Narmer, first King of the Two Lands."

Hapusoneb appears dubious, then relieved. After all, he can scarcely overrule Pharaoh-to-be, no matter what his misgivings.

And as I am resolved to be as resolute, as forceful as any king, I will begin by donning full regalia[2] for my coronation. Around my waist, over the short kilt, I fasten a broad belt adorned with a metal buckle in the form of my personal cartouche.[3] Tied to it in front is an apron of beads, in back a bull's tail. A girl attaches the beard to my chin. Over my wig is fitted the *nems*, the leather headcloth with the two striped lappets falling forward over my shoulders.

For the ceremony I have ordered a dazzling gold-and-jeweled pectoral[4] suspended from a double gold chain. On each of my arms a girl clasps a pair of wide bracelets, another on each wrist, a third pair on my ankles. On my fingers rings are strung like chunks of beef on skewers. Surely I must weigh twice as much as usual.

As I take a final peek in my silver mirror, I gasp to Henut,[5] "But I look a

---

[2] **regalia:** symbols of royalty
[3] **cartouche** (kar•TOOSH): An Egyptian decoration with the name of a ruler written in hieroglyphics
[4] **pectoral:** an object worn on the chest
[5] **Henut** (HEN•uht): Hatshepsut's servant

Pectoral, or chest plate, worn by a pharaoh of Dynasty 19

mummy! One can hardly see the flesh for the gold."

"Very appropriate, Highness." Henut nods approvingly. "Egypt is wealthy beyond measure. You are the symbol of that wealth."

Perhaps so, but wealth, I find, does not always signal comfort.

The ceremony goes off with fanfare. Although the coronation of my husband occurred fifteen years before, the rites are still clear in my memory.

I sit on a light throne borne by six slaves from the Great House to the royal barge, which carries us down the river. From the shore to the temple the procession is headed by heralds crying, "Earth, beware! Your god comes!" Rows of soldiers pace before and behind my carrying chair, and in back of them hundreds of priests.

Behind my chair a servant supports a long-handled sunshade to provide me some relief from the sun, and beside me two young pages wave fans of ostrich plumes. (Vizier has promised boys with endurance and dedication enough not to whack off my headpiece.) The tail of the procession—a very long tail—is made up of government dignitaries,[6] the nobility, and foreign envoys.[7]

Most of the spectators sink to their knees, heads in the dust, although a few bewildered country folk stand gaping in amazement. A guard motions them sternly to bow, or even strikes one or two with his spear. As Hapusoneb says, "Manners grow more and more out of fashion." Still, the atmosphere is a happy mixture of reverence and rejoicing.

---

[6]**dignitaries:** persons holding high office
[7]**envoys:** persons sent to another place or country as representatives

In the main hall of the temple my litter is lowered and I walk, accompanied by the High Priest, to the gleaming gilded throne set on a dais.[8] After prayers and hymns to Amon, the Priest makes an address in which he repeats my father's words uttered in the dream: "I have appointed her to be my successor upon my throne. She it is, assuredly, who shall sit upon my glorious throne; she shall order all matters for the people in every department of the state; she it is who shall lead you."

---

[8]**dais** (DAY•uhs): a raised platform

Thutmose III, who followed Hatshepsut as pharaoh, destroyed many statues of her. This statue of Hatshepsut in the form of a sphinx—a creature half human and half animal—remained untouched.

Finally he pronounces me Lord of the Two Lands, seated on the Horus-throne, and living forever and ever. Into my hands he puts the two scepters, emblems of Osiris: the golden crook, and the golden flail with its handle carved in the form of a lotus flower. And on my head he places one symbolic crown after another, ending with the double crown, combining the white crown of Upper Egypt and the red of Lower Egypt, with the golden uraeus, or cobra, attached to the front. The cobra has the reputation of spitting poisonous fire at anyone venturing too near to Pharaoh. (Someday for amusement I must persuade Vizier to test this.) The whole contraption is so heavy that my neck soon aches with the weight.

During the crowning I notice my daughter and the Prince standing beside each other. As Nefrure refused to ride in a carrying chair for fear of falling, the two march (when Nefrure is not being carried by a guard) in the procession, close behind my litter. Nefrure beams at me, proud and excited, while Thutmose's gaze is as blank as when he viewed the gems and vases at the reception of ambassadors. Lost in his own world (perhaps a world where his stepmother is either feeble or dead), he seems oblivious of all movement about him.

The return journey to the palace is agonizing, so that I have to grit my teeth and lock my neck in position. What if suddenly my neck were to bend—or break—and the unwieldy crown bounce off onto the pavement and into the crowd? King Hatshepsut would have to fabricate a glib story; else all of Egypt would believe that Amon had sent a warning that I was unfit to be Pharaoh. I shudder and lock my neck even more tightly.

Finally it is over. I am home in my suite, resting, my head and neck painful but still intact. The reception and banquet lie ahead, but those I can manage easily. In the distance I hear the celebration of the people, with their eating and drinking, their singing and dancing, their roars of amusement at the acrobats and jugglers and clowns provided for their entertainment. Egypt's treasury will sink this day like the Nile during harvest, but then coronations do not happen every day, that of a queen practically never.

I, Makare Hatshepsut, am Pharaoh of all of Egypt! The thought is too stupendous to fit into my head just yet. First I must view it from all sides . . . and stroke it . . . and shape it . . . till it can slip naturally into place.

LITERATURE REVIEW

1. In what ways did Hatshepsut both keep to and change Egyptian tradition by taking on the role of ruler?

2. What do you think caused Hatshepsut to challenge tradition and seek to become pharaoh?

3. Use what you have learned about Hatshepsut to write a character sketch of the female pharaoh. Be sure to mention any leadership qualities you think she showed.

Follow Routes

1. Why Learn This Skill?

Suppose that on your next vacation, you are traveling in a car with your family. You know the name of the highway you are on, but you don't know in which direction you are traveling. You have a map that shows where your family wants to end up. If your family stopped in a town to eat lunch, would you be able to figure out the direction in which you would have to travel to reach your destination? If your map had a compass rose, you would be able to.

A compass rose is a symbol that shows directions on a map. It shows the main directions—north, south, east, and west. It also shows the directions in between—northeast, northwest, southeast, and southwest. The compass rose makes it possible to relate the map to the real world and find directions.

To figure out the direction in which your family would have to travel, you would start by finding on the map the town you are stopped in. Next, you would find your family's destination on the map. The compass rose would show you in which direction your destination is from the town where you stopped. This is the direction in which you and your family will have to travel to reach your destination.

2. Understand the Process

The map shows the **trade routes**, paths that traders use as they exchange goods, of Egypt during the New Kingdom. Some of these routes show travel over land, while others show travel over water. A dashed line shows a route that may have been used by traders in ancient Egypt. Use the compass rose to answer the questions:

1 An Egyptian trader's route begins at Thinis. In which direction will the trader have to travel to connect with another trade route shown on the map?

2 In Memphis another Egyptian trader is preparing to leave. In which different directions do major trade routes go from that city?

3 Some Egyptian traders want to travel from Byblos to Enkomi on the island of Cyprus. In which direction must they go? Will they travel by land or by sea?

4 Egyptian traders can take several routes to travel from Memphis to Mycenae. Identify the routes by naming the directions in which the traders will travel, whether the trade route is by water or over land, and listing the cities they will pass through.

on a Map

5 A group of Egyptian traders from Memphis has passed through Byblos and Kadesh. If they continue to follow the trade routes, what city will they come to next? In which direction are they traveling, north or south?

6 An Egyptian trader wants to travel from Buhen to Hattusas without traveling by sea. What routes must the trader take?

7 In which direction is the Hittite Empire from Egypt? In which direction is Kush from Egypt? Punt from Kush? Egypt from Arabia? Crete from Cyprus?

8 What body of water would traders use to travel from Sawu to Punt? What body of water would traders use to travel from Byblos to Mycenae?

3. Think and Apply

Imagine that you are a trader in Egypt during the New Kingdom. Plan a trip from your home in Thebes to Mycenae. Draw your own map showing the routes you would like to take. Put a compass rose on your map in the correct position. Is most of your travel over land or water? What cities will you pass through during your journey? In which general direction must you travel to reach Mycenae?

Egyptian Trade Routes

Hattusas
HITTITE EMPIRE
Mycenae
Carchemish
MITTANI
Crete
Rhodes
Enkomi
Ugarit
Knossos
Cyprus
Kadesh
Byblos
Mediterranean Sea
Kyrene
Megiddo
Qantir
Memphis
ARABIA
EGYPT
Akhetaton
Western Desert
Thinis
Sawu
Coptos
Thebes
Quseir
Red Sea
Elephantine
SAHARA
Berenice
Buhen
Nile River
PUNT
KUSH
Napata

N
W E
S

0   150   300 Miles
0   150   300 Kilometers
Lambert Conformal Conic Projection

New Kingdom Egypt → Land trade route
Oasis → Water trade route
---→ Possible trade route

CONNECT MAIN IDEAS

Use this organizer to describe the ancient Egyptian civilization that arose in northern Africa. Write two details to support each main idea. A copy of the organizer appears on page 32 of the Activity Book.

Geography of Northern Africa

The changing environment of the Sahara and the Nile Valley helped Egypt prosper.

1. _____
2. _____

Importance of the Nile River

The Nile River affected the development of Egyptian society and religion.

1. _____
2. _____

Ancient Egypt

Early Egyptian Rule

Egyptian pharaohs used different methods to build political power and religious authority.

1. _____
2. _____

Later Egyptian Rule

The Egyptians kept their civilization as it was for thousands of years yet also changed some things to meet new conditions.

1. _____
2. _____

WRITE MORE ABOUT IT

Write a Description Imagine that you are the son or daughter of an Egyptian farmer. You are living beside the Nile in about the year 2000 B.C. Describe what your life is like. Use these questions to help you plan what you will write: How does the Nile River affect you? What do you do each day? What is important to you and your family? What are your plans for the future?

Write a News Report Think about how the environment has affected people's lives. Then imagine that you are a reporter for the *Ancient Egyptian Times* and the Nile River is flooding. Write a news article about what is happening in your area. Describe both the good and the bad results of the flooding. Answer these questions: Who? What? Why? Where? When? and How?

| 3000 B.C. | 2000 B.C. | 1000 B.C. | B.C. | A.D. |

About
3000 B.C.
• Egypt is
united

2625 B.C.
• Old
Kingdom
begins

1980 B.C.
• Middle
Kingdom
begins

1539 B.C.
• New
Kingdom
begins

30 B.C.
• Egyptian
dynasties
end

USE VOCABULARY

For each group of terms, write at least one sentence that shows how the terms are related.

1 delta, cataract

2 dynasty, pharaoh, decree

3 papyrus, hieroglyphics

4 pyramid, mummy

5 bureaucracy, vizier

CHECK UNDERSTANDING

6 Why was silt important to early Egyptian farmers?

7 How did nature affect the religion of the ancient Egyptians?

8 Who does legend say united the Two Lands of Egypt?

9 How did the pharaohs of Egypt make sure that Egyptian life would continue unchanged?

10 How did the Egyptian religion influence the way the tombs of the pharaohs were built?

11 How did Egyptian government and religion change during the Middle Kingdom?

12 Why was the reign of Pharaoh Hatshepsut important?

13 What areas did Egypt conquer during the New Kingdom?

14 How did Akhenaton try to change the Egyptian religion?

15 What peoples conquered Egypt after the end of the New Kingdom?

THINK CRITICALLY

16 **Cause and Effect** What is the Rosetta Stone? What effect did its discovery and decoding have?

17 **Think More About It** Why do you think Akhenaton's religious reforms failed to last?

18 **Past to Present** What might archaeologists find 2,000 years from now that would give them clues about our culture?

APPLY SKILLS

Solve a Problem Ask an adult family member about a problem he or she has had to solve. What steps did that person take? Compare those steps with the ones listed on pages 148 and 149.

Follow Routes on a Map Look at the map on page 163. In which directions would you go to travel from Memphis to Thinis? Byblos to Knossos?

READ MORE ABOUT IT

Pepi and the Secret Names by Jill Paton Walsh. Lothrop, Lee & Shepard Books. An Egyptian boy uses his special knowledge to help his father paint a prince's tomb.

HARCOURT
BRACE

Visit the Internet at
http://www.hbschool.com
for additional resources.

ANCIENT NUBIA

"Here gold is found in great abundance and huge elephants, and ebony, and all sorts of trees growing wild."

Greek historian Herodotus, writing about Nubia, 450 B.C.

Silver and gold mask of Kushite Queen Malaqaye, made about 500 B.C.

Nubia: Egypt's Rival

| 6000 B.C. | 4000 B.C. | 2000 B.C. | B.C. | A.D. |

The land of Nubia stretched along the Nile River from Egypt's southern border almost to where the city of Khartoum (kar•TOOM), Sudan, stands today. Beneath Nubia's rocky soil were many resources, such as copper and gold. Cliffs made of granite and other kinds of rock used in building rose high above the landscape. Animals of many kinds roamed the land. The many resources of Nubia made life comfortable for its people. Nubia's resources also caused other peoples, such as the Egyptians, to want control of the land. Many conflicts arose as a result. The close contact of the Egyptians and the Nubians caused them to influence each other's religion, government, and culture. Each adopted some of the ideas and customs of the other. Still, over thousands of years, each held on to its own identity.

The Land and People of Ancient Nubia

The geography of Nubia was very different from the geography of Egypt. Nubia was much rockier than Egypt. In some places high cliffs rose straight up from the Nile River.

Even the Nile River took on a different shape as it traveled through Nubia. The Nile's course was not as smooth in ancient Nubia as it was farther north in ancient Egypt. Large granite boulders blocked parts of the river in the south, causing rapids and waterfalls. These groups of rocks formed the six large areas of cataracts found along the southern, or upper, part of the Nile.

Archaeologists believe that people migrated to Nubia at least 8,000 years ago. Evidence of an early culture from this time has been uncovered near the modern city of

FOCUS

How can contact between neighboring groups lead to both cooperation and conflict?

Main Idea   Look for ways in which the people of Nubia and the people of Egypt affected each other.

Vocabulary

annex
independence
ally

Khartoum. Like the ancient Egyptians, the Nubians usually lived alongside the Nile.

The earliest people of Nubia lived just as the Egyptians lived before the dynasties. Some experts believe that the ancient Nubians provided some of the basic ideas of Egyptian culture. For example, some Egyptian gods may have been first worshipped in Nubia.

To survive, the early people of Nubia fished and hunted and gathered wild grains. In time, the ancient Nubians began to grow their own grain and raise cattle, sheep, and goats. These Nubian farmers and herders found it best to stay in one place all year round rather than travel from place to place.

As settled people, the ancient Nubians began to make pottery to store grains and carry supplies. People on the move could not use pottery because it would get broken on long trips. For settled people, however, pottery was very useful.

The Nubians were among the first people to make pottery. Nubian craftworkers worked with clay as early as 6000 B.C. Nubian bowls and jars are among the most beautiful and best-made of all early objects.

Over time, pottery became a trade item offered by the Nubians. The Nubians also traded goods that came to them from several places in central and southern Africa. These goods were in great demand by the Egyptians and the peoples of southwestern Asia.

Nubia's location between Egypt and southern Africa made it an ideal trading center. The Nubians served as go-betweens for trade between northern and southern Africa. Among the many trade items the

While under the rule of the Egyptians, ancient Nubians were often required to offer tribute to the Egyptian pharaoh. This wall painting shows a Nubian princess riding in a chariot and four Nubian princes on foot. The group is on its way to offer gold to the pharaoh.

Egypt and Nubia: Conflicts and Conquests

2100 B.C.	1850 B.C.	1600 B.C.	1350 B.C.	1100 B.C.	850 B.C.	600 B.C.

About 1935 B.C.
- Pharaoh Amenemhet conquers Nubia
- Independent Kush establishes capital at Kerma

About 1650 B.C.
- Nubia regains independence

About 1465 B.C.
- Pharaoh Thutmose III claims Nubia
- Independent Kush establishes capital at Napata

750 B.C.
- King Kashta conquers Upper Egypt

730 B.C.
- King Piye conquers Lower Egypt

671 B.C.
- Kushite rule in Egypt ends
- Independent kingdom of Kush continues

LEARNING FROM TIME LINES This time line shows that Egypt and Nubia often were in conflict with one another.

■ *According to the time line, during what years was Kush in control of Egypt?*

Nubians sent northward were leopard skins, ostrich eggs, feathers, ivory, ebony, spices, and gold.

Archaeological evidence suggests that Egypt and Nubia traded peacefully at first. The Egyptians realized, though, that they could gain greater wealth if they had control of Nubia's trade routes, the paths that traders use as they exchange goods.

By 2600 B.C. Egyptian kings succeeded in claiming all the trade routes in northern Nubia. The Egyptians also began helping themselves to Nubia's rich natural resources. Egyptians cut blocks of stone such as granite, which they used for statues and buildings. They also mined Nubian copper and gold. After years of controlling much of northern Nubia, Egypt moved to **annex**, or take over, the land. About 1900 B.C. the Egyptian pharaoh ordered forts built near the second cataract to protect the newly annexed land from enemies.

REVIEW *Why did Egypt want control of Nubia's trade routes?*

Freedom and Reconquest

Egyptian control of ancient Nubia did not last long. A powerful kingdom began to grow in Upper Nubia. This kingdom soon gained the strength to drive the Egyptians out of Nubia.

The ancient Egyptians called the new kingdom Kush. Modern archaeologists call the people of this kingdom the Kerma culture. Its center was near the third cataract, where the modern town of Kerma, Sudan, is today.

By 1650 B.C. the people of Nubia had regained their **independence**, or complete freedom, from Egypt. Free from Egyptian rule, the Kerma culture grew. The ancient town of Kerma became a main stopping point for both river and overland trade. Goods such as gold, salt, spices, elephants, and rhinoceros horns moved through Kerma to markets all over Africa and across the Red Sea. This trade brought great wealth to the people of Kerma.

The ancient burial grounds of the Kerma kings provide evidence of their wealth. To bury a king, the people of Kerma dug a large round pit. They then placed a gold-covered wooden funeral bed at the bottom. They dressed the king in his finest clothes and laid him on the funeral bed. Around him they placed his weapons, his treasures of gold and ivory, and his jewelry. Then they covered the pit with a mound of earth and outlined the mound with skulls of cattle.

During Kerma's days of prosperity, its kings gained power as well as wealth. Over time they were able to gain control of much of northern Sudan and even some parts of southern Egypt.

The same period was not as good for the Egyptians. At this time the Hyksos held control of much of Egypt. Kerma's leader decided that it would be best to become an **ally**, or supporter, of the Hyksos. After all, the Hyksos controlled most of the land to the north of Nubia. The Kerma king did not know that the Egyptians would soon regain the land. The victorious Egyptians forced the Hyksos out of their country and into

southwestern Asia. Then the Egyptians turned south and destroyed Kush's capital city of Kerma. They took this action to punish the people of Kerma for helping the Hyksos.

Following their military successes, the Egyptians claimed control of much of Nubia. This time Egypt's control of Nubia reached past the fourth cataract. As a show of strength, the Egyptians built cities and temples all over Nubia.

Egypt's rule over Nubia lasted for about 550 years. During that time the Egyptian pharaoh created a special position called the King's Son of Kush. This person was responsible for the day-to-day governing of Nubian lands and for collecting taxes.

Under Egyptian rule, the people of Nubia were encouraged to become like Egyptians. Many Nubians adopted Egyptian religious beliefs, writing, customs, and ways of dress.

REVIEW *How did the decision to side with the Hyksos affect the people of Kerma?*

Pyramids built during the time of the kingdom of Kush are reminders of the civilizations that developed in ancient Nubia.

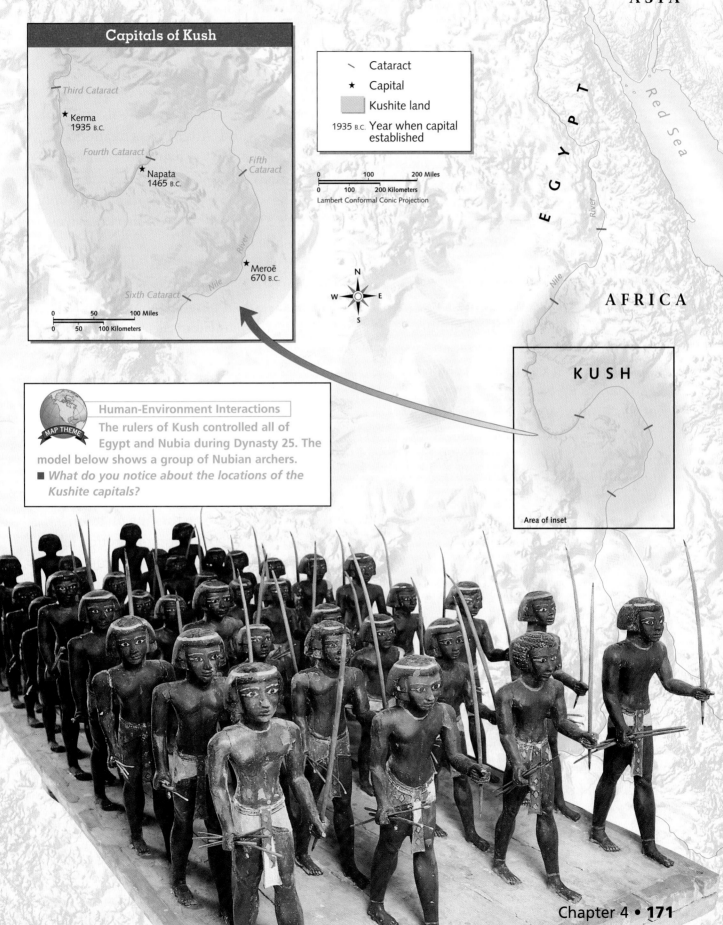

Kingdom of Kush

Capitals of Kush

Third Cataract

Kerma
1935 B.C.

Fourth Cataract

Napata
1465 B.C.

Fifth Cataract

River

Meroë
670 B.C.

Sixth Cataract

Nile

0   50   100 Miles
0   50   100 Kilometers

— Cataract
★ Capital
▢ Kushite land
1935 B.C. Year when capital established

0   100   200 Miles
0   100   200 Kilometers
Lambert Conformal Conic Projection

N
W   E
S

ASIA

E G Y P T

Red Sea

River

Nile

AFRICA

KUSH

Area of inset

Human-Environment Interactions

The rulers of Kush controlled all of Egypt and Nubia during Dynasty 25. The model below shows a group of Nubian archers.

■ *What do you notice about the locations of the Kushite capitals?*

PIYE'S ATTACK ON EGYPT

These words, which appear on an ancient stela, describe Piye's capture of the Egyptian city of Memphis:

When day broke, at early morning his majesty reached Memphis. When he had landed on the north of it, he found that the water had approached to the walls, the ships mooring at (the walls of) Memphis....

Then his majesty was enraged against it like a panther; he said: "I swear, as Re loves me, as my father, Amon (who fashioned me) favors me.... I will take it like flood of water..." Then he sent forth his fleet and his army to assault the harbor of Memphis.

Conquest of Egypt

Beginning about 1075 B.C. several weak dynasties brought the Egyptian Empire into a time of disorder. By 800 B.C. Egyptian soldiers had to leave Nubia to take care of troubles at home. At the same time, the kingdom of Kush started to regain its strength. The Kushites built a new capital city farther south on the Nile called Napata (NA•puh•tuh), near the fourth cataract.

King Aspelta, shown in this statue, ruled Kush from 593 B.C. to 568 B.C.

Kush's king, Kashta (KASH•tuh), kept a careful watch on events taking place in Egypt. About 750 B.C. Kush attacked Upper Egypt. About 20 years later Kashta's son Piye (PEE•yeh), also known as Piankhi (PYANG•kee), conquered most of Lower Egypt. Piye's conquest brought all of Egypt under his control. After Piye's death his brother Shabaka (SHA•bah•kah) claimed the pharaoh's throne. He and the Kushite pharaohs who followed him ruled as Egypt's Dynasty 25. This dynasty is also known as the Kushite dynasty.

Perhaps the most successful of all the Dynasty 25 pharaohs was Taharka (tuh•HAR•kuh). Pharaoh Taharka is remembered for the many temples and pyramids he ordered built.

The Kushite pharaohs ruled Egypt from about 730 B.C. to 660 B.C. and helped restore Egypt to its former glory. Temples that had been destroyed in earlier invasions of Egypt were rebuilt and new temples were constructed. The Kushite pharaohs brought back long-forgotten religious ceremonies and ordered scribes to copy and save ancient Egyptian books.

The kings of Dynasty 25 learned to write in Egyptian hieroglyphics. For the first time, the people of Nubia began to write about themselves. They recorded their achievements in writing on temple walls and stelae. Their writings give us a first-hand look at their way of life.

REVIEW *How was Dynasty 25 different from other Egyptian dynasties?*

Kushite Rule Ends in Egypt

The Kushites' powerful rule over Egypt came to an end in 671 B.C., when the Assyrians invaded Egypt. The Assyrians' iron weapons overpowered the bronze weapons used by the Kushites. The Assyrians destroyed the combined Kushite and Egyptian armies. This forced Taharka and the Kushite army to retreat to Napata.

King Taharka died in Napata, and soon after, the Kushites lost their control of Egypt. However, the Kushites had learned from the Assyrians how to make iron. This skill would help them as they set about building a new kingdom.

REVIEW *What caused the Kushites to lose control of Egypt?*

HERITAGE

The Temples of Abu Simbel

About 1279 B.C. Pharaoh Ramses II had two temples built at Abu Simbel in Nubia. In 1959 Egypt announced plans to build the Aswan High Dam. The lake formed by the dam would cover much of Lower Nubia. A worldwide effort was made to save the temples. The temples were cut into blocks—some weighing as much as 30 tons—and moved slightly farther away from the Nile and at a higher elevation.

Workers move a massive statue of Ramses II at Abu Simbel.

LESSON 1 REVIEW

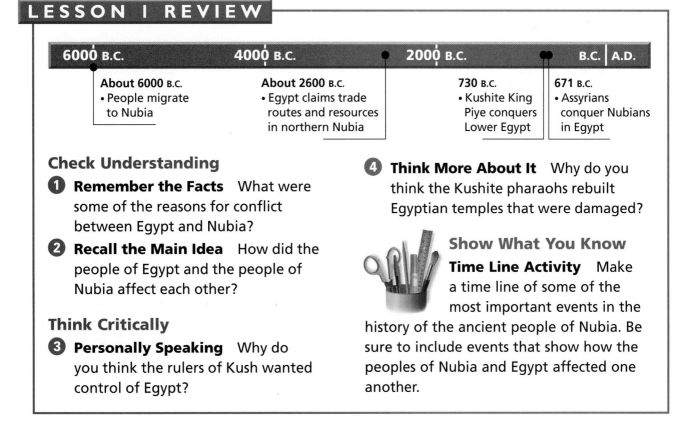

6000 B.C.	4000 B.C.	2000 B.C.	B.C.	A.D.
About 6000 B.C. • People migrate to Nubia	**About 2600 B.C.** • Egypt claims trade routes and resources in northern Nubia	**730 B.C.** • Kushite King Piye conquers Lower Egypt	**671 B.C.** • Assyrians conquer Nubians in Egypt	

Check Understanding

1 Remember the Facts What were some of the reasons for conflict between Egypt and Nubia?

2 Recall the Main Idea How did the people of Egypt and the people of Nubia affect each other?

Think Critically

3 Personally Speaking Why do you think the rulers of Kush wanted control of Egypt?

4 Think More About It Why do you think the Kushite pharaohs rebuilt Egyptian temples that were damaged?

Show What You Know

Time Line Activity Make a time line of some of the most important events in the history of the ancient people of Nubia. Be sure to include events that show how the peoples of Nubia and Egypt affected one another.

Which Civilization Came First: Nubia or Egypt?

For many years archaeologists and other scholars knew little about either the Egyptians or the Nubians. Then, in 1822, Jean-François Champollion used the Rosetta Stone to decode the language of the ancient Egyptians. His work gave the world the key to understanding their written records. These writings, however, gave only the Egyptians' view of the Nubians. For nearly 150 years, most scholars believed that the Nubians were of little importance.

It was not until the 1960s that archaeologists and scholars began to learn more about ancient Nubia. They have uncovered and studied artifacts and monuments that show that Nubia had a highly developed civilization.

Now some scholars wonder which civilization, the Nubian or the Egyptian, affected the other more. One topic of the debate centers on which civilization was the first to have a unified government ruled by a single king. The opinions of two scholars follow on page 175.

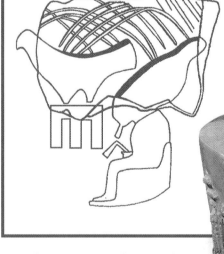

At near right is an incense burner. This artifact was found among the remains of ancient Nubia. The sketch above shows a portion of the incense burner which has an image of a falcon and a king.

Bruce Williams

Bruce Williams, an archaeologist at the University of Chicago, believes that Nubian artifacts from 3300 B.C. show the world's earliest representations of kings. One of the artifacts Williams has studied is a stone incense burner that shows a falcon and a human figure.

❝The falcon means a god. . . . That [figure] is definitely a representation of a king, and he's wearing a crown. . . . The burner is definitely a typical Nubian, not an Egyptian, object.❞

David O'Connor

David O'Connor of the University of Pennsylvania believes that the Nubians copied many Egyptian ideas, including that of having a united government ruled by a king.

❝I think there may well have been an elite group in Nubia at the time, in charge of a complex chiefdom. But the artifacts Williams's argument depends on are almost certainly Egyptian, not Nubian—traded to Nubia in early . . . times. The kings he sees were Egyptian kings.❞

Compare Viewpoints

1. Why does Bruce Williams believe that Nubia was the first civilization to have kings?

2. Why does David O'Connor disagree with Bruce Williams?

3. How might knowing which culture made the incense burner help archaeologists settle this disagreement?

Think and Apply

People often use evidence to support their views. However, people do not always agree on what the evidence means. What situations today deal with the meaning of evidence? Does everyone agree on what that evidence means?

Nubian pyramids are generally much steeper and smaller than Egyptian pyramids.

FOCUS

How can the location and the natural resources of a place help shape its history and culture?

Main Idea Think about how the location and the natural resources of Meroë affected its rise and fall.

Vocabulary

trade network

Kush and the World

| 400 B.C. | 200 B.C. | B.C. | A.D. | A.D. 200 | A.D. 400 |

Attacked but not defeated, Kushite leaders moved their capital south to Meroë (MAIR•oh•wee), near the sixth cataract of the Nile River. There, farther from Egypt, the Kushite culture continued. This time of great achievement lasted from 270 B.C. to A.D. 350 and is known as the Meroitic period.

During the Meroitic period, Kush included most of Nubia as well as regions far south of Khartoum. Across the empire the Kushites built temples to their own gods as well as palaces and pyramids for their own kings and queens. They also created many new customs of their own. Once again the Kushites became known for trade.

Trade Links

One of Meroë's greatest advantages was its location. The city was not only on the Nile River but also at the meeting point of several overland trade routes. In Meroë, Kushite merchants once again set up their old **trade network**, or group of buyers and sellers. Traders from southwestern Asia and from all parts of Africa came to Meroë. Along with gold and spices, the Kushites began to offer iron products.

The knowledge of ironmaking proved very important to the people of Kush. Under their new land lay much iron ore. In mining pits near Meroë, Kushite workers dug the iron ore from beneath the rock and sand. Iron-workers melted the ore in furnaces and removed the minerals that could not be used.

This beautiful Nubian necklace was found in a pyramid at Meroë.

The pure iron was then hauled to the city, where craftworkers used it to make iron tools and weapons.

Meroë was one of the earliest centers for ironmaking in Africa. Today huge heaps of slag, the waste from the melted iron ore, are evidence of this important economic activity of long ago.

Meroë won fame in much of the ancient world as a center of trade. The city became an artistic and cultural meeting ground for travelers from all parts of Africa. The Meroitic trade network even reached to the Mediterranean. We know this because artifacts from all parts of the Mediterranean region have been found in graves and tombs excavated in and around ancient Meroë.

The need to keep records of their trade led the people of Meroë to create the first Nubian written language. Before this time the Nubian language was only spoken. Any written communication had used Egyptian hieroglyphics. The new alphabet had 23 symbols, which stood for sounds in the Nubian language. Today the sounds of the symbols are known, but no one has been able to figure out the meaning of the words. The Meroitic language is still a mystery. Until this mystery is solved, much of the ancient history of the people of Meroë will remain unknown.

REVIEW *Why was Meroë's location important?*

Meroitic Rulers

Trade brought the Meroitic culture much wealth, but its rulers gave it its strength. Just as the pharaohs of Dynasty 25 had claimed to be sons of the god Amon, so too did the leaders of the Meroë culture.

Early Ironworking
in Kush

LEARNING FROM DIAGRAMS This diagram shows how iron ore may have been ❶ mined, ❷ melted, and ❸ worked in Kush during the Meroitic period.
■ *Why do you think the furnaces for melting iron ore were partially buried?*

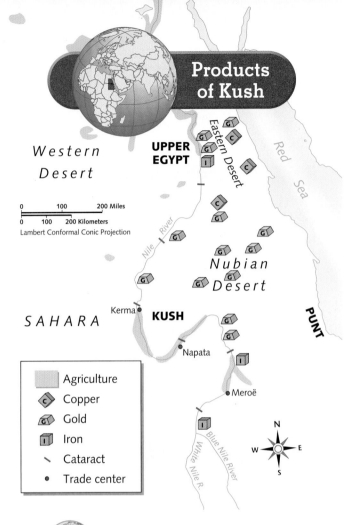

Products of Kush

Western Desert

UPPER EGYPT

Eastern Desert

Red Sea

Nile River

0   100   200 Miles
0   100   200 Kilometers
Lambert Conformal Conic Projection

Nubian Desert

SAHARA   Kerma   KUSH

Napata

• Meroë

PUNT

Agriculture
Copper
Gold
Iron
Cataract
Trade center

Blue Nile River

White Nile R.

N W E S

Place Kush was rich in natural resources, including minerals, metals, and agricultural products.

■ *What resources could be found in the Nubian Desert?*

Meroitic queens are pictured as warriors holding swords. These powerful queens are even known to have led their own troops in battles. One queen was Amanitore (uh•MAN•uh•tawr•ee). Queen Amanitore led her army against the Romans in 24 B.C.

The carvings also show how Meroitic rulers dressed. A king or queen wore a long robe with a cloak over it. Often this outfit was draped with a fringed shawl and long bands of cloth with tassels that hung almost to the floor. Kings and queens wore jewelry. Sometimes they placed a whole series of thick bracelets on their lower and upper arms and as many as ten rings on each hand. Large pendants were worn on chains around their necks.

REVIEW *In what ways did women take part in ruling Meroë?*

In some ways, however, the rulers of Meroë were quite different from Egyptian rulers. In Meroë, women played an important role in governing. In fact, many historians believe that the right to rule was passed on through the queen, not the king. Women could also be rulers themselves, and many queens ruled Meroë.

Much of what we know about the women who ruled Meroë comes from ancient carvings on Nubian temples. Many of the

Nubians and Egyptians placed small sculpted figures called shawabtis inside their tombs. They believed that shawabtis would work as servants for a deceased person in the afterlife.

178 • Unit 2

The Fall of Meroë

During the 200s B.C., Greek rulers in Egypt ordered ports built on the Red Sea. Traders began to use sea routes rather than the overland routes that passed through the once thriving city of Meroë. No longer a center of trade, Meroë lost much of its power, wealth, and importance.

Also, soldiers from the African kingdom of Axum began making raids on Kushite towns. By about A.D. 350 the people of Axum had defeated the Kushites. The king of Axum wrote,

66 I burned their towns, both those built of bricks and those built of reeds. 99

By the end of the fourth century A.D., the Kushite culture had disappeared.

Between A.D. 500 and A.D. 600, missionaries from Egypt and southeastern Europe brought Christianity to the Nubians. Christianity remained the main religion of the region until the 1300s. During this time, the religion of Islam was introduced.

REVIEW *What caused Meroë to lose much of its power, wealth, and importance?*

LESSON 2 REVIEW

400 B.C.	200 B.C.	B.C.	A.D.	A.D. 200	A.D. 400

270 B.C.
• Meroitic period begins

24 B.C.
• Queen Amanitore leads Nubian army against Rome

A.D. 350
• Meroitic period ends

Check Understanding

1 **Remember the Facts** Where was the city of Meroë located?

2 **Recall the Main Idea** How did the location and natural resources of Meroë affect its rise and fall?

Think Critically

3 **Think More About It** Why do you think the people of Axum were able to do so much damage to Kushite towns?

4 **Past to Present** How has the location of your community affected its growth?

Show What You Know

Journal Activity Imagine that you are a trader from southwestern Asia who has just arrived at Meroë. Write a journal entry that describes the activities taking place in the city. Exchange journal entries with a classmate, and compare your descriptions.

Use a Historical

1. Why Learn This Skill?

One way to learn about history is by using historical maps. A **historical map** gives information about the past. A historical map can show you where trade routes once were and where battles were fought. It can also tell you who controlled the resources of a place. Knowing how to use a historical map can help you understand what a place was like in ancient times.

2. Understand the Process

The two maps on page 181 show part of northern Africa. Map A is a historical map. It shows the land controlled by Kush around 730 B.C. Map B is a current political map of the same region. Both maps show physical features, such as rivers, seas, and mountains.

Physical features usually change little over time. However, the names they go by may change. For example, the Eastern Desert of the past is now also known as the Arabian Desert. Political borders and the names of regions, cities, and towns also may change. Look closely at the differences between Map A, which shows Egypt and Nubia as they were in the past, and Map B, which shows a present-day view of the same area. Then answer these questions:

1 What cities and towns are shown on Map A? What cities and towns are shown on Map B? Why do you think

the cities and towns shown on the two maps are different?

2 What ancient city was built near where the city of Cairo is today?

3 What two ancient kingdoms are identified on Map A?

4 What present-day countries are identified on Map B?

5 What other ancient kingdom did the Kingdom of Kush control in about 730 B.C.? How do you know?

6 What present-day countries occupy land once controlled by the ancient Kingdom of Kush?

7 How many tributaries appear near the mouth of the Nile River in Map A? How many tributaries appear near the mouth of the Nile in Map B? Why do you think the maps show a different number of tributaries?

8 Why do you think the relief shown on the two maps is the same?

9 Which map shows a reservoir and a dam built along the Nile River? Why do a reservoir and a dam appear on this map only?

3. Think and Apply

Find another historical map in this textbook. How do you know that it shows information about the past? What kind of information does it show? How would a present-day map of the same area be different?

Map

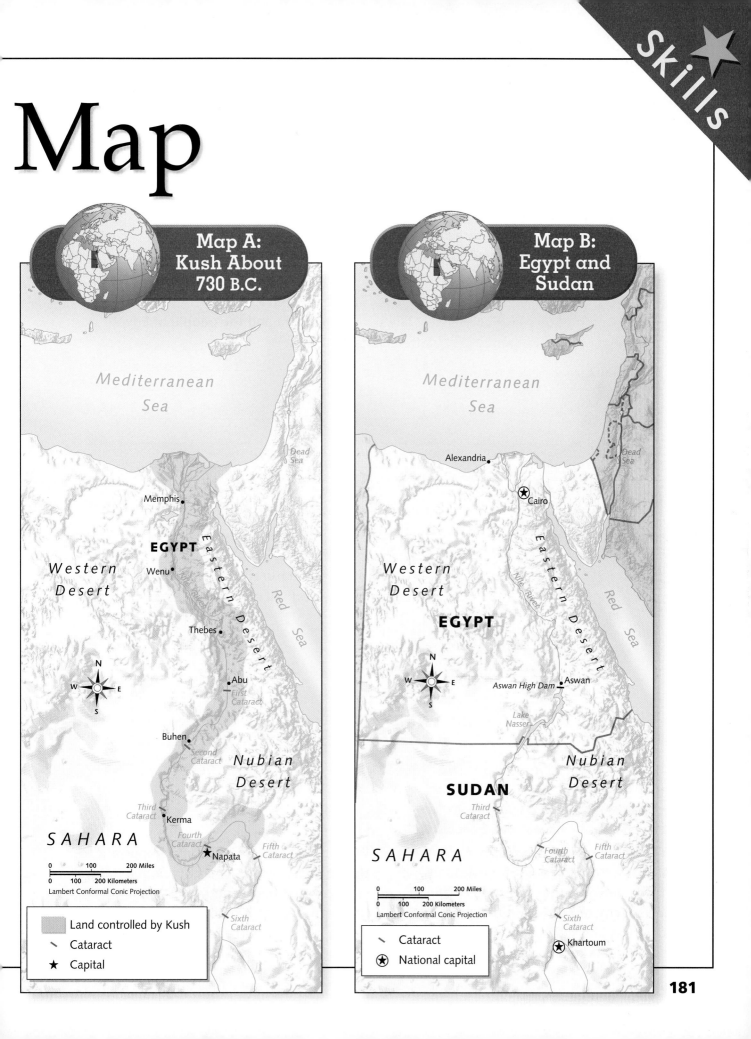

Map A: Kush About 730 B.C.

Mediterranean Sea

Dead Sea

Memphis

EGYPT

Eastern Desert

Red Sea

Western Desert

Wenu

Thebes

Abu
First Cataract

Buhen
Second Cataract

Nubian Desert

Third Cataract
Kerma

Fourth Cataract

S A H A R A

★ Napata

Fifth Cataract

Sixth Cataract

Nile River

0   100   200 Miles
0   100   200 Kilometers
Lambert Conformal Conic Projection

Land controlled by Kush

\ Cataract

★ Capital

Map B: Egypt and Sudan

Mediterranean Sea

Dead Sea

Alexandria

⊛ Cairo

EGYPT

Eastern Desert

Red Sea

Western Desert

Nile River

Aswan High Dam • Aswan

Lake Nasser

Nubian Desert

SUDAN

Third Cataract

Fourth Cataract

Fifth Cataract

S A H A R A

Sixth Cataract

⊛ Khartoum

0   100   200 Miles
0   100   200 Kilometers
Lambert Conformal Conic Projection

\ Cataract

⊛ National capital

CHAPTER 4
REVIEW

6000 B.C.   5000 B.C.   4000 B.C.

About 6000 B.C.
• People migrate
  to Nubia

CONNECT MAIN IDEAS

Use this organizer to tell about the ancient people of Kush and about their achievements. Write three details to support each main idea. A copy of the organizer appears on page 37 of the Activity Book.

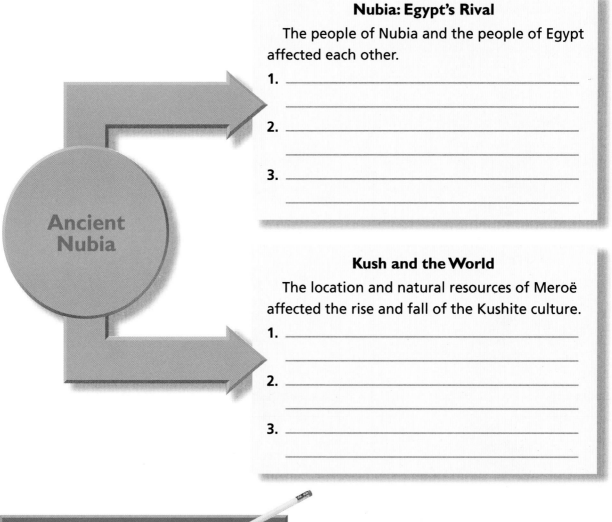

Ancient Nubia

Nubia: Egypt's Rival

The people of Nubia and the people of Egypt affected each other.

1. _____

2. _____

3. _____

Kush and the World

The location and natural resources of Meroë affected the rise and fall of the Kushite culture.

1. _____

2. _____

3. _____

WRITE MORE ABOUT IT

Write a Descriptive Paragraph Ancient Kerma was a stopping point for overland and river trade. Imagine that you are a citizen of the ancient city of Kerma. Write a paragraph that describes the sights, sounds, smells, and tastes of the marketplace.

Write a Report Iron was very important to the people of Kush. Find out about a natural resource that has helped your community grow. Then write a report about the ways in which this resource has affected your community.

About 2600 B.C.
• Egypt claims trade routes and resources in northern Nubia

730 B.C.
• Kushite king Piye conquers Lower Egypt

270 B.C.
• Meroitic period begins

About A.D. 200
• Meroë declines as traders use Roman sea routes

USE VOCABULARY

Write a word or phrase from this list to complete each of the sentences that follow.

ally   independence

annex   trade network

1 The people of Nubia celebrated their _____, or complete freedom, from Egypt.

2 Kerma became an _____, or supporter, of the Hyksos.

3 Egypt decided to _____, or take over, Nubia after years of controlling much of its northern area.

4 A group of buyers and sellers can be called a _____.

CHECK UNDERSTANDING

5 Why did Egypt want to gain control of the land of Nubia?

6 How was the geography of ancient Nubia different from the geography of ancient Egypt?

7 Where was Nubia located? Why was this location helpful to Nubia as a trading center?

8 How did Meroë's location affect the city?

9 What evidence tells historians that Meroë was one of the earliest centers for iron-making in Africa?

10 How were the lives of women in Meroë different from the lives of women in Egypt?

11 What were some of the reasons the Kushite culture disappeared?

THINK CRITICALLY

12 **Past to Present** The need to keep trade records led the people of Meroë to create the first written Nubian language. How do you think life would be different without written languages?

13 **Cause and Effect** How did Egypt's desire for Nubia's resources affect the relationship between Egypt and Nubia?

14 **Personally Speaking** What do you think scholars may learn about the Nubians in the future?

APPLY SKILLS

Use a Historical Map Look at the maps on page 181. Then answer these questions.

15 Was Buhen part of the land once controlled by Kush? How do you know?

16 What country would the town of Napata be in today?

READ MORE ABOUT IT

The Nubians: People of the Ancient Nile by Robert Steven Bianchi. Millbrook. The history of the ancient Nubians is traced in this interesting book.

HARCOURT BRACE

Visit the Internet at **http://www.hbschool.com** for additional resources.

Why Preserve the Past?

To some people in the United States, building a shopping mall on a Civil War battle site or knocking down an old school to put in a parking lot is making progress. To others, it is destroying a memory from a community's past.

Ancient buildings, monuments, and other structures link the world of today with history. They are reminders that people who lived long ago achieved important things. As long as the structures that they built remain, those people will not be forgotten.

One of the most remarkable of the world's monuments is the Great Sphinx of Egypt. It reminds people of the powerful Egyptian pharaohs who ruled more than 4,000 years ago. These pharaohs ordered thousands of workers to labor for years to build huge structures such as the pyramids and the Sphinx.

In recent years the Sphinx has shown much damage from pollution, weather, and age. The present-day Egyptian people might have lost this link with their past. To keep this from happening, they began a costly project to save the Sphinx. Adam Henein, an artist, explained his reason for giving long hours to restore and protect the Sphinx. "To me," said Henein, "[the Sphinx] is the soul of Egypt."

Think and Apply

Think about why it is important to preserve the memories of our past. What objects would you leave behind so that people in the future could remember what you achieved? Work with your class to prepare a time capsule that contains these objects. Find a safe place to keep the capsule so that it can be opened by students in your school many years from now.

Visit the Internet at **http://www.hbschool.com** for additional resources.

Check your media center or classroom video library for the Making Social Studies Relevant videotape of this feature.

Scaffolds help workers restore the Great Sphinx (top). Workers are also trying to preserve Kushite pyramids (bottom).

VISUAL SUMMARY

Summarize the Main Ideas
Study the pictures and captions to help you review the events you read about in Unit 2.

Formulate a Generalization
Study the scenes in the visual summary. Formulate a generalization about what life was like in ancient Egypt and Nubia based on what you see.

1 The early Egyptians lived in villages along the Nile River. The Nile shaped life, farming, trade, and religion in Egypt.

3 Egypt expanded its borders and traded with distant lands during the Middle Kingdom and New Kingdom.

5 Nubian culture developed south of Egypt, in what is today Sudan. Nubian and Egyptian culture influenced each other.

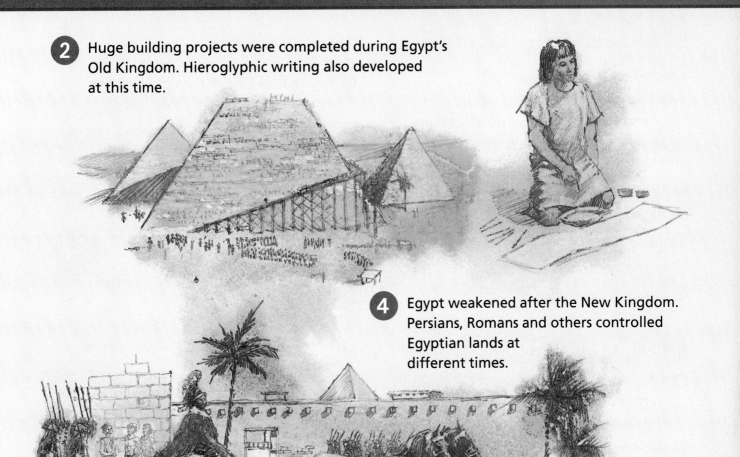

2 Huge building projects were completed during Egypt's Old Kingdom. Hieroglyphic writing also developed at this time.

4 Egypt weakened after the New Kingdom. Persians, Romans and others controlled Egyptian lands at different times.

6 The Nubian kingdom of Kush conquered Egypt in 730 B.C. Egypt's twenty-fifth Dynasty was made up of Kushite pharaohs.

7 The production of iron helped Kush establish a vast trade network centered in Meroë. Kushites were among the first ironworkers in Africa.

UNIT 2 REVIEW

USE VOCABULARY

For each pair of terms, write at least one sentence that shows how the terms are different from each other.

1. delta, cataract
2. nation-state, dynasty
3. vizier, bureaucracy
4. decree, pharaoh
5. annex, independence

CHECK UNDERSTANDING

6. Why did the people of Egypt call the land in the north Lower Egypt and the land in the south Upper Egypt?

7. What was the name of the most important of the Egyptian gods?

8. What were some of the daily activities of the ancient Egyptians?

9. What religious change was made during the time of Pharaoh Akhenaton?

10. How did Pharaoh Sesostris III change the Egyptian government?

11. For what important achievement is the Kushite leader Piye known?

12. How did the Kushite pharaohs help restore Egypt to its former glory?

13. What Nubian city became an artistic and cultural meeting ground for travelers from all parts of Africa?

THINK CRITICALLY

14. **Think More About It** Why do you think conquest was so important to some of the New Kingdom pharaohs?

15. **Cause and Effect** How did Egyptian control affect the people of Nubia?

16. **Explore Viewpoints** Egyptian scribes often described the Nubians in negative ways. Why do you think they did this?

APPLY SKILLS

Use a Historical Map Read the map and answer the questions.

17. What time period does this historical map cover?

18. What cities in the New Kingdom were located near cataracts?

19. On what two continents did Egypt control land during the New Kingdom?

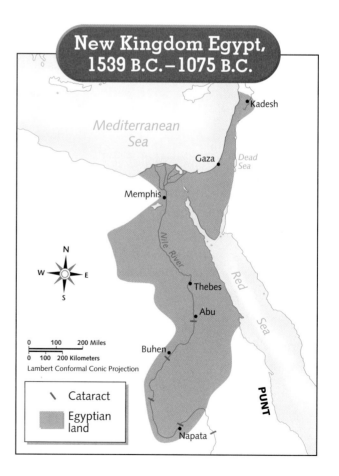

New Kingdom Egypt, 1539 B.C.–1075 B.C.

Mediterranean Sea

Kadesh

Gaza
Dead Sea

Memphis

Nile River

Thebes

Abu

Red Sea

0   100   200 Miles
0   100   200 Kilometers
Lambert Conformal Conic Projection

Buhen

PUNT

Napata

⟍ Cataract
◻ Egyptian land

188 • Unit 2

REMEMBER

- Share your ideas.
- Cooperate with others to plan your work.
- Take responsibility for your work.
- Help one another.
- Show your group's work to the class.
- Discuss what you learned by working together.

Hold a Round-table Discussion

With a group of four or five classmates, hold a round-table discussion between leaders of ancient Egypt and leaders of today's world. Talk about the qualities that were needed to lead well as a pharaoh long ago and the qualities that are needed to lead well today. Then compare the qualities good leaders needed then with those needed now.

Make a Poster

Work with two classmates to create a poster that shows the seasons of the ancient Egyptian calendar. Draw a large circle divided into three equal parts. Label each part with the name of a season and illustrate it.

Act as Merchants

Your class will divide into two groups. One group will be Nubian traders traveling to Egypt. The other group will be Egyptian merchants. Each group should create a list of goods that it will have to trade and then write each item on a separate index card. The traders will then meet to exchange goods. The goal for each group is to come away pleased with the trade it has made.

Unit Project Wrap-Up

Make a Scroll It is time to complete your scroll. Study your notes to decide what information you will include on the scroll. You might tell about the effect of geography on the people of Egypt and Nubia, the work of the Egyptians and Nubians, and the early ways each group governed. Write a rough draft of what you want to say. Then prepare a final copy in the form of a scroll. Be sure to illustrate your scroll.

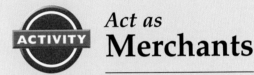

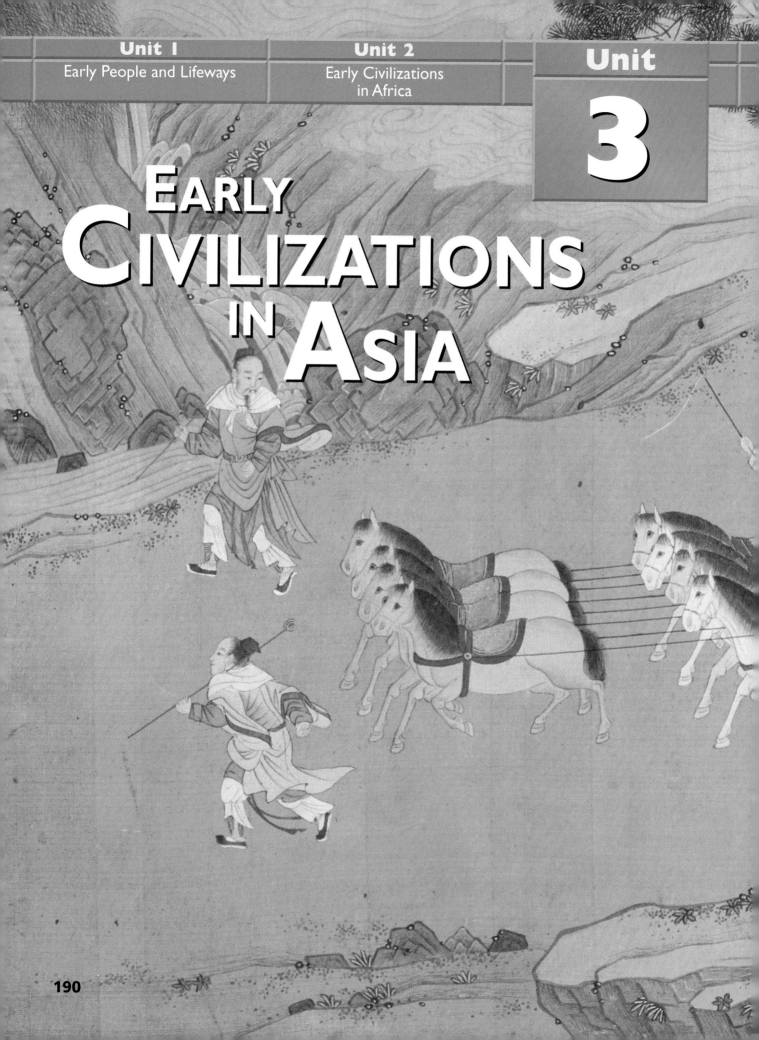

Unit 1
Early People and Lifeways

Unit 2
Early Civilizations
in Africa

Unit

3

EARLY CIVILIZATIONS IN ASIA

Between 1500 B.C. and A.D. 200, the foundations of Asia's major civilizations were laid. Political, social, and economic conditions created traditions that have lasted for thousands of years. Asia's Classical Age also saw the rise of new religions and new ideas about life. These continue to affect the ways of life of people in Asia and in other parts of the world.

◄ The emperors of ancient China greatly affected the way of life of the people. In this miniature painting Emperor Mu of the Zhou dynasty travels in fine style.

UNIT THEMES

- Continuity and Change
- Interaction Within Different Environments
- Conflict and Cooperation

Unit Project

Publish a Booklet Complete this project as you study Unit 3. With a group, plan to make a booklet about ancient India and China. As you read the unit, make a list of important people, places, and events of India and China long ago. This information will help you publish your booklet.

UNIT 3 PREVIEW

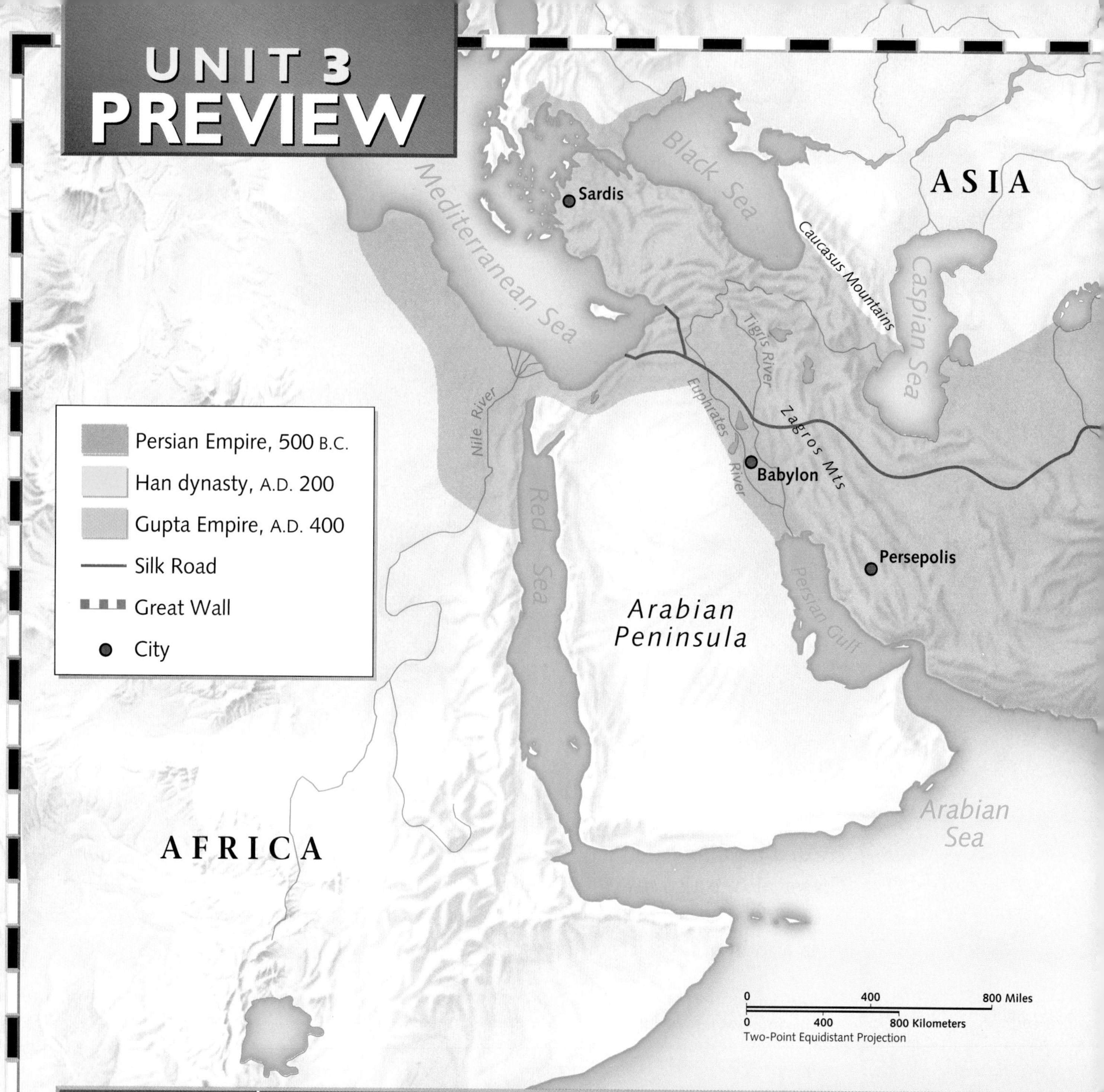

Persian Empire, 500 B.C.
Han dynasty, A.D. 200
Gupta Empire, A.D. 400
Silk Road
Great Wall
City
ASIA
AFRICA
Black Sea
Mediterranean Sea
Caspian Sea
Caucasus Mountains
Sardis
Tigris River
Euphrates River
Zagros Mts
Babylon
Persepolis
Persian Gulf
Nile River
Red Sea
Arabian Peninsula
Arabian Sea
0 400 800 Miles
0 400 800 Kilometers
Two-Point Equidistant Projection

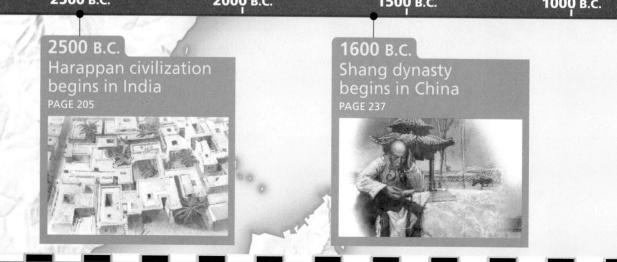

2500 B.C. | 2000 B.C. | 1500 B.C. | 1000 B.C.

2500 B.C.
Harappan civilization begins in India
PAGE 205

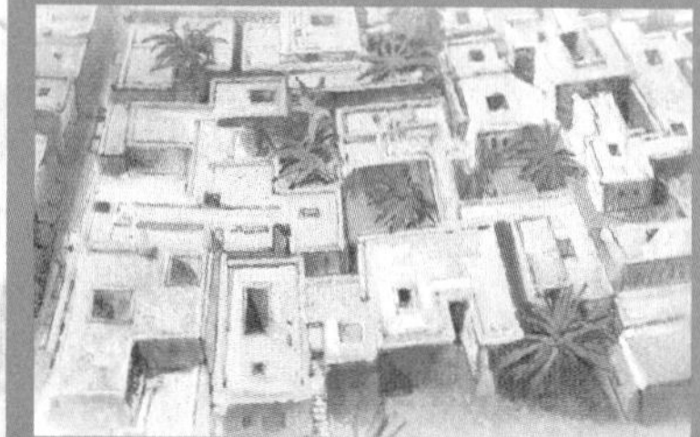

1600 B.C.
Shang dynasty begins in China
PAGE 237

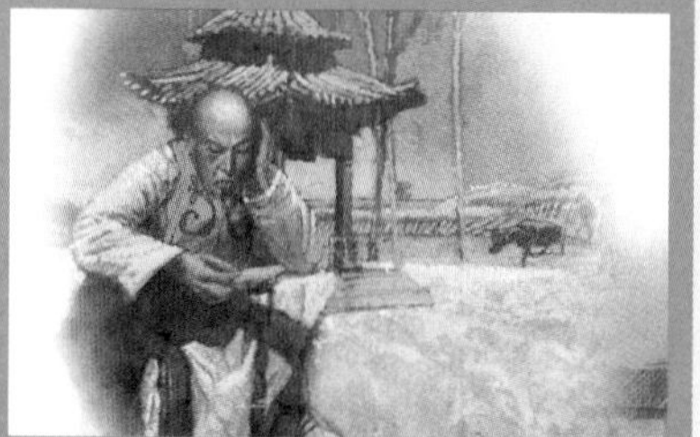

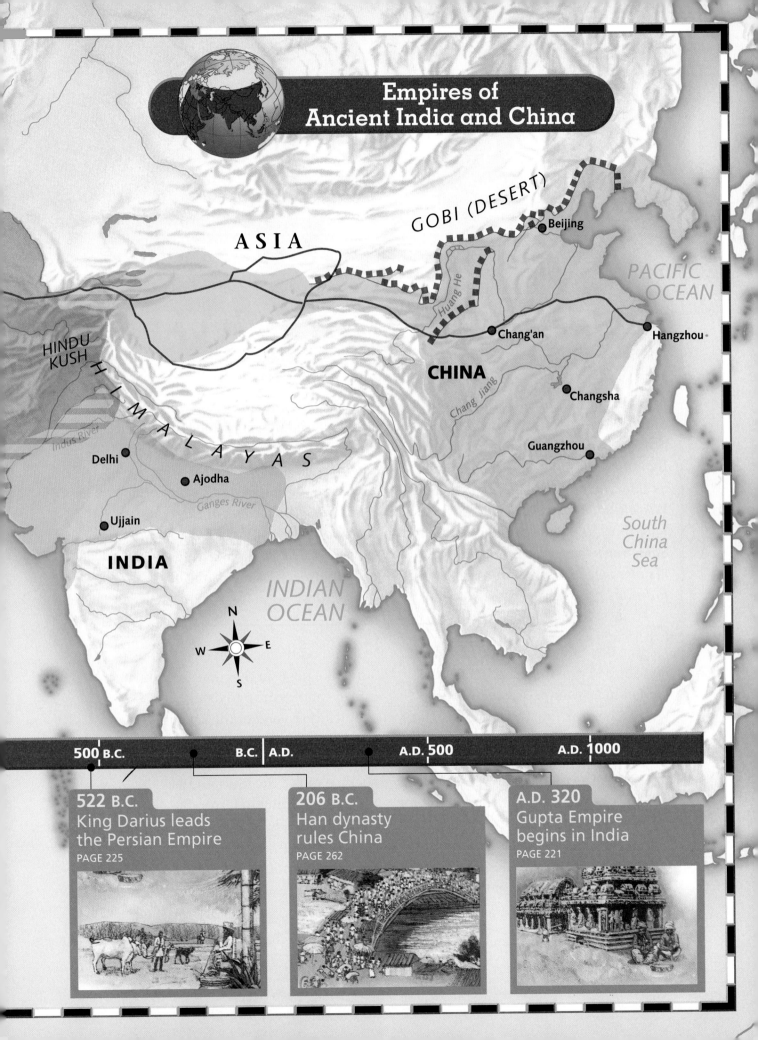

Empires of Ancient India and China

ASIA

GOBI (DESERT)

Beijing

PACIFIC OCEAN

Huang He

Chang'an

Hangzhou

CHINA

Chang Jiang

Changsha

HINDU KUSH

HIMALAYAS

Indus River

Delhi

Ajodha

Ganges River

Guangzhou

Ujjain

INDIA

South China Sea

INDIAN OCEAN

N
W E
S

| 500 B.C. | | B.C. | A.D. | | A.D. 500 | A.D. 1000 |

522 B.C.
King Darius leads
the Persian Empire
PAGE 225

206 B.C.
Han dynasty
rules China
PAGE 262

A.D. 320
Gupta Empire
begins in India
PAGE 221

Jataka Tales
Friends and Neighbors

edited by Nancy DeRoin • illustrated by Navin Patel

In this unit, you will read about Siddhartha Gautama (sih•DAHR•tuh GOW•tuh•muh), the founder of the Buddhist religion. He became known as Buddha, or "The Enlightened One." When Buddha taught, he spoke in a way that all people could understand. Sometimes he used folktales to get his message across. A number of these folktales were fables, short stories that use animal characters to teach a lesson. Buddha's followers believed that he remembered these fables from past lives, when his soul was in the bodies of animals. Many years after Buddha's death, some of these fables were collected and written down in a book called the **Jataka Tales,** *or "Birth Stories." Here is one of those tales.*

One day while hunting deer, a big lion slipped down a steep hill and landed in a swamp. Due to his great weight, he sank into the mud up to his neck. Try as he might, he could not get out. As soon as he lifted one foot, the other three sank in deeper. Finally, afraid to struggle any more for fear of sinking in above his head, he stood as still as a stone with only his huge head sticking out of the mud.

He stood there for seven days, his feet sunk like posts in the mud, without a bite to eat or a drop to drink.

Toward the end of the seventh day, a jackal, who was hunting for food, came upon him. Seeing a lion's head sticking out of the mud, the jackal ran away yelping in terror. But the lion called after him:

"I say, jackal. Stop! Don't run away. Here am I, caught fast in the mud. Please save me!"

The jackal came back slowly, looked at the lion, and said, "I could get you out I think, but I am afraid that once free you would eat me."

"Do not fear," the lion said. "If you save me, I will be your friend for life."

The jackal decided to trust him. He dug a hole around each of the lion's four feet. From these holes, he dug trenches out to the nearby pond. Water from the pond filled the trenches and ran into the holes at the lion's feet. It made the mud very soft, indeed. Then the jackal said:

"Now, make one great effort!"

The weakened lion strained every nerve, every muscle, every bone in his body. At last his feet broke loose from the mud with a loud slurp! The lion crawled onto dry land.

After washing the mud from his golden body, the great lion killed a buffalo and said to the jackal, "Help yourself, friend."

As the jackal ate, the lion noticed that he saved part of the meat.

"Why do you not eat your fill?" the lion asked.

"I am saving some to take to my mate," the jackal replied.

"I, too, have a mate," said the lion. "I will go with you." When they neared the jackal's den, his mate almost died of fright to see a huge lion heading straight toward her cave. But the jackal called out:

"Fear nothing. This lion is my friend."

And the lion said to her,

"Now, my lady, from this day on I am going to share my life with you and your family." He led the jackals to the place where he lived, and they moved into a cave next to his own.

After that, the jackal and the lion would go hunting together, leaving their mates at home. Soon, cubs were born to both families, and as they grew, they played together.

But one day, quite suddenly, the lioness thought, "My mate seems very fond of those jackals. It does not seem natural to me. They are different, after all." This thought stuck firmly in her mind, and she could think of nothing else. "We are lions and they are jackals," she thought. "I must get rid of them."

So, whenever the lion and the jackal were away on the hunt, the lioness began to frighten her neighbor. The lioness would spring from hiding and snarl, "Why do you stay where you are not wanted?" Or she would creep up on the sleeping jackal and hiss in her ear, "Do you not know when your life is in danger?" Then again, she would say under her breath, "Such darling little jackal cubs. Too bad their mother does not care about their safety."

Finally, the mother jackal told her mate all that had been happening. "It is clear," she said, "that the lion must have told his wife to do this. We have been here a long time and he is tired of us. Let us leave, or those lions will be the death of us."

Hearing this, the jackal went to the lion and said:

"Friend lion, in this world the strong will always have their way. But, I must say, even if one does not like a neighbor, it is cruel to frighten his wife and children half to death."

"Why, what are you talking about?" the lion asked in surprise.

Then the jackal told him how the lioness had been scaring his wife and cubs. The lion listened very carefully; then he called his wife before him. In front of everyone he said:

"Wife, do you remember long ago when I was out hunting and did not come back for a week? After that, I brought this jackal and his wife back with me."

"Yes, I remember very well," the lioness replied.

"Do you know why I was gone for a week?"

"No, I do not," she answered.

"I was ashamed to tell you then," the lion said, "but I will now. I was trying to catch a deer, and I jumped too far, slipped down a hill, and got stuck fast in the mud. There I stayed for a week without food or water. Then along came this jackal and saved my life. This jackal is my friend."

From that day on, the lions and jackals lived in peace and friendship. Furthermore, after their parents died, the cubs did not part. They, too, lived together in friendship, always remembering the words of the great lion:

A friend who truly acts like one,
Whomever he may be,
Is my comrade and my kin,
He is flesh and blood to me.

◆

As you read this unit, you will find out more about the history, beliefs, and ways of life of ancient Asian peoples.

INDIA
AND
PERSIA

"An age like this one, which is golden while it lasts and proves a culture's greatness forever after, is never a sudden or rootless event."

Lucille Schulberg,
Historic India

Young girl from Chennai (Madras), India, in traditional dress

Geography of Ancient India

The present-day countries of India, Bangladesh, and Pakistan are located in southern Asia. The area these countries fill is called the Indian subcontinent. A **subcontinent** is a large area of land that is separated by geography from the rest of a continent. To the north of the Indian subcontinent lie the tallest mountains in the world, the Himalayas (hih•muh•LAY•uhz). The Himalayas form a natural barrier between the Indian subcontinent and the rest of Asia.

The Land of India

The two great rivers of the Indian subcontinent, the Indus and the Ganges (GAN•jeez), begin in the snowy peaks of the Himalayas. Many tributaries flow into the Indus and the Ganges rivers. The Indus River and its tributaries begin in the western Himalayas and move southward through Pakistan to empty into the Arabian Sea.

FOCUS

How do elevations and climates affect the lives of people today?

Main Idea Read to find out how the elevations and climates of India affected the lives of the ancient people who lived there.

Vocabulary

subcontinent
monsoon
deforestation

The Himalayas stretch for about 1,500 miles (2,414 km) and are divided into three ranges—the Greater, Lesser, and Outer Himalayas.

Indian Subcontinent

IRAN

AFGHANISTAN

HINDU KUSH

CHINA

PAKISTAN

Indus River

H I M A L A Y A S

NEPAL

BHUTAN

OMAN

Tropic of Cancer

20°N

Vindhya Range

INDIA

Ganges River

BANGLADESH

BURMA (MYANMAR)

Arabian Sea

Godavari River

20°N

Bay of Bengal

THAILAND

Western Ghats

Krishna River

Eastern Ghats

10°N

INDIAN OCEAN

Andaman Islands

100°E

10°N

60°E

70°E

SRI LANKA

90°E

Nicobar Islands

Two-Point Equidistant Projection

0   200   400 Miles
0   200   400 Kilometers

Place   This map shows present-day India and Pakistan.

■ *Where are most of the mountains located in India?*

MAP THEME

The Indus is one of the longest rivers in the world, with a length of about 1,800 miles (2,900 km). The Ganges River and its tributaries start in the middle of the Himalayas and flow eastward through India to the Bay of Bengal.

Today much of the Indian subcontinent is part of the country of India. For the most part northern India is covered by wide river plains. The plain that surrounds the Indus River and its four main tributaries is called the Punjab, or "Five Rivers." East of the Punjab, the Ganges River flows through the large Ganges Plain. This region of the Indian subcontinent is often called the North Indian Plain.

No large mountains like the Himalayas rise in southern India. This area also lacks the wide river plains found in northern India. Instead, southern India is a land of varying heights, with many large rugged hills. This region is known as the Deccan (DEH•kuhn). Travel is more difficult in this hilly land than in northern India.

Rivers in southern India are fed by rainfall, not by melting snow as in northern India. Because of this, many of southern India's smaller streams are dry except during the rainy season. While the rivers of northern India are often used for transporting people and goods, boats are rarely used on southern India's rivers.

The greater ease of travel in northern India made it easier for people to unite there. This may help explain why the large empires of ancient India were all located in the north.

REVIEW *How is the geography of northern India different from that of southern India?*

Rivers and Rainfall

An ancient Indian text says this about rivers and rainfall: "Waters, you are the ones who bring us the life force. Help us to find nourishment so that we may look upon great joy." The people of ancient India knew that their rivers made life possible. Because of water's importance, India's people have always thought of their rivers as holy.

Ancient India's holiest river, the Ganges, is also one of the longest rivers on the Indian subcontinent. This river stretches for 1,560 miles (2,512 km). An Indian poet named Jagannatha (JAHG•nuh•tuh), who lived in the 1500s, called its water the "blessing of the world," which would "soothe our troubled souls." Even today followers of the Hindu religion come to bathe in the Ganges River. They believe that its waters will wash away their sins.

Besides rivers, the other major source of water for India is rain. Almost all of India's rain falls during the summer **monsoon**, the season when moist winds blow from the Indian Ocean toward the subcontinent. In the winter, the winds reverse direction. The

The fertile plains of the Indus River Valley (right) are surrounded by mountains, such as the Karakoram Range in Pakistan (below).

winter winds bring no rain, because they come from a dry inland area of Asia.

The shifting of the winds usually follows a regular pattern. But some years the monsoon rains begin late or never arrive at all. This affects crops and sometimes leads to famine. At these times, the people of India turn to the gods they believe in. One of the most important gods is Indra, the god of thunderstorms. When rain is needed, they ask the god to "draw up the enormous bucket and pour it down."

Once the monsoon rains begin, they continue for four months. This constant rain has surprised visitors to India for centuries. One such visitor to the land was Aristobulus (uh•ris•tuh•BYOO•luhs), from Greece, who traveled there in 327 B.C. He wrote that in India the rains poured "violently from the clouds both day and night." Even armies at war in ancient India stopped fighting during the monsoon season because the roads got so muddy.

REVIEW *Why did the people of ancient India think of rivers as holy?*

Farming in Ancient India

All rivers in India carry more water in the monsoon season because of local rainfall. The rivers of northern India also get extra water from rainfall over the Himalayas. This often causes the northern rivers to overflow their banks and flood the surrounding land. Flooding can sometimes be destructive and lead to the loss not only of crops but of human lives as well. At the same time, floods in India are also much needed, because they leave fresh silt on the land they cover. This silt makes the land fertile for growing crops.

The early farmers of the Indus Valley made good use of the yearly floods. They

This woman is picking tea leaves. Today India is one of the world's largest producers of tea.

planted cotton and sesame seeds just before the monsoon began. By the time the rain stopped and the Indus River shrank to its normal size, the crops would be ready to harvest. The farmers grew barley and wheat during the winter and harvested it in the spring. The ground was moist enough from the summer flooding that no more water was needed.

Early farmers in India also raised livestock, such as cattle, sheep, and goats. However, for making clothing they used the cotton plant instead of animals. Cotton is a plant native to India.

Although it was a good region for agriculture, the area near the Indus River also had drawbacks. The river often flooded and also shifted its course because of the buildup of silt. Some villages had to be abandoned when the Indus River moved too far away.

Still, life was good for the early settlers in the Indus Valley. The importance of the Indus River can be seen in the fact that the entire subcontinent is named after it.

Today flooding still causes problems in northern India. **Deforestation**, or the widespread cutting down of trees, has led to larger floods than in ancient times. The worst flooding happens in the Ganges Plain. This region once had thick forests, but now there are few trees left. In the last 50 years, many of the forests in the Himalayas have also been cleared. These forests used to help soak up some of the heavy rains. Without the forests, water rushes quickly downhill and causes flooding.

REVIEW *How did river flooding help the early farmers of the Indus River Valley?*

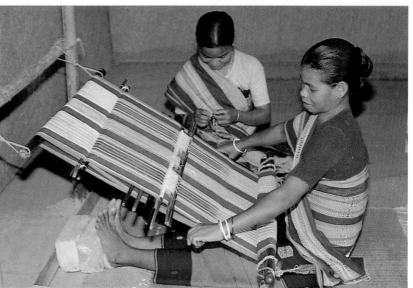

The people of India have long used cotton to make clothing. In this photograph a weaver in Manipur, India, uses a hand loom to create cloth.

LESSON I REVIEW

Check Understanding

1 **Remember the Facts** What are the main sources of water in India?

2 **Recall the Main Idea** What effect did rivers and the monsoon have on ancient India?

Think Critically

3 **Past to Present** Do you think rivers still make life better for the people of India? Do you think rivers still cause problems?

4 **Think More About It** How would the landscape and rivers of India be different without the Himalayas?

Show What You Know

Map Activity Think about a single raindrop falling onto the Himalayas and being carried from there all the way to the Arabian Sea. Make a map of some of the possible routes that the raindrop might take.

Civilization
in the
Indus Valley

3000 B.C.	2000 B.C.	1000 B.C.

FOCUS

Why do some civilizations last a long time, while others do not?

Main Idea As you read, think about how the physical setting of the Indus Valley civilization affected its development and survival.

Vocabulary

fortress
inscription
assimilate

Archaeologists estimate that this sculpture from Mohenjo-Daro was created around 2000 B.C. The subject of the sculpture may have been a priest. An ancient toy ram is shown above.

The Indus Valley offered the best conditions for agriculture on the Indian subcontinent. At first, people built small villages and farmed the surrounding land. By about 2500 B.C., not long after people in the Fertile Crescent and the Nile Valley had developed civilizations, the early people of the Indus Valley built cities and formed a civilization of their own.

Settling the Indus Valley

Fed by melting snows, the Indus River tumbles down from the high mountains, carrying rocks, gravel, and silt. It flows south and west onto a hot, dry plain in present-day Pakistan. Each spring, the Indus River spills over its banks and the old soil is made fertile by a new layer of silt. Another river, the Sarasvati (SAR•ahs•vuh•tee), once flowed parallel to the Indus. A series of earthquakes shifted the waters of its tributaries to other rivers. Today the Sarasvati is a dried-up riverbed. Early farmers in these river valleys grew barley and other grains in the rich soil. These grains supplemented, or added to, the food people got by hunting animals and gathering wild plants.

People in the Indus Valley built their villages on large mounds made from mud and stones. The purpose of the mounds was to keep the villages above the flooded land. Over time these villages grew to become cities. Eventually, a great civilization formed—one that would cover present-day Pakistan and parts of what are now Afghanistan and northern India.

Some of the largest and most important early cities in the Indus Valley were Harappa (huh•RA•puh), Lothal, and Mohenjo-Daro (moh•HEN•joh DAR•oh).

Harappa is named after a Pakistani town where the first evidence of the civilization was found. It became so important that this early civilization is often called the Harappan civilization. Many archaeological discoveries have also been made at Lothal, which lies near the coast of the Arabian Sea. However, the most complete evidence of city life in the early Indus Valley has been found at Mohenjo-Daro.

REVIEW *What were Mohenjo-Daro and Harappa?*

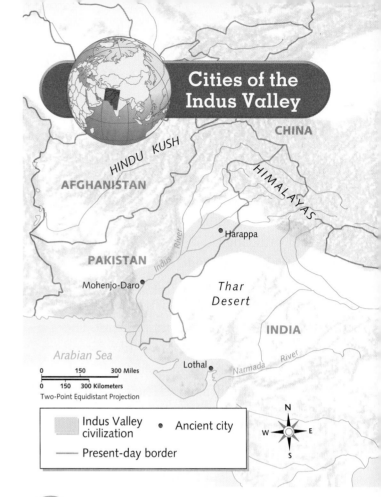

Cities of the Indus Valley

CHINA

HINDU KUSH

HIMALAYAS

AFGHANISTAN

Harappa

PAKISTAN

Indus River

Mohenjo-Daro

Thar Desert

INDIA

Arabian Sea

0   150   300 Miles
0   150   300 Kilometers
Two-Point Equidistant Projection

Lothal

Narmada River

N W E S

Indus Valley civilization

Ancient city

Present-day border

Regions Excavations have revealed that the three ancient cities shown on this map—Mohenjo-Daro, Harappa, and Lothal—looked almost identical.

■ *Why is it interesting that these ancient cities were so much alike?*

Archaeologists (below) continue to study Mohenjo-Daro and other Harappan cities in what are today the countries of Pakistan and India. Artifacts such as this vase (left) provide clues as to what life was like in these ancient cities.

The City of Mohenjo-Daro

In its time, Mohenjo-Daro was a model of city planning. Straight, wide streets, some as wide as 30 feet (about 9 m), crisscrossed the city. These streets were carefully laid out to form rectangular blocks for houses and other buildings.

On a hill at the end of the city nearest the Indus River, a walled fortress was built on a platform of bricks. A **fortress** is a building designed to protect a city or army. The fortress of Mohenjo-Daro—like fortresses in all Harappan cities—was built in the western part of the city. The thick walls of the ancient fortress protected government buildings, a bathhouse, and a huge storage shed. The shed stood 30 feet (about 9 m) tall and 1,200 feet (about 366 m) long. It held more than enough grain to feed the city's population, which by 1500 B.C. was about 45,000. The grain in the storage shed was also used to pay many of the workers in Mohenjo-Daro.

Most of the buildings in Mohenjo-Daro, including the huge grain shed, were made of bricks. Instead of sun-drying their bricks, as people in the Fertile Crescent and the Nile Valley did, people of the Indus Valley baked their bricks in ovens. These baked bricks were harder and lasted longer than sun-dried bricks.

Only the wealthiest families in the Indus Valley lived in the city's brick buildings. Most people lived in small huts in villages surrounding Mohenjo-Daro. Some city houses were two stories high and were large enough to have a courtyard and rooms for servants. The doors of most city houses opened onto alleys rather than onto the busy main streets. The fronts of the houses, which had no windows, looked much alike.

Even the smallest city houses had separate rooms inside for cooking, sleeping, and bathing. Some even had a separate room for a well. Almost every house in Mohenjo-Daro had its own bathroom, some with polished brick floors. Family members showered by pouring fresh water over themselves with jugs. The runoff water flowed through brick pipes into a city drain system running along the main streets. The streets had covered openings that let workers get to the drains to fix problems.

Each house also had a chute through which trash could be emptied into a bin in the street. The garbage was then collected by city workers.

Within Mohenjo-Daro's fortress was a large bathhouse. The main tank was 40 feet (12 m) long and 8 feet (2 m) deep. The bathhouse may have been used by people in the practice of their religion. It may also have been a gathering place where people exchanged news and conducted business.

REVIEW *What were the streets like in Mohenjo-Daro?*

LEARNING FROM DIAGRAMS The great bath (bottom) is among the ruins of Mohenjo-Daro that are still being explored. The diagram (top) gives a view of daily life in the Harappan civilization. The main diagram shows some of Mohenjo-Daro's features:
1. Fortress
2. Mats for resting
3. Palm trees for shade
4. Paved road
■ *Where do most of the roads in the city seem to lead?*

Mohenjo-Daro

City People

Most people in Mohenjo-Daro were craft-workers or merchants. For the most part, craftworkers wove cotton cloth, shaped clay pots, or made metal items such as silver jewelry. As early as 2300 B.C., Indus Valley merchants traded with settlements as far away as the Fertile Crescent.

Many of the craftworkers and merchants in Mohenjo-Daro knew how to read and write. We know this because stone seals marked their clay pots and other items. These seals showed who owned the items.

Pictures of animals such as elephants and tigers were often carved onto the seals. Many seals also had an **inscription**, or written message. By putting a string through a hole at the back, a merchant could tie the seal to bales of grain and other goods.

An interesting fact about Harappan cities is that they were all very much alike. Their street layouts were similar. People in each city used the same kinds of weights, measures, and tools.

REVIEW *What facts about the people of Mohenjo-Daro do their artifacts reveal?*

To identify goods and crafts, Indus Valley merchants marked their property with seals. The seals were either stamped onto goods or tied to them with string. The seal on the right shows the Sumerian ruler Gilgamesh. The seal on the left shows an elephant.

ECONOMICS

Trade Beyond the Indus Valley

Indus Valley seals have been uncovered in the ancient city of Ur and in other Mesopotamian cities. Seals from Mesopotamia have also been found in the ruins of the Indus Valley port city of Lothal. Sea-going Indus Valley traders may have made use of the strong monsoon winds to cross the Arabian Sea from Lothal. Their ships probably carried gems, sesame oil, and cotton. The Sumerians most likely sailed to Lothal with barley, wool, and silver.

The Mystery of Mohenjo-Daro

No one has lived in Mohenjo-Daro for more than 3,000 years. How the city and all the rest of Harappan civilization ended is still a mystery. We do know that the end came quickly, probably around 1500 B.C.

Looking for evidence of ancient life in the city of Mohenjo-Daro, archaeologists found signs of sudden death. They discovered many unburied human skeletons. The poses of the skeletons suggested that the people had been running from something. Houses and other buildings appear to have been abandoned suddenly. Perhaps the people of Mohenjo-Daro were victims of an earthquake or a flood. Some skeletons showed evidence of sword cuts, however. This suggests that Mohenjo-Daro may have been attacked by invaders.

Games and toys were just as popular in the Indus Valley long ago as they are today. At left is a two-wheeled toy cart. At right is an ancient board game played with pegs and stones.

There is also evidence that underground water in the Indus Valley had become salty. This would have made the farmland salty too. It would have been difficult for farmers to continue growing crops.

Without food many people would have starved. The rest of the people probably deserted their cities and moved somewhere else. In time they may have been **assimilated** (uh•SIH•muh•lay•tuhd), or accepted into the general population of other cultures.

What we know today about Mohenjo-Daro comes from evidence that archaeologists have pieced together. Only ruins and small artifacts remain as proof of a civilization that no longer exists.

REVIEW *What are some possible reasons for the end of the Harappan civilization?*

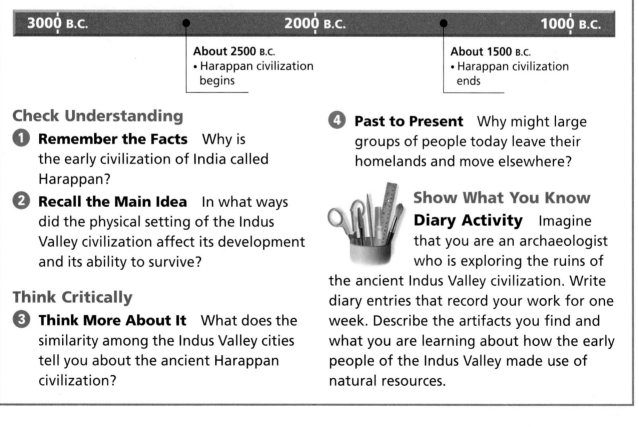

LESSON 2 REVIEW

3000 B.C.   2000 B.C.   1000 B.C.

About 2500 B.C.
• Harappan civilization begins

About 1500 B.C.
• Harappan civilization ends

Check Understanding

1 Remember the Facts Why is the early civilization of India called Harappan?

2 Recall the Main Idea In what ways did the physical setting of the Indus Valley civilization affect its development and its ability to survive?

Think Critically

3 Think More About It What does the similarity among the Indus Valley cities tell you about the ancient Harappan civilization?

4 Past to Present Why might large groups of people today leave their homelands and move elsewhere?

Show What You Know

Diary Activity Imagine that you are an archaeologist who is exploring the ruins of the ancient Indus Valley civilization. Write diary entries that record your work for one week. Describe the artifacts you find and what you are learning about how the early people of the Indus Valley made use of natural resources.

LESSON 3

Aryans Bring Changes to India

1500 B.C.	1000 B.C.	500 B.C.

FOCUS

How does the movement of people into an area affect those already living there?

Main Idea As you read, think about how the arrival of the Aryans changed life for the people of ancient India.

Vocabulary

Aryan
Sanskrit
Vedas
Hinduism
reincarnation
caste
untouchable
Buddhism

Around 1500 B.C. large numbers of people began to migrate into India. These migrations lasted for more than 3,000 years. They were important because they introduced to the region people with different customs and ideas. The earliest immigrants are known as **Aryans** (AIR•ee•uhnz). The word *Aryan* means "noble." The Aryans were warriors and herders from eastern Europe and western Asia. Many came from areas near the Black and Caspian seas. Their arrival on the Indian subcontinent caused many changes to the way of life of the people of India.

Aryan Immigrants

The earliest Aryan migrations took place over hundreds of years. They were part of a larger southward movement of people called Indo-Europeans. Why the Aryans and others left their original home is not known. Overpopulation in

Travelers in present-day Pakistan make their way through a Hindu Kush mountain pass. The Aryans used these same mountain passes to immigrate to the Indian peninsula.

210

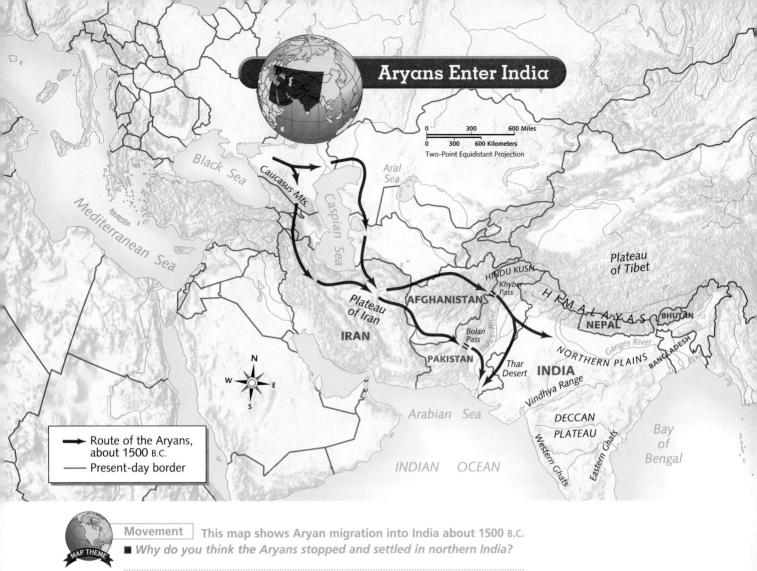

Aryans Enter India

Route of the Aryans, about 1500 B.C.
Present-day border

Two-Point Equidistant Projection

Movement This map shows Aryan migration into India about 1500 B.C.
■ *Why do you think the Aryans stopped and settled in northern India?*

their homeland may have forced the Aryans to migrate.

Some Aryans moved west, into Europe. Others pushed south, through the mountain passes of the Hindu Kush, a part of the Himalayas. These Aryans moved to the Punjab, which is now part of Pakistan. Aryans eventually occupied much of northern India as well.

Each wave of migration brought more Aryans to the subcontinent. Soon the Aryans competed with the native people of India for land. The Aryans were stronger fighters because they had horses. Until the Aryans arrived, there were no horses in India. The Aryans also introduced the chariot to India.

Before coming to India the Aryans had lived as herders. They raised cattle, goats, and sheep. From these animals, the Aryans got meat, milk products, and wool for their clothing. Over time, the Aryans shifted from herding to farming. Crops such as barley and possibly wheat were first grown in India by the Aryans.

The Aryans lived in small villages in the countryside. In the following centuries life and work in India came to center on the villages. Present-day India has huge cities. Many Indian people, however, still live in small villages. In fact, India is often called "a nation of villages."

REVIEW *What may have caused the Aryans to leave their homeland?*

A Selection from the Bhagavad Gita

The Bhagavad Gita, *or Song of the Lord,*
is part of a larger ancient Indian poem
called the Mahabharata. *In this selection,*
the Hindu god Vishnu speaks to Arjuna, a
main character in the Bhagavad Gita:

There is no doubt that you will know me
   in my total being when you persist
In discipline, and rely on me,
   and when your thought clings to me. Listen.

Without holding back anything, I shall teach you
   wisdom, and explain how it can be attained,
Knowing which,
   there is nothing left to be known.

One out of thousands
   may strive for success.
And even of these only a few
   may know me as I really am.

Hinduism

The ideas of the Aryans can be seen in present-day Indian culture and beliefs. For example, the Aryans brought their language, **Sanskrit**, to India. Many Indian languages of today, including the one most widely spoken, Hindi, are based on Sanskrit.

The Aryans believed that Sanskrit was a holy language. To them it was the language spoken by the gods. The Aryans' holiest books, the **Vedas** (VAY•duhz), are written in Sanskrit. These four books of sacred writings describe the Aryan religion.

The Aryan religion developed into the religion of Hinduism. **Hinduism** is one of the oldest religions still practiced today. Believers in Hinduism worship three main gods—Brahma the Creator, Vishnu the Preserver, and Shiva the Destroyer. Below these gods are many other lesser gods.

Hinduism teaches that people live many lives until they reach spiritual perfection. They believe that the soul lives on after death and returns to life in a new body. This rebirth is called **reincarnation**. According to Hinduism, those who obey their religious teachings and lead good lives will be reborn into higher social positions. Those who do not will return as lower life-forms. Hindus also believe that animals have souls and that cows are holy. For this reason, many do not eat beef.

The Hindu god Shiva

REVIEW *What religion of today comes from the religion of the Aryans?*

Classes

For hundreds of years Aryan priests used the Vedas to give order to their society. Following the teachings of the Vedas, the Aryans divided their society into four social classes. Each class, or *varna* in the Sanskrit language, had a special job to do.

To the people of ancient India, the different social classes worked together like the different parts of the human body. The Brahmans (BRAH•muhnz), who were the priests and scholars, made up the head. The Kshatriyas (KSHAH•tree•uhz), who were the rulers, made up the arms. The Vaisyas (VYSH•yuhz), who were the merchants and professionals, made up the legs. The Sudras (SOO•druhz), who were the laborers and servants, made up the feet.

The Aryans' social classes led to India's caste system. A **caste** is a group within a social class. A person born into one caste could not become a member of another caste. Caste members worked within their own group and could marry only others from their caste.

Below all the other castes were the **untouchables**. These people did all the unpleasant jobs in Indian society. They picked up garbage, cleaned stables, and handled the dead. Untouchables were thought to be impure. They had to avoid all contact with the rest of society. An untouchable could not even let his or her shadow fall on a person of a higher caste.

Hinduism required people to accept the caste into which they were born. Each person had a place in society and a job to do. Life might be hard, but if people did the work of their caste, there was hope that the next life would be better.

Around the sixth century B.C., a new religion appeared in India. This new religion challenged the rituals and caste system of Hinduism.

REVIEW *What was the ancient Indian caste system?*

The Origins of Buddhism

An Indian story tells that a traveling Brahman met a stranger one day. The Brahman asked the stranger's name and received this answer:

> 66 Although born in the world, grown up in the world, having overcome the world, I abide unsoiled by the world. Take it that I am Buddha. 99

This statue (below left) made in the A.D. 100s shows a young female servant of the Sudra caste. Above left are two members of the Brahman caste.

On the right is a Buddhist wall painting found in the Ajanta Caves in Hyderabad, India. At left is a Buddhist monk.

LEARNING FROM CHARTS Buddhists follow these eight points, called the Noble Eightfold Path, in their search for nirvana—a feeling of happiness, peace, and complete understanding.

■ *Why would practicing proper concentration be important?*

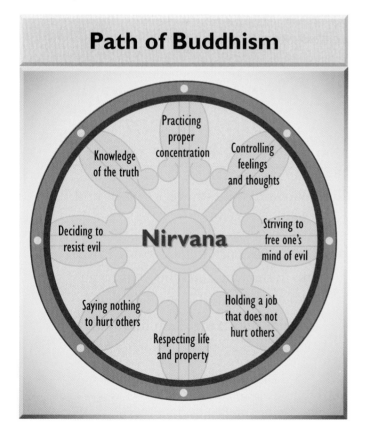

Path of Buddhism

Practicing proper concentration

Knowledge of the truth

Controlling feelings and thoughts

Deciding to resist evil

Nirvana

Striving to free one's mind of evil

Saying nothing to hurt others

Holding a job that does not hurt others

Respecting life and property

We know little of this man who called himself Buddha, or the "Enlightened One." What we do know comes from information written many years after his death. These writings tell us that his real name was Siddhartha Gautama. Born in northern India in 563 B.C., Gautama lived a comfortable life as the son of an Indian prince. His father gave him everything he wanted and kept him from seeing the suffering of the common people.

At about age 30, Gautama went outside the walls of his palace for the first time. First he saw an old man bent over with age. Then he came upon a man too sick to care for himself. Finally he saw a dead body. Gautama asked a servant to explain what he had seen. The servant said that age, sickness, and death come to us all. This answer was not enough for Gautama. Why, he asked, was there so much suffering? How might this suffering be ended? Gautama decided to spend the rest of his life searching for the answers to his questions.

He left his father's palace and lived the life of a wandering beggar.

For years Gautama continued his search for knowledge by studying and praying with Brahman priests. Nothing helped him find answers. One day Gautama sat down to rest and think under a tree. After several hours of deep thought, Gautama felt that he understood the meaning of life. He decided that people should seek love, truth, the joy of knowledge, and a calm mind. At that moment he became Buddha.

Gautama spent the rest of his life teaching his message, which centered on Four Noble Truths: (1) Suffering is a part of life.

The lotus flower is often associated with Buddhism.

(2) Wanting things brings suffering. (3) People can find peace by giving up wants. (4) Following eight basic rules, called the Eightfold Path, can lead to peace.

After his death in 483 B.C., his followers told of his teachings. **Buddhism**, the religion based on those teachings, eventually spread across Asia.

Neither Buddha nor his followers organized a church or wrote holy books like the Vedas. They wished only to set an example for others through peaceful behavior.

REVIEW *Why did Gautama begin a search for truth?*

LESSON 3 REVIEW

1500 B.C.	1000 B.C.	500 B.C.

About 1500 B.C.
• Aryan migrations to India begin

563 B.C.
• Buddha is born

483 B.C.
• Buddha dies

Check Understanding

1 **Remember the Facts** Where did the Aryans come from? Where did they migrate to?

2 **Recall the Main Idea** How did the Aryan migrations affect civilization in India?

Think Critically

3 **Past to Present** Today India is an industrialized country. What effect do you think the development of industry has had on the caste system?

4 **Explore Viewpoints** If you had been a Brahman in early Indian society, how might you have felt about the teachings of Buddha? How might you have felt about his teachings if you had been an untouchable?

Show What You Know

Research Activity Create a chart comparing Indian civilization before and after the arrival of the Aryans. Topics you might present in your chart include how people lived, where people lived, and what the social classes were. Use your textbook, encyclopedias, and almanacs to gather information.

Use a Cultural Map

1. Why Learn This Skill?

Symbols on road signs give people information without using words. They show information in a way that lets people understand it quickly. For example, a road sign showing a picture of a leaping deer tells you that deer cross the road there. On maps, too, symbols show information in a way that lets people understand it quickly. Map symbols might tell where certain products are made or where battles were fought.

Like other kinds of maps, cultural maps can give you a general picture of a region of the world. Cultural maps may use symbols that show places where most of the people speak a certain language or follow a certain religion. These maps can help you understand more about the people and cultures in those places.

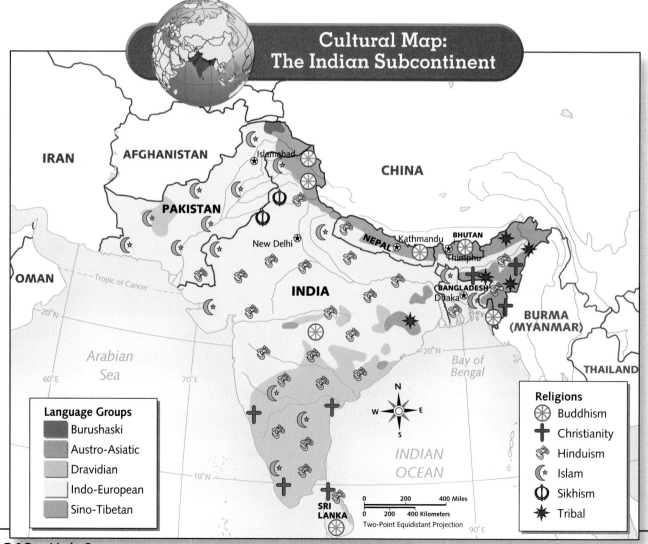

Cultural Map:
The Indian Subcontinent

Language Groups
- Burushaski
- Austro-Asiatic
- Dravidian
- Indo-European
- Sino-Tibetan

Religions
- ⊛ Buddhism
- ✝ Christianity
- ॐ Hinduism
- ☾ Islam
- ☬ Sikhism
- ✳ Tribal

Notice that this map of the present-day Indian subcontinent has two map keys. The key on the left uses colors as symbols. The colors divide the subcontinent into regions based on language. The key tells you that there are five main language groups on the Indian subcontinent.

The map key on the right of the map uses pictures as symbols. Each picture symbol stands for a religion and is shown in the middle of an area where that religion is followed.

2. Understand the Process

Now that you know about the symbols in the map keys, use these questions as a guide for making generalizations about the present-day cultures on or near the Indian subcontinent.

1 What color covers most of the northern half of India? What generalizations can you make about the language of the people who live there?

2 What is the main language group in southern India?

3 What is the main language group in Pakistan?

4 What do the picture symbols in Pakistan tell you?

5 In what country do most of the people follow Buddhism?

6 Do all the people in Bangladesh follow the same religion? Explain your answer.

7 Make a generalization about language and religion in each of these countries: Bangladesh, India, Pakistan, Bhutan.

3. Think and Apply

Draw a cultural map of all of Asia. Use an encyclopedia, atlas, or almanac to gather the information you will need. Use colors to show language groups and use picture symbols to show different religions. Be sure to label the countries. What language groups and religions will appear on your map that do not appear on the map on page 216? Have a classmate use your map to make some generalizations about the cultures of present-day Asia.

Sikh "Golden Temple" at Amritsar, India, near the India-Pakistan border

FOCUS

What causes people to unite?

Main Idea As you read, think about what the Maurya and Gupta rulers did to unite India.

Vocabulary

rajah
assassination
turning point
missionary
Arabic numeral
inoculation

United Rule in India

| 400 B.C. | | B.C. | A.D. | | A.D. 400 |

During the time of Buddha, India was a divided land. Princes called **rajahs** ruled over large city-states rich in foods, jewels, and metals. This wealth brought invaders—first the Persians from Asia and then the Greeks from Europe. For more than 200 years after the death of Buddha, parts of the Indian subcontinent were held by outsiders. Finally, a young Indian leader drove the invaders out of India and conquered all the rajahs.

India's First Empire

About 320 B.C. a ruler named Chandragupta Maurya (chuhn•druh•GUP•tuh MOW•ree•uh) united India and formed the Maurya Empire. Chandragupta Maurya ruled the new empire harshly. He made peasants work as slaves to chop down forests, drain swamps, and farm the newly cleared land. He then taxed the crops that were grown.

Chandragupta's cruelty made him many enemies in the empire. He feared for his own safety. Because of this he appeared in public only during a few important festivals. He also had servants taste all his food before he ate it. To protect himself from assassination, Chandragupta slept in a different room every night. **Assassination** (uh•sa•suh•NAY•shun) is murder for a political reason. No attack came, however. In 297 B.C. Chandragupta quietly gave up the throne to his son.

Both Chandragupta and his son governed the empire according to a book called the *Arthashastra* (ar•thuh•SHAH•struh). The *Arthashastra* said that rulers should govern with a firm hand. "Government is the science of

This Mauryan artwork is part of a series of tablets that describe ancient rulers.

punishment," it stated. It also said that war was an acceptable way for rulers to reach their goals. Ruling by the *Arthashastra*, both Chandragupta and his son expanded the Maurya Empire to include what is today western Pakistan and southern India.

REVIEW *What kind of ruler was Chandragupta?*

The Reign of Ashoka

Chandragupta's grandson, Ashoka (uh•SHOH•kuh), became Maurya emperor about 273 B.C. The new emperor ruled as firmly as his father and grandfather had. "Any power superior in might to another should launch into war," Ashoka believed.

About 265 B.C. Ashoka's army marched into the kingdom of Kalinga on the empire's southern border. There the Maurya forces defeated the Kalingans. Ashoka recorded that "150,000 people were deported, 100,000 were killed, and many times that number died."

During the time of the Mauryas, Buddhists built large stupas, or religious shrines. The Great Stupa (below) at Sanchi, India, still stands today. This stupa, like most stupas, is covered with ancient drawings and carvings (left). Buddhists show respect for a stupa by walking around the outside of it.

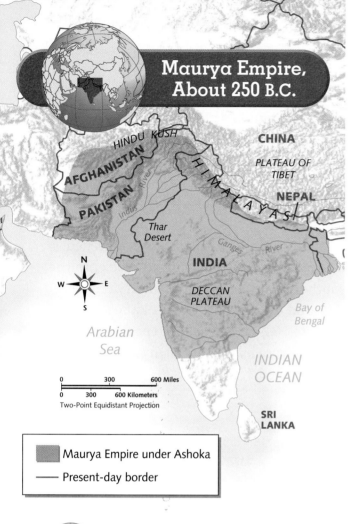

Maurya Empire, About 250 B.C.

HINDU KUSH

AFGHANISTAN

PAKISTAN

Indus River

CHINA

PLATEAU OF TIBET

HIMALAYAS

NEPAL

Thar Desert

Ganges River

INDIA

DECCAN PLATEAU

Bay of Bengal

Arabian Sea

INDIAN OCEAN

SRI LANKA

0   300   600 Miles
0   300   600 Kilometers
Two-Point Equidistant Projection

Maurya Empire under Ashoka

Present-day border

MAP THEME

Place The Maurya Empire reached its largest size under the reign of Ashoka. ■ *What part of the Indian subcontinent was not ruled by the Mauryas?*

The invasion of Kalinga was a turning point in Ashoka's life. A **turning point** is a time of important change. The bloody invasion of Kalinga turned Ashoka against violence. He began to follow the teachings of Buddha. He refused to eat meat or to hunt and kill animals. His change led many of his people to adopt peaceful ways, too.

To spread the message of Buddhism, Ashoka issued a number of edicts, or commands. He had these edicts carved on rocks and stone pillars along main roads. Many of these pillars can still be read. One of Ashoka's edicts called on people to show "obedience to mother and father." Ashoka

also sent **missionaries**, or people who teach about their religion, to spread Buddhism to other parts of Asia.

Ashoka used his power to make the lives of his people better. During his rule, people began to place less importance on the caste system.

So fair was Ashoka that he is known in history as "the greatest and noblest ruler India has known." Not long after his death in 232 B.C., India again became a land of several smaller kingdoms.

Today the people of India still honor Ashoka. The lion and the wheel, two designs Ashoka used to decorate his edicts, are symbols of present-day India.

REVIEW *What principles guided Ashoka's government after the invasion of Kalinga?*

BIOGRAPHY

Ashoka
ruled 273 B.C.–232 B.C.

Ashoka inherited the rule of India from his father, Bindusara. Before becoming emperor, Ashoka served as governor in two large cities, Taxilla and Ujjain. When he began following Buddhist teachings, his government followed a policy of *ahimsa*, or peace and nonviolence. Ashoka ruled according to *dharma*, or "principles of right life."

Ashoka placed sculptures of lions and wheels on top of pillars along ancient Indian roads.

The Guptas Come to Power

Only 50 years after Ashoka's death, the Maurya Empire broke up into quarreling city-states. About 500 years passed before another great empire, the Gupta Empire, united India once again.

In A.D. 320 Chandragupta I became ruler of a small kingdom in the Ganges Valley. Chandragupta I soon controlled much of the valley. His son Samudra (suh•MUH•druh) Gupta and grandson Chandragupta II enlarged the empire, but it never grew as large as the Maurya Empire had been. Gupta rule ended centuries of fighting between the many city-states throughout India. For 200 years India enjoyed peace and economic growth.

Much of what we know about Gupta society comes from the writings of Faxian (FAH•SHYUHN), a Chinese Buddhist monk who went to India about A.D. 400. Faxian stayed in India for 10 years, collecting Buddhist writings to take back to China. Faxian also wrote about his travels. His writings are collected in the book *Fo Kuo Chi*, known in English as the *Record of Buddhist Kingdoms*.

The people, he observed, "are very well off." They had such freedom that "if they desire to go, they go; if they like to stop, they stop." Faxian marveled at the well-kept roads and the beautiful temples, monuments, and palaces. He also wrote of the free hospitals to which people went for treatment. India during the Gupta

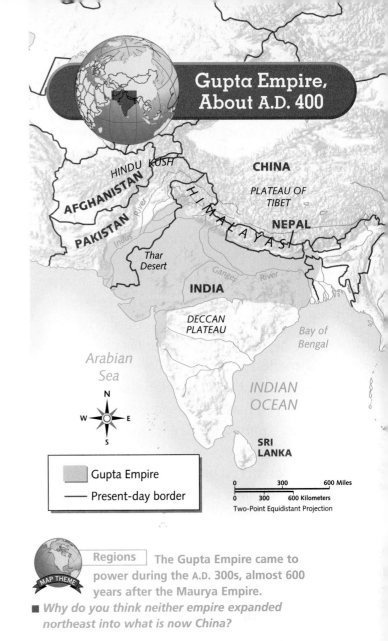

Gupta Empire, About A.D. 400

Regions The Gupta Empire came to power during the A.D. 300s, almost 600 years after the Maurya Empire.

■ *Why do you think neither empire expanded northeast into what is now China?*

Empire, Faxian concluded, seemed to be a safe and happy place.

Faxian also traveled to what is now Sri Lanka to learn more about Buddhism. He returned to China and translated the important Buddhist texts he collected. His journey to India strengthened Buddhism in China and may have helped improve India–China relations.

REVIEW *What was life like during Gupta times?*

This coin shows Chandragupta II, who led ancient India during its Golden Age.

The Golden Age of India

Faxian visited India during the rule of Chandragupta II. Historians call this period India's Golden Age. It was a time of peace, growth, and great advances in art and science.

Chandragupta II supported many artists and writers. Perhaps the most famous of these was Kalidasa (kah•lih•DAH•suh), an author known for his poems and plays.

During this time writers collected a series of folktales called the *Panchatantra* (pahn•chah•TAHN•truh). Over the centuries these popular tales traveled through the world. You may know some of the stories, such as "Sinbad the Sailor" and "Jack the Giant-Killer."

Artists carved beautiful sculptures in stone and made fantastic objects from metal during the Golden Age. One such object is a pillar of pure iron, made for Chandragupta II about A.D. 400. The pillar stands 23 feet (7 m) tall near the town of Delhi, and shows hardly any signs of rust to this day.

Many important advances were also made in Indian mathematics and medicine. As early as A.D. 595, Indian mathematicians developed the base-ten number system: 1 through 9 and the zero. Now known as **Arabic numerals**, these numerals were used in India long before they were borrowed by Arab traders.

During the Golden Age, Indian doctors discovered ways to set broken bones and to help women give birth. Like surgeons today, they used skin from other parts of the body to mend ears and noses. Understanding the need for cleanliness in surgery, they sterilized their cutting tools. Indian

The ruins of an ancient Buddhist university in what is now Nalanda, India

The Ajanta Caves in India are actually Buddhist temples that were carved from solid rock sometime between 200 B.C. and A.D. 600. These caves have given much information about the ancient cultures of India.

doctors also used **inoculation**, giving a person a mild form of a disease so that he or she would not get sick with a more serious form. European and American doctors did not use inoculation until the 1700s.

Many of the ideas of India were carried to other lands by traders. Arab merchants took Indian spices, cloth, carpets, and jewelry west to the Mediterranean. They carried Indian books and ideas to distant places such as Europe and Africa. News of India's innovations reached many parts of the world.

REVIEW *What important advances in learning took place during the time of Gupta rule?*

LESSON 4 REVIEW

400 B.C.	200 B.C.	B.C.	A.D.	A.D. 200	A.D. 400

About 320 B.C.
• Maurya Empire begins

About 273 B.C.
• Ashoka begins rule in India

A.D. 320
• Gupta Empire begins

Check Understanding

1 Remember the Facts Who created India's first empire? What ruler turned against violent ways?

2 Recall the Main Idea What methods did Maurya and Gupta rulers use to unite India? How were their methods similar? How were they different?

Think Critically

3 Personally Speaking Which ruler do you think was a better leader, Chandragupta Maurya or Ashoka? Why?

4 Think More About It Why do historians refer to the period of the Gupta kings as India's Golden Age?

Show What You Know

Oral Presentation Activity
Ashoka ruled his empire by following Buddhist teachings. Imagine that you are a visitor to the India of Ashoka's time. Describe to several classmates the effect of Ashoka's actions on the Indian people. Then listen as they offer their own descriptions.

FOCUS

How do powerful
leaders create change?

Main Idea As you
read, think about how
strong leaders affected
the development of the
Persian Empire.

Vocabulary

cavalry
tribute
courier
prophet
Zoroastrianism

The Persian Empire

| 1000 B.C. | 500 B.C. | B.C. | A.D. | A.D. 500 | A.D. 1000 |

Some of the Aryans migrated to lands west of India and settled in what is now the country of Iran around 900 B.C. The name *Iran* may have come from the word *Aryan*. The Aryan people of Iran came to be known as Persians.

Cyrus, the Empire Builder

The Persians of long ago lived on the Plateau of Iran, a large area stretching from India to the Zagros Mountains. From the plateau the Persians spread out in all directions. They conquered the Babylonians in 539 B.C. and the Egyptians in 525 B.C. Over the years, they formed the largest empire the world had seen.

The Persian army was huge. Its size and advanced war technology overwhelmed its enemies. Persian footsoldiers were well protected by bronze helmets and shields. This protection often made them the winners in hand-to-hand combat. The Persians also fought well at sea.

The Persians used **cavalry**, soldiers who rode horses and camels, to make swift attacks. Horses were also used to pull Persian war chariots, which had sharp knives attached to the wheels. In less than 20 years, the Persian army conquered lands from northern India to North Africa.

The leader who built the Persian Empire was Cyrus the Great. Cyrus was born between 590 B.C. and 580 B.C. The only battle he ever lost was his last. In that battle he led his army to fight people who lived near the Caspian Sea. Their ruler was Queen Tomyris (tuh•MY•ruhs). She led her smaller army against Cyrus's fighting force. One historian,

This sculpture (right) is possibly of Cyrus the Great, who founded the ancient Persian Empire. The image above shows King Darius on his throne.

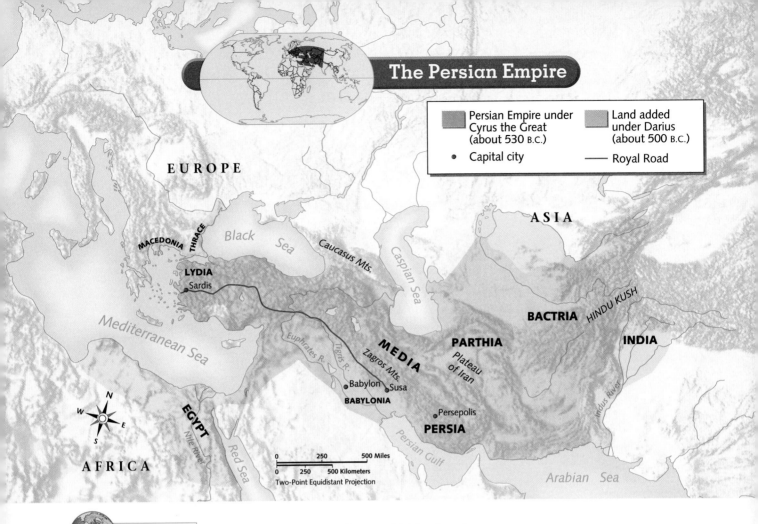

The Persian Empire

Legend:
- Persian Empire under Cyrus the Great (about 530 B.C.)
- Land added under Darius (about 500 B.C.)
- • Capital city
- —— Royal Road

EUROPE

ASIA

MACEDONIA
THRACE
Black Sea
Caucasus Mts.
Caspian Sea

LYDIA
Sardis

BACTRIA
HINDU KUSH

Mediterranean Sea

Euphrates R.
Tigris R.
MEDIA
Zagros Mts.
Babylon • Susa
BABYLONIA

PARTHIA
Plateau of Iran

INDIA
Indus River

Persepolis •
PERSIA
Persian Gulf

EGYPT
Nile River
Red Sea

AFRICA

Arabian Sea

N W E S

0   250   500 Miles
0   250   500 Kilometers
Two-Point Equidistant Projection

MAP THEME | **Movement**   The Persian Empire gained most of its land under Cyrus the Great.
■ *On what continents did Darius add new territories?*

Herodotus (hih•RAH•duh•tuhs) of Greece, later described the battle this way:

> First the two armies stood apart and shot their arrows at each other. Then, when their quivers were empty, they closed and fought hand-to-hand with lances and daggers. And thus they continued fighting for a length of time, neither choosing to give ground. "

In the end most of the Persians were killed, including Cyrus the Great. Persia's time of great growth had ended.

REVIEW   *Who created the Persian Empire?*

Darius, the Organizer

Darius (duh•RY•uhs), the Persian emperor from 522 B.C. to 486 B.C., faced the task of organizing the large empire. Darius was a successful organizer. He let the different peoples in the empire keep their own customs and also chose local leaders to rule. Darius also completed many projects to improve trade and travel. One of these projects was a canal in Egypt that linked the Red Sea and the Nile River.

The people conquered by the Persians were expected to send **tribute**, or yearly

The ruins of Darius's palace in Persepolis. Today Persepolis is part of Iran.

payments, to the emperor. At Persepolis (per•SEH•puh•luhs), the capital built by Darius, artists left a record in stone of people paying tribute. Babylonians are shown bringing livestock, and Assyrians are shown bringing hides of tanned leather. Indians carry containers of gold dust. Other people offer fine cloth, pottery, horses, and camels.

Darius faced a great problem in ruling his empire. How could he communicate with people a thousand miles from his capital? To solve this problem, Darius started a pony-express system for delivering messages. Riders called **couriers** galloped across the Persian Empire, changing horses at stations along the way.

With couriers, information could travel 1,677 miles (2,699 km) in seven days. "There is nothing in the world that travels faster than these Persian couriers," wrote the Greek historian Herodotus about 440 B.C. "Nothing stops these couriers from covering their allotted stage in the quickest possible time—neither snow, rain, heat, nor darkness." Words like these are used today by the United States Postal Service to describe its mail carriers.

REVIEW *How did Darius communicate with the different parts of his empire?*

Zarathustra, the Prophet

The earliest Persians worshipped many gods. But a prophet named Zarathustra (zar•uh•THOOS•trah) changed that. A **prophet** is a person who others believe speaks or writes with a divine message. Zarathustra began a religion called **Zoroastrianism** (zohr•uh•WASS•tree•uh•nih•zuhm), which taught a belief in two gods.

One god was the good and kind Ahura Mazda, or "Wise Lord." Ahura Mazda stood for truth. The other god, Ahriman, was his enemy. Zoroastrians believed that good and evil fought each other but that one day

This stone carving from about 800 B.C. shows Ahura Mazda, the Zoroastrian god of truth and kindness.

good would win. "The Earth is a battleground, a struggle between forces of light and forces of darkness," said Zarathustra. People who followed Zoroastrianism believed that they would live in a paradise after they died.

Persian religion, customs, and culture spread as the Persian Empire grew. When the empire began to decline, Persians had to fight their conquerors to hold on to their heritage. The fighting continued until the Arabs conquered the region in about A.D. 750. They brought their culture and the religion of Islam to the region.

REVIEW *What is Zoroastrianism?*

LESSON 5 REVIEW

1000 B.C.	500 B.C.	B.C.	A.D.	A.D. 500	A.D. 1000

About 900 B.C.
• Aryans arrive in what is now Iran

522 B.C.
• Rule of Darius begins

486 B.C.
• Rule of Darius ends

About A.D. 750
• Arabs conquer the Persian Empire

Check Understanding

1 Remember the Facts Who expanded the Persian Empire to its largest size?

2 Recall the Main Idea What was one accomplishment of each of these people: Cyrus, Darius, and Zarathustra?

Think Critically

3 Think More About It Why was it important for messages to reach all parts of the Persian Empire quickly?

4 Cause and Effect What might have happened if Cyrus had won his battle against Queen Tomyris?

Show What You Know

Simulation Activity Congratulations! You have been elected president of your class. Prepare an acceptance speech in which you describe the changes you plan to make as a strong but fair leader. Be sure to explain how your changes are going to work and why you think your changes are necessary. If a tape recorder is available, you may want to record your speech and play it back to hear how it sounds. Present your speech to your family or to your classmates.

CHAPTER 5
REVIEW

3000 B.C.   2000 B.C.

About 2500 B.C.
• Harappan civilization
  begins

CONNECT MAIN IDEAS

Use this organizer to describe the cultures of ancient India and Persia. List three details to express each main idea listed below. A copy of the organizer appears on page 46 of the Activity Book.

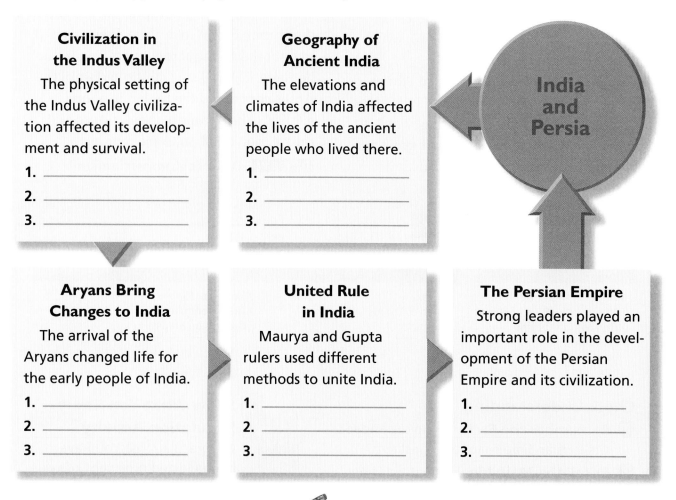

Civilization in the Indus Valley

The physical setting of the Indus Valley civilization affected its development and survival.

1. _____
2. _____
3. _____

Geography of Ancient India

The elevations and climates of India affected the lives of the ancient people who lived there.

1. _____
2. _____
3. _____

India and Persia

Aryans Bring Changes to India

The arrival of the Aryans changed life for the early people of India.

1. _____
2. _____
3. _____

United Rule in India

Maurya and Gupta rulers used different methods to unite India.

1. _____
2. _____
3. _____

The Persian Empire

Strong leaders played an important role in the development of the Persian Empire and its civilization.

1. _____
2. _____
3. _____

WRITE MORE ABOUT IT

Write Questions Write five questions you would like to ask someone who practices the religion of Hinduism today.

Write to Compare and Contrast Write several paragraphs that tell ways the religions of Hinduism and Buddhism are similar and ways they are different.

Write a Description This quotation from the *Arthashastra* describes how some rulers govern: "Government is the science of punishment." Do you agree that punishing citizens is a good way for rulers to govern? Why or why not? Write your own brief description of a good government.

About 1500 B.C.
• Aryan migrations to India begin

563 B.C.
• Buddha is born

About 320 B.C.
• Maurya Empire begins

A.D. 320
• Gupta Empire begins

About A.D. 750
• Arabs conquer the Persian Empire

USE VOCABULARY

For each group of terms, write a sentence or two that explain how the terms are related.

1 Sanskrit, Vedas

2 Hinduism, caste, untouchables

3 Arabic numerals, inoculation

4 prophet, Zoroastrianism

CHECK UNDERSTANDING

5 What advantage did the Aryans have over the native people of India in the competition for farmland?

6 What were some of the things the Aryans brought to India?

7 Who are the three main gods of the Hindu religion?

8 How did the caste system affect early Indian society?

9 What caused Siddhartha Gautama to begin his search for knowledge?

10 What event caused Ashoka to change his way of ruling?

11 What important contributions were made during India's Golden Age?

12 How did Darius's pony-express system affect Persia?

THINK CRITICALLY

13 **Think More About It** How might a belief in reincarnation affect people who live in the Indian subcontinent and are part of the Hindu caste system?

14 **Explore Viewpoints** How would a Hindu priest probably view the caste system? How might an untouchable view it?

15 **Past to Present** Buddhism has spread to many countries with very different cultures. Why do you think Buddhism is followed in so many different places?

16 **Personally Speaking** Imagine that you are a member of the Sudra class. Do you plan to willingly accept your place in society? Explain why or why not.

APPLY SKILLS

Use a Cultural Map Select a present-day country. Use an encyclopedia to find out which religions and languages are most common in different parts of the country. Make a map that shows this information. Use colors and symbols to show different religions and languages. Then exchange maps with a classmate. Write a paragraph describing the information on your classmate's map.

READ MORE ABOUT IT

Come with Me to India by Sudha Koul. Cashmir. This book covers many subjects, including the government, cultures, and religions of present-day India.

Visit the Internet at **http://www.hbschool.com** for additional resources.

CHINA

Life-size statue of a
Chinese soldier, carved
about 210 B.C.

*"Eastward goes the great river,
its waves have swept away
a thousand years of gallant men."*

Chinese poet Su Shi,
1037–1101

Geography of Ancient China

FOCUS

How does geography create differences among regions in the United States today?

Main Idea Think about how mountains and rivers have divided China into several regions, each with its own unique culture.

Vocabulary

loess
basin
dialect

In ancient times the geography of China separated it and its people from the rest of the world. Mountains, deserts, and large bodies of water made travel to and from China difficult. This led the people of China to develop a unique respect for the land around them. China's geography helped shape the civilization, culture, and beliefs of the people who lived there.

The Land of China

China is located at the far-eastern end of the continent of Asia. Present-day China covers more than 3,696,100 square miles (9,572,160 sq km) and is the third-largest country in the world. It stretches about 3,100 miles (4,989 km) from east to west and about 3,400 miles (5,472 km) from north to south. The entire United States mainland could fit inside China's borders.

China has many long and wide rivers that flow across the country. The largest of these rivers are the Huang He (HWAHNG HUH), or "Yellow River," in the north and the Chang Jiang (CHAHNG JYAHNG), or "Long River," in the south.

The Huang He twists and turns about 2,900 miles (4,667 km) from its source in the high plateaus of western China to its mouth at the Yellow Sea. It picks up **loess** (LOH•uhs), a yellow silt, as it flows through China's northern deserts. This yellow silt colors the water and gives the Huang He, or "Yellow River," its name.

The largest tributary of the Huang He is the Wei River. The Wei River begins in central China and travels to the east until it empties into the Huang He.

A farmer watering his vegetables north of Canton, China

The Chang Jiang, also called the Yangtze (YAHNG•SEH), is the third-longest river in the world. Only the Nile River in Africa and the Amazon River in South America are longer. The Chang Jiang flows about 3,430 miles (5,520 km) from the highlands of Tibet to the Pacific Ocean. It winds through mountains and plunges through deep gorges before it reaches the ocean.

China is known not only for its mighty rivers but also for its rugged mountains. Most of China's many mountain ranges are high, rocky, and hard to cross. One such mountain range—the Taihang Mountains— runs north and south through the center of northern China. Another range, the Qinling (CHIN•LIN) Mountains, runs east and west.

REVIEW *What are some of China's most important waterways and mountains?*

China's Land Regions

Rivers and mountains divide China into different areas. The Qinling Mountains divide China into two main parts— northern China and southern China. Both northern and southern China can be divided into smaller regions.

Among the major regions of northern China are the North China Plain, the

The Huang He winding through mountains (left) and a recent photo of Beijing (below) show that China is a land both old and new.

China

KAZAKHSTAN
RUSSIA
MONGOLIA
KYRGYZSTAN
TIAN SHAN
Takla Makan (Desert)
GOBI (DESERT)
KUNLUN SHAN
Plateau of Tibet
CHINA
Huang He
NORTH KOREA
SOUTH KOREA
Sea of Japan
JAPAN
Yellow Sea
HIMALAYAS
NEPAL
BHUTAN
BANGLADESH
INDIA
Chang Jiang
East China Sea
PACIFIC OCEAN
Bay of Bengal
BURMA (MYANMAR)
LAOS
VIETNAM
Xi Jiang
TAIWAN
Tropic of Cancer
South China Sea
0   250   500 Miles
0   250   500 Kilometers
Two-Point Equidistant Projection

50°N
140°E
40°N
30°N
20°N
90°E
120°E
130°E

Regions China has many different regions.
■ *Why do you think that early Chinese civilization developed in the eastern part of what is now China rather than in the western part?*

Shandong Peninsula, and the Huang He Valley. Some of the major land regions of southern China are the Szechwan Basin, the Southeast Mountains, and the Chang Jiang Basin. A **basin** is a bowl-shaped area of land surrounded by higher land.

To the west of the Qinling Mountains lies the Plateau of Tibet. This plateau in southwestern China occupies about one-fourth of the whole country. The plateau's elevation ranges from about 13,000 feet (3,962 m) to 26,000 feet (7,925 m). North of the Qinling Mountains is the enormous Gobi desert. This 500,000-square-foot (46,450-sq-m) area is dry and has very few plants.

Each of China's regions has a different geography and climate. Many also have their own local culture. Each region has its own **dialect**, or way of speaking, the Chinese language. The dialect of one region often cannot be understood in another.

China's mountains and rivers are one reason for the great differences between regions. For centuries these mountains and rivers have separated groups of people. Without much contact from outsiders, the people of each region developed their own way of life.

REVIEW *How are China's regions different from each other?*

Chapter 6 • **233**

Loess

The enriched sandy soil of the Huang He Valley is called loess. Loess is different from other soils because it never stops collecting and then shifting in the howling winds. Loess can build up in the Huang He, causing the river to flood. Mounds of loess in the river can even cause the river to change course, drowning people and destroying homes. Since the earliest days, people have had good reason to call the Huang He "The River of Sorrows." However, the same destructive floods also deposit loess along the riverbanks of the Huang He. This has enriched the soil there, making it perfect for growing crops. In this way, "The River of Sorrows" makes agriculture possible in the area.

Loess colors the water of the Huang He yellow. The name Huang He means "Yellow River." The loess collected in the river has caused the Huang He to change its course many times.

Farming in China

The North China Plain and the Huang He Valley have had large populations for thousands of years. These regions have also long been among China's most important food-producing regions. Growing food in northern China has always been a challenge. The climate is cold and dry, and the growing season is short. However, the land alongside the Huang He has been made rich by the river's deposits of silt. This fertile soil has allowed northern farmers to grow wheat, other grains, and a variety of vegetables.

Southern China has warmer climates and longer growing seasons. Farmers in the Chang Jiang Basin produce about three-fourths of all the rice eaten in China. Wheat, corn, and beans are just a few of the other crops that grow well in the Chang Jiang Basin.

REVIEW *What are some of the crops that grow in China?*

LESSON 1 REVIEW

Check Understanding

1 **Remember the Facts**   What are the two major rivers in China?

2 **Recall the Main Idea**   How have mountains and rivers affected China?

Think Critically

3 **Past to Present**   How do you think living in a country of many cultures affects Chinese people today?

4 **Think More About It**   How might China have been different if it did not have mountains and wide rivers?

Show What You Know
Map Activity   Imagine that you are traveling by boat from the source of the Huang He to its mouth. Make a map that shows the route you will take.

Early Chinese Civilization

5000 B.C.	3000 B.C.	1000 B.C.

FOCUS

How can people's attitudes toward the past affect the way they live?

Main Idea Read to find out how respect for ancestors influenced the lives of the ancient Chinese.

Vocabulary

legend
ritual
ancestor
oracle bone
oracle
character

Chinese civilization has a long and complex history. Over the years, historians have kept an almost complete record of rulers, cultures, and events. Today the chain of Chinese history directly links present-day China with China's earliest civilizations. Two of the most important early civilizations were located in river valleys. One was in the valley of the Huang He. The other was in the valley of the Chang Jiang.

Legends and Facts About China's Origins

Like many other people, the Chinese have often used **legends**, or stories handed down from earlier times, to explain the distant past. One Chinese legend tells that the goddess Nugua (NEW•GWAY) made the first humans out of clay. Another story tells that her husband, Fuxi (FOO•SHEE), invented writing by studying the scratches of birds and other animals.

The story of Yu the Great and the Great Flood may be the most famous Chinese legend of all. This legend tells of a time when floods covered much of China. To save China, Yu the Great dug deep rivers to hold the extra water. Yu worked for 13 years to remove floodwaters from the land. When his work was done, the farmers could once again plant their crops. Even today Chinese students say, "If it were not for Yu the Great, we would all be fishes."

Historians may never know if Yu the Great helped farmers control floods. There is no proof that he even existed. Still, the ancient legend tells us a lot about the early Chinese. It helps show the importance that they placed on agriculture.

This ax head may have been used for religious ceremonies in ancient China.

This pot was used for cooking food during the Shang dynasty. Its shape allowed it to stand easily over a small fire.

As early as 5000 B.C., farmers were growing crops in both northern and southern China. There is also evidence that dogs and pigs were domesticated at this time. In northern China early farmers grew grains such as millet, as well as fruits and green vegetables. At the same time, farmers in southern China were growing rice. By 3000 B.C. cattle were being raised in northern and southern China.

In both parts of China, the settled farmers began to make pottery. Bowls, jugs, and other pieces of pottery were used to store and transport rice and other grains. Some pottery was decorated with simple designs and placed in graves during burials. Beautiful objects made of jade—a very hard, usually green stone—have also been found in graves of this period.

REVIEW *Why is the story of Yu the Great important?*

The Xia and Shang Dynasties

By about 2000 B.C. there were hundreds of settlements near the Chang Jiang and the Huang He. As in other civilizations, some of these settlements grew into towns. Later these towns developed into powerful kingdoms that competed for resources. This competition often led to fights between kingdoms.

According to early legends, Yu the Great ruled a number of kingdoms after he found a way to control

The Shang also made weapons such as this sword and dagger out of bronze.

Human-Environment Interactions   The Shang claimed land in eastern Asia.
■ *Why do you think other groups may have wanted the land controlled by the Shang?*

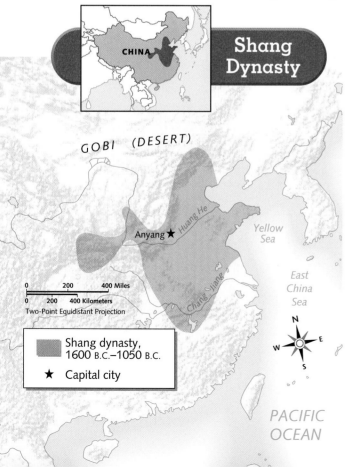

CHINA

Shang Dynasty

GOBI (DESERT)

Anyang ★

Huang He

Yellow Sea

Chang Jiang

East China Sea

0   200   400 Miles
0   200   400 Kilometers
Two-Point Equidistant Projection

▨ Shang dynasty, 1600 B.C.–1050 B.C.
★ Capital city

PACIFIC OCEAN

the floods. The stories say that when he died, his son took over as ruler. In this way Yu and his family created the first Chinese dynasty, the Xia (SYAH). Because no archaeological evidence from the Xia has been found, we do not know if they really existed. Experts do know that many different families ruled China through the centuries. Dynasties continued to rule China for almost 4,000 years.

Early legends tell us that the Xia dynasty ruled for many years. However, by about 1600 B.C., another kingdom had gained power. Its king, Tang the Successful, supposedly conquered the Xia and began a new ruling dynasty. This dynasty is remembered as the Shang. The Shang used war chariots and weapons made of bronze—a metal made by combining copper, lead, and tin. This technology may have helped them take control of China.

Over the years the Shang added land to their kingdom. As the size of the Shang kingdom grew, its rulers moved the Shang capital farther north. The Shang may have had as many as five different capitals during their rule. At one of the capitals, Zhengzhou, workers built enormous walls around the city. They made the walls by pounding thin layers of earth together inside a movable frame. After this was done several times, the frame was removed. Using this method, the Shang created walls as hard as cement. The walls were 60 feet (18.3 m) wide, 30 feet (9.1 m) tall, and

2,385 feet (727 m) long. The last Shang capital was near the present-day city of Anyang (AHN•YAHNG), not very far from the Huang He.

REVIEW *What was the first Chinese dynasty?*

Bronze Vessels and Oracle Bones

Most people during the Shang dynasty lived in small farming villages. The farmers grew grain, kept chickens and pigs, and raised silkworms for silk cloth. Craftworkers made bronze tools, weapons, and beautiful vessels used for rituals. A **ritual** is a set way of conducting a ceremony.

The Shang people used bronze ritual vessels in ceremonies to honor their ancestors who had died. **Ancestors** are relatives further back than grandparents. Because of the importance of the rituals, the Shang devoted much skill, energy, and time to making bronze ritual vessels. Sometimes the maker of a bronze vessel would carve an inscription into it that told who made it and which ancestor it honored. Such inscriptions are among the earliest examples of Chinese writing.

The ancient Chinese worshiped their ancestors and several gods. Ancestors were worshipped because they were thought to be very wise and able to guide the lives of the living. Most of the gods Shang people worshipped were nature gods. The Shang prayed to the gods of wind, rain, and fire, as well as to the gods of directions—north,

Lady Hao (About 1250 B.C.)

Much of the information we have about the Shang people comes from their tombs. Unfortunately, most Shang tombs were robbed before they were discovered by archaeologists. The only royal Shang tomb not robbed before its discovery is Lady Hao's tomb. It contained over 460 bronze objects and several sculptures in jade and ivory.

Little is known about Lady Hao. Some researchers believe she is mentioned in oracle bone inscriptions of the time as a wife of the king Wu Ding. According to these inscriptions, Lady Hao handled certain rituals and managed an estate outside the capital. She also led military campaigns—once with more than 13,000 soldiers.

Chinese artifacts found in Lady Hao's tomb, such as this ivory and turquoise cup, are admired today because of their beauty and strength.

south, east, and west. The chief god of the Shang was called Shang Di, which means "God-on-High." This god's name suggests that the people believed he lived in the sky and oversaw everything they did.

The ancient Shang thought that their ancestors could communicate with the gods. Ancestors were asked to encourage the powerful gods of nature to be kind to humankind. The Shang feared that angry gods might bring disasters, diseases, or enemy attacks.

Shang kings would often ask their ancestors for advice on a wide variety of subjects. To learn the answers to his questions, the king needed the help of a diviner. A diviner was a person who, it was believed, could communicate with the spirits of the dead.

The diviner would lay out animal bones or turtle shells. Then, the diviner would touch the bones or shells with hot metal sticks. The heat caused cracks to form on the bones and shells. The diviner then gave the bones and shells to the king. The Shang king "read" the cracks to find out the answers to his questions.

The ancient Chinese looked to oracle bones for the answers to both major and minor problems. What sources do people today turn to for help in solving problems?

After the Shang king received answers from his ancestors, a scribe wrote the answers on the bones or shells. Like the inscriptions on Shang bronze vessels, these inscriptions on bones and shells are among the earliest known examples of Chinese writing.

About 100 years ago farmers near Anyang began to find the animal bones and turtle shells the Shang had used long ago. The farmers could not read the writing on them. They mistakenly believed the bones were dragon bones. They sold these "dragon bones" to local drugstores, where they were used to make medicines.

The silk on this model shows little damage though it is over 2,000 years old.

In time, archaeologists heard about the farmers' discoveries. Only then were the "dragon bones" correctly identified. The world learned that the bones show answers to questions that the ancient Shang kings asked their ancestors. Today scholars who study ancient China call the shells and bones **oracle bones**. An **oracle** is a person who gives wise advice.

Oracle bones give important clues to the way of life of the Shang people. They help give an idea of the problems the Shang people faced and how they sought solutions to their problems. Oracle bones also show what daily life was like in ancient China.

REVIEW *How did the Shang people use oracle bones?*

HISTORY

The Legend of Silk

Silk has long been used in China to weave beautiful clothing, fine ribbons, and colorful decorations. A legend tells that the Chinese discovered silk in 2700 B.C., when Xilingshi (SEE•LING•SHIR), a ruler's wife, noticed worms eating a prized mulberry tree. She took a cocoon spun by a worm, dropped it into hot water and watched the thread unwind. Xilingshi then used the thread to weave a beautiful piece of cloth. No one knows whether this story is true or false, but silk has been produced throughout the Huang He Valley since the time of the Shang and probably earlier.

Silk cloth has long been a prized product of China. Eighteenth-century Chinese craftworkers weave silk on a large loom (right).

Chinese Writing

WRITING FROM SHANG PERIOD	ENGLISH WORD	CURRENT CHINESE WRITING
⊙	Sun	日
☽	Moon	月
⼨	Tree	木
⾬	Rain	雨
⼭	Mountain	山
⽔	Water	水

LEARNING FROM TABLES This table shows the development of the Chinese language from ancient times to the present day.

■ *What similarities can you see between the characters of the past and those of the present?*

Chinese Writing

The Shang dynasty contributed many inventions to early Chinese civilization. Bronze ritual vessels, bronze weapons, chariots, and walled cities were just a few of their innovations. Of all the Shang advances, the most important was the development of Chinese writing.

Legend says that people of the Shang period wrote in books made of bamboo and wood. Yet none of these have ever been found. Books made of such materials would not have lasted through the centuries.

The only evidence of Shang writing can be found on oracle bones and bronze ritual vessels. These artifacts make it clear that the Shang were the earliest people east of the Indus Valley to read and write. Writing would have allowed the Shang government to keep records and to work better.

The writing system created by the Shang was adopted by later Chinese dynasties. It forms the base of all later Chinese writing. Shang writing is different from the writing of many other peoples in one important way. The **characters**, or symbols, used in Shang writing represent whole words. They

Chinese artists (below) use inkstones (below left) and brushes (right) to create calligraphy, or "beautiful writing."

are not like the letters of the English alphabet, which represent parts of words. Shang characters are more like Egyptian hieroglyphs, which also stand for whole words. Like hieroglyphs, many Shang characters began as drawings of the things they name.

Oracle bones and bronze vessels show that the Shang people used a very large number of characters. Only about 1,000 of these have been figured out.

Chinese writing has changed over the years. Chinese civilization developed many new ideas and came into closer contact with other peoples and traditions. Because of these changes, some old characters have changed in meaning and new ones have been added. However, present-day Chinese writing has strong roots in Shang characters.

REVIEW *How is Shang writing different from other types of writing?*

Chinese calligraphy atop the mountain Tai Shan.

LESSON 2 REVIEW

5000 B.C.		3000 B.C.		1000 B.C.

About 5000 B.C.
• Agriculture begins in China

About 2700 B.C.
• Silk produced in the Huang He Valley

About 1600 B.C.
• Shang dynasty begins

Check Understanding

1 Remember the Facts What were the names of the first two Chinese dynasties?

2 Recall the Main Idea How did respect for the past affect Chinese civilization?

Think Critically

3 Personally Speaking The ancient Chinese respected family traditions and the opinions of the oldest members of their families. Does our society show respect for tradition and for the wisdom of older people? Explain.

4 Past to Present Inscriptions on oracle bones show some of the problems the Shang kings faced. What sources might give clues to the problems leaders face today?

Show What You Know

Role-Play Activity With a partner, plan and act out two dramatic scenes about people finding oracle bones. First, act out a scene between two farmers who are amazed to find "dragon bones" in their fields. Then, act out a scene in which two archaeologists uncover oracle bones while on a dig. After you have acted out the scenes, think about how the two scenes were alike and different. Compare and contrast the differing views each group had about the oracle bones.

Chapter 6 • **241**

Use Elevation Maps

1. Why Learn This Skill?

Different kinds of maps provide different kinds of information. A road map, for example, shows which routes go from one place to another and how far it is between places. Sometimes, however, people need information that is not given on a road map. If you wanted to know how high or low the land is, you would need an elevation (eh•luh•VAY•shuhn) map. **Elevation** is the height of the land. Elevation maps help city planners decide where to lay water pipes or build a shopping mall. Elevation maps can also help you choose a good place for skateboarding or riding your bike.

2. Contour Lines and Color

To find out how tall you are, you must measure the distance from your base (the bottom of your feet) to your top (the top of your head). Land is also measured from the base to the top. The base for all landforms is sea level, or 0 feet (0 m). Find sea level on Drawing A to the left of the elevation map of the southeastern part of Asia on page 243.

The lines on this drawing of a hill are contour lines. A **contour line** connects all points of equal elevation. Find the 400-foot (122-m) contour line on Drawing A. This line connects all the points that are exactly 400 feet (122 m) above sea level.

Imagine that you are flying in an airplane over the hill shown in the drawing. Picture the drawing as a rising hill. As you look down on it from above, you can see the contour lines as loops. If you flew over the hill in Drawing B, you would see each contour line labeled with its elevation. You would see that the contour lines are not evenly spaced. On the steeper side of the hill, the contour lines are closer together. On the gently sloping side, the contour lines are farther apart.

On some elevation maps, color is added between the contour lines. Drawing C is an example of this type of elevation map. A key is used instead of labels. The key shows that everything green is between sea level and 100 feet (30 m). The line between green and yellow on the map is a 100-foot (30-m) contour line. The lines bordering the other colors are also contour lines.

Most elevation maps use a few important contour lines with colors added between the lines. Look at the elevation map on the next page. The map key shows the range of elevation that each color stands for. Land that is 13,120 feet (4,000 m) above sea level or higher is shown in purple. Green is used for land in the range between sea level and 655 feet (200 m). When you study the map, you cannot tell whether land in the green areas is at sea level, at 655 feet (200 m) above sea level, or at some elevation in between.

3. Understand the Process

Use these questions as a guide for better understanding elevation maps.

1. What is the difference between what a contour line shows on a map and what an area of color shows?

2. To find the exact elevation of a place, should you look for a contour line or a band of color? Why?

3. How high are the highest areas of Burma? How can you tell? Where are these areas located?

4. Where are the lowest areas in Vietnam? How can you tell?

5. Is most of the land in Cambodia high or low? Explain your answer.

4. Think and Apply

Around 2000 B.C. people living in northeastern and central Thailand began making bronze objects. They made tools and weapons, ornaments, and drums. They traded these objects with people in nearby settlements. Imagine that you are a Thai trader traveling from central Thailand to the coast of the South China Sea. Use your finger to trace the route. Describe the land you pass along the way.

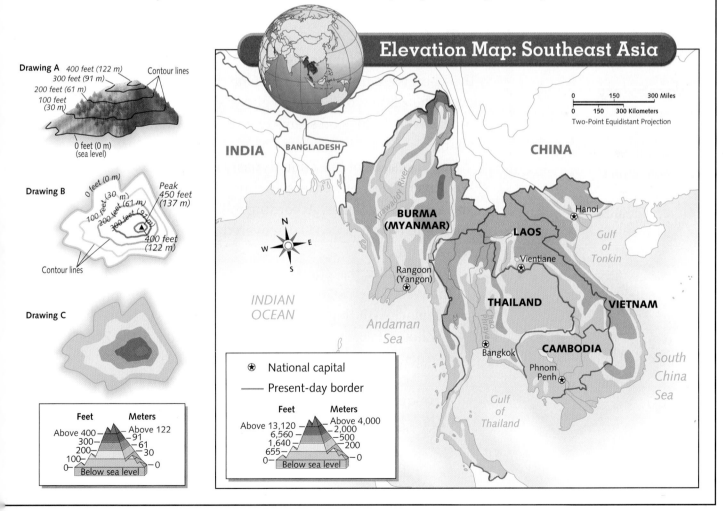

Drawing A
400 feet (122 m)
300 feet (91 m)
200 feet (61 m)
100 feet (30 m)
Contour lines
0 feet (0 m) (sea level)

Drawing B
0 feet (0 m)
100 feet (30 m)
200 feet (61 m)
300 feet (91 m)
400 feet (122 m)
Peak 450 feet (137 m)
Contour lines

Drawing C

Feet | Meters
Above 400 — Above 122
300 — 91
200 — 61
100 — 30
0 — 0
Below sea level

Elevation Map: Southeast Asia

0   150   300 Miles
0   150   300 Kilometers
Two-Point Equidistant Projection

INDIA
BANGLADESH
CHINA
Irrawaddy River
BURMA (MYANMAR)
LAOS
Hanoi
Gulf of Tonkin
Rangoon (Yangon)
Vientiane
INDIAN OCEAN
THAILAND
VIETNAM
Andaman Sea
Chao Phraya
Bangkok
CAMBODIA
Phnom Penh
South China Sea
Gulf of Thailand

✳ National capital
—— Present-day border

Feet | Meters
Above 13,120 — Above 4,000
6,560 — 2,000
1,640 — 500
655 — 200
0 — 0
Below sea level

Chapter 6 • 243

The Zhou Dynasty

| 1250 B.C. | 1000 B.C. | 750 B.C. | 500 B.C. |

The Classical Age in China began with the conquest of the Huang He Valley in 1050 B.C. by the Zhou (JOH) dynasty. Under the Zhou and the dynasties that followed, China became powerful. These dynasties left a heritage that has lasted for thousands of years. A **heritage** is a set of ideas that have been passed down from one generation to another.

Winning the Mandate of Heaven

The beginnings of the Zhou people are not entirely clear. Even experts in Chinese history are not sure how different the Zhou were from the Shang. One difference is clear, however. The Zhou worshipped a god they called Tian (TYEN), or "Heaven." This god seems to have been unknown to the Shang.

The ancestors of the Zhou dynasty may have lived in the Wei River Valley as herders. In time, they learned to farm and settled in villages. According to legend, the founder of the Zhou, Hou Ji (HO GEE) discovered agriculture when he was a child.

Gradually, the Zhou began to move farther east in the Wei River Valley. As they moved, they came into contact with the Shang. Around the year 1150 B.C., the Zhou attacked the Shang. In about 1050 B.C. the Zhou ruler, King Wu, claimed victory over the Shang.

According to the Zhou, Heaven ordered King Wu to conquer the Shang and begin a new dynasty. The early Zhou kings believed that the god Heaven disapproved

FOCUS
How do ideas and values affect societies today?

Main Idea As you read, think about the ideas that first arose during the Zhou dynasty and still define Chinese civilization.

Vocabulary
heritage
virtue
Mandate of Heaven
philosopher
filial piety
Confucianism

The sacred bi, or ring of heaven, was a symbol of the bond between the Chinese gods and the leaders chosen to carry out the Mandate of Heaven.

of the Shang king. They thought that the Shang did not have the **virtues**, or good qualities, needed to lead the people.

The Book of Documents, an early Chinese text, calls Heaven's order to claim rule over China the **Mandate of Heaven**. The Zhou kings believed that they would be able to keep the mandate as long as they continued to show virtues. The Zhou kings believed that virtues kept order in their society.

REVIEW *What was the Mandate of Heaven?*

Division of Classes

The family was the basic unit of Zhou society. During Zhou times, society was divided into three classes of families— the king and his family, noble families, and peasant families. Families of each class were expected to show virtues by performing services for other classes.

The king showed that he had virtues by giving land to the noble families. Land given to a noble by the king is called a fief. Fiefs remained the property of the noble families and were passed down from generation to generation. In return for this land, the noble families showed loyalty to the king by paying him tribute. Tribute was paid in the form of valuable gifts or by supplying an army to help the king fight battles.

Peasants lived on the fiefs owned by the nobles. Nobles allowed the peasants to farm part of their fiefs. In return, the peasants had to serve in the nobles' armies and pay taxes by sending the nobles some of their crops.

The lives of peasants were filled with hardships. Some landlords were greedy and demanded that the peasants pay more taxes than they could afford. However, the

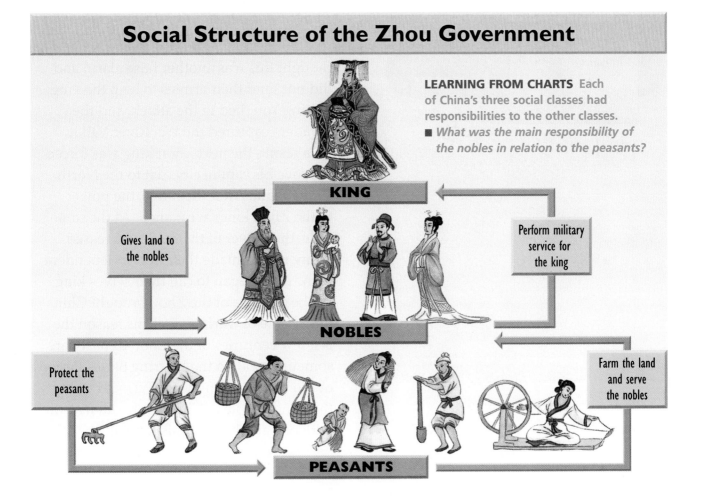

Social Structure of the Zhou Government

LEARNING FROM CHARTS Each of China's three social classes had responsibilities to the other classes.
■ *What was the main responsibility of the nobles in relation to the peasants?*

KING

Gives land to the nobles

Perform military service for the king

NOBLES

Protect the peasants

Farm the land and serve the nobles

PEASANTS

peasant farmers were not slaves and could leave. A peasant complains about his landlord in one of the earliest books of Chinese poetry, the *Book of Songs*:

66 Big rat! Big rat!

Don't eat our millet!

For three years we've spoiled you, you haven't paid us back.

It's got to the point where we'll leave you and go to that happy land.

Happy land! Happy land!

There we'll find a place. 99

REVIEW *What were the three classes of Zhou society?*

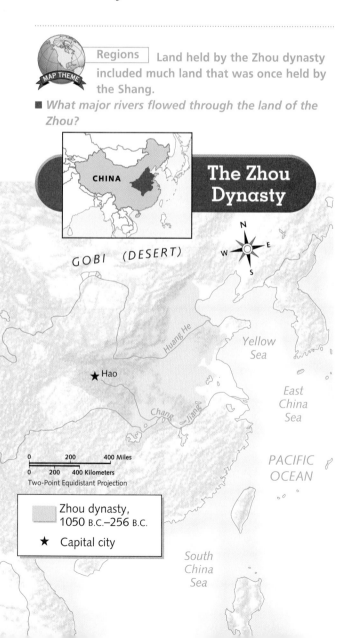

Regions Land held by the Zhou dynasty included much land that was once held by the Shang.

■ *What major rivers flowed through the land of the Zhou?*

CHINA

The Zhou Dynasty

GOBI (DESERT)

Huang He

Yellow Sea

★ Hao

East China Sea

Chang Jiang

PACIFIC OCEAN

0   200   400 Miles
0   200   400 Kilometers
Two-Point Equidistant Projection

Zhou dynasty, 1050 B.C.–256 B.C.

★ Capital city

South China Sea

The Decline of the Zhou

King Wu and the kings who followed him were all strong rulers. *The Book of Documents* says that the Zhou governed carefully because they feared losing the Mandate of Heaven. The power and good standing of the Zhou kings, however, eventually weakened. Soon, people to the north and to the west of the Zhou kingdom invaded the valley of the Wei River.

In 771 B.C. the people of the Zhou capital city of Hao (HOW) got ready for an attack by the invaders. A legend tells that the Zhou leader, King You (YOO), ordered fires lighted on hills around the capital when an attack seemed likely. However, several times he lit the fires when there was no invasion. He just wanted to see if the nobles would come. Finally, there really was an attack. King You ordered the fires to be lit, in hopes of bringing the nobles' armies. The nobles thought this was another false alarm and did not send their armies to help the king.

King You died in the attack, and the invaders captured the Wei River Valley. As a result, the next Zhou king was forced to move his capital city east to the North China Plain. After the move, the power of the Zhou kings weakened. At the same time, the power of the nobles increased. Many nobles made their fiefs independent. Some even began to call themselves king.

The collapse of the Zhou brought China into a time of warfare. For this reason the last few centuries of the Zhou dynasty are sometimes called the Warring States Period, or the Warring Kingdoms Period. During this time people in China were often at war with one another. Yet this time of war also

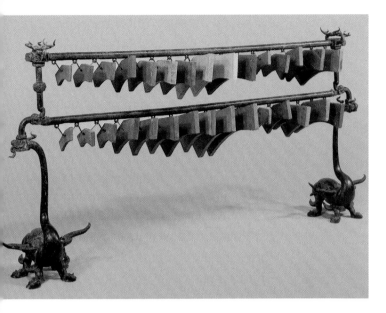

This set of chimes was made during the Warring Kingdoms Period. The chimes are made of jade. Bronze animal sculptures form the rack.

brought the development of new forms of government to bring back law and order.

As early as the 600s B.C., the kingdom of Chu (JOO) had invented a new way of dividing and governing land. The Chu kings did not give out land to noble families. Instead they created counties and picked people to govern them. The people who governed these counties were chosen because of their abilities. The Chu system of governing counties is one of

This bronze and jade statue of a peasant child is from the time of the Zhou dynasty. Why do you think statues like this were made?

the earliest examples in world history of a bureaucracy. In the Chu bureaucracy, a network of appointed government officials did specific jobs. The idea of bureaucracy spread rapidly throughout ancient China.

In 535 B.C. the king of Zheng (ZHENG), a small kingdom in the North China Plain, wrote down a set of laws. These were the earliest written laws in China. The Zheng ruler no longer believed that having virtues was enough to keep order in society. He believed that specific laws were needed. The laws were meant to explain clearly what was right and what was wrong. The ruler of Zheng inscribed his new laws on the outside of a giant bronze vessel so that everyone could see the laws.

REVIEW *How was the kingdom of Chu governed?*

The Ideas of Confucius

One of China's most important thinkers, Confucius, lived during the Warring Kingdoms Period. Confucius is often called China's first philosopher. A **philosopher** is a person who studies the meaning of life. Confucius spent much of his time thinking about ways to improve society and restore order in China.

Confucius is also remembered as China's first teacher. Many people sought Confucius so that they could study the ancient traditions with him. Often he used short sayings to teach his ideas. After Confucius died, his students grouped all his sayings into a huge collection. Many later followers argued that some of the sayings were not from Confucius. A book was then made

Confucius (551–479 B.C.)

Confucius is believed to have been born in 551 B.C. The name *Confucius* is a Latin form of the philosopher's name—Kong Fuzi (KOONG FOO•zuh), which means Master Kong. Confucius' father was a government official. By the time Confucius was 25 years old, he also worked in the Lu government. Perhaps because he had offended powerful noble families, Confucius was exiled from Lu. According to legend, Confucius wandered for 25 years. During this time, he formed his ideas about government and society. Many of his ideas are still respected and used today.

No one knows for sure what Confucius looked like. A portrait of him from A.D. 1734 (above) and an ivory statue from about A.D. 1000 (above right) provide very different views.

containing the sayings most people agreed were really spoken by Confucius. This book is called *Lunyu* (LUN•YOO) in Chinese and the *Analects* in English. The Chinese word *lunyu* means "discussions."

The *Analects* tell much about the philosopher's ideas. He opposed the new forms of government that the Chu, Zheng, and other kingdoms were practicing. Confucius did not agree with the idea of bureaucracy. He also thought that the use of written laws and punishments was not the best way to bring back order. Instead, Confucius supported the old Zhou dynasty idea that a ruler should set a good example for his people.

Many of Confucius' thoughts about government seem to be based on his views about families. In ancient China, children were expected to treat their parents with great honor and respect. The ancient Chinese called this kind treatment of parents *xiao* (SHOW), or **filial piety** (FIH•lee•uhl PY•uh•tee). Confucius told his followers that by studying filial piety they could learn how to become loyal subjects. Confucius also taught that rulers could gain loyalty only by treating their subjects with the same love that parents show to their children. He called such love *ren*, or kindness.

For the most part, the teachings of Confucius were ignored during his lifetime. In time, however, his ideas, which came to be called **Confucianism**, spread throughout eastern Asia.

REVIEW *What qualities did Confucius believe that rulers and subjects should have?*

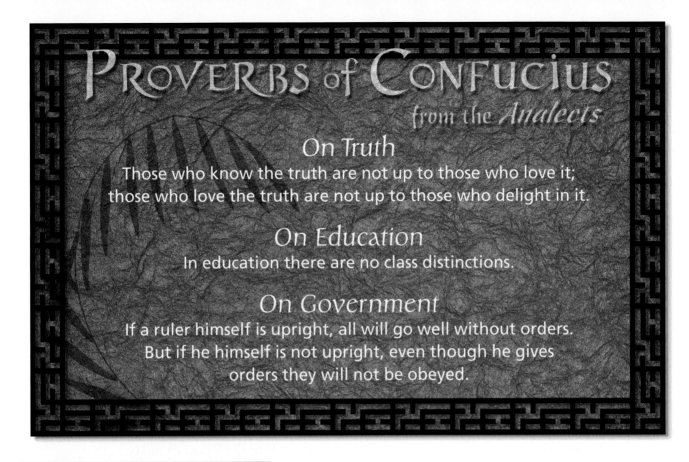

PROVERBS of CONFUCIUS
from the *Analects*

On Truth
Those who know the truth are not up to those who love it;
those who love the truth are not up to those who delight in it.

On Education
In education there are no class distinctions.

On Government
If a ruler himself is upright, all will go well without orders.
But if he himself is not upright, even though he gives
orders they will not be obeyed.

LESSON 3 REVIEW

1250 B.C.	1000 B.C.	750 B.C.	500 B.C.

About 1050 B.C.
• Zhou dynasty defeats the Shang dynasty

About 770 B.C.
• Warring Kingdoms Period begins

551 B.C.
• Confucius is born

535 B.C.
• Earliest written laws in China

Check Understanding

❶ Remember the Facts   What teacher and philosopher of ancient China developed an important system of ideas and values?

❷ Recall the Main Idea   How did the Chinese people's shared belief in a set of ideas strengthen their civilization?

Think Critically

❸ Think More About It   In what ways did Confucianism support the idea of the Mandate of Heaven?

❹ Personally Speaking   Zhou society was divided into three classes, each with different responsibilities. In your opinion, would such a system be more likely to lead to cooperation or to conflict? Explain.

Show What You Know
Creative Writing Activity
Confucius often presented his ideas about society as proverbs, or short sayings. Some examples can be found in the Proverbs of Confucius from the *Analects,* shown above. Using those examples as models, write your own proverbs about the need for order and cooperation in your school or community.

Identify Causes

1. Why Learn This Skill?

To find links between different events in history, you need to understand causes and their effects. A cause is something that makes something else happen. What happens is an effect. Knowing about causes and effects is important not only for understanding history but also for making personal decisions. It can help you think about the consequences of your actions. In that way you can make more thoughtful decisions.

2. Remember What You Have Read

Before the decline of the Zhou, their society was divided into three levels. The king was at the top, nobles were in the middle, and peasants were at the bottom. For the structure to work, the king had to be virtuous. In return, the nobles had to remain loyal to the king, and the peasants had to obey the nobles. You read the legend of King You. His story gives an example of what happened when a king was not thought to be virtuous.

3. Understand the Process

Many events in history have more than one cause and more than one effect. Follow the arrows on the chart on the next page to help you understand the causes and effects of the fall of the Zhou dynasty.

1. What caused King You to send signals to the nobles? What was the effect?
2. Why did the nobles not respond when the Zhou capital was invaded?
3. What happened as a result of the nobles failing to respond?
4. What caused the Zhou to move their capital? What was the effect?

4. Think and Apply

Identify an event that took place in your community or was reported in the news. Perhaps there was a bad storm or a community clean-up day. Link the event's causes and effects on a chart like the one shown. Use your chart to explain the event to a classmate or family member.

A Chinese artist may have been thinking about the legend of King You when making this statue of a man holding a huge lamp.

and Their Effects

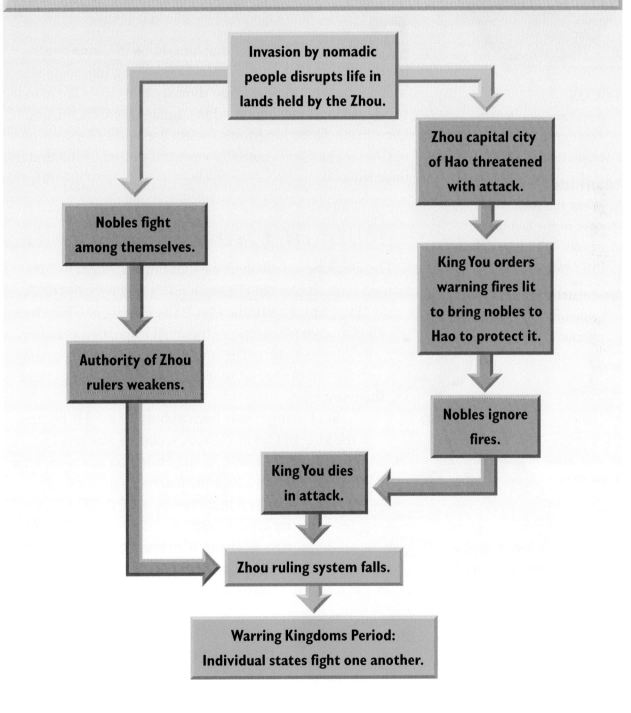

The Fall of the Zhou Dynasty: Cause and Effect

Invasion by nomadic people disrupts life in lands held by the Zhou.

Zhou capital city of Hao threatened with attack.

Nobles fight among themselves.

King You orders warning fires lit to bring nobles to Hao to protect it.

Authority of Zhou rulers weakens.

Nobles ignore fires.

King You dies in attack.

Zhou ruling system falls.

Warring Kingdoms Period: Individual states fight one another.

FOCUS

How can people with different backgrounds be united today?

Main Idea Read about the ways the ruler of the Qin united people and created the first Chinese empire.

Vocabulary

Legalism
standardization
province

The Qin dynasty used their army to conquer the other kingdoms in what is now China.

The Qin Dynasty

300 B.C.	200 B.C.	100 B.C.

During the 300s B.C., large kingdoms in China began to conquer smaller ones. The last Zhou kingdom met its end in 256 B.C., bringing the Zhou dynasty to a close. Three independent kingdoms remained in China—the Qi, Chu, and Qin (CHIN). These kingdoms fought each other for control of China. The Qin eventually won and united China under their rule.

Rule of Qin Shi Huangdi

The Qin king established the Qin Empire in 221 B.C. He named himself Qin Shi Huangdi (CHIN SHIR HWAHNG•DEE), or "First Emperor of the Qin." The uniting of China by the Qin dynasty is one of the most important events in all Chinese history. The importance of the Qin dynasty is reflected in the fact that the name *China* comes from the word *Qin*.

Shi Huangdi was born about 259 B.C. He became the king of Qin in 246 B.C., when he was just 13 years old. At first, he depended on advisors, who told him to adopt the teachings of Confucius. When he reached the age of 20 in 239 B.C., the young king rejected this advice. He appointed new advisors who taught him other ideas about governing. These other ideas included the strict following of laws.

The most powerful of Shi Huangdi's new advisors was Li Si (LEE SUH). Shi Huangdi made Li Si his prime minister in 237 B.C. Some Chinese scholars believe that Li Si deserves much of the credit for uniting China.

To be sure that his subjects learned little of ideas other than those used by the Qin, Shi Huangdi ordered book burnings throughout the empire. This painting by Hung Wu, an artist from a later period, shows one of the book burnings.

Later Chinese historians often described the Qin government as cruel and uncaring. According to these historians, all those who were foolish enough to challenge Shi Huangdi were killed along with their families to warn others to obey.

REVIEW *Why is the Qin dynasty remembered today?*

Legalism

To help him rule his empire, Shi Huangdi put into place both written laws and a bureaucracy. The strict following of laws and use of bureaucracy is known as **Legalism**. Legalism taught that people obeyed their rulers out of fear, not out of respect. Under a system of Legalism, people who obey receive rewards. Those who do not obey are punished.

The most well-thought-out writings about Legalism were done by Master Han Fei (HAHN FAY). Han Fei's ideas were different from those of Confucius. Han Fei believed that a government based on virtues and respect would not work. Instead, he urged rulers to rely on laws and on the "two handles" of reward and punishment. Eventually, Han Fei introduced Shi Huangdi to his thoughts on Legalism.

REVIEW *What were the "two handles" Han Fei thought rulers should use?*

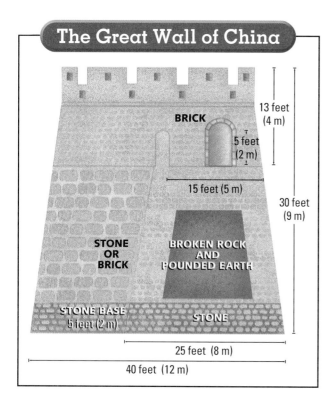

The Great Wall of China

BRICK

13 feet (4 m)

5 feet (2 m)

15 feet (5 m)

30 feet (9 m)

STONE OR BRICK

BROKEN ROCK AND POUNDED EARTH

STONE BASE 5 feet (2 m)

STONE

25 feet (8 m)

40 feet (12 m)

LEARNING FROM DIAGRAMS This diagram shows a cross-section of the Great Wall.

■ *Why do you think builders used a variety of materials to build different parts of the wall?*

The Great Wall of China as it appears today. Much of the wall that stands today was built in the 1300s.

The Great Wall

The First Emperor not only united China, but also extended the borders of the Qin Empire. As the empire grew, communication became more difficult. To solve this problem, Shi Huangdi used prisoners as workers to build new roads and canals. These workers built more than 4,000 miles (6,437 km) of roads. This linked even the distant parts of the empire to the center of the Qin government at Xianyang (shee•AHN•yahng).

Shi Huangdi found that protecting his large empire was not easy. To the north of the empire lived large tribes of fierce warriors who rode horses. In earlier times, the people of the northern kingdoms of China had built walls of rammed earth to protect their borders from these people. But these walls did not keep the invaders away for long. Shi Huangdi ordered his workers to link together the existing walls. Using this forced labor, the Qin created a long, single wall—a Great Wall.

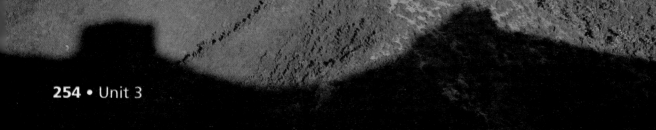

The Great Wall stood 30 feet (9 m) high, with 40-foot (12-m) towers. The long wall twisted and turned through mountains, valleys, marshes, and deserts for more than 1,500 miles (2,414 km). Yet in spite of its size, the Great Wall was built in just seven years.

The Great Wall not only kept invaders out of China, it warned people when invasions were taking place. Soldiers on the Great Wall communicated with each other by using signals. Smoke was used as a signal during the day, while fire was used as a signal at night. Signals would travel from tower to tower along the Great Wall, until they reached the Qin capital.

The cost of building the wall was high in terms of human life. Some estimates say that more than 500,000 workers died during the building of the wall. Some were buried between its stones.

REVIEW *Why did the Qin build the Great Wall?*

GEOGRAPHY

The Great Wall Today

Today visitors to China marvel at the Great Wall. The Great Wall seen today is a result of construction started in 1368 by the Ming dynasty. This construction lasted for 200 years and extended the wall. The Great Wall now runs for more than 3,700 miles (5,954 km), over twice its original size. The original wall was not maintained after the Qin dynasty. The Ming dynasty found it necessary to rebuild the wall to defend themselves from invaders known as the Mongols.

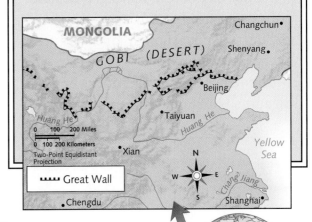

A Program of Standardization

Walls, canals, and roads helped unite China. So, too, did Shi Huangdi's program of standardization. **Standardization** means making all things of a certain type alike. The use of standardized coins, weights, and writing helped make trade and communication easier throughout China. Use of the same standards also helped the many peoples of the empire think of themselves as one.

Writing was also standardized in China during the time of the Qin. There were two official kinds of Chinese writing. One kind of writing was used for stone carvings and official documents. Another kind was used for everyday writing.

Education became another focus of standardization. Shi Huangdi wanted tight control of all the books used to teach. Li Si complained that too many books praised the Zhou and questioned the ideas of the Qin. In 213 B.C. Shi Huangdi ordered the burning of certain books. Many of the books destroyed were about Confucianism. Legends say that teachers who refused to give up their Confucian writings were taken prisoner and buried alive.

As part of his program of standardization, Shi Huangdi also did away with the fiefs created during the Zhou dynasty. The smaller ones became counties. The larger ones became provinces. **Provinces** are political regions of a country, similar to the states of the United States.

Shi Huangdi ordered the noble families who had owned the fiefs to move to Xianyang, the Qin Empire's capital. This forced move helped end any loyalty peasants had felt toward their nobles. In addition, Shi Huangdi made it illegal for people not in the army to carry weapons. Any weapons that did not belong to the army were collected and melted down.

Shi Huangdi then appointed government officials to run the counties and provinces. These officials reported directly to the central government in Xianyang. In this way, the Qin created a single bureaucracy for the entire empire. To support this bureaucracy, the people of China were required to pay heavy taxes.

REVIEW *What were some things that were standardized during the time of the Qin dynasty?*

Qin Dynasty

CHINA

0   200   400 Miles
0   200   400 Kilometers
Two-Point Equidistant Projection

GOBI (DESERT)

YAN
ZHAO
WEI
QIN   ★ Xianyang
HAN
CHU

Huang He
Chang Jiang
Xi Jiang

Yellow Sea

South China Sea

N W E S

▨ Qin dynasty, 221 B.C.–206 B.C.
★ Capital city
┅ Existing walls
QI Warring state

Human-Environment Interactions
Several independent warring kingdoms were united under the Qin dynasty.
■ *In what directions would the Qin most likely have traveled to expand their empire?*

MAP THEME

The End of the Qin

The Qin government was designed to place all power in the hands of the emperor. The emperor had to be strong, however, to maintain rule over China. Many people in China were unhappy with the Qin but were too afraid of Shi Huangdi to rebel.

Shi Huangdi, the First Emperor, died in 210 B.C. His favorite son became the Second Emperor, but he proved to be a weak ruler. Soon civil war broke out. In a civil war, different groups of people from the same place or country fight one another. By 206 B.C., the Qin had collapsed. After four more years

of civil war, the king of the Han, Liu Bang, defeated all other rival powers in 202 B.C.

Most of what we know about Shi Huangdi, Li Si, and the Qin Empire comes from historians and scholars of the Han dynasty. The Han did not agree with the way the Qin had ruled. Because the Han government closely followed the teachings of Confucius, they disapproved of the Qin government for adopting Legalism.

There is no doubt that the Qin could be cruel as they created their Legalist society. Newly discovered Qin laws prove that the government treated people very harshly. However, many of the Han claims of Qin cruelty may be based more on the rivalry between the Qin and the Han than on historical facts.

REVIEW *Why did the Qin Empire collapse?*

Standard weights helped the Chinese measure like goods, such as pieces of jade, the same way. Why was it important that like goods be measured the same way?

LESSON 4 REVIEW

300 B.C.   200 B.C.   100 B.C.

221 B.C.
• Qin Shi Huangdi establishes Qin Empire

206 B.C.
• Qin Empire ends

Check Understanding

1 Remember the Facts Did the Qin dynasty use Legalism or Confucianism to unite and rule China?

2 Recall the Main Idea What were some of the ideas and projects that helped unite China under the Qin?

Think Critically

3 Cause and Effect What do you think happened when the Qin government took fiefs away from nobles?

4 Past to Present What are some ways leaders today bring together the people they govern?

Show What You Know

Poster Activity Divide a sheet of posterboard into two columns. In one column, list the ideas used by the Zhou dynasty when they governed. In the other column, list the ideas the Qin used in place of those of the Zhou.

Discovery and Excavation of Shi Huangdi's Tomb

from *Calliope* magazine

written by Helen Wieman Bledsoe
illustrated by Higgins Bond

Qin Shi Huangdi, China's first emperor, united China in 221 B.C. His rule became known as a time of great cruelty by later historians. It is known that Shi Huangdi forced peasant farmers to complete large construction projects such as the Great Wall, roads, canals, and several new palaces. Shi Huangdi also made many enemies during his rule. He was almost assassinated three times.

After Shi Huangdi survived the assassination attempts, he became determined to find a way to live forever. For example, he sent groups of men and women out to sea to look for a land where people did not die. Realizing that he might not live forever, Shi Huangdi ordered the building of an elaborate tomb. If he had to die, he wanted his afterlife to be comfortable. Read now to find out why his tomb, the ruins of which were discovered in 1974, has fascinated people around the world.

In March of 1974, Chinese peasants digging a well near Xi'an in the central province of Shaanxi found some unusual pottery fragments. Then, deeper down at eleven feet, they unearthed a head made of terra cotta (baked earth or clay). They notified the authorities and excavation of the site began immediately. To date, workers have dug up about eight thousand sculpted clay soldiers, and the site has proved to be one of the greatest archaeological discoveries of all time.

For over two thousand years, these clay warriors have been guarding the tomb of Shi Huangdi, the First Emperor of China. Tradition says that the First Emperor began building his tomb when he ascended to the throne at age thirteen, and that it was unfinished at his death, thirty-six years later. The Chinese historian Sima Qian wrote in the *Shiji*, "Historical Records," that the emperor forced 700,000 laborers to work on his elaborate tomb.

The warriors stand guard in three pits (a fourth was found to be empty) that cover five-and-a-half acres and are sixteen to twenty-four feet deep. The largest one contains six thousand terra-cotta soldiers marching in military formation in eleven trenches, each as long as a football field. At the western end of the formation is a vanguard of archers and bowmen. At the head of six of the trenches stand the remnants of chariots, each with four life-size horses and eighteen soldiers. The wooden chariots have largely disintegrated, unlike the well-preserved terra-cotta horses and men. Last come row upon row of soldiers. Despite the enormous number of men, no two faces are alike. Their expressions display dignity, steadfastness, and intelligence. Each is tall, standing five-and-a-half to six feet high. Some people think the terra-cotta soldiers portray real-life men from the vast army of the First Emperor.

The warriors' legs are solid columns of clay, with squared-toed sandals on their feet. The hollow bodies are of coiled clay. The head and hands of each soldier were carefully molded and attached to the body in assembly-line fashion. Traces of pink, yellow, purple, blue, orange, green, brown, and black pigment show that the figures were once brightly painted. The horses were roan (reddish-brown, brown, or black) with pink mouths.

The warriors' hair styles and topknots, and the tassels trimming their garments, denote their military rank. Many do not wear helmets or carry shields, a mark of bravery in battle. Their armor was probably of lacquered leather; some pieces look like baseball catchers' pads. The soldiers' hands are positioned to hold weapons, but most of the weapons have disappeared. Very likely they were stolen when the pits were looted after the fall of the Qin dynasty (the dynasty founded by Shi Huangdi). Even so, bronze spears, halberds (a combination spear and battle-ax), swords, daggers, and about fourteen hundred arrowheads remain. Some of the blades are still very sharp.

A second pit, only partially excavated, contains about fourteen hundred more soldiers. While the first pit holds mostly infantry, the second has a more mobile attack force of horses and chariots. A third pit is thought to hold the high command of the army. The chariot of the Commander-in-Chief survives, with men surrounding it in protective formation.

Covered by a wooden roof and ten feet of earth, these figures were not intended to be seen. When the pits were looted and burned, the roof fell in and damaged most of the sculptures. Reconstruction is a slow, delicate task. Today, a visitor to the site can walk on long wooden platforms sixteen feet above the pits and gaze down with astonishment at the thousands of sculptured soldiers below.

Approximately a mile away from the pits is a gently sloping, rounded mountain covered with trees—the burial mound of the First Emperor. The four-sided, rammed-earth mound covers three quarters of a square mile and is one hundred fifty-six feet high. It once stood at four hundred feet. Of the two great walls that enclosed the funerary park only rubble remains. The perimeter of the outer wall is almost four miles. Set into the strong thick walls were four gates and four corner towers. Inside the walls were gardens, pavilions, and a sacrificial palace, in addition to the burial mound. The burial chamber itself is still untouched, its contents as yet unknown.

Tradition based on the *Shiji* says that the emperor's body was buried in a suit of small jade pieces sewed together with gold thread and covered with a pearl and jade shroud. Also in the burial mound were bronze models of Shi Huangdi's palaces and government offices. The replicas featured such details as pearls to represent the sun and moon, and pools of mercury to recreate rivers and seas.

According to the ancient Chinese, the soul of the dead continued living and therefore required all of life's necessities within the tomb. Kings especially needed many luxuries and that is why their tombs are treasure houses of jewels, gold, silver, and bronze.

The *Shiji* states that in order to prevent people from robbing the tomb, "Craftsmen built internal devices that would set off arrows should anyone pass through the tunnels." Because Sima Qian wrote his history a century after the death of the First Emperor, the accuracy of his statements is questionable. In fact, grave robbers did enter and loot Shi Huangdi's tomb for thirty years after the fall of the Qin dynasty (four years after the Emperor's death). During this time, many precious relics most likely were stolen.

In 1980, additional smaller pits were discovered. One contains pottery coffins with bones of exotic birds and animals, probably from the royal zoo. Another has vessels inscribed with the words, "Belonging to the Officials in Charge of Food at Mount Li," and must be where food and sacrifices were offered to the dead emperor. Uncovered in the nearby Hall of Slumber were clothes and everyday objects for use by the soul of the Emperor.

As the excavations continue, each find serves to remind us of the tremendous energy and genius of Shi Huangdi and his people.

LITERATURE REVIEW

1. From what ancient Chinese source do we get most of our information about the tomb of Shi Huangdi?

2. Why do you think Shi Huangdi had a large life-size clay army buried with him?

3. Imagine that you are Shi Huangdi. Write a set of instructions for the craftworkers who will make your clay army. Clearly explain each specific thing you want, and tell why you want it. Share your completed instructions with a classmate.

The Han Dynasty

| 300 B.C. | | B.C. | A.D. | A.D. 300 |

L iu Bang, the founder of the Han dynasty, came from a peasant background. Unlike the nobles of the time, Liu Bang wanted the kingdoms of China to be united under one government. As the first ruler of the Han dynasty, he achieved this goal and more. The dynasty he founded lasted for more than 400 years, from 206 B.C. until A.D. 220.

Gaozu, First Ruler of the Han

After claiming control of China, Liu Bang took the name of Han Gaozu (GOW•ZOO), or "High Ancestor." He located his capital city at Chang'an (CHANG•AHN) in the valley of the Wei River, not far from the old Qin capital of Xianyang. Gaozu made sure that his government differed from that of Shi Huangdi. He feared that the Chinese people would turn against him if he set up a Legalist government. In place of Legalism, Gaozu turned to Confucianism.

Gaozu also hoped to win the support of the nobles of China. To do this, Gaozu did away with the provinces of the Qin and restored the kingdoms of the Zhou dynasty. He appointed nobles as rulers of these kingdoms. The later Han dynasty emperors took back the kingdoms Gaozu had given to the nobles and appointed government officials to rule them. The officials reported only to the emperor. In this way, the Han formed a bureaucracy like the Qin dynasty.

Han government began to use both Confucian and Legalist ideas. While Han leaders

FOCUS

How do governments today build on the ideas of the governments of the past?

Main Idea As you read, think about how the Han dynasty blended ideas from Confucianism and Legalism to create a strong government.

Vocabulary

civil service   ambassador
Daoism   Silk Road
import   profit
export   caravan

This Han bronze horse sculpture was made during the A.D. 100s.

believed that a ruler should set an example for the people, they also saw a need for strong central government and an all-powerful leader.

The Han dynasty emperors came to be as feared and respected as Shi Huangdi had been. Yet they did not use the detailed laws of the Qin. Instead, they relied on the Confucian idea that people should obey their rulers in the same way that children obey their parents.

REVIEW *Who was the founder of the Han dynasty?*

Wu Di and Civil Service

In 140 B.C. Wu Di (WOO DEE) came to the Han throne. The name Wu Di, or "Warlike Emperor," was a good title for this leader. He created large armies, some with as many as 300,000 soldiers, to conquer new lands and expand the borders of the empire.

Wu Di's empire faced a tremendous threat from the north. A nomadic people called the Xiongnu (shee•UNG•noo) often made raids into China. Much later the Xiongnu, also known as the Huns, would attack Europe. To guard against attack by the Xiongnu, Wu Di extended the Great Wall. He also sent his armies north against the nomadic warriors. Wu Di's actions restored some peace to the distant regions of China.

Wu Di also brought peace to the empire by making some changes in government.

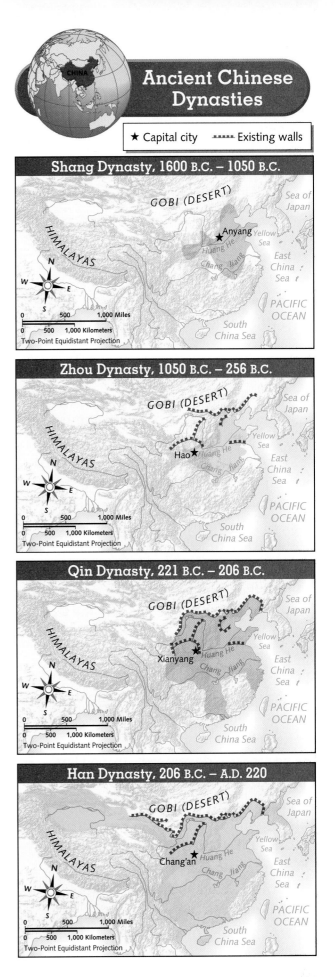

Ancient Chinese Dynasties

★ Capital city ▪▪▪▪▪ Existing walls

Shang Dynasty, 1600 B.C. – 1050 B.C.

Zhou Dynasty, 1050 B.C. – 256 B.C.

Qin Dynasty, 221 B.C. – 206 B.C.

Han Dynasty, 206 B.C. – A.D. 220

Regions Ancient China grew steadily under the rule of various dynasties. Compare the size of China during the Shang dynasty to its size during the Han dynasty.
■ *In what directions did the empire expand during the Han dynasty?*

Wu Di set up China's first civil service. A **civil service** is a part of a bureaucracy that oversees the day-to-day business of running a government.

As in the Qin government, many Han government jobs were given as a reward for loyalty. Some jobs, however, could be earned by performing well on tests. The tests measured a person's ability to do government work. Many of these tests were open to people of all classes.

REVIEW *How did Wu Di protect his empire and run it?*

Han Contributions

The Han people made many lasting contributions to Chinese society. A number of their innovations were related to technology. In A.D. 132 a Han inventor created the world's first seismograph, an instrument that detects and measures earthquakes. Han scientists also made tools that allowed them to study the movement of the planets.

Of all their innovations, the Han are perhaps best known for developing the technology of papermaking. People living in the western regions of the Han Empire probably made the first paper about 100 B.C. It came to the attention of the imperial court about A.D. 100. A court official took credit for its invention.

The arts also developed during Han times. Advances were made in both landscape and portrait painting. Han dynasty authors wrote many essays and poems that are still studied in China's schools. One Han writer, Sima Qian (SOO•MUH CHIH•YIHN), wrote the first history of China. Much of what we know about the Shang, Zhou, and Qin dynasties comes from Sima Qian's work.

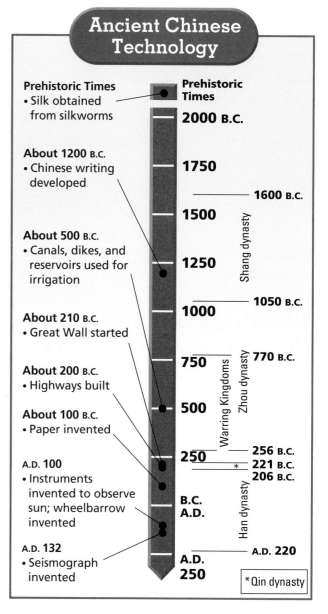

Ancient Chinese Technology

Prehistoric Times
• Silk obtained from silkworms

About 1200 B.C.
• Chinese writing developed

About 500 B.C.
• Canals, dikes, and reservoirs used for irrigation

About 210 B.C.
• Great Wall started

About 200 B.C.
• Highways built

About 100 B.C.
• Paper invented

A.D. 100
• Instruments invented to observe sun; wheelbarrow invented

A.D. 132
• Seismograph invented

Prehistoric Times
2000 B.C.
1750
1600 B.C.
1500
1250
1050 B.C.
1000
770 B.C.
750
500
256 B.C.
250
221 B.C.
206 B.C.
B.C.
A.D.
A.D. 220
A.D. 250

Shang dynasty
Zhou dynasty
Warring Kingdoms
Han dynasty
*Qin dynasty

LEARNING FROM TIME LINES The ancient Chinese made many advances in technology from prehistoric time to A.D. 220.

■ *Which was invented first, an instrument for detecting earthquakes or the wheelbarrow?*

The Han are also remembered for philosophy. Confucianism became the official Han teaching. Han rulers also supported such teachings as Daoism (DOW•ih•zuhm). **Daoism** teaches that the key to happiness is accepting life as it is. Daoism developed into a religion, with its own rituals and houses of worship.

Seismograph

About A.D. 132 Chang Heng invented China's first seismograph. A modern seismograph tells the location and strength of earthquakes. The early seismograph worked in much the same way. A rod inside the seismograph fell toward the dragon nearest the earthquake, making a loud noise. A ball then dropped from the dragon's mouth into a bronze frog below. The noise let the Chinese emperor know that there had been an earthquake in his empire. The direction in which the ball fell told him the general location of the earthquake.

Chang Heng's seismograph not only worked well but also was beautifully crafted.

The Han dynasty ended in A.D. 220. However, Han ideas lived on and can still be seen today in the culture of the present-day Chinese people. It is no wonder that the Chinese people still call themselves the children of the Han.

REVIEW *What are some of the lasting contributions the Han made to Chinese civilization?*

The Silk Road

Even before the Han dynasty, Chinese traders **imported**, or brought in, goods for sale from other lands. They also **exported**, or sent out, their own goods for sale in other places. However, during the time of the Han dynasty, trade with the outside world grew dramatically.

In 139 B.C. Wu Di sent an **ambassador**, or government representative, to talk to enemies of the Xiongnu about becoming allies. The ambassador, Zhang Qian (JAHNG CHIH•yihn), did not succeed in this. However, he did learn about some of the civilizations to the west of China. Zhang Qian came back with tales of resources unknown to the people of China. The Chinese people were especially interested in stories of magnificent horses. The stories led Chinese traders to travel in search of these horses and other goods.

Most of China's trade was done by land. The trade route used the most began near the Han capital of Chang'an. It continued through the deserts and

Wealthy Chinese during the Han dynasty lived in large houses like this one. The poor usually lived in small, one-story houses.

high plains of central Asia. The route finally ended at the shores of the Mediterranean Sea.

The Chinese product most in demand was silk. In fact, it was silk that gave the trade route its nickname—the **Silk Road**. Traders traveled west with products made from silk. They returned with lumber, horses, and other products that the Chinese people needed.

The journey on the Silk Road was sometimes dangerous. However, the **profits**, or money gained, more than made up for the risks. Camel **caravans**, or groups of traders, became common sights on the Silk Road.

Chinese traders easily found buyers for their silk. Those who bought silk directly from the Chinese traded it to others farther west. Chinese traders did not go all the way to Africa and Europe, but their goods did.

REVIEW *What was the Silk Road?*

Kashgar

Samarkand

Merv

EUROPE

Trebizond

Byzantium

Rayy

Antioch

Baghdad

Rome

ARABIA

The Silk Road

Turpan · Hani · Jiayuguan · Shandan · Wuwei
Anxi · Dunhuang · Lanzhou · Tianshui · Baoji · Chang'an
Khotan
Aksu
INDIA
CHINA

LESSON 6 REVIEW

| 300 B.C. | | 150 B.C. | | B.C. | A.D. | | A.D. 150 | | A.D. 300 |

206 B.C.
• Han dynasty begins

140 B.C.
• Rule of Wu Di begins

A.D. 220
• Han dynasty ends

Check Understanding

1 **Remember the Facts** What were the major achievements of Gaozu and Wu Di?

2 **Recall the Main Idea** What ideas from Legalism and Confucianism did the Han blend in order to create a strong government?

Think Critically

3 **Think More About It** Why was the Silk Road important?

4 **Past to Present** In what ways does the government of your community blend ideas?

Show What You Know

Collage Activity Some people say that the twentieth century has been a century of innovations. Using pictures and headlines from newspapers and magazines, create a collage that illustrates this idea. Show recent inventions and discoveries in your collage.

Use a Table to

1. Why Learn This Skill?

Imagine that you are looking through a pile of papers on your desk. Your home-work, book reports, and other assignments are mixed together in a big jumble. You cannot quickly find what you need. In the same way, it can be hard to search through jumbled information. Like a pile of papers, information is easier to use if it is classified, or sorted. Knowing how to classify infor-mation can make it easier for you to find the facts you need.

2. Remember What You Have Read

When you read about the dynasties of the Classical Age in China, you were given a lot of information. You learned when the Zhou, Qin, and Han dynasties ruled China, when the Warring Kingdoms Period was, who the important leaders were, and what con-tributions each dynasty made to Chinese civilization. These and other facts can be classified by using a table. A table is a chart that lists information in classes.

3. Understand the Process

In the table on page 269, China's early history is classified according to its dynas-ties and its Warring Kingdoms Period. The years for each period are in the first column. The years are listed in order, with the ear-liest first.

Each row gives facts about a single period in Chinese history. Suppose you want to find information about the Qin dynasty. Move your finger down the Name column until you find the Qin. Then move your finger across that row to the Contributions column. What was a contribution of the Qin dynasty? Now go to the next column to find out who led the Qin.

This painting from the time of a later Chinese dynasty shows hopeful Chinese officials taking the civil service examinations.

Classify Information

China's Early History

YEARS	NAME	CONTRIBUTIONS	IMPORTANT LEADERS
1600 B.C. to 1050 B.C.	Shang dynasty	Writing Use of bronze	
1050 B.C. to 256 B.C.	Zhou dynasty	Idea of Mandate of Heaven Improved ways of farming Division of Classes	Wu
770 B.C. to 221 B.C.	Warring Kingdoms Period	New forms of Government	
221 B.C. to 206 B.C.	Qin dynasty	Building of Great Wall Standardization of weights and measures Creation of road system	Shi Huangdi
206 B.C. to A.D. 220	Han dynasty	Civil service examinations Invention of paper Invention of seismograph Beginning of trade on the Silk Road Advances in medicine and mathematics	Gaozu Wu Di

Use the table to answer the following questions:

1. What were some of the contributions of the Shang dynasty?
2. What dynasty is the leader Gaozu associated with?
3. During what period of time did the Qin dynasty rule China?
4. During what period were new forms of government introduced to China?
5. Who was an important leader of China during the Zhou dynasty?
6. What group controlled China about 1300 B.C.?
7. During what period in Chinese history were important contributions to agriculture and division of classes made?
8. Which of the periods shown on the table overlap?

4. Think and Apply

Make your own table to show information about ancient China. Use the information in the table on this page, but classify it differently. Share your table with a partner as you review the chapter.

CHAPTER 6

REVIEW

5000 B.C.   4000 B.C.   3000 B.C.

Around 5000 B.C.
• Agriculture begins
  in China

CONNECT MAIN IDEAS

Use this organizer to show that you understand the beginnings of Chinese civilization. Write a sentence or two that describes each topic listed below. A copy of the organizer appears on page 61 of the Activity Book.

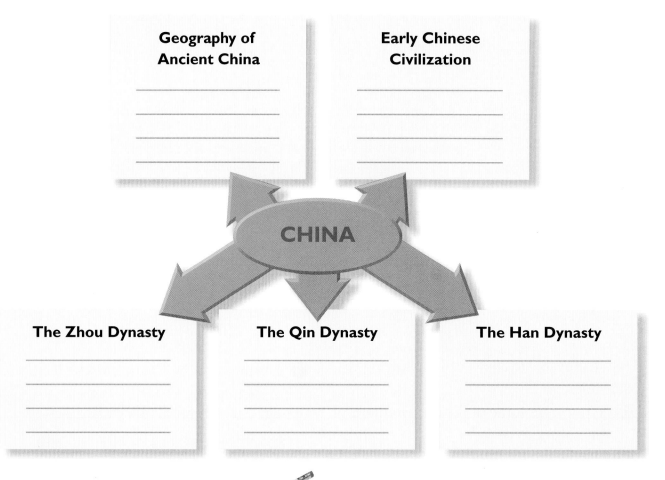

Geography of Ancient China

Early Chinese Civilization

CHINA

The Zhou Dynasty

The Qin Dynasty

The Han Dynasty

WRITE MORE ABOUT IT

Write Your Opinion Throughout many periods of ancient Chinese history, peasant farmers were forced to work on building projects and to serve as soldiers. In return, they were given land to farm and settle by the noble class. Do you think that this was a fair arrangement? Explain.

Write a Short Report Compare and contrast the ruling methods of Shi Huangdi and Gaozu.

Write a Description Look at the map on page 233. Use the information on the map to write two or three paragraphs that describe China's physical features.

| 2000 B.C. | | 1000 B.C. | | B.C. | A.D. | | A.D. 1000 |

Around 2700 B.C.
• Silk produced in the Huang He Valley

About 1600 B.C.
• Shang dynasty begins

About 770 B.C.
• Warring Kingdoms Period begins

221 B.C.
• Shi Huangdi establishes Qin Empire

206 B.C.
• Han dynasty rules China

A.D. 220
• Han dynasty ends

USE VOCABULARY

Write the term that correctly matches each definition. Then use each term in a complete sentence.

civil service   dialect   loess

Mandate of Heaven   oracle   philosopher

1 a person who studies the meaning of life

2 a way a language is spoken in a region

3 a person who gives advice based on signs

4 a heavenly order to claim rule in China

5 part of a bureaucracy that oversees the business of running a government

6 yellow silt

CHECK UNDERSTANDING

7 What role did the Huang He and the Chang Jiang play in China's early history?

8 What metal did Shang craftworkers form from copper, lead, and tin? What items did they make with this metal?

9 How did the Zhou kings explain their conquest of the Shang in 1050 B.C.?

10 How did Confucius say a ruler must act to be successful?

11 What was Legalism?

12 For what is Shi Huangdi remembered?

13 Why was standardization important to China?

14 What was the Silk Road?

15 What was the most important innovation of the Han dynasty? Why was it important?

THINK CRITICALLY

16 **Past to Present** The ancient Chinese looked to Confucian sayings to guide their behavior. What kinds of guides for behavior do people follow today?

17 **Personally Speaking** Whose ideas do you prefer, those of Confucius or those of Han Fei? Explain.

18 **Cause and Effect** What effect do you think outside interest in Chinese resources had on China after the Han dynasty ended?

APPLY SKILLS

Identify Causes and Their Effects
Look in a newspaper or magazine for an article that describes an event. List at least one cause mentioned in the article and one effect.

Classify Information Interview several classmates, asking each to name a favorite food, song, book, and subject in school. Then make a table that classifies the information.

READ MORE ABOUT IT

Ancient China by Brian Williams. Viking. History, rulers, cities, and inventions are some of the topics included in this book.

HARCOURT BRACE

Visit the Internet at
http://www.hbschool.com
for additional resources.

Chapter 6 • **271**

RELIGION in the WORLD TODAY

Religion has always played an important part in people's lives. Religion connects people who share beliefs. Many countries have a national religion or have one religion that most of its people follow. More than 80 percent of the people in India today are Hindus. In Japan most people are Buddhists and Shintoists.

Unlike other countries in the world, the United States was founded on the idea of religious freedom. The Bill of Rights of the United States Constitution gives citizens the freedom to follow their own religious beliefs, whatever they may be. Members of religions that have been followed for centuries— Christianity, Islam, Hinduism, Buddhism, and Judaism—live together in the United States today. Followers of many newer religions live here, too. In fact, there are more than 1,000 different religious groups in our country!

Think and Apply

Read a number of news sources to learn how differences in religious beliefs are affecting people's lives today—in schools, government, and other parts of society. Look for examples from our country and from other countries. Then, with a partner, make a visual display of your information and share it with classmates.

HARCOURT BRACE

Visit the Internet at **http://www.hbschool.com** for additional resources.

CNN Turner Le@rning

Check your media center or classroom video library for the Making Social Studies Relevant videotape of this feature.

VISUAL SUMMARY

Summarize the Main Ideas
Study the pictures and captions to help you review the events you read about in Unit 3.

Examine the Scenes
Look closely at each scene. What details are shown for each period? After you have looked at all the scenes, write your own description for each.

1 The physical setting of the Indus Valley civilization affected the development and survival of its well-planned cities.

5 The beliefs of the ancient Chinese people affected the growth of their civilization.

6 The Chinese philosopher Confucius lived during a time of disorder known as the Warring Kingdoms Period. Confucius taught that certain virtues were needed to bring order in society.

2 The religions of Hinduism and Buddhism began in ancient India. These religions have affected life in Asia for centuries.

3 The Gupta Empire in India brought about a time of growth in the arts, writing, mathematics, and medicine.

 4 Strong leaders such as King Darius helped the Persian Empire grow.

7 The emperor Shi Huangdi united many independent states to create China's first empire. Shi Huangdi is remembered for his Great Wall and for bringing standardization to China.

8 The Han dynasty was a time of great achievement for the Chinese in government, the arts, the recording of history, and trade.

UNIT 3
REVIEW

USE VOCABULARY

Write a term from this list to complete each of the sentences that follow.

courier   Legalism   reincarnation
ritual   virtues

1 A _____ is a set way of conducting a ceremony.

2 A rider who delivered messages on horseback in the Persian Empire was called a _____.

3 The belief that the soul lives on after death and returns to life in a new body is called _____.

4 _____ is a form of governing that involves the strict following of laws and the use of bureaucracy.

5 Good qualities are known as _____.

CHECK UNDERSTANDING

6 Who were the untouchables?

7 Who was Zarathustra?

8 What caused the breakdown of China's ruling system in the 700s B.C.?

9 What Chinese philosopher compared society to a family?

10 What were some of the innovations of the Han dynasty?

THINK CRITICALLY

11 **Past to Present** The Aryan immigrants changed the culture of ancient India. How do immigrants affect cultures today?

12 **Personally Speaking** What do you think it would have been like to live during the time of the Zhou? the Qin? the Han?

276 • Unit 3

13 **Cause and Effect** What effect did the conflicts of China's Warring Kingdoms Period have on Chinese society?

APPLY SKILLS

Use a Cultural Map The labels on the map show the locations of cultural groups in China. The colors show the languages spoken. Use the map to answer the questions.

14 In what parts of China are languages other than Chinese spoken?

15 Why do you think different cultural groups live mainly on the edges of China?

16 Which groups live along the western and southern borders of China?

Present-Day China: Cultural Groups and Languages

Chinese and Tibetan languages
- Mandarin
- Southern
- Tibetan
- Kam-Tai
- Miao-Yao

Other languages
- Tajik
- Turkic
- Mongolian
- Manchu-Tungus
- Korean

HAN Cultural group

REMEMBER

- Share your ideas.
- Cooperate with others to plan your work.
- Take responsibility for your work.
- Help one another.
- Show your group's work to the class.
- Discuss what you learned by working together.

 ACTIVITY

Make a
Class Collage

As a class, make a collage that illustrates some of the ideas of Confucianism. Cut out magazine and newspaper pictures of people doing things that show each idea. Place pictures showing the same idea near each other in the collage. Then label each idea. Display the collage outside your classroom.

 ACTIVITY

Tell a
Fable

With three or four classmates, think of a message you would like to give to the world. Then, with your group, write a fable that tells the message in an interesting way. Present your fable orally to the class.

 ACTIVITY

Make a
Travel Plan

Imagine that you have a chance to visit China. Make a list of the ancient Chinese sites you would most like to visit. Beside each entry, explain why you would want to visit that site. Describe each site in detail and tell why it is important in Chinese history. Compare your list with those of your classmates.

Unit Project Wrap-Up

Publish a Booklet Now you are ready to make your booklet about ancient India and China. To complete your booklet, you will work in a small group. First write an outline. Each group member should have a different job. One member could be the researcher, another could be the artist, and still another could be the writer. All group members should review the writing and illustrations and proofread the completed booklet. When you are finished, pass your booklet around the classroom for all to read.

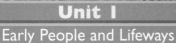

Unit 1	Unit 2	Unit 3
Early People and Lifeways	Early Civilizations in Africa	Early Civilizations in Asia

EARLY CIVILIZATIONS IN EUROPE

278

Many civilizations developed in the Mediterranean region between 3000 B.C. and A.D. 500. Among these peoples were the ancient Greeks and Romans. The Greeks and the Romans borrowed ideas from other societies that existed during their time. The Romans, in fact, built much of their civilization on the learning of the Greeks. Both of these peoples developed new ways of thinking and new ideas about science, politics, literature, language, and the arts. Many of the achievements of the Greeks and Romans are still admired today.

◄ The ancient Minoan religious ceremony of leaping over bulls is shown in this painting made about 3,500 years ago.

UNIT THEMES

- Continuity and Change
- Conflict and Cooperation
- Individualism and Interdependence
- Interaction Within Different Environments

Unit Project

Build an Ancient City Complete this project as you study Unit 4. With your classmates, plan and build a model of an ancient Greek or Roman city. As you read the unit, make a list of important features of Greek cities and Roman cities. Your list will help you plan how to build your own model.

UNIT 4
PREVIEW

BRITAIN

EUROPE

GAUL

Loire River

ALPS

Po River

Apennines

ATLANTIC
OCEAN

Ebro
River

Pyrenees

Adriatic Sea

SPAIN

Corsica

Rome

Tagus   River

Sardinia

Tyrrhenian
Sea

New Carthage

Mediterranean

Sicily

Carthage

Atlas Mountains

N
W   E
S

AFRICA

0   250   500 Miles
0   250   500 Kilometers
Azimuthal Equal-Area Projection

| 1750 B.C. | 1500 B.C. | 1250 B.C. | 1000 B.C. | 750 B.C. |

1600 B.C.
Minoan culture
flourishes
PAGE 291

800 B.C.
Greek city-states
begin to form
PAGE 300

280

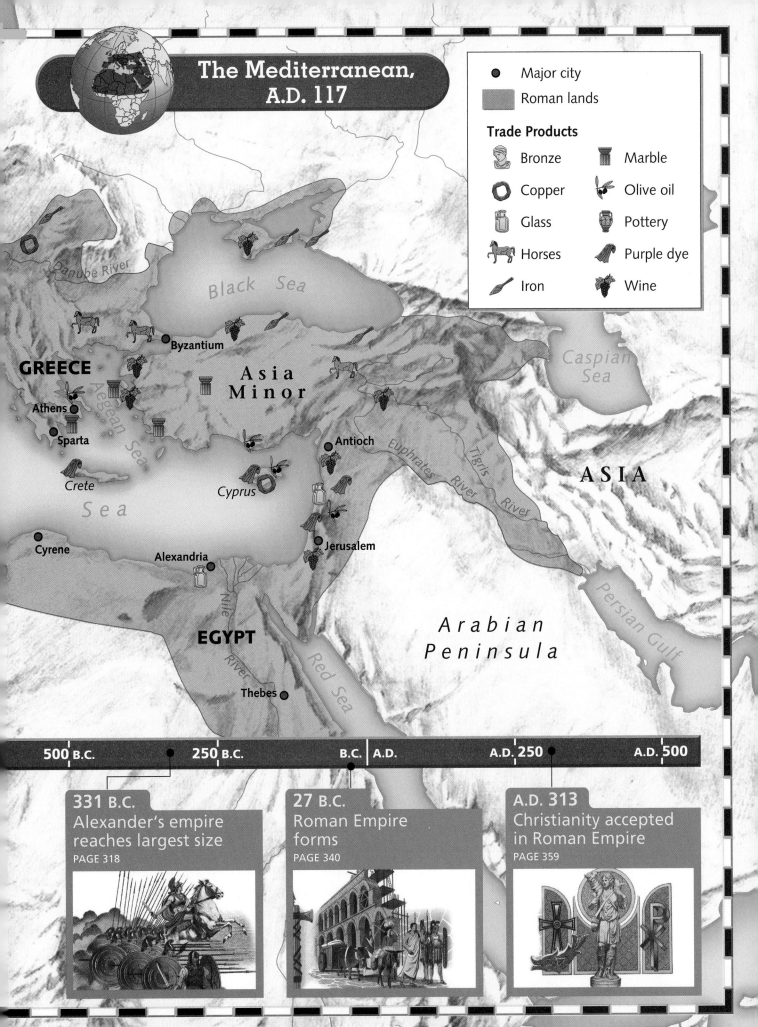

The Mediterranean, A.D. 117

- ● Major city
- ▨ Roman lands

Trade Products

- Bronze
- Marble
- Copper
- Olive oil
- Glass
- Pottery
- Horses
- Purple dye
- Iron
- Wine

Danube River

Black Sea

Caspian Sea

GREECE

Byzantium

Asia Minor

Aegean Sea

Athens

Sparta

Crete

Sea

Cyprus

Antioch

Euphrates River

Tigris River

ASIA

Cyrene

Alexandria

Jerusalem

Nile River

EGYPT

Red Sea

Arabian Peninsula

Persian Gulf

Thebes

500 B.C. 250 B.C. B.C. | A.D. A.D. 250 A.D. 500

331 B.C.
Alexander's empire reaches largest size
PAGE 318

27 B.C.
Roman Empire forms
PAGE 340

A.D. 313
Christianity accepted in Roman Empire
PAGE 359

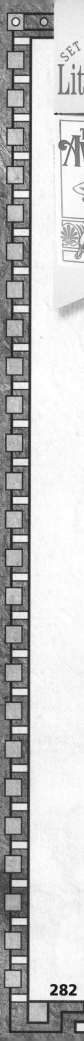

THE AVENGER

BY MARGARET HODGES

INTRODUCING THE CHARACTERS:

Alexis: *a young athlete from Asini*

Lampis: *a rival athlete from Sparta*

Dion: *Alexis's brother*

Niki: *Alexis's sister*

Aristes: *Alexis's father*

Telamon: *Alexis's trainer*

Like many people living today, the people of the ancient Mediterranean civilizations enjoyed sports. They believed in "a sound mind in a sound body." The ancient Greeks, for example, included athletic contests in their religious festivals. The most famous contests in Greece were the Olympic Games.

The Greeks held the Olympic Games every four years to honor Zeus, who was believed to be the most powerful of the Greek gods. Cities and towns sent their finest young athletes to take part in the games. They came from such places as Athens, Sparta, Elis, and Delphi to run, throw, and wrestle. Like Olympic athletes today, they competed for the honor of their hometowns, their families, and themselves.

Read now about a 15-year-old athlete named Alexis, who competed in the Olympic Games in 492 B.C. for his hometown of Asini in Greece. As you read, imagine the sights, sounds, and feelings you would have experienced while watching or taking part in the Olympic Games long ago.

In the first light the athletes came again to the Altis[1] and gathered around the altar of Zeus at the center of the sacred olive grove. It towered high, filled with the ashes of sacrifices offered for more years than any living man could remember or even guess. A priest moved through the crowd, carrying a torch from the eternal fire that burned on the altar of Hestia, goddess of the hearth. He climbed the steps to the top of the altar of Zeus and set fire to the wood piled there. The smell of blazing poplar and of incense filled the grove. Then the Olympic flame burst through the smoke and the crowd gave a sigh like the sound of a wave breaking on a long beach. Officials were coming with this year's sacrifices for the Games, baskets of meat cut from the thighs of a hundred cattle that had been brought to the slaughter with their horns gilded[2] and with wreaths of flowers about their necks. At last the fire died down and was quenched with water from the Alpheus.[3] When the ashes were cold, they would be hard and smooth, and the altar of Zeus would have mounted even closer to heaven; earth, air, fire, and water mingled[4] to praise him who ruled all things. On the last night of the Games, after the gods were satisfied, the crowds would feast.

Alexis remembered what followed as if it had been a dream. Somehow he got to the stadium for the boys' race. The slopes were filling, many of last night's revelers[5] having stretched out to sleep there. Alexis drew his lot. Luckily, he was to run in the first heat[6] and would have time to rest while four other heats were run, supposing that he survived to run in the finals. There were fifteen boys in the first heat, but Lampis was not among them.

He remembered very little from the moment he toed the starting line and heard the trumpet until he reached the finish. He only knew that another runner had been ahead of him almost to the end. Then, with the blood beating in his ears and his lungs bursting, he had somehow closed the gap. But he did not know that he had won until he fell into the crowd at the finish line and felt himself being pounded on the back to shouts of "Asini! Asini has won the first heat! Alexis of Asini!"

His mouth was dry, his head throbbing. Then his father and Dion were breaking a path for him through the crowd to a stone water basin where he took a long drink and sank

---

[1] **Altis:** name for the sacred olive grove
[2] **gilded:** coated with gold
[3] **Alpheus:** a river in Greece
[4] **mingled:** mixed together
[5] **revelers:** party-goers

[6] **heat:** a round or part of a contest

down on the grass. He could not believe that he had won. His legs were numb. Could he run again? He needed time, and it would not take much time to run off four more heats.

Telamon was rubbing him down and gently kneading the muscles of his legs. "There will be time enough. The managers will be announcing the name and town of each contestant, you know, and the umpires usually argue about who has won, and there may be some false starts. It all takes time. You will be ready."

It was as Telamon had predicted. Twice the heats were delayed when runners made false starts and were punished by sharp blows from officials with long forked sticks. But Lampis won his heat easily, and all too soon they were announcing the final race for boys.

Aristes and Dion embraced Alexis. Above the noise of the crowd he could not hear what they were saying—something about Lampis, something about Asini—but he knew what

they meant, and nodded as he went to the starting line.

"Eucles of Athens . . ." All over the stadium Athenians shouted encouragement to their runner. "Sotades of Elis . . . Lampis of Sparta . . . Alexis of Asini . . . Troilus of Delphi . . ." Each name was followed by cheers from some parts of the stadium and silence from others whose own champions had been beaten by one of the finalists or whose own city had been at war with one of these cities.

Alexis stared down the length of the stadium to the finish line. Lampis was the one to beat and he had to do it for Asini. But Lampis always went into the lead from the very start. If Alexis held himself back this time, tired as he was, he would never be able to close the gap at the end. He must start fast and stay even with Lampis all the way, then do even better in the last stretch. He drew a deep breath, let it out, and leaned forward, his toes gripping the starting stone. The trumpet blared and the runners shot forward.

Out of the corner of his eye Alexis saw to his left Lampis and the boy from Elis, running smoothly. On his right, no one. Athens and Delphi were somewhere behind. Another glance showed him that Lampis was going into the lead. Alexis felt his lungs and his legs laboring painfully. Then suddenly he heard, as if the words were spoken, "I belong to Zeus." He saw in his mind the beach at Asini, and he felt his breath coming easily and powerfully. His leg muscles were obeying his will and he was overtaking, passing Lampis. The crowd at the finish line loomed up and overwhelmed him.

It was over. Alexis had won. Sprays of flowers and olive branches flicked his shoulders. Arms pummeled him. And then, while faces were still a blur, he saw one familiar face that made him think he had gone mad. It happened in a flash. Slender arms were around his neck and a girl's voice spoke into his ear. "You won and I saw you win! Oh, you are excellent!"

It was Niki. Niki where no girl was allowed to be on pain of death, Niki with her hair cropped so like a boy's and wearing one of his old tunics that she must have brought from home, planning this trick all along. No one seemed to be giving her even a second glance, but his blood froze.

"You fool!" he said under his breath. "Quick! Leave, before it's too late. You know the penalty."

"I don't believe in the penalty." She gave him a flashing smile and slipped away into the crowd.

Telamon was wiping the sweat from Alexis's face, his father and brother lifted him shoulder-high, and his townsmen put a crown of flowers on his head. They tied a ribbon on his arm, another on his thigh, and so carried him to the stone seat of the judges to receive the palm branch that would serve as a token of victory until the final night when victors were crowned with wild olive. As Alexis looked down, dazed and smiling, from his high perch, he saw Lampis, his cheeks white and tear-stained, leaving the crowd, followed by his grim-faced trainer. Again, in the midst of his own triumph, Alexis felt pity. It was a weakness, one he must try to overcome. He did not allow himself to picture the arrival of Lampis in Sparta.

As you read more about the ancient people of the Mediterranean, you will discover why Alexis felt pity for Lampis, the runner from Sparta. You also will learn that the ancient Greeks are remembered today for more than the Olympic Games.

CHAPTER 7

ANCIENT GREECE

"Here each individual is interested not only in his own affairs, but in the affairs of state as well."

Pericles,
leader of Athens,
430 B.C.

Statue of a young
Greek charioteer,
made about 470 B.C.

Geography of Ancient Greece

The ancient Greeks were fascinated by geography. In fact, the word *geography* was first spoken by these people. The word comes from two Greek words—*gaia*, meaning "the earth," and *graph*, meaning "a drawing or a picture." The Greeks wanted to find out all they could about the "earth picture," or geography, of their land.

The Land of Greece

Present-day Greece occupies a large peninsula on the southern edge of Europe. This peninsula—the Balkan Peninsula—curves south and east into the Mediterranean Sea toward a part of Asia called Asia Minor, or "Little Asia." Today the country of Turkey fills Asia Minor. Turkey and Greece are separated by an island-dotted arm of the Mediterranean called the Aegean (ih•JEE•uhn) Sea.

West of present-day Greece is the Ionian Sea. To the south is the Mediterranean. These seas cut deeply into Greece, nearly splitting it in two. The southern part, called the Peloponnesus (peh•luh•puh•NEE•suhs), is connected to the rest of the mainland by a small strip of land, or **isthmus** (IS•muhs). Surrounding Greece are as many as 2,000 islands. The largest of these islands is Crete, located southeast of the Greek mainland.

Ancient Greek settlement was not limited to the land we call Greece today. Instead, early settlement spread across the Aegean, Ionian, and Mediterranean seas. Colonies thrived on several islands and on the coasts of northern Africa, Spain, Italy, and Asia Minor.

REVIEW *Where is Greece located?*

FOCUS
How have landforms and resources helped shape the history of your community?

Main Idea Read to find out how the mountains and the sea have affected ancient Greek history and culture.

Vocabulary
isthmus
harbor
trireme

This ancient Greek vase shows olive pickers at work.

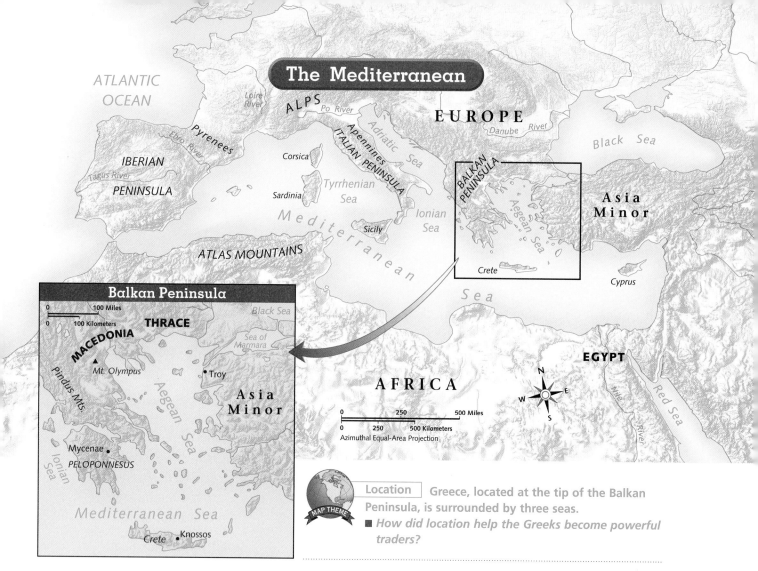

The Mediterranean

ATLANTIC OCEAN

EUROPE

Loire River

ALPS
Po River

Pyrenees

Ebro River

IBERIAN PENINSULA

Tagus River

Corsica

Apennines
ITALIAN PENINSULA

Adriatic Sea

Danube River

Black Sea

Sardinia

Tyrrhenian Sea

BALKAN PENINSULA

Aegean Sea

Asia Minor

Mediterranean

Sicily

Ionian Sea

ATLAS MOUNTAINS

Crete

Cyprus

Sea

AFRICA

EGYPT

Nile River

Red Sea

Balkan Peninsula

0   100 Miles
0   100 Kilometers

THRACE

MACEDONIA

Black Sea

Sea of Marmara

Mt. Olympus

Pindus Mts.

Troy

Aegean Sea

Asia Minor

Mycenae

PELOPONNESUS

Ionian Sea

Mediterranean Sea

Crete   Knossos

0   250   500 Miles
0   250   500 Kilometers
Azimuthal Equal-Area Projection

Location | Greece, located at the tip of the Balkan Peninsula, is surrounded by three seas.
MAP THEME
■ *How did location help the Greeks become powerful traders?*

A Land of Mountains

Mountains cover nearly three-fourths of Greece. The Pindus Range runs north and south through the center of Greece. Between the mountains lie narrow valleys and small areas of plains.

The geography of Greece made inland travel difficult and trade nearly impossible for the ancient Greeks. Dirt paths provided the only way to travel on land. The rivers of Greece were of no use for travel because they often dried up.

Mount Olympus

Because it was so hard to travel and trade inland, the people of each village had to survive on only the food they raised. Since the villages had little direct contact with each other, each one formed its own government and became fiercely independent. The mountainous land kept the people of this area from uniting under one government for many centuries.

The rugged land greatly affected the way of life of the ancient Greeks. Mountains were even a part of the religion of the Greeks. Mount Olympus, Greece's highest and most famous mountain, was said to be the home of Zeus and the other gods the ancient Greeks believed in.

Because Greece is so mountainous, the ancient people found few places suitable for farming. In fact, the rocky land provided very few natural resources.

REVIEW *What effect did the mountains of Greece have on the Greek people?*

The Sea Around

While the mountains separated people, the seas brought people together. Greece has many fine natural **harbors**, sheltered places with deep water close to shore. The ancient Greeks used these natural harbors to explore the seas.

The ancient Greeks first used the sea as a source of food. Later the Greeks traveled the seas to trade for resources they did not have at home. In time, the sea led Greek adventurers to new lands, where they started colonies. Across the sea, colonists found better farmland and new resources.

Through sea trade, the Greeks gained not only resources and products but also ideas. Phoenician traders probably introduced the Greeks to their alphabet, which became the basis for the Greek alphabet. Greek artists borrowed ideas from Egyptian sculpture. Many Greek ideas were also carried across the seas to distant lands.

Contact with people across the seas sometimes brought conflict. Over time, the ancient Greeks became skilled at fighting on the seas. In the late sixth century they began to make large fighting ships called **triremes** (TRY•reemz), borrowing the technology from peoples located near the eastern Mediterranean. Their skill at protecting themselves allowed their sea trade to grow.

Throughout the centuries the Greeks have adapted to a rugged land. This twelfth-century monastery (inset) is just one example of how the Greeks made the most of their rocky land.

Olive trees grow well in Greece because of the dry climate.

also became a major export for Greek traders.

The ancient Greeks ate both grapes and grape leaves. They also squeezed grapes to make wine. Much of the wine was poured into clay jars and exported to places along the Mediterranean.

A meal in ancient Greece might have included olives and grapes, dried fish, vegetables, and crusty bread made from imported grain. Meat was usually eaten only at special times.

REVIEW *Why were grapes and olives important to the ancient Greeks?*

The Greeks believed that the seas had their own god. According to the Greeks Poseidon watched over sailors. Even so, they did not really feel at home on the open sea. Usually they stayed close to shore.

REVIEW *How was Greek culture affected by the sea?*

Farming in Ancient Greece

In Greece's thin soil and dry climate, few kinds of crops could be grown in ancient times. Only one-fifth of the land was good for farming. Small amounts of wheat and barley were raised. However, the ancient Greeks found it better to import, or bring in, these grains since they could grow so little of their own.

Grapes and olives, which do well in a dry climate, became the main crops of the ancient Greeks. The Greeks used olives for things other than food. They crushed them to make olive oil, which they used for cooking and for fuel for lamps. Olive oil

LESSON 1 REVIEW

Check Understanding

1 Remember the Facts   What kinds of landforms are found in Greece?

2 Recall the Main Idea   How did the sea and the mountains affect Greek history and culture?

Think Critically

3 Past to Present   Do you think people today are as affected by Greece's mountains as they were long ago? Explain.

4 Think More About It   How might ancient Greek life have been different if Greece had been a flat land?

Show What You Know
Map Activity   Imagine that you are an ancient geographer traveling through the land now known as Greece. Make a map that shows the main landforms there. Then share your map with a classmate.

Early People of Greece

2000 B.C. | 1400 B.C. | 800 B.C.

O ver the centuries, peoples of many cultures settled on the land now known as Greece. Among the earliest peoples were the Minoans (muh•NOH•uhnz), who settled on the island of Crete, and the Mycenaeans (my•suh•NEE•uhnz), who settled on the Greek mainland. For centuries legends have told about the first people to live in and around Greece. Some of the tales may be based on truth. Others, however, may have come from the imaginations of those who first told the stories years ago. Today most of what we know about the Minoans and the Mycenaeans comes from the work of archaeologists. Their studies are based on the actual remains of the Minoan and Mycenaean civilizations.

FOCUS
What could cause a culture to gain or lose control of an area?

Main Idea As you read, think about the reasons different cultures began and later weakened in Greece.

Vocabulary
cultural borrowing
epic

The Minoans

The island of Crete lies about 60 miles (97 km) south of the Peloponnesus. The Greek poet Homer described Crete as "a rich and lovely land, washed by the waves on every side." Today Crete is still much as Homer described it so many years ago.

For centuries the people of Greece told stories of a long-lost civilization on the island of Crete. Experts, however, could find no proof of this ancient civilization. Then, at the beginning of the twentieth century, British archaeologist Arthur Evans announced an amazing discovery. He had found the ruins of an ancient kingdom. He called this kingdom the Minoan civilization, in honor of a legendary king of Crete called Minos (MY•nuhs). Today we still call the people of ancient Crete Minoans.

This gold Minoan pendant from about 1500 B.C. shows two bees and a honeycomb.

Chapter 7 • 291

Minoan Trade, 1450 B.C.

Black Sea

Sea of Marmara

Ionian Sea

Pindus Mountains

Mt. Olympus ▲

Troy

Thermi

Karditsa

Iolkos

Aegean Sea

Asia Minor

Ithaca

Delphi

Gla

Marathon

Zakynthos

Olympia

Corinth

Mycenae

Tiryns

PELOPONNESUS

Pylos

Vapheio

Naxos

Miletus

tin from Sicily

to Italian Peninsula and Sicily

pottery

Kastri

Mediterranean

Thera

pottery, stone vases to mainland Greece

pottery, stone vases to Aegean islands

pottery, stone vases to Asia Minor

Sea

copper, ivory, bronze daggers from Cyprus and the eastern Mediterranean

pottery, woolens, herbs, stone bowls, bronze weapons to Cyprus and the eastern Mediterranean

Knossos

Mallia

pottery, herbs, wool, oil, bronze weapons, wood to Egypt

Phaistos

Crete

Gournia

stone vases, charms, ivory, gold, gems, linen from Egypt

0   50   100 Miles

0   50   100 Kilometers

Lambert Conformal Conic Projection

← Trade route

Movement The ancient Minoans traded with many different cultures around the Mediterranean.

■ *What were the main Minoan exports? the main imports?*

For many years Minoans lived in small farming communities. As the population grew, so did the communities.

Around 1900 B.C. the people of Crete began building palaces. These huge buildings were centers for governing and controlling the neighboring countryside. The palaces may also have been centers of religion. The palaces seemed like mazes, with many rooms and winding passages. Many houses were built around the palaces. Beyond the palaces and houses were small towns, villages, and farmland.

The remains of four Minoan palaces have been uncovered. The largest, called Knossos (NAHS•uhs), stood at least three stories high. Knossos probably covered 185 acres of land. That is the size of 20 football fields. Archaeologists believe that as many as 12,000 people lived in and around this palace.

Beautiful paintings showing peaceful scenes decorated the walls of the

The Minoans will long be remembered for their beautiful wall paintings.

ancient palaces. The paintings tell much about the Minoans. These works of art show that the Minoans loved dancing, music, and sports. In many of the paintings, both women and men have long, flowing hair and wear gold jewelry. The wall paintings also show that religion was an important part of Minoan life.

The paintings and other archaeological evidence also suggest that the Minoans were expert sailors and sea traders. They traded with peoples in ancient Africa, Asia, and Europe. Egypt, in Africa, and Syria, in southwestern Asia, were just two of their many trading partners. Minoan trading ships carried olive oil, wine, wool, pottery, and other goods from Crete to ports across the seas. The ships returned with supplies of copper, tin, and gold. The people of Crete mixed copper and tin to form the metal bronze. Using bronze, they crafted bowls, axes, and other objects.

The Minoans developed a system of writing as a way of keeping records. Unfortunately, some Minoan writings may have been destroyed by a fire that swept through the kingdom in about 1370 B.C. Only records that were written on clay tablets remain. So far, no one has been able to translate the writing on these tablets. Once experts learn how to read this early Minoan writing, we may learn more about the way of life of the ancient Minoans.

No one knows for sure what caused the decline of Minoan civilization. Some historians believe that a large fire burning out of control may have caused the civilization's end. Others believe that a powerful earthquake struck the island. Still others think that invaders from the Greek mainland stopped the growth of Minoan civilization.

REVIEW *What were Minoan palaces like?*

Parts of the city-like palace of Knossos (below) were restored in the beginning of the twentieth century. This wall painting of dolphins (inset) once decorated the Queen's Hall in the palace.

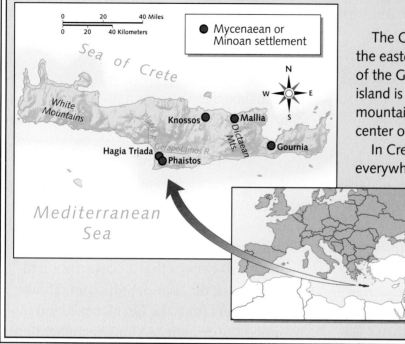

Crete

The Greek island of Crete is located in the eastern Mediterranean, just southeast of the Greek mainland. This long, narrow island is rugged. In fact, a breathtaking mountain chain runs right through the center of the island.

In Crete olive trees grow almost everywhere. Orange groves are also common sights.

Crete's weather is almost never very hot or very cold. It is easy to see why people today are just as enchanted with the island as the people of Homer's time were.

The Mycenaeans

During the last years of their kingdom, Minoan merchants started trading with the people of Mycenae (my•SEE•nee), a city near the coast of the mountainous Peloponnesus. The Mycenaeans seem to have been a warlike people who measured their wealth by the number of weapons they owned.

The Mycenaeans learned many Minoan customs and adapted Minoan ways to fit their own culture. The process by which a culture takes ideas from other cultures is known as **cultural borrowing**. The Mycenaeans borrowed Minoan religious beliefs. They changed Minoan art styles and pottery designs to make them more warlike. They also changed Minoan writing to match the Mycenaean language. Historians now know that the Mycenaean language is an early form of Greek.

These vases show Minoan influence on Mycenaean culture. The vases are Minoan (left), early Mycenaean (center), and late Mycenaean (right).

In 1450 B.C., after the Minoan kingdom weakened, the Mycenaeans invaded Crete. Mycenae controlled Crete and much of the Peloponnesus from about 1450 B.C. to 1100 B.C.

Like the Minoans, the Mycenaeans built large palaces. However, the Mycenaeans put up walls to protect their palaces. The Minoans had not seen a need to guard themselves with walls. The fact that the Mycenaeans built walls shows that they often fought with others.

For many years the Mycenaeans sailed the seas in search of new trade just as the Minoans had done. Mycenaean trade and travel led to the founding of colonies all along the Mediterranean coast. However, after several centuries of strength, the Mycenaean civilization weakened about 1100 B.C.

No one knows why Mycenaean control of Greece weakened. For many years historians believed that other Greek warriors called Dorians marched southward and burned palaces and villages in their path. Now some historians believe that invaders called the Sea Peoples attacked the Mycenaeans. They think that the Dorians had long lived side by side with the Mycenaeans or moved into the area after the attack. Other historians believe that disagreements among the Mycenaeans themselves weakened them.

Most historians do believe that some great change must have happened or the Mycenaeans would not have given up their writing, art, and trade. Between 1100 and 800 B.C., much Minoan and Mycenaean learning was lost. The ancient people of Greece returned to a simpler way of life.

The work of archaeologists has helped us learn about the Mycenaeans. In 1876 German archaeologist Heinrich Schliemann found the first signs of Mycenaean civilization. He uncovered many Mycenaean riches, including golden cups, weapons, and masks.

REVIEW *From whom did the Mycenaeans borrow ideas about art, writing, and religion?*

Mycenaean warriors wore bronze armor with helmets (far right) made from boars' tusks. Mycenaean vases (near right) often showed warlike scenes.

Ancient Legends

Four centuries after the Mycenaean civilization lost its strength, the poet Homer created long story-poems, or **epics**, that kept its memory alive. His poems were based on old stories that had been retold through the centuries. Homer built on these stories to give a powerful picture of a society in which honor and courage were everything.

Today, people around the world read Homer's works to find out more about the early Greeks. The *Iliad* is a story about people's actions during a great war. Homer's next epic, the *Odyssey*, follows the hero Odysseus (oh•DIH•see•uhs) as he returns from that war. During his ten-year journey home, Odysseus has many strange adventures, among them a fight with a one-eyed giant. At the same time, his wife, Penelope (puh•NEH•luh•pee), deals with problems caused by his absence.

Tradition says the war that Homer described in the *Iliad* was fought between

The ODYSSEY

In this passage from the Odyssey, *Odysseus' boat is overturned by rough ocean waves.*

"As he spoke, a mountainous wave, advancing with majestic sweep, crashed down upon him from above and whirled his vessel round. The steering-oar was torn from his hands, and he himself was tossed off the boat, while at the same moment the warring winds joined forces in one tremendous gust, which snapped the mast in two and flung the sail and yard far out into the sea."

BIOGRAPHY

Homer
700s B.C.

Historians know very little about Homer, the author of the *Iliad* and the *Odyssey*. He probably grew up in Ionia in Asia Minor sometime between the years 800 B.C. and 700 B.C. Tradition says that Homer was blind and that he recited from memory the 28,000 verses of his epic poems. Some historians now believe that Homer may have been only one of several authors of the *Iliad* and the *Odyssey*.

Statue of Homer

the Mycenaeans and the Trojans. The Trojans lived in the city of Troy, in what is now northwestern Turkey. The war has become known as the Trojan War.

According to legend the war began when a Trojan prince named Paris kidnapped Helen, the wife of a Mycenaean king. The king's brother, Agamemnon, took soldiers to Troy to get Helen back.

The conflict continued with no end in sight. Then the Mycenaeans came up with a plan to trick the Trojans. The legend tells how they built a huge, hollow wooden horse and dragged it to the gates of Troy during the night. The curious Trojans pulled the large horse into the city the next

This gold mask, made by a Mycenaean artist, is a reminder of the early people who once lived in what is now Greece.

morning. Mycenaean soldiers hiding inside the hollow horse crawled out late at night. They opened the city gates to other Mycenaean soldiers waiting outside. By the following morning, the Mycenaeans had rescued Helen and set fire to the city of Troy.

The legend of the Trojan War, Homer's epics, and other stories left a lasting record of the early people of Greece. From this beginning, the Greek civilization continued to grow and change.

REVIEW *How did Homer keep alive the memory of Mycenae?*

LESSON 2 REVIEW

2000 B.C.	1400 B.C.	800 B.C.

1900 B.C.
• Minoans begin to build palaces on Crete

1450 B.C.
• Mycenaeans invade Crete

800 B.C.
• Much of Minoan and Mycenaean learning has been lost

Check Understanding

1 Remember the Facts Who were the Minoans and the Mycenaeans? Which civilization settled on Crete first?

2 Recall the Main Idea What is one explanation for the end of the Minoan kingdom? What may have caused the Mycenaeans to lose their strength?

Think Critically

3 Past to Present What might cause a culture of today to first gain and then lose strength?

4 Think More About It Why did the Mycenaeans change the ideas they borrowed from the Minoans rather than use them just as they were?

Show What You Know

Art Activity Make a painting that shows what you think may have caused the Minoans or the Mycenaeans to lose their power. Display your finished painting in your classroom with the work of other students to form a row of "wall paintings."

Compare Different

1. Why Learn This Skill?

There are many kinds of maps, and each kind shows different information. For example, historical maps give information about a place as it was in the past. Political maps mark present-day cities and borders. Elevation maps show the height of the land.

Understanding how to read different kinds of maps is useful, but knowing how to use different kinds of maps together can help you even more. It allows you to make connections between the history, geography, economics, government, and culture of a country or region. For example, using a physical map and a political map together can help you see why cities began in some places but not in others.

2. Understand the Process

The maps on these pages show the elevations of Greece and the early settlements of the ancient Greeks. Using the two maps together can help you understand more about the settlement patterns of the early Greeks.

Look first at the elevation map. Are the elevations of Greece mostly high or low? Do you think it would have been easy or difficult for people long ago to travel across this land? By studying the elevation map and its key, you can see that Greece has many high areas. Because of this, travel across the land long ago was often difficult.

Next, look at the historical map. Were the Mycenaean settlements on the Balkan

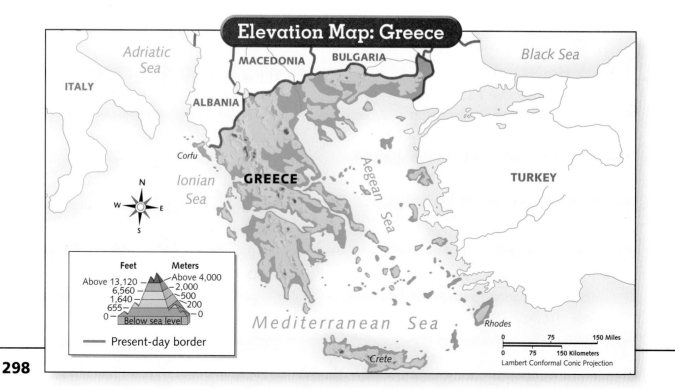

Elevation Map: Greece

Adriatic Sea · MACEDONIA · BULGARIA · Black Sea · ITALY · ALBANIA · Corfu · Ionian Sea · GREECE · Aegean Sea · TURKEY · Mediterranean Sea · Rhodes · Crete

N W E S

Feet | Meters
Above 13,120 — Above 4,000
6,560 — 2,000
1,640 — 500
655 — 200
0 — 0
Below sea level

— Present-day border

0 75 150 Miles
0 75 150 Kilometers
Lambert Conformal Conic Projection

Kinds of Maps

Peninsula mostly inland or on the coast? Were Mycenaean settlements located only on the Balkan Peninsula? Do you think the early Mycenaeans traveled mainly by sea or by land to build new settlements? The map shows that most settlements on the Balkan Peninsula were along the coast. You can see that the Mycenaean settlements in Asia Minor were also on the coast. This shows that the people from the Balkan Peninsula traveled to these locations to begin new settlements. You can infer that Mycenaeans traveled across the Aegean Sea to begin these settlements. Why did they sail east across the sea to build settlements rather than travel west across the land? By studying the two maps, you can see that the early Greeks migrated by sea rather than inland because of the mountainous land.

3. Think and Apply

Use library resources to find a population map and a physical map of the United States. On the population map, find a large city and a small town. Then use the maps together to answer these questions.

A. What physical features surround the large city? Do you think these features affected the city's growth? Explain.

B. From the physical map, can you tell why the small town has not grown larger? What physical features may have made its growth difficult? Explain.

Historical Map: Early Greek Settlements, 1150 B.C.

- Mycenaean settlements

FOCUS

Why might people in different places have different ways of life?

Main Idea Think about why ancient Greeks in different places developed different ways of life.

Vocabulary

polis	helot
acropolis	oligarchy
agora	democracy
tyrant	majority rule
aristocracy	myth
assembly	

City-States and Greek Culture

| 800 B.C. | 700 B.C. | 600 B.C. | 500 B.C. |

Around 800 B.C. the people of Greece started building settlements once again. The settlements began as small farming villages, but some grew to become cities. Often, a city joined with small towns, villages, and nearby farms to form a kind of large community called a **polis**, or city-state. Sparta, Athens, Argos, and Aegina were all ancient Greek city-states.

Rise of City-States

To protect themselves from invaders, most Greek communities built a fort on top of a large hill. Farmers from the countryside moved to this protected area for safety during enemy attacks. Later this secure place, called an **acropolis** (uh•KRAH•puh•luhs), also became a center of religion in many city-states.

Outside the acropolis stood houses, temples, and an open-air market and gathering place called an **agora** (A•guh•ruh). People met in the agora to trade and to discuss the news of the day.

At first a king or tyrant ruled each city-state. In ancient Greece a **tyrant** was someone who took control of a government by force or other means and ruled alone. Today the word *tyrant* refers to a cruel ruler.

Over time each city-state formed its own way of governing. In some city-states the richest men shared authority with a king. This wealthy ruling class, or **aristocracy**, was made up of powerful landowners and merchants. In other city-states all free men took part in government. These men met in an **assembly**, or lawmaking group, to make decisions.

Most city-states had fewer than 5,000 people. As the population of a city-state grew, overcrowding forced some people to look for new places to live. Many city-states set up colonies in Asia Minor, northern Africa, and southern Europe.

Besides providing space for more people, the colonies brought the Greeks new natural resources and trade markets. This also helped spread Greek ideas and customs through the Mediterranean region.

Soon the city-states began to compete for land and trade. Sparta and Argos both

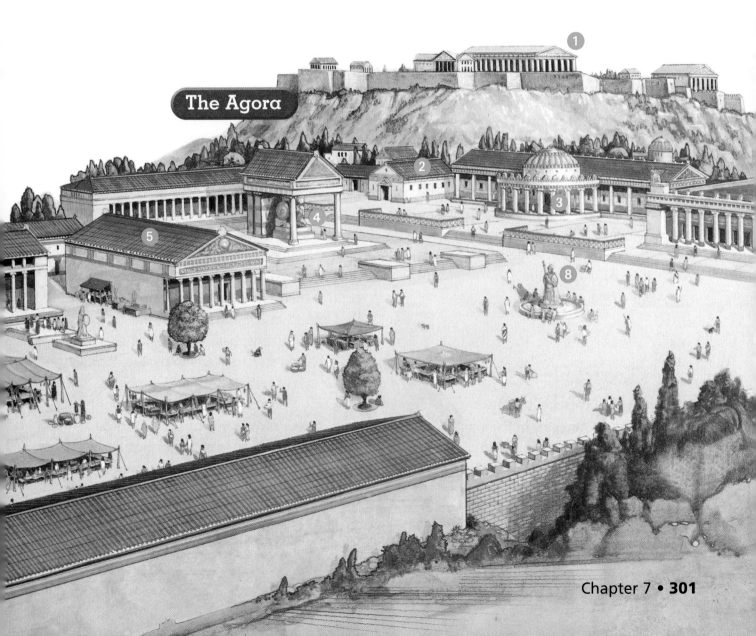

The Agora

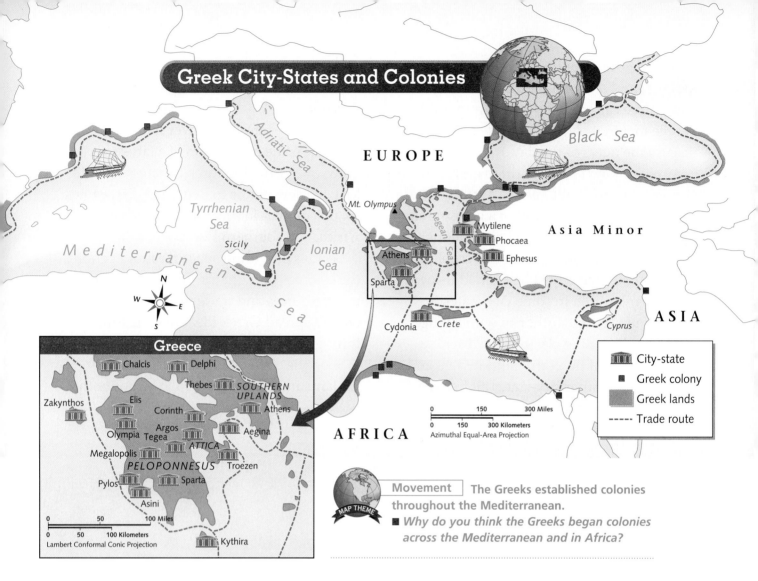

Greek City-States and Colonies

EUROPE

Black Sea

Tyrrhenian Sea

Adriatic Sea

Mt. Olympus

Aegean Sea

Mytilene

Asia Minor

Phocaea

Ephesus

Athens

Sparta

Sicily

Ionian Sea

Mediterranean Sea

Cydonia

Crete

ASIA

Cyprus

AFRICA

Greece

Chalcis

Delphi

Thebes

SOUTHERN UPLANDS

Zakynthos

Elis

Corinth

Athens

Olympia

Argos

Tegea

Aegina

Megalopolis

ATTICA

PELOPONNESUS

Troezen

Pylos

Sarta

Asini

Kythira

0   50   100 Miles
0   50   100 Kilometers
Lambert Conformal Conic Projection

0   150   300 Miles
0   150   300 Kilometers
Azimuthal Equal-Area Projection

Legend:
- 🏛 City-state
- ■ Greek colony
- ▨ Greek lands
- ---- Trade route

Movement The Greeks established colonies throughout the Mediterranean.

■ *Why do you think the Greeks began colonies across the Mediterranean and in Africa?*

---

wanted control of the Peloponnesus. Athens and Thebes were rivals for control of the land northeast of the Peloponnesus. Sparta and Athens, while not rivals at first, had very different ways of life.

REVIEW *How were city-states alike?*

Sparta

Sparta was located in the southern Peloponnesus. In this city-state soldiers marching and young boys and girls exercising were common sights. Spartan citizens led a simple life filled with physical activity.

The Spartans were descendants of Dorian settlers. They conquered the earlier people of the area and made them **helots**—slaves owned by the state, not by private citizens.

Spartan leaders used military strength to control their city-state. Historians believe that Sparta may have had ten times as many slaves as citizens. Fear that the slaves would rebel led the Spartans to protect themselves with a military way of life.

Spartan children went through long physical-training programs. Boys had to leave their families at age 7 to attend training camps. Girls

Physical training was an important part of life for both women and men in ancient Sparta.

stayed at home but received training in gymnastics and running. Boys continued training until age 18 and served in the Spartan army until age 30.

The army camps taught Spartans to obey their leaders without question. Spartans believed that they must never give up a battle, even when wounded. The Spartans believed that there was no greater honor than to die defending their city-state.

The women of Sparta had fewer rights than men but more rights than women in other Greek city-states. Spartan women managed the household and often handled business matters. However, the main duty of women, according to Spartan leaders, was to raise strong children.

All Spartans followed a simple way of life. By law everyone ate "in common, of the same bread and same meat." Spartan leaders feared that new ideas would bring unwanted changes to their society. For this reason, citizens were rarely allowed to travel outside Sparta and were discouraged from trading with outsiders. This meant that the Spartans could use only their own resources. Because they kept to themselves, their way of life changed little over time.

Sparta had two kings, each from a different royal family. Except in times of war, the kings had little authority. Both kings served as part of a 30-member senate. The other members of the senate—all over the age of 60—were elected by an assembly of citizens. All male Spartans were allowed to be part of the assembly. The assembly elected five wealthy landowners called *ephors* (EH•ferz) to handle daily governing.

Only the senate or the ephors could suggest new laws in Sparta. The assembly of citizens voted for or against new laws, but their votes could be ignored by the ephors

and the senate. This meant that the ephors and the senators held most of the power in Sparta. Any small ruling group such as this is called an **oligarchy**.

Although strict, Spartan government was among the most admired governments in all of Greece. Many Greeks thought that the Spartan government's tight control over its citizens made it a strong city-state.

REVIEW *Why did Spartans believe they needed a strong army?*

Spartan soldiers were fierce and disciplined. This bronze warrior still guards the tomb of King Leonidas, who lived during the 400s B.C.

Athens

Athens was located in Attica (A•tih•kuh), the ancient name for part of the Greek peninsula northeast of the Peloponnesus. Life in Athens was very different from life in Sparta. Unlike Sparta, Athens required its young men to serve in its army only during times of war. The government of Athens also encouraged citizens to take part in decisions affecting the community. This civic participation grew into a system of **democracy**, or rule by the people. The Greek historian Thucydides (thoo•SIH•duh•deez) said about Athens, "Its administration favors the many instead of the few."

The Athenian leader Solon led the Athenian government toward democracy

Paintings on Greek pottery show stories of history and legend, religious ceremonies, or daily life.

around 594 B.C. Under his leadership male Athenians were able to take a greater part in government. Then, in 508 B.C., a leader named Cleisthenes (KLYS•thuh•neez) changed the form of Athenian government to a full democracy. By 500 B.C., every free man over age 20 had full political rights.

All male citizens of Athens took part in the city-state's assembly, or Ecclesia (ih•KLEE•zee•uh). Every member of the assembly was allowed one vote. All decisions were made by **majority rule**. In other words, the idea that received the most votes became law.

The reforms of Cleisthenes kept any one person from controlling Athens. To get rid of a troublesome person, citizens held a special meeting. Any citizen who received the most votes out of a total of 6,000 was forced to leave Athens for ten years. The candidates' names were written on broken pieces of pottery called *ostraca* (AHS•truh•kuh). This ancient practice gave us the English word *ostracize*, which means "to shut out."

The changes made by Cleisthenes let more people take part in government. But Athenian democracy did not include everyone. Women could not take part in government even though they were considered citizens. Athens's enslaved people, who made up about one-third of the population, also had no voice in government. For the most part, Athens's slaves were people from neighboring areas who had been captured in war. The slaves did much of the work in Athens, giving citizens the time to take part in their democracy. Unlike the

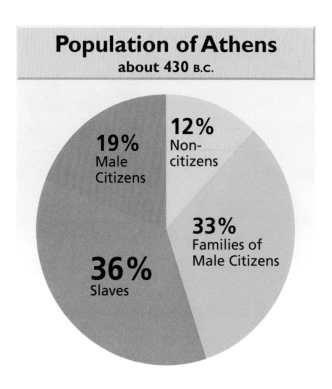

Population of Athens
about 430 B.C.

- 12% Non-citizens
- 19% Male Citizens
- 33% Families of Male Citizens
- 36% Slaves

LEARNING FROM GRAPHS Male citizens with the right to vote made up only a small part of Athens's population.
■ *Athens's population was about 285,000. About how many male citizens were there? About how many slaves were there?*

helots of Sparta, the enslaved people of Athens could be bought and sold by private citizens.

REVIEW *How were government decisions made in Athens?*

Greek Identity

During the time of the city-states, Greeks did not think of themselves as belonging to a single country. People identified only with their city-state. However, the Greek people did feel a strong cultural connection, or cultural identity, with one another. Having a common ancestor, language, and religion brought the Greeks together.

The hero Hellen was believed to have been the ancestor of all Greek people. A Greek **myth**, or story passed down about

LEARNING FROM TABLES The Greek alphabet borrowed many letters from the Phoenicians but added its own vowels to form a 24-letter alphabet.
■ *In what ways is the ancient Greek alphabet similar to today's English alphabet?*

The Greek Alphabet

GREEK LETTER	WRITTEN NAME	ENGLISH SOUND
A	alpha	a
B	beta	b
Γ	gamma	g
Δ	delta	d
E	epsilon	e
Z	zeta	z
H	eta	e
Θ	theta	th
I	iota	i
K	kappa	c, k
Λ	lambda	l
M	mu	m
N	nu	n
Ξ	xi	x
O	omicron	o
Π	pi	p
P	rho	r
Σ	sigma	s
T	tau	t
Y	upsilon	y, u
Φ	phi	ph
X	chi	ch
Ψ	psi	ps
Ω	omega	o

HERITAGE

The First Olympics

The first Olympic Games were held in the valley of Olympia near the city-state of Elis in 776 B.C. As many as 40,000 people watched athletes from city-states all over Greece compete in one event— a footrace. Women were not allowed to enter the stadium at Olympia to compete or even to watch. Later, however, women in Elis held their own footraces to honor the goddess Hera.

This sculpture is of a boxer who competed in the Olympic Games of long ago. How do the modern Olympics connect different cultures today?

a god or a hero, said that Hellen alone survived an ancient flood. The religion the Greeks shared also set them apart, in their minds, from other peoples who lived along the Mediterranean.

The Greek cultural identity was seen in various activities. The Olympic Games, for example, brought the city-states together in peace. Beginning about 776 B.C. Greeks met every four years to honor the god Zeus by competing in athletic contests. The Greeks believed that Zeus and their other gods controlled daily events in the world.

A common written language also helped bring the city-states closer together. In the 700s B.C. the Greeks developed an alphabet based on the alphabet of the Phoenicians. Like the Minoans long before them, the Phoenicians were traders and needed a writing system to keep track of their trade. Phoenician writing used symbols to stand for single sounds rather than whole ideas.

Greek Gods

Aphrodite	Goddess of love
Apollo	God of music and poetry
Ares	God of war
Athena	Goddess of war and wisdom
Hera	Protector of marriage and women
Hermes	Messenger for the gods
Hestia	Goddess of the home
Poseidon	God of the sea
Zeus	Ruler of the gods

LEARNING FROM TABLES The ancient Greeks believed that different gods controlled different areas of human life.
■ *What areas of life did Athena oversee?*

The Greeks changed this system to fit their needs. They called their first letter *alpha* and their second letter *beta*. Our word *alphabet* comes from the names of those Greek letters.

REVIEW *What helped the Greeks feel a cultural identity?*

LESSON 3 REVIEW

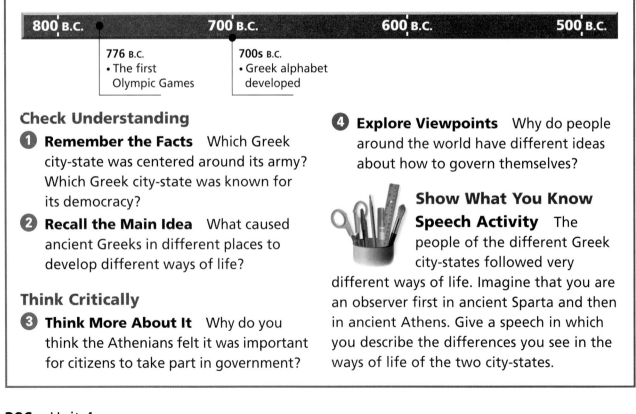

800 B.C.   700 B.C.   600 B.C.   500 B.C.

776 B.C.
• The first Olympic Games

700s B.C.
• Greek alphabet developed

Check Understanding

1 Remember the Facts Which Greek city-state was centered around its army? Which Greek city-state was known for its democracy?

2 Recall the Main Idea What caused ancient Greeks in different places to develop different ways of life?

Think Critically

3 Think More About It Why do you think the Athenians felt it was important for citizens to take part in government?

4 Explore Viewpoints Why do people around the world have different ideas about how to govern themselves?

Show What You Know
Speech Activity The people of the different Greek city-states followed very different ways of life. Imagine that you are an observer first in ancient Sparta and then in ancient Athens. Give a speech in which you describe the differences you see in the ways of life of the two city-states.

The
Golden Age
of Athens

`500 B.C.` `400 B.C.`

FOCUS

How do times of war and times of peace affect societies today?

Main Idea   Look for ways war and peace affected the lives of the ancient Greeks.

Vocabulary

league
tragedy
comedy
plague
demagogue

For centuries the Greek city-states fought over land and trade. Then, beginning early in the fifth century B.C., a common enemy brought the Greek people together.

The Persian Wars

Beginning about 540 B.C., armies from Persia conquered Babylon, Assyria, Egypt, and other lands around the Mediterranean. They also captured the Greek cities in Asia Minor. Soon Persian armies crossed the narrow Aegean Sea separating Europe from Asia and invaded the northern Balkans. About 500 B.C. the Greeks of Asia Minor rebelled against the Persians. Although the Athenians sent help, the Greeks in Asia Minor could not defeat the Persians.

In 490 B.C. the Persian king, Darius I, turned his soldiers toward Athens because Athens had helped the colonies fight the Persians. The Athenians met the Persians on the plain of Marathon, not far from Athens. Although the Persians had more soldiers, the Athenians managed to defeat them in just one day of fighting. Later, people told a story of a messenger running all the way to Athens from Marathon to report the amazing victory. Athletes in today's Olympic Games re-create this action in the long-distance running event called the marathon.

Darius I died in 486 B.C. After his death, his son Xerxes (ZERK•seez) took control of the Persian kingdom. Xerxes never forgot his father's defeat at the hands of the Greeks. In 480 B.C. he sent 200,000 soldiers in 800 ships to attack Greece. This

The Athenian leader Pericles lived from about 495 B.C. to 429 B.C.

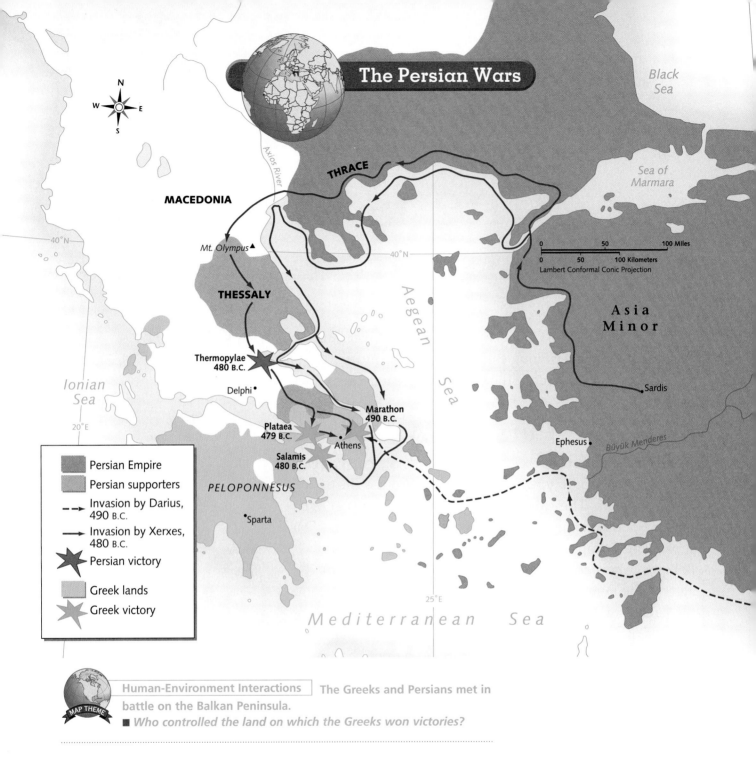

The Persian Wars

Black Sea

Sea of Marmara

THRACE

MACEDONIA

Axios River

Mt. Olympus ▲

THESSALY

40°N

Aegean

Sea

Asia
Minor

Sardis

Thermopylae
480 B.C.

Delphi •

Ionian
Sea

20°E

Marathon
490 B.C.

Plataea
479 B.C.

Athens •

Ephesus •

Büyük Menderes

Salamis
480 B.C.

PELOPONNESUS

• Sparta

Persian Empire

Persian supporters

Invasion by Darius,
490 B.C.

Invasion by Xerxes,
480 B.C.

Persian victory

Greek lands

Greek victory

25°E

Mediterranean   Sea

MAP THEME
Human-Environment Interactions   The Greeks and Persians met in
battle on the Balkan Peninsula.
■ *Who controlled the land on which the Greeks won victories?*

time the Persians met Greek forces made up
of armies and navies from many city-states,
including Athens and Sparta. The Persians
still had more soldiers and sailors than the
Greeks. Yet in a sea battle near the island
of Salamis (SAL•uh•muhs), the Greeks
defeated the Persians. The Persians were
forced to return home. Greek civilization
was able to continue undisturbed.

After the Persian Wars, the Greek city-
states feared future attacks. They banded
together to form **leagues**, or groups of
allies, for protection. Sparta led city-states
in the Peloponnesian League. Athens led
the city-states of Asia Minor and the Aegean
islands in the Delian League.

REVIEW *What caused the Greek city-
states to band together?*

308 • Unit 4

The Golden Age

The Greeks felt great pride after defeating the Persians. From about 479 B.C. to 431 B.C., Athenians turned their pride into a time of achievement known as the Golden Age. Athens was the cultural center of this important period.

A member of the aristocracy named Pericles (PAIR•uh•kleez) led Athens during much of this time. Pericles was elected leader for 15 years in a row. He believed in the saying "Nothing to excess," meaning that a person should not overdo anything.

Pericles led Athens with the help of an assembly made up of thousands of male citizens. Any member could speak to the assembly, and each had the right to vote. Assembly members usually voted by raising their hands.

A group called the Council of 500 decided what would be discussed at each assembly meeting. Council members were chosen from the assembly each year by drawing names from a bowl. Many other government officials, as well as the jury members for court cases, were also chosen this way.

Although Pericles strongly supported the Athenian democracy, he believed it could be made even better. He felt that every citizen had a right to take part in government, not just wealthy citizens. Pericles arranged for jurors to be paid a salary for the days they served.

CITIZENSHIP

Direct Democracy

Unlike the democracy of the United States, the democracy of Athens was a direct democracy. Each citizen took a direct role in government decisions. Today most countries have too many people to have a direct democracy.

The United States has a representative democracy. In such a democracy, large numbers of citizens elect other citizens as representatives to make governmental decisions for them.

This pay made up for the money they would lose by not being at their regular jobs. Even the poorest citizens of Athens could now afford to serve the city-state. As Pericles explained,

66 With us, poverty does not stand in the way. No one is prevented from being of service to the city-state. 99

REVIEW *How did Pericles improve Athenian democracy?*

The most remarkable building of the Golden Age in Athens was the Parthenon, which was built on the city's acropolis. This marble temple celebrated Greek victories in the Persian Wars and honored the Greek goddess Athena. The Parthenon was completed in 432 B.C. Its ruins still stand.

Achievements of the Golden Age

Pericles wanted Athens to become "the school of Greece." He offered support to Athenians working in the arts and the building trades. He also invited artists from other Greek city-states to come to Athens.

Architects and builders set about making Athens more beautiful. Architects designed new temples, gymnasiums, theaters, and other public buildings. Artists decorated the new buildings with murals, or wall paintings, showing scenes from Athens's history and from Greek myths.

Writers also contributed to the Golden Age. Herodotus (hih•RAH•duh•tuhs), whom some call the first historian and one of the earliest geographers, wrote about the Persian Wars. Herodotus explained that he wrote the history to put on record "the astonishing achievements of our own and of other peoples." Even today many people read his works. Sophocles (SAHF•uh•kleez) wrote **tragedies**, or serious plays in which the main character comes to an unhappy end. Aristophanes (air•uh•STAHF•uh•neez) wrote **comedies**, or humorous plays. His comedies usually made fun of political leaders or traditional ideas.

Greek amphitheaters, such as this one in Delphi, were designed so that even a whisper could reach the seats farthest from the stage.

Greek Columns

Doric   Ionic   Corinthian

LEARNING FROM DIAGRAMS The ancient Greeks used three different styles, or orders, of columns in their buildings.
■ *What can you learn about the ancient Greeks by studying these columns?*

During the time of Pericles, scientists who studied nature and human life came to Athens from all around the Mediterranean. Their findings changed the way people saw their world. One of the great scientists of the Golden Age was Hippocrates (hih•PAH•kruh•teez). Hippocrates and his followers showed that illnesses came from natural causes. Before Hippocrates' time, many people believed that diseases were punishments from the gods.

Doctors in Athens used the ideas of Hippocrates. They advised the Greeks that to stay healthy, "wheaten bread is to be preferred to barley cake, and roasted to boiled meats." While many of their ideas made sense, they also thought that "vegetables should be reduced to a minimum."

Hippocrates is perhaps best remembered for the rules of behavior he wrote for doctors. Today, doctors still promise to follow these rules when they graduate from medical school.

REVIEW *What kinds of people worked in Athens during the Golden Age?*

The End of the Golden Age

During the time of the Golden Age, Athens and Sparta became the most powerful city-states in Greece. Yet neither was satisfied. Athens wanted to become even stronger. Sparta wanted to weaken Athens. The city-states of the Peloponnesian League supported Sparta, while those of the Delian League supported Athens. In 431 B.C. the Peloponnesian War broke out. The war lasted 27 years.

After Sparta attacked Attica, many people from the countryside moved into Athens. Because of the crowding, diseases swept

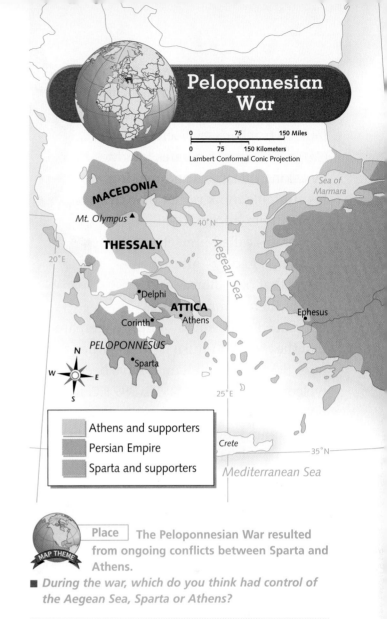

Place The Peloponnesian War resulted from ongoing conflicts between Sparta and Athens.

■ *During the war, which do you think had control of the Aegean Sea, Sparta or Athens?*

through the city-state. One-fourth of the Athenian army died from an outbreak of a **plague**, or deadly sickness. Pericles also died at this time.

Without the wise leadership of Pericles, the members of the assembly began to follow bad leaders, or **demagogues** (DEH•muh•gahgz). These demagogues made promises they could not keep and led the assembly to make poor decisions. Faced with ruin, Athens surrendered to Sparta in 404 B.C. Sparta quickly replaced the Athenian assembly with an oligarchy like its own. However, the Athenians soon rebelled and brought democracy back to Athens.

Great thinkers and teachers lived in Athens during the last days of the Golden Age and after. One famous teacher was Socrates (SAH•kruh•teez). Socrates taught by asking questions and making his students think rather than by telling them information.

Socrates called himself Athens's "gadfly," after an insect that bites horses and makes them jump. Socrates often used criticism to "sting" Athenians so that they would return to their earlier greatness. Such criticism would have been more welcome in Pericles' day. In 399 B.C. it was not. An Athenian court convicted Socrates of teaching dangerous ideas to the city's young people. The court sentenced Socrates

The ideas of Socrates are still studied today.

to end his own life by drinking poison. He did so, because he believed it was more important to obey the law than to save his own life by running away.

One of Socrates' students was Plato. Like Socrates, Plato was disappointed in the leaders who came after Pericles. Plato said that a ruler should be a good person, because good people are just and wise. He believed that it was possible to become a good person by studying hard and loving wisdom. He felt that philosophers, or "lovers of wisdom," would make the best rulers. In 385 B.C. Plato started a

At Plato's Academy, philosophers studied the responsibilities of citizens and leaders. The school gained its name from its location near an olive grove planted in honor of the Greek hero Academus. Over the years the word *academy* has come to mean "school."

school called the Academy. There philosophers could learn the lessons they would need to live and govern well.

Plato also thought about what it takes to be a good citizen. He decided that a good citizen is someone who thinks and feels and then takes action. He felt that it was important for people to be informed, to understand other viewpoints, and to be responsible for their own actions. This idea of citizenship is shared by many people today.

Aristotle (AIR•uh•stah•tuhl), a student of Plato's, was more interested in how things were rather than in how he would like them to be. Aristotle entered Plato's Academy at age 18 and studied there for

Aristotle, who lived from 384 B.C. to 322 B.C., loved all knowledge.

about 20 years. He left when Plato died in 347 B.C.

Aristotle's wide search for knowledge covered many subjects including law, economics, astronomy, science, and sports. Aristotle was also a pioneer in zoology—the study of animals— and botany—the study of plants.

Aristotle and Plato disagreed about many things. However, they both thought that the best life was one spent in search of knowledge and truth.

REVIEW *What brought an end to the Golden Age of Athens?*

LESSON 4 REVIEW

500 B.C.		400 B.C.

480 B.C.
• Greeks defeat Persians at Salamis

479 B.C.
• Golden Age of Athens begins

385 B.C.
• Plato starts the Academy in Athens

Check Understanding

1 Remember the Facts What wars did the Athenians fight in the 400s B.C.?

2 Recall the Main Idea How did periods of war and peace affect the way of life of the ancient Greeks?

Think Critically

3 Past to Present Do people's ways of life change during times of war? Explain.

4 Think More About It How did the Persian Wars help bring the Greeks together? How did the Peloponnesian War tear the Greeks apart?

5 Personally Speaking Socrates taught by asking questions. Which do you think is a better way to teach—by asking or by telling? Explain.

Show What You Know

Poster Activity After the defeat of the Persians, the Athenians showed their pride in being Greek through great works in art and science. Think about the pride you feel in the United States. Make a poster that explains why you feel proud to be a citizen. Display your poster in your classroom or another part of your school.

Were Greek Women

Were women in ancient Athens made to stay in their homes and kept out of society? This question is hard to answer. We have almost no archaeological record of women's activities—the crafts they made have been lost to time. No words come from the women themselves either—almost all ancient records of Greece were written by men and for men.

Ancient Greek artwork adds to the confusion. While some writings state that women were not allowed to go outside, some vase paintings show women gathered at fountains, talking together. From studying such writings and artworks, some scholars believe that women had little social or public life. Others disagree.

The following statements are by four experts on ancient Greek culture. Each expert tells his or her ideas about the role of women in ancient Greek society. Their ideas are based on years of study, which has led them to differing opinions about how Greek women lived long ago. Read each statement, and then answer the questions under Compare Viewpoints.

This detail from a fifth-century B.C. Greek vase shows women preparing for a wedding.

Sarah Pomeroy

Sarah Pomeroy, a historian who focuses on women, writes,

66 Free women were usually secluded so that they could not be seen by men who were not close relatives. An orator [a speaker in the courts] could maintain that some women were too modest to be seen by men who were not relatives. 99

Active Citizens?

François Lissarrague

François Lissarrague, an art historian, writes about a vase that shows women at a fountain:

66 Here, then, the fountain is portrayed as the female equivalent of what the public square represents for men. It was a public place where one saw mainly women (or so the painters would have us believe). 99

Elizabeth Wayland Barber

Elizabeth Wayland Barber, a professor of archaeology, writes,

66 Women were virtually household prisoners in fifth-century Athenian society in particular, as the legal orations of Lysias show, and this seems to have been the typical state of affairs from shortly before the time of Homer onward. 99

David Cohen

David Cohen, a Greek historian, writes,

66 Husbands expected wives to go out and those wealthy enough gave them slaves to accompany them. . . . Indeed, one of the most important activities of women included visiting or helping friends and relatives. As men had their circle of friends, there is considerable evidence to indicate that women formed . . . friendships with neighbors, and visited one another frequently— whether to borrow salt or a dress. 99

The Greek women in this clay scene are playing a game similar to jacks.

Compare Viewpoints

1. Which writers believe that ancient Greek women could not leave their homes? How do you know?
2. Which writers mention physical evidence to support their viewpoint?

Think and Apply

Pictures and texts can be used to support views that differ greatly. Think of a time when two people or two countries have looked at the same evidence and drawn different conclusions.

Skills

Predict a Likely Outcome

1. Why Learn This Skill?

When you make a prediction, you are not just guessing about what will happen in the future. Rather, you are using what you already know along with new information to predict a probable, or likely, outcome.

2. Remember What You Have Read

The Persians fought the Greeks to try to gain more land. Although the Greeks won the Battle of Marathon, the Persians returned. The Persian king, Xerxes, sent 800 ships to attack Greece.

3. Apply New Information

The Greek ships sailed into the narrow strait at Salamis. In the strait they had the chance to rest while they waited. As the Greeks hoped, the 800 Persian ships followed. The Persians had to row for 12 hours before they reached the Greek fleet in the small body of water. Imagine that you are one of the Greek sailors. What do you predict will happen next?

4. Understand the Process

To make a prediction, you can follow these steps:

1. Think about what you already know. *The Persians wanted more land and sent a fleet of ships to attack the Greeks.*

2. Review any new information you have learned. *The Persians rowed their large fleet into a narrow body of water where the Greeks were rested and waiting.*

3. Make a prediction.

Here's what happened when the Persian fleet followed the Greeks. After more than 12 hours of rowing, the tired Persian sailors met the Greek fleet. The huge Persian fleet was too large to move around in the narrow strait. The smaller Greek fleet, with its well-rested sailors, was easily able to ram and sink most of the Persian ships.

5. Think and Apply

As you read the next lesson, follow the steps listed above to predict how Greek culture would influence other cultures.

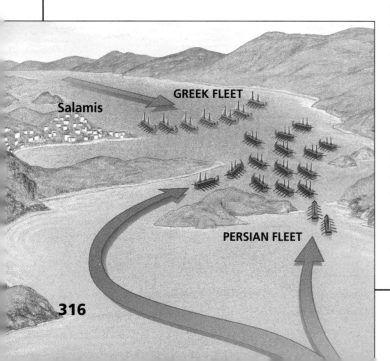

The battle of Salamis

Alexander's Great Empire

400 B.C.	300 B.C.

No one leader had ever ruled over the many different Greek city-states. That would soon change, however. In time, young Alexander the Great controlled lands that stretched from the Greek peninsula to northern India. This leader created the largest empire the world had known.

Conquest of Greece

Conflict and distrust grew among the ancient Greeks after the Peloponnesian War. City-states formed **alliances**, or agreements to help each other, but most of these alliances did not last long. A friend in one conflict became an enemy in the next. Each city-state put its own interests above the common good of Greece. Sparta lost all of its power during this period, while Athens became the leader of a second Delian League.

Meanwhile, in Macedonia, an area north of the Greek city-states on the Balkan Peninsula, a strong king came to the throne. Philip II had brought his own people together under one rule. He wanted to do the same for the rest of the Greek mainland.

Even the combined armies of Athens and Thebes could not stop Philip's well-trained Macedonian soldiers. Philip's armies moved south through northern and central Greece. In 338 B.C. his army defeated Athens and its allies in an important fight known as the Battle of Chaeronea (ker•uh•NEE•uh). With this victory Philip gained control of most of the Greek peninsula.

FOCUS

How can one person affect the course of history?

Main Idea   As you read, look for ways in which Alexander the Great changed the Mediterranean region forever.

Vocabulary

alliance
Hellenistic
multicultural

Alexander the Great was only 20 when he became king of Macedonia. This marble sculpture is a Roman copy of the original, which was made in 320 B.C.

317

The Macedonians did not take over Greece to destroy it. Philip greatly respected Greek culture and sought to preserve it, not end it.

With Greece under his control, Philip required that the city-states join the League of Corinth, which he headed. To join the League of Corinth, each city-state had to promise not to fight any other member of the league.

With Greece under his control, Philip looked toward Asia. He wanted to free all Greek cities under Persian control. In 336 B.C. Philip sent a small army to Asia. He planned to send his entire army there later.

King Philip did not live to fight the Persians. The king was assassinated by a Macedonian in 336 B.C. while attending his daughter's wedding. His rule passed to his 20-year-old son Alexander.

REVIEW *What ruler united Greece and where was he from?*

Building an Empire

Alexander's parents had prepared him well for his new role. Philip, who had spent part of his boyhood in Greece, wanted to pass on his love of Greek culture to his son. To do this, he hired the Greek philosopher Aristotle to be Alexander's teacher. From Aristotle, the future leader learned knowledge. From his father, he learned to be a fearless warrior. Stories say that Alexander slept with a dagger and a copy of Homer's *Iliad* under his pillow.

As king, Alexander wanted to complete his father's plan to rule not only the Greeks and the Macedonians but the whole world. The world known to Alexander was eastern Europe, northern Africa, and western Asia.

Trouble in his own kingdom delayed Alexander's plans. Neighboring peoples began to attack Macedonia along its northern border. Alexander had to make

This mosaic is a Roman copy of a Greek painting. It was found in the ancient Roman city of Pompeii and shows Alexander (left) charging into battle against King Darius III and the Persians.

sure his homeland was safe before he could set out for distant lands.

Alexander and his army defeated the invaders quickly. During the battle, however, a rumor started that Alexander had been killed. Hearing this, some Greek city-states rebelled against Macedonian rule. Alexander returned to southern Greece and ended the rebellion by force.

In 334 B.C. Alexander returned to his dream of world conquest. He and his army crossed the Hellespont Strait between Europe and Asia Minor, attacking the Persian Empire, ruled by King Darius III. Alexander's army was made up of more than 35,000 well-trained soldiers.

One by one Alexander freed the Greek colonies of the region from Persian control. For the most part, Alexander established democratic rule in the Greek cities he freed. However, this did not mean that they had full independence. The Greek city-states of Asia Minor were forced to accept Alexander as their new ruler.

After this, Alexander continued his bloody conquest. One by one, new peoples and places fell under his control. All across his growing empire Alexander the Great, as he came to be called, built new cities. Alexander named many of these cities Alexandria, after himself. The cities became centers of learning and helped spread Greek culture. In time Alexandria, Egypt, rivaled Athens as the center of Greek culture.

This gold leaf crown was worn by Alexander the Great.

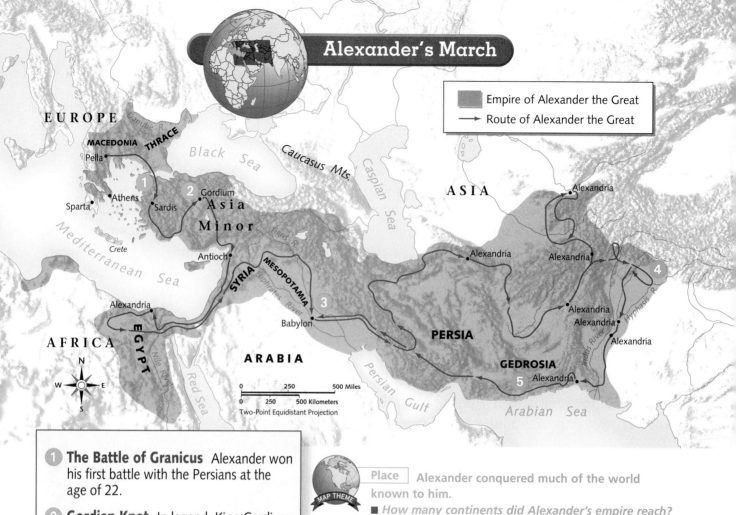

Alexander's March

Legend:
- Empire of Alexander the Great
- → Route of Alexander the Great

EUROPE
MACEDONIA
THRACE
Pella
Athens
Sparta
Sardis
Gordium
Asia Minor
Crete
Antioch
SYRIA
MESOPOTAMIA
Mediterranean Sea
Alexandria
AFRICA
EGYPT
Nile River
Red Sea
ARABIA
Babylon
Persian Gulf
ASIA
Caucasus Mts.
Caspian Sea
Black Sea
Danube R.
Tigris R.
Euphrates River
Alexandria
Alexandria
Alexandria
Alexandria
Alexandria
Hyphasis R.
Indus River
PERSIA
GEDROSIA
Alexandria
Arabian Sea

1
2
3
4
5

0   250   500 Miles
0   250   500 Kilometers
Two-Point Equidistant Projection

N W E S

Place — Alexander conquered much of the world known to him.
■ **How many continents did Alexander's empire reach?**

1 The Battle of Granicus Alexander won his first battle with the Persians at the age of 22.

2 Gordian Knot In legend, King Gordius, father of Midas, tied a difficult knot to his chariot. It was said that whoever untied it would rule all of Asia. Alexander went to Gordium, cut the knot with his sword, and was crowned king.

3 Babylon The city was seized easily by Alexander. Later, after returning from the East, Alexander returned to Babylon, where he became ill from traveling and died in 323 B.C.

4 Hyphasis River Alexander had planned to cross into India, but his troops stopped here and refused to go any farther. Alexander had to turn back after conquering most of the world known to him.

5 Desert of Gedrosia As much as one-half of Alexander's army died crossing this desert as they headed west to Babylon.

Greek soldiers and settlers spread throughout the empire. The different peoples of Alexander's empire learned to speak the Greek language and began to worship Greek gods. Because of this, the period of Alexander's rule and the next several centuries after his death became known as the **Hellenistic**, or "Greek-like," Age.

Alexander's conquests made him the ruler of a **multicultural** empire, or an empire of many cultures. As the ruler of many different peoples, Alexander felt it was wise to adopt some of their customs as

This silver coin made in Babylon honors Alexander's battle against soldiers on elephants in India.

well as introduce them to Greek culture. This helped the Persians and other conquered people accept his rule. By 331 B.C. Alexander's empire stretched from the Danube River in Europe south to the Nile River in Africa, and from Greece east beyond the Tigris and Euphrates rivers in Asia. Alexander had conquered Asia Minor, Syria, Egypt, Mesopotamia, and other parts of the once-mighty Persian Empire—all without losing a single major battle!

REVIEW *How did Alexander build his empire?*

The Breakup of the Empire

Alexander the Great now ruled a wide area, but he still wanted more lands. Beyond Persia lay India. Alexander led his soldiers east from Persia to the Indus River. There he fought Porus, an Indian king.

Porus's army had more than 300 chariots and 200 war elephants. King Porus himself fought from high atop a large elephant. Though these beasts were a terrifying sight, they were not enough to win the battle. After being wounded, Porus surrendered to Alexander's forces. Alexander allowed Porus to continue as ruler of his kingdom.

Alexander planned to push on from the Indus

Valley to the Ganges River. However, his conquest-weary soldiers refused to follow. Bitterly disappointed, Alexander turned back to Babylon in 326 B.C.

Shortly after he returned to Babylon, in 323 B.C., Alexander became ill with a fever. He died a few days later, not long before his thirty-third birthday. Legend says that before Alexander's death, a soldier asked, "To whom will rule of the great empire go?" Alexander answered, "To the strongest!"

No one leader proved strong enough to replace Alexander. His empire broke up quickly after his death as his generals fought for control. The empire split into many parts. The largest of these parts were Macedonia, Syria, and Egypt. These three kingdoms were often at war with one another. Even so, these Hellenistic kingdoms continued and built upon many of Alexander's ideas.

REVIEW *Why did Alexander's empire break up after his death?*

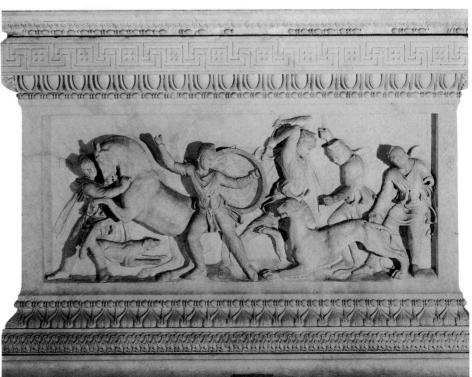

The scenes on this limestone coffin show Alexander in battle.

Alexander's Legacy

The empire may not have lasted, but the Hellenistic culture that started with Alexander did. As in the time of Pericles, great thinkers of the Hellenistic Age changed people's understanding of the world.

Alexandria, Egypt, became the leading center of learning in the Hellenistic world. The huge library at Alexandria contained more than 500,000 scrolls, rolled-up sheets of papyrus with writing on them. The goal of its librarians was to collect every text in the world!

Connected to the library was a building known as the Museum. There scholars wrote books and exchanged ideas. Today museums are places that preserve history and offer knowledge.

Hellenistic teachers worked out new ideas in mathematics. Euclid (YOO•kluhd) of Alexandria, Egypt, conducted the first work in geometry, the study of lines and angles. Archimedes (ar•kuh•MEE•deez) of Syracuse, on the island of Sicily, used mathematics to build many useful machines.

Hellenistic scientists also made use of mathematics as they began to think about the universe. For example, Aristarchus (air•uh•STAR•kuhs) used mathematics to discover that Earth moves in a path around the sun.

Hellenistic scientists built on the knowledge of medicine that Hippocrates had introduced. Alexandria, Egypt, became the center

Hellenistic advances in architecture can be seen in these tombs (above), carved around the year 7 B.C. The tombs, in what is now Turkey, were cut out of rock. This stone figure (right) from India shows how far Hellenistic influences in art had reached.

for the study of medicine and surgery. Doctors there learned that the brain was the center of the nervous system.

Scientists of the Hellenistic period also focused on the study of geography. They not only improved the way maps were drawn but also made new discoveries about the Earth.

By 146 B.C. another group of people, the Romans, had grown strong enough to gain control of the Mediterranean world. But the knowledge the Greeks had gained was not forgotten. The Romans borrowed from the religion, art, architecture, philosophy, and language of the Greeks to build their own civilization. For many years after the Romans took control, Alexandria, Egypt, remained a center for Greek medical learning.

REVIEW *What city was considered the center of learning during the Hellenistic Age?*

This Persian miniature painting shows how Alexander was admired by the people he ruled.

LESSON 5 REVIEW

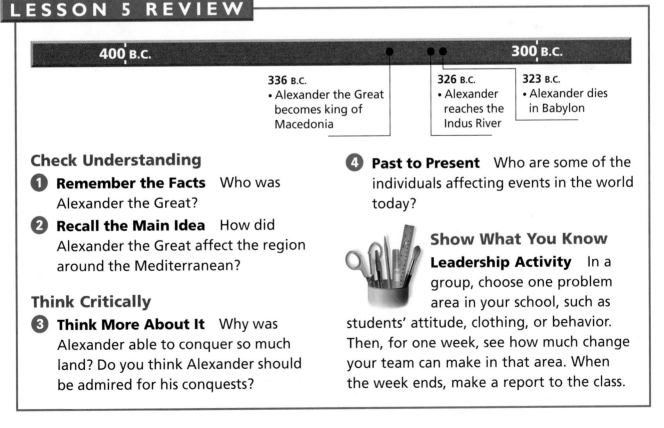

400 B.C.   300 B.C.

336 B.C.
• Alexander the Great becomes king of Macedonia

326 B.C.
• Alexander reaches the Indus River

323 B.C.
• Alexander dies in Babylon

Check Understanding

1 Remember the Facts Who was Alexander the Great?

2 Recall the Main Idea How did Alexander the Great affect the region around the Mediterranean?

Think Critically

3 Think More About It Why was Alexander able to conquer so much land? Do you think Alexander should be admired for his conquests?

4 Past to Present Who are some of the individuals affecting events in the world today?

Show What You Know

Leadership Activity In a group, choose one problem area in your school, such as students' attitude, clothing, or behavior. Then, for one week, see how much change your team can make in that area. When the week ends, make a report to the class.

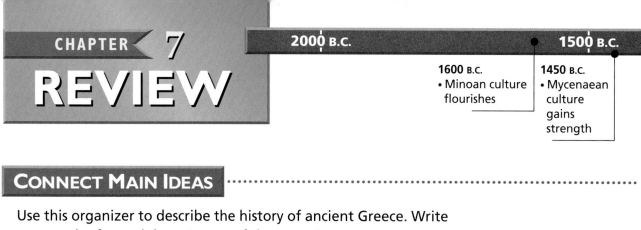

2000 B.C.

1500 B.C.

1600 B.C.
• Minoan culture flourishes

1450 B.C.
• Mycenaean culture gains strength

CONNECT MAIN IDEAS

Use this organizer to describe the history of ancient Greece. Write two examples for each box. A copy of the organizer appears on page 71 of the Activity Book.

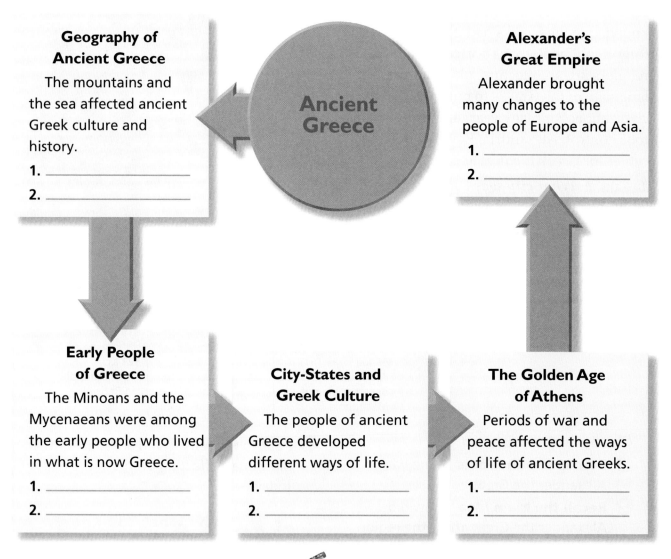

Geography of Ancient Greece

The mountains and the sea affected ancient Greek culture and history.

1. _____
2. _____

Ancient Greece

Alexander's Great Empire

Alexander brought many changes to the people of Europe and Asia.

1. _____
2. _____

Early People of Greece

The Minoans and the Mycenaeans were among the early people who lived in what is now Greece.

1. _____
2. _____

City-States and Greek Culture

The people of ancient Greece developed different ways of life.

1. _____
2. _____

The Golden Age of Athens

Periods of war and peace affected the ways of life of ancient Greeks.

1. _____
2. _____

WRITE MORE ABOUT IT

Write a Compare-and-Contrast Report
Write a report that compares and contrasts the city-states of Athens and Sparta. Discuss their governments and achievements.

Write a Description The poet Homer described Crete as "a rich and lovely land, washed by the waves on every side." Write your own description of Greek lands.

1000 B.C.   500 B.C.   B.C. | A.D.

800 B.C.
• Greek city-states begin to form

479 B.C.
• Golden Age of Athens begins

331 B.C.
• Alexander's empire reaches largest size

USE VOCABULARY

For each pair of terms, write at least one sentence that shows how the terms are different from each other.

1. epic, myth

2. acropolis, agora

3. aristocracy, oligarchy

4. league, alliance

CHECK UNDERSTANDING

5. Why was Greece a good center for trade?

6. Who was Homer?

7. For what did the Minoans use their huge palaces?

8. Why did the Spartans form a military culture?

9. What were three ways in which the people in the different Greek city-states felt a cultural connection with one another?

10. What people were not included in Athenian democracy?

11. How did winning the Persian Wars affect Athens?

12. Why is the period of Alexander's rule known as the Hellenistic Age?

13. What happened to Alexander's empire after his death? Why?

THINK CRITICALLY

14. **Past to Present** How is the present-day government of the United States like the Athenian government under Pericles? How is it different?

15. **Personally Speaking** Why do you think Alexander the Great wanted to control a large empire?

16. **Cause and Effect** How did the thinkers of the Hellenistic Age change people's understanding of the world?

APPLY SKILLS

Predict a Likely Outcome During the time of Alexander the Great, Greek culture strongly affected the Mediterranean region. Before you read Chapter 8, predict how the death of Alexander would change this. Be sure to use the three-step process listed on page 316. Write down your prediction. Then, as you read Chapter 8, see whether the information you learn supports your prediction.

READ MORE ABOUT IT

Alexander the Great by Robert Green. Franklin Watts. This biography tells details about the life of the conqueror, who built an empire in Europe and Asia. The author not only describes Alexander's early days but also provides a look at his life as a military leader.

HARCOURT BRACE

Visit the Internet at
http://www.hbschool.com
for additional resources.

ANCIENT ROME

"Veni, vidi, vici."

(I came,
I saw,
I conquered.)

Julius Caesar,
after a victory
in battle in 46 B.C.

Geography of Ancient Rome

After the death of Alexander in 323 B.C., control in the Mediterranean slowly shifted from the Balkan Peninsula to the peninsula of Italy. Over the centuries, many peoples had settled there, among them the Latins. The Latins migrated across the Alps from central Europe. These farmers and herders founded Rome in the eighth century B.C.

The Peninsula of Italy

The Italian peninsula lies just west of the Balkan Peninsula. It is shaped like a long, high-heeled boot. The peninsula is about 700 miles (1,127 km) long and only about 100 miles (161 km) wide for much of its length. The "toe" of the boot seems aimed to kick the nearby island of Sicily. Beyond Sicily, less than 100 miles (161 km) across the Mediterranean Sea, lies the northern coast of Africa.

Seas surround Italy on all sides except the north. The Tyrrhenian (tuh•REE•nee•uhn) lies to the west, the Adriatic to the east, and the Mediterranean to the south.

Along the northern border of Italy rises a range of snow-capped mountains called the Alps. The Alps separate the Italian peninsula from the rest of Europe. The steepest peak of the Alps rises as high as 15,771 feet (4,807 meters). Another range of mountains, the Apennines (A•puh•nynz), runs the length of the peninsula. Between these two high ranges lies an area of lower land called the Po Valley.

FOCUS

How does geographical location affect people and cities today?

Main Idea As you read, look for ways in which the geography of Italy contributed to the rise of the ancient Roman civilization.

Vocabulary

arable land
extinct volcano
forum

The Apennine Mountains stretch for 875 miles (1,408 km) northwest to southeast and then west to the southern tip of the Italian peninsula.

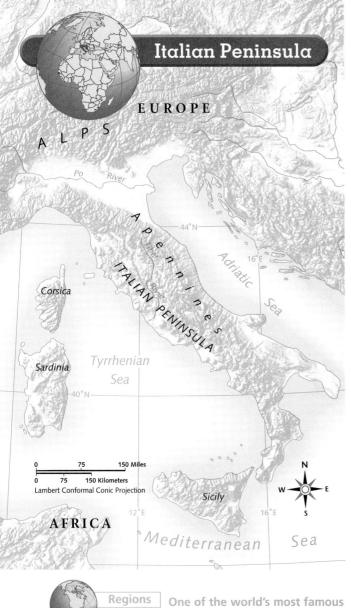

Italian Peninsula

EUROPE

ALPS

Po River

44°N

16°E

Adriatic Sea

Corsica

Apennines

ITALIAN PENINSULA

Sardinia

Tyrrhenian Sea

40°N

0   75   150 Miles
0   75   150 Kilometers
Lambert Conformal Conic Projection

Sicily

12°E   16°E

AFRICA

N
W   E
S

Mediterranean   Sea

Regions One of the world's most famous mountain ranges, the Alps, separates Italy from the rest of Europe.

■ *What other natural features separate Italy from neighboring lands?*

While some of Italy is made up of valleys and plains, most has higher elevations. However, the hills and mountains in Italy are less rugged than those in Greece. So land travel and trade were easier for the early people of Italy than for the early Greeks. Travel and trade by sea were more difficult, however. Although Italy has a long coastline, the peninsula has few good harbors. Because of this, the early people of

Italy traded more with each other than with outsiders across the seas.

REVIEW *How did geography affect the way early people of the Italian peninsula traded?*

Rich Farmland

"Tell me, all you who have journeyed through many lands, have you seen a more richly farmed land than Italy?" asked the Roman writer Varro in the first century B.C. From earliest times, the fertile land and mild climate of Italy attracted many settlers. The Italian peninsula had more arable (AIR•uh•buhl) land than the Balkan Peninsula, where the ancient Greeks lived. **Arable land** is land that can be used to grow crops. Early settlers were able to grow many different crops instead of importing them from other places.

Many rivers in Italy carry mineral-rich silt that creates good farmland. The peninsula's volcanoes have also made much of Italy's soil rich with volcanic ash. Most of the volcanoes have been extinct for a long time. An **extinct volcano** is a volcano that will never again erupt.

Around 1000 B.C. people from central Europe began migrating into the Italian peninsula. These people, who became known as the Latins, settled on land south of the Tiber River. There they raised crops, such as wheat and barley; peas, beans, and other vegetables; and figs, grapes, and olives. They also herded sheep, goats, and cattle. Latin women spun sheep's wool and wove it into fabric for clothing. These early farmers and herders were the ancestors of the Romans.

REVIEW *Why was the area along the Tiber River a good place to settle?*

The Founding of Rome

Around the eighth century B.C., a Latin community started on a hill overlooking a bend in the Tiber River. The area proved to be an excellent site, and the village grew into the city of Rome.

The land around Rome offered good soil for farming. It was also near supplies of wood and stone for building. The seven hills on which Rome was built could easily be defended. A stretch of level ground near the river provided a **forum**, a public place where people could meet and exchange goods and ideas.

Rome's inland location protected the city from pirates. Yet with the sea only about 15 miles (24 km) away, the Romans were close to sources of salt and fish.

Rome's location in the center of the peninsula was ideal for communication and trade with the rest of Italy. The Tiber River gave the Romans a route to the sea so that they could also trade with other Mediterranean civilizations. In time, partly because of its location, Rome gained control of sea routes linking Europe, Asia, and Africa. "Not without good reason did gods and men choose this spot as the site of a city," a Roman historian wrote.

Early settlers of Rome told colorful legends to explain how their city began. One legend told of the cruel brother of a Latin king who seized the throne from the rightful leader. When the real king's daughter gave birth to twin boys, the tyrant feared that the boys would grow up to take the throne from him. He left the babies to die on the banks of the Tiber River, but a mother wolf saved the twins and raised them. When Romulus and Remus grew to be adults, they defeated their great-uncle and made their grandfather king again.

Rome began alongside the Tiber River (below). According to legend, Romulus personally drew Rome's ancient boundaries (left).

Some of Italy's rich farmland can be seen in the Tuscany region (above). Many crops, including grapes (left), have been grown in Italy for centuries.

In 753 B.C., the legend says, the brothers set out to build their own city on the Tiber River near where they had been rescued long ago. They quarreled, however, over which hill to build the new city on, and Remus was killed. Romulus became the first ruler of the new city he founded. His followers named the city Rome in his honor. Romulus promised that the small city would someday rise to greatness. "My Rome shall be the capital of the world," Romulus said.

REVIEW *What advantages did the site of Rome offer?*

LESSON I REVIEW

Check Understanding

1 **Remember the Facts**   How is the Italian peninsula shaped? Where is it located?

2 **Recall the Main Idea**   How did geography contribute to the rise of Roman civilization?

Think Critically

3 **Think More About It**   What might be some of the advantages of having a capital located in the center of a country?

4 **Past to Present**   How do climate and the amount of arable land affect the way people live in your community today?

Show What You Know

Speech Activity   Imagine that you are an early Roman trader visiting a far-off land. Give a speech in which you describe the geography around Rome and how it helps your city. You may want to make a map that you can refer to as you speak.

The Roman Republic

| 600 B.C. | 300 B.C. | B.C. | A.D. |

From its beginning as a small village on the peninsula of Italy, Rome grew to control a great empire. Early Rome was ruled as a monarchy. As Rome grew, however, its form of government changed.

From Monarchy to Republic

In about 600 B.C. the Etruscans, a people from Italy's northern region, took control of Rome. The Etruscans, who often traded with the Greek colonies, brought Greek ideas and customs to the Romans.

After almost 100 years of Etruscan rule, the Romans rebelled. They ended the monarchy and started a new kind of government. Wealthy Romans elected leaders to make all government decisions. They called their new government a **republic**.

As in Athens, free men in the Roman Republic formed an assembly of citizens. Both assemblies had the right to declare war, make peace treaties, and build alliances. Unlike the assembly in Athens, however, the Roman assembly elected officials to represent Roman government.

FOCUS

What causes change in governments today?

Main Idea As you read, think about what caused changes in the government of ancient Rome.

Vocabulary

republic	patrician
consul	plebeian
dictator	tribune
senate	veto

The ancient Etruscans are particularly remembered for their fine art. This stone coffin, with the images of an Etruscan husband and wife, was made about 2,600 years ago. The Etruscans lived side by side with the Latins in ancient Italy. The people of Rome borrowed the Etruscan alphabet, technology, art, and customs as their own culture developed.

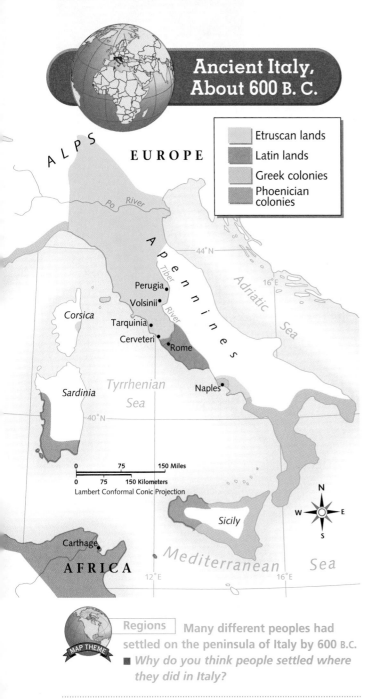

Ancient Italy, About 600 B. C.

EUROPE

ALPS

Po River

Apennines

44°N

Tiber River

Perugia
Volsinii
Tarquinia
Cerveteri
Rome

Corsica

Adriatic Sea

16°E

Naples

Sardinia

Tyrrhenian Sea

40°N

Sicily

Carthage

AFRICA

Mediterranean Sea

12°E   16°E

	Etruscan lands
	Latin lands
	Greek colonies
	Phoenician colonies

0   75   150 Miles
0   75   150 Kilometers
Lambert Conformal Conic Projection

N W E S

Regions Many different peoples had settled on the peninsula of Italy by 600 B.C.
■ *Why do you think people settled where they did in Italy?*

Each year the Roman assembly elected two chief officials called **consuls**. Having two consuls meant that no one person would gain too much power. The consuls led the armies, served as judges, and acted for the citizens of Rome. In an emergency, Romans could appoint a dictator for a six-month term. A **dictator** is a ruler with complete authority. In Rome a dictator could give orders that even the two consuls had to obey.

The elected consuls were advised by a governing body called the **senate**. Only some of Rome's citizens could hope to become senators. Early Roman citizens were divided into two groups. **Patricians** (puh•TRIH•shuhnz), who were the descendants of Rome's earliest settlers, formed one group. All other Roman citizens including farmers, merchants, soldiers, and craftworkers, made up the other group, called **plebeians** (plih•BEE•uhnz). The patricians controlled Rome's government and considered the plebeians to be less important.

In 494 B.C. the plebeians rebelled. They marched out of Rome to set up their own assembly. They then elected their own special officials called **tribunes**. The patricians realized that Rome's economy would suffer without the plebeians. They agreed to let the plebeians keep their assembly and tribunes. The tribunes could attend meetings

Slaves' Room

Kitchen

of the senate and **veto**, or refuse to agree to, any laws they did not like.

The plebeians also protested Rome's unwritten laws. Only patrician leaders knew exactly what the laws were. In 451 B.C. and 450 B.C., the Roman government began recording its laws on tablets called the Twelve Tables. The laws were posted in Rome's forum, or public square. Many plebeians could not read the laws. However, the fact that they were now written down meant that what they said was no longer hidden from the plebeians.

Because the laws were now common knowledge, the plebeians knew how their rights differed from those of the patricians. More and more, they began to ask for changes. In time the rights of plebeians and patricians became more nearly equal.

REVIEW *What form of government did the Romans set up after they freed themselves from Etruscan rule?*

Roman Society

Just as Roman citizens were divided into groups, so, too, was Roman society. A person's family and amount of wealth determined his or her class.

The Roman upper class was made up of wealthy patricians and wealthy plebeians. This class enjoyed the best Rome had to offer. Its members held jobs as government officials. Members of the upper class lived in large homes with many rooms, and their needs were taken care of by slaves. A large family of Rome's upper class might have owned 500 or more slaves.

LEARNING FROM DIAGRAMS Wealthy Romans lived in houses that also served as their place of business. It was not uncommon to find offices or stores inside Roman homes.

■ *What rooms shown below probably would not be part of a home of a less wealthy Roman? How is this home similar to a home of today? How is it different?*

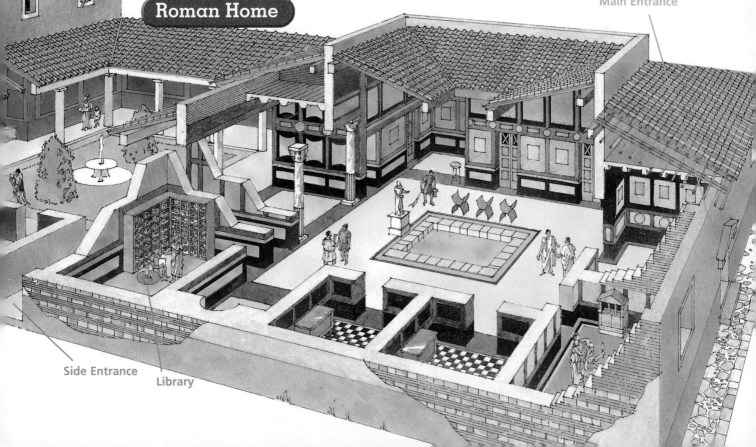

Roman Home

Main Entrance

Side Entrance

Library

This wall sculpture shows a group of Roman senators and a Roman woman and her servant. While Roman women did enjoy some freedoms, they were not allowed to take part in government.

The Roman lower classes were made up of all other citizens, ranging from the fairly wealthy to the very poor. Soldiers, farmers, merchants, and craftworkers all belonged to these groups. Unlike the very rich, these Romans lived in apartment-style dwellings. In some cases, entire families lived in one room.

As in other ancient civilizations, slaves were at the bottom of society. In Rome they were not counted as Roman citizens and were not as well protected by Roman law as Roman citizens were. They did have more rights than enslaved peoples in other parts of the world, however. Many were freed upon their owner's death or were given the chance to buy their freedom. Even so, living conditions for slaves depended completely on their owners.

In all classes, men ruled Roman households. Women did help make household decisions and often gave advice to their husbands. They were also allowed to own property. However, women took no direct part in government decision making.

REVIEW *How was Roman society divided?*

The Path of Roman Conquest

Starting in 500 B.C. the Romans extended their power through the whole peninsula of Italy. The Romans fought many wars to defend themselves from attack. With each victory the area under their control grew. By 272 B.C. all of the Italian peninsula belonged to Rome.

During this time, a strong rivalry developed between Rome and Carthage. Carthage was a city-state in northern Africa founded by the Phoenicians. Between 264 B.C. and 146 B.C., Rome fought three wars with Carthage. These wars are called the Punic (PYOO•nik) Wars, from the Roman word for Phoenician—*Punicus*.

One reason the wars started was because both Rome and Carthage wanted to control sea trade in the western Mediterranean. After a long fight Rome won the first Punic War. In the second Punic War, the city of Rome itself was threatened. Led by a general named Hannibal, Carthage's army marched on Rome. Starting in what is now Spain, Hannibal led his soldiers and war elephants over high, snow-covered mountains into Italy. A Roman historian wrote about Hannibal,

66 No work could tire his body or his spirit. Heat and cold were the same to him. . . . He was always the first into battle and the last to leave. 99

Although tired, the soldiers of Carthage surprised the Romans with sudden and violent attacks. They fought so fiercely that they nearly defeated Rome. Then a Roman general named Scipio (SIH•pee•oh) made a clever move. He left the Italian peninsula and attacked lands in northern Africa that were under the control of Carthage. Hannibal was forced to return to Africa to defend his home city. In 202 B.C. Hannibal lost an important battle in the town of Zama near Carthage, and Carthage had to give up.

In 146 B.C. the third and final Punic War left the city of Carthage in ruins. The Romans destroyed the entire city and sold many Carthaginians into slavery.

By this time Greece, Macedonia, and parts of southwestern Asia were also under Roman control. The Romans divided the land they now ruled into provinces. A Roman governor ruled each province. The people had to pay taxes to Rome, and some of them were taken there as slaves.

REVIEW *What lands did Rome conquer between 500 B.C. and 146 B.C.?*

From Republic to Dictatorship

The tax money that came from the provinces made the upper class richer, but the slaves who came made the lower classes poorer. Many plebeians lost their jobs or land because their work was turned over to slaves. This caused conflicts between the rich and the poor. Two brothers, Tiberius and Gaius Gracchus, tried to change the laws to help the poor. However, the senate would not agree to these changes. Both brothers were killed for their ideas.

For the next 50 years, many leaders tried to gain control of the republic. In 82 B.C., after a bloody civil war, Lucius Sulla became dictator. He ruled for three years, not for just the six months Roman law allowed. Sulla retired in

Hannibal's war methods are still studied by army leaders.

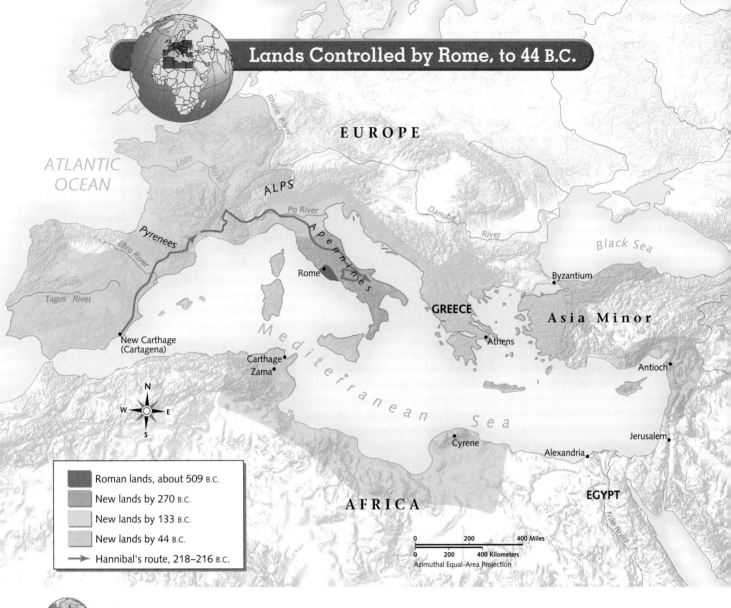

Lands Controlled by Rome, to 44 B.C.

EUROPE

ATLANTIC OCEAN

Rhine River

Loire River

ALPS

Po River

Pyrenees

Ebro River

Apennines

Danube River

Black Sea

Byzantium

Tagus River

Rome

GREECE

Asia Minor

New Carthage (Cartagena)

Athens

Carthage

Zama

Antioch

Mediterranean Sea

Cyrene

Jerusalem

Alexandria

AFRICA

EGYPT

Nile River

Roman lands, about 509 B.C.

New lands by 270 B.C.

New lands by 133 B.C.

New lands by 44 B.C.

Hannibal's route, 218–216 B.C.

0   200   400 Miles
0   200   400 Kilometers
Azimuthal Equal-Area Projection

Movement   By 44 B.C. Rome controlled much of Europe as well as parts of Africa.

■ *What advantages did Rome gain by conquering all the land around Italy?*

79 B.C., and the government was returned to consuls. Pompey and Cicero (SIH•suh•roh) were among those who served as consuls after Sulla gave up his power.

In 59 B.C. Julius Caesar, a Roman general, was elected consul. Caesar put together a careful plan to rule all Roman lands. His first move was to form an army and capture Gaul (what is now France). His success in winning Gaul for the Romans proved his military ability. As governor of the new province of Gaul, Caesar kept close watch on Rome.

In 49 B.C. Caesar prepared to return to Rome. By this time the senate feared that he would try to take over the Roman government. The senate warned Caesar not to bring his soldiers past the Rubicon River, the border between Gaul and Italy. "The die is cast," Caesar said as he crossed the Rubicon with his army and declared war on his enemies in Rome. Civil war raged for three years while Caesar fought his enemies for power.

In 46 B.C. Julius Caesar was appointed dictator for ten years. Caesar proved to be a strong leader. He improved many lives by making laws to help the poor. He also created new jobs and gave citizenship to more people.

In 44 B.C. Caesar became dictator for life. The republic had become a dictatorship. But Caesar's time of glory was short. Some senators and citizens feared that Caesar would make himself king. On March 15, known as the Ides of March on the Roman calendar, Caesar went to the senate without his bodyguards. He was stabbed to death by a group of senators. Caesar's death in 44 B.C. led to another time of civil war.

REVIEW *What kind of ruler was Julius Caesar?*

HISTORY

Roman Calendar

July, the seventh month of our modern calendar year, is named for Julius Caesar. Before Caesar's time, the calendar was not long enough to match the 365 days it takes Earth to orbit the sun. To solve this problem, Caesar added 67 days to the calendar. Then he made the first year of the new calendar very long to get the new calendar back on track. The year 46 B.C. had 445 days! The Romans called this unusual year "the year of confusion."

Julius Caesar

LESSON 2 REVIEW

| 600 B.C. | | 300 B.C. | | B.C. | A.D. |

500 B.C.
• Roman Republic begins

264 B.C.
• First Punic War begins

46 B.C.
• Julius Caesar becomes dictator of Rome

Check Understanding

1 Remember the Facts What three forms of government did Rome have between about 600 B.C. and 44 B.C.?

2 Recall the Main Idea What caused each change in Rome's government?

Think Critically

3 Past to Present Has our country ever changed its form of government? If so, describe the changes.

4 Explore Viewpoints Only patricians could become senators and consuls in the early Roman Republic. How might a patrician have felt about this? Why might a plebeian have felt differently?

Show What You Know

Writing Activity Imagine that you are a Roman citizen trying to get people to vote for you for a government office. Write a speech promising good government for Rome. Tell what you would do to help each class in society. Present your speech to a small group of classmates.

Make a Thoughtful

1. Why Learn This Skill?

Every action you take has a consequence, or result. Some consequences are short-term—they happen right away and last a short time. Other consequences are long-term—they happen in the future and last a long time. An action can also have either positive or negative consequences—or both. To make a thoughtful decision, you need to think about all the possible consequences before you take action.

2. Remember What You Have Read

You have read that between 264 B.C. and 146 B.C. Rome and Carthage fought three wars, called the Punic Wars, over control of the sea trade in the western Mediterranean. In the second Punic War, Carthage's army marched on Rome. Both Hannibal of Carthage and Scipio of Rome had important decisions to make.

Hannibal had to decide how he would attack Rome. He could make the easier, but expected, sea attack. Or he could travel to Spain and cross the Pyrenees and the Alps mountain ranges to attack from the north. Traveling over the high mountains and attacking from the north would be difficult. The Alps contained many dangers, including extreme cold and deep snow. Hannibal risked losing many soldiers. But

the advantage would be that Carthage's army could surprise the Roman army. Hannibal decided to take the risk and cross the mountain ranges. He set out on his dangerous journey with about 50,000 soldiers on foot, 9,000 cavalry, and 37 war elephants. Hannibal reached the Roman army with only about 26,000 of his soldiers left. However, the surprise attack was so successful that Carthage's army came close to defeating Rome in one battle. Hannibal's attack from the north gave Carthage an advantage over Rome.

The Roman general Scipio had to decide what to do in response to Hannibal's success. Scipio could stand and fight, or he could try a surprise move to catch Hannibal off guard.

Scipio realized that an unexpected action would be the best way to counter Hannibal's attack. Scipio had to think carefully about what that action would be. He decided to attack Carthage itself. This decision forced Hannibal to leave the Italian peninsula to fight Scipio's army in northern Africa.

Scipio's army defeated Hannibal at Zama in northern Africa in 202 B.C. The second Punic War ended in 201 B.C. with Rome the winner.

3. Understand the Process

To make a difficult decision, you can follow a set of steps that many people use

Decision

in their business and personal life. Following these steps can help you make your decision more thoughtfully.

1 Identify your goal.

2 Think about the problem that is keeping you from reaching your goal.

3 List the actions you could take. Begin with those you think would have the most positive consequences, and end with those you think would have negative consequences.

4 Make the choice that seems best.

5 Put your choice into action.

6 Think about whether your choice helped you reach your goal.

4. Think and Apply

Think about a decision that you have recently made at school. What steps did you follow to make your decision? What choice did you make? What were the consequences? Do you think you made a thoughtful decision? Explain.

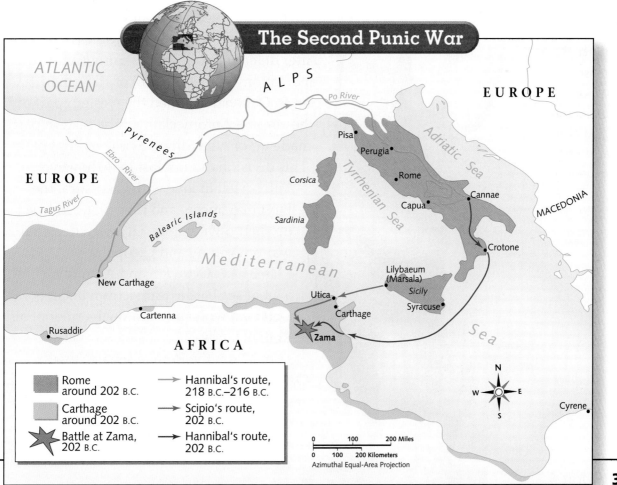

The Second Punic War

Legend:
- Rome around 202 B.C.
- Carthage around 202 B.C.
- ★ Battle at Zama, 202 B.C.
- → Hannibal's route, 218 B.C.–216 B.C.
- → Scipio's route, 202 B.C.
- → Hannibal's route, 202 B.C.

0 100 200 Miles
0 100 200 Kilometers
Azimuthal Equal-Area Projection

339

The Roman Empire

| 100 B.C. | | B.C. | A.D. | | A.D. 100 | | A.D. 200 |

After Julius Caesar's death a new leader rose up to rule the Roman lands. This new leader brought many different peoples into the Roman culture. Over the next few hundred years, more than 75 million people came to call themselves Romans.

FOCUS

What factors help unite many different peoples under one government today?

Main Idea
As you read, look for reasons that many peoples united under the Roman Empire.

Vocabulary

census
legion
basilica
gladiator
acid rain
aqueduct

Rome Becomes an Empire

After the death of Julius Caesar, the Roman senate and Caesar's supporters waged a civil war. Caesar's grand-nephew, Octavian (ahk•TAY•vee•uhn), and Mark Antony, a Roman general, led Caesar's armies into battle. After defeating the senate's army, Octavian and Antony gained control of all Roman lands. Octavian claimed the western part of the empire. Antony claimed the eastern part, made up of Asia Minor, Syria, and Egypt.

This division did not last long, however. Antony fell in love with Cleopatra, the Egyptian queen, and they planned to set up their own empire. Octavian declared war on Antony and Cleopatra.

In 31 B.C. Octavian and Antony met in a great sea battle near Actium in Greece. Octavian won and became the ruler of all Roman lands.

In 27 B.C. the Roman senate gave Octavian the title *Augustus*. The title means "respected one" or "holy one." Octavian has been known ever since as Augustus Caesar, or simply Augustus.

Julius Caesar's grandnephew, Octavian, later known as Augustus

This nineteenth-century watercolor shows how an Italian artist imagined daily events at the Roman Forum. Wealthy Romans built monuments in front of the forum as a display of wealth and to honor gods, events, or people.

Upon gaining control of Rome, Augustus boasted,

> ❝ I freed the Roman Republic from the control of those who assassinated Julius Caesar. . . . The Roman senate . . . and all the Roman people have called me 'Father of the Country.' ❞

Augustus was Rome's first true emperor, but he never used this title. He adopted the title *princeps*, meaning "first citizen," instead. Augustus knew that the idea of a republic was important to the Roman people, so he made sure his government seemed to be representative. But in fact, the Roman Republic ended when Augustus's long rule began.

REVIEW *Who became Rome's first emperor?*

The Age of Augustus

Augustus turned out to be both a strong and skilled leader. Under Augustus a *Pax Romana*, or Roman Peace, spread across the empire. This time of peace and unity for the

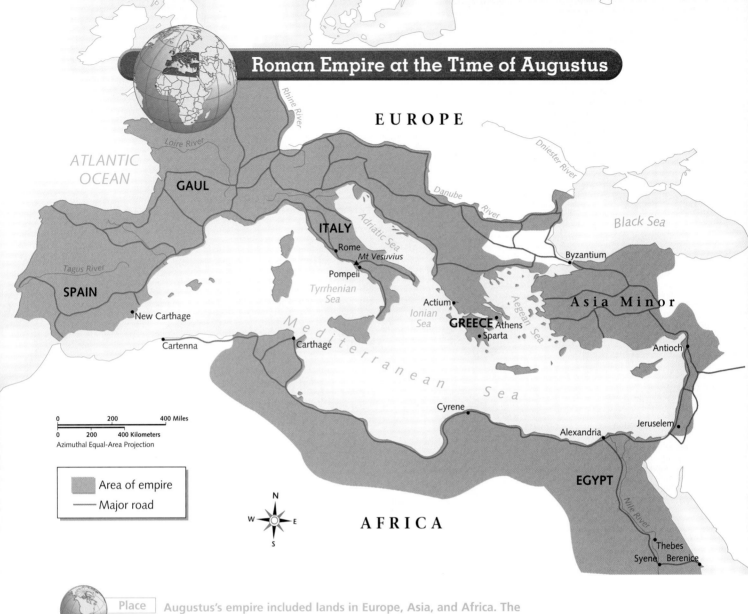

Roman Empire at the Time of Augustus

EUROPE

ATLANTIC OCEAN

GAUL

Rhine River

Loire River

Danube River

Dniester River

Black Sea

ITALY

Adriatic Sea

Rome
Mt Vesuvius
Pompeii

Byzantium

SPAIN

Tagus River

New Carthage

Cartenna

Carthage

Tyrrhenian Sea

Mediterranean Sea

Ionian Sea

Actium

GREECE Athens
Sparta

Aegean Sea

Asia Minor

Antioch

Cyrene

Alexandria

Jeruselem

0   200   400 Miles
0   200   400 Kilometers
Azimuthal Equal-Area Projection

Area of empire
Major road

N
W   E
S

AFRICA

EGYPT

Nile River

Thebes
Syena   Berenice

Place Augustus's empire included lands in Europe, Asia, and Africa. The Roman Empire stretched for thousands of miles.
■ *How do you think ancient Romans traveled to Carthage, by land or water?*

Romans lasted for more than 200 years—from 27 B.C. to A.D. 180. The empire grew to about 2½ million square miles (6½ million sq km) during this time.

Augustus carefully chose the people who would be the governors for the provinces. Like Julius Caesar, he passed laws that gave more people citizenship. These policies helped create a government that the people liked and that was strong enough to hold the empire together.

Before Augustus and after, new laws were created so that people would be treated more fairly. One law said that people could not be forced to speak against themselves in a court of law. This and other principles established by the Romans are important to our legal system today.

The Romans also were the first to take a **census**, a count of a country's people. The census helped the government make sure that all the people paid their taxes.

To protect his large empire, Augustus depended on the Roman army. This well-trained army was divided into large groups called **legions** (LEE•juhnz). A legion might have as many as 6,000 soldiers. Augustus ordered that legions stand guard along the borders of the empire to keep enemies out.

The roads the army built and traveled on united the Roman peoples. These Roman roads were built to help legions move quickly from province to province, but traders and travelers used them too. The roads connected almost all parts of the empire to Rome. This is where the saying "All roads lead to Rome" comes from. The Roman roads made possible the exchange of goods and ideas from all over the empire. This movement of ideas led to cultural borrowing between provinces.

REVIEW *How did the army's roads unite the peoples of the Roman Empire?*

Pride in Rome

Augustus felt that the city of Rome did not look grand enough for the center of a great empire. He built new government offices, libraries, temples, and public baths and rebuilt existing buildings. "I found Rome a city of bricks and left it a city of marble," he said.

Around the Palatine (PA•luh•tyn), the hill in the center of Rome, stood huge marble government buildings called **basilicas** (buh•SIL•ih•kuhz). New temples and other buildings rose beside them. In this area merchants sold fresh meats and vegetables, cloth, and pottery. The rich could buy fine things from faraway parts of the empire such as Egypt and Spain. For those who

---

HISTORY

Pompeii

The ancient Roman city of Pompeii was a successful trade center for many years. Then Mount Vesuvius, a volcano very near the city, erupted in A.D. 79. Lava and rocks covered the city, reaching depths of up to 9 feet (about 3 meters). Not long after, an additional 9 feet of ash fell on the city. People, houses, theaters, and forums were completely buried. For 17 centuries the city remained untouched. In the 1700s archaeologists began to dig up Pompeii. They found the ancient Roman city, left as it was in A.D. 79. Because Pompeii was trapped in time, we now know a great deal about the daily life of the ancient Romans.

This portrait of a young couple was found among the ashes of Pompeii. What do you think this portrait says about the people of Pompeii?

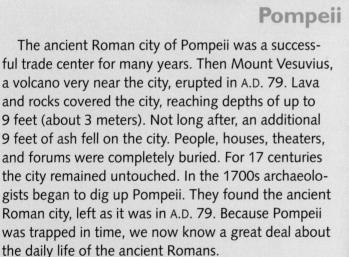

100 B.C.		B.C.	A.D.		A.D. 100

27 B.C.
• Roman Empire established

A.D. 79
• Eruption of Mt. Vesuvius

Colosseum

could read, there were papyrus scrolls filled with writing.

Ideas from Greek architecture could be seen in every building. Roman builders admired the beauty of Greek architecture and used Greek columns and beams in their own buildings. They also used arches, an idea they borrowed from the Etruscans. In addition, Roman architects added ideas of their own, such as domes.

Roman Road

The Romans enjoyed entertainment, so some of the new buildings were theaters and sports arenas. The largest arena, the Colosseum (kah•luh•SEE•uhm), was completed in A.D. 80, after Augustus's death. There as many as 50,000 Romans watched battles between gladiators. **Gladiators** were slaves and prisoners who were forced to fight, often to the death.

Rome's new look made leaders all over the empire want to rebuild their cities in the same way. As far away as Britain and Syria, people built forums in the centers of their cities. Around the forums they built temples, baths, libraries, and arenas.

Some of Rome's ancient buildings still stand. Acid rain has put the survival of these buildings in question, however. **Acid rain** is rainwater mixed with gases from burning fossil fuels, such as coal and oil. The gases and water form an acid that falls with rain and damages the stone of buildings and monuments.

Aqueduct

Ancient Rome

LEARNING FROM DIAGRAMS
Rome grew from a village of huts to become one
of the grandest cities the world has ever known. Below are
some of the main structures of Rome around A.D. 320.

1. Pantheon
2. Temple of Jupiter
3. Forum
4. Circus Maximus
5. Aqueduct of Claudius
6. Temple of the Divine Claudius
7. Arch of Constantine
8. Temple of Venus and Rome
9. Colosseum
10. Baths of Titus

■ *What two structures held sporting events in ancient Rome?*

Public Baths

The Romans built many large pools and baths. There people could take hot or cold baths. The baths also were places where people could meet friends or discuss business. Some Roman baths even contained libraries, gardens, theaters, and shops. The Romans built baths all over the lands they conquered. Ruins of Roman baths can be found in places such as Britain, France, Israel, Syria, Tunisia, and Algeria.

The Roman baths shown here are located in Bath, England.

All across the empire, the Romans built aqueducts (A•kwuh•duhkts). An **aqueduct** is a system of bridges and canals used to carry water from place to place. The stone aqueducts of the Roman Empire carried water from faraway rivers to the cities.

REVIEW *What kinds of buildings were put up in Rome?*

Arts, Literature, and Language

Rome controlled the Mediterranean region but often looked to Greece for cultural ideas. Roman artists, sculptors, and writers adopted the Greek styles. The ideas of the Greek philosophers Socrates, Plato, and Aristotle also spread to Rome. In fact, the children of many wealthy families were taught by Greek scholars. As the Roman poet Horace said,

66 Conquered Greece conquered its uncultured conqueror and brought the arts to Rome. 99

Augustus asked Roman artists and writers to create works that would bring out patriotic feelings among the Roman people. Above all Augustus wanted someone to write an epic to glorify Rome as the *Iliad* and the *Odyssey* had glorified Greece. A poet named Virgil (VER•juhl) did just that. Virgil wrote the *Aeneid* (ih•NEE•uhd), a story about a Trojan, Aeneas, who escapes during the Greek attack on Troy and finds a new home in Italy. In Virgil's telling of early Roman history, Romulus and Remus—the legendary founders of Rome—are descendants of Aeneas. The *Aeneid* stirred the feelings of Romans everywhere.

Other writers also made important contributions during this time. Among these were the historian Livy and the poet Horace.

Language also helped bring together the peoples of the Roman Empire. As Roman soldiers traveled through the provinces, they used the Latin language. The Latin alphabet came from the Etruscan alphabet, which was based on the Greek alphabet. Latin came to be used in government and education in all the Roman provinces.

REVIEW *In what ways did the arts and literature help unite the peoples of the Roman Empire?*

The Romans often borrowed many ideas from the Greeks. This statue of the Greek goddess Athena is a Roman copy of an early Greek statue.

LESSON 3 REVIEW

| 100 B.C. | B.C. | A.D. | A.D. 100 | A.D. 200 |

27 B.C.
• Pax Romana begins under Augustus

A.D. 180
• Pax Romana ends

Check Understanding

1 Remember the Facts What changes were made in Roman government and in the arts after Augustus became emperor of Rome?

2 Recall the Main Idea What helped unite the many different peoples of the Roman Empire?

Think Critically

3 Explore Viewpoints Why do you think Augustus liked to use peaceful methods to bring together the different people and cultures of his vast empire?

4 Past to Present Like the Roman Empire, the United States is a land of many cultures. What unites the people of the United States?

Show What You Know

Map Activity Using the map on page 342 as a guide, make a model or a relief map of the Roman Empire. Show the borders of the countries that now occupy these lands, and write in the names of the countries. Color in all the lands that made up the Roman Empire. Have a "showing" of student relief maps in your classroom.

Compare

1. Why Learn This Skill?

In Chapter 4 of Unit 2, you learned how to use a historical map. Some historical maps show where events in the past took place. Others show how places were in the past. Knowing how to compare historical maps can help you discover how a place was and how it has changed over time.

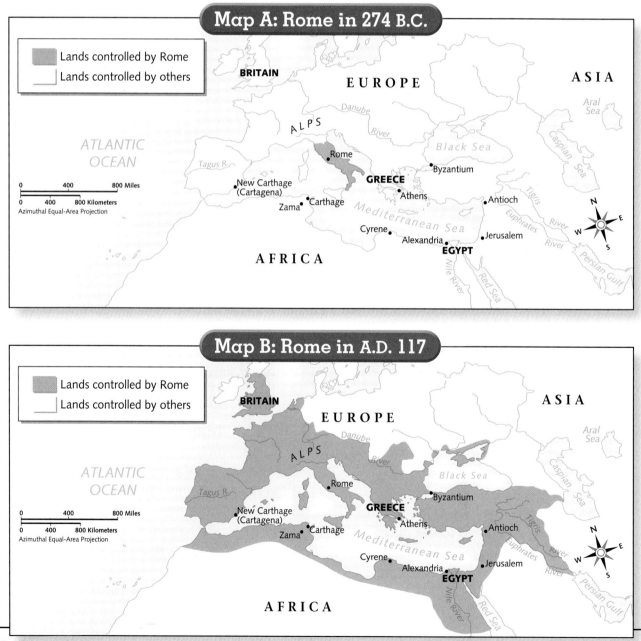

Map A: Rome in 274 B.C.

Lands controlled by Rome
Lands controlled by others

ATLANTIC OCEAN

BRITAIN
EUROPE
ASIA
Aral Sea
Danube River
ALPS
Black Sea
Caspian Sea
Rome
Byzantium
Tagus R.
GREECE
Athens
New Carthage (Cartagena)
Antioch
Zama • Carthage
Euphrates River
Mediterranean Sea
Tigris River
Cyrene
Jerusalem
Alexandria
EGYPT
AFRICA
Nile River
Red Sea
Persian Gulf

0   400   800 Miles
0   400   800 Kilometers
Azimuthal Equal-Area Projection

Map B: Rome in A.D. 117

Lands controlled by Rome
Lands controlled by others

ATLANTIC OCEAN

BRITAIN
EUROPE
ASIA
Aral Sea
Danube River
ALPS
Black Sea
Caspian Sea
Rome
Byzantium
Tagus R.
GREECE
Athens
New Carthage (Cartagena)
Antioch
Zama • Carthage
Euphrates River
Mediterranean Sea
Tigris River
Cyrene
Jerusalem
Alexandria
EGYPT
AFRICA
Nile River
Red Sea
Persian Gulf

0   400   800 Miles
0   400   800 Kilometers
Azimuthal Equal-Area Projection

Historical Maps

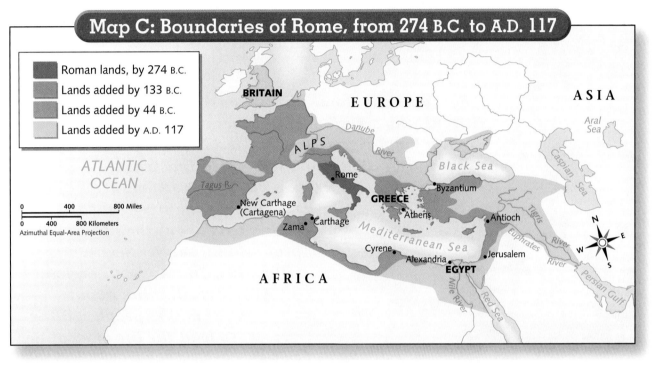

Map C: Boundaries of Rome, from 274 B.C. to A.D. 117

Roman lands, by 274 B.C.
Lands added by 133 B.C.
Lands added by 44 B.C.
Lands added by A.D. 117

ATLANTIC OCEAN

0   400   800 Miles
0   400   800 Kilometers
Azimuthal Equal-Area Projection

BRITAIN

EUROPE

ASIA

Aral Sea

Danube River

ALPS

Black Sea

Caspian Sea

Rome

Tagus R.

New Carthage (Cartagena)

Zama   Carthage

GREECE

Athens

Byzantium

Antioch

Tigris River

Euphrates River

Persian Gulf

Mediterranean Sea

Cyrene

Alexandria   Jerusalem

EGYPT

Nile River

Red Sea

AFRICA

N E S W

2. Understand the Process

Often the title or the key of a historical map tells what year or time period is shown on the map. Map A shows ancient Roman lands in 274 B.C. The purple areas on the map show lands governed by Rome. The cream-colored areas show lands controlled by other groups.

The Roman Empire grew until it reached its greatest size under the emperor Trajan in A.D. 117. As on Map A, the purple areas on Map B show lands governed by Rome. The cream-colored areas show lands controlled by other groups.

Now look at Map C. It combines information from Map A and Map B. It also shows how the boundaries of Rome changed from

274 B.C. to A.D. 117. Study the map key to learn what each color means. Then answer the questions below.

1 What lands did Rome add to its empire by 133 B.C.?

2 By what year did Rome take control of Britain?

3. Think and Apply

Use an atlas to find a historical map that shows the growth of the United States. Then write a paragraph that describes how and when your state became part of the United States. Draw your own map to go with your paragraph. Use different colors to show how the United States looked before and after your state joined it.

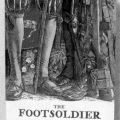

THE
FOOTSOLDIER
Martin Windrow & Richard Hook
OXFORD

THE FOOTSOLDIER

WRITTEN BY
MARTIN WINDROW AND RICHARD HOOK
ILLUSTRATED BY ANGUS MCBRIDE

For centuries Rome's army consisted of volunteers, citizens who served only in times of need. As the Roman Empire grew, leaders decided that the army needed professional soldiers—full-time trained fighters paid by the Roman government. The story that follows tells about the life of professional soldier Sextus Duratius, 2nd Augusta Legion. As you read, think about what makes people willing to lead the life of a soldier.

Roman soldiers protected
themselves with body
armor similar to the suit
shown above.

As a soldier, in what he considered the finest legion in the Empire, Sextus could hope for travel, adventure, and promotion: promotion, perhaps, to the unapproachable godlike status of a senior centurion, commanding a cohort[1] of 500 men. In return for hard knocks and unquestioning obedience he would receive 337½ silver pennies a year, in three installments—less compulsory[2] deductions for rations, boots, replacement of lost kit,[3] burial insurance, and anything else the penny-pinching clerks could think up. He might get handsome[4] bonuses from time to time—if he was in an important victory, or if a new Emperor came to power. Part of his pay would be safely banked for him, and if he survived his term of enlistment he would get a generous lump-sum pension, or a grant of land instead. It was not at all a bad deal—provided you lived to collect it.

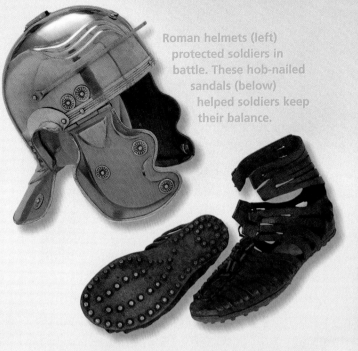

Roman helmets (left) protected soldiers in battle. These hob-nailed sandals (below) helped soldiers keep their balance.

During the first months Sextus often doubted that he would survive his first year. He learned the soldier's trade the hard way, harried about the parade ground and practice field by the brazen[5] tongues and vine-wood cudgels[6] of the instructing

---

[1]**cohort:** a part of a legion
[2]**compulsory:** required
[3]**kit:** supplies
[4]**handsome:** generous

[5]**brazen:** bold
[6]**cudgels:** heavy clubs

A legion of the Roman army on the move

centurions. He learned how to keep his armor clean and bright, even if it meant sitting up half the night. He learned how to march twenty-five miles a day in full kit, rain or shine, with hob-nailed sandals raising blisters on his blisters. As often as not he reeled back to barracks only to be herded straight off to the practice ground to dig ditches and build ramparts[7]— and to see them filled in again, ready for tomorrow's session. He learned to handle javelin, sword and shield. He suffered more bruises and grazes than he could count from the double-weight wooden swords they practiced with before being trusted with Roman steel in their shaky hands. He learned to recognize the signals for the different battle formations—the "wedge," the "saw," and all the other tricks of combat. And he learned just who, when, and how much to bribe, in order to avoid the frequent appearance of his name on the

centurion's little lists for latrine-cleaning, cookhouse-cleaning, camp-cleaning, and a dozen other traps for the unwary recruit. Before two years had passed he was a thoroughly trained, disciplined, and dangerous professional soldier.

It had been eight years before Sextus and his comrades started their long journey by foot and barge and ship from the familiar surroundings of Strasbourg, with its stone barracks and lively civilian town, to the empty beaches and rolling, forested hills of Britain. In that time he had served on two or three short local expeditions on the German frontier—nothing serious, not much more than tax-gathering trips enlivened by the occasional brisk skirmish.[8] He discovered that his training really worked, and that gave him confidence.

He had needed it, on this rather frightening expedition into the far northern mists. Only the gods knew what horrors awaited a man in these black woods and wind-haunted uplands, to say nothing of the dangers of drowning in the choppy grey seas or dying under the spears of the Britons. They were only savages, of course, but there had been a lot of them in some of the early battles of the invasion. But the magic of Roman arms and discipline worked again, and Sextus soon forgot his doubts and fears.

[7]**ramparts:** walls of earth

[8]**skirmish:** brief fight

Throughout the Roman Empire, soldiers built forts from which they could defend the land they had conquered.

When the Augusta was detached from the other legions and marched westwards things improved even more. Away from the eyes of the generals and staff officers, the Legate Vespasian proved a fair and decent commander. He expected his legionaries to do their duty, and do it quickly and thoroughly; but he didn't nag at men who were fighting almost every day.

Tonight, for instance, when the battle was over—and to judge from the thickening smoke and the noise from beyond the gateway it wouldn't be long now—Sextus could hope for a good night's rest. Perhaps the auxiliary cohorts which hadn't been in action would be ordered to dig the ramparts and pitch the tents for the men who had fought today? At any rate, Sextus probably wouldn't have to stand guard.

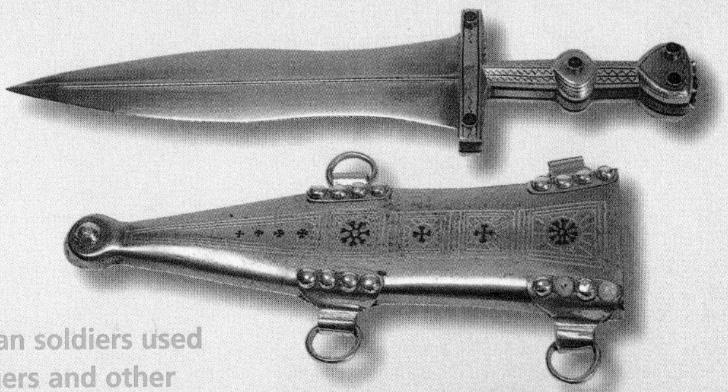

Roman soldiers used daggers and other weapons to win victory over their enemies. Shown above is a Roman dagger (top) and a dagger cover (bottom).

LITERATURE REVIEW

1. What was daily life in the Roman army like for Sextus?
2. Why do you think Sextus joined the army?
3. Do you think Sextus would want his son to join the army? Make a list of the good points and bad points Sextus might mention about serving as a Roman soldier.

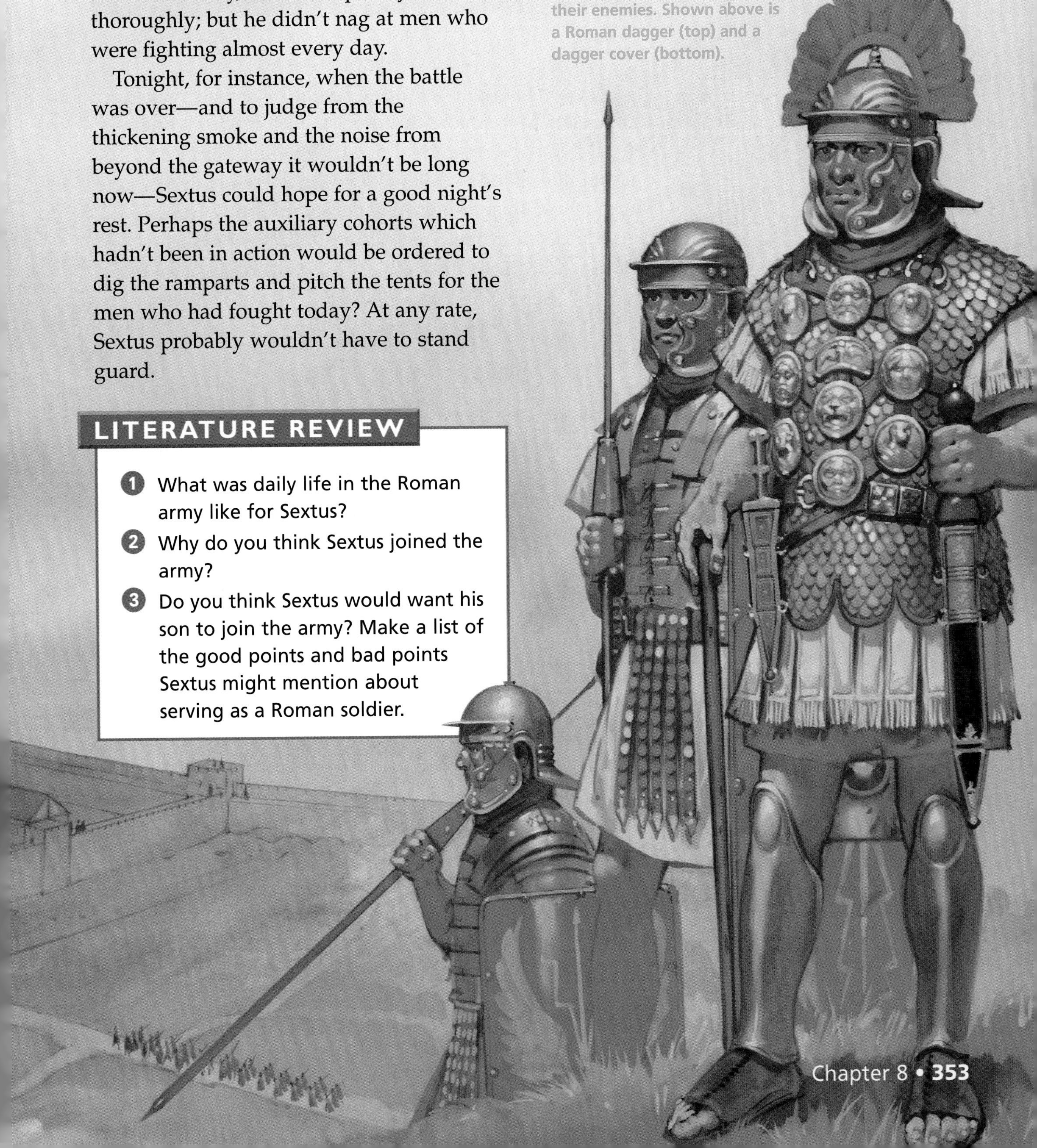

FOCUS

How do religions and
societies affect each
other today?

Main Idea As you
read, look for ways the
Christian religion and
Roman society affected
each other.

Vocabulary

parable
messiah
disciple
crucifixion
Christianity
apostle
persecute
martyr
Gospels
New Testament
Old Testament
pope

The Chi-Rho design (above)
was made during the early
days of Christianity. Chi and
Rho are the first two letters
of the word *Christ* in Greek.

Beginnings of
Christianity

B.C.	A.D.		A.D. 200	A.D. 400

Parts of the Roman Empire lay far from the city of
Rome itself. More than 1,200 miles (1,932 km) from their
central city, the Romans claimed the region of Judaea,
once known as Judah. Many Jews, the descendants of
the Israelites, lived in this distant region. Today, Judaea
is remembered by many people around the world as the
birthplace of Christianity.

Religion and the
Roman Empire

Augustus was not only the ruler of the Roman Empire
but also a leader of Rome's religion. As a religious leader,
he wanted all citizens to take part in religious ceremonies.
He believed that this would help unite the many groups
of Romans.

Like most cultures of long ago, the Romans worshipped
many gods. Of all their gods, Jupiter was believed to be the
most powerful. Other Roman gods included Mars, the god
of war, and Ceres, the goddess of the harvest.

Although the Romans had their own religion, they often
adopted the gods and the beliefs of the people whom they
conquered. The Romans also came to identify some of the
gods they already believed in with the gods of other peoples. For example, the Roman goddess Juno, who protected
marriage and women, came to be like the Greek goddess
Hera. Jupiter, the main Roman god, began to match Zeus,
the ruler of the Greek gods. The Roman religion even
included myths borrowed from the Greeks.

Belief in the gods was an important part of Roman life.
The Romans thought that harm would come to the empire
if people did not respect the Roman gods. So Roman law
punished those who discouraged worship of Roman gods.

As time passed, the Romans began to treat their emperor as a god. Anyone who refused to worship the emperor was considered an enemy of the empire.

Roman control over religion was not always carried out, however. For example, the Romans allowed the Jewish people to follow their own religious leaders, laws, and teachings. Jews lived not only in the Roman-controlled land of Judaea but also throughout the Roman Empire. Although Jews were allowed to live among the Romans, they were often mistreated.

REVIEW *Why did the Romans want everyone to respect the Roman gods?*

Jesus and His Teachings

In Judaea events were happening that would affect the whole Roman Empire. A child named Jesus was born to a woman named Mary in the village of Bethlehem in Judaea. For much of his early life, Jesus lived in the town of Nazareth (NA•zuh•ruhth). Later there were reports that he was teaching new ideas and performing miracles.

As he traveled through Judaea, Jesus taught belief in one God and in the Ten Commandments just as other Jewish teachers did. Yet in some ways his teachings were very different from theirs. Jesus told of the coming of the kingdom of God. He called on people to turn away from sin, or going against the word of God, so that they could be a part of God's kingdom. Jesus explained that God was loving and would forgive those who were sorry for their sins.

Jesus also encouraged his listeners to love one another, saying, "You shall love your neighbor as yourself." Enemies, too, were to be forgiven and loved. He said,

> 66 You have heard it said, 'You shall love your neighbor and hate your enemy.' But I say to you, 'Love your enemies and pray for those who persecute you.' 99

To make his ideas clear, Jesus often used parables. A **parable** (PAIR•uh•buhl) is a story that teaches a religious idea. One of Jesus' parables is about a prodigal, or wasteful, son. It tells the story of a young man who demanded his share of his father's wealth. With this wealth the young man left home to travel. After he had spent all his money, the young man realized that he had acted foolishly. He decided to return home and seek work on his father's farm. The father forgave his son immediately and welcomed him back into the family. Jesus used the parable of the prodigal son to make the point that God forgives and that people should do the same.

Jesus called himself the Good Shepherd because he tended human souls as one might tend sheep.

Chapter 8 • **355**

THE BEATITUDES

The Beatitudes (bee•A•tuh•toodz) are groups of statements made by Jesus. They appear in the New Testament. The following beatitudes are in the Sermon on the Mount, a lesson he gave on a hillside. (Matthew 5:3-12)

Blessed are the poor in spirit, for theirs is the kingdom of heaven.

Blessed are those who mourn, for they will be comforted.

Blessed are the meek, for they will inherit the earth.

Blessed are those who hunger and thirst for righteousness, for they will be filled.

Blessed are the merciful, for they will receive mercy.

Blessed are the pure in heart, for they will see God.

Blessed are the peacemakers, for they will be called children of God.

Blessed are those who are persecuted for righteousness' sake, for theirs is the kingdom of heaven.

Blessed are you when people revile you and persecute you and utter all kinds of evil against you falsely on my account.

Rejoice and be glad, for your reward is great in heaven.

Wherever Jesus spoke, he gained new followers. One belief of Judaism is that a **messiah** (muh•SY•uh) will come to bring justice to the world. Some people believed Jesus was the messiah.

Many people, however, did not believe this and did not accept Jesus' ideas. Some Jewish leaders disliked the fact that Jesus and his **disciples** (dih•SY•puhlz), or followers, did not strictly follow Jewish law. Often the teachings of Jesus caused great debate among the Jewish people living in the Roman Empire.

REVIEW *How did Jesus spread his ideas?*

Jesus' Teachings Spread

Like Jewish leaders, Roman leaders also became concerned as more and more people listened to the words of Jesus. They thought that Jesus might take over the empire and set up his own kingdom. In about A.D. 30 Pontius Pilate, the Roman governor of Judaea, ordered that Jesus be put to death by **crucifixion** (kroo•suh•FIK•shuhn). This meant that Jesus was to be nailed to a cross and left to die.

Jesus' message did not end with his death, however. On the third day after his death, Jesus' disciples reported that he had risen from the dead and appeared to them. The disciples were sure from this that Jesus was the messiah. They began to tell of Jesus' resurrection, or return from death, as well as his teachings.

Soon the Roman roads that connected the empire carried the story of Jesus and his teachings far and wide. Wherever Jesus' disciples traveled, they gained new believers. Later followers preached

Catacombs (above) were underground tunnels used as burial places for Christians persecuted and killed by the Romans. Many catacombs were decorated with paintings of early Christian scenes (above inset) or funeral writings (left).

in Greek in the eastern part of the Roman Empire. The Greek word for *messiah* was *christos*. Jesus came to be known as Jesus Christus, or Jesus Christ. His growing number of followers became known as Christians and their religion as **Christianity**.

Among the first to spread the word of Jesus were the **apostles**, a group of twelve men who had been Jesus' closest followers, plus one who joined them later. Peter, the leader of the apostles, was very courageous in spreading the word of Jesus. He talked first to the Jews in Jerusalem and then to both Jews and non-Jews in other parts of the empire.

Paul, a later apostle, was another important teacher of Christianity. Paul was a new believer in Christianity. After he became a convert, he spent the rest of his life explaining the teachings of Jesus to others, converting both Jews and non-Jews to Christianity. Wherever he went in the empire he began Christian communities.

REVIEW *How did the teachings of Jesus continue to spread after his crucifixion?*

Rome and the New Religion

Christianity caused concern for Roman leaders. The Romans allowed people to have other religious beliefs as long as they also worshipped the Roman gods. The Roman leaders believed that their gods would become angry because the Christians did not worship them. Therefore, they began to persecute the Christians. To **persecute** someone is to punish him or her for following certain religious beliefs. Often they ordered the death of Christians who would not worship the

The Spread of Christianity

EUROPE

ATLANTIC OCEAN

Rhine R.

Danube River

Black Sea

Caspian Sea

Rome

Constantinople

Asia Minor

Edessa

Antioch

Granada

Mediterranean Sea

Damascus

Carthage

Jerusalem

AFRICA

Cyrene

Alexandria

Nile R.

Red Sea

ASIA

N
W — E
S

▨ Converted to Christianity before Constantine, about A.D. 312

▨ Converted to Christianity after Constantine, about A.D. 400–A.D. 600

— Roman Empire, about A.D. 400

0   250   500 Miles
0   250   500 Kilometers
Azimuthal Equal-Area Projection

Movement Constantine helped Christianity grow by making it the official religion of the Roman Empire.
■ *How many continents had Christianity reached by A.D. 400?*

MAP THEME

Roman gods. Christians were killed in cruel ways such as by crucifixion.

Pliny the Younger, a Roman government official in Asia Minor around A.D. 112, explained his actions in this way:

❝ With those who have been brought before me as Christians, I have acted as follows: I asked them whether they were Christians. If they answer yes twice, I threaten to punish them and ask a third time. Those who continue to say yes, I order executed. . . . I dismissed those who said they had never been Christians and those who offered sacrifices to our gods. ❞

Roman persecution did not stop Christianity. In fact, the persecutions made many Christians more determined to hold on to their beliefs. Many Christians became **martyrs** (MAR•terz), or people who willingly died for their beliefs. Polycarp (A.D. 69–155), an 86-year-old bishop from Asia Minor, was one such martyr. When he was brought before the Roman governor, he was given several chances to give up his beliefs. Polycarp refused, saying he had served Jesus for many years and would not stop. The example of Polycarp and other martyrs helped other Christians to remain strong in their beliefs.

In A.D. 313 the persecution of Christians came to an end. This happened because of

358 • Unit 4

the actions of the new Roman emperor, Constantine (KAHN•stuhn•teen).

The year before, Constantine, then a general in the Roman army, had fought another general for the right to become emperor. Their armies faced each other at Rome's Milvian Bridge. Just before the battle something happened that changed Constantine's life. He reported that the Greek letters for the word *Christ*—*chi rho*—appeared in the sky above him. Over these letters were written the Latin words *in hoc signo vinces*, which means "In this sign you will conquer." So Constantine ordered his soldiers to paint crosses—symbols for Jesus—on their shields. Constantine won the battle and became emperor.

Because of this victory, Constantine believed that the God of the Christians was a powerful god. In A.D. 313 he issued the Edict of Milan, which made Christianity an accepted religion. Throughout his reign as emperor, Constantine supported Christianity.

REVIEW *How did Roman persecution affect the Christians?*

The Growth of Christianity

In A.D. 392, Christianity became the official religion of the Roman Empire under the rule of the Roman emperor Theodosius (thee•uh•DOH•shuhs). From this time on, the number of Christians steadily grew.

Writings by Christians played an important role in the growth of the new religion. Many of the letters that Paul wrote to members of the communities he founded were saved and shared with other Christians.

Today Christianity is practiced throughout the world. At right is a service in Lewisburg, Pennsylvania. Below, Christians worship in Nairobi, Kenya.

Other Christian writings were grouped to form the **Gospels**, which describe Jesus' life, death, and resurrection. The word *gospel* means "good news." The Gospels are made up of four books: Matthew, Mark, Luke, and John. These and other Christian writings were combined to form the **New Testament**. This part of the Christian Bible tells about the life and teachings of Jesus and about his followers. The first part of the Bible, the **Old Testament**, contains the books of the Hebrew Bible.

As Christianity grew, it became more organized. Each group chose a single leader called a bishop. Some people believe Peter served as an early bishop. Over time, the role of the bishop of Rome grew into the position of pope, the leader of all the bishops. Today the **pope** is the head of the Roman Catholic Church. The pope oversees the Catholic Church from the smallest country in the world—Vatican City, in Rome.

After the Edict of Milan, Roman emperors and society supported and even encouraged the growth of Christianity. Emperors helped Christians build churches and supported their work.

Since Christianity's early days, there have been many divisions. The first of these was when the Christian Church split into the Roman Catholic Church in the west and the Eastern Orthodox Church in the east. Another important split came with the beginning of Protestantism in the 1500s. At the same time, the religion has seen tremendous growth. Today almost 2 billion people around the world follow the religion of Christianity.

REVIEW *How did the support of Roman emperors affect Christianity?*

LESSON 5 REVIEW

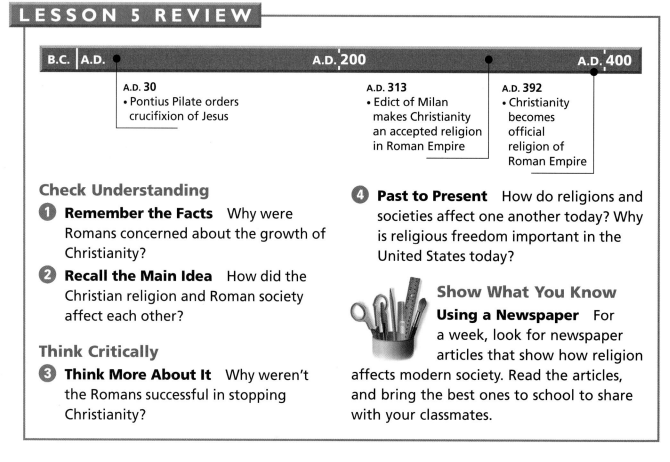

B.C. | A.D. — A.D. 200 — A.D. 400

A.D. 30
• Pontius Pilate orders crucifixion of Jesus

A.D. 313
• Edict of Milan makes Christianity an accepted religion in Roman Empire

A.D. 392
• Christianity becomes official religion of Roman Empire

Check Understanding

1 **Remember the Facts**   Why were Romans concerned about the growth of Christianity?

2 **Recall the Main Idea**   How did the Christian religion and Roman society affect each other?

Think Critically

3 **Think More About It**   Why weren't the Romans successful in stopping Christianity?

4 **Past to Present**   How do religions and societies affect one another today? Why is religious freedom important in the United States today?

Show What You Know

Using a Newspaper   For a week, look for newspaper articles that show how religion affects modern society. Read the articles, and bring the best ones to school to share with your classmates.

Read Telescoping Time Lines

1. Why Learn This Skill?

Just as a telescope helps you take a closer look at a faraway object, a **telescoping time line** helps you take a closer look at a long-ago time. Knowing how to read a telescoping time line can help you learn the details of events in history.

2. Understand the Process

The time line of early Christianity on this page shows the years between A.D. 1 and A.D. 350. Each date on the main part of the time line marks a period of 50 years.

Many important events happened between the years A.D. 310–330. To show these events clearly, part of the time line was expanded, or enlarged. The expanded part of the time line gives a "telescope" view of that time period. Each of its dates marks a period of only 5 years.

Use the information on both parts of the time line to answer these questions:

1. Which event took place first, the issuing of the Edict of Milan or the death of Constantine? How do you know?

2. Was the Edict of Milan issued before or after Constantine became emperor? How do you know?

3. Did Constantinople become the capital of the Roman Empire before or after Constantine's death? How do you know?

3. Think and Apply

Use events of your school year to make your own telescoping time line. Show one month in detail by including an expanded section. Share your time line with a family member.

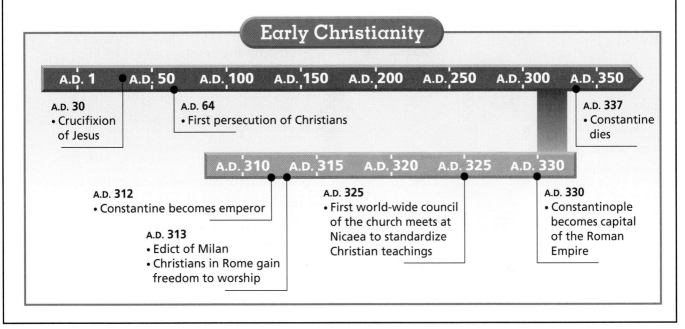

Early Christianity

A.D. 1 | A.D. 50 | A.D. 100 | A.D. 150 | A.D. 200 | A.D. 250 | A.D. 300 | A.D. 350

A.D. 30
• Crucifixion of Jesus

A.D. 64
• First persecution of Christians

A.D. 337
• Constantine dies

A.D. 310 | A.D. 315 | A.D. 320 | A.D. 325 | A.D. 330

A.D. 312
• Constantine becomes emperor

A.D. 313
• Edict of Milan
• Christians in Rome gain freedom to worship

A.D. 325
• First world-wide council of the church meets at Nicaea to standardize Christian teachings

A.D. 330
• Constantinople becomes capital of the Roman Empire

FOCUS

What forces could cause a country today to break apart?

Main Idea Look for reasons Roman rule weakened in the western half of the empire.

Vocabulary

barbarian
vandal

Rome's Decline in the West

| A.D. 200 | A.D. 300 | A.D. 400 | A.D. 500 |

By the middle of the second century A.D., the Roman Empire faced many problems. For one thing, several emperors, including Constantine, tried to keep the Roman Empire strong. However, even the efforts of strong rulers could not protect the empire from decline. It had grown too large to be managed easily. In addition, the empire's rule was being challenged by peoples both outside and within.

Trouble in the Roman Empire

A Roman historian living in the third century A.D. contrasted the period he lived in with the earlier days of the empire. "Our history," he wrote, "now plunges from a kingdom of gold to one of iron and rust."

The *Pax Romana*, which brought peace for two centuries, ended during the A.D. 160s. At this time outsiders began to attack the empire along its borders. These people were known to the Romans as **barbarians**. The Greeks had developed this term because they thought the speech of outsiders sounded like "bar, bar, bar."

Throughout much of the A.D. 200s, outsiders threatened the empire on three sides. Germanic tribes from the north attacked Greece and Gaul. In the east the Persians attacked Roman territory in Asia. In the south an African people called the Berbers (BER•berz) raided Roman lands in northern Africa.

Roman emperor Constantine

To make matters worse, many Roman emperors ruled poorly during these uneasy times. No one seemed to be able to govern such a large region, and civil wars often broke out. Tyrants seized control of the government in Rome, but they often ruled only a short time before being overthrown and killed. Twenty-five different emperors ruled in less than 50 years.

Roman citizens began to lose respect for their rulers during this time. Even the soldiers who fought to keep the Roman Empire together felt little loyalty toward it. Instead they gave their loyalty to their generals, who were fighting one another.

The political conflicts within the Roman Empire caused its economy to suffer. Trade declined, and Roman money lost value. The prices of food rose dramatically, bringing many hardships to the Roman people.

REVIEW *What problems did the Romans face during much of the A.D. 200s?*

The Roman Empire Splits in Two

As the third century drew to a close, better times returned to the Roman Empire. In A.D. 284, a leader named Diocletian (dy•uh•KLEE•shuhn) came to power. Emperor Diocletian made many changes to strengthen the government. A fourth-century writer described him as "the man whom the state needed."

One of his changes was to divide the leadership of the Roman Empire. Diocletian put a trusted friend in charge of the western part. He then gave most of his attention to the eastern part.

Diocletian's actions led the way for other strong leaders to rebuild the strength of the empire. One of these was Constantine. Constantine not only made Christianity an accepted religion but also helped keep the Roman Empire alive.

The Hagia Sophia, built from A.D. 532 to A.D. 537 in Constantinople, gives evidence of the wealth of the eastern part of the Roman Empire.

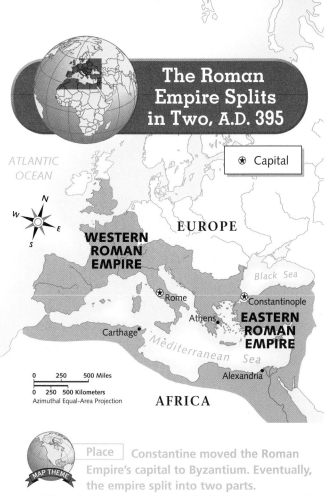

The Roman Empire Splits in Two, A.D. 395

● Capital

ATLANTIC OCEAN

EUROPE

WESTERN ROMAN EMPIRE

Black Sea

● Rome

⊛ Constantinople

Athens

EASTERN ROMAN EMPIRE

Carthage

Mediterranean Sea

Alexandria

AFRICA

0 250 500 Miles
0 250 500 Kilometers
Azimuthal Equal-Area Projection

MAP THEME | Place | Constantine moved the Roman Empire's capital to Byzantium. Eventually, the empire split into two parts.

■ *Which city became the capital of the eastern part?*

Like Diocletian, Constantine focused on the eastern part of the empire. In A.D. 330 Constantine moved the empire's capital from Rome to the eastern city of Byzantium (buh•ZAN•tee•uhm). A Roman historian boasted,

❝ Byzantium occupies a position the most secure and in every way the most advantageous of any town in our quarter of the world. ❞

Nearly surrounded by water, Byzantium was easy to defend against attack and was well-located for trade. Constantine renamed the city Constantinople in his own honor. Soon Constantinople replaced Rome as the most important city of the Roman Empire. Today, Constantinople is known as Istanbul (is•tuhn•BOOL), Turkey.

In A.D. 395, the empire officially split in two. The east would see the growth of cities and trade. The west would see decline.

REVIEW *How did the Roman Empire divide into two parts?*

A Time of Invasions

During the late 300s and the 400s, the Romans faced more attacks by Germanic tribes. Even the huge Roman army could not guard all of the border of the empire.

Many different Germanic tribes began to enter Roman territory. Their goal was to find new lands to settle on. Their own lands were being taken over by the Huns, a people from central Asia who were migrating westward.

The Visigoths invaded the Danube River region in A.D. 378. Led by Alaric (A•luh•rik), they captured Rome in A.D. 410 and looted the city.

Another tribe, the Vandals, crossed the Rhine River into Gaul in A.D. 406 and spread southwest into what is now Spain. They crossed the Mediterranean into northern Africa and from there attacked Rome in A.D. 455. In Rome they stole items of value and destroyed monuments. Today we use the word **vandal** to describe someone who purposely damages property.

In A.D. 476, a Germanic chief named Odoacer (OH•duh•way•ser) overthrew the Roman emperor in the west.

This helmet, found in Britain, belonged to an Anglo-Saxon king.

A Roman emperor continued to rule—but only from Constantinople.

Germanic tribes continued to claim Roman lands in the west. The Angles and the Saxons attacked and conquered Britain. The Franks invaded northern Gaul. In A.D. 486 Clovis, a leader of the Franks, captured the last Roman territory in Gaul.

By A.D. 500, the western part of the Roman Empire had separated into several kingdoms. Visigoths ruled in Italy, Spain, and southern Gaul. Franks held northern Gaul. Angles and Saxons were spreading out through Britain.

REVIEW *How did Roman rule end in the western part of the Roman Empire?*

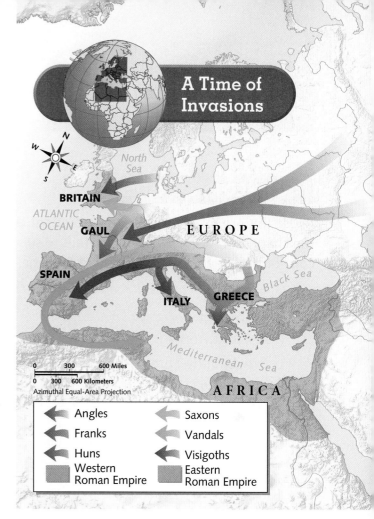

A Time of Invasions

Angles	Saxons
Franks	Vandals
Huns	Visigoths
Western Roman Empire	Eastern Roman Empire

Movement **Many different Germanic tribes invaded the western Roman Empire.**
■ *Which tribes invaded Britain? North Africa? Greece?*

LESSON 6 REVIEW

A.D. 200   A.D. 300   A.D. 400   A.D. 500

A.D. 200s
• Invaders threaten Roman Empire

A.D. 284
• Diocletian takes throne as strong emperor

A.D. 395
• Roman Empire splits in two

A.D. 476
• Odoacer overthrows western Roman emperor

Check Understanding

1 **Remember the Facts** What Germanic tribes attacked the Roman Empire?

2 **Recall the Main Idea** Why did Roman rule weaken in the western part of the empire?

Think Critically

3 **Think More About It** The eastern Roman Empire continued to prosper under strong leaders. Do you think strong leaders could have saved the western empire? Explain.

4 **Cause and Effect** What do you think caused the Roman Empire to split apart?

Show What You Know

Role Play Imagine that you are the Roman emperor Diocletian. Make a list of ways you believe you can improve the empire. Pair up with another student. Present a brief speech that outlines your suggested improvements. Then listen as your partner acts as Diocletian.

CHAPTER 8
REVIEW

600 B.C.		400 B.C.	

500 B.C.
• Roman Republic
  begins

264 B.C.
• First Punic
  War starts

CONNECT MAIN IDEAS

Use this organizer to show the growth of the Roman Empire and the changes it faced. Write two details to support each main idea. A copy of the organizer may be found on page 82 of the Activity Book.

**Geography of
Ancient Rome**

The geography of the Italian peninsula contributed to the rise of ancient Roman civilization.

1. _____

2. _____

The Roman Republic

Over the years the government of Rome changed.

1. _____

2. _____

Ancient Rome

The Roman Empire

Many peoples were united under the Roman Empire.

1. _____

2. _____

**Beginnings of
Christianity**

Christianity spread throughout the Roman Empire.

1. _____

2. _____

**Rome's Decline
in the West**

Roman rule weakened in the western half of the Roman Empire.

1. _____

2. _____

WRITE MORE ABOUT IT

Write a Speech Write a speech that you, as Roman emperor, will give about why Romans were able to unite many different peoples under one empire.

Write a Diary Entry Imagine that you are a Roman soldier during the time of the Punic Wars. Write a diary entry that describes your thoughts about fighting Hannibal's army.

| 200 B.C. | B.C. | A.D. | A.D. 200 | A.D. 400 |

27 B.C.
• Roman Empire forms

A.D. 30
• Crucifixion of Jesus

A.D. 313
• Christianity becomes an accepted religion in the Roman Empire

A.D. 395
• Roman Empire splits

USE VOCABULARY

For each pair of terms, write at least one sentence that shows how the terms are related.

1. patrician, plebeian
2. tribune, veto
3. republic, consuls
4. Christianity, New Testament

CHECK UNDERSTANDING

5. Who were Romulus and Remus?
6. Why did the Romans set up a republic?
7. How did Julius Caesar plan to rule Rome?
8. Why did Augustus call for new buildings in Rome?
9. Which culture's ideas could be seen in every new Roman building?
10. Why did Roman leaders persecute Christians?
11. What made Constantine begin to support Christianity?

THINK CRITICALLY

12. **Personally Speaking** Do you think that Julius Caesar was right to declare himself dictator of Rome? Explain your answer.
13. **Past to Present** What Roman principles are still important to the United States legal system?
14. **Think More About It** Why did the cruel actions of Roman leaders make many Christians hold on to their beliefs more strongly?

APPLY SKILLS

Compare Historical Maps Use Map C on page 349 and the map on page 358 to answer these questions.

15. Was the Roman Empire larger in A.D. 400 or in A.D. 117?
16. By A.D. 600 had Christianity come to all the lands that had belonged to the Roman Empire in A.D. 117?

Read Telescoping Time Lines Use the information on the time line on page 361 to answer the questions.

17. Did Constantine become emperor nearer to when Jesus was crucified or to when Constantinople became the capital of the Roman Empire? How do you know?
18. About how long after their first persecution did Christians in Rome gain freedom to worship? How do you know?
19. Why is there a telescoping view of the time period between A.D. 310 and A.D. 330?

READ MORE ABOUT IT

Ancient Rome by Simon James. Viking. This fact-filled book explores the many different parts of ancient Roman life, including food and dining, homes, work, and entertainment.

Visit the Internet at
http://www.hbschool.com
for additional resources.

Chapter 8 • **367**

THE GIFTS OF CIVILIZATIONS

You can find many signs of earlier cultures in your life today. Look for the Latin words *e pluribus unum*, "out of many, one," on a coin. You might also find words written in Latin on government buildings. Look at such buildings in your town. They may look like those built by the Greeks and Romans long ago.

The ancient Greek and Roman cultures have affected present-day American life in many ways, especially in government and law. Many of our ideas about democracy came from the Greeks. And law students still study the ideas of Cicero, a Roman lawyer who lived from 106 B.C. to 43 B.C. United States citizens also elect national, state, and local representatives much as the Romans chose representatives during the time of the Roman Republic.

Just as Americans have built on the achievements of Greek and Roman civilizations, the Greeks and Romans built on the achievements of earlier civilizations in Africa and Asia. This cultural borrowing links us with the ancient past and explains how some of our ways of life came to be.

LONG AGO

Think and Apply

With a partner, make an illustrated booklet titled *Cultural Borrowing*. Show some ways in which different cultures from the past and present affect you. Include architecture, holidays, names, ideas, literature, clothing, art, music, and ways of daily life. Share your booklet with the class. Then take it home and discuss it with family members.

Visit the Internet at
http://www.hbschool.com
for additional resources.

Check your media center or classroom video library for the Making Social Studies Relevant videotape of this feature.

VISUAL SUMMARY

Summarize the Main Ideas
Study the pictures and captions to help you review the events you read about in Unit 4.

Illustrate the Story
Make your own visual summary for one of the following: 1) the development of democracy in Greece, 2) the growth of Rome, or 3) the beginning and growth of Christianity.

 The seagoing Minoans and the Mycenaeans were among the earliest people to live in the land now known as Greece.

3 Times of peace in the Greek city-state of Athens led to growth and the development of new ideas.

5 Roman government changed from a monarchy to a republic to an empire.

2 Later, the peoples of ancient Greece developed different ways of life. The Spartans built a military culture. The Athenians developed a democratic government.

4 The conquests of Alexander the Great introduced Greek culture to the peoples of the Mediterranean.

6 Augustus united many groups of people under the Roman Empire.

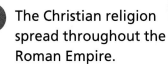

7 The Christian religion spread throughout the Roman Empire.

USE VOCABULARY

Write the term that correctly matches each meaning.

gladiator   isthmus   republic

Hellenistic   martyr

1 a small strip of land that connects two larger pieces of land

2 Greek-like

3 a form of government in which citizens elect leaders to make all government decisions

4 a slave or prisoner forced to fight, often to the death

5 a person who suffers for his or her beliefs

CHECK UNDERSTANDING

6 What do historians think brought an end to Minoan civilization?

7 Who was allowed to take part in Athenian democracy?

8 Why did the early people of Italy trade more with one another than with outsiders?

9 What were the Punic Wars?

10 What effects did the teachings of Jesus have on the Roman Empire?

THINK CRITICALLY

11 **Past to Present** Why might people today be interested in learning how the Minoan and Mycenaean civilizations ended?

12 **Think More About It** Do you think that it is a good idea for people to obey leaders without question, as citizens were taught to do in Sparta? Explain your answer.

APPLY SKILLS

Compare Historical Maps Look closely at the two maps. Then use them to answer the questions.

13 Why are there more colors on the second map than on the first map?

14 What kingdoms formed on the land once ruled by Alexander?

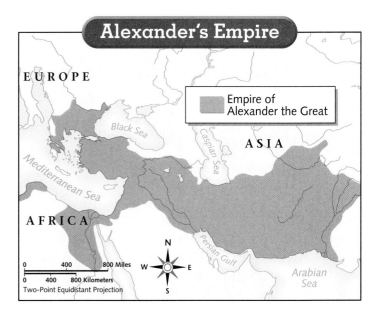

Alexander's Empire

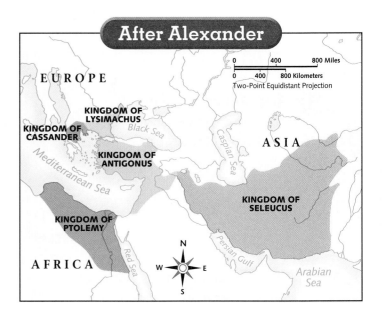

After Alexander

REMEMBER

- Share your ideas.
- Cooperate with others to plan your work.
- Take responsibility for your work.
- Help one another.
- Show your group's work to the class.
- Discuss what you learned by working together.

ACTIVITY

Make a
Time Line

With two or three classmates, make a list of important events that you have read about in this unit. For each, write the date and a description of the event at the top of a separate sheet of paper. Below the description, draw a picture to illustrate the event. Then tape the sheets in the correct time order to create a fold-out time line of Greek and Roman history.

ACTIVITY

Paint a
Mural

Work with a group of classmates to paint a mural that shows some of the people and the achievements of the Golden Age of Athens.

ACTIVITY

Plan a
Book

Imagine that you have been asked to write a book about ancient civilizations of the Mediterranean. Your publisher says that you may include any topics you like. Work in a group to prepare an outline for the book. Once you have a rough draft, use it to write your outline on a piece of posterboard.

Unit Project Wrap-Up

Build an Ancient City With your classmates, plan and build a model of an ancient Greek or Roman city. Study the notes you made as you read what features to include. For example, a Greek city might include an acropolis, an agora, and a theater. A Roman city might include a forum, a temple, a bath, an arena, and aqueducts. To complete this project, the class could divide into several groups. Each group would then work on one part of the city.

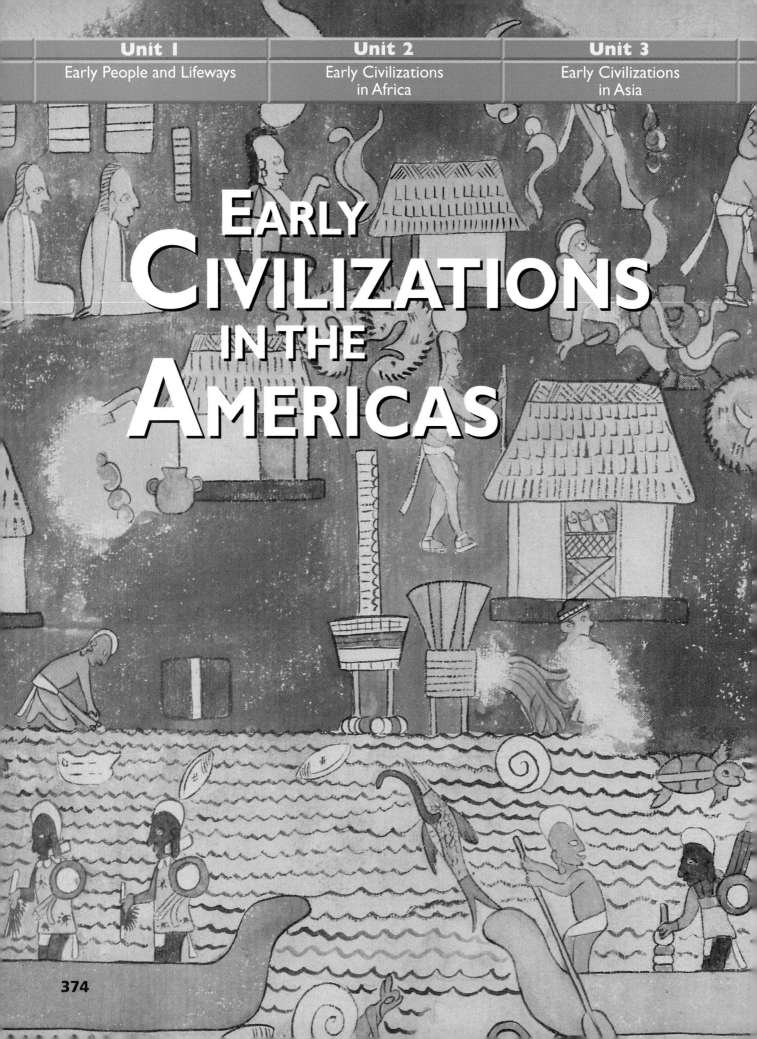

EARLY CIVILIZATIONS IN THE AMERICAS

During the same centuries in which the peoples of Greece and Rome formed their civilizations, other peoples were forming civilizations in the Americas. Between 1500 B.C. and A.D. 1500, complex societies developed in Mexico, Central America, and the highlands of Peru. The unique conditions in each region helped shape these societies in different ways.

◄ This mural was found in southeastern Mexico among the ruins of the ancient Mayan city of Chichén Itzá.

UNIT THEMES

- Continuity and Change
- Conflict and Cooperation
- Commonality and Diversity
- Interaction Within Different Environments

Unit Project

Make a Map Complete this project as you study Unit 5. With two or three classmates, draw a map that shows Mexico, Central America, and South America. Then, as you read the unit, take notes on the ways of life of each early civilization in the Americas. Later you will illustrate your map with scenes that show how different peoples lived in the Americas.

375

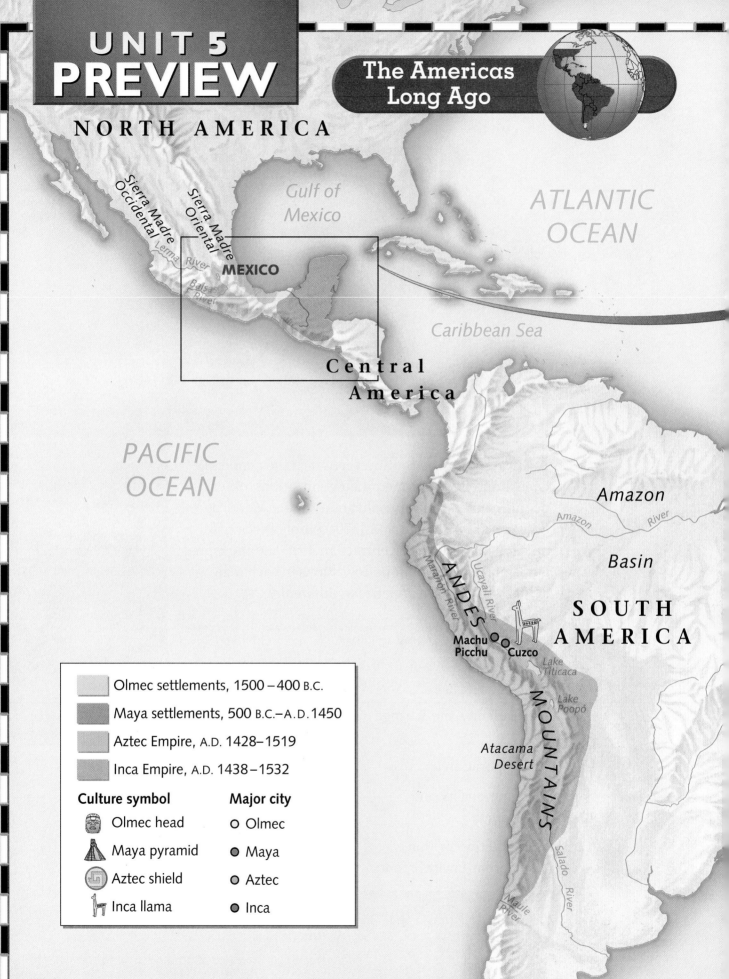

UNIT 5
PREVIEW

The Americas Long Ago

NORTH AMERICA

Sierra Madre Occidental

Sierra Madre Oriental

Lerma River

Balsas River

MEXICO

Gulf of Mexico

ATLANTIC OCEAN

Caribbean Sea

Central America

PACIFIC OCEAN

Amazon

Amazon River

Basin

SOUTH AMERICA

ANDES

Marañón River

Ucayali River

Machu Picchu

Cuzco

Lake Titicaca

Lake Poopó

MOUNTAINS

Atacama Desert

Salado River

Maule River

Olmec settlements, 1500–400 B.C.

Maya settlements, 500 B.C.–A.D.1450

Aztec Empire, A.D. 1428–1519

Inca Empire, A.D. 1438–1532

Culture symbol

Olmec head

Maya pyramid

Aztec shield

Inca llama

Major city

O Olmec

● Maya

O Aztec

● Inca

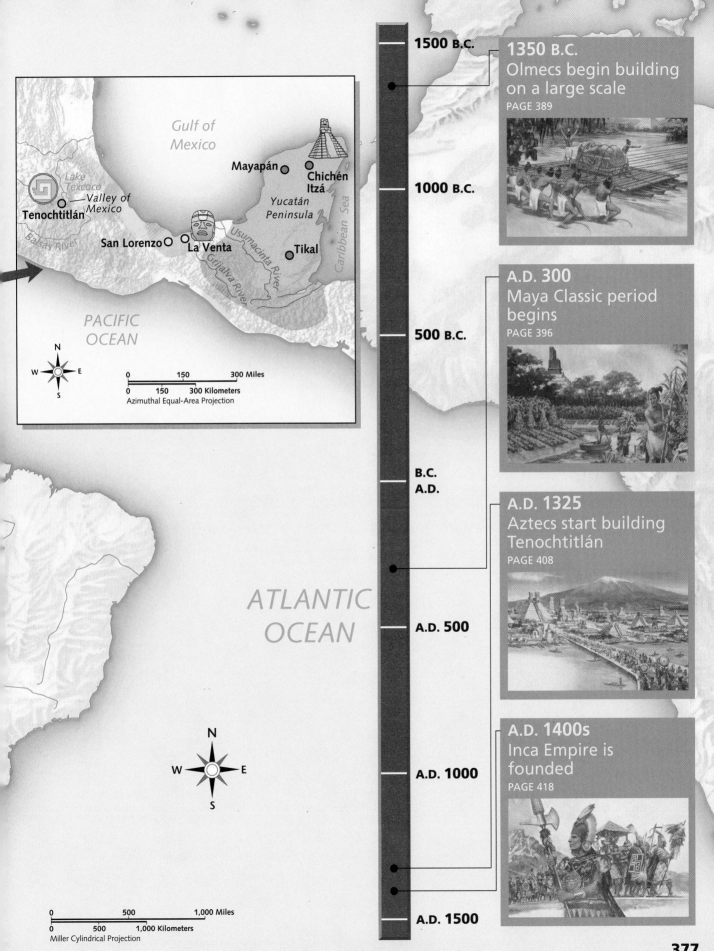

Gulf of
Mexico

Mayapán
Chichén
Itzá

Lake
Texcoco
Valley of
Mexico
Tenochtitlán

Yucatán
Peninsula

San Lorenzo
La Venta

Usumacinta River

Tikal

Caribbean Sea

Balsas River

Grijalva River

PACIFIC
OCEAN

N
W   E
S

0   150   300 Miles
0   150   300 Kilometers
Azimuthal Equal-Area Projection

ATLANTIC
OCEAN

N
W   E
S

0   500   1,000 Miles
0   500   1,000 Kilometers
Miller Cylindrical Projection

1500 B.C.

1000 B.C.

500 B.C.

B.C.
A.D.

A.D. 500

A.D. 1000

A.D. 1500

1350 B.C.
Olmecs begin building
on a large scale
PAGE 389

A.D. 300
Maya Classic period
begins
PAGE 396

A.D. 1325
Aztecs start building
Tenochtitlán
PAGE 408

A.D. 1400s
Inca Empire is
founded
PAGE 418

SPIRIT OF THE MAYA

A BOY EXPLORES HIS PEOPLE'S MYSTERIOUS PAST

written by Guy Garcia

illustrated by Manuel Garcia

This story, set in present-day Mexico, tells much about the peoples who lived there long ago. Kin, a twelve-year-old boy living in Palenque (pah•LAYN•kay), Mexico, feels little connection with his ancestors, the ancient Mayas (MY•yahs). Read now to see what brings about a change in his feelings.

Grandfather is wearing a white tunic, which is the traditional clothing of the Lacando'n (lah•kahn•DOHN) Indians, who once roamed the green forests around Palenque. Grandfather remembers the old ways of his people. When he talks to Kin, he uses the Maya language. Kin understands his grandfather because he also speaks Maya. But he prefers to speak Spanish, which is the national language of Mexico. Kin would like to cut his hair short like other Mexican boys, but his father won't let him because it's traditional for the Lacando'n to wear their hair long.

Kin has never shown much interest in the old Maya traditions. But now that Kin is twelve, his father, Chan Kin, feels that he's ready to begin learning the ancient ways. Chan Kin is an artisan who sells his wares to tourists at the pyramids outside of town. Kin would rather be out playing soccer, but he reluctantly agrees to stay home and help his father make the ceremonial clay figures.

Using clay that comes from a special place in the jungle, Chan Kin expertly molds a figure. In a few minutes his fingers have turned the ball of clay into a little man with thick arms and legs. Kin picks the man up, and the small eyes seem to be staring back at him.

Seeing that Kin is interested, his father tells him to sit down and pay attention. "You make a picture here," Chan Kin says, pointing to his head. "And then you let your fingers do the work."

After the figures are formed, Kin's father lets them dry for a month. Then, when the time is right, he builds a fire and puts the figures into the hot coals to bake.

While they're baking, Chan Kin shows his son how to make hunting arrows with parrot feathers and stone tips. Using a steel knife, he carefully splits the bamboo shaft and ties on the flint blade with wire. Then he glues on the feathers, and the arrow is ready to be tested.

"The arrows and clay figures are part of our past," Kin's father says. "It's important to keep our aim true, even if the world has changed."

Kin's father goes out into the yard and puts a new arrow into his bow. His target is a tree about twenty yards away. He pulls back on the bow, takes aim, and—*boing!*—the arrow flies through the air. Kin's father laughs because he has missed the target. He tries again; this time the arrow sticks in the tree.

Chan Kin explains how their ancestors used bows and arrows to hunt for food, and how they placed clay statues inside the pyramids to honor their gods.

That night, Kin's grandfather shows him a book about the pyramids that tells about a king named Pacal (pah•CAHL), which means "Shield." Like all Maya kings, Pacal had the power to speak to

the gods through dreams and sacred visions.

Pacal was twelve years old—the same age as Kin—when he became the king of Palenque. He ruled for sixty-seven years and built many pyramids. His tomb is buried deep inside the pyramid called the Temple of Inscriptions.

"I wish I could see Pacal's tomb," Kin says.

"You can," his grandfather replies. "The tomb is open for the tourists every day. Tomorrow is Saturday. Ask your father to take you to the ruins with him, and you can visit Pacal's tomb yourself."

Kin is up extra early the next morning. At first, his father is surprised to see him waiting by the family's Volkswagen van, but when Kin explains that he wants to see Pacal's tomb his father smiles and tells him to jump in. It only takes a few minutes to drive through town and past the statue that marks the turn-off leading to the ruins, but to Kin it seems like forever. At last they arrive at the pyramids, but there are too many trees for Kin to see anything. Kin's father parks the van in the parking lot, and Kin helps him carry the boxes of arrows he has brought to sell to an area near the entrance gate. Then his father buys him a ticket and tells him he'll be waiting to drive him home. "I knew that one day you'd come," Kin's father says proudly. Still, Kin feels a twinge of sadness at seeing his father sell trinkets to tourists at the gates of the great city that his ancestors once ruled.

Passing through the gate, Kin follows a tree-covered path to a plaza surrounded by incredible buildings. The pyramids are so tall that he has to bend his head all the way back to see the tops. Some of the pyramids are still half-covered by the

jungle, and others have steps like long ladders leading up the sides. It took the Maya hundreds of years to build the pyramids with stones that they cut from solid rock and carried through the jungle.

* * * *

Kin looks at Pacal's tomb for a long time, marveling at the beauty of the carvings. The symbols and drawings tell the story of Pacal, who received the crown of Palenque from his mother in A.D. 615. He ruled until the age of eighty and was buried in this very spot. His grave was decorated with beautiful pottery and jewelry made from

gold and precious stones. Many years later, archaeologists discovered the tomb and moved Pacal's bones and many other objects to a museum near the ruins.

Afterward, Kin walks over to the Palenque museum, where he learns that Pacal was part of a long dynasty of rulers that lasted until the reign of Snake-Jaguar II, who died in A.D. 702. Pacal's jade-covered skeleton and death mask are on display in the National Museum of Anthropology in Mexico City.

As Kin leaves the museum, he feels a stab of sorrow. He climbs to the top of a nearby ruin, but doesn't feel the same excitement he felt before. He knows now that he will never meet Pacal or the amazing Maya who built these pyramids. Kin wishes that he could travel back in time to visit the city during the height of its imperial glory.

Kin's father is waiting for him near the entrance to the ruins. When he asks Kin how he liked the pyramids, Kin tells him that they made him feel lonely and that he never wants to come back.

Chan Kin doesn't say anything, but Kin can tell that his father is disappointed.

Kin's father drives home silently. Then, without explaining why, he parks near the traffic circle that leads into town. In the center of the circle is a large statue of a man's head. Kin has looked at it a thousand times without knowing who it was, but now he recognizes it as the face of Pacal.

Kin runs out to get a closer look at the statue. It looks just like him! Suddenly, he understands why his father has brought him here. Even though he and Pacal live in worlds that are centuries apart, they are still brothers. Their skin and features are the same, and the same Maya blood runs in their veins.

As Kin and his father head home, he sees everything through new eyes. His Maya ancestors no longer seem so distant, and he no longer feels alone. Because, for the first time in his life, he knows how it feels to be a king.

As you continue reading this unit, you will learn about Kin's ancestors, the ancient Mayas, and those who came before them, the ancient Olmecs (OHL•mehks).

THE OLMECS AND THE MAYAS

"Only a century ago, the Olmecs were entirely unknown, yet today they are regarded as the creators of the first civilization of America."

Henri Stierlin,
The World's Last Mysteries

Wood and jade mask from the time of the Olmec culture of the Americas

Geography
of the Americas

North and South America were the last of the world's continents, except for Antarctica, to be settled by people. Not until nature provided a bridge were people able to cross from Asia to North America. As they migrated through the Americas, the early people found a wide variety of climates and landforms.

North America

Third in size of all the continents, North America is a land of many different environments. Forests and plains cover the center of North America. Cutting through the woods and grasslands are many rivers. The largest of these is the Mississippi.

Oceans lap the shores of the continent—the Pacific on the west and the Atlantic on the east. Mountain ranges separate both coasts of the continent from the middle. The very old Appalachian (a•puh•LAY•chee•uhn) Mountains follow the eastern coast. On the western coast, the newer and taller Alaska Range and Sierra Madre Occidental rise above the land. Slightly inland stand the Rocky Mountains and the Sierra Madre Oriental.

Today almost all parts of North America show signs of human life. Roads and highways crisscross the continent, connecting hundreds of cities large and small.

REVIEW *What are some important land and water features of North America?*

FOCUS
How does the environment affect the movement of people today?

Main Idea Think about how the environment affected the movement of early people into the Americas.

Vocabulary
cordillera
active volcano
tropical zone
temperate zone

Above is a scene at Arches National Park in the United States. The photograph below shows part of the Great Plains, where farmers grow wheat, barley, and other grains.

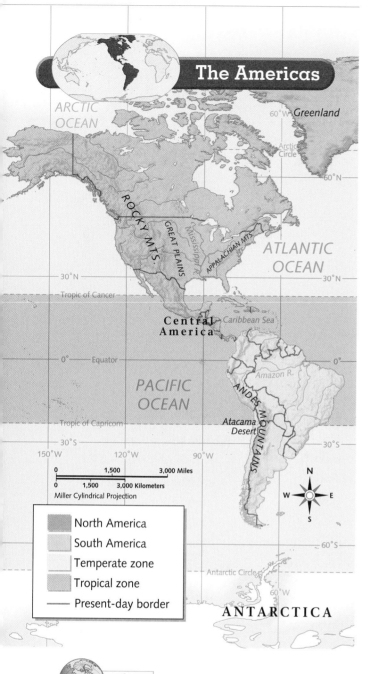

The Americas

ARCTIC OCEAN

Greenland

Arctic Circle

60°W

60°N

ROCKY MTS.

GREAT PLAINS

Mississippi

APPALACHIAN MTS.

ATLANTIC OCEAN

30°N

Tropic of Cancer

Central America

Caribbean Sea

0° Equator

Amazon R.

ANDES MOUNTAINS

PACIFIC OCEAN

Tropic of Capricorn

Atacama Desert

30°S

150°W   120°W   90°W

0   1,500   3,000 Miles
0   1,500   3,000 Kilometers
Miller Cylindrical Projection

N   W   E   S

60°S

Antarctic Circle

60°W

ANTARCTICA

North America
South America
Temperate zone
Tropical zone
— Present-day border

Place The Americas stretch through the tropical zone and the temperate zones.
■ Which zones are the Andes Mountains located in?

MAP THEME

Central America

Farther to the south, North America gets narrower and narrower. This region, often called Central America, is actually part of the continent of North America.

Central America is bordered on the west by the Pacific Ocean and on the east by the Caribbean (kair•uh•BEE•uhn) Sea, which is a part of the Atlantic Ocean. East of Central America are the many islands of the Caribbean.

Running north and south through much of Central America are very long mountain ranges called **cordilleras** (kawr•dee•YAY•rahs). Many of Central America's mountains are **active volcanoes**, or volcanoes that still erupt. Ash from eruptions of the active volcanoes has made the soil nearby very fertile. Because of the fertile soil, people often farm near volcanoes in spite of the dangers they may face.

On both sides of the mountains are regions of lowlands. Rain forests and swamps cover much of the lowlands in eastern Central America. Forests of evergreen trees grow along the lowlands in the west. The thick forests make farming difficult in the lowlands regions.

REVIEW *Where in Central America is farming better, near the mountains or in the lowlands?*

The city of San Pedro la Laguna is located at the base of a Central American volcano.

South America

At the southern end of Central America is the Isthmus of Panama, which connects North America with the continent south of it—South America. South America is the fourth-largest continent in the world. Most of South America lies in the part of the Earth called the **tropical zone**, or "the tropics." This region lies between the Tropic of Cancer, 23½ degrees north of the equator, and the Tropic of Capricorn, 23½ degrees south of the equator. The areas north and south of the tropical zone are called the **temperate zones**.

A chain of mountains called the Andes runs along South America's western coast. These are the highest mountains in the Americas and the second highest in the world. Only the Himalayas in Asia are taller. Many of the highest peaks of the Andes are topped with snow all year. Even the mountain valleys are thousands of feet above sea level.

To the west of the Andes, in the country of Chile, lies one of the world's driest regions, the Atacama Desert. To the east of the Andes is the huge basin of the Amazon River. The world's largest tropical rain forest is also located in this part of South America. North and south of the rain forest are vast tropical grasslands. Near the cold southern tip of South America, the grasslands give way to a rocky area with few plants and trees.

REVIEW *What large river and large mountain range are located in South America?*

Iguaçú Falls in South America is about 2.5 miles (4 km) wide and features more than 20 cataracts.

Migrating to the Americas

At the time of the last Ice Age, much of the world was covered by huge glaciers. So much water was frozen in the glaciers that the world's oceans became shallower. As ocean levels dropped, land that had been underwater was uncovered. Between what is today Alaska and the easternmost part of Russia, dry land connected the continents of Asia and North America. Today scholars and archaeologists call this land bridge of long ago Beringia (bair•IN•gee•uh).

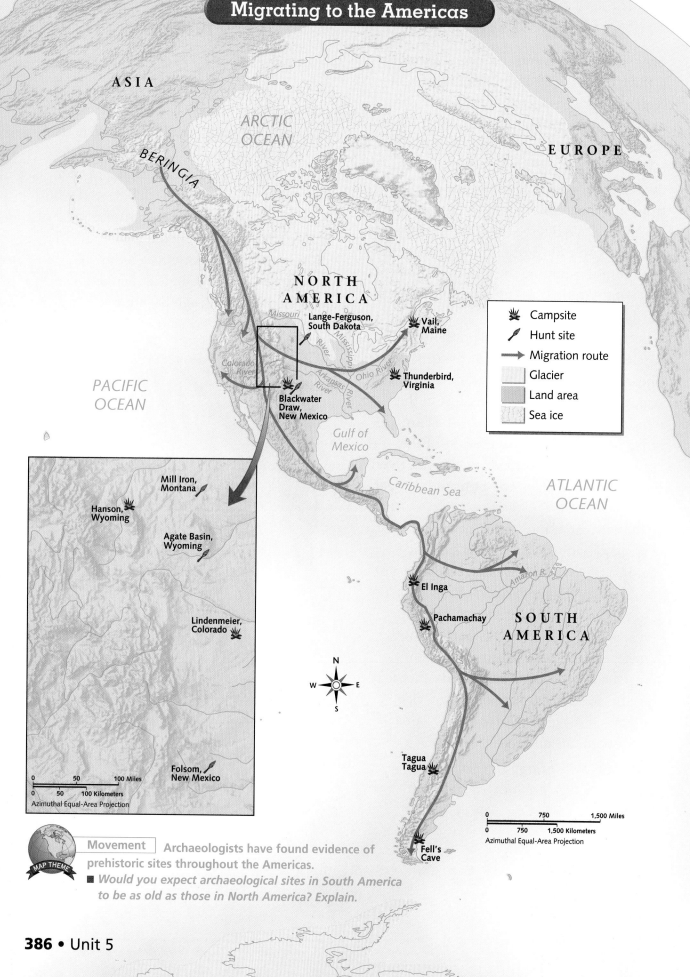

ASIA

ARCTIC OCEAN

EUROPE

BERINGIA

NORTH AMERICA

Missouri

Lange-Ferguson, South Dakota

Vail, Maine

Colorado River

PACIFIC OCEAN

Mississippi River

Arkansas River

Ohio River

Thunderbird, Virginia

Blackwater Draw, New Mexico

Gulf of Mexico

Caribbean Sea

ATLANTIC OCEAN

	Campsite
	Hunt site
→	Migration route
	Glacier
	Land area
	Sea ice

Mill Iron, Montana

Hanson, Wyoming

Agate Basin, Wyoming

Lindenmeier, Colorado

El Inga

Pachamachay

Amazon R.

SOUTH AMERICA

Folsom, New Mexico

| 0 | 50 | 100 Miles |
| 0 | 50 | 100 Kilometers |

Azimuthal Equal-Area Projection

Tagua Tagua

N
W · E
S

| 0 | 750 | 1,500 Miles |
| 0 | 750 | 1,500 Kilometers |

Azimuthal Equal-Area Projection

Fell's Cave

Movement Archaeologists have found evidence of prehistoric sites throughout the Americas.

■ *Would you expect archaeological sites in South America to be as old as those in North America? Explain.*

Beringia

Beringia is the name scientists of today call the ancient land bridge between northern Asia and North America. It linked the regions that are now Siberia—a part of Russia—and Alaska. Beringia was uncovered only during the Ice Ages. This land bridge was about 1,000 miles (1,609 km) wide. Its landscape was a combination of tundra and steppe, or grassy plain. The plain provided rich grazing land for woolly mammoths, mastodons, horned bison, and other plant-eating mammals. When the world's glaciers melted at the end of the last Ice Age, the oceans rose, and Beringia disappeared once again.

Early people from Asia crossed Beringia into the Americas.

Many scientists believe that the first people to reach the Americas were nomads who hunted the huge mammals of the Ice Age. Over thousands of years they probably followed the mammals across Beringia.

Once in the Americas, groups of nomads began to travel south and east in search of food. This slow migration of people took many more thousands of years. In time, however, people had reached almost every part of the Americas.

In their new homelands, the different groups learned to adapt to different environments. A variety of cultures developed across the Americas. Each culture had its own tools, language, religion, and art.
REVIEW *How and why did the first people come to the Americas?*

LESSON 1 REVIEW

Check Understanding

1 Remember the Facts Where is the tropical zone located?

2 Recall the Main Idea How did the environment affect the movement of early people into the Americas?

Think Critically

3 Think More About It Why do you think early people migrated into areas with harsh environments?

4 Past to Present For what reasons do people today migrate in the Americas?

Show What You Know
Diorama Activity Think about the landforms and waterways of the Americas. Choose one such landform or waterway and make a diorama that shows what it looks like. Display your finished diorama in your classroom.

The Olmecs

1600 B.C.	1200 B.C.	800 B.C.	400 B.C.

Olmec civilization began along the coast of the Gulf of Mexico in what are now the Mexican states of Veracruz and Tabasco. This civilization is remembered for its many ideas and inventions. Its innovations were used and added to by later civilizations in **Mesoamerica**, or Middle America, a region that includes central and southern Mexico and Central America. For this reason, the Olmec civilization is called the "mother civilization" of the Americas.

FOCUS

Why are the ideas and inventions of one culture often adopted by other cultures?

Main Idea Read to learn how the ideas and inventions of the Olmec culture affected the development of other civilizations.

Vocabulary

Mesoamerica
intercropping
obsidian
elite
ceremonial
  center
tumpline

Early Olmec Farmers

The Olmec civilization began in the coastal lowlands of what is today eastern Mexico. By the early 1500s B.C. the Olmecs had begun planting maize, beans, squash, and other crops in the rich soil along the banks of the area's rivers. Olmec farmers planted their maize, beans, and squash together. The bean vines grew around the stalk, or stiff stem, of the maize. The squash vines spread out on the ground between the stalks. The bean plants gave the soil nitrogen, an important nutrient that the maize and squash needed. By **intercropping**, or planting different crops together, Olmec farmers made the best possible use of the small amount of fertile soil they had.

Crops grew quickly in the area's warm climate, and large amounts of rainfall kept the ground moist year-round. Two or more harvests were possible each year, giving the Olmecs a surplus of food.

Like other ancient civilizations, the Olmecs depended on the resources around them. They fished in the rivers and hunted animals such as deer, wild pigs, and jaguars in the rain forests. They built their homes of reeds from the rivers and grasses from the savannas. They made pots and bowls from clay they found near the rivers.

Olmec clay figure crafted around 100 B.C.

388 • Unit 5

The Olmecs did not use only the resources available in their own coastal region. When they traveled inland to trade, they exchanged resources from their region for resources from the mountains, such as **obsidian**, a volcanic glass they used for cutting.

One of the resources the Olmecs traded was rubber, which they gathered from trees in the rain forest. In fact, it was rubber that gave them the name Olmec, which means "People from the Land of Rubber."

REVIEW *What advantages did the coastal lowlands offer early Olmec farmers?*

Olmec Centers

The earliest Olmec farmers lived in small communities. By around 1500 B.C. Olmec society had split into classes. About 150 years later the **elite**, or ruling class, had enough power to order the construction of large building projects. These projects required the labor of many people.

One building project took place at San Lorenzo, the oldest known Olmec city.

There, around 1150 B.C., workers carried baskets of dirt up a large hill. They used the dirt to make a platform more than 20 feet (6 m) high and as long as eight basketball courts placed end to end.

On this platform the Olmecs built an area for religious ceremonies called a **ceremonial center**. Among the ruins of San Lorenzo, archaeologists have uncovered the remains of stone columns and more than 70 stone monuments. The center also includes the oldest known ball court in Mesoamerica.

Temples and palaces where rulers lived probably also once stood on the ceremonial center. Nothing remains of these buildings today. Archaeologists believe that invaders destroyed San Lorenzo around 900 B.C.

Another Olmec center, called La Venta, grew up after San Lorenzo ended. From 800 B.C. to 400 B.C. most Olmec activity took place in this center.

Many large Olmec statues can still be seen at the site of the ancient Olmec city of La Venta (below). A museum that preserves ancient Olmec artifacts now sits where La Venta once flourished. A variety of smaller Olmec figures (top) are also on display at the museum.

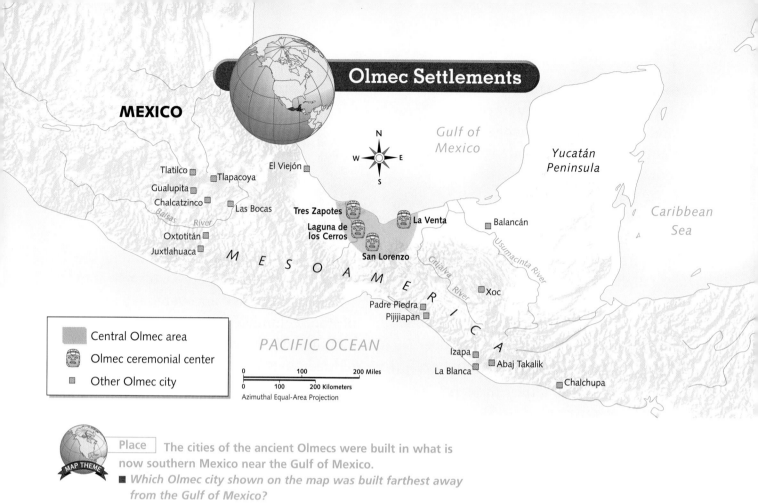

MEXICO

Gulf of Mexico

Yucatán Peninsula

Caribbean Sea

Tlatilco
Tlapacoya
Gualupita
Chalcatzinco
El Viejón
Las Bocas
Balsas River
Tres Zapotes
Laguna de los Cerros
La Venta
Balancán
Oxtotitán
Juxtlahuaca
San Lorenzo

Usumacinta River

M E S O A M E R I C A

Grijalva River

Xoc

Padre Piedra
Pijijiapan

PACIFIC OCEAN

Izapa
Abaj Takalik
La Blanca
Chalchupa

Central Olmec area

Olmec ceremonial center

Other Olmec city

0   100   200 Miles
0   100   200 Kilometers
Azimuthal Equal-Area Projection

Place   The cities of the ancient Olmecs were built in what is now southern Mexico near the Gulf of Mexico.
■ *Which Olmec city shown on the map was built farthest away from the Gulf of Mexico?*

At La Venta, Olmec workers formed an earthen mound 110 feet (34 m) tall. Some archaeologists refer to this mound as the first Mesoamerican pyramid, or the Great Mound. Many of the pyramids the Olmecs built contained hidden tombs. However, archaeologists do not yet know if the Great Mound at La Venta contains a tomb.

REVIEW *What were Olmec ceremonial centers like?*

Olmec Art

Ancient Olmec artists created what archaeologist Michael D. Coe describes as "magnificent and awe-inspiring sculptures." The artists carved their works from some of the hardest rock in the Americas, even though they did not have metal tools.

The Olmecs made tools out of materials that were available to them. They used drills made of bone to cut into basalt, greenstone, jade, and other rocks. They used sand and reeds to carve the finer lines of their artwork.

The Olmecs are perhaps best known for the giant heads they carved from basalt rock. They cut out large pieces of the basalt from mountains that were many miles away from their ceremonial centers. They probably moved the stones to their centers by floating them downriver on rafts made of balsa, a very lightweight wood.

A number of the ancient carved heads still exist. Some of them are more than 9 feet (2.7 m) tall and weigh as much as 20 tons each. Modern archaeologists marvel at the finely carved lines of the ancient stone faces. Experts believe that each face is a portrait of a different Olmec ruler.

Olmec artists also used basalt to carve thrones for their rulers. On the front of many of these thrones is a carved opening with a small stone figure inside. Some archaeologists think that the stone figure represented the ruler returning from a trip to the "otherworld." The otherworld was the place where the Olmecs believed their people went after they died. The Olmecs thought that if their king survived a trip to the otherworld, he would bring back life and good fortune for his people.

Not all Olmec art showed real people. Some pictured the many gods worshipped by the Olmecs. The Olmec religion was based on the forces in nature that affected farming. The most important god to the Olmecs was the jaguar god, a cat god they believed brought the rain. The image of the jaguar appears often in Olmec art. Some Olmec art shows figures that are half-jaguar and half-human. Other gods that the Olmecs worshipped included a fire god, a corn god, and a feathered serpent. Many of these gods are also found in later Mesoamerican cultures.

Not all Olmec art is huge like the stone heads. In fact, the Olmecs made some sculptures that were only a few inches tall. Tiny masks and jade statues have been found. The Olmecs did not display their smaller works of art as they did the huge stone heads. Instead they buried them, probably as offerings to their gods.

REVIEW *What were some of the subjects of Olmec sculptures?*

This large head and others carved by the Olmecs long ago still amaze visitors to Mexico today. The heads, carved from basalt rock, weigh as much as 20 tons. Olmec artists used simple stone tools to create the basalt heads.

The Oldest Ball Game in the Americas

The Olmecs made great use of the resource of rubber. They even used rubber to make balls for a game that they played on an outdoor court. Two teams competed in the ancient game. Players wore heavy padding to protect them from injury by the fast-moving ball.

A game played in Mexico today is much like the Olmec game. In the modern game, players cannot hit the ball with their hands or feet. Instead, they use other parts of their body such as their hips. Because the ball is very hard and travels at high speeds, all players wear protective clothing, just as their ancestors did.

In 1989, archaeologists found three rubber balls in a bog near San Lorenzo. Each of the ancient balls is 3 to 5 inches (7.6 to 12.7 cm) across. These balls are believed to be the only ones to have survived from Olmec times. They are probably more than 3,000 years old.

This statue of an ancient ballplayer shows the heavy padding the players wore around their waists and arms during a game.

The "Mother Civilization"

In many parts of Mexico and Central America, far from Olmec centers, traces of Olmec civilization have been found. In southwestern Mexico, cave paintings show scenes of Olmec gods. In El Salvador, 500 miles (about 800 km) southeast of Olmec lands, a boulder is carved in the Olmec style.

Since the first discovery of the remains of Olmec civilization, archaeologists have tried to figure out how Olmec ideas spread throughout Mesoamerica. Most experts believe that Olmec ideas spread through Mesoamerica by cultural diffusion. You have already learned that cultural diffusion is the spreading of new ideas to other places.

No evidence has been found that suggests that the Olmecs conquered a large area and forced other peoples to follow their ways. Instead, Olmec ideas probably spread as different cultures came in contact with the Olmecs through trade. Other peoples may have adopted many Olmec ways because they admired Olmec innovations.

Some of the Olmec innovations included the use of hieroglyphic writing and a number system. The Olmecs were also among the first Mesoamerican peoples to use a calendar. Other Olmec innovations helped make everyday life easier. For example, the Olmecs made mirrors by polishing iron ore.

Some Olmec innovations are still used in modern Mexico. The early people of Mesoamerica did not use animals or wheeled carts to carry loads. Instead, workers or slaves used tumplines to carry trade goods and workloads. A **tumpline** (TUHM•plyn) is a kind of sling that makes it easier to carry heavy loads. A strap placed over the forehead helps support the load carried in the sling on the person's back.

A number of customs shared by later Mesoamerican peoples began with the Olmecs. These include their art and architecture, their religion, and their ball game. In fact, Olmec culture is in many ways the base of other Mesoamerican cultures. Richard E. W. Adams, who studies and writes about ancient Mesoamerica, notes, "Olmec culture did not die out but was absorbed and passed on in [different ways]." The way in which Olmec culture was passed on to other cultures has caused many scholars to call it the "Mother Civilization" of Mesoamerica.

REVIEW *How did Olmec ideas spread to other peoples?*

This girl from Mexico is using a tumpline to carry wood. Tumplines have been used by people in Mesoamerica since the time of the Olmecs.

LESSON 2 REVIEW

1600 B.C.	1200 B.C.	800 B.C.	400 B.C.
1500 B.C. • Olmec society becomes organized into classes	**1350 B.C.** • Olmecs start building on a large scale	**800 B.C.** • La Venta begins to flourish	**400 B.C.** • La Venta declines

Check Understanding

1 Remember the Facts When and where did Olmec civilization develop?

2 Recall the Main Idea How did the ideas and inventions of the Olmec culture influence the development of other civilizations in Mesoamerica?

Think Critically

3 Think More About It Why do you think the Olmecs carved huge stone portraits of their rulers?

4 Past to Present What are some examples of cultural diffusion in the world today?

Show What You Know

Descriptive Writing Activity Imagine that you are an archaeologist at the site of an ancient Olmec center such as La Venta. Write several paragraphs that describe what you see. Then read your description to classmates.

Learn from Artifacts

1. Why Learn This Skill?

Artifacts are objects people make and use. You have seen many artifacts made by people who lived long ago in different places. You know that artifacts can be large, like the Olmec head on page 391, or small, like the Olmec figures on page 388. Ancient tools, weapons, coins, jewelry, toys, and cooking pots are all artifacts. The artifacts of a society of long ago can tell us much about how its people lived and worked and about what they thought was important.

Artifacts do not have to be ancient. Televisions, computers, automobiles, and watches are artifacts, too. The things we make and use today may tell future generations what our time was like.

2. Understand the Process

Although early civilizations around the world were different from one another, many had things in common. Most early societies depended on agriculture. They also built cities, set up governments, and followed religions. Many used some form of money for exchange.

Some early societies produced artifacts much like those of other societies. People both in the Nile Valley and in Middle America built pyramids. What does this tell you about the two cultures?

Three artifacts are shown below and on the next page. One was made in Egypt, one in the Americas, and one in China. They look different, yet they are alike in important ways. Study the pictures and their

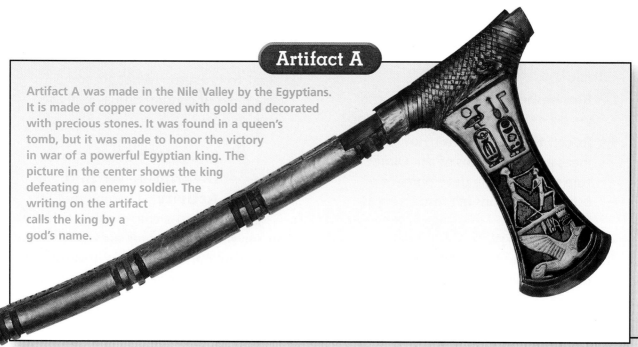

Artifact A

Artifact A was made in the Nile Valley by the Egyptians. It is made of copper covered with gold and decorated with precious stones. It was found in a queen's tomb, but it was made to honor the victory in war of a powerful Egyptian king. The picture in the center shows the king defeating an enemy soldier. The writing on the artifact calls the king by a god's name.

Artifact B

Artifact B was made in Mesoamerica by the Olmecs. It is crafted of jade, a stone the Olmecs valued more than gold. The artifact is shaped like a creature part human and part jaguar. Such objects have been found in the tombs of kings and other leaders. The jaguar may have been a symbol of authority for the Olmecs.

Artifact C

Artifact C was made in China during the Shang dynasty. It is made of bronze, a metal with which the Shang formed objects used in public ceremonies. This artifact was found in the tomb of a Shang lord or king. To the Shang, it may have been a symbol of political strength.

captions. Then use the questions as a guide in comparing these early civilizations.

1. How do you know what each artifact is?

2. How was each artifact used by the people who made it?

3. What tells you that each artifact was important to the people who made it?

4. How are the three artifacts alike? In what ways do you think the societies that made them may have been alike?

5. Why do you think the artifacts do not look exactly alike?

6. What do the materials used to make the artifacts say about each of the societies?

3. Think and Apply

The Olmec artifact gives information through its shape and its material. It is shaped like a jaguar and made of jade. To the Olmecs, the jaguar was a god and jade was valuable. This information suggests that this artifact could have been used in religious ceremonies. Look back at the illustrations in this chapter and in previous chapters to find other artifacts. Remember that artifacts are items that people make and use. With a partner, make a list of the artifacts you have found. Then discuss what these artifacts seem to tell you about the societies that made them. Share your findings with the class.

FOCUS

How do people today adapt to changes in government?

Main Idea Read to learn how the Mayas adapted to change.

Vocabulary

regent
slash-and-burn farming
glyph
cenote

Ancient Mayan carving (above)

LEARNING FROM DIAGRAMS
The ruins of the Mayan city of Tikal (inset) give clues to what the ancient city may have looked like long ago (right). Important features included the following:
1 Temple I
2 Temple II
3 The Great Plaza
■ *What do you think made the Great Plaza an important place for the people of Tikal?*

The Mayas

| 500 B.C. | B.C. | A.D. | A.D. 500 | A.D. 1000 | A.D. 1500 |

The civilization of the Mayas was one of the longest-lasting civilizations of the ancient Americas. The Mayan way of life began to form around 500 B.C. The earliest Mayas lived as farmers in the tropical rain forests of southern Mexico and Central America. By building on ideas borrowed from the Olmecs, the Mayan civilization grew strong.

The "Lost Cities" of the Mayas

The Mayas built more than 100 cities and towns deep in the rain forests of the region that today includes Mexico, Guatemala, Belize, Honduras, and El Salvador. Their culture was strong during the time between A.D. 300 and A.D. 900. This time has become known as the Classic period of the Mayas.

The Mayas were skilled architects and builders. Their cities had temples, pyramids, ball courts, palaces, and plazas. At the height of the Classic period, some Mayan cities had huge populations.

After A.D. 900 the Mayan civilization fell into decline. For many centuries the cities and towns of the Classic period lay in ruins, hidden by thick rain forests. Then, in the nineteenth and twentieth centuries, the "lost cities" were rediscovered. Even today, archaeologists are making new finds at the sites of these ancient cities.

The largest of the ancient Mayan cities was Tikal (tih•KAHL). At the site of the ancient city, the remains of about 3,000 temples and other buildings have been found. Scientists estimate that as many as 100,000 people lived in Tikal.

Located at the center of Tikal are the ruins of six tall stone temples. Each is made of huge blocks of limestone and shaped like a pyramid. The tallest is 299 feet (91 m) in height—as high as a 30-story building. On its top still sits a carved jaguar with sharp, curving claws. This temple is sometimes called the Temple of the Giant Jaguar.

The cities of the Mayas were alike in many ways. All had stone temples, which shows that religion was important to the Mayas. Like the Olmecs, the Mayas worshipped many gods. They believed in gods of the sun, the rain, and many other aspects of nature.

The Mayan City of Tikal

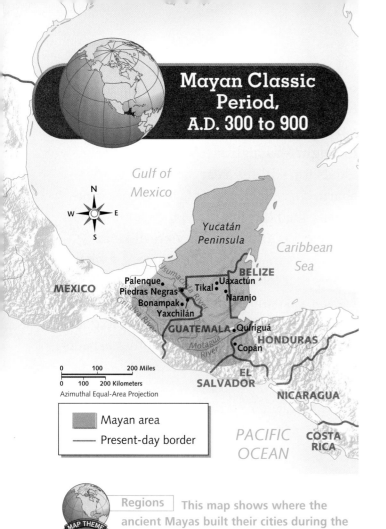

Mayan Classic Period, A.D. 300 to 900

Gulf of Mexico

Yucatán Peninsula

Caribbean Sea

BELIZE

MEXICO
Palenque
Piedras Negras
Bonampak
Yaxchilán
Tikal
Uaxactún
Naranjo

GUATEMALA · Quiriguá
Copán
HONDURAS

EL SALVADOR

NICARAGUA

PACIFIC OCEAN

COSTA RICA

0   100   200 Miles
0   100   200 Kilometers
Azimuthal Equal-Area Projection

■ Mayan area
— Present-day border

Regions This map shows where the ancient Mayas built their cities during the Classic period.
■ *Which present-day countries claim land settled by the Mayas during their Classical period?*

Near the stone temples was a palace for the city's leader. Each city had its own king and its own government. The king also controlled the smaller towns near his city. From time to time, one powerful Mayan king may have claimed control of several cities.

Each king also had a temple built in his honor. Later the temple would serve as the tomb for the king. Stelae in front of the temple gave information about the king, including the dates of his birth, his time of rule, and his death.

Stelae from the temples often described more than just the men who served as kings. Women were pictured and written about, since they, too, were important in noble families. For example, some women served as **regents**, or temporary rulers. They acted as leaders until young heirs to the throne were old enough to rule.

In the Mayan cities the temples and palaces were surrounded by workshops and homes. Paved courtyards provided space for markets and public gatherings. Most cities also featured ball courts like the ones at the Olmec centers.

For much of the year, Mayan farmers lived near their fields, in one-room mud huts. Between growing seasons they came to the city to build temples and palaces and to participate in ceremonies.

REVIEW *What were Mayan cities like?*

Changing the Environment

Some archaeologists believe that the Mayan population may have grown to 14 million people by the end of the Classic period. There may have been as many as 500 people per square mile (200 per sq km) in some places. The ancient region where the Mayas lived could have been more crowded than present-day China.

Feeding such a large population took a lot of thought and planning. The Mayas had to find ways to use their tropical rain forest environment to meet their needs for food.

The ancient Mayas, like their modern descendants, cut and burned parts of the rain forest to provide land for growing crops. This **slash-and-burn farming**, however, can support only small communities. This is because the ashes fertilize the soil for no more than three years. Then the land must lie free of crops for several years until the soil regains the nutrients needed for growing plants.

As their population increased, the Mayas invented new ways to grow more crops. In swampy areas, they built raised fields. On hillsides, they made terraces, or ledges, they could use for farmland.

Like the Olmec farmers, Mayan farmers used intercropping to grow maize, beans, and squash in the same field. They also grew avocados, a starchy food called ramon, and cacao beans.

REVIEW *How did the Mayas produce enough food to support a large population in the rain forest?*

Mayan Learning

The ancient Mayas studied many different subjects, including mathematics and astronomy. They made use of mathematics both to record trade and to keep track of days. The Mayan number system was different from those of other ancient cultures in one important way. It had a symbol that stood for zero. It also used just three symbols to make all the numbers. Shells stood for zeros, dots for ones, and bars for fives. Combinations of these three symbols allowed the Mayas to make all the other numbers. For example, a 6 was made by placing a dot over a bar. The Mayas showed numbers higher than 19 by using position much as we use position to show numbers higher than 9.

The ancient Mayas were fascinated not only by mathematics but also by astronomy. They watched the night sky closely, following the movements of the planets. One planet they carefully tracked was Venus, which they could see both in the morning and at night.

From their study of the skies, the Mayas developed two very accurate calendars. One had a 365-day year, just like our modern calendar. They used this one to keep track of planting, harvesting, and seasonal flooding. The Mayas' other calendar had 260 days and was used to keep track of religious events.

The Mayas also created an advanced system of writing. Mayan writing consisted of a type of hieroglyphics called glyphs (GLIFS). **Glyphs** were picture-symbols that

These farmers are planting corn on recently cleared land in Mexico. Intercropping is still used by Mayan descendants to grow crops.

Mayan Glyphs

Jaguar	Water
North	South
East	West

LEARNING FROM CHARTS Archaeologists have discovered that some Mayan glyphs represent sounds while other glyphs stand for objects and ideas.
■ *Which glyph in the chart looks most like the object or idea that it represents?*

represented objects, ideas, and sounds. Only recently have archaeologists begun to be able to read the Mayan language.

For writing material, the Mayas made paper from the bark of wild fig trees. Using this paper, they created codices (KOH•duh•seez)—books containing Mayan glyphs. Only four codices of Mayan writing have survived. They tell about such subjects as Mayan religion and astronomy.

The Mayas also carved their glyphs on stone monuments, murals, pottery, and wooden beams. Most of these glyphs are records of dates and events in Mayan history. They provide archaeologists with their main source of information on the ancient Mayas.

REVIEW *What were some of the achievements of the ancient Mayas?*

The ancient Mayas threw offerings of gold and jade into this natural well, or cenote, at Chichén Itzá.

Continuity and Change

During the A.D. 900s, the Mayan people began to leave their cities in the rain forests of the southern lowlands. Some archaeologists believe that the cities became too crowded. Others think that war between the Mayan cities caused the Mayan civilization of the Classic period to collapse.

Some Mayas migrated north and west. During the A.D. 900s a new Mayan civilization grew up in the northern part of the Yucatán Peninsula. This region has no rivers, so the Mayas built their new cities near **cenotes** (sih•NOH•teez)—deep natural wells. One of these cities, Chichén Itzá (chee•CHEHN it•SAH), became the Mayas' new capital.

The Mayas of the northern Yucatán Peninsula continued to use the writing, astronomy, and mathematics of the Mayan Classic period. However, they had lost trust in individual kings. Instead, they set up ruling councils to govern their cities.

Regions The Mayas migrated north after the Classic period ended.
■ *What was the land of the Mayas' new location like?*

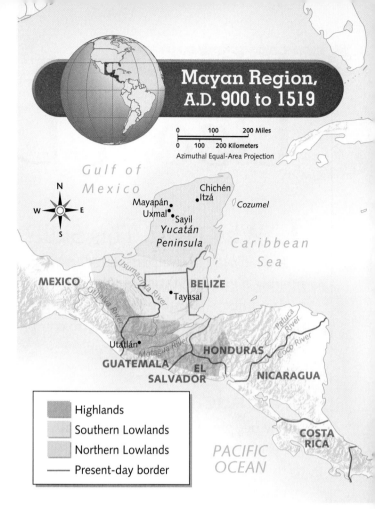

Mayan Region, A.D. 900 to 1519

0   100   200 Miles
0   100   200 Kilometers
Azimuthal Equal-Area Projection

Gulf of Mexico

Chichén Itzá
Cozumel
Mayapán
Uxmal
Sayil
Yucatán Peninsula

Caribbean Sea

MEXICO

Usumacinta River

BELIZE

Tayasal

Grijalva River

Utatlán

Motagua River

HONDURAS

Patuca River

Coco River

GUATEMALA

EL SALVADOR

NICARAGUA

COSTA RICA

PACIFIC OCEAN

Highlands
Southern Lowlands
Northern Lowlands
— Present-day border

In 1187 the rulers of the Mayan city Mayapán (my•ah•PAHN) captured Chichén Itzá. Mayapán then became the Mayan capital until 1450.

At the time of his fourth voyage to the Americas, Christopher Columbus encountered the Mayas. Later Spanish contact brought European diseases to Mesoamerica. Many Mayas died during this time. Others were enslaved. However, one group of Mayas—the Itzas—fought Spanish rule for almost 200 years. Today, nearly 3 million Mayas speak Mayan languages and farm the lands where their ancestors once lived.

REVIEW *Where did the Mayas migrate after they left their cities in the rain forest?*

LESSON 3 REVIEW

A.D. 300   A.D. 600   A.D. 900   A.D. 1200

A.D. 300
• Mayan Classic period begins

A.D. 900
• New Mayan culture at Chichén Itzá

A.D. 1187
• Rulers of Mayapán overthrow Chichén Itzá

Check Understanding

1 Remember the Facts What happened to the Mayas of the Classic period during the A.D. 900s?

2 Recall the Main Idea How did Mayan society change during the A.D. 900s?

Think Critically

3 Think More About It What sources might tell you more about why the Mayan cities of the rain forest were abandoned?

4 Past to Present Is overcrowding caused by population growth a problem in today's world? Explain.

Show What You Know

Research Activity Find out more about Mayan writing, Mayan religion, Mayan numbers, Mayan astronomy, or Mayan cities. Then write a brief research report describing your findings. Add your report to a class booklet entitled "More About the Mayas."

Use a Double-Bar

1. Why Learn This Skill?

A good way to compare statistics is by making a graph. **Statistics** are facts shown with numbers. **Double-bar graphs**, such as those in this lesson, make it easy to compare two sets of statistics.

2. Understand the Process

The people in Mexico and Central America were once mostly farmers, just as the ancient Mayas had been. In the twentieth century, more and more people moved out of the countryside, or rural areas, and into the cities, or urban areas. People stopped being farmers because they thought life would be better in the cities. The double-bar graphs on the next page show, by country, the number of people who lived in the rural areas and the number of people who lived in cities. Graph A shows the percentages in 1950, and Graph B shows the percentages in 1997. Use these steps as a guide to study the graphs.

1 Look at the words and numbers along the bottom and left-hand side of each graph. Countries are listed along the bottom, and population measured in percentage is listed along the left-hand side.

2 Notice that there are two different kinds of bars for each country. The solid bar shows the percentage of people living

in the countryside. The striped bar shows the percentage living in the cities.

3 Read each graph by running your finger up to the top of each bar and then left to the number. If the top of the bar is between two numbers, the exact number is between those two.

4 Compare the heights of the solid bars for the countries on Graph A. Which country had the most people living in the countryside in 1950?

5 Compare the heights of the striped bars for the countries on Graph B. Which country had the highest percentage of people living in the cities in 1997?

6 Compare the heights of the solid bar and the striped bar for any one country on Graph A. Which bar is higher? How much higher is one bar than the other?

7 Compare the heights of the solid bar and the striped bar for any one country on Graph B. Which bar is higher? How much higher is one bar than the other?

8 Now compare all the bars on both graphs. In which year, 1950 or 1997, did more people live in the cities? In which year did more people live in the countryside? How do the double-bar graphs help you understand the growth of city population in Honduras, Mexico, and Nicaragua from 1950 to 1997?

Graph

3. Think and Apply

Make a double-bar graph of your test scores in social studies and in your other subjects. Begin by listing the subjects along the bottom of your graph. Along the left-hand side of your graph, list a range of your possible test scores by tens from 0 percent on the bottom to 100 percent at the top. For each subject, make two bars to show your next two test scores. Remember to use different colored bars or solids and stripes for the first and second tests. You should also make a key showing what each kind of bar in your graph represents. Study your completed graph. What does it tell you?

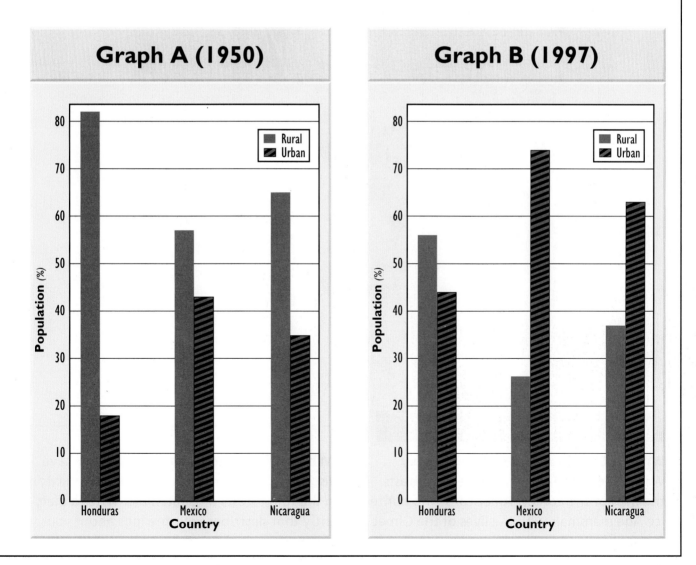

Graph A (1950)

Graph B (1997)

1500 B.C.	1000 B.C.

1500 B.C.
• Olmec society is
  organized into classes

CONNECT MAIN IDEAS

Use this organizer to tell about early civilizations in the Americas.
Write two examples for each main idea. A copy of the organizer may
be found on page 89 of the Activity Book.

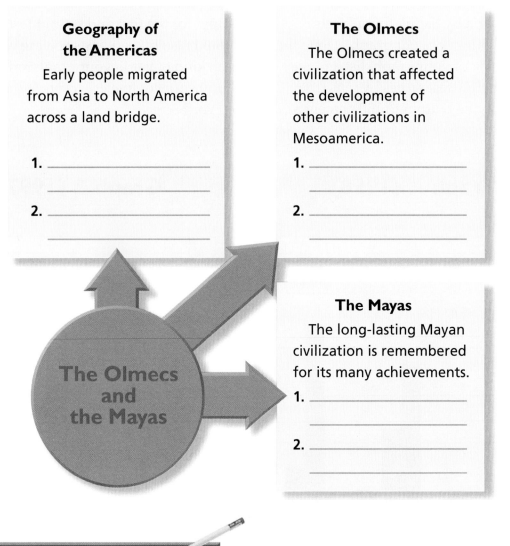

Geography of the Americas

Early people migrated from Asia to North America across a land bridge.

1. _____
   _____
2. _____
   _____

The Olmecs

The Olmecs created a civilization that affected the development of other civilizations in Mesoamerica.

1. _____
   _____
2. _____
   _____

The Olmecs and the Mayas

The Mayas

The long-lasting Mayan civilization is remembered for its many achievements.

1. _____
   _____
2. _____
   _____

WRITE MORE ABOUT IT

Write a Compare-and-Contrast Essay
Write an essay that compares and contrasts the lives of the earliest Americans who hunted Ice Age mammals with the lives of the Olmec farmers.

Write a Diary Entry Imagine that you have discovered the ruins of an ancient Mayan city in the rain forests of Guatemala. Write a diary entry that describes your feelings about your discovery.

500 B.C.		B.C. A.D.		A.D. 500		A.D. 1000

400 B.C.
• La Venta begins to decline

A.D. 300
• Mayan Classic period begins

A.D. 900
• New Mayan culture emerges at Chichén Itzá

USE VOCABULARY

For each pair of terms, write at least one sentence that shows how the terms are related.

1. temperate zone, tropical zone
2. elite, ceremonial center
3. intercropping, slash-and-burn farming
4. Mesoamerica, cenote

CHECK UNDERSTANDING

5. Which continent is larger, North America or South America?
6. Which continent is Central America a part of?
7. Where are the Andes located?
8. What was Beringia? Why does it no longer exist?
9. In which part of the Americas did the Olmecs live?
10. Why did the Olmecs build large platforms of earth?
11. Why has the Olmec culture been called the "Mother Civilization" of Mesoamerica?
12. Where did the Mayas of the Classic period build their cities?
13. What methods of farming did the Mayas use to grow more food?
14. What is interesting about the Mayas' number system?
15. What are glyphs?
16. How did the Spanish conquest of parts of the Americas affect the Mayas?

THINK CRITICALLY

17. **Think More About It** Why do you think the early people of the Americas spoke many different languages?
18. **Cause and Effect** How did the environment affect the early civilizations of the Americas?
19. **Past to Present** How are present-day problems caused by population growth like the problems faced by the Mayas? How are they different?

APPLY SKILLS

Learn from Artifacts Imagine that you are an archaeologist in the year A.D. 2999. What would an artifact such as a car from the 1990s tell you about the society that used it?

Use a Double-Bar Graph Use the double-bar graphs on page 403 to find out which country had the highest percentage of its people living in rural areas in 1997.

READ MORE ABOUT IT

Tombs of the Ancient Americas by Jeanne Bendick. Franklin Watts. Learn more about the ancient civilizations of the Americas in this book.

HARCOURT BRACE

Visit the Internet at **http://www.hbschool.com** for additional resources.

Chapter 9 • **405**

THE AZTECS AND THE INCAS

"Your people are protected by your shade, for you are like the silk-cotton tree or the bald cypress which gives a great round shadow; and the multitudes are protected by your branches."

Speech made in honor of a new Aztec emperor

This woman from Peru is a descendant of an ancient people of the Americas called the Incas.

The Aztecs

| 1300 | 1400 | 1500 |

Neither the Olmecs nor the Mayas built empires. It was not until the 1400s that a large empire formed in Mesoamerica. The people who built this empire were the Aztecs.

The Arrival of the Aztecs

Around 1200, nomads from the north came to the area of central Mexico now known as the Valley of Mexico. There they settled near other communities of native peoples that had been built along the lakes in the center of the valley. These newcomers were the Aztecs. The already settled people of the valley, which they called Anahuac (AH•nah•wahk), thought of the Aztecs as uncivilized. The newcomers did not speak Nahuatl (NAH•waht•uhl), the language used in the valley. Also, they wore animal skins rather than clothes woven from cotton. In addition, they used bows and arrows. These weapons helped make them better warriors than others in the valley.

The Aztec people called themselves the Mexica rather than the name by which they are now known. Because of this, the land all around them has become known as Mexico.

Many experts believe that the ancient Aztecs came from what is now northern Mexico. The Aztecs moved south in search of a new homeland. According to legend, the Aztec war god, Huitzilopochtli (wee•see•loh•PAWCH•tlee), had promised that they would find their homeland where they saw an eagle with a snake in its mouth, sitting on a cactus. The Aztecs saw this sign on a small, swampy island in Lake Texcoco (tes•KOH•koh) and settled there. Today the eagle with the snake is a symbol of Mexico and appears on the Mexican flag.

REVIEW *Where did the Aztec people settle?*

FOCUS
How can one group of people gain political control over other groups?

Main Idea Read to learn how the Aztecs gained control over other Mesoamerican peoples.

Vocabulary
causeway
chinampa
conquistador

An Aztec god (right); an Aztec calendar (above).

The Building of Tenochtitlán

About 1325, the Aztecs began building a capital city on the island in Lake Texcoco. They called the new capital Tenochtitlán (tay•nohch•teet•LAHN). In some ways the place said to be chosen by Huitzilopochtli was a good one. Having water all around made the island city easy to defend against attack. Also, the lake offered fish, water birds, and frogs for food.

However, the island had no farmland and no stone or wood for building. Flooding, too, was a problem.

The Aztecs found ways to solve all the problems caused by their location. First, they built **causeways**, or land bridges, to connect the island capital to the mainland. Then they made a dike, or earthen wall, 9 miles (14 km) long to protect the city from floods. They drove large posts deep into the ground and built reed houses on top of them. They traded with other peoples to get the wood and stone they needed for palaces and temples.

To solve the problem of not having enough farmland, the Aztecs built **chinampas** (chee•NAHM•pahz) in their lake. Chinampas were human-made islands formed by weaving branches

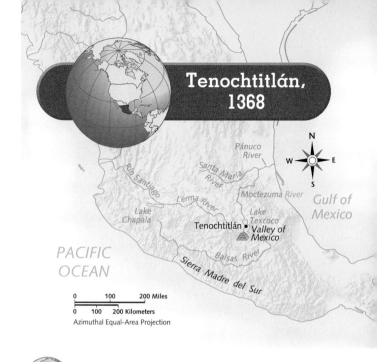

Tenochtitlán, 1368

Pánuco River
Río Santiago
Santa María River
Lerma River
Moctezuma River
Lake Chapala
Lake Texcoco
Tenochtitlán • Valley of Mexico
Gulf of Mexico
PACIFIC OCEAN
Balsas River
Sierra Madre del Sur

0   100   200 Miles
0   100   200 Kilometers
Azimuthal Equal-Area Projection

Location The Aztecs built their city Tenochtitlán in a valley in what is now central Mexico.
■ *What physical features might have made living in Tenochtitlán difficult?*

together to make huge underwater baskets. Trees planted around the baskets helped keep them in place. Workers then filled the baskets with mud from the lake's bottom. New islands of farmland now rose above the water. On these "floating gardens," farmers grew corn, beans, peppers, and avocados.

All these changes to the environment helped Tenochtitlán grow. By the 1400s Tenochtitlán had become a huge city of more than 300,000 people.

REVIEW *How did the Aztecs solve the problems caused by Tenochtitlán's location?*

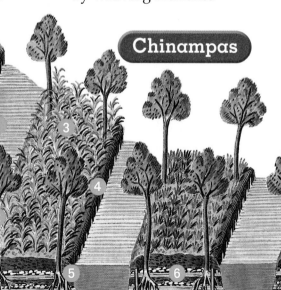

Chinampas

LEARNING FROM DIAGRAMS
Chinampas are human-made islands for farming. Each chinampa contained the following:
1 canal   4 topsoil
2 tree   5 stake
3 crop   6 plant fiber
■ *What might Aztec farmers have done when their chinampas flooded?*

Creating an Empire

In 1428 the Aztecs of Tenochtitlán joined the people of the city-states of Texcoco and Tlacopán to form a triple alliance. This united group quickly became the strongest fighting force in the Valley of Mexico. Together the three city-states built an empire. It is often called the Aztec Empire because the Aztecs were the most powerful of the three allies.

During the 1400s, Aztec warriors began to march across the Valley of Mexico and over the mountains to the south and the east. The soldiers conquered many other native peoples. From all the conquered people, the Aztecs demanded tribute, or payment. The tribute brought large amounts of food, precious stones and metals, and clothing into the Aztec capital of Tenochtitlán. Maize, beans, chilis, cotton, rubber, jaguar skins, feathers of tropical birds, gold, silver, jade, and cacao beans were all part of the tribute.

By 1500 the Aztec Empire covered more than 200,000 square miles (517,960 sq km) of Central America. As many as 5 million people lived under the rule of the Aztecs. From the peoples they conquered, the Aztecs borrowed many new ways of doing things. They also learned new ideas from the Mayas, just as the Mayas had from the Olmecs. Together the ideas helped the Aztecs build a strong empire.

REVIEW *How did the Aztecs gain their power and wealth?*

Location The Aztecs built an empire by conquering the city-states of neighboring peoples.

■ *What city-states shown on the map were independent within the Aztec Empire?*

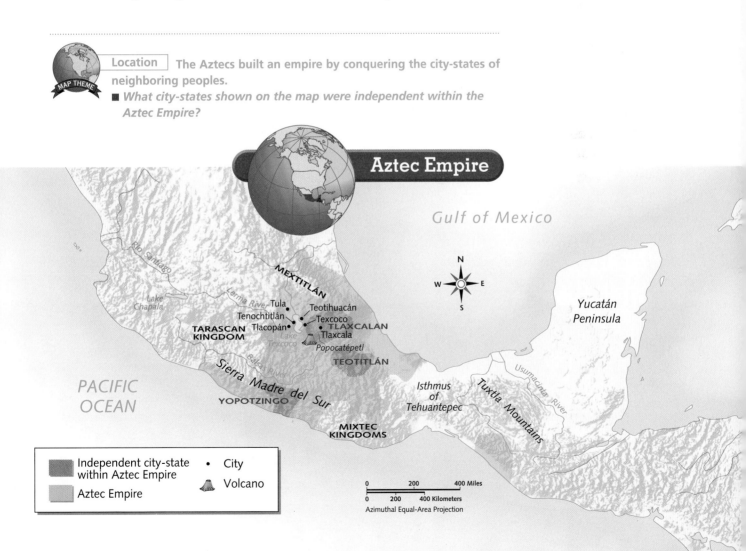

Aztec Empire

Gulf of Mexico

Río Santiago

MEXTITLÁN

Lake Chapala

Lerma River

Tula

Teotihuacán

Tenochtitlán

Texcoco

TARASCAN KINGDOM

Tlacopán

TLAXCALAN

Tlaxcala

Lake Texcoco

Popocatépetl

TEOTITLÁN

Yucatán Peninsula

Balsas River

Sierra Madre del Sur

YOPOTZINGO

Isthmus of Tehuantepec

Usumacinta River

Tuxtla Mountains

PACIFIC OCEAN

MIXTEC KINGDOMS

N W E S

Independent city-state within Aztec Empire

City

Aztec Empire

Volcano

0   200   400 Miles
0   200   400 Kilometers
Azimuthal Equal-Area Projection

Aztec Way of Life

Like the Mayas, the Aztecs had a calendar, a number system, and a way of writing. They also built many large cities, just as the Mayas had.

All the Aztec cities were ruled by one emperor, who was believed to talk to the gods. The emperor ruled over both military and religious matters. Assisted by a council of four high-ranking officials, the emperor made all Aztec laws and saw that they were followed. This leader stood at the top of Aztec society. People were not allowed to turn their back on the emperor or look directly at his face.

Below the emperor in society were the nobles, who helped him rule, and the soldiers. Then came the farmers, artisans, and merchants. Aztec women in these classes were allowed to own property and manage businesses. Aztec girls attended school. Some grew up to become religious leaders or healers, while many others farmed.

At the bottom of Aztec society were the slaves. Some Aztecs became slaves because their parents were too poor to support them. Others were enslaved as adults because they had broken Aztec laws. Some captured enemies also became slaves.

Not all captives became slaves, however. Many were sacrificed, or killed as offerings, to the Aztec gods. In fact, one reason the Aztecs fought wars was to capture enemy warriors to sacrifice.

Like other ancient cultures, the Aztecs worshipped many gods. One of the most important gods was Quetzalcoatl (ket•zahl•koo•WAH•tahl), the god of knowledge and creation. The Aztecs believed the world would end if they did not make sacrifices to their gods. Thousands of people died each year as sacrifices. Because human sacrifice was so important to the Aztecs, the goal in battle was to capture enemies, not to kill them.

REVIEW *What was the connection between religion and war in Aztec life?*

This pyramid is part of the ruins at Teotihuacán, Mexico. Once the largest city in Mesoamerica, it was abandoned about A.D. 700. When the Aztecs saw Teotihuacán about 600 years later, they thought it was the burial place of their gods.

The End of the Aztec Empire

By the early 1500s the Aztecs ruled over many city-states. Yet some city-states in the region remained independent. When the Spanish landed in Mexico in 1519, these independent city-states helped the Spanish conquer the Aztec Empire.

The Spanish conquerors, or **conquistadors** (kahn•KEES•tah•dawrz), seemed strange to the Aztecs. The conquistadors rode horses and had weapons unknown to the Aztecs, such as cannons, steel swords, and crossbows.

When the Aztec ruler Motecuhzoma (maw•tay•kwah•SOH•mah) heard descriptions of the Spanish, he thought they might be Aztec gods. According to the Aztec religion, Quetzalcoatl would return one day to rule the Aztecs. The Aztecs believed that the Spanish conquistador Hernando Cortés (kawr•TEZ) might be Quetzalcoatl.

The Aztec people did not know that the Spanish were interested only in their gold.

This stone, known as the Calendar Stone, was found in Mexico City in 1790. Mexico City was built on top of the ruins of the Aztec capital, Tenochtitlán.

The Aztecs found out too late that the newcomers were men, not gods. The Spanish kidnapped Motecuhzoma and demanded that control of Tenochtitlán be turned over to them.

The Aztecs did not give up their city without a fight. However, in 1521 the Aztec capital finally fell to the Spanish. The Spanish built a new city over the ruins of Tenochtitlán. This city became the center of Spain's new empire in the Americas. Today the city is known as Mexico City.

REVIEW *What caused the end of the Aztec Empire?*

LESSON 1 REVIEW

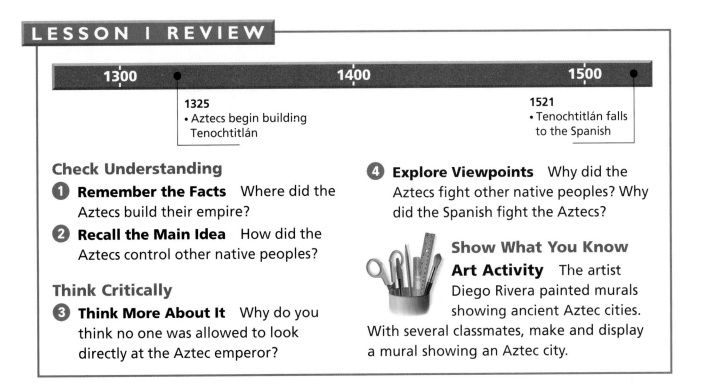

```
1300 ———————————— 1400 ———————————— 1500
        •                                      •
       1325                                   1521
       • Aztecs begin building                • Tenochtitlán falls
         Tenochtitlán                            to the Spanish
```

Check Understanding

1 **Remember the Facts** Where did the Aztecs build their empire?

2 **Recall the Main Idea** How did the Aztecs control other native peoples?

Think Critically

3 **Think More About It** Why do you think no one was allowed to look directly at the Aztec emperor?

4 **Explore Viewpoints** Why did the Aztecs fight other native peoples? Why did the Spanish fight the Aztecs?

Show What You Know

Art Activity The artist Diego Rivera painted murals showing ancient Aztec cities. With several classmates, make and display a mural showing an Aztec city.

Compare Maps with

1. Why Learn This Skill?

The size in which places are drawn on maps depends on how large an area is to be shown. Maps that show a large area must use a small scale—that is, places must be drawn small to fit everything in. Maps that show a small area use a larger scale—places are drawn larger because there is less to fit in. Knowing about map scales can help you choose the best map for gathering the information you need.

2. Understand the Process

The maps on these two pages use different scales to show different views of the same area. Map A shows the Aztec Empire in North America at the height of its power. Map B shows the Valley of Mexico. Map C shows the area around Lake Texcoco. Map A has the smallest scale of these maps. Small-scale maps show large areas. Map C has the largest scale. Large-scale maps show small areas in detail.

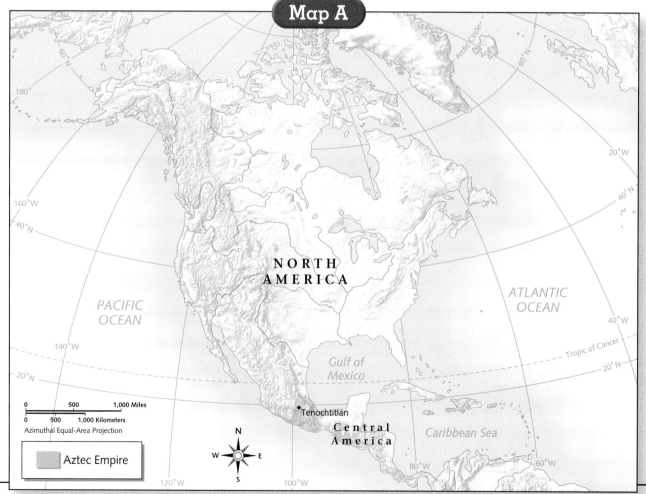

Map A

Aztec Empire

Azimuthal Equal-Area Projection

Different Scales

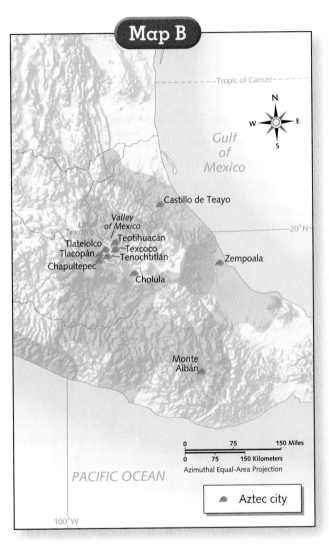

Map B

Tropic of Cancer

Gulf
of
Mexico

N
W   E
S

Castillo de Teayo

Valley
of Mexico

Lake
Texcoco

Teotihuacán

Tlatelolco

Texcoco

20°N

Tlacopán

Tenochtitlán

Chapultepec

Zempoala

Cholula

Monte
Albán

0   75   150 Miles
0   75   150 Kilometers
Azimuthal Equal-Area Projection

PACIFIC OCEAN

100°W

🔺   Aztec city

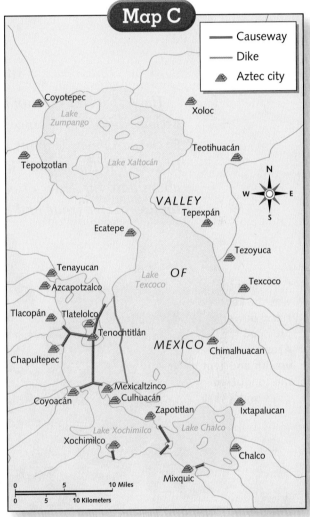

Map C

— Causeway
— Dike
🔺 Aztec city

Coyotepec

Lake
Zumpango

Xoloc

Teotihuacán

Tepotzotlan

Lake Xaltocán

VALLEY

Tepexpán

Ecatepe

N
W   E
S

Tezoyuca

Tenayucan

Lake
Texcoco

OF

Azcapotzalco

Texcoco

Tlacopán

Tlatelolco

Tenochtitlán

MEXICO

Chapultepec

Chimalhuacan

Mexicaltzinco

Coyoacán

Culhuacán

Zapotitlan

Ixtapalucan

Lake Xochimilco

Lake Chalco

Xochimilco

Chalco

Mixquic

0   5   10 Miles
0   5   10 Kilometers

Use the maps to answer these questions:

1. Find Tenochtitlán on all three maps, and notice other cities near it. Which map shows the most cities?

2. Suppose that you wanted to travel from Tenochtitlán to the Gulf of Mexico. Which map would best help you? Explain.

3. Suppose that you wanted to measure the length of Lake Texcoco. Which map would you use?

3. Think and Apply

Think about how you use maps when you travel. Find two road maps with different scales—such as one of your state and one of a large city in your state. When would it be more helpful to use the state map? When would it be more helpful to use the city map? Which of the maps has a smaller scale? Which of the maps has a larger scale?

THE AZTECS

written by Tim Wood
illustrated by Philip Hood

The Aztec civilization has held the interest of historians and archaeologists ever since the ruins of their first cities were uncovered. Even today people want to find out all they can about the Aztec way of life. Author Tim Wood's book **The Aztecs** *helps to answer many questions about how the Aztecs lived. The selection that follows describes two topics—Aztec trade and Aztec writing.*

Collecting tribute was the key to Aztec power. It provided the Aztecs with great wealth and kept the conquered cities under their control.

TRADE AND TRIBUTE

Much of the wealth of the Aztecs came from tribute sent to Tenochtitlán by the other cities in the Empire. Gathering tribute was very well organized, with Aztec tax gatherers, called calpixques, stationed at key points throughout the Empire to supervise the system's operation.

Gathering Tribute

Every few months, lists of the tribute required from each city were sent out from the capital. If the cities refused to send the tribute, war was declared. Throughout the year, but especially at harvest time, a constant stream of goods was carried into Tenochtitlán to be stored in the city's warehouses.

Merchants

The Aztecs also acquired the goods they needed by trade. The traveling merchants, called pochteca, led very different lives from those of other Aztecs. They lived in separate areas in the city and all belonged to a merchant guild. They had their own laws and judges and worshipped their own god, Yacatecuhtli—the "Lord Who Guides" or "Lord Nose"—to whom they made offerings so he would protect them on their journeys. The children of merchants were allowed to marry only the children of other merchants.

Merchants were afraid of being envied by the nobles, so they hid their great wealth, dressing in plain cloaks and headdresses made of cactus fiber.

Trading Expeditions

The pochteca went on long trading journeys to all corners of the Empire. When preparing for an expedition, great care was taken. They chose a lucky date and cut their hair for the last time until they returned. Their departure was announced in the marketplace so that other people could join the trading expedition. The merchants left the Valley of Mexico carrying goods belonging to many different merchants, each of whom shared in the profits—or losses—of the venture. The pochteca were heavily armed and took large numbers of soldiers with them.

Since the Aztecs had no pack animals—they had never even seen horses or oxen—all their trade goods were carried by porters in bundles on their backs. They returned with luxury goods from all corners of the Empire, such as fine cloth, dyes, cacao beans, gold, cotton, feathers, jade beads, and copper.

Spying

As well as adding to the great wealth of the Aztecs, the merchants were useful in other ways. Some acted as spies, reporting to Aztec generals about the wealth of other cities and the size of their armies. Sometimes they were told to cause trouble in an area that the Aztecs wanted to attack. They would find a way to insult a local chief so that their expedition would be attacked. The Aztec armies would then march in to restore order and make sure the trade routes were safe—and to collect prisoners for sacrifice.

Hiding Their Wealth

The merchants always returned secretly, arriving at night with the goods in their canoes or packs, well covered. Everything was then hidden in the house of another trader. Merchants were always very careful to keep their enormous wealth and trade secrets hidden from other Aztecs.

Stripping bark from a fig tree to make into paper. Other forms of paper were made from cactus fibers or animal skins. Paper-making was a complicated process that required a lot of hard work.

WRITING

The Aztecs did not have an alphabet. Instead, they wrote in pictures, or glyphs. Some glyphs were simply pictures of objects, such as a tree or a knife. Other glyphs represented ideas. War, for example, was shown by a picture of a shield and a club. Speech was represented by small scrolls coming out of the mouth of the speaker. Motion was shown by a line of footprints. The glyphs were drawn first in black and then colored in.

Sound Signs

Some glyphs came to represent the sound of the object they showed. These glyphs were called phonograms and could be put together to spell out the sound of a word. This method was often used for writing the names of places. For example, by combining the glyph for a tree (quauitl) with the glyph for teeth (tlantli), the scribe created a new glyph that sounded like the city of Quauhtitlán.

An Aztec codex. Most early Mexican cultures had paper and writing, and made codices. Some codices tell stories from Mexican history. Others are religious almanacs containing weather forecasts, and prophecies that named lucky and unlucky days for farming and fighting. These concertina-like books provide much information for historians studying Mexican civilization.

Reading Pictures

Glyphs were not written on a page in regular order. They were drawn to make a scene that had to be interpreted by the reader, in the same way that we might try to solve a picture puzzle. The position and size of the glyphs were important. Things that were supposed to be further away were drawn at the top of the page, with nearer things at the bottom. Glyphs that were more important would be drawn larger.

This type of picture writing is not easy to understand, nor is it easy to use. It is not surprising that only a few skilled scribes, usually priests, could read and write.

Paper

Paper was made from the bark of wild fig trees, which was soaked in lime water and beaten to separate the fibers. The pulp was mixed with gum and beaten into thin sheets. The sheets were often stuck together to make a long concertina-like book called a codex. Some codices were painted on parchment made of animal skin.

Official Paperwork

Ruling the vast Aztec Empire required large numbers of written records dealing with tribute owed and collected, orders given to officials, and reports from other cities. In addition, each calpulli kept detailed maps and records of the land held by its members. Every temple had a large library of religious and astrological books. Priests believed the stars and planets affected the lives of their people, and they kept records of eclipses, planetary events, and star movements. All this writing meant that a lot of paper was used, and nearly half a million sheets were sent as tribute each year.

Counting

The Aztecs were also able to write numbers. Their counting system was based on 20, the number of fingers and toes each person has. The numbers 1 to 19 were represented by fingers; the number 20 was shown by a flag; the number 400 (20×20) was a feather; and the number 8,000 ($20 \times 20 \times 20$) was a bag, which could hold that number of cacao beans.

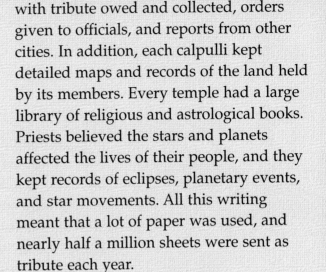

LITERATURE REVIEW

1. How were the lives of merchants different from the lives of the other Aztecs?

2. How was the Aztec number system like the Maya number system, which you read about earlier? How was it different?

3. Write a review of the selection you have just read. Tell about the information it gives and whether you would recommend the selection to others.

FOCUS

How can a small group of people rule over a large area?

Main Idea   Read to find out how the Incas created a strong central government for their empire.

Vocabulary

quinoa   mitima
Quechua   quipu

The Incas

1200   1400   1600

Between the snow-capped peaks of the high Andes Mountains, early peoples found a few wide and fertile valleys. The rich land was perfect for growing corn, potatoes, and **quinoa** (KEEN•wah), a grain high in protein. This highland region also offered the settlers stones for building and llamas for carrying loads. Other animals called alpacas (al•PAH•kahz) and vicuñas (vih•KOON•yahz) provided wool.

In time, people known as the Incas moved into the area and formed a remarkable civilization. Over the years they claimed the entire area and formed an empire.

The Incas Rise to Power

The first Incas settled in the Cuzco (KOOS•koh) Valley around 1200. They took their name from their ruler, who was known as the Inca.

Legends tell of the founding of the city of Cuzco by the first Inca, Manco Capac (MAHNG•koh KAH•pahk). One legend says that the sun god sent his son and daughter to bring civilization to the world. The Incas believed that they were descended from this god and goddess.

The Incas began to farm in their new home and to build communities. They did not, however, live peacefully with the native peoples around them. By the early 1400s, they began to conquer their neighbors. Under the leadership of Pachacuti (pah•chah•KOO•tee), the ninth Inca, Inca rule spread far beyond the Cuzco Valley. Pachacuti conquered some groups by military force. Others he won over through peace talks.

Pachacuti's son and grandson expanded the empire even farther. By the time the Spanish arrived in Peru in

Most Inca gold was melted down by the Spanish conquistadors who conquered the Incas. This knife (above) and this llama (left) are among the few gold Inca artifacts left.

1532, the Inca Empire covered an area of almost half a million square miles (1.3 million sq km). It stretched through what is today Peru, Ecuador, Bolivia, Argentina, and Chile. The Incas ruled over more than 9 million people. The conquered peoples spoke at least 20 different languages and belonged to many ethnic groups.

REVIEW *When and where did the Inca people first settle?*

Governing an Empire

The Inca Empire covered three very different environments: the dry Pacific coast, the hot and humid eastern foothills of the Andes, and several highland plateaus surrounded by rugged mountains.

To link the many regions of their empire, the Incas built more than 14,000 miles (22,526 km) of roads. Two main roads ran the length of the empire, one through the mountains and the other along the coast. Many smaller roads connected the two at different points along the way.

Inca roads were built differently, depending on the environment. Stone causeways led over swampy areas along the coast. On steep mountainsides, roads took the form of stone steps. In the highlands,

Expansion of the Inca Empire

VENEZUELA
COLOMBIA
GUYANA
Angasmayo River
Quito
ECUADOR
Amazon River
PERU
Urubamba R.
Marañón R.
BRAZIL
SOUTH AMERICA
Huánuco Pampa
Lima
Machu Picchu
Cuzco
Abancay
Lake Titicaca
Chuquiabo (La Paz)
BOLIVIA
Lake Poopó
PACIFIC OCEAN
ANDES
MOUNTAINS
Atacama Desert
PARAGUAY
Copiapo
CHILE
Salado
Paraná River
URUGUAY
Santiago
Talca
Maule River
ARGENTINA

0   300   600 Miles
0   300   600 Kilometers
Modified Chambers Trimetric Projection

— Present-day border
Lands added, 1438–1463
Lands added, 1463–1493
Lands added, 1493–1525

Regions The Inca Empire closely followed the coast of the Pacific Ocean.
■ *Which Inca cities were built near the Pacific coast?*

These ancient Inca ruins were found outside of what is today the city of Cuzco, Peru.

swaying rope bridges hung across deep canyons.

Along the Inca roads relay teams of runners carried messages, and llamas moved goods. Inca transportation worked so well that Incas in Cuzco could enjoy fresh fish caught in the Pacific Ocean.

Roads could connect the many parts of the empire, but roads alone could not bring the people together. To win loyalty, the Incas showered newly conquered peoples with gifts of cloth and food. They also allowed those peoples' former chiefs to take part in governing.

The Incas made sure, though, that the conquered people learned Inca ways. They brought the sons of conquered chiefs to Cuzco. There they taught them Inca ways to take back to their people. **Quechua** (KECH•wah), the Inca language, became the official language all through the empire. People were free to worship their own gods only after saying that the Inca gods were more powerful.

To support Inca rule, each household in the empire had to pay a labor tax. For part of each year, all men had to work for the government. They served in the army, cared for government-owned farms and herds, and built roads, bridges, or cities. Most conquered people were able to stay in their homelands. However, some were sent to live in new places. This practice was called **mitima** (mee•TEE•mah). Mitima helped the Incas begin new communities. It also prevented rebellion by breaking up large groups of conquered people and spreading them throughout the Inca Empire.

REVIEW *What steps did the Incas take to make newly conquered peoples part of the empire?*

Movement Many roads crisscrossed the Inca Empire. Some of the ancient roads, such as the one shown above, are still in use today.

■ *About how far was it from Quito to Cuzco using the ancient Inca roads?*

Inca Roadways

Orinoco River

AMAZON

Quito

Chimborazo
20,561 ft.
(6,267 m)

Huancabamba

BASIN

Amazon River

SOUTH
AMERICA

Chan Chan

Huascarán
22,205 ft.
(6,768 m)

Huánuco

Jauja Machu
Picchu

Vilcas Cuzco

Lake Titicaca

Volcán Misti
19,101 ft.
(5,822 m)

Illimani
20,741 ft.
(6,322 m)

Lake
Poopó

N
W E
S

ANDES

MOUNTAINS

Atacama
Desert

Mt. Acay

PACIFIC
OCEAN

Copiapo

Paraná River

0   300   600 Miles
0   300   600 Kilometers
Modified Chambers Trimetric Projection

Santiago Aconcagua
22,834 ft.
(6,960 m)

Talca

Maule River

Inca Empire
— Inca roadways

Pachacuti
(Ruled 1438–1471)

Many legends tell about the life of Pachacuti, the ninth Inca ruler. One says that when enemies threatened Cuzco, the eighth ruler and his older son fled. Only the younger son stayed to defend the city. His prayers to the Inca god Viracocha were said to turn stones on the hillside into a fierce army. After defeating the enemy, the prince took the name Pachacuti— "Transformer of Earth."

Other legends tell about Pachacuti's achievements. These legends claim that Pachacuti began the Inca Empire in 1438 and organized the government that ruled over the newly conquered lands.

Inca ruler Pachacuti, by an eighteenth-century artist who lived in Cuzco, Peru

Inca Life and Work

In the center of each Inca city was a main square, with large government buildings all around it. To construct their buildings, Inca workers cut large stone blocks and stacked them to form walls. They fit the blocks so closely that cement was not needed to hold them together. Many Inca walls still stand in areas where earthquakes have toppled later buildings.

Inside the government buildings nobles and others did many jobs. Accountants kept track of numbers of people and goods in the empire. They also kept lists that told who owed labor taxes and where and when they would work. Because the Incas did not have hieroglyphics or an alphabet, all this information was stored on groups of colored, knotted strings known as **quipus** (KEE•pooz). The different-colored knots on the quipus stood for different words or ideas. For example, the color yellow was the word *gold*. The color white was the word *peace*.

All the people wore beautiful, finely made clothing. Some of the clothing was made from cotton raised by Inca farmers. Some was woven from yarn made from alpaca hair. Only Inca nobles could own jewelry made of gold or silver.

Away from the busy streets of the city's center were the Inca homes. Three

Inca accountants were trained to record and read records kept on quipus (left). Inca craftworkers wove fine cloth (above).

generations of the same family usually lived together. Most people lived in small mud houses with thatched roofs. The richest nobles had their own palaces.

Some Incas worked as craftworkers, traders, or merchants. Most, however, worked on government-owned farms.

REVIEW *What were some of the jobs in Inca society?*

LEARNING FROM DIAGRAMS The Incas built their buildings with stone blocks cut to fit together closely.
■ *Why do you think the Incas cut the stones they used?*

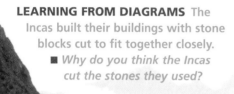

Inca Stonework

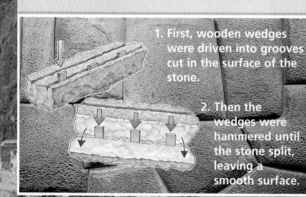

1. First, wooden wedges were driven into grooves cut in the surface of the stone.

2. Then the wedges were hammered until the stone split, leaving a smooth surface.

The Surviving Inca Empire

In 1532 conquistador Francisco Pizarro (pee•ZAR•oh) and a group of Spanish conquistadors landed on the Pacific coast of Peru. Their goal was to claim the wealth of the Americas.

Not long before the arrival of the Spanish, the Inca ruler died. Two of his sons, Huascar (WAHS•kar) and Atahuallpa (ah•tah•WAHL•pah), were fighting over which of them would become the new leader of the Incas.

Atahuallpa's forces finally defeated their enemy, killing Huascar in the fight. Pizarro invited the new emperor to his camp. Once there, Pizarro's forces captured him. Atahuallpa promised Pizarro a room full of gold and silver in exchange for his freedom. The Incas brought Pizarro these riches, but the conquistador ordered his soldiers to kill Atahuallpa anyway. Then Pizarro and his army captured Cuzco. Inca attempts to

The ruins of the Inca city of Machu Picchu rest high in the Andes Mountains. Built around 1490, Machu Picchu was never discovered by the Spanish conquistadors.

take Cuzco back from the Spanish failed. The Incas outnumbered the Spanish, but their wooden swords were no match for Spanish guns.

The Spanish claimed control of the Inca Empire. Many Incas became slaves and were forced to work on Spanish farms and in Spanish mines.

Spanish ways began to replace Inca ways. Christianity replaced the worship of the Inca gods. The Spanish began to import resources from their homeland. Cows, sheep, chickens, and wheat and barley were introduced as new foods to the Americas. The Spanish exported native resources to Spain.

Spanish culture did not replace all of the Inca culture. In the highlands, many Incas hid from the Spanish. They continued to live much as they had before Pizarro landed. They secretly kept their religion

alive. Even today, Peruvian highlanders often wear traditional clothing woven in the old style. The Inca language, Quechua, is an official language of present-day Peru, along with Spanish.

REVIEW *How and when did the Inca Empire end?*

Inca descendants in present-day Peru

LESSON 3 REVIEW

1200		1400		1600

1200
• Incas first settle in the Cuzco Valley

1438
• Pachacuti founds Inca Empire

1532
• Spanish arrive in Peru

Check Understanding

1 **Remember the Facts** Where was the Inca Empire located?

2 **Recall the Main Idea** How did the Incas create a strong central government for their empire?

Think Critically

3 **Think More About It** Do people have much personal freedom in a highly organized society? Explain.

4 **Explore Viewpoints** Why might an Inca noble have felt differently about Spanish rule than an Inca farmer? Explain.

Show What You Know
Multimedia Activity
Work in a group to prepare and present a multimedia report to your class. Research an ancient native group of the Americas before 1500 that is not discussed in this unit. Find out about the civilization's lifeways, environment, government, religion, and economy. Use any of the following as part of your report: computers, posters, charts and graphs, slides, overhead transparencies, speeches, models, music, dance, art.

Evaluate Information

1. Why Learn This Skill?

You can get information from many sources, such as radio, newspapers, the Internet, and television. Before you use this information, however, you need to evaluate it. To **evaluate** information is to decide whether you can trust it.

2. Information and Sources

One kind of information is **facts**, or statements that can be proved to be true. Other kinds of information cannot be proved so easily. Archaeologists study ancient cultures about which little is known. Based on their studies, they form opinions. An **opinion** is a statement of someone's belief or judgment. Although some opinions are supported by fact, most cannot be trusted as much as facts.

For historians, written or picture records are important sources of information to find out about the people and events of the past. These records may be firsthand accounts, or **primary sources**, that tell the authors' own ideas. Other records are secondhand accounts, or **secondary sources**, that tell about other people's ideas.

Picture A shows Motecuhzoma urging the Aztecs to surrender as the Spanish hold him prisoner. A Spanish artist painted this scene during the 1500s.

Picture A

and Sources

3. Understand the Process

To evaluate information and its sources, you can follow these steps:

- Study the material carefully.
- Think about the audience.
- Check for **bias**, a leaning toward or against someone or something.
- When possible, compare sources.

Now see how well you can evaluate the pictures that appear on these pages. Both pictures show a different battle between the Spanish and the Aztecs. Picture A was drawn by a Spanish artist. Picture B was drawn by an Aztec artist. Use what you know about evaluating sources to answer the questions.

1 What audience do you think Picture A was drawn for? Explain how you know.

2 Does Picture A show bias? Explain how you know.

3 In what ways is Picture A like Picture B? How is it different?

4. Think and Apply

With a partner, look again at some of the pictures in this unit. Identify each as being a primary source or a secondary source. Then follow the steps in Understand the Process to study the pictures closely. Discuss how much you could trust these pictures as sources of information.

Picture B

Picture B shows Aztec warriors defending Motecuhzoma's palace from Spanish attackers. An Aztec artist painted this scene during the 1500s. The scene appears in a Mexican manuscript.

1200   1300

1200
• Incas first settle in the Cuzco Valley

1325
• Aztecs begin building Tenochtitlán

CONNECT MAIN IDEAS

Use this organizer to show how the Aztecs and the Incas built their empires. Write two examples for each main idea. A copy of the organizer may be found on page 95 of the Activity Book.

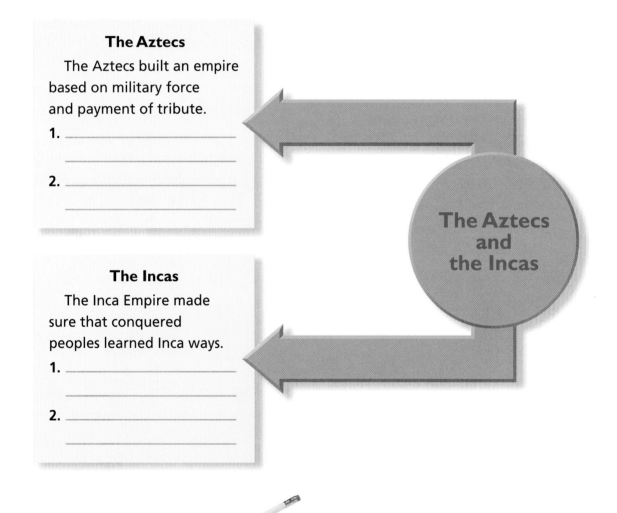

The Aztecs

The Aztecs built an empire based on military force and payment of tribute.

1. _____

2. _____

The Incas

The Inca Empire made sure that conquered peoples learned Inca ways.

1. _____

2. _____

The Aztecs and the Incas

WRITE MORE ABOUT IT

Write a Short Story Write a short story about an ancient Aztec family. Before you write, be sure to plan what your setting will be, who your characters will be, and what your plot will be. Mention Aztec innovations and ways of life in your story.

Write a Letter Imagine that you are a conquistador first with Cortés in Mexico and later with Pizarro in Peru. Write a letter to your family in Spain, telling them about the similarities and differences between the Aztecs and the Incas.

USE VOCABULARY

Write a word from this list to complete each of the sentences that follow.

chinampa   quipu

Quechua   quinoa

1 _____ is a protein-rich grain that is native to the Andes.

2 The Incas recorded information on a set of knotted strings called a _____.

3 The Inca language called _____ became the official language of the Inca Empire.

4 An Aztec "floating garden," or _____, provided additional farmland.

CHECK UNDERSTANDING

5 Why did the Aztecs settle where they did?

6 What symbol of Mexico appears on the Mexican flag?

7 What was the Aztecs' capital city called?

8 What caused the Aztec Empire to end?

9 Where in the Americas did the Incas settle?

10 Who was Pachacuti?

11 Why did the Incas build so many roads?

THINK CRITICALLY

12 **Think More About It** Both the Aztecs and the Incas believed they had a duty to rule other people. How did this affect their civilizations?

13 **Cause and Effect** What are some problems that can occur when people from different cultures first meet?

14 **Past to Present** The Aztec Empire was supported by tribute, while the Inca Empire was supported by a labor tax. How are most governments supported today?

APPLY SKILLS

Compare Maps with Different Scales Use the maps on pages 412 and 413 to answer these questions.

15 Suppose you want to find the distance between Texcoco and Chapultepec. Which map would you use? Why?

16 What might a map of Tenochtitlán look like at an even larger scale?

Evaluate Information and Sources
Imagine that you have been asked to write a report on how the Spanish affected the native peoples of the Americas. Would you use primary sources, secondary sources, or both? Do you think you might find bias in sources on this topic? Explain.

READ MORE ABOUT IT

Aztec Times by Antony Mason. Simon & Schuster. Read this book to learn more about the Aztec way of life including Aztec art, science, and schools.

Visit the Internet at **http://www.hbschool.com** for additional resources.

F·O·O·D
America Gave the World

Who could imagine Italian food without tomatoes? Irish stew without potatoes? Indian curry without chili peppers to make it hot? Or Ghanaian stew without peanuts?

Yet none of these traditional foods of Europe, Asia, and Africa could have developed without ingredients that came from the Americas. When the earliest Americans began to farm, they domesticated many wild plants unknown in other parts of the world. Throughout both continents, they developed corn, several kinds of beans, including kidney beans, snap beans, and lima beans, and squashes like zucchini and pumpkins. North American Indians called corn, beans, and squash the "three sisters." Together these foods gave Native Americans a balanced diet.

Different areas of the Americas made their own contributions to the world's dinner tables. On islands throughout the Caribbean, native peoples raised peanuts and sweet potatoes. In the eastern woodlands of North America, peoples collected sap from maple trees and boiled it down into maple syrup and sugar. In the jungles of Central America, other peoples found cacao beans and vanilla pods. In the high Andes, still others grew potatoes and preserved them by freeze-drying. Chili peppers, avocados, cranberries, tomatoes, and eggplants are all foods that originated in the Americas.

So next time you enjoy popcorn, spaghetti, bean soup, a baked potato, or hot chocolate, think about the Native American farmers. It was they who gave key ingredients to these popular foods.

Think and Apply

Think about the different foods you eat during one week. Then use library resources to find out where key ingredients of these foods first came from. Using this information, create a quiz on these foods and places for friends and family members.

Visit the Internet at **http://www.hbschool.com** for additional resources.

Check your media center or classroom video library for the Making Social Studies Relevant videotape of this feature.

Summarize the Main Ideas
Study the pictures and captions to help you review the events you read about in Unit 5.

Write Creatively
Imagine that you could visit one of the civilizations shown in this visual summary. Now imagine meeting a person from that civilization. Write about that meeting.

1 As the great animal herds disappeared, early people began hunting smaller game and foraging for food. In time, bands settled in different parts of the Americas.

3 The Mayas adapted to change in many ways. They used unique ways of farming to grow food in the rain forests.

5 The Incas created a strong central government by building roadways and by making sure their conquered subjects learned Inca customs.

2 Olmec culture, religion, and government influenced later Mesoamerican civilizations.

4 The Aztecs conquered other Mesoamerican peoples. The conquered peoples gave the Aztecs tribute to keep peace.

USE VOCABULARY

Write each term in a sentence that will explain its meaning.

1 conquistador **4** Quechua

2 intercropping **5** quipu

3 Mesoamerica **6** slash-and-burn farming

CHECK UNDERSTANDING

7 How do scientists think the first people reached the Americas?

8 What innovations of Olmec civilization were adopted by the Mayas?

9 What were the Mayan temples of Tikal made of and what did they look like?

10 How did the Aztecs change their environment as they built Tenochtitlán?

11 How did the Incas overcome the problem of high mountains dividing their empire?

12 What areas of South America did the Inca Empire cover?

13 What is so remarkable about the ancient walls of the Incas?

THINK CRITICALLY

14 **Past to Present** Why might people today be interested in learning what caused the collapse of Mayan civilization?

15 **Think More About It** How do you think the Americas might be different today if the Spanish had not conquered the Aztecs and the Incas?

16 **Personally Speaking** Which of the cultures you read about in this unit interests you the most? Why?

APPLY SKILLS

Compare Maps with Different Scales Use Map A and Map B to answer the questions.

17 Which map would you use to identify ancient cities fewer than 100 miles from Chichén Itzá?

18 Which map would you use to find the distance from the Chichén Itzá market to each of the ball courts?

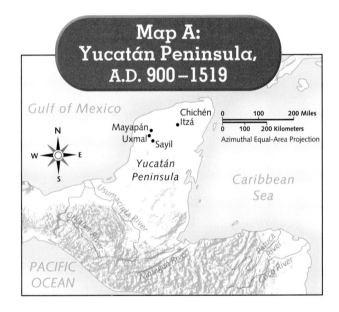

Map A: Yucatán Peninsula, A.D. 900–1519

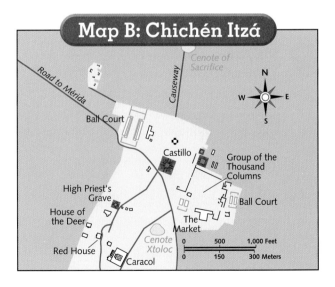

Map B: Chichén Itzá

REMEMBER

- Share your ideas.
- Cooperate with others to plan your work.
- Take responsibility for your work.
- Help one another.
- Show your group's work to the class.
- Discuss what you learned by working together.

ACTIVITY

Make a Model

In a group, think about the monuments and structures built by early civilizations in the Americas. Then choose one to build as a model. You and your group might make an Olmec head, an Aztec or Maya temple, or an Inca rope bridge. Whatever you build, include a human figure to show the scale. Display your finished model in the classroom.

ACTIVITY

Tell a Story

Imagine that you and your group are Aztec storytellers. It is your responsibility to remember and retell the history of the Aztecs. Plan a retelling of the story of the way the Aztecs found their island home. Then take turns telling this story to another group.

Unit Project Wrap-Up

Make a Map Now that you have completed Unit 5, you and your classmates can complete your map of early civilizations of the Americas. First, label the regions where the Olmecs, Mayas, Aztecs, and Incas lived. Then use the notes you have gathered to illustrate one or two scenes that show the culture of each civilization. Include one or two sentences to describe each scene. You may wish to draw your scenes and write your sentences on separate sheets of paper. You can then display these papers alongside your map. Place your completed map on a classroom wall.

THE WORLD TODAY

In many ways, the present-day world is different from the world of long ago. New ways of governing, manufacturing, traveling, and communicating make ancient days seem far away. Yet it was the ideas of past civilizations that laid the foundation for the modern world. Much of our present-day thinking about laws, religious beliefs, art, literature, and science has its roots in the distant past.

◄ These modern communications satellites orbiting the Earth use solar cells for power.

UNIT THEMES

- Individualism and Interdependence
- Interaction Within Different Environments
- Commonality and Diversity
- Continuity and Change

Unit Project

Hold a World Summit At the end of the unit, you and your classmates will hold a world summit—a meeting of the highest-level world leaders. The topic will be "Challenges for the Twenty-First Century." As you read this unit, choose a present-day country that interests you and take notes as you learn more about that country. Use other references to find out more about your chosen country as well. Your notes will help you represent your chosen country at the class world summit.

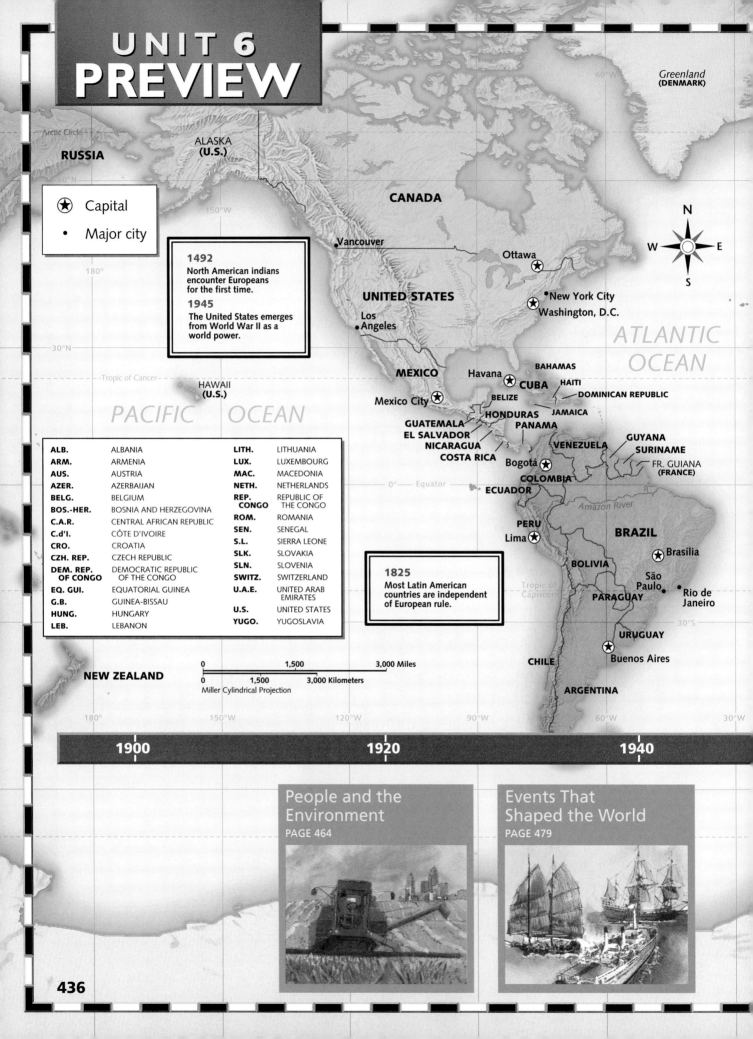

Greenland
(DENMARK)

Arctic Circle

RUSSIA

ALASKA
(U.S.)

CANADA

⭐ Capital
• Major city

1492
North American indians
encounter Europeans
for the first time.

1945
The United States emerges
from World War II as a
world power.

Vancouver

Ottawa ⭐

UNITED STATES

Los
•Angeles

•New York City
⭐ Washington, D.C.

ATLANTIC
OCEAN

30°N

Tropic of Cancer

HAWAII
(U.S.)

PACIFIC   OCEAN

MEXICO   Havana ⭐

BAHAMAS

CUBA   HAITI

Mexico City ⭐   BELIZE   DOMINICAN REPUBLIC
JAMAICA

GUATEMALA   HONDURAS
EL SALVADOR   PANAMA
NICARAGUA   VENEZUELA   GUYANA
COSTA RICA   SURINAME
Bogotá ⭐   FR. GUIANA
COLOMBIA   (FRANCE)

0° — Equator   ECUADOR

ALB.	ALBANIA	LITH.	LITHUANIA
ARM.	ARMENIA	LUX.	LUXEMBOURG
AUS.	AUSTRIA	MAC.	MACEDONIA
AZER.	AZERBAIJAN	NETH.	NETHERLANDS
BELG.	BELGIUM	REP.	REPUBLIC OF
BOS.-HER.	BOSNIA AND HERZEGOVINA	CONGO	THE CONGO
C.A.R.	CENTRAL AFRICAN REPUBLIC	ROM.	ROMANIA
C.d'I.	CÔTE D'IVOIRE	SEN.	SENEGAL
CRO.	CROATIA	S.L.	SIERRA LEONE
CZH. REP.	CZECH REPUBLIC	SLK.	SLOVAKIA
DEM. REP.	DEMOCRATIC REPUBLIC	SLN.	SLOVENIA
OF CONGO	OF THE CONGO	SWITZ.	SWITZERLAND
EQ. GUI.	EQUATORIAL GUINEA	U.A.E.	UNITED ARAB
G.B.	GUINEA-BISSAU		EMIRATES
HUNG.	HUNGARY	U.S.	UNITED STATES
LEB.	LEBANON	YUGO.	YUGOSLAVIA

PERU
Lima ⭐

Amazon River

BRAZIL

⭐ Brasília

BOLIVIA

São
Paulo
• Rio de
Janeiro

1825
Most Latin American
countries are independent
of European rule.

Tropic of
Capricorn

PARAGUAY

30°S

URUGUAY

CHILE   ⭐ Buenos Aires

ARGENTINA

NEW ZEALAND

| 0 | | 1,500 | 3,000 Miles |
| 0 | 1,500 | 3,000 Kilometers | |

Miller Cylindrical Projection

180°   150°W   120°W   90°W   60°W   30°W

1900   **1920**   **1940**

People and the Environment
PAGE 464

Events That Shaped the World
PAGE 479

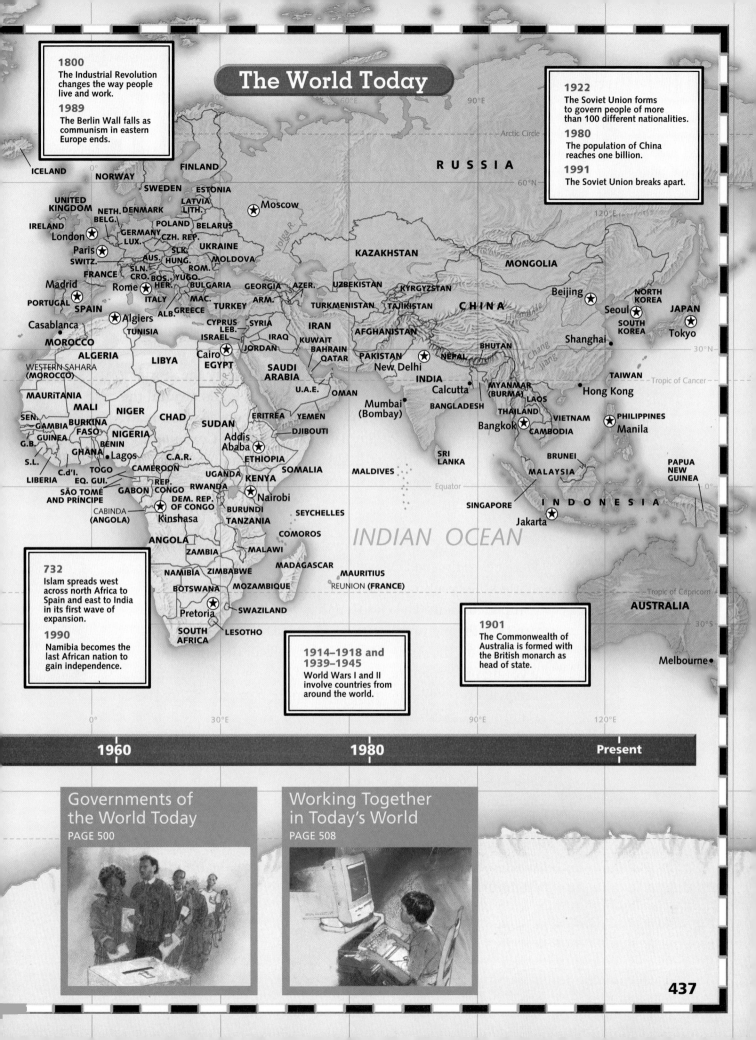

The World Today

1800
The Industrial Revolution changes the way people live and work.

1989
The Berlin Wall falls as communism in eastern Europe ends.

1922
The Soviet Union forms to govern people of more than 100 different nationalities.

1980
The population of China reaches one billion.

1991
The Soviet Union breaks apart.

732
Islam spreads west across north Africa to Spain and east to India in its first wave of expansion.

1990
Namibia becomes the last African nation to gain independence.

1914–1918 and 1939–1945
World Wars I and II involve countries from around the world.

1901
The Commonwealth of Australia is formed with the British monarch as head of state.

1960   1980   **Present**

Governments of the World Today
PAGE 500

Working Together in Today's World
PAGE 508

437

Talking Walls
The Stories Continue

written by Margy Burns Knight • illustrated by Anne Sibley O'Brien

Author Margy Burns Knight is fascinated by the stories that ancient walls tell. She has researched walls around the world and has written two books about them. As you read this selection from *Talking Walls: The Stories Continue*, think about how the walls she describes, though built so long ago, still affect people today.

Bonampak

No one knows why the murals in Bonampak, Mexico, were never finished. Maya children know that their ancestors started the paintings about 1,000 years ago, but they never completed them. The children that visit the murals today can't see the pictures very well because the ancient paint is chipping off the walls. One painting tells of the coronation of a young prince, but no one knows if he grew up to be king because his people disappeared from Bonampak before the painting was finished.

Today, archaeologists study the murals at Bonampak. They use computers to imagine what the colors might have looked like in the paintings and to find clues about why the Maya left Bonampak. Perhaps it was a war or a famine; the answer remains a mystery. Archaeologists hope that Maya children and other visitors will be able to see the paintings for generations to come. They are working hard to save the murals from further disintegration.

Prayer Wheels

Om mani padme hum—"Hail the jewel in the lotus"—can be heard throughout the day and night as Tibetans turn prayer wheels. This prayer, repeated over and over, is called a *mantra*. Tibetans believe that as the wheel is turned, the special power of the mantra is released. Some prayer wheels are very small and can be hand-held. Others are built along walls near monasteries or temples. Children and grownups spin them as they walk past.

Many Tibetans are not able to spin prayer wheels in their own country because they have been forced to leave Tibet and now live elsewhere. In 1959 China invaded Tibet, and thousands of Tibetans fled from their homes. Many went to India, including the Dalai Lama, the leader of the Tibetan Buddhist people.

Tibetans want independence from China. The Dalai Lama doesn't believe that violence should be used to win back his country. He teaches people to be kind and forgiving, even with people who seem to be enemies. He and many others are working for peace in Tibet.

Hadrian's Wall

Once a year English children dress up as Roman soldiers and pretend to march and guard Hadrian's Wall. They are reenacting[1] a time about 2,000 years ago when Roman Emperor Hadrian ordered his soldiers to build a 74-mile-long wall across England to mark the northern boundary of his empire. About 10,000 soldiers spent six years building the wall.

Once the wall was completed, the soldiers guarded the Roman territory from atop the turrets[2] and towers along the wall. Before the Roman invasion, the Picts, a tribe from Scotland, lived in Northern England. They tried to keep the Romans from taking their land, but the Roman army was too strong for them.

Today much of Hadrian's Wall is in ruins, but people are trying to preserve parts of it. The historians and archaeologists who study the wall think at one time it was painted white, but they are not sure why. They hope that some of the Roman artifacts that they have found near the ruins— jewelry, toys, sandals, and games—will be the clues they need to piece together more stories about Hadrian's Wall.

Read now to find out more about how the past has helped shape the present-day world and its people. As you continue to read Unit 6, you will also learn about the governments, economies, and ways of life of many different groups of people in the world today.

---

[1] **reenacting:** repeating the actions of an earlier time
[2] **turrets:** small towers

PEOPLE AND PLACES

"There are no such things as limits to growth, because there are no limits on the human capacity for intelligence, imagination, and wonder."

Ronald Reagan, governor of California from 1967 to 1975 and President of the United States from 1981 to 1989

Young girl from the country of Senegal in Africa

Countries of the World Today

About 10,000 years ago the world had no political borders and no countries. Today almost 200 countries of different sizes exist. On every continent except Antarctica, borders have been drawn to bring people together or to separate them.

FOCUS

How have geography and the events of the past helped create the borders of today's countries?

Main Idea Look for ways both geography and history have helped form the countries of the world today.

Vocabulary

bilingual
communism

The Americas

When people think of North America, they usually think of three large countries—Canada, the United States, and Mexico. However, North America also includes the smaller countries that make up Central America and the Caribbean.

The northernmost country in North America is Canada. Canada is a country that is large in area but small in population. It covers 3,851,809 square miles (9,975,415 sq km), but it has just 29 million people.

Most of Canada's population lives in the southern part of the country, where the climate is warmer. Canada's large cities and most of its population are located along its border with the United States. However, some Canadians do live in the far north. For example, the native Inuit (IN•yoo•wit) people have lived in the harsh climate of Canada's arctic tundra for centuries.

Each year millions of people visit Niagara Falls on the border of Canada and the United States.

Independence in the Americas

ARCTIC OCEAN

Greenland (DENMARK)

ALASKA (U.S.)

CANADA 1867 (Britain)

UNITED STATES 1776 (Britain)

ATLANTIC OCEAN

GUATEMALA 1821 (Spain)

BELIZE 1981 (Britain)

HONDURAS 1821 (Spain)

MEXICO 1823 (Spain)

NICARAGUA 1821 (Spain)

VENEZUELA 1821 (Spain)

EL SALVADOR 1821 (Spain)

GUYANA 1966 (Britain)

COSTA RICA 1821 (Spain)

PANAMA 1821 (Spain)

PACIFIC OCEAN

ECUADOR 1830 (Spain)

COLOMBIA 1819 (Spain)

SURINAME 1975 (Netherlands)

PERU 1821 (Spain)

BRAZIL 1822 (Portugal)

BOLIVIA 1825 (Spain)

CHILE 1818 (Spain)

PARAGUAY 1811 (Spain)

URUGUAY 1825 (Spain)

ARGENTINA 1816 (Spain)

0   1,500   3,000 Miles
0   1,500   3,000 Kilometers
Miller Cylindrical Projection

ECUADOR 1830 (Spain) | Present-day country, with date of independence and former ruling country

Place Most of the countries in North and South America gained their independence by 1825.

■ *What was the first country to gain its independence?*

Canada was settled and ruled by both the British and the French. Because of this, Canada is a **bilingual**, or two-language, country. Both French and English speakers make up large parts of the population.

Like Canada, the United States is a large country in area. However, it is also large in terms of population. With more than 267 million people, the United States has about 10 times the number of people Canada has. People from all over the world came to the United States in the past, and they continue

to come today. Because of this, every one of the United States' 50 states has people of different backgrounds.

To the south of the United States is Mexico. In some ways, Mexico is like the United States. It is made up of states, elects a president, and has a congress. Yet its culture is very different. Although Mexico is part of North America, it is also part of the cultural region of Latin America.

Latin America is made up of Mexico, Central America, South America, and many nearby islands. It gets its name from the Latin-based languages, Spanish and Portuguese, spoken in the region. These languages were introduced during the 1500s, when the first Spanish and Portuguese colonies were built there.

The Spanish greatly influenced the culture of Latin America. The culture also has deep roots in ancient native groups such as the Olmecs, Mayas, Aztecs, and Incas.

The countries of Latin America are very different geographically. For example, the country of Chile has the driest desert in the world, the Atacama Desert, while much of the country of Brazil is covered by lush tropical rain forests.

REVIEW *How has settlement by different groups affected the cultures of the Americas?*

Europe

The cultures of Europe have affected—and been affected by—other cultures around the world. Europeans began colonies in the Americas, Asia, Australia, and Africa. Most of these colonies are now independent. Yet the contact between cultures can still be seen in such things as clothing, food, architecture, art, and music.

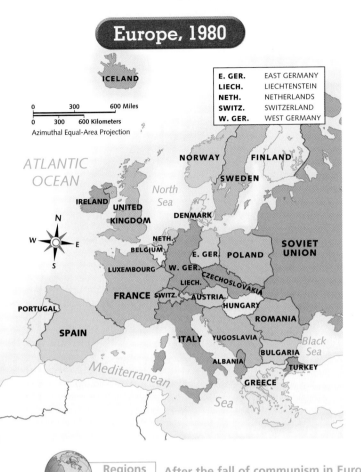

Europe, 1980

E. GER.	EAST GERMANY
LIECH.	LIECHTENSTEIN
NETH.	NETHERLANDS
SWITZ.	SWITZERLAND
W. GER.	WEST GERMANY

Europe, 1998

BOS.-HERZ.	BOSNIA-HERZEGOVINA
LIECH.	LIECHTENSTEIN
MAC.	MACEDONIA
NETH.	NETHERLANDS
SLOV.	SLOVENIA
SWITZ.	SWITZERLAND
YUGO.	YUGOSLAVIA

Regions After the fall of communism in Europe, new countries came into being as ethnic groups gained their independence.
■ *What countries were created after 1980?*

Europe today is very different from how it was 20 years ago. Some European countries that existed in the 1980s no longer exist. Others have changed in size. New ones have formed as well.

Most of these changes came about with the fall of communism in eastern Europe. **Communism** is a form of government in which a country owns all property and businesses. Under communism, people have little freedom. Today no country in Europe has a communist government.

About 500 million people live in Europe though its area is just 4 million square miles (10,359,200 sq km). The continent of North America is more than twice the size of Europe and has fewer people.

With more than 40 countries, Europe has many different cultures. More than 50 languages are spoken throughout the continent.

Some countries of Europe are very small, while others are quite large. Russia is Europe's largest country. It covers land in both Europe and Asia. Europe's smallest country is Vatican City, with an area of less than 1 square mile (2.6 sq km). It is the smallest country in the world.

Present-day Europe has many large industrial cities. Among the best-known European cities are London, in Great Britain; Paris, in France; St. Petersburg, in Russia; Vienna, in Austria; and Rome, in Italy.

REVIEW *How has the geography of Europe changed in the past 20 years?*

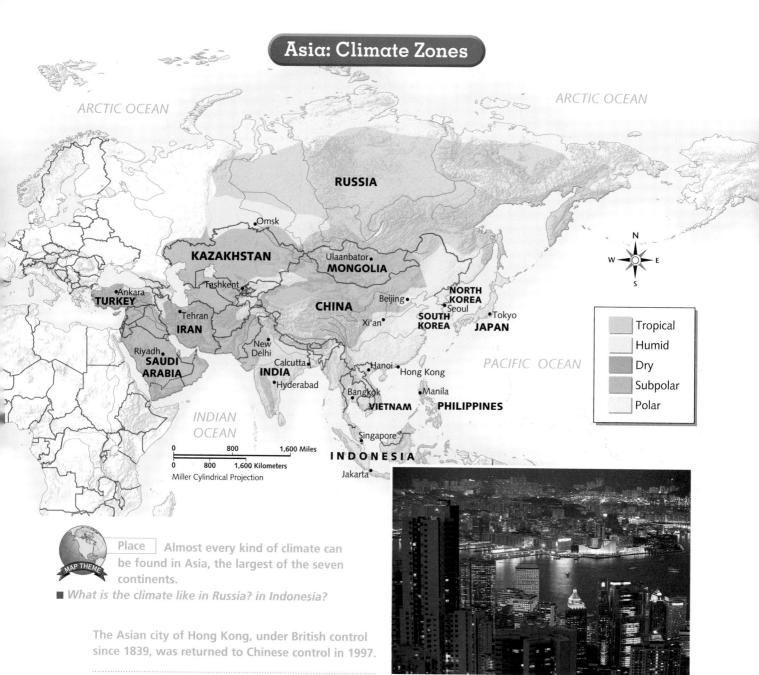

Asia: Climate Zones

ARCTIC OCEAN

ARCTIC OCEAN

RUSSIA

•Omsk

KAZAKHSTAN

Ulaanbator•
MONGOLIA

•Tashkent

•Ankara
TURKEY

CHINA

Beijing•

NORTH
KOREA

•Tehran
IRAN

Xi'an•

Seoul•
SOUTH
KOREA

•Tokyo
JAPAN

Riyadh•
SAUDI
ARABIA

New
Delhi

Calcutta•

Hong Kong•

PACIFIC OCEAN

INDIA
•Hyderabad

•Hanoi

•Manila

INDIAN
OCEAN

Bangkok•

VIETNAM

•Manila
PHILIPPINES

	Tropical
	Humid
	Dry
	Subpolar
	Polar

0   800   1,600 Miles
0   800   1,600 Kilometers
Miller Cylindrical Projection

•Singapore

I N D O N E S I A

Jakarta•

Place Almost every kind of climate can be found in Asia, the largest of the seven continents.
■ *What is the climate like in Russia? in Indonesia?*

The Asian city of Hong Kong, under British control since 1839, was returned to Chinese control in 1997.

Asia

Asia was the birthplace of the world's major religions—Christianity, Islam, Judaism, Buddhism, and Hinduism. More people live in Asia than on any other continent. The country of China alone has more than 1 billion people. It is the world's most heavily populated country.

Asia is huge not only in population but also in physical size. Asia is the largest continent, with an area of more than 17 million square miles (44,026,600 sq km). Because

Asia is so large, geographers usually divide it into several regions.

Part of the huge country of Russia forms the entire region of northern Asia. The present-day countries of Pakistan, Bangladesh, and India form a large part of the region known as southern Asia. Cultures in southern Asia trace their heritage back thousands of years, but their countries are fairly new. India and Pakistan became independent countries in 1947. When colonial India gained its independence from Britain, it split in two. The part where most Hindus lived became India. The part where most Muslims lived became Pakistan.

The towering Himalayas separate the regions of southern and central Asia. A large part of China, Kazakhstan (ka•zak•STAN), Kyrgyzstan (kir•gih•STAN), Turkmenistan (terk•meh•nuh•STAN), and Uzbekistan (uhz•beh•kih•STAN) make up the region of central Asia.

Bordering central and southern Asia to the west is southwestern Asia. This area is also known as the Middle East. The ancient civilizations of the Fertile Crescent began in this region. Today all the countries in southwestern Asia are Muslim countries, except for Israel, which is a Jewish state.

Far to the east of central Asia lies eastern Asia. It includes part of China, North Korea, South Korea, and Japan. All of these countries border the Pacific Ocean. China is the largest country in the world that remains communist.

To the south of China is southeastern Asia. This region includes the island countries of the Philippines and Indonesia and the mainland countries of Vietnam, Laos, Cambodia, and Thailand.

REVIEW *What was one of the reasons India and Pakistan separated?*

Africa

As you have read, most experts believe that the world's earliest people lived in Africa. Some of these people migrated from Africa into Asia and Europe.

The ancient Egyptian and Nubian civilizations developed in northern Africa. Africa was where important trade routes were started and where Ghana and Mali, large empires based on trade, first grew.

The events that would lead to the creation of Africa's present-day countries took place just 500 years ago. At that time, European countries were beginning to build colonies in Africa. The borders of these colonies were formed by the Europeans' desire for resources rather than by the location of the different African cultural groups. For

GEOGRAPHY

The Continent of Antarctica

Antarctica is made up of the land over and around the South Pole. Most of the continent is covered in deep snow and ice all year long. Antarctica is the world's coldest continent. The temperature there once reached −128.6°F (−89.2°C)—the world's lowest recorded temperature. Scientists from several countries conduct research in Antarctica on weather, animal life, and other subjects.

Penguins in Antarctica have adapted to the cold climate there.

Africa offers a diverse landscape—from modern cities such as Nairobi, Kenya (left), to the grasslands of the savanna, populated by unique wildlife (above).

Place Independence came to the countries of Africa at different times.
■ *What countries became independent during the 1990s?*

Independence in Africa

1960	Date of independence
	Not independent

ATLANTIC OCEAN

Madeira Islands (PORTUGAL)

Canary Islands (SPAIN)

ASIA

TUNISIA

MOROCCO 1956

Mediterranean Sea 1956

WESTERN SAHARA (Morocco)

ALGERIA 1962

LIBYA 1951

EGYPT 1922

CAPE VERDE 1975

MAURITANIA 1960

MALI 1960

NIGER 1960

CHAD 1960

SUDAN 1956

ERITREA 1993

DJIBOUTI 1977

SENEGAL 1960

THE GAMBIA 1965

BURKINA FASO 1960

GUINEA-BISSAU 1974

GHANA 1957

NIGERIA 1960

CENT. AFRICAN REP. 1960

ETHIOPIA

SOMALIA 1960

GUINEA 1958

SIERRA LEONE 1961

LIBERIA 1847

BENIN 1960

CAMEROON 1960

UGANDA 1962

KENYA 1963

Equator 0°

CÔTE D'IVOIRE (IVORY COAST) 1960

TOGO 1960

GABON 1960

DEM. REP. OF CONGO 1960

RWANDA 1962

SÃO TOMÉ AND PRÍNCIPE 1975

EQUATORIAL GUINEA 1968

BURUNDI 1962

TANZANIA 1964

SEYCHELLES 1976

REP. OF THE CONGO 1960

ANGOLA 1975

ZAMBIA 1964

MALAWI 1964

COMOROS 1975

ATLANTIC OCEAN

NAMIBIA 1990

ZIMBABWE 1980

BOTSWANA 1966

MOZAMBIQUE 1975

MADAGASCAR 1960

RÉUNION (FRANCE)

Tropic of Capricorn

N
W E
S

SOUTH AFRICA 1910

SWAZILAND 1968

LESOTHO 1966

MAURITIUS 1968

INDIAN OCEAN

0   500   1,000 Miles
0   500   1,000 Kilometers
Azimuthal Equal-Area Projection

example, the land of the Somali people and other groups was divided among several different colonies. These colonies later became the independent countries of Somalia, Kenya, and Ethiopia. Today Somali people live in all three countries.

Present-day countries of Africa are still feeling the effects of the European divisions. In some cases, people of the same ethnic group are separated by the boundary lines of countries. In other cases, enemy groups must live together in the same country. In the 1990s, conflicts arose in Rwanda and Burundi because of the European divisions. Fighting broke out between two rival ethnic groups, the Hutu and the Tutsi.

Conflict between peoples also led to the forming of Africa's newest country. This country, Eritrea (air•ih•TREE•uh), was once the northeastern part of Ethiopia. After a 30-year civil war, the Eritreans gained their freedom from Ethiopia in 1993.

In 1997, another change came about in Africa, when a new government was formed in Zaire. At that time the country changed its name to become the Democratic Republic of the Congo.

REVIEW *How were the borders of Africa's countries formed?*

Australia and Oceania

Australia is the world's smallest continent. This continent plus Oceania—all the islands of the central and south Pacific Ocean—would fill an area of just 3.3 million square miles (8.5 million sq km). Yet more than 20,000 islands make up the watery region of Oceania.

Australia is the only continent that holds just one country, also called Australia. Its name means "southern land," and its nickname is "the land down under."

The population of Australia is unevenly spread. The coastal plain in the east is very dry, so most people live near the eastern coast. A range of mountains called the Great Dividing Range runs north and south through Australia. Today most Australians live in the large cities of Brisbane, Sydney, Canberra (KAN•ber•uh), Newcastle, and Melbourne on the continent's eastern coast.

For thousands of years the native peoples of Australia were the only ones who knew about Australia's resources and beauty. Then the Dutch began to explore Australia in the early 1600s. In the late 1700s, Britain claimed Australia and started a colony there. In 1901, Australia became an independent country.

Ayers Rock in Australia is a popular tourist attraction. It has many caves with paintings made by early native Australians.

East of Australia is New Zealand, which is made up mainly of two long, narrow islands. New Zealand was colonized by the British in 1840, and gained its independence in 1907.

The other islands of Oceania are usually divided into three groups—these are called Melanesia (meh•luh•NEE•zhuh), Micronesia (my•kruh•NEE•zhuh), and Polynesia (pah•luh•NEE•zhuh). All are located northeast of Australia.

REVIEW *How have natural features affected the location of Australia's population?*

LESSON 1 REVIEW

Check Understanding

1 **Remember the Facts**   What is the main language spoken in Latin America? How was this language introduced?

2 **Recall the Main Idea**   How have geography and history helped form the countries of the world today?

Think Critically

3 **Think More About It**   Why might Asia cause great changes in the world if all its countries united? Why will this probably not happen?

4 **Cause and Effect**   How might the way European colonies were set up long ago cause political conflict in Africa today?

Show What You Know
Writing Activity
Select a country of today, and use an encyclopedia to find out how it got its borders. Write a report based on your findings, and present it to the rest of your class.

Compare Population

1. Why Learn This Skill?

Like most other geographic information, facts about population can be shown on maps. Using maps, geographers can show which parts of the world have the most people and which have the fewest. They can also show the number of people living in cities of the world. Population can be shown on maps in many ways. Most population maps use dots or color, but different kinds of maps use these in different ways. Knowing how to read all kinds of population maps will make it easier for you to find out where few or many people live in the world and how many people live in each place.

find out how many people live in each city shown on the map.

Map B shows different information about population. It shows India's **population distribution**, or how many people live in each part of the country. On Map B, population distribution is shown by dots. Each dot stands for 100,000 people. The dots run together in some places on the map. In these places many people live close together. In other places there are fewer dots. In these places people live farther apart. In still other places, there are no dots. These places have either fewer than 100,000 people or no people at all.

2. Understand the Process

India, in Asia, is one of the most crowded countries in the world, with almost 1 billion people. Suppose that you wanted to find out more about India's population. You could do this by studying population maps. Map A shows the population of certain cities in India. It does this with dots of different sizes and colors. Look at the map key for Map A. Each dot stands for a different range of population according to its size. The dots get larger and larger to show more and more people. You can use the key to

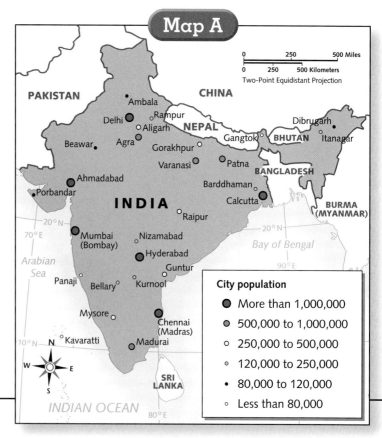

Map A

City population
- ● More than 1,000,000
- ● 500,000 to 1,000,000
- ○ 250,000 to 500,000
- ○ 120,000 to 250,000
- • 80,000 to 120,000
- ○ Less than 80,000

Maps

Where there are a great many people living close together, the population is *dense*. Where there are only a few people living far apart, the population is *sparse*. Both these terms describe population density. **Population density** is the average number of people living on a square unit of land. You can find this figure by dividing the number of people living on a given amount of land by the area of that land. For example, if 5,000 people live on 10 square miles (26 sq km) of land, the population density is 500 people per square mile.

Map C uses color to show the population density of India. Using the key, you can see where the population density in India is high and where it is low. Compare all three maps as you answer these questions:

1. About how many people live in the city of Mumbai? Which map did you use to find out?
2. Do people live closer together in northwestern or northeastern India? Which map did you use to find this out?
3. Which has the greater population density—the area of India around Delhi (DEH•lee) or the area around Hyderabad (HY•duh•ruh•bad)? Which map did you use to find out?

3. Think and Apply

With a partner, study the population maps on these pages. Together, prepare a list of five questions you might ask to see how well other classmates know how to use population maps. Exchange lists with other partner pairs, and answer their questions.

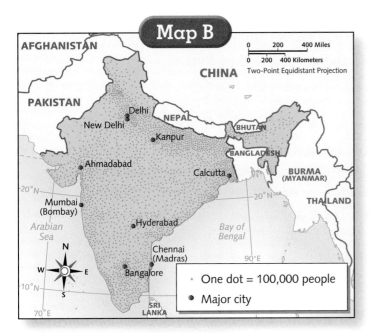

Map B

AFGHANISTAN

CHINA

PAKISTAN

Delhi
New Delhi
NEPAL
BHUTAN
Kanpur
BANGLADESH
Ahmadabad
Calcutta
BURMA (MYANMAR)
20°N
20°N
THAILAND
Mumbai (Bombay)
Arabian Sea
Bay of Bengal
Hyderabad
Chennai (Madras)
90°E
Bangalore
10°N
70°E
SRI LANKA

0   200   400 Miles
0   200   400 Kilometers
Two-Point Equidistant Projection

· One dot = 100,000 people
● Major city

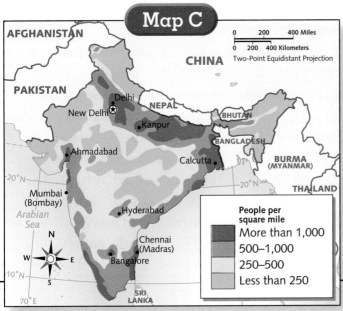

Map C

AFGHANISTAN

CHINA

PAKISTAN

Delhi
New Delhi
NEPAL
BHUTAN
Kanpur
BANGLADESH
Ahmadabad
Calcutta
BURMA (MYANMAR)
20°N
20°N
THAILAND
Mumbai (Bombay)
Arabian Sea
Hyderabad
Chennai (Madras)
Bangalore
10°N
70°E
SRI LANKA

0   200   400 Miles
0   200   400 Kilometers
Two-Point Equidistant Projection

People per square mile
More than 1,000
500–1,000
250–500
Less than 250

FOCUS

Why do people migrate from one country to another country?

Main Idea As you read, think about why people migrate from one part of the world to another.

Vocabulary

refugee
famine
urbanization
Islam
Muslim
Qur'an
mosque
suburbs
metropolitan
    area
megalopolis

People and the World Today

People can affect places, and places can affect people. It is easy to see how people affect places. They build houses and streets, carve tunnels in mountains, and make dams and reservoirs. But places can also change people or cause them to act in certain ways. The resources of an area affect what people eat, what they wear, and how they build. Physical features of an area affect where people build and how they travel. Through all of history, there has been a connection between people and the places they live.

People on the Move

From earliest times to the present, nomads have been on the move in search of new grasslands for their herds, or new animals to hunt and plants to gather. There are still a few nomadic peoples, such as the Fulanis (FOO•lah•neez) of western Africa and the Bedouins (BEH•duh•winz) of southwestern Asia. Unlike these present-day nomads, most people of the modern world are not always on the move. However, many people do make at least one major move in their lifetime.

Often people who migrate to another country or continent do so because of a problem. For example, they may move to escape the effects of war. In 1997 many Africans left the country that was then called Zaire to escape war. People who leave their homes to escape from war or other danger are called **refugees**.

Drought and times of **famine**, or shortage of food, may also cause people to leave a place. During the mid-nineteenth century, Ireland's potato crop failed for several

The Statue of Liberty was one of the first sights for many early immigrants arriving by ship in the United States.

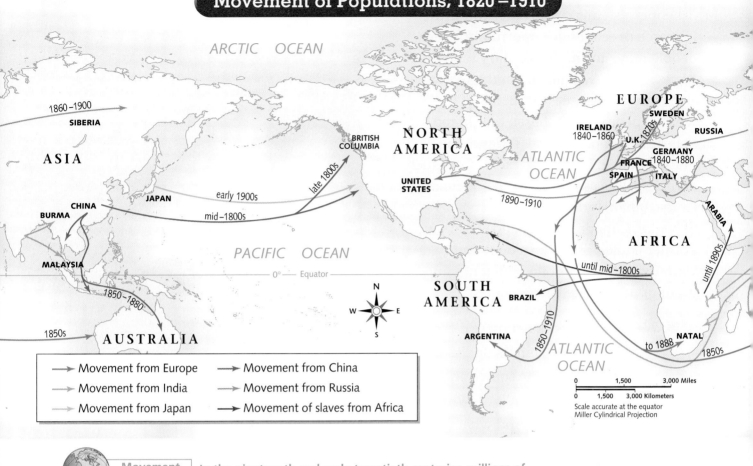

Movement of Populations, 1820–1910

ARCTIC OCEAN

1860–1900
SIBERIA

ASIA

EUROPE
SWEDEN
IRELAND 1840–1860
U.K. 1870s
RUSSIA
GERMANY 1840–1880
FRANCE
SPAIN
ITALY

CHINA
BURMA
JAPAN
early 1900s
mid–1800s
late 1800s

NORTH AMERICA
UNITED STATES

ATLANTIC OCEAN

1890–1910

ARABIA

MALAYSIA

PACIFIC OCEAN

0° — Equator

AFRICA

until mid–1800s

until 1890s

SOUTH AMERICA
BRAZIL

1850–1880

1850s

AUSTRALIA

N
W E
S

ARGENTINA

1850–1910

ATLANTIC OCEAN

NATAL
to 1888
1850s

Scale accurate at the equator
Miller Cylindrical Projection
0   1,500   3,000 Miles
0   1,500   3,000 Kilometers

→ Movement from Europe   → Movement from China
→ Movement from India   → Movement from Russia
→ Movement from Japan   → Movement of slaves from Africa

MAP THEME — **Movement**   In the nineteenth and early twentieth centuries, millions of people migrated from their home countries in search of a better life.
■ *Who immigrated to North America during this period? to South America?*

years in a row. This time became known as the Potato Famine. A large number of Irish people starved to death. Many others moved to Britain, the United States, or other countries. During the 1930s a severe drought caused thousands of people to leave the Great Plains area of the United States.

The search for more freedoms is another reason people migrate. Many of the early colonists in what became the United States left their homelands for religious freedom. When India and Pakistan became independent in 1947, thousands of Hindus left Pakistan for the mainly Hindu India. At the same time, thousands of Muslims left India for Pakistan.

People also migrate to escape persecution. In the 1930s Germany's leader Adolf Hitler took away rights from European Jews and other groups. Many were killed. Those who could escape left Europe for other places.

Each year many people, such as these at Ellis Island in New York, become United States citizens.

Chapter 11 • 455

People also migrate to other countries in search of economic opportunity. These people move to another country with the hope that they will make a better living.

Whatever their reasons, many of the world's people have chosen the United States as their new home. Today, immigrants come to the United States from such diverse places as Mexico, Cuba, Vietnam, China, Japan, India, the Philippines, El Salvador, Canada, Russia, and Germany. Former United States President Jimmy Carter said this about the different immigrant groups in the United States:

❝ We are of course a nation of differences. Those differences don't make us weak. They're the source of our strength. The question is . . . why our families came here. And what we did after we arrived. ❞

REVIEW *What are some reasons people migrate to other countries?*

To the Cities

Often people move not to a new country but to a new place in their own country. All over the world, people in rural areas move to cities because they cannot make a living farming. They may have heard of people who moved to the city and became successful. Many times, the newcomers find that city living does not match their dreams.

People who migrate to the cities sometimes face a life of poverty in their new home. These people often cannot find jobs or housing.

The movement of people to the cities has led to rapid urbanization. **Urbanization** is the changing of rural areas to cities. Some

Many Mexican farmers (inset) who can no longer earn a living from their land are moving to cities, such as Mexico City (above), to look for jobs.

cities, such as Calcutta in India, Manila in the Philippines, Caracas in Venezuela, and São Paulo in Brazil, already have millions of people. Yet each year millions more crowd into their city limits.

Such cities cannot handle all the newcomers. They cannot provide services such as garbage collection, fire and police protection, and public transportation for so many people. For the newcomers, city life is often worse, not better, than the life they left.

REVIEW *What problems do people sometimes face in moving to the cities?*

These photographs show the diversity of cultures around the world. Two men from Nigeria wear traditional dress (top left); a farmer and his family stand outside their house in Syria (below); two children play at their rural French home (bottom left).

World Cultures

Cultures around the world have very different beliefs, customs, and languages. The almost 4 billion people who live in Asia belong to many different cultures. Japanese, Chinese, Arab, Israeli, Indian, Turkish, and Tibetan are only a few of these cultures. Many of these cultures have continued unchanged in the same areas for centuries. Thousands of different languages and dialects are spoken in Asian lands.

Africa is home to more than 750 million people and at least 800 different cultures. In northern Africa, many people are Arab or have Arab ancestors. South of the Sahara, most people are descendants of native Africans, though some are descendants of European and Asian settlers. Today almost

900 languages are spoken in Africa. Among these are many African Bantu languages. Ever since the time of the European colonies in Africa, English, French, and Afrikaans—a language created by early Dutch settlers—have also often been spoken.

Europe's 500 million people also belong to many different cultural groups. Some, such as the French, the Greeks, the Italians, and the Germans, have their own country. Not all the different peoples of Europe have their own countries, however, and in some cases this has led to conflict. In the United Kingdom, for example, fighting has often flared between the English and the people of Northern Ireland.

North America and South America have been affected by several cultures. Early

European migrations led to large European populations in both places. Both places also have rich native cultures.

In North America, many people have British ancestors. Many others have an African heritage. In South America and Latin America, many people have Spanish ancestors.

Today the cultures of the world are in closer contact than ever before because of improved communication and transportation. In some ways many of the world's cultures are blending. At the same time, many are seeking ways to preserve their own heritages.

REVIEW *What are some of the cultures of Asia?*

World Religions

Many of the world's major religions had their roots in ancient times. The Israelites in southwestern Asia were the first to practice Judaism. Today about 14 million Jewish people live in all parts of the world. Almost 6 million Jews live in North America, many of them in the United States. Many people consider the country of Israel to be the homeland of the Jewish people. More than 80 percent of Israel's 5 million people are Jewish.

The beginnings of Hinduism and Buddhism can be traced to the continent of Asia. Most of the world's 322 million Buddhists live in Asia, but Buddhists can be found in most parts of the world. Almost 1 million people in North America alone follow the Buddhist religion.

The Hindu religion is followed mainly in Asia, where about 790 million Hindus live. Another 6 million Hindus live in other parts of the world.

The religion of Christianity has grown since the days of Jesus Christ and his early followers. Today almost 2 billion Christians live around the world. More than 700 million Christians live in North and South America. In the rest of the world, Christians include about 361 million Africans, 303 million Asians, and 555 million Europeans.

The religion of **Islam** (is•LAHM) is practiced by over 1 billion people. Followers of Islam are called **Muslims**. About half of all Muslims live in southern, central, and

Muslim pilgrims at Sacred Mosque in Mecca, Saudi Arabia (below left); Jain Temple in Ranakour, India (below)

southeastern Asia. Many others live in Europe. In Africa, Muslims make up about half of the total population. About 6 million Muslims live in the United States.

Muslims believe that a man named Muhammad (moh•HA•muhd), born in A.D. 570, was the last in a series of messengers from God. Among the first messages that Muhammad gave people was that there is only one God, or *Allah* in Arabic. The messages of Muhammad form the holy book of Islam, known as the **Qur'an** (kuh•RAN).

Muslims follow five basic acts of worship, known as the five pillars. The first pillar is belief in one God, and that Muhammad is the last of many messengers from God. The second pillar is the Muslim practice of praying five times a day and visiting a **mosque**, or house of worship, on Fridays. The third pillar is the act of giving a fixed part of yearly savings to the needy. The fourth pillar is the Muslim practice of fasting, or not eating and drinking, in the daytime during Ramadan (RAH•muh•dahn), the ninth month of the Islamic calendar. The fifth pillar is the making of at least one pilgrimage, or religious visit to Mecca, a holy Islamic city in Saudi Arabia. All Muslims face toward the city of Mecca when they pray.

REVIEW *What five religions that began long ago are still followed today?*

Russian Orthodox leader blesses the congregation on Easter (above left); Congregational church in Williamstown, Massachusetts (left); synagogue, New York City, New York (below)

Megalopolis

The Tokyo Metropolitan Region can truly be called a megalopolis. This region is made up of the metropolitan areas of Tokyo, Yokohama (yoh•kuh•HAH•muh), Osaka (oh•SAH•kuh), Chiba (CHEE•buh), and Kawasaki (kah•wuh•SAH•kee). It also includes 25 suburban cities west of Tokyo, several towns, and the Izu islands. Home to about 27 million people, the Tokyo Metropolitan Region is the largest urban center in the world.

JAPAN

Kawanishi • Ikeda
Kawanishi — Expressway
Takarazuka•
•Ibaraki
•Hirakata
Itami ✈ •Toyonaka
Expressway •Neyagawa
Suita
Moriguchi •Kadoma
Nishinomiya• •Daito Kongo-Ikoma Park
•Amagasaki
OSAKA
Expressway •Higashiosaka
KOBE
•Yao
Osaka Bay Sakai•
•Matsubara
Habakino•
N
W E
S
•Izumi
Kishiwada• Kongo-Ikoma Park

0   5   10 Miles
0   5   10 Kilometers

Cities of the World

Cities are not a new development. As long ago as 3500 B.C., the ancient Sumerians built the world's first cities. Today only the remains of those cities can be found. Some ancient cities, however, are still alive with people and activity. Rome, in Italy, has grown from its ancient beginnings to a modern city with a population of about 2,800,000 people. The ruins of its early times stand side by side with its modern buildings. In North America, Mexico City is built over the ancient Aztec city of Tenochtitlán.

History does not run so deep in other cities. Brasília, the capital of Brazil, is only about 50 years old. The sprawling city of Miami, Florida, was just a small settlement in 1895.

Cities around the world have grown dramatically. London, England (inset), and Rio de Janeiro, Brazil (below), are two of the largest cities in the world.

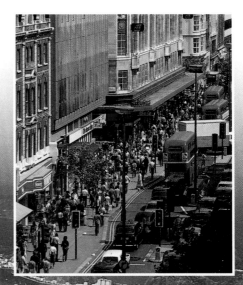

Today many cities have grown amazingly large. Japan, a very small country, has the world's largest city—Tokyo. About 27 million people live and work in this city. Other very large cities around the world include Buenos Aires (BWAY•nohs EYE•rays) in Argentina; Shanghai (shang•HY) in China; New York City, New York, and Los Angeles, California, in the United States; and Lagos (LAY•gahs) in Nigeria.

Many large cities have areas around them that have been developed as well. These areas where many people live are called **suburbs**. A city and its surrounding suburbs make up a **metropolitan area**. A metropolitan area usually has at least 50,000 people.

Some metropolitan areas are so close to one another that they blend together. The term **megalopolis** (meh•guh•LAH•puh•luhs) describes a region where this has happened. One megalopolis stretches from Boston, Massachusetts, to Washington, D.C., on the east coast of the United States.

REVIEW *What is a metropolitan area?*

Top Ten Urban Centers

Chart showing population of cities (in millions):
- Tokyo, Japan
- Mexico City, Mexico
- São Paulo, Brazil
- New York City, United States
- Mumbai (Bombay), India
- Shanghai, China
- Los Angeles, United States
- Calcutta, India
- Buenos Aires, Argentina
- Seoul, Korea

Population axis: 0 4 8 12 16 20 24 28 32
Population (in millions)

LEARNING FROM GRAPHS More than 10 million people live in each of these urban centers.
■ *About how many more people live in New York than in Calcutta?*

LESSON 2 REVIEW

Check Understanding
1. **Remember the Facts** What is meant by the term *refugee*?
2. **Recall the Main Idea** What are some things that cause people to migrate?

Think Critically
3. **Cause and Effect** What are some effects, other than overpopulation, that migration might have on cities?
4. **Think More About It** In what ways can newcomers of different cultures bring positive changes to United States cities?

Show What You Know
Plan a Web Page Imagine that your class wants to create an Internet site that describes many cities of the world. Each student in the class will write a Web page for one city. Choose a city and plan how you will describe that city on your Web page. Write a rough draft of the information you will show. Be sure to include the city's population, its size in area, a brief history, and a list of its places of interest. You may want to include maps of the different cities in your Web pages.

Understand a

1. Why Learn This Skill?

Time on Earth cannot be the same everywhere, since not all places face the sun at the same time. So time is divided by meridians, or lines of longitude. The prime meridian, or line of 0° (degrees) longitude, passes through Greenwich (GREH•nich), a

Clocks Around the World

NEW YORK
7:00 A.M.

CAIRO
2:00 P.M.

BUENOS AIRES
9:00 A.M.

DELHI
5:30 P.M.

LONDON
NOON

TOKYO
9:00 P.M.

suburb of London, England. Many years ago, Greenwich was chosen as the location for the prime meridian, which is the starting point for the world's time zones.

There are 24 standard zones, 12 of them to the east of Greenwich and 12 to the west. Each time zone covers 15 degrees of longitude. Every 15 degrees east or west, the time changes by one hour.

All time zones to the east of the prime meridian are ahead of Greenwich time. All zones to the west are behind Greenwich time. The meridian where the eastern and western time zones meet is known as the international date line. It is 12 time zones from the prime meridian, so when it is noon in the city of Greenwich, it is midnight at the international date line, the time when the date changes.

Today it is not unusual for people on different sides of the world to communicate with one another. More than ever it is necessary to know how to read time zone maps.

2. Understand the Process

The map on the next page shows all 24 time zones. It tells what time it is in each zone when it is noon at the prime meridian. Look at the times at the top of the map. The time in each zone is one hour ahead of the time in the zone to the west and one hour behind the time in the zone to the east. As you go east from Greenwich, the time in each zone you come to is one hour later

Time Zone Map

than the last. When it is noon in Greenwich, it is 1:00 P.M. in Vienna, Austria. Vienna is in the first time zone to the east of Greenwich. As you go west from Greenwich, the time in each zone is one hour earlier. When it is noon in Greenwich, it is 6:00 A.M. in Mexico City, which is in the sixth time zone to the west.

You can also see on the time zone map that the boundary between two time zones does not always follow the meridian exactly. The boundary may zigzag in places so that neighboring cities and towns can keep the same time. In some places the people in a time zone have chosen not to use the time of their zone. Such places are shown on the map as having nonstandard time zones.

3. Think and Apply

Write five word problems about time zones, and give them to a partner to solve. Here is an example: "At 9:00 P.M. Maria, who lives in Mexico City, Mexico, telephones her sister in Buenos Aires, Argentina. What time is it in Buenos Aires?"

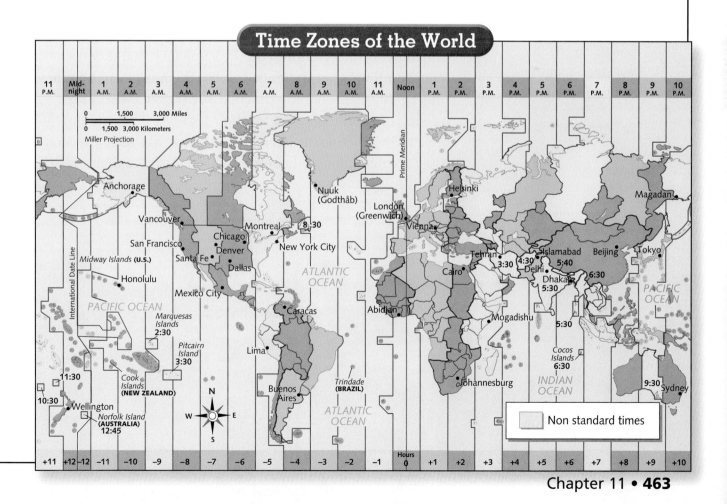

Time Zones of the World

FOCUS

How do people interact with their environments today?

Main Idea As you read, look for ways people around the world affect and are affected by their environments.

Vocabulary

economic system
traditional economy
subsistence farming
command economy
market economy
free enterprise
standard of living
gross domestic product
developing country
developed country
pollution

People and the Environment

Ancient civilizations developed their own ways of interacting with their environment. Today's peoples must also find the best ways to work with their environment.

Meeting Needs

Every country of the world must think about its economy, or the way its people use resources to meet their needs. A booming economy will bring a good life to many of a country's citizens. A poor economy will bring hardships.

Each country has an **economic system**, or way that it produces and uses goods and services. There are three main kinds of economic systems—traditional, command, and market.

A **traditional economy** is one that has not changed much over time. Children do the same jobs that their parents and their grandparents did. For the most part, people in a traditional economy practice **subsistence farming**, raising only enough food for their families. They are not able to produce a surplus to sell. Because of this limitation, they are not able to buy better tools to improve their way of

These farmers in Vietnam, in southeastern Asia, are part of a traditional economy.

Throughout the world, societies have different economies. For many years, Ukraine, in the former Soviet Union, had a command economy (top right). In the Valley of the Incas, Peru (above), a traditional economy exists. The Mall of the Americas, in St. Paul, Minnesota (left), illustrates the United States market economy.

farming. They must work as they always have. Traditional economies are still found in many countries of Africa, Asia, and South America.

In a **command economy** the government makes most economic decisions. It controls both farms and factories so it can decide the direction the economy will take. Cuba is an example of a country with a command economy. China, which once had a command economy, is now changing to a market economy.

In a **market economy** people make their own choices about which goods and services they will buy. They decide how they will spend their money and what kind of work they will do. The freedom of individuals to choose how they will make and spend money is called **free enterprise**. Most countries, such as the United States, Canada, and Mexico, have market economies.

There are several ways to measure a country's economy. One way is to look at a country's **standard of living**, a measure of how well its people live. Another way is to look at a country's gross domestic product. The **gross domestic product (GDP)** is the total value of the goods and services a country produces.

Countries with high gross domestic products include the United States, Japan, and Germany. The GDP of the United States is more than 7 trillion dollars. The

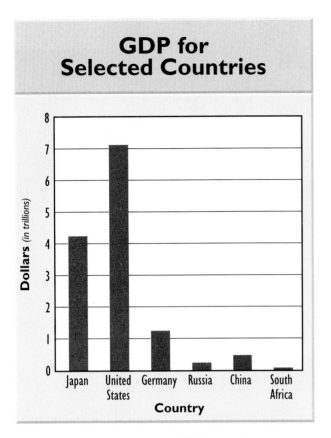

GDP for Selected Countries

Dollars *(in trillions)* / **Country**: Japan, United States, Germany, Russia, China, South Africa

LEARNING FROM GRAPHS This bar graph compares the gross domestic products of countries around the world.

■ *How much higher is Japan's GDP than China's GDP?*

small country of Santa Lucia in the Caribbean has a low GDP of just over 600 million dollars.

REVIEW *What is the difference between a command economy and a market economy?*

World Resources

The world is a treasure chest of resources. It has air to breathe, water to drink, and soil to plant crops in. It also has minerals, rocks, fuels, trees, plants, and animals.

However, these resources are not evenly spread around the world. No country has all the natural resources its people need. For example, many of the countries of southwestern Asia have large amounts of oil but little farmland for growing crops. In contrast, the people of central Africa have much farmland but hardly any fuel. The uneven spread of resources means that countries must depend on one another for what they need or want.

Wind is used as a resource by these turbines, which generate power for California.

Many countries understand the importance of forests and have begun reforestation projects to help the environment.

The countries of the world must also be careful to safeguard their treasure chest of natural resources. They must find ways to use resources while protecting them so that they will be there in the future.

REVIEW *Why do countries trade their resources?*

Population

Since agriculture began, the world's population has grown steadily. In 10,000 B.C., before agriculture, there were only about 4 million people on the Earth. After farming began, population skyrocketed, reaching about 84 million by 4000 B.C. By 1900 the number of people had reached about 1.6 billion. In 1990, less than 100 years later, census figures showed world population at more than 5 billion! At this rate of growth, nearly 8 billion people will be living on the Earth by the year 2025.

Population, like resources, is not evenly spread around the world.

Less than 20 percent of the Earth's land is lived on, since high plateaus, mountains, and deserts are not easy places to live. Population also is not divided evenly among the seven continents.

Countries, too, have different populations. China has the most people—with about 1.2 billion people—while tiny Nauru (nah•OO•roo), in Oceania, has just 10 thousand. It is important to remember that a country's size in population may not match its size in area. The huge country of Russia covers an area of 7 million square miles (18,128,600 sq km), but its population is only about 150 million. By contrast, Japan is small in area, covering only about 146,000 square miles (378,111 sq km), but it has a population of more than 125 million people.

Population growth is not the same in different countries. At present, population is growing faster in some countries than in others. Geographers often speak of developing countries and developed countries. A **developing country** is one whose economy is still being developed. It usually has a low food supply and uses few resources. It also has little high technology and has a low standard of living.

This overcrowded bus in India is just one indication of the large population there.

467

In contrast, a **developed country** is one that already has a successful economy. A developed country usually has enough food for its people, uses many resources and high technology, and has a high standard of living.

The population of developing countries is growing much faster than that of developed countries. An increasing population adds to the challenges these countries already face.

REVIEW *How has the physical environment affected population?*

Environment

People have lived on Earth for thousands of years. From the start people have changed the environment to meet their needs. Often these changes have helped people live better lives but have also caused damage to the land, air, and water.

People today understand that they must find ways to preserve and protect the world they live in. Many countries are now researching ways to protect their environment while still using the resources they need.

LEARNING FROM GRAPHS The population of the world is made up of many different people. World population has been growing rapidly during the past century. This line graph shows how the world population has increased since 1900.

■ *What was the world population increase between 1900 and 1950? What is the projected increase between 1950 and 2000?*

World Population Growth

Many different environmental issues face the people of the world today. Perhaps the most important of these is pollution. **Pollution** is anything that makes a natural resource, such as air, soil, or water, dirty or unsafe to use.

Air pollution is a major problem in and around large cities. The great number of cars, trucks, and factories in cities contribute to air pollution.

Mexico City has a very serious problem with air pollution. The mountains that surround the city keep the pollution from moving away. Mexico City's government has taken steps to improve its air quality. It has limited the number of cars that can enter the city each day. Once a week, every car owner must take a day off from driving. In addition, the government has made rules about the smoke allowed from factories in Mexico City.

Mexico City is not alone in its fight for cleaner air. Other cities with serious air pollution problems include London, Los Angeles, São Paulo, Mumbai (Bombay), Athens, and Beijing.

Problems caused by air pollution include acid rain and smog. You have read that acid rain, produced by chemicals in the air, threatens to destroy ancient buildings. Acid rain can also destroy forests, kill fish, and pollute rivers. Smog is formed when polluted air mixes with fog. This kind of pollution is most often found in large cities. Breathing smog can harm people's lungs.

Other kinds of pollution, such as water pollution, also affect people and places around the world. The world's rivers and lakes become polluted when chemicals and wastes are released into the water. Polluted rivers and lakes mean fewer fish and less drinking water.

Deforestation can cause landslides by removing the tree roots that hold the soil in place. Without the roots the soil is washed downhill by the rain.

Soil pollution is also a serious problem. The world's soil is affected by pesticides and other chemicals. Such pollution makes soil less fertile. Because less food grows on polluted soil, food shortages may occur.

In recent years much attention has been given to another environmental problem—the destruction of rain forests. People in areas with rain forests have often cleared the land to make room for building and agriculture. This deforestation can have many negative effects. It may cause landslides, flooding, and other disasters.

Land Use: South America

Caribbean Sea

VENEZUELA
Caracas
Lake Maracaibo

GUYANA
Georgetown **SURINAME**
Paramaribo
**FRENCH GUIANA
(Fr.)**

ATLANTIC OCEAN

Bogotá
COLOMBIA

Quito
ECUADOR
Chimborazo
20,561 ft.
(6,267 m)

Negro R.
Amazon
Putumayo
Juruá R.
Purus R.
Madeira R.

PERU

Huascarán
22,205 ft.
(6,763 m)
Lima

Tapajós R.
Xingu R.
Tocantins R.
São Francisco R.

BRAZIL

PACIFIC OCEAN

Lake Titicaca
La Paz
Lake Poopó
BOLIVIA
Volcán Misti
19,101 ft.
(5,822 m)
Sucre
Illimani
20,741 ft.
(6,322 m)

Guaporé R.
Paraguay R.
Araguaia R.

Brasília

PARAGUAY
Grande R.
Paraná R.
Pilcomayo R.
Asunción

CHILE
Aconcagua
22,831 ft.
(6,959 m)
Santiago
Buenos Aires
Río de la Plata
Uruguay R.

URUGUAY
Montevideo

ARGENTINA

N
W   E
S

0   500   1,000 Miles
0   500   1,000 Kilometers
Modified Chambers Trimetric Projection

Legend

	Manufacturing
	Farming
	Grazing
	Forest
	Little-used land
B	Bauxite
C	Copper
	Gemstones
G	Gold
	Iron ore
L	Lead
A	Oil
S	Silver
T	Tin
Zn	Zinc

Human-Environment Interactions More and more rain forests in South America (inset) are being used for farming.
■ *How is most land used in Peru? in Argentina?*

In rain forest areas, workers usually clear the land by burning the trees. The fires cause pollution and leave the soil bare. The rain forest's soil has few nutrients. When heavy rains fall on the bare soil, the nutrients are washed away. This means that farmers can grow crops on the cleared land for only about two or three years. People must clear more land if they want to continue farming.

The loss of rain forests also changes the world's air and climate. Trees produce oxygen, which we need in order to breathe. Trees also take in carbon dioxide. With fewer trees, there is more carbon dioxide in the atmosphere, and the burning of the trees adds even more. The increase in carbon dioxide may be causing a warming of Earth's atmosphere.

Some scientists refer to the possible warming of Earth's atmosphere as the "greenhouse effect," or "global warming." Rising temperatures and drier conditions could hurt farming around the world. Global warming might also cause polar ice to melt, raising the water level of oceans and flooding coastal lands.

Not everyone agrees that global warming will cause problems. Some experts say that climate changes are a natural part of Earth's history and environment. These people say that no action needs to be taken.

Most scientists agree, however, that people should take steps to decrease pollution and to solve other problems affecting the environment. These steps include using less energy, developing nonpolluting energy sources, and planting new trees when forests are cut down. Today some governments are taking steps to protect the environment. These governments have signed agreements to cut back pollution and to search for new energy sources.

REVIEW *What are some environmental problems faced by people of the world?*

The Three Gorges Dam on the Yangtze River in China will generate a record amount of power. However, no one knows for certain what effect it will have on the environment.

LESSON 3 REVIEW

Check Understanding

1 **Remember the Facts** What are the three main types of economic systems used by countries today?

2 **Recall the Main Idea** What are some ways in which people are affecting the environment?

Think Critically

3 **Personally Speaking** What do you think is the most important environmental problem today?

4 **Cause and Effect** What effect do you think continued population growth will have on the world in the year 2100?

Show What You Know
Simulation Activity
With a group of classmates, make up your own country. Give it a name, a location, and a population size. List your country's resources, and describe the type of economy it has. Draft a plan for using your country's resources in ways that will harm the environment the least.

Read and Compare

1. Why Learn This Skill?

Climate affects the kinds of foods people can grow in a place and the kinds of shelter and clothing they need to live there. One way to learn about the climate of a place is to study a climograph. A **climograph** is a kind of graph that shows the average monthly temperature and precipitation for a place. Knowing about the climate can help you understand more about a place and its people.

2. Understand the Process

A climograph is a line graph and a bar graph in one. Temperatures are shown as a line graph. Amounts of precipitation are shown as a bar graph. Along the bottom of a climograph are the months of the year.

Along the left-hand side of a climograph is a scale to measure temperature. A dot is placed to show the average temperature for each month. These dots are connected with a line. By studying the line, you can see

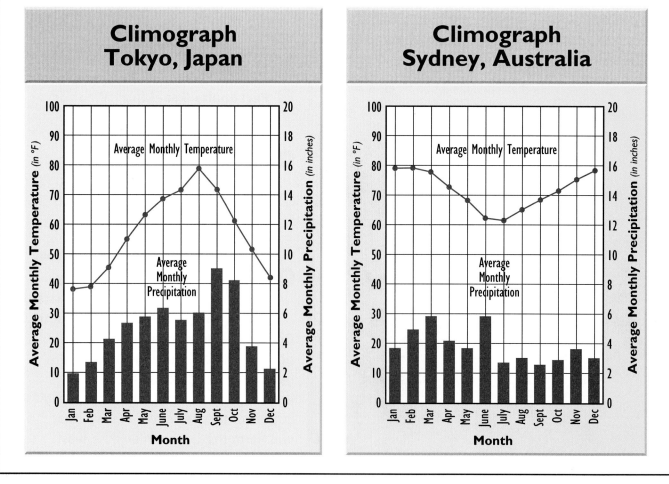

Climographs

which months are hotter and which are colder.

Along the right-hand side of a climograph is a scale to measure precipitation. A bar is drawn up to the average amount for each month. By studying the heights of the bars, you can see which months are drier and which are wetter.

The climographs shown on these pages give weather averages for Tokyo, Japan; Sydney, Australia; and San Francisco in the United States. Study the climographs. Then use them to answer the questions:

1. Which are the warmest and coldest months in Tokyo? in Sydney? in San Francisco?

2. Which are the wettest and driest months in Tokyo? in Sydney? in San Francisco?

3. Which city has the lowest average temperature in January?

4. Which city has the warmest average temperature in September?

5. Which city has the highest average precipitation in February? in July? in September?

6. How would you describe the climate of Tokyo? of Sydney? of San Francisco?

7. Which of the three cities has the greatest change in temperature from January to July?

8. Which of the three cities has the least amount of rain in a year?

3. Think and Apply

Use an almanac to create a climograph for your city or a city near you. Compare your climograph with those for Tokyo, Sydney, and San Francisco. Share your climograph with a friend or a family member. What does the information tell you about the area where you live?

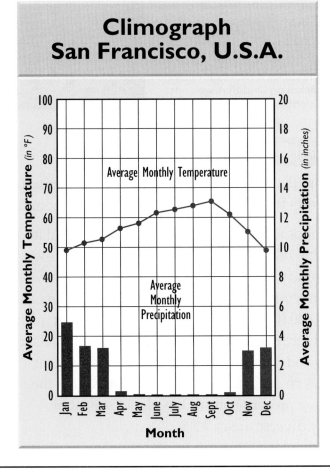

How Should World

To help their economies grow, all countries need to decide on the best uses for their resources. To use their resources one way, they give up the possibility of using them in other ways. This is called a **trade-off**. If countries clear parts of their rain forests in order to use the land, the trade-off is that they will no longer have the forests.

When a country makes an economic choice, what it gives up is the **opportunity cost** of what it gets. If countries keep their rain forests, it costs them the opportunity to use the land for farming, mining, or logging. If they clear their rain forests, it costs them the use of the forests and the benefits of the forests to the Earth itself.

People have many different viewpoints about the economic choices countries should make about their rain forests. Some people think that rain forests should be preserved at all costs, and that development should not be allowed in them. Others argue that not using the natural resources found in rain forests is unfair to the people who need them.

How and whether to use rain forests is often the subject of debate. El Yunque rain forest in Puerto Rico (above) remains undisturbed. Work on a mining project continues in Brazil on land that was once a rain forest (right).

Jonathan Burton

Writer Jonathan Burton believes in finding ways to use the rain forests that will make money for the economy:

66 One proposal is to harvest the forests for useful and renewable resources instead of cutting them down. A 1989 study showed that an acre in the Peruvian Amazon would be worth $148 if used for cattle pasture, $1,000 if cut for timber, and $6,820 if selectively combed for fruits, rubber, and other products. Using this method, known as 'sustainable development,' countries could gain economic benefits and at the same time preserve one of the planet's most biologically diverse areas. 99

Resources Be Used?

Zoran Bosnic

Zoran Bosnic, who works for the Brazilian government, believes that Brazil must be free to clear parts of its rain forests for industrial use.

66 Europe and America [the United States] destroyed their forests to become industrial powers, but when it comes to the Amazon they say, 'Stop!' Brazil has a debt, people to feed and employ. The economy is under terrific pressure. It must industrialize as soon as possible. 99

Santos Adam Afsua

Santos Adam Afsua, a Peruvian Indian, believes that the people who live in the rain forests should be the ones to make decisions about them.

66 We live to protect the forest with the best ecological and environmental knowledge that we possess, a knowledge we inherited from our ancestors. We do this with the understanding that we will continue living there, and we have to protect this forest because we have to think of future generations. . . . We have come to meet with the different environmental organizations to tell them, first of all, that the only people that can really conserve the environment are our people. 99

This rain forest is in Marenco, Costa Rica.

Compare Viewpoints

1. Why does Jonathan Burton believe that sustainable development is the best use of rain forest resources?

2. Why does Zoran Bosnic believe that it is necessary to clear parts of rain forests for industrial use?

3. How is the viewpoint of Santos Adam Afsua different from those of Jonathan Burton and Zoran Bosnic?

Think and Apply

People often have different viewpoints about the best way to solve a problem. Which of the three ideas given do you think is the best? Why? What other ideas do you have about using the resources of rain forests?

CONNECT MAIN IDEAS

Use this organizer to describe the countries and peoples of the world today and the challenges they face. Write two details to support each main idea. A copy of the organizer appears on page 106 of the Activity Book.

People and Places

Countries of the World Today

Both geography and history have helped form the countries of the world today.

1. _____

2. _____

People and the Environment

People of the world today affect and are affected by their environments.

1. _____

2. _____

People and the World Today

People migrate from one place to another to change their way of life.

1. _____

2. _____

WRITE MORE ABOUT IT

Write to Compare and Contrast Think about the cities of the past that you have learned about. Then think about what you know about present-day cities. Write several paragraphs that compare and contrast ancient cities and present-day cities.

Write Questions This chapter probably answered many questions you had about the world today. It probably also caused you to wonder about many new things. Write five questions that you now have about the world today.

For each pair of terms, write a sentence or two that explain how the terms are related.

1. metropolitan area, megalopolis
2. market economy, free enterprise
3. communism, command economy
4. urbanization, suburbs

CHECK UNDERSTANDING

5. What are three ways in which the United States and Mexico are alike?
6. How would you describe Europe in terms of size and population?
7. What is the difference between nomads and refugees?
8. Which city is the largest in the world? What problems does it probably face?
9. How is a developed country different from a developing country?

THINK CRITICALLY

10. **Personally Speaking** Suppose that you were the leader of a new country. Which kind of economy would you want your country to use? Explain.
11. **Explore Viewpoints** Some people believe that environmental damage is a necessary cost of using resources. Others disagree. What reasons might each group give to support its view?
12. **Think More About It** How might the world be different if every country had all the resources its people needed or wanted?

APPLY SKILLS

Compare Population Maps
Use the maps on pages 452–453 to answer these questions.

13. About how many people live in the city of Rampur?
14. Do more people live along India's border with Nepal or along its border with Pakistan?

Understand a Time Zone Map
Use the map on page 463 to answer these questions.

15. You make a telephone call from Helsinki to Chicago. It is 3:00 P.M. in Helsinki. What time is it in Chicago?
16. If you travel west from Cairo to Santa Fe, how many time zones will you cross?

Read and Compare Climographs Choose one of the world's large cities. Find that city's average temperature and precipitation for each month of the year and make a climograph. Trade climographs with a classmate, and write a paragraph describing the climograph you receive.

READ MORE ABOUT IT

Around the World in 80 Pages: An Adventurous Picture Atlas of the World by Antony Mason. Millbrook. This book follows Philip S. Flogg and his dog, Passport, as they travel around the world.

HARCOURT BRACE

Visit the Internet at **http://www.hbschool.com** for additional resources.

HISTORY, GOVERNMENT, AND ECONOMY

"I believe in democracy because it releases the energies of every human being."

United States President Woodrow Wilson, 1856–1924

Young boy from the former Yugoslavia

Events That
Shaped the World

500	1250	Present

During the centuries that followed the Roman Empire, people became more aware of other peoples and other places. Peoples who lived far from each other began trading and affected each other's ways of life.

A World of Trade

Between 500 and 1500, empires based on trade grew up around the world. You have read that the Roman Empire split into two parts. The western part fell to Germanic invaders. In contrast, the eastern part became the Byzantine (BIH•zuhn•teen) Empire, beginning in the 500s. Its capital, Constantinople, became a crossroads for travel, trade, and the exchange of technology and ideas.

In the 600s another empire—the Muslim Empire—rose in southwestern Asia. This empire, which was based on the religion of Islam, grew to include Egypt and Persia as well as ancient Arabia.

Farther east in Asia lay still another large empire, the Mongol Empire. Under the leadership of Genghis Khan, the Mongol people conquered China in the 1200s. Genghis Khan's sons and grandsons continued to claim more lands. In just 50 years the Mongol Empire spread across much of Asia. The European explorer Marco Polo visited China during the time of Mongol control. After Polo's return to Europe, reports of his travels caused much interest in China. Soon European merchants began searching for ways to trade with Asia.

The people of Africa, too, took part in world trade and empire building. Between the years 700 and 1500, powerful kingdoms based on trade developed in western Africa. The Ghana (GAH•nuh) Empire ruled over many peoples of western Africa. This empire was followed by the Mali

FOCUS

How does contact between peoples affect cultures today?

Main Idea As you read, look for ways contacts between cultures affected world history.

Vocabulary

crusades
Columbian exchange
triangle trade
Magna Carta
Industrial Revolution
imperialism
nationalism
armistice
Great Depression
Holocaust
arms race
Cold War

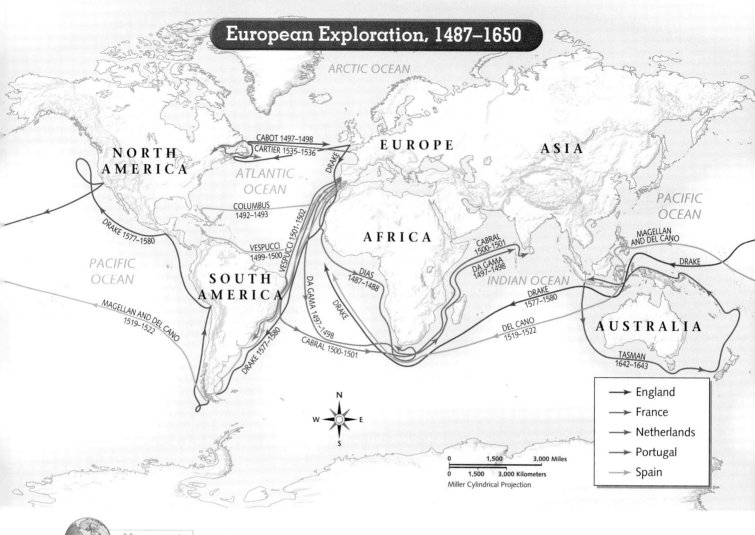

European Exploration, 1487–1650

ARCTIC OCEAN

NORTH AMERICA

ATLANTIC OCEAN

CABOT 1497–1498
CARTIER 1535–1536

EUROPE

ASIA

PACIFIC OCEAN

COLUMBUS 1492–1493

VESPUCCI 1501–1502

AFRICA

CABRAL 1500–1501

DA GAMA 1497–1498

INDIAN OCEAN

MAGELLAN AND DEL CANO

DRAKE

DRAKE 1577–1580

PACIFIC OCEAN

VESPUCCI 1499–1500

SOUTH AMERICA

DA GAMA 1497–1498

DIAS 1487–1488

DRAKE 1577–1580

DEL CANO 1519–1522

AUSTRALIA

MAGELLAN AND DEL CANO 1519–1522

DRAKE 1577–1580

CABRAL 1500–1501

TASMAN 1642–1643

N
W E
S

0   1,500   3,000 Miles
0   1,500   3,000 Kilometers
Miller Cylindrical Projection

→ England
→ France
→ Netherlands
→ Portugal
→ Spain

Movement   At the end of the fifteenth century, European sailors set off to explore the world.
■ *Which explorers sailed around the world?*

Empire, which, in turn, was replaced by the Songhay (SAWNG•hy) Empire. Contact with the Muslim Empire brought many changes to the peoples of western Africa, including the introduction of Islam.

Meanwhile, unknown to the peoples of Asia, Africa, and Europe, the Aztecs and the Incas were conquering their neighbors to build empires in the Americas. All through the Aztec Empire and the Inca Empire, native peoples of the Americas traded goods and ideas.

REVIEW *What important empires rose up in the world between the years 500 and 1500?*

Worlds Collide

Increasing contact between cultures brought new trade goods and new ways of thinking to many peoples. This contact, however, also brought conflict.

One important conflict arose between the people of Europe and the Seljuk (SEL•jook) Turks, a Muslim people from southwestern Asia. Even though western Europe was no longer part of a single empire, most Europeans still felt connected to one another. They shared the same religion—Christianity. Beginning in 1095, Christian Europeans joined together to fight the Muslim Seljuk

Turks, who had captured the city of Jerusalem. This city was holy to Christians, Muslims, and Jews. The battles that were fought to free Jerusalem from Muslim control are known as the **crusades**.

The crusades caused much loss of life for both Christians and Muslims. Yet they also brought the two peoples closer together. During the crusades the Christians and the Muslims learned about each other's ways of life and resources. Europeans returned from the crusades with spices, silks, and other goods from Asia. A demand for these goods developed, and trade began between Europe and Asia.

As trade continued, Europeans began to look for new water routes to Asia. Christopher Columbus was sure that he could reach Asia by sailing west across the Atlantic Ocean. On October 12, 1492, he landed on the island of San Salvador in the Caribbean Sea. Columbus believed that he had reached the Indies, in Asia, so he called the island's people Indians. Columbus

This Spanish cannon was made during the sixteenth century.

made three more trips, never realizing that he had reached the Americas.

After Columbus's voyages several other Europeans traveled to, explored, and settled in the Americas. The Europeans and the native peoples introduced each other to new foods, animals, ideas, and ways of doing things. For example, the Europeans learned about corn, beans, and potatoes. The peoples of the Americas saw cattle and horses for the first time. Today, historians call the movement of people, animals, plants, and ideas between Europe and the Americas the **Columbian exchange**.

In the Americas some Europeans created huge farms called plantations. Others started gold and silver mines. Plantation and mine owners turned to the continent of Africa for the many workers they needed. Africans were enslaved and brought to the Americas to work.

This painting, called *The Conquest of Mexico,* shows the Spanish battling against native Indians of Mexico. Throughout the Americas, Europeans often won battles with native peoples because of their advanced weapons.

481

Slavery had long been known in Africa. Enemies captured in wars between rival African peoples were often enslaved. They usually regained their freedom at a later time. Slavery in the Americas was different. Slaves in America were thought of as property, to be bought and sold as their owners wished. A slave in the Americas had little hope of ever becoming free.

The sale of human life was part of a system called the **triangle trade**. First, traders sailed from Europe to Africa with iron, cloth, guns, and liquor. In Africa the traders exchanged these goods for enslaved people. Next, during what is sometimes called the Middle Passage, the enslaved people were carried across the Atlantic to the Americas. There the traders sold the Africans for products from the plantations. The traders took these goods back to Europe, completing the triangle.

In time many people in the Americas began to feel that slavery was cruel and wrong. However, it was not until the 1860s that slavery ended in much of the Americas.

REVIEW *How did European settlement in the Americas affect the peoples of Africa?*

A Call for Freedom

As people moved from place to place, their ways of thinking changed. The thoughts of many people began to focus on freedom.

In Britain in 1215, a group of nobles presented King John with a list of 63 demands and forced him to sign it. This document came to be called the **Magna Carta**, or "Great Charter." By signing it, King John agreed that he, too, had to obey the laws of the land. The Magna Carta was a first step in moving power from rulers to citizens.

This print made by Currier & Ives in 1876 shows American patriots rushing to battle during the American Revolution.

By the 1700s, a new time of thought called the Enlightenment was changing people's ideas about art, science, religion, and law. People began to believe that governments should protect the rights of individuals.

In the British colonies in North America, Thomas Jefferson was well aware of the ideas of the Enlightenment. Jefferson and other colonists wrote the Declaration of Independence in 1776. In this document the colonists declared themselves independent of Britain. The British, they felt, did not care about the rights of the American colonists.

To win independence from Britain, the colonists fought a long war. That war is remembered as the American Revolution. In 1781 the former British colonies in North America became the United States of America. The first United States President, George Washington, was elected in 1789. The creation of the United States led other peoples to dream of greater freedom.

In France, many people suffered under the French system of government. Peasants and workers paid heavy taxes but had little voice in how the government was run. In 1789 the middle class of French society created its own government body called the National Assembly. Soon the French government was overthrown. By 1793 the monarch, Louis (LOO•ee) XVI, and Queen Marie Antoinette (an•twuh•NET) had been executed. France had become a republic. By 1800, however, France was once again controlled by a single person—the leader of the French army, Napoleon Bonaparte.

In the early 1800s the desire for freedom had spread to Mexico, Central America, and South America. People in these places fought for independence from their

A large group of French people attacked the Bastille, a French state prison, hoping to find weapons to use during the French Revolution.

European rulers. By 1830 many independent countries had formed in these regions.

REVIEW *In what way were the American Revolution and the French Revolution alike?*

Industrial Revolution

In the late 1700s another kind of revolution began to take place. The change this revolution caused was not in government but in the way people lived and worked. Machines came into the lives of people in this period, which is known as the **Industrial Revolution**.

The Industrial Revolution began in Britain with the textile, or cloth, industry. Until the Industrial Revolution the textile industry had been a cottage industry. This meant that families worked together in their own homes, or cottages, to spin thread and weave cloth.

Soon people looked for ways to produce these goods faster. Machines were invented that made it possible to weave cloth more quickly. However, families could not afford to buy these machines. Also, the machines were too big to fit into a house. Rich textile merchants bought many machines and put them in large buildings, creating the first factories. Workers were forced to move to be near these workplaces.

By the middle of the 1800s, the Industrial Revolution was well under way in Britain. Huge factories produced more and more goods. Cities became crowded because many people came from the country in search of work. They jammed into poorly built houses. The streets were filthy, and the air was full of smoke from the factory chimneys. People faced difficult working conditions as well. Many men, women, and children worked at least 12 hours a day, six days a week, for very low pay.

The Industrial Revolution did improve the lives of workers in some ways, however. Although wages were low, they were steady. Workers could buy meat and vegetables once in a while to go with their daily bread and cheese. They also had enough money to buy better clothes.

Over time the Industrial Revolution spread to such places as the United States, Japan, Germany, France, and Belgium. In all these industrialized countries, cities became centers of industry and grew quickly. The wave of invention and the shift to factory work brought many new inventions. Among these inventions were the telephone, the automobile, and the radio.

REVIEW *How did the Industrial Revolution affect people's lives?*

Imperialism and Nationalism

To keep their factories producing, the industrialized countries needed many kinds of raw materials, such as wood and rubber. To get these materials, European countries began colonies in Africa and Asia. As time passed, the Europeans took control of more lands in the two continents to protect their trading interests. Soon the European countries began to compete with one another to add more lands to their colonial empires. Many people in Asia and Africa came under the rule of European governments. Such empire building is called **imperialism**.

The manufacturing of cloth shifted from small families (below) to large mills (left) during the Industrial Revolution.

484

As imperialism grew, so did another idea—nationalism. **Nationalism** is loyalty to one's nation or country, based on religious or cultural ties. In the 1800s, nationalism brought some people together, but it also created many conflicts. European leaders began to build up their nations' armies and create alliances with each other. The alliances were not strong enough to keep peace in Europe, however. When Archduke Francis Ferdinand, the future ruler of Austria-Hungary, was assassinated on June 28, 1914, it started what is known as World War I.

REVIEW *What effect did imperialism and nationalism have on the world's people?*

International Conflicts

By early August 1914 most of Europe was at war. In time, other countries all over the world joined the conflict. On one side were the Allies, which included Britain, France, Russia, and the United States. On the other side were the Central Powers, which included Germany, Austria-Hungary, and the Ottoman Empire.

The Great War, as it was called at the time, was a new kind of war. For the first time deadly weapons such as machine guns, tanks, and poison gas were used. More than 8 million soldiers from several countries lost their lives.

On November 11, 1918, Germany signed an **armistice** (AR•muh•stuhs), or agreement to stop fighting. In 1919 the Treaty of Versailles (ver•SY) brought an end to the war.

Queen Victoria used imperialism to gain resources for England.

In the 1920s and 1930s most countries of the world suffered through a period of economic hard times called the **Great Depression**. Things were especially bad in Germany. The German people wanted a strong leader who would make Germany a powerful country again.

Adolf Hitler quickly took control of Germany as a dictator. He told the Germans that their political and economic troubles were the fault of the Jewish people. Hitler passed laws taking away the rights and property of Jewish citizens.

During this time, Germany, Italy, and Japan began building empires. At first, European leaders did little to stop this. They did not want to risk starting another world war. This policy of not opposing the takeovers by Germany, Italy, and Japan became known as appeasement.

As Germany continued to attack and conquer its neighbors, it became clear that appeasement would not work. Once again many countries of the world entered into war. During World War II the Allies—Britain, France, the Soviet Union (formerly Russia), and the United States—faced the Axis Powers—Germany, Italy, and Japan.

War quickly spread through Europe, Asia, and northern Africa. The United States entered the war when Japan attacked a United States naval base at Pearl Harbor in Hawaii in December 1941. Over time, the Allies began to get ahead. On May 7, 1945, Germany surrendered, ending the war in Europe. On August 6, 1945, the United States dropped an atomic bomb on

Europe in 1944

Legend:
- Allied countries
- Axis countries
- Axis-occupied areas
- Neutral countries

0 — 250 — 500 Miles
0 — 250 — 500 Kilometers
Azimuthal Equal-Area Projection

NORWAY
FINLAND
SWEDEN
IRELAND
DENMARK
North Sea
Baltic Sea
SOVIET UNION
BRITAIN
NETHERLANDS
BELGIUM
GERMANY
Elbe River
Rhine R.
ATLANTIC OCEAN
Loire River
FRANCE
SWITZERLAND
Danube River
SLOVAKIA
HUNGARY
ROMANIA
PORTUGAL
Douro R.
SPAIN
Corsica
ITALY
YUGOSLAVIA
ALBANIA
BULGARIA
GREECE
Black Sea
TURKEY
Sardinia
Mediterranean Sea
Sicily
SPANISH MOROCCO (SPAIN)
MOROCCO (FRANCE)
ALGERIA (FRANCE)
TUNISIA (FRANCE)

Human-Environment Interactions Europe was divided during World War II.
■ *Which European countries were neutral in 1944?*

Hiroshima (hir•uh•SHEE•muh), Japan. Two days later a bomb was dropped on Nagasaki (nah•guh•SAH•kee), Japan. The Japanese surrendered soon after.

After the war ended, the terrible effects of Hitler's time of rule became clear. Under his command European Jews had been shipped to prison camps and killed. This mass killing of the Jewish people is known as the **Holocaust**. In addition to 6 million Jews, Hitler ordered the killing of 6 million others.

REVIEW *What two twentieth-century conflicts affected the entire world?*

Allied troops prepare to make the largest invasion ever, D-day, which took place on June 6, 1944.

A Cold War

World War II took 50 million lives and left Europe in ruins. As the war ended, world leaders began to plan for the future. The Soviet Union, however, had its own plans. It had already begun to set up communist governments in several eastern European countries which had been freed from Hitler's control. Americans and Europeans feared that the Soviets wanted to force communism on the rest of the world.

With the recent invention of the atomic bomb, people worried that any outward conflict between the Soviet Union and the United States might result in nuclear war. Therefore, the two countries did not fight each other directly. Instead, they became rivals in an **arms race**, or competition to have the most weapons. This conflict

Many Americans built underground bomb shelters during the Cold War.

became known as the **Cold War**. The Cold War finally ended in December 1991, when a chain of events led to the breakup of the Soviet Union.

REVIEW *What was the reason for the Cold War?*

LESSON 1 REVIEW

500	1000	1500	Present
About 500 • Byzantine Empire is formed	**1095** • First crusades begin	**1492** • Columbus reaches the Americas	**About 1800** • Industrial Revolution in Britain **1939** • World War II begins

Check Understanding

1 Remember the Facts What was the Columbian exchange?

2 Recall the Main Idea In what ways did contacts between cultures affect world history between 500 and 1500? between 1900 and 1990?

Think Critically

3 Think More About It How do you think the world might be different today if Europeans had not come to the Americas until a much later time?

4 Personally Speaking Which do you think had the greater effect on people in the period covered by this lesson—trade relations or wars? Explain your answer.

Show What You Know

Compose a Ballad A ballad is a story-song. Many ballads have been written about historical events. Choose a tune that you enjoy and write words to it about an event covered in this lesson.

Read a Cartogram

1. Why Learn This Skill?

One interesting way to compare countries is to use a kind of map called a **cartogram**. A cartogram is based on a map of the world. A cartogram displays information about countries by showing them as a certain size. On a cartogram, the size of states, countries, or continents is based on a geographical statistic. A country that has a lot of something, such as rainfall or oil, is drawn larger than countries that have less. Knowing how to read a cartogram can help you quickly compare facts about countries.

2. Population Cartograms

A cartogram is not like most maps. On most maps the size a country is drawn is based on its land area. On a cartogram the size of the country is based on a certain kind of information. For example, on the cartogram on page 489, the size of countries is based on population. Countries are shown as if everyone had the same amount of land. A country with many people is shown much larger than a country with few people. When countries are shown in this way, you can quickly compare populations around the world.

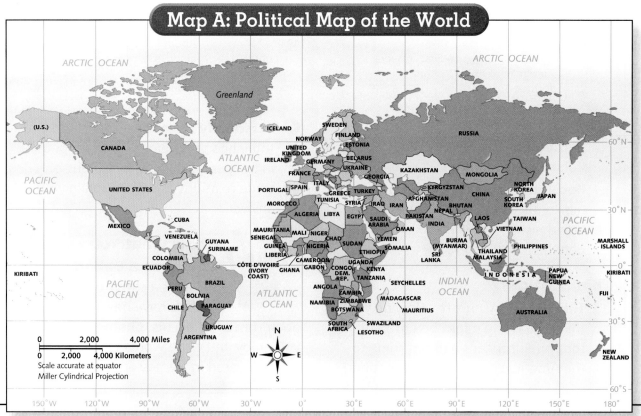

Map A: Political Map of the World

3. Understand the Process

Map A is a political map of the world. The size each country is drawn is based on its land area. Compare the size of Russia with the size of China. Which is larger? Map B is a population cartogram. The size each country is shown is based on its population. Compare the sizes of Russia and China again. Although China has a smaller land area than Russia, it is shown larger than Russia on the cartogram because it has more people.

Locate Australia and Japan on Map A. You can see that Australia has a much larger land area than Japan. Now find Australia and Japan on the cartogram. Which of these countries has the larger population?

Continue to compare land area and population by answering these questions.

① Which country in Africa has the greatest land area?

② Which country in Africa has the largest population?

③ Which country in North America has the second-largest population?

④ Which country in North America has the second-largest land area?

4. Think and Apply

With a partner, think of other kinds of world information that could be shown using cartograms. Choose one kind of information, and locate figures for it in your local library. Then make your own cartogram. Next, write questions that could be answered by looking at your cartogram. Ask other students to take your cartogram quiz while you and your partner take theirs.

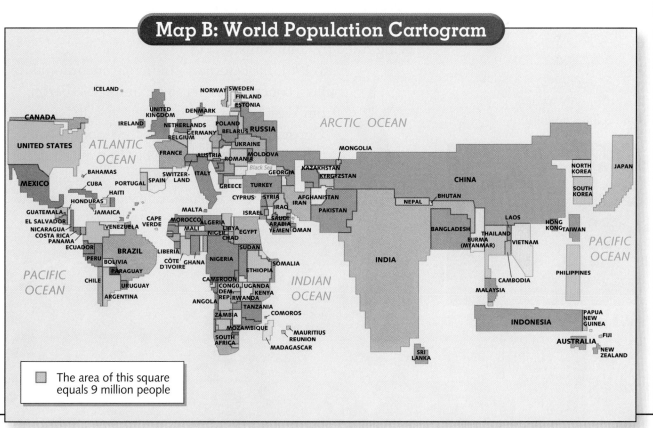

Map B: World Population Cartogram

The area of this square equals 9 million people

Recent Events in the World

FOCUS

How have present-day countries tried to resolve their conflicts?

Main Idea Read to learn about conflicts that have existed between countries of the world in recent years.

Vocabulary

apartheid
perestroika
glasnost
dissident
terrorism
ethnic cleansing
intifada

1980	1990	Present

Recent history has been about people wanting to change their lives for the better. People around the world have searched for ways to gain more personal and economic freedom. Some, but not all, of the recent changes in the world have been peaceful.

New Democracies

In the closing days of World War II, the Soviet Union set up communist governments in many eastern European countries. Poland, Czechoslovakia, Hungary, Yugoslavia, Romania, and Bulgaria all came under communist rule. The end of the war also saw a split in Germany. The newly formed East Germany became communist, while West Germany became democratic. The city of Berlin also divided, with East Berlin being ruled by communists.

In 1961, East German soldiers were ordered to build a concrete barrier to separate East Berlin from West Berlin. The goal was to stop East Germans from escaping to freedom in West Berlin. This barrier, the Berlin Wall, showed plainly the division between democratic western Europe and communist eastern Europe.

Berliners celebrate the end of the Berlin Wall by climbing it (below) and chipping pieces from it (inset).

For almost 30 years, the two parts of Europe remained divided. Then, in the late 1980s, democracy began to appear in eastern Europe. Poland held free elections in June 1989. Hungary declared itself a noncommunist republic in October of that same year.

For a while the leaders of East Germany stood solidly against the idea of change. In October 1989, these leaders were forced from power. On November 9, 1989, the East German government said that it would open its borders. In Berlin joyous demonstrators gathered at the hated wall that had divided the city. They climbed on top of it, breaking off chunks of concrete, as if they would tear it down with their bare hands. Openings were made in the wall which allowed people to travel freely between East and West Germany once again. In October 1990 the two countries united to form the Federal Republic of Germany, with a democratic government.

In 1990, African peoples faced their own struggle for human rights. The South African government was made up of white South Africans. These people were mostly Afrikaners (a•frih•KAH•nerz), or descendants of Dutch settlers. In 1948 the Afrikaners began a policy of **apartheid** (uh•PAR•tayt), or "apartness." Under this policy white people and black people were to have as little contact with one another as possible.

Life under apartheid was hard for black South Africans. Although they made up more than two-thirds of South Africa's population, they had few rights.

Thabo Mbecki (left) and Nelson Mandela (right) were both elected to serve as leaders in the democratic South African government.

Black South Africans had long dreamed of making changes in the way they were treated. The African National Congress (ANC) was founded in 1912 to work for the rights of black South Africans. In 1960, however, the South African government banned the ANC and jailed many of its leaders.

Many countries stopped trading with South Africa because of the policy of apartheid. Even so, the government of South Africa continued apartheid.

At last things changed after Frederik Willem de Klerk, an Afrikaner, became president of South Africa in 1989. De Klerk met with black leaders to work out a way to share power. By November 1993 the leaders agreed to open South African elections to all races. The election held on April 27, 1994, resulted in victory for the ANC and its leader, Nelson Mandela. In one of his first speeches as president of South Africa, Mandela described a new South Africa, "in which all South Africans, both black and white, will be able to walk tall, without any fear in their hearts."

Democracy had also won out across the Atlantic in Latin America. During much of the twentieth century, the peoples of many Latin American countries lived under the rule of military dictators. One by one these dictatorships began to fall in the 1980s and 1990s. Today, every Latin American country but Cuba is a democracy.

Not all struggles for rights have been successful. In 1989, college students across China were calling for democracy and more human rights. Thousands of them gathered at Tiananmen Square in Beijing to protest against their government. Many people around the world believed that the Chinese government would make some political changes to give its people greater freedoms.

On June 4, 1989, the Chinese government did take action, but not the kind many people had hoped for. It ordered Chinese soldiers to remove the students. When the students did not leave, the troops began firing on them. As many as 5,000 students were killed. Many others were put in prison.

These actions quickly ended many demands for democracy in China. Today China seems to be changing economically to include more free enterprise. Politically, however, the country remains a long way from becoming a democracy.

REVIEW *How did South Africa change in the 1990s?*

New Countries on the Map

The late 1980s and early 1990s saw changes that no one could have guessed just a few years earlier. Some European countries ceased to exist, and others that had been taken over were restored to their former state. Among these restored countries is the Federal Republic of Germany.

A major event in Europe was the collapse of communism after more than 70 years. The Soviet Union dissolved in 1991. Fifteen independent European nations now exist where the former Soviet Union was.

One of the most important figures in this historical drama was Mikhail Gorbachev (mee•kah•EEL gawr•buh•CHAWF). Gorbachev served as the president of the Soviet Union from 1985 until 1991. During

College students protesting for human rights and democracy in Tiananmen Square, Beijing.

The Collapse of Communism

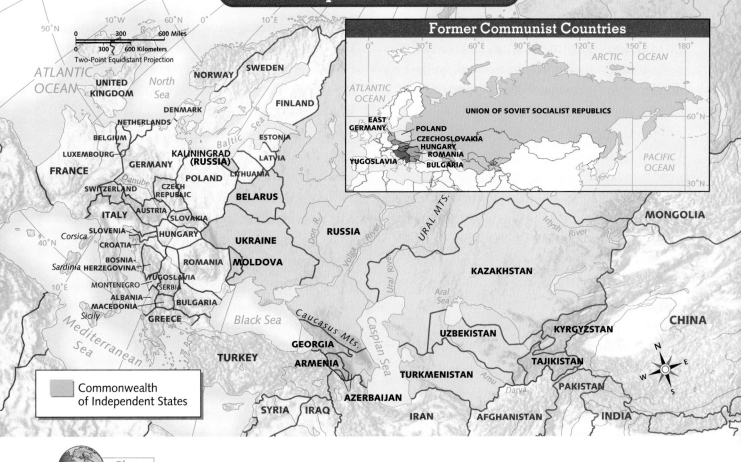

Former Communist Countries

Place The Soviet Union broke up into 15 independent countries.
■ *What are four of the countries formed from the former Soviet Union?*

Boris Yeltsin campaigned for the presidency of the Russian Republic in 1991. When Russia became an independent country, Yeltsin continued as its president.

these years he brought many changes to Soviet society.

Gorbachev put into action a new economic plan that he called **perestroika** (pair•uh•STROY•kuh), or "rebuilding." *Perestroika* took some of the economic decision-making power away from the central government and gave it to local manufacturers and consumers.

Gorbachev also began a new political plan called **glasnost** (GLAHS•nohst), which means "openness." *Glasnost* gave Soviet citizens the freedom to speak out without fear of being punished. It also gave a certain amount of religious freedom to Soviet citizens. The news media gained the freedom to report information that had

been hidden. As part of glasnost, Gorbachev freed political **dissidents**— people who had spoken out against the government.

People in the Soviet Union and around the world watched the changes in amazement. "Our jaws cannot drop any lower," wrote one journalist.

Boris Yeltsin was the president of Russia, which at that time was still a part of the

Soviet Union. In December 1991, he and the presidents of other Soviet republics made a startling announcement. They declared that the Soviet Union no longer existed. In its place they set up a loose association, or group, called the Commonwealth of Independent States, or CIS.

From its beginning, the CIS set out to build a market economy for its member countries. By 1995, 12 of the 15 former Soviet republics had joined the CIS as independent countries. These countries are Armenia, Azerbaijan (a•zer•by•JAHN), Belarus (byeh•luh•ROOS), Georgia, Kazakhstan, Kyrgyzstan, Moldova (mahl•DOH•vah), Russia, Tajikistan (tah•jih•kih•STAN), Turkmenistan, Ukraine (yoo•KRAYN), and Uzbekistan.

REVIEW *What loose association of independent states replaced the Soviet Union?*

Conflict in Europe

History has shown that when two groups claim the same piece of land, a struggle may result. When differences in religious beliefs are involved, emotions become even stronger.

The conflict between Ireland and England is an example of a political and religious struggle. Today England is a part of the United Kingdom of Great Britain and Northern Ireland. As this name tells you, Northern Ireland is also part of this country. The rest of Ireland is an independent country.

A look back in history can explain much about the conflict between the Irish and the English. In the 1500s the kingdom of England invaded Ireland. For 400 years the mostly Catholic Irish lived under the rule of the mostly Protestant English. Then, in 1920, Ireland began to seek independence. After years of on-and-off fighting, much of the Irish land became independent Ireland in 1922. Just six northern counties remained a part of Britain. Today these counties are known as Northern Ireland.

For many years fighting has taken place over the question of freedom for Northern Ireland. Sometimes **terrorism**, or acts of violence to further a cause, has been used in this conflict. The Irish Republican Army, or IRA, has been responsible for several of these terrorist attacks. The main goal of the IRA is to reunite the two parts of Ireland. Many people in Northern Ireland, however, want to remain part of Britain.

As a result of peace talks, the Irish Republican Army declared a cease-fire, an order to stop fighting, on August 31, 1994. In spite of flare-ups of violence, more peace talks were held in 1998. The agreements reached in these talks are believed by many to be meaningful steps toward peace.

This mural in Belfast, Northern Ireland, illustrates the tensions in the region.

The Former Yugoslavia

AUSTRIA

HUNGARY

SLOVENIA

CROATIA

ROMANIA

BOSNIA-
HERZEGOVINA

SERBIA

Adriatic Sea

YUGOSLAVIA

MONTENEGRO

BULGARIA

ITALY

MACEDONIA

TURKEY

GREECE

Aegean
Sea

ALBANIA

| | Border of Yugoslavia in 1991 |
| | Present-day borders |

Main ethnic groups, 1991

	Albanians
	Croats
	Macedonians
	Montenegrins
	Muslims
	Serbs
	Slovenes
	Other ethnic groups

0   50   100 Miles
0   50   100 Kilometers
Azimuthal Equal-Area Projection

N
W E
S

Regions This map shows the culture groups living in the former Yugoslavia.
■ *What groups live in what is now Bosnia-Herzegovina?*

On the other side of Europe, cultural and religious differences have also caused conflict. After World War I, some countries in the Balkan region were forced to become republics of Yugoslavia. After World War II, Yugoslavia came under communist control. Differences among the country's three main ethnic groups—Muslims, Serbs, and Croats (KROH•ats)—made it difficult for these people to settle down together in one country.

In 1991, people in the Yugoslavian republics of Slovenia (sloh•VEE•nee•uh) and Croatia (kroh•AY•shuh) voted to break away from Yugoslavia. The Serbs in Croatia feared living under the rule of the Croats. They called on the Yugoslavian republic of Serbia for help. In 1991, Serbia attacked

A Bosnian man repairs his war-damaged house in Stup, a suburb of Sarajevo.

Croatia and eventually took over about one-third of Croatia's territory.

In 1992 the republic of Bosnia also declared its independence. Right away, people from each ethnic group in Bosnia—Muslims, Serbs, and Croats—began using violence to drive out people from other groups. Sometimes the Serbs killed large numbers of their enemy ethnic group, the

The Persian Gulf War

In August 1990 Saddam Hussein (suh•DAHM hoo•SAYN), the president of Iraq, ordered the Iraqi army to invade the oil-rich country of Kuwait. To help the Kuwaitis push Iraq out, the United States and other countries began a series of bombing attacks. The Iraqis were quickly forced to leave Kuwait. This war was unlike wars of the past. Television reports brought people the latest war news, high-technology weapons were used, and American women took part in the war as soldiers.

American soldiers at camp during the Persian Gulf War

Muslims. They thought of this type of killing as **ethnic cleansing**, or "cleaning" their area of the "wrong" people.

The United Nations sent troops to Bosnia to restore peace. Leaders representing Serbs, Croats, and Muslims agreed to stop fighting in 1995. However, much work remains to be done to form a truly lasting peace. Though a new democratic government has been formed in Bosnia, many of the same problems still exist between the Serbs, Croats, and Muslims. The fighting in the region has also led to many economic problems.

REVIEW *What happened when the republic of Bosnia declared independence?*

Arab-Israeli Conflict

Both Jews and Arabs claim the piece of land that is present-day Israel. No way of living together peacefully has been accepted by both sides.

The Jewish Israelis and the Muslim Arabs were already in conflict when Israel became a country in 1948. During one of several wars between Israel and the Arab countries, Israel captured much Arab land. With the new land, 1 million Arabs came under Israeli control. A group called the Palestine Liberation Organization, or PLO, headed by Yasir Arafat (AH•ruh•faht), was formed to gain a homeland for these Arabs.

In the late 1980s the Palestinians began an **intifada** (in•tee•FAH•duh), or uprising, in the Arab land occupied by Israel. The intifada gave many Palestinians a sense of unity. At the same time, it caused many Israelis to want an end to the fighting. Many countries, including the United States, urged both sides to compromise.

In 1992 Yitzhak Rabin (rah•BEEN) was elected prime minister of Israel. Soon the Israelis and the Palestinians began secret peace talks.

In August 1993 an agreement was reached. Under the terms of the agreement, Israelis and Palestinians had a five-year period in which to settle the major disagreements that

Place The shape of the land controlled by Israel has changed since 1947.

■ *Why do you think Israelis and Palestinians disagree about control of Jerusalem?*

Israel: 1947 to Present

0   25   50 Miles
0   25   50 Kilometers
Transverse Cylindrical Projection

N W E S

LEBANON
SYRIA

Security zones

GOLAN HEIGHTS

Land gained after Six-Day War, 1967, and still occupied

Acre
Haifa
Nazareth

Lake Tiberias (Sea of Galilee)

Land gained after Six-Day War, 1967; some Palestinian self-rule

Mediterranean Sea

Tel Aviv

WEST BANK

Amman

Jericho

Land gained after Six-Day War, 1967

Jerusalem
Bethlehem

Hebron

Dead Sea

GAZA STRIP
Gaza

Land gained after 1948 War

Beersheba

ISRAEL

JORDAN

Israeli troops have withdrawn from area

EGYPT
Sinai Peninsula

Negev

Jewish state under 1947 partition plan

Under Palestinian control

Land gained after Six-Day War, 1967, and returned to Egypt

---

divided them. As part of the agreement, the Palestinians would gain control of some land.

In 1995 Yitzhak Rabin was assassinated by an Israeli who was against the peace process. The country, and the entire world, were stunned. In 1996, Benjamin Netanyahu (neh•tahn•YAH•hoo) was elected as Israel's prime minister.

In recent years, progress toward a compromise has been slow. Terrorist attacks have increased in Israel, and Israeli pullouts from areas planned for Palestinian control have been delayed. Many countries are now involved in searching for a solution to this conflict.

REVIEW *How has land affected the relationship between the Israelis and the Palestinians?*

LESSON 2 REVIEW

1980 ● 1990 ● ● Present

1989
• Students demonstrate for democracy in China

1991
• The Soviet Union breaks up

1994
• Free elections are held in South Africa

Check Understanding

1 **Remember the Facts** What major communist country collapsed in 1991?

2 **Recall the Main Idea** What are some of the conflicts in the world today?

Think Critically

3 **Think More About It** What other actions might Chinese leaders have taken at Tiananmen Square?

4 **Personally Speaking** What issues do you think cause the most disagreements?

Show What You Know

Make a Map of Europe
Trace the outlines of European countries from a present-day map. Label each country, and color in all that are new since 1989. Choose one country, and write several paragraphs to tell its story.

Resolve Conflict

1. Why Learn This Skill?

When a disagreement arises, there are many ways to handle it. You can walk away and let your strong feelings fade. You can explain your ideas and try to get the other side to agree with them. You can also compromise, or give up some of what you want in order to reach an agreement that will work for both sides. Knowing how to compromise to resolve conflicts will help you settle problems all your life.

2. Understand the Process

To work out a compromise, you can follow steps like these:

1 Think about what each of you wants. Realize that the other person probably values his or her ideas as much as you do yours.

2 Be prepared to give up some things you want, if necessary.

3 Tell the other person what you want. Listen to what the other person wants.

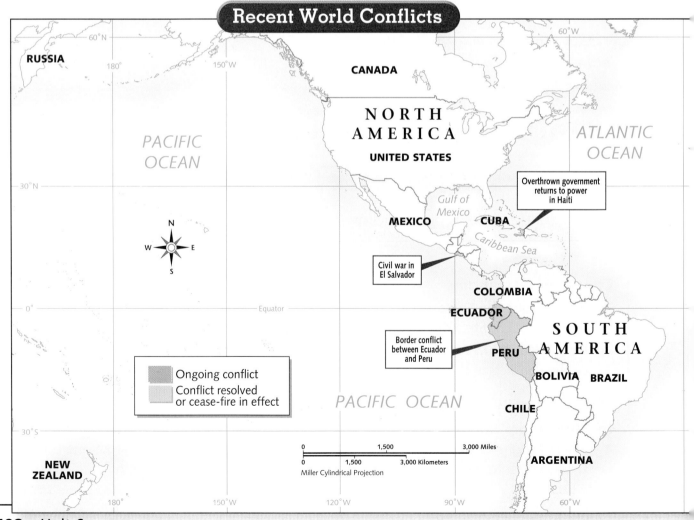

Recent World Conflicts

Overthrown government returns to power in Haiti

Civil war in El Salvador

Border conflict between Ecuador and Peru

Ongoing conflict
Conflict resolved or cease-fire in effect

0   1,500   3,000 Miles
0   1,500   3,000 Kilometers
Miller Cylindrical Projection

4 Present your plan for a compromise, and pay attention as the other person shares ideas.

5 Talk about how the two plans are alike and how they are different. Try to resolve the differences between the plans.

6 Be patient. A good compromise takes time. If either of you becomes angry, take a break to calm down.

7 Keep talking until you reach a solution that satisfies both of you.

3. Think and Apply

Think of something the students in your class disagree about. Join one of two teams to discuss the problem. Follow the steps to work out a compromise that will settle the disagreement. After both sides have reached a compromise, write a paragraph or two explaining it. Tell whether or not you think the compromise is fair and list any ideas you may have for improving the compromise.

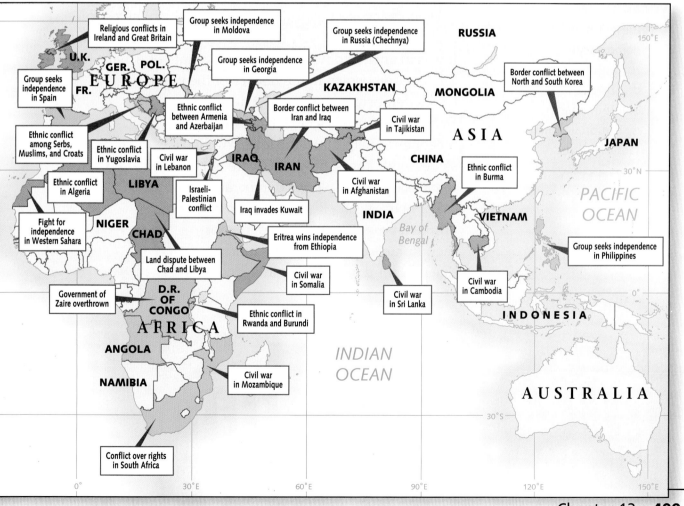

FOCUS

How are government
systems of today
different from one
another?

Main Idea Think
about the ways in
which different systems
of government work.

Vocabulary

representative
  democracy
constitutional
  democracy
absolute monarchy
constitutional monarchy
totalitarianism

The Capitol building in Washington,
D.C., is a symbol of United States
democracy. The United States
Congress meets in the Capitol.

Governments
of the
World Today

Governments are frameworks of societies. They run
the countries and make the laws. Governments also see that
the laws are obeyed, control business, and protect citizens.
All governments do these things, but different governing
systems do them in different ways. Today there are four main
governing systems in the world: democracy, monarchy,
dictatorship, and oligarchy.

Democracy

Democracy is a governing system in which the people
of the country take part. You have read about democracy as
it was in ancient days. The Greek city-state of Athens had
the first democracy in the history of the world.
Greek democracy was a direct democracy.
Everyone who was a citizen could attend
meetings to help make the laws. Women,
slaves, and others, however, were not allowed
to participate in Greece's democracy.

For many years, Rome, too, had a government based on the ideas of democracy. Rome's democracy was more
like present-day democracies—

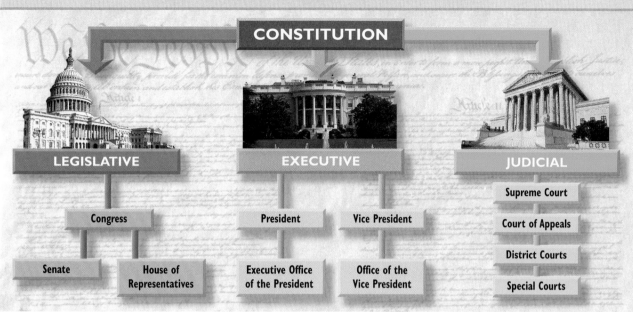

The United States Government

CONSTITUTION

LEGISLATIVE
- Congress
  - Senate
  - House of Representatives

EXECUTIVE
- President
  - Executive Office of the President
- Vice President
  - Office of the Vice President

JUDICIAL
- Supreme Court
- Court of Appeals
- District Courts
- Special Courts

LEARNING FROM CHARTS This chart illustrates the structure of the United States government.
■ *What are the three branches of the United States government?*

it was a representative democracy. In a **representative democracy**, citizens elect people to make laws and decisions for them. Another name for this kind of democracy is *republic*.

In the first century A.D., the Roman government changed from a democracy to a monarchy and later to a military dictatorship. For centuries after, democracy was not used as a governing system.

Then, in 1215, the government of England began developing in a democratic direction with the signing of the Magna Carta. As time passed, the number of people allowed to take part in English government increased. A group of lawmakers known as a parliament was set up, and it began to gain more authority. This was important because

the parliament was a branch of government separate from the king.

Today democracy has spread around the world. More than 140 countries have some form of democracy. Present-day democracies include the United States, Venezuela, Australia, Argentina, Canada, Mexico, Israel, Egypt, India, and Germany.

United States President Abraham Lincoln spoke of "Government of the people, by the people, and for the people." By this, Lincoln meant a government created by citizens and run by citizens for the good of citizens. Lincoln's words described the democracy of the United States of America and all democracies.

Campaign posters in democratic South Korea

Like ancient Rome, the United States has a representative democracy. The United States' democracy is also a constitutional democracy. In a **constitutional democracy**, the goals of the government and the ways it will work to achieve them are laid out in a constitution, or plan for governing. Today most countries have constitutions. Yet not all countries with constitutions are democracies.

Many countries now are democracies, but not all democracies are alike. For example, Canada's democracy differs in many ways from that of the United States. Unlike the United States, Canada has a democracy with a parliament. In Canada the prime minister and the members of the Cabinet are part of the government's executive branch, just as the President and the Cabinet are in the United States. At the same time they are also members of Parliament, the legislative branch. The Canadian Parliament, like the United States Congress, has two houses. Members of one house, the Senate, are appointed. Members of the other house, the House of Commons, are elected.

Democracies require effort on the part of the citizens of a country. For a democracy to work well, citizens need to participate, stay informed, and vote. A democracy can be overthrown by a dictator, can be voted out of existence, or can last for centuries—as the United States' democracy has.

REVIEW *How would you describe the democracy of the United States?*

The Canadian Parliament building is located in Canada's national capital, Ottawa.

An example of a constitutional monarch is Queen Elizabeth II of Britain (above). An example of an absolute monarch is Sultan Qaboos bin Said (right), the ruler of present-day Oman.

Monarchy

As you have already read, a monarchy is any government that is ruled by a monarch, such as a king or queen or an emperor. In fact, the word *monarchy* means "rule by one." A monarch usually inherits power and rules for life.

For many centuries monarchy was the most common governing system. The governments of ancient Egypt, China, and India were all monarchies.

There are still some monarchies, but most monarchs today do not have as much power as monarchs did in the past. Long ago every monarchy was an **absolute monarchy**. The monarch had absolute, or complete, authority. Today very few countries have absolute monarchies. One present-day absolute monarchy is in the country of Oman (oh•MAHN) in southwestern Asia.

The Magna Carta, signed in 1215, cut back the power of monarchs for the first time. Later, the British Bill of Rights and the American and French revolutions all helped end the absolute authority of monarchs.

In most present-day monarchies, the monarch is limited by laws. Such a monarchy is called a constitutional monarchy. A **constitutional monarchy** is actually run by a prime minister and a cabinet, and its laws are passed by the legislative branch of the government. Instead of controlling their governments, most modern monarchs represent the history of their country. King Hussein of Jordan and Queen Elizabeth II of Britain are two such monarchs.

REVIEW *Who makes the laws in a constitutional monarchy?*

German citizens salute the Nazi party during this parade in Germany before World War II. Such parades were meant to strengthen support for the Nazi party.

Dictatorship

Though the age of the absolute monarch is over, there are still leaders who want to rule in this way. A governing system in which one person claims absolute authority is called a dictatorship. The difference between absolute monarchs and dictators is that dictators do not inherit their power. Instead they take power for themselves, often violently and suddenly.

Dictatorship began in ancient Rome. At first, Roman dictators served for only brief times during emergencies. Later, however, some Roman dictators refused to give up their control.

Dictators do not belong only to the past. Several have ruled in the twentieth century. Adolf Hitler in Germany, Pol Pot in Cambodia, and the Ayatollah Khomeini (eye•uh•TOH•luh koh•MAY•nee) in Iran are all examples of dictators in recent history.

Most dictatorships are examples of the kind of government called **totalitarianism** (toh•ta•luh•TAIR•ee•uh•nih•zuhm). That is, the government has total authority over people's lives. In many dictatorships the government controls all land, schools, and newspapers. Dictators, like absolute monarchs, often rule until their deaths or until they are overthrown.

The only dictatorship in the Americas is in Cuba, an island nation located less than 100 miles (161 km) off the coast of Florida. In 1959 Fidel Castro took over Cuba's government. Soon after, Castro began to make Cuba into a communist country, like the Soviet Union.

In 1962 the world came close to war when United States pilots discovered that Soviet missile launching sites were being built in Cuba. President John F. Kennedy

Fidel Castro

demanded that Nikita Khrushchev—who was then the communist leader of the Soviet Union—remove the sites. When he finally did, war was prevented. Castro continues to rule in Cuba as a communist dictator, even though communism collapsed in the Soviet Union.

Cuba is not the only dictatorship in the world. A few countries that claim to be republics are actually dictatorships. Though they may have elections and a legislative branch of government, all real power is in the hands of a single person. One such country is Iraq.

REVIEW *How is a dictatorship like an absolute monarchy?*

Oligarchy

Not all dictatorships are run by one individual. Sometimes a small group of people controls the government of a country. Such a governing system is called an oligarchy.

You have read that in Sparta a small group of landowners controlled the government. At many other times in history, small groups have ruled countries. Sometimes the rulers have been members of one class of people or one political party. Perhaps the most famous oligarchy of all time was the government of the former Soviet Union. Only members of the Communist party could take part in governing.

Human-Environment Interactions Dictators have risen on almost every continent during the twentieth century.
■ *Who were four twentieth-century African dictators?*

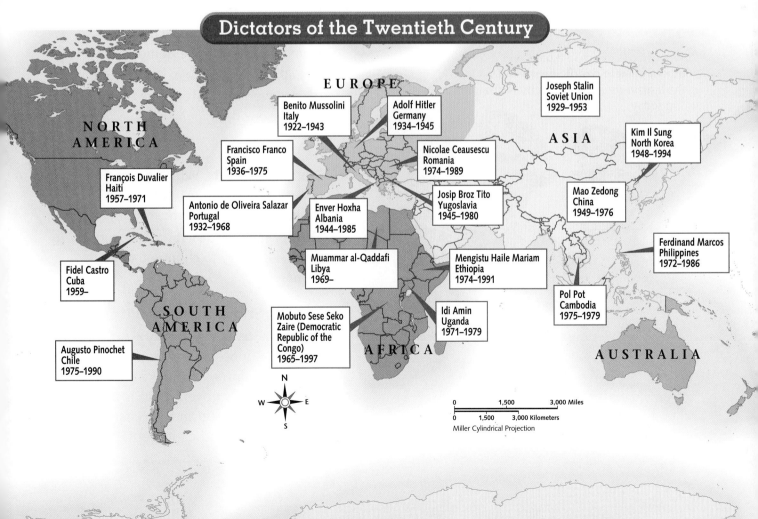

Dictators of the Twentieth Century

Benito Mussolini
Italy
1922–1943

Adolf Hitler
Germany
1934–1945

Joseph Stalin
Soviet Union
1929–1953

Francisco Franco
Spain
1936–1975

Nicolae Ceausescu
Romania
1974–1989

Kim Il Sung
North Korea
1948–1994

François Duvalier
Haiti
1957–1971

Josip Broz Tito
Yugoslavia
1945–1980

Mao Zedong
China
1949–1976

Antonio de Oliveira Salazar
Portugal
1932–1968

Enver Hoxha
Albania
1944–1985

Ferdinand Marcos
Philippines
1972–1986

Muammar al-Qaddafi
Libya
1969–

Mengistu Haile Mariam
Ethiopia
1974–1991

Fidel Castro
Cuba
1959–

Mobuto Sese Seko
Zaire (Democratic Republic of the Congo)
1965–1997

Idi Amin
Uganda
1971–1979

Pol Pot
Cambodia
1975–1979

Augusto Pinochet
Chile
1975–1990

0   1,500   3,000 Miles
0   1,500   3,000 Kilometers
Miller Cylindrical Projection

Today's communist-controlled People's Republic of China fits the definition of an oligarchy. The Chinese government has executive, legislative, and judicial branches. However, the real power of Chinese government is in the hands of a few committees which are controlled by the Chinese Communist Party, or CCP.

China's constitution divides the government into four main parts. The largest of these is the National People's Congress, which has over 1,900 members elected from regions all over China. The next-largest part of the government is the Central Committee. Its 300 members are elected by the National People's Congress. The Central Committee, in turn, elects 20 members for another committee—the Politburo. Part of the Politburo is made up of a committee of important party leaders. This committee elects the members of the five-member

Secretariat. Much of the power to make government decisions rests with the Politburo and the Secretariat. The amount of power that these small groups have is what makes the Chinese government an oligarchy.

Although China is an oligarchy, often one person has steered China's course. From 1980 until his death in 1997, Deng Xiaoping (DUHNG SHOH•PING) was the real leader of China, even after he retired in 1990. Since Deng's death, President Jiang Zemin (JEE•AHNG zuh•MIN) has taken over leadership in China. Deng personally trained Jiang to follow him.

REVIEW *Why is China considered an oligarchy?*

Chinese troops march in a parade in the southern Chinese city of Shenzhen. China is the largest communist country in the world today.

LESSON 3 REVIEW

Check Understanding

1 **Remember the Facts**   How is a constitutional monarchy different from a representative democracy?

2 **Recall the Main Idea**   What four main governing systems are used in the world today?

Think Critically

3 **Past to Present**   Which governing system was used most in the past? Which system is used most today?

4 **Think More About It**   What might cause a country to change from a monarchy?

Show What You Know
Poster Activity
Choose a present-day country, and make a poster that shows how its government is set up. Display your poster in the classroom with the posters of other students.

Form a Logical Conclusion

1. Why Learn This Skill?

A **logical conclusion** is a decision or an idea formed as the result of a study of all the known facts. Knowing how to form logical conclusions will help you understand events of both the past and the present.

The Declaration of Independence, written in 1776, states the reasons why the American colonists decided to separate from Britain.

2. Understand the Process

Read the following passage. What system of government do the words describe?

> 66 That, to secure these rights, Governments are instituted among Men, deriving their just powers from the consent of the governed,
>
> That, whenever any Form of Government becomes destructive of these ends, it is the Right of the People to alter or to abolish it, and to institute new Government, laying its foundation on such principles, and organizing its powers in such form, as to them shall seem most likely to effect their Safety and Happiness. 99

The phrases *to secure these rights* and *deriving their just powers from the consent of the governed* tell you that the passage describes a democracy. In fact, this passage is from the Declaration of Independence of the United States.

Here are some steps you can follow to form a logical conclusion:

1. Form a question about the passage you are reading. A question for this passage might be *Why are democracies formed?*
2. Think about evidence you already have that might help you answer the question.
3. Gather new evidence to help you answer your question.
4. Form a conclusion based on the strongest evidence.

3. Think and Apply

Write five clues that lead to the identification of a system of government. Read the clues one by one to a partner. How many clues does it take before he or she can form a logical conclusion as to what kind of government you are describing? Discuss with your partner how each clue led to the conclusion.

Working Together in Today's World

Working together has been important through the many different time periods of world history. Ancient people depended on one another to survive in their natural environment. In the modern world, working with others is still an important part of life.

Revolution in Technology

Today, technology affects the lives of people in most parts of the world. Electronic communication, once just a dream, is now a reality almost everywhere. Keeping in touch around the world is faster and easier than ever before.

The word that describes all the electronic ways of sending and receiving information is **telecommunications**. *Tele* is from a Greek word that means "far away." It makes sense, then, that *telecommunications* means "communications over a distance." Telephones, fax machines, e-mail, and computer networks are all used in telecommunications.

One kind of telecommunications that is growing in use is the **Internet**. The Internet is a large computer network made up of thousands of smaller networks that are all linked with each other. People use the Internet to buy things, conduct business, gather information, and communicate.

In many ways new technology has brought the people of the world closer together. People in different countries and on different continents can communicate quickly and easily by computer. Letters and documents can be sent from one place to another in seconds. News that happens far away can be heard in the United States almost instantly. All this has helped to make cultures more aware of each other than at any other time in the past.

FOCUS

How do people in different countries work together in the modern world?

Main Idea
As you read, think about how and why present-day countries work together.

Vocabulary

telecommunications
Internet
protectionism
OPEC
common market
NAFTA
bloc

Technological innovations such as compact discs, or CDs, allow information to be stored faster and more easily.

Students in downtown St. Paul, Minnesota, use the Internet to examine a Hmong-English "talking dictionary."

New technologies are also affecting the way we explore the world and beyond. Since 1981, the United States has used space shuttles for many kinds of missions. One of these missions was to repair the Hubble telescope, which orbits the Earth. In 1996, a different kind of spacecraft carried a remote-control vehicle to Mars. The United States, Russia, Canada, Europe, and Japan are now working together to build an international space station for scientific research.

REVIEW *How is telecommunications bringing people closer together?*

World Trade

Today it is not unusual to find products from all over the world right in your own home. This is possible because countries all over the world are trading with one another. Telecommunications and other new technologies have made international trade much easier.

It might seem that every country in the world would trade with every other country. Sometimes, however, countries cut back or cut off trade with another country because of that country's actions or beliefs. For example, many countries stopped trading with South Africa because of its policy of apartheid.

Sometimes a country uses a policy of **protectionism** in its dealings with other countries to help the sale of its own products. It may add a tariff, or import charge, to the price of another country's product, such as cars. This protects its own market for that product. For example, cars made within the country will cost less than cars from other places. This influences buyers to choose the country's own cars.

LEARNING FROM GRAPHS The amount of United States imports and exports have grown over the years.
■ *During what years shown were United States exports greater than imports?*

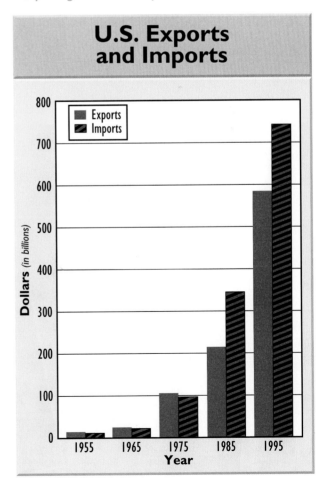

U.S. Exports and Imports

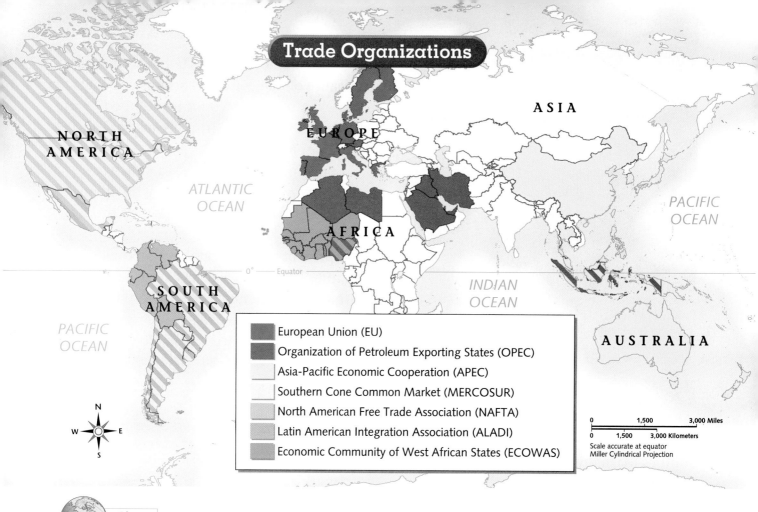

Trade Organizations

ASIA

EUROPE

NORTH AMERICA

ATLANTIC OCEAN

PACIFIC OCEAN

AFRICA

SOUTH AMERICA

PACIFIC OCEAN

0° — Equator

INDIAN OCEAN

AUSTRALIA

- European Union (EU)
- Organization of Petroleum Exporting States (OPEC)
- Asia-Pacific Economic Cooperation (APEC)
- Southern Cone Common Market (MERCOSUR)
- North American Free Trade Association (NAFTA)
- Latin American Integration Association (ALADI)
- Economic Community of West African States (ECOWAS)

| 0 | 1,500 | 3,000 Miles |
| 0 | 1,500 | 3,000 Kilometers |

Scale accurate at equator
Miller Cylindrical Projection

MAP THEME

Place Many countries with the same economic interests have formed trade organizations.

■ *What trade organizations is the United States a member of?*

Lately countries have found it better to work with one another. Many countries have come together to form the World Trade Organization (WTO). This group has the authority to decide trading disagreements between member countries.

In recent years many countries have also joined to form groups that trade freely with one another. Often the groups are made up of countries in the same region of the world. Some of these

Much oil is drilled from platforms (far left). Oil is transported over water by enormous ships called supertankers (near left).

510

A meeting of the European Union in Strasbourg, France

groups are the Asia-Pacific Economic Cooperation (APEC), the Latin American Integration Association (ALADI), and the North American Free Trade Agreement (NAFTA) members.

At times countries might also form a group because they share a common interest. The countries that make up the Organization of Petroleum Exporting Countries, or **OPEC**, formed their organization to gain control of the price of their oil in other parts of the world. The greater part of the world's oil is located in countries such as Algeria, Libya, Kuwait, Iran, Iraq, and Saudi Arabia. Venezuela, Indonesia, Nigeria, and Ecuador are also OPEC members. OPEC allows member countries to set standard prices for oil.

REVIEW *Why did OPEC form?*

The European Union

Europe is made up of many different countries and cultures, all located in a small region. Each country has its own money, laws, and economic policies. Because people and goods are constantly moving across their national borders, these countries have joined together to form a trading and economic association known as the European Union (EU).

The idea of European countries joining is not new. Several western European nations formed a **common market**, a group of countries that has free trade among its members and a single trade policy, in 1957. The purpose of the European common market, called the European Economic Community (EEC), was to make sure that the economic policies of its members did not work against one another. The EEC set as its goal the creation of the European Union. In 1993 the European Union became a reality.

The European Union is divided into five branches. Four of these branches—the European Council, the European Commission, the Council of Ministers, and the European Parliament—decide policy and make laws for the EU. The fifth branch, the European Court of Justice, sees that the branches follow the rules and laws of the EU.

Today the EU is the world's largest trading power, with 15 trading partners. EU members do not add tariffs to goods they import from one another. Future goals of the EU include a common unit of money and a central bank.

REVIEW *What is the European Union?*

NAFTA

In 1994 a trade arrangement was made that affects Canada, Mexico, and the United States. It is called the North American Free Trade Agreement, or **NAFTA**. Under the agreement these three countries would, over a 15-year period, remove all tariffs and other forms of protectionism among them.

The goal of the agreement is to encourage the three countries to buy more of one another's goods.

Mexican pesos

Some labor leaders and farmers in Canada and the United States were against NAFTA. They thought that large companies might move to Mexico so they could hire people for less money. If this happened, many workers in Canada and the United States might lose their jobs. They also feared that Mexican crops would replace American and Canadian crops in the stores, hurting American and Canadian farmers.

Business leaders claimed that NAFTA would actually strengthen the economies of Canada and the United States. They said that a better Mexican economy would increase the Mexican demand for goods from Canada and the United States.

Business leaders in all three countries hope NAFTA will lead to a powerful North American free-trade **bloc**, or group of countries with the same interests. This free-trade bloc, they believe, will help North American companies compete against Asian and European companies.

In 1993 a number of Central American countries signed their own free-trade agreement. Some South American countries have done the same. Business leaders from places as far north as Canada and as far south as Argentina believe that one day all the countries of the Western Hemisphere will be part of a single free-trade agreement.

REVIEW *What do North American business leaders hope NAFTA will achieve?*

A Mexican electrical worker

Uniting for Peace

Countries often unite for reasons other than economic success. Most countries in the world today want to live together in peace. Many countries belong to organizations whose goals are to help make this possible.

Almost all of the world's countries belong to the organization known as the United Nations (UN). Some of the main goals of the United Nations are to bring peace to the world and to improve the lives of the world's people.

One part of the United Nations is the World Court. This international court is located in The Hague, the capital of the Netherlands. The World Court was set up to solve conflicts between countries. Countries do not have to agree to have their cases heard in the World Court, but if they do, the Court's decisions are final.

United Nations flag

During the time of the Cold War, two rival organizations formed. Countries that strongly supported democracy united to form the North Atlantic Treaty Organization (NATO). Some communist countries united to form the Warsaw Pact. The first members of NATO included the United States, France, Britain, West Germany, Italy, and Greece. Warsaw Pact members included the Soviet Union, East Germany, Poland, Czechoslovakia, and Hungary.

The fall of communism in Europe has brought an end to the Warsaw Pact. In contrast, NATO has grown. NATO has invited some former members of the Warsaw Pact to join it. The new members are the Czech Republic, Hungary, and Poland. More formerly communist countries may be invited to join NATO in the future.

REVIEW *What are the goals of the United Nations?*

LESSON 4 REVIEW

Check Understanding

1 **Remember the Facts**   What are NAFTA and OPEC?

2 **Recall the Main Idea**   What are some reasons present-day countries form groups?

Think Critically

3 **Cause and Effect**   What effect does telecommunications have on relations between countries?

4 **Speaking Personally**   How do you think countries around the world should work together to solve problems? Explain.

Show What You Know
Write a Letter   In a letter to a local business leader, ask whether NAFTA has changed his or her business and, if so, what changes it has brought. Report to your classmates on what you learn.

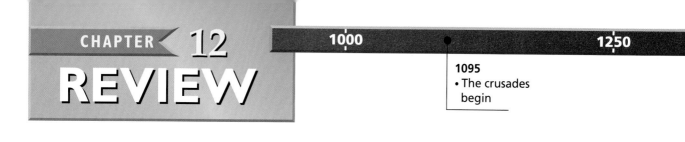

CONNECT MAIN IDEAS

Use this organizer to describe history, government, and economy in today's world. Write two details to support each main idea. A copy of the organizer appears on page 115 of the Activity Book.

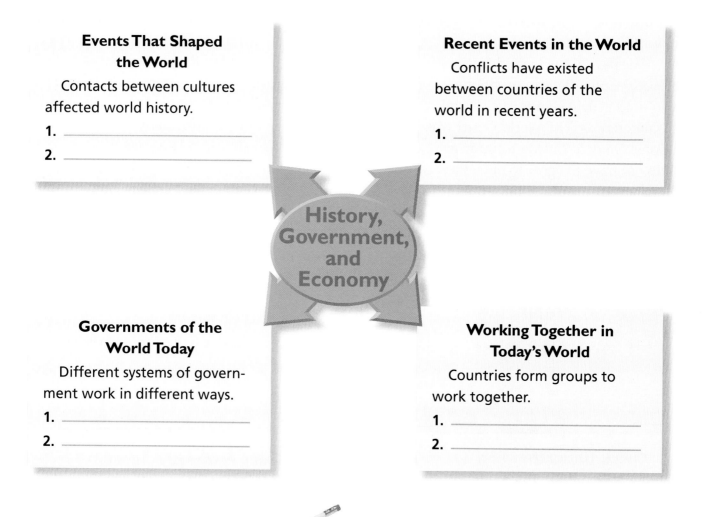

Events That Shaped the World

Contacts between cultures affected world history.

1. _____
2. _____

Recent Events in the World

Conflicts have existed between countries of the world in recent years.

1. _____
2. _____

History, Government, and Economy

Governments of the World Today

Different systems of government work in different ways.

1. _____
2. _____

Working Together in Today's World

Countries form groups to work together.

1. _____
2. _____

WRITE MORE ABOUT IT

Write a News Story Imagine that you are a news reporter in the 1930s. The newspaper you write for has sent you to Europe to cover recent events there. Write a news story that describes the events leading up to World War II.

Write a Description Write a short description of a technology you are familiar with. Explain how the technology works. At the end of your description, name some technologies you would like to see invented in the future.

1500   1750   Present

1492
• Columbus reaches
  the Americas

About 1700
• The Enlightenment
  begins

1991
• Soviet Union
  collapses

USE VOCABULARY

Write a word or phrase from this list to complete each of the sentences that follow.

imperialism   absolute monarchy

bloc   protectionism

1 A _____ is a group of nations with the same interests.

2 One ruler has complete authority in an _____.

3 Creating colonies to build an empire is _____.

4 A country may use _____ to help the sale of its own products.

CHECK UNDERSTANDING

5 How did the Enlightenment affect governments in the 1700s?

6 Why was the Berlin Wall built?

7 Which governing system does Canada have? Cuba? China?

8 What was one of the reasons the Internet was invented?

THINK CRITICALLY

9 **Personally Speaking** What do you think is the greatest environmental problem?

10 **Cause and Effect** What were some effects of the collapse of the Soviet Union?

11 **Explore Viewpoints** How is protectionism good for countries? How is it bad for countries they trade with?

APPLY SKILLS

Read a Cartogram Draw a cartogram that compares the populations of Arizona, Nevada, New Mexico, California, and Texas. To find the population of each state, look in an almanac. Once you have drawn your cartogram, answer these questions:

12 Which state has the largest population? Which state has the smallest population?

13 How do the sizes of states on your cartogram compare to their actual sizes?

Resolve Conflict Think about a conflict that exists in your community. Then, using the steps on pages 498–499, write down possible solutions to this conflict.

Form a Logical Conclusion Use the steps on page 507 to support this conclusion: Conflicts between the United States and the Soviet Union led to the Cold War. Use this book and other sources to support the conclusion. Make a list of supporting evidence, and give your sources.

READ MORE ABOUT IT

The DK Visual Timeline of the 20th Century by Sam Adams. DK Publishing. In this book, events are illustrated and displayed along a time line for easy reference.

Visit the Internet at
http://www.hbschool.com
for additional resources.

The International

A thousand years ago the Chinese city of Chang'an (now Xian) lay at the eastern end of the Silk Road, the main world trade route of its day. In the city market, merchants sold goods from distant lands—sandalwood from Indonesia, cloves from India, and incense from eastern Africa. Some merchants offered Persian dates and pistachios. The smells of Burmese pepper and Tibetan mustard rose from the marketplace.

In the United States today, any shopping mall has more kinds of goods from more places in the world than the Chang'an marketplace offered. Present-day mall merchants might sell coffee and fruit grown in South America, cotton shirts from India, athletic shoes made in South Korea, compact disc players from Japan, and American products from nearly every state in the Union.

The international exchange of goods that is now a part of everyday life began hundreds of years ago with the traders who traveled the world. It was their idea to find new products and bring them to market. Thanks to those daring adventurers, you can choose among basketball shoes made in many places—some as far away as South Korea!

Marketplace

Container ships from around the world use the port of Hong Kong to distribute and receive their goods.

Think and Apply

Like an early trader, search for products made in other parts of the world. Look around your home for such products, and mark on a world map the places where they were made. Then, look closely at your map. Where were most of the products you found made? Were certain kinds of goods more likely to come from certain areas? Work with a partner to write a short report that explains your findings.

HARCOURT BRACE
Visit the Internet at **http://www.hbschool.com** for additional resources.

CNN Turner Le@rning
Check your media center or classroom video library for the Making Social Studies Relevant videotape of this feature.

UNIT 6 REVIEW

Summarize the Main Ideas
Study the pictures and captions to help you review the events you read about in Unit 6.

Formulate a Generalization
Look at the present-day scenes in this visual summary. How do you think they will change by the year 2010? Re-create each of the present-day scenes to show the year 2010, and write a brief description below.

1 People's lives are affected by their culture and the places they live.

3 People changed when they went to new places and affected the lives of the people they met.

5 People take actions to better their lives within different kinds of government systems.

518 • Unit 6

People interact with their environment to meet their needs, and those interactions affect their environment.

 As new nations come into being, relationships between all the world's nations adjust and change.

 New technologies are affecting the lives of people today.

USE VOCABULARY

For each pair of terms, write at least one sentence that shows how the terms are related.

1. Qur'an, mosque
2. standard of living, developed country
3. arms race, Cold War
4. dissident, totalitarianism
5. telecommunications, Internet

CHECK UNDERSTANDING

6. What recent change took place in the country formerly called Zaire?
7. How have improved communications and transportation affected world cultures?
8. What actions has Mexico City taken to relieve its air pollution problems?
9. What was an effect of the crusades?
10. What happened to the ANC in South Africa during 1960?
11. What is a representative democracy? What is a constitutional democracy?
12. What is the difference between a constitutional monarchy and an absolute monarchy?
13. What is the purpose of the World Court?

THINK CRITICALLY

14. **Think More About It**   What do you think former U.S. President Carter meant when he said that differences in the United States were a source of strength?
15. **Past to Present**   In what ways are the Industrial Revolution of the 1800s and today's revolution in technology alike?

16. **Explore Viewpoints**   How do you think the upper class felt about revolutions against monarchies? How do you think the other classes felt about them?

APPLY SKILLS

Understand a Time Zone Map

Time zones are an important part of international trade. For example, time may change several times for a ship crossing the Pacific Ocean. Use the time zone map below to answer the questions.

17. When a ship leaves Lima, Peru, at 7:00 A.M., what time is it in Los Angeles?
18. If a ship leaves Tokyo, Japan, at 9:00 P.M. on Monday, what is the time and what is the day in Hawaii?

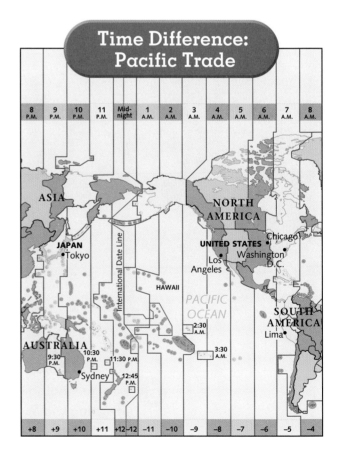

Time Difference: Pacific Trade

REMEMBER

- Share your ideas.
- Cooperate with others to plan your work.
- Take responsibility for your work.
- Help one another.
- Show your group's work to the class.
- Discuss what you learned by working together.

ACTIVITY

Make a Scrapbook

Important events happen daily throughout the world. As part of a group, select one of these continents: Africa, Asia, Australia, Europe, North America, or South America. Then, look through recent newspapers and magazines for articles and pictures about the latest political events in countries on the continent you selected. With your group, make a scrapbook that contains the most important articles along with pictures the group has found. For each article, write a brief description.

ACTIVITY

Present a Report

Work in groups to learn more about one of the African countries that became independent during the twentieth century. Find out about the country's languages, people, colonial history, present-day government, and other topics of interest. Present a report to your class.

ACTIVITY

Plan a Trip

You are about to complete the last unit of this book. Now you know all about the world, past and present. Imagine that you and a group of classmates have the chance to travel to five places in the world. Together, decide the five places you will travel to. Make a travel plan that tells why you want to go to those places. Then make a map that identifies the places and shows your travel route.

Unit Project Wrap-Up

Hold a World Summit Review the notes you have written about your selected country and write a list of concerns you want to discuss. Make a sign that shows the country you represent. Then, either with your whole class or as part of a small group, take part in a world summit meeting.

For Your Reference

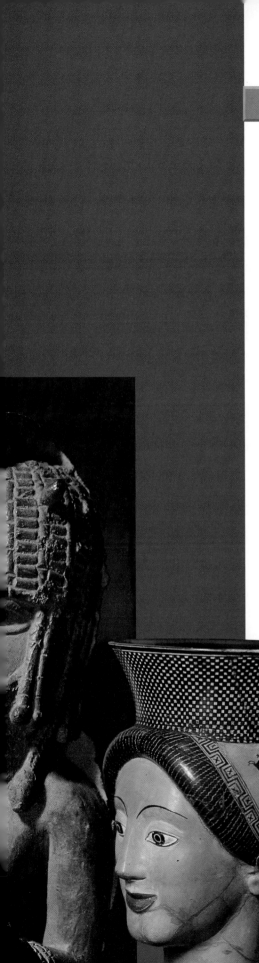

Contents

How to Gather and Report Information

To write a report, make a poster, or do many other social studies projects, you may need information that is not in your textbook. You would need to gather this information from reference books, electronic references, or community resources. The following guide can help you in gathering information from many sources and in reporting what you find.

HOW TO USE REFERENCE TOOLS

Reference works are collections of facts. They include books and electronic resources, such as almanacs, atlases, dictionaries, and encyclopedias. In a library a reference book has *R* or *REF*—for *reference*—on its spine along with the call number. Most reference books may not be taken home. They are for use only in the library. Many libraries also have electronic references on CD-ROM and the Internet.

▶ WHEN TO USE AN ENCYCLOPEDIA

An encyclopedia is a good place to begin to look for information. An encyclopedia has articles on nearly every subject. The articles are in alphabetical order. Each gives basic facts about people, places, and events. Some electronic encyclopedias allow you to hear music and speeches and see short movies.

▶ WHEN TO USE A DICTIONARY

A dictionary can give you information about words. Dictionaries explain word meanings and show the pronunciations of words. A dictionary is a good place to check the spelling of a word. Some dictionaries also include the origins of words and lists of foreign words, abbreviations, well-known people, and place names.

▶ WHEN TO USE AN ATLAS

You can find information about places in an atlas. An atlas is a book of maps. Some atlases have road maps. Others have maps of countries around the world. There are atlases with maps that show crops, population, products, and many other things. Ask a librarian to help you find the kind of atlas you need.

▶ WHEN TO USE AN ALMANAC

An almanac is a book or electronic resource of facts and figures. It shows information in tables and charts. However, the subjects are not in alphabetical order. You will need to use the index, which lists the subjects in alphabetical order. Most almanacs are brought up to date every year. So an almanac can give you the latest information.

These students are researching information that they need to prepare a report on ancient civilizations in the Americas.

Skills Handbook • **R3**

▶ HOW TO FIND NONFICTION BOOKS

Nonfiction books give facts about real people and things. In a library all nonfiction books are numbered and placed in order on the shelves. To find the nonfiction book you want, you need to know its call number. You can find the call number by using a card file or a computer catalog, but you will need to know the book's title, author, or subject. Here are some sample entries for a book on the early Mayas, a Native American people.

Subject Card

INDIANS OF CENTRAL AMERICA.

REF
972.81
MEYE
Meyer, Carolyn.
    The mystery of the ancient Maya / Carolyn Meyer and Charles Gallenkamp. -- New York : Atheneum, 1985.

    ix, 159 p. : ill. ; 24 cm.

    ISBN 0-689-50319-9

Title Card

The mystery of the ancient Maya

REF
972.81
MEYE
Meyer, Carolyn.
    The mystery of the ancient Maya / Carolyn Meyer and Charles Gallenkamp. -- New York : Atheneum, 1985.

    ix, 159 p. : ill. ; 24 cm.

F1435.M56 1985

    ISBN 0-689-50319-9

REF
972.81
MEYE
Meyer, Carolyn.
    The mystery of the ancient Maya / Carolyn Meyer and Charles Gallenkamp. -- New York : Atheneum, 1985.

    ix, 159 p. : ill. ; 24 cm.

F1435.M56 1985

    "A Margaret K. McElderry book."
    Includes index.
    SUMMARY: Explores the advanced civilization and unsolved mysteries of the Mayas, who reigned for six centuries and then disappeared.
    ISBN 0-689-50319-9

Author Card

F1435.M56 1985   REF 972.81
84-24209 /AC/r9(

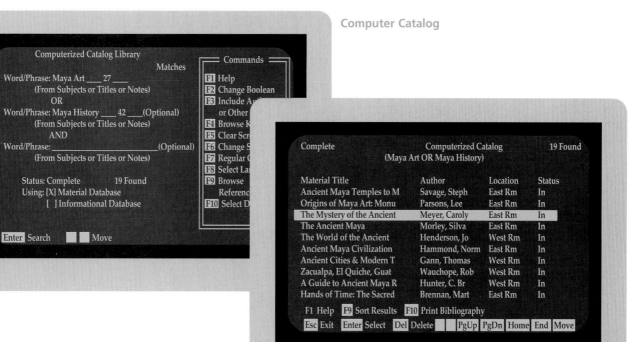

Computer Catalog

▶ HOW TO FIND PERIODICALS

Libraries have special sections for periodicals—newspapers and magazines. Periodicals are good sources for the latest information and for topics not covered in books. New issues of periodicals are usually displayed on a rack. Older issues are stored away, sometimes on film. Most libraries have an index or guide that lists magazine articles by subject. The most widely used guides are the *Children's Magazine Guide* and the *Readers' Guide to Periodical Literature*.

The entries in these guides are usually in alphabetical order by subject, author, or title. Abbreviations may be used for many parts of an entry, such as the name of the magazine and the date of the issue. Here is a sample entry for an article about prehistoric sculptures found in the country of Jordan.

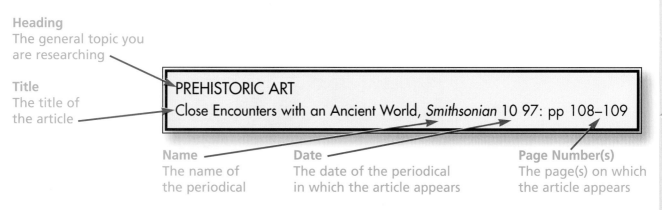

Heading
The general topic you are researching

Title
The title of the article

PREHISTORIC ART

Close Encounters with an Ancient World, *Smithsonian* 10 97: pp 108–109

Name
The name of the periodical

Date
The date of the periodical in which the article appears

Page Number(s)
The page(s) on which the article appears

HOW TO FIND INTERNET RESOURCES

The World Wide Web, part of the Internet, is a rich resource for information. You can use the World Wide Web to read documents, see photographs and artworks, and examine other primary sources. You can also use it to listen to music, read electronic books, take a "tour" of a museum, or get the latest news.

Information on the World Wide Web changes all the time. What you find today may not be there tomorrow, and new information is always being added. Much of the information you find may be useful, but remember that some of it may not be accurate.

▶ PLAN YOUR SEARCH

1. Make a list of your research questions.
2. Think about possible sources for finding your answers.
3. Identify key words to describe your research topic.
4. Consider synonyms and variations of those terms.
5. Decide exactly how you will go about finding what you need.

▶ SEARCH BY SUBJECT

To search for topics, or subjects, choose a search engine. You can get a list of available search engines by clicking the SEARCH or NET SEARCH button at the top of your screen.

If you want to find Web sites for baseball, for example, enter "baseball" in the search engine field. Then click SEARCH or GO on the screen. You will see a list of sites all over the World Wide Web having to do with baseball. Because not all search engines list the same sites, you may need to use more than one search engine.

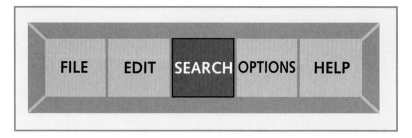

▶ SEARCH BY USING ADDRESSES

Each site on the World Wide Web has an address called a Uniform Resource Locator, or URL for short. A typical URL is shown in the box below.

To find URL listings, look in manuals, books, newspapers, magazines, and television and radio credits. To use a URL to go to a Web site, type the URL in the LOCATION/GO TO or NETSITE box in the upper left corner of the screen.

Go To   http://www.hbschool.com

▶ BOOKMARK YOUR RESOURCES

Once you have found a site that you think will be helpful, you can bookmark it. Bookmarking makes a copy of a URL and keeps a record of it so you can easily go back to the site later.

While you are at the site you want to bookmark, click BOOKMARKS at the top of your screen and choose ADD BOOKMARK. Your list of bookmarks might look like this:

BOOKMARKS

■ Harcourt Brace School Publishers: The Learning Site

■ Library of Congress Home Page

■ The Smithsonian Institution Home Page

■ National Archives Online Exhibit Hall

Knowing how to use the Internet can help you find a wide range of information on a subject quickly and easily.

Skills Handbook • **R7**

Interviewing can be a good way to gather firsthand information about a topic.

HOW TO CONDUCT AN INTERVIEW

Conducting interviews, or asking people questions, is a good way to get facts and points of view.

▶ PLANNING AN INTERVIEW

1. Make a list of people to interview.
2. Call or write to each person to request an interview. Identify yourself, and let the person know what you want to talk about.
3. Ask the person you will interview to set a time and place to meet.

▶ BEFORE THE INTERVIEW

1. Read more about your topic, and, if possible, about the person. That way, you will be better able to talk with the person about your topic.
2. Make a list of questions to ask.

▶ DURING THE INTERVIEW

1. Listen carefully. Do not interrupt or argue with the person.
2. Take notes, and write down the person's exact words.
3. If you want to use a tape recorder, first ask the person if you may do so.

▶ AFTER THE INTERVIEW

1. Before you leave, thank the person you interviewed.
2. Follow up by writing a thank-you note.

HOW TO CONDUCT A SURVEY

A good way to get information about the views of people in your community is to conduct a survey.

1. Identify your topic, and make a list of questions. Write them so that they can be answered with "yes" or "no" or with "for" or "against." You may also want to give a "no opinion" or "not sure" choice.
2. Make a tally sheet for recording the responses.
3. Decide how many people you will ask and where you will conduct your survey.
4. During the survey, record the responses carefully.
5. When you have finished your survey, count the responses and write a summary statement or conclusion that your survey supports.

HOW TO WRITE FOR INFORMATION

People in places far away can also give you information. You can write a letter to ask for it. When you write, be sure to do these things:

- Write neatly by hand or use a computer.
- Say who you are and why you are writing.
- Make your request specific and reasonable.
- Provide a self-addressed, stamped envelope for the answer.

HOW TO WRITE A REPORT

You may be asked to write a report on the information you have gathered. Most reports are 300 to 500 words long.

▶ GATHER AND ORGANIZE YOUR INFORMATION

Gather information about your topic from reference books, electronic references, or community resources. Then organize the information you have gathered.

- Take notes as you find information for your report.
- Review your notes to make sure that you have all the information you need.
- Outline your information.
- Make sure the information is in the right order.

▶ DRAFT YOUR REPORT

- Review your information. Decide whether you need more.
- Remember that the purpose of your report is to share information about your topic.
- Write a draft of your report. Put all your ideas on paper.

▶ REVISE

- Check that you have followed the order of your outline. Move sentences that seem out of place.
- Add any information that seems needed.
- Add quotations that show people's exact words if you can.
- Reword sentences if too many follow the same pattern.

▶ PROOFREAD AND PUBLISH

- Check for errors.
- Make sure nothing has been left out.
- Write a clean copy of your report by hand, or use a computer.

A good report is well-organized, informative, and error-free.

Almanac

Country Flag	Country	Capital	Population*	Area (sq. mi.)	Economy
Africa					
	Algeria	Algiers	29,830,000	918,497	oil, natural gas, light industry, food processing, grains, iron
	Angola	Luanda	10,624,000	481,351	textiles, coffee, sugarcane, bananas, iron, diamonds
	Benin	Porto-Novo	5,902,000	43,483	palm products, peanuts, cotton, corn, oil
	Botswana	Gaborone	1,501,000	219,916	livestock processing, corn, coal, copper, tourism
	Burkina Faso	Ouagadougou	10,891,000	105,869	agricultural processing, textiles, millet, sorghum, manganese
	Burundi	Bujumbura	6,053,000	10,759	food processing, coffee, cotton, tea, nickel
	Cameroon	Yaoundé	14,678,000	183,591	oil products, food processing, cocoa, coffee
	Cape Verde	Praia	394,000	1,557	bananas, coffee, sweet potatoes, salt
	Central African Republic	Bangui	3,342,000	240,376	textiles, cotton, coffee, diamonds

Country Flag	Country	Capital	Population*	Area (sq. mi.)	Economy
	Chad	N'Djamena	7,166,000	495,752	cotton, sorghum, millet, uranium
	Comoros	Moroni	590,000	863	perfume, textiles, vanilla, coconut oil, perfume, plants, fruits
	Congo Republic	Brazzaville	2,583,000	132,047	oil, wood products, cocoa, coffee, potash
	Côte d'Ivoire (Ivory Coast)	Yamoussoukro	14,986,000	124,503	food processing, coffee, cocoa, oil, diamonds
	Democratic Republic of the Congo	Kinshasa	47,440,000	905,356	mining, food processing, sugar, rice, cobalt
	Djibouti	Djibouti	434,000	8,880	mainly service activities
	Egypt	Cairo	64,792,000	386,900	textiles, tourism, chemicals, cotton, rice, beans, oil, gas
	Equatorial Guinea	Malabo	443,000	10,825	fish, cocoa, coffee, bananas, oil
	Eritrea	Asmara	3,590,000	45,405	food processing, cotton, coffee, tobacco, gold, potash
	Ethiopia	Addis Ababa	58,733,000	471,775	food processing, textiles, coffee, grains, platinum, gold
	Gabon	Libreville	1,190,000	102,317	textiles, cocoa, coffee, oil, manganese, uranium

*These population figures are from the most recent available statistics.

Almanac

Country Flag	Country	Capital	Population*	Area (sq. mi.)	Economy
	The Gambia	Banjul	1,248,000	4,003	tourism, peanuts, rice, fish
	Ghana	Accra	18,101,000	92,100	aluminum, cocoa, gold, manganese
	Guinea	Conakry	7,405,000	94,925	mining, bananas, pineapples, iron, bauxite, diamonds
	Guinea-Bissau	Bissau	1,179,000	13,948	peanuts, cashews, cotton, rice, bauxite
	Kenya	Nairobi	28,803,000	224,960	tourism, oil refining, coffee, corn, gold, limestone
	Lesotho	Maseru	2,008,000	11,716	food processing, textiles, corn, grains, diamonds
	Liberia	Monrovia	2,602,000	43,000	mining, rice, cassava, coffee, iron, diamonds, gold, rubber, timber
	Libya	Tripoli	5,648,000	679,358	oil, food processing, dates, olives, gypsum
	Madagascar	Antananarivo	14,062,000	226,657	textiles, meat processing, coffee, cloves, vanilla, chromite, graphite
	Malawi	Lilongwe	9,609,000	45,747	agricultural processing, sugar, tea, tobacco, coffee

Country Flag	Country	Capital	Population*	Area (sq. mi.)	Economy
	Mali	Bamako	9,945,000	478,652	millet, rice, peanuts, cotton, gold, phosphates
	Mauritania	Nouakchott	2,411,000	397,955	fish processing, dates, grains, iron ore, gypsum
	Mauritius	Port Louis	1,154,000	720	tourism, textiles, sugarcane, tea
	Morocco	Rabat	30,391,000	172,413	carpets, clothing, leather goods, grains, fruits, phosphates, iron ore
	Mozambique	Maputo	18,165,000	297,846	chemicals, petroleum products, cashews, cotton, sugar, coal, titanium
	Namibia	Windhoek	1,727,000	318,321	diamonds, copper, gold, fish
	Niger	Niamey	9,389,000	459,073	peanuts, cotton, uranium, coal, iron
	Nigeria	Abuja	107,129,000	356,669	oil, gas, textiles, cocoa, palm products
	Rwanda	Kigali	7,738,000	10,169	coffee, tea, tin
	São Tomé and Príncipe	São Tomé	148,000	372	cocoa, coconuts
	Senegal	Dakar	9,404,000	76,124	food processing, fishing, peanuts, millet, phosphates

*These population figures are from the most recent available statistics.

Country Flag	Country	Capital	Population*	Area (sq. mi.)	Economy
	Seychelles	Victoria	78,000	107	food processing, tourism, coconut products, cinnamon, vanilla
	Sierra Leone	Freetown	4,892,000	27,699	mining, cocoa, coffee, diamonds, titanium
	Somalia	Mogadishu	9,940,000	246,154	sugar, bananas, iron, tin
	South Africa	Cape Town	42,327,000	471,445	steel, automobiles, corn, other grains, gold, diamonds, platinum
	Sudan	Khartoum	32,594,000	967,500	textiles, gum arabic, cotton, chromium, copper
	Swaziland	Mbabane	1,032,000	6,705	wood pulp, sugar, corn, cotton, asbestos, clay, coal
	Tanzania	Dar es Salaam	29,461,000	364,900	agricultural processing, cotton, tin, diamonds
	Togo	Lomé	4,736,000	21,853	textiles, coffee, cocoa, yams, phosphates
	Tunisia	Tunis	9,183,000	63,378	food processing, textiles, oil products, grains, olives, dates, phosphates
	Uganda	Kampala	20,605,000	91,134	textiles, cement, coffee, cotton, tea, copper, cobalt

Almanac

Country Flag	Country	Capital	Population*	Area (sq. mi.)	Economy
	Zambia	Lusaka	9,350,000	290,585	corn, cassava, sugar, cobalt, copper, zinc, emeralds, gold, silver
	Zimbabwe	Harare	11,423,000	150,820	clothing, steel, chemicals, tobacco, sugar, chromium, gold, nickel

Asia

Country Flag	Country	Capital	Population*	Area (sq. mi.)	Economy
	Afghanistan	Kabul	23,738,000	250,775	textiles, furniture, wheat, fruits, copper, coal, wool
	Armenia	Yerevan	3,466,000	11,506	vegetables, grapes, copper, gold
	Azerbaijan	Baku	7,736,000	33,436	oil, grains, cotton, iron, cattle
	Bahrain	Manama	603,000	255	oil, gas, fruits, vegetables
	Bangladesh	Dhaka	125,340,000	55,126	jute, textiles, fertilizers, rice, tea
	Bhutan	Thimphu	1,865,000	16,000	rice, corn, timber
	Brunei	Bandar Seri Begawan	308,000	2,226	petroleum, rice, bananas, cassava
	Burma (Myanmar)	Rangoon (Yangôn)	46,822,000	261,789	textiles, petroleum, rice, sugarcane, lead, gemstones

*These population figures are from the most recent available statistics.

Almanac

Country Flag	Country	Capital	Population*	Area (sq. mi.)	Economy
	Cambodia	Phnom Penh	11,164,000	69,898	rice, wood, rubber, corn, gemstones
	China	Beijing	1,221,600,000	3,700,000	iron, steel, textiles, tea, rice and other grains, cotton
	Cyprus	Nicosia	753,000	3,572	barley, grapes, olives, copper
	Georgia	Tbilisi	5,175,000	26,911	manganese, citrus fruits, potatoes, corn
	India	New Delhi	967,613,000	1,195,063	textiles, steel, rice and other grains, tea, spices, coal, iron
	Indonesia	Jakarta	209,774,000	779,675	textiles, rice, cocoa, peanuts, nickel, tin, oil
	Iran	Tehran	67,540,000	635,932	sugar refining, carpets, rice and other grains, oil, gas
	Iraq	Baghdad	22,219,000	168,927	textiles, grains, dates, oil
	Israel	Jerusalem	5,535,000	7,992	diamond cutting, textiles, electronics, citrus fruits, copper, phosphates
	Japan	Tokyo	125,717,000	143,619	electronics, automobiles, fishing, rice, potatoes
	Jordan	Amman	4,325,000	34,575	oil refining, cement, grains, olives, phosphates

Country Flag	Country	Capital	Population*	Area (sq. mi.)	Economy
	Kazakhstan	Aqmola	16,899,000	1,048,300	steel, grains, cotton
	Kuwait	Kuwait	2,077,000	6,880	oil, oil products, gas
	Kyrgyzstan	Bishkek	4,540,000	76,641	textiles, mining, tobacco, cotton, sugar beets, gold
	Laos	Vientiane	5,117,000	91,428	wood products, mining, sweet potatoes, corn, cotton, gypsum
	Lebanon	Beirut	3,859,000	3,949	banking, textiles, oil refining, fruits, olives, vegetables
	Malaysia	Kuala Lumpur	20,376,000	128,727	rubber goods, logging, steel, electronics, palm oil, tin, iron
	Maldives	Male	280,000	115	fish processing, tourism, coconuts, sweet potatoes, corn
	Mongolia	Ulaanbaatar	2,538,000	604,247	food processing, mining, grains, coal, oil
	Nepal	Kathmandu	22,641,000	54,362	sugar, jute, tourism, rice and other grains, quartz
	North Korea	P'yongyang	24,317,000	46,609	textiles, corn, potatoes, coal, lead
	Oman	Muscat	2,265,000	82,000	dates, vegetables, limes, oil, gas

*These population figures are from the most recent available statistics.

Country Flag	Country	Capital	Population*	Area (sq. mi.)	Economy
	Pakistan	Islamabad	132,185,000	310,403	textiles, petroleum products, rice, wheat, natural gas, iron ore
	Palau	Koror	17,000	191	tourism, fish, coconuts, copra, cassava, sweet potatoes
	Philippines	Manila	76,104,000	115,651	textiles, clothing, wood products, sugar, cobalt, copper
	Qatar	Doha	665,000	4,400	oil, petroleum products
	Saudi Arabia	Riyadh	20,088,000	865,000	oil, oil products, gas, dates, wheat
	Singapore	Singapore	3,462,000	225	shipbuilding, oil refining, electronics, banking, tourism
	South Korea	Seoul	45,949,000	38,022	electronics, automobiles, textiles, clothing, rice, barley, tungsten
	Sri Lanka	Colombo	18,762,000	25,332	clothing, textiles, tea, coconuts, rice, graphite, limestone
	Syria	Damascus	16,138,000	71,498	oil products, textiles, cotton, grains, olives
	Taiwan	Taipei	21,656,000	13,887	textiles, clothing, electronics, rice, fruits, coal, marble

Almanac

Country Flag	Country	Capital	Population*	Area (sq. mi.)	Economy
	Tajikistan	Dushanbe	6,014,000	55,251	aluminum, cement, barley, coal, lead
	Thailand	Bangkok	59,451,000	198,455	textiles, tourism, rice, corn, tapioca, sugarcane
	Turkey	Ankara	63,528,000	301,380	steel, textiles, grains, mercury
	Turkmenistan	Ashgabat	4,225,000	188,455	oil, mining, textiles, grains, cotton, coal, sulfur, salt
	United Arab Emirates	Abu Dhabi	2,262,000	32,280	oil, vegetables, dates
	Uzbekistan	Tashkent	23,860,000	173,591	machinery, natural gas, vegetables, cotton
	Vietnam	Hanoi	75,124,000	130,468	food processing, textiles, rice, sugar, phosphates
	Yemen	Sanaa	13,972,000	203,849	oil, grains, fruits, salt

Australia and Oceania

Country Flag	Country	Capital	Population*	Area (sq. mi.)	Economy
	Australia	Canberra	18,439,000	2,967,909	iron, steel, textiles, electrical equipment, wheat, cotton, fruits, bauxite, coal
	Fiji	Suva	792,000	7,055	tourism, sugar, bananas, gold, timber

*These population figures are from the most recent available statistics.

Country Flag	Country	Capital	Population*	Area (sq. mi.)	Economy
	Kiribati	Tarawa	82,000	277	fishing, coconut oil, breadfruit, sweet potatoes
	Marshall Islands	Majuro	61,000	70	agriculture, tourism
	Micronesia	Palikir	128,000	1,055	tourism, tropical fruits, vegetables, pepper
	Nauru	Yaren	10,000	8.5	phosphates
	New Zealand	Wellington	3,587,000	103,736	food processing, textiles, machinery, fish, forest products, grains, potatoes, gold, gas, iron, coal
	Papua New Guinea	Port Moresby	4,496,000	178,260	coffee, coconuts, cocoa, gold, copper, silver
	Samoa	Apia	220,000	1,100	timber, tourism, coconuts, yams, hardwoods, fish
	Solomon Islands	Honiara	427,000	11,500	fishing, coconuts, rice, gold, bauxite
	Tonga	Nuku'alofa	107,000	270	tourism, fishing, coconut products, bananas
	Tuvalu	Funafuti	10,000	9	coconut products, coconuts

Almanac

Country Flag	Country	Capital	Population*	Area (sq. mi.)	Economy
	Vanuatu	Portvila	181,000	5,700	fish processing, meat canneries, tourism, coconut products, manganese

Europe

Country Flag	Country	Capital	Population*	Area (sq. mi.)	Economy
	Albania	Tiranë	3,293,000	11,100	cement, textiles, food processing, corn, wheat, chromium, coal
	Andorra	Andorra la Vella	75,000	180	tourism, sheep, tobacco products, iron, lead
	Austria	Vienna	8,054,000	32,375	steel, machinery, automobiles, grains, iron ore
	Belarus	Minsk	10,440,000	80,154	manufacturing, chemicals, grains, vegetables
	Belgium	Brussels	10,204,000	11,781	steel, glassware, diamond cutting, automobiles, wheat, coal
	Bosnia and Herzegovina	Sarajevo	2,608,000	19,904	steel, mining, textiles, timber, corn, wheat, berries, bauxite, iron
	Bulgaria	Sofia	8,653,000	42,823	chemicals, machinery, metals, textiles, grains, fruits, bauxite, copper, zinc
	Croatia	Zagreb	5,027,000	21,829	chemicals, plastics, steel, paper, olives, wheat, oil, bauxite

*These population figures are from the most recent available statistics.

Country Flag	Country	Capital	Population*	Area (sq. mi.)	Economy
	Czech Republic	Prague	10,319,000	30,450	machinery, oil products, glass, wheat, sugar beets, rye, coal, kaolin
	Denmark	Copenhagen	5,269,000	16,629	food processing, machinery, textiles, furniture, grains, potatoes, dairy products, oil, salt
	Estonia	Tallinn	1,445,000	17,413	shipbuilding, electric motors, potatoes, oil
	Finland	Helsinki	5,109,000	130,128	metal, wood products, grains, copper, iron
	France	Paris	58,470,000	210,918	steel, textiles, tourism, wine, perfume, grains, fruits, vegetables, bauxite, iron
	Germany	Berlin	84,068,000	137,735	shipbuilding, automobiles, grains, potatoes, coal, potash, steel
	Greece	Athens	10,583,000	50,944	textiles, tourism, chemicals, wine, grains, olives, grapes, citrus fruits, bauxite
	Hungary	Budapest	9,936,000	35,919	iron, steel, wheat, corn, sunflowers, bauxite, coal
	Iceland	Reykjavik	273,000	39,702	fish, aluminum, potatoes

Country Flag	Country	Capital	Population*	Area (sq. mi.)	Economy
	Ireland	Dublin	3,556,000	26,600	food processing, textiles, chemicals, tourism, potatoes, grains, zinc, lead
	Italy	Rome	57,534,000	116,313	tourism, steel, machinery, automobiles, textiles, shoes, grapes, olives and olive oil, mercury, potash, sulfur
	Latvia	Riga	2,438,000	24,595	machinery, train cars, grains, sugar beets
	Liechtenstein	Vaduz	31,461	62	electronics, textiles, ceramics, vegetables, wheat
	Lithuania	Vilnius	3,636,000	25,174	machinery, shipbuilding, grains, potatoes, vegetables
	Luxembourg	Luxembourg	422,474	999	steel, chemicals, food processing, grains, potatoes, grapes
	Macedonia	Skopje	2,114,000	9,928	mining, textiles, wheat, rice, chromium, lead
	Malta	Valletta	379,365	122	textiles, tourism, potatoes, tomatoes
	Moldova	Chisinau	4,475,000	13,012	canning, wine, textiles, grains, lignite, gypsum
	Monaco	Monaco	32,000	370 acres	tourism, chemicals, plastics

*These population figures are from the most recent available statistics.

Country Flag	Country	Capital	Population*	Area (sq. mi.)	Economy
	Netherlands	Amsterdam The Hague	15,653,000	16,033	metals, machinery, chemicals, grains, potatoes, flowers, oil, gas
	Norway	Oslo	4,404,000	154,790	paper, shipbuilding, grains, potatoes, copper
	Poland	Warsaw	38,700,000	120,756	shipbuilding, chemicals, grains, potatoes, sugar beets, coal, copper, silver
	Portugal	Lisbon	9,868,000	35,383	textiles, footwear, cork, fish, grains, potatoes, tungsten, uranium, iron
	Romania	Bucharest	21,399,000	91,699	mining, machinery, oil, oil products, grains, grapes, gas, coal
	Russia**	Moscow	147,987,000	6,592,812	steel, machinery, motor vehicles, chemicals, textiles, grains, sugar beets, mercury, manganese, potash, bauxite, cobalt
	San Marino	San Marino	25,000	24	tourism, postage stamps, woolen goods, wheat, grapes
	Slovakia	Bratislava	5,393,000	18,923	iron, steel, glass, grains, potatoes
	Slovenia	Ljubljana	1,946,000	7,819	electronics, vehicles, coal, lead, zinc

**in both Asia and Europe.

Country Flag	Country	Capital	Population*	Area (sq. mi.)	Economy
	Spain	Madrid	39,244,000	194,881	machinery, textiles, grains, olives, grapes, lignite, uranium, lead
	Sweden	Stockholm	8,946,000	173,665	steel, machinery, vehicles, grains, potatoes, zinc, iron, lead
	Switzerland	Bern	7,249,000	15,941	machinery, chemicals, watches, cheese, chocolate products, tourism, salt
	Ukraine	Kiev	50,685,000	233,089	chemicals, machinery, grains, sugar beets, potatoes, iron, manganese
	United Kingdom	London	58,610,000	94,251	steel, vehicles, shipbuilding, banking, textiles, grains, sugar beets, coal, tin, oil, gas, limestone
	Vatican City	—	840	109 acres	tourism, postage stamps
	Yugoslavia	Belgrade	10,655,000	39,449	steel, machinery, corn and other grains, oil, gas, coal

North America

Country Flag	Country	Capital	Population*	Area (sq. mi.)	Economy
	Antigua and Barbuda	St. John's	66,000	171	manufacturing, tourism
	Bahamas	Nassau	262,000	5,386	tourism, rum, banking

*These population figures are from the most recent available statistics.

FACTS ABOUT THE WORLD

Country Flag	Country	Capital	Population*	Area (sq. mi.)	Economy
	Barbados	Bridgetown	258,000	166	sugar, tourism
	Belize	Belmopan	225,000	8,867	sugar
	Canada	Ottawa	29,123,000	3,851,809	nickel, zinc, copper, gold, livestock, fish
	Costa Rica	San José	3,534,000	19,652	furniture, aluminum, textiles, fertilizers, coffee, gold
	Cuba	Havana	10,999,000	41,620	food processing, tobacco, sugar, rice, coffee, cobalt, nickel, iron, copper, salt
	Dominica	Roseau	83,226	289	tourism, bananas, citrus fruits, pumice
	Dominican Republic	Santo Domingo	8,228,000	18,657	cement, tourism, sugar, cocoa, coffee, nickel, bauxite
	El Salvador	San Salvador	5,662,000	8,260	food products, tobacco, coffee, corn, sugar
	Grenada	St. George's	96,000	120	textiles, spices, bananas, cocoa
	Guatemala	Guatemala City	11,558,000	42,042	furniture, rubber, textiles, coffee, sugar, bananas, oil
	Haiti	Port-au-Prince	6,611,000	10,714	textiles, coffee, sugar, bananas, bauxite

Country Flag	Country	Capital	Population*	Area (sq. mi.)	Economy
	Honduras	Tegucigalpa	5,751,000	43,277	textiles, wood products, bananas, sugar, gold, silver, copper, lead
	Jamaica	Kingston	2,616,000	4,471	tourism, sugar, coffee, bananas, potatoes, bauxite, limestone
	Mexico	Mexico City	97,563,000	759,530	steel, chemicals, textiles, rubber, petroleum, tourism, cotton, coffee, wheat, silver, lead, zinc, gold, oil, gas
	Nicaragua	Managua	4,386,000	49,579	food processing, chemicals, textiles, cotton, fruits, coffee, gold, silver, copper
	Panama	Panama City	2,693,000	33,659	oil refining, international banking, bananas, rice, copper, mahogany, shrimp
	Saint Kitts and Nevis	Basseterre	42,000	104	sugar, tourism
	Saint Lucia	Castries	160,000	238	clothing, tourism, bananas, coconuts, forests
	Trinidad and Tobago	Port-of-Spain	1,273,000	1,980	oil products, chemicals, tourism, sugar, cocoa, asphalt, oil, gas
	United States of America	Washington, D.C.	267,955,000	3,619,969	wheat, coal, lead, uranium, iron, copper, gold, computers, electronics, machinery

*These population figures are from the most recent available statistics.

Country Flag	Country	Capital	Population*	Area (sq. mi.)	Economy

South America

Country Flag	Country	Capital	Population*	Area (sq. mi.)	Economy
	Argentina	Buenos Aires	35,798,000	1,072,156	food processing, automobiles, chemicals, grains, oil, lead
	Bolivia	La Paz/Sucre	7,670,000	424,162	mining, tobacco, coffee, sugar, potatoes, soybeans, tin, tungsten
	Brazil	Brasília	164,511,000	3,284,426	steel, automobiles, textiles, coffee, soybeans, sugar, iron, manganese
	Chile	Santiago	14,508,000	292,257	fish, wood, grains, grapes, beans, copper
	Colombia	Bogotá	37,418,000	439,735	textiles, food processing, coffee, rice, bananas, emeralds, oil, gas
	Ecuador	Quito	11,691,000	109,483	food processing, bananas, coffee, oil, gas, copper, zinc, silver, gold
	Guyana	Georgetown	706,000	83,000	mining, textiles, sugar, bauxite, diamonds, gold
	Paraguay	Asunción	5,652,000	157,043	food processing, textiles, cement, corn, cotton, iron, manganese, limestone
	Peru	Lima	24,950,000	496,222	fishing, mining, textiles, cotton, sugar, coffee, rice, copper, silver, gold, oil

Country Flag	Country	Capital	Population*	Area (sq. mi.)	Economy
	Saint Vincent and the Grenadines	Kingstown	119,000	150	tourism, bananas, arrowroot, coconuts
	Suriname	Paramaribo	443,000	63,251	aluminum, food processing, rice, sugar, fruits, bauxite, iron
	Uruguay	Montevideo	3,262,000	68,039	meat packing, textiles, wine, corn, wheat, oil refining
	Venezuela	Caracas	22,396,000	352,143	steel, textiles, coffee, rice, corn, oil, gas, iron

*These population figures are from the most recent available statistics.

Almanac

Biographical Dictionary

The Biographical Dictionary lists many of the important people introduced in this book. The page number tells where the main discussion of each person starts. See the Index for other page references.

A

Abraham *c. 2000s B.C.* Earliest ancestor of the Israelites, according to the Bible. p. 105

Ahmose *c. 1500s B.C.* Egyptian pharaoh who defeated the Hyksos and reclaimed Egypt. p. 152

Akhenaton (ahk•NAHT•uhn) *c. 1300s B.C.* Egyptian ruler who changed his name from Amenhotep IV. He and Nefertiti, his wife, urged the Egyptians to worship only one god, the Aton. p. 153

Alaric (AL•uh•rik) *c. 370–410* King of the Visigoths who crossed the Alps and attacked the city of Rome in 410. p. 364

Alexander the Great *356 B.C.–323 B.C.* Son of Philip II. He was tutored by Aristotle and became king of Macedonia in 336 B.C. As ruler, Alexander built a huge empire. p. 318

Amanitore (uh•MAN•uh•tawr•ee) *first century B.C.* Queen of ancient Meroë, in Nubia. p. 178

Amenemhet (AHM•uhn•em•HET) *1991 B.C.– 1962 B.C.* Vizier who made Egypt an empire. This started the period called the Middle Kingdom, which lasted for 200 years. p. 150

Arafat, Yasir (AH•ruh•faht) *1929–* Palestinian political leader, chairperson of the Palestine Liberation Organization, and President representing the Palestinian people. p. 496

Archimedes (ar•kuh•MEE•deez) *c. 287 B.C.– 212 B.C.* Greek teacher and inventor who used mathematics to build many useful machines. p. 322

Aristarchus (air•uh•STAR•kuhs) *c. 200s B.C.* Greek teacher who used mathematics to discover that the Earth moves in a path around the sun. p. 322

Aristobulus (uh•ris•tuh•BYOO•luhs) *c. 300s B.C.* Greek traveler to ancient India. p. 202

Aristophanes (air•uh•STAHF•uh•neez) *c. 450 B.C.–c. 388 B.C.* Ancient Greek writer of comedies, or humorous plays. p. 310

Aristotle (AIR•uh•stah•tuhl) *384 B.C.–322 B.C.* Greek philosopher and tutor of Alexander the Great. He is considered one of the greatest thinkers of all time. p. 313

Ashoka (uh•SHOH•kuh) *c. 200s B.C.* Maurya emperor remembered as "the greatest and noblest ruler India has known." p. 219

Atahuallpa (ah•tah•WAHL•pah) *1502?–1533* Inca ruler who was killed in the Spanish conquest of the Incas. p. 422

B

Bonaparte, Napoleon (BOH•nuh•part, nuh•POH•lee•uhn) *1769–1821* French military leader and emperor of France. p. 483

C

Caesar, Julius *100 B.C.–44 B.C.* Roman general and statesperson. He was dictator of Rome until he was murdered by a group of nobles. p. 336

Cambyses II (kam•BY•seez) *500 B.C.* Persian king who made Egypt a part of his empire in 525 B.C. p. 155

Castro, Fidel *1926–* Cuban revolutionary leader, prime minister, and president. p. 504

Champollion, Jean-François *1790–1832* Person who unlocked the secret of Egyptian hieroglyphics by decoding them. p. 154

Chandragupta I (chuhn•druh•GUP•tuh) *c. 300s* Maurya emperor of India. He gave up his throne to his son Samudra Gupta. p. 221

Chandragupta II *c. 400s* Son of Samudra Gupta of India's Maurya dynasty. He encouraged learning during his reign, which lasted from about 380 to 415. p. 221

Chandragupta Maurya (chuhn•druh•GUP•tuh MOW•ree•uh) *?–c. 297 B.C.* Emperor who united India. He gave up the throne to his son in 297 B.C. p. 218

Chang Heng *c. A.D. 100.* Inventor of China's first seismograph. p. 265

Cicero (SIH•suh•roh) *106 B.C.–43 B.C.* Roman orator, statesperson, and philosopher. He served as a consul of Rome. p. 336

Cleisthenes (KLYS•thuh•neez) *c. 570 B.C.–508 B.C.* Athenian leader who is regarded as the founder of democracy. p. 304

Cleopatra *69 B.C.–30 B.C.* Egyptian queen who, with Mark Antony, planned to set up an independent empire until the Roman leader Octavian defeated them. p. 340

Clovis *c. 466–551* Leader of the Franks who captured the last Roman territory in Gaul. p. 365

Columbus, Christopher *1451–1506* Italian-born Spanish explorer. In 1492 he sailed from Spain and thought he had reached Asia. Actually, he had reached islands near the Americas, lands that were unknown to Europeans. p. 401

Confucius *551 B.C.–479 B.C.* Philosopher who is considered to be the most revered person in Chinese history. His philosophy, known as Confucianism, became a guide for the way people lived. p. 247

Constantine (KAHN•stuhn•teen) *c. 280–337* Roman general and emperor. The Edict of Milan, which was issued in 313 (during his reign), made Christianity an accepted religion within the Roman Empire. p. 359

Cortés, Hernando (kawr•TEZ) *1485–1547* Spanish conquistador who conquered the Aztec Empire. p. 411

Cyrus the Great *c. 585 B.C.–529 B.C.* Leader who built the Persian Empire. p. 224

D

Darius I (duh•RY•uhs) *550 B.C.–486 B.C.* Persian ruler who brought order to the Persian Empire. He also built roads; established a postal system; and standardized weights, measures, and coinage. p. 225

Dart, Raymond *1893–1988* South African scientist who was the first to discover an australopithecine fossil. p. 51

David *c. 1025 B.C.–960 B.C.* Second king of Israel; defeated the Philistines. p. 107

Deng Xiaoping (DUHNG SHOW•PING) *1904–1997* Deputy premier and leader of the Chinese Communist party during the 1970s. His major influence on economic changes helped make China an industrial power. p. 506

Diocletian (dy•uh•KLEE•shuhn) *c. 245–c. 313* As Roman emperor he tried to strengthen the struggling empire. p. 363

Dubois, Eugene (dyoo•BWAH) *1858–1940* Dutch surgeon who was the first to discover the remains of a *Homo erectus* skeleton. p. 51

E

Elizabeth II *1926–* Queen of Britain for much of the latter half of the twentieth century. p. 503

Enheduanna (en•hay•doo•AHN•ah) *c. 2700s B.C.* Sumerian remembered for the many religious songs that she composed. p. 94

Euclid (YOO•kluhd) *c. 300s B.C.* Greek teacher who began the study of geometry. p. 322

Evans, Arthur *1851–1941* Archaeologist who discovered the ruins of a kingdom of the ancient Minoans. p. 291

F

Faxian (FAH•SHYUHN) *c. 400s* Buddhist missionary from China who traveled in India and wrote about the scenes he observed. p. 221

Francis Ferdinand *1863–1914* Archduke of Austria, whose assassination in 1914 is considered to be the cause of World War I. p. 485

G

Gaozu (GOW•ZOO) *256 B.C.–195 B.C.* Ruler during the Han dynasty of China. He was a respected leader who combined ideas from Legalism and Confucianism. p. 262

Gautama, Siddhartha *563 B.C.–c. 483 B.C.* Known as the Buddha, or the Enlightened One, he gave up worldly goods to search for enlightenment and truth. He founded the religion of Buddhism in India. p. 214

Genghis Khan *c. 1162–1227* Mongol leader who built the Mongol Empire. p. 479

Gilgamesh *c. 2700s B.C.* King of the ancient Sumerian city-state of Uruk. He is the subject of one of the world's oldest stories. p. 92

Gorbachev, Mikhail (gawr•buh•CHAWF, mee•kah•EEL) *1931–* Secretary general of the Communist party of the Soviet Union from 1985 to 1991. He supported new ideas that included restructuring the government and making it more open to Soviet citizens. p. 492

Gracchus, Gaius *153 B.C.–121 B.C.* Ancient Roman who, like his brother, Tiberius, died while working to change Roman law to help the plebeian class. p. 335

Gracchus, Tiberius *163 B.C.–133 B.C.* Ancient Roman who, like his brother, Gaius, died while working to change Roman law to help the plebeian class. p. 335

H

Hammurabi (hah•muh•RAH•bee) *c. 1792 B.C.–1750 B.C.* King of the city-state of Babylon. He compiled the set of laws known as the Code of Hammurabi. p. 98

Han Fei (HAHN FAY) *c. 260s B.C.* Ancient Chinese writer of materials relating to the idea of Legalism. p. 253

Hannibal *247 B.C.–183 B.C.* Carthaginian general who attacked Rome during the Second Punic War. p. 335

Hatshepsut (hat•SHEP•soot) *1503 B.C.–1482 B.C.* Female Egyptian pharaoh who expanded Egyptian trade routes. p. 153

Herodotus (hih•RAH•duh•tuhs) *c. 484 B.C.–430 B.C.* Greek historian who traveled through most of the world known to the Greeks during his time. p. 310

Hippocrates (hih•PAH•kruh•teez) *c. 460 B.C.–c. 377 B.C.* Greek physician known as the Father of Medicine. p. 311

Hitler, Adolf *1889–1945* German politician and *führer*, or leader. As Nazi dictator of Germany, he planned to conquer the world and claimed that the German people were superior to all others. During his time of power, he ordered 12 million people killed. p. 485

Homer *c. 700s B.C.* Greek poet and author of the *Iliad* and the *Odyssey*. Much of what we know of the Mycenaeans comes from his stories. p. 291

Horace *8 B.C.–A.D. 65* Roman poet. p. 347

Huascar (WAHS•kar) *c. 1500s* Inca prince who fought his brother for control of the Inca Empire in its final days. p. 422

Hussein (hoo•SAYN) *1935–* King of Jordan. p. 503

Hussein, Saddam (hoo•SAYN, suh•DAHM) *1935–* Military ruler of Iraq since 1979. His 1990 invasion of Kuwait led to the defeat of Iraq in the Persian Gulf War. p. 496

I

Imhotep *c. 2600s B.C.* Royal architect of Egypt who built Pharaoh Zoser's step pyramid around 2650 B.C. p. 144

Isaac *c. 2000s B.C.* Son of Abraham. p. 106

Ishmael *c. 2000s B.C.* Son of Abraham. p. 106

J

Jacob *c. 2000s B.C.* Early leader of the people who became the Israelites. Later called Israel, he was a son of Isaac and grandson of Abraham. p. 106

Jefferson, Thomas *1743–1826* Third President of the United States and the main writer of the Declaration of Independence. p. 483

Jesus *c. 6 B.C.–c. A.D. 30* The person whose life and teachings are the basis of Christianity. Believing him to be the Son of God, his disciples proclaimed him the Messiah and savior of humankind. p. 355

Jiang Zemin (JEE•AHNG zuh•MIN) *1926–* President of China, who followed Deng Xiaoping as leader. p. 506

Johanson, Don *1943–* Paleoanthropologist who discovered the australopithecine nicknamed Lucy. p. 52

John *1167–1216* King of England, who was made to sign the Magna Carta. p. 482

K

Kalidasa (kah•lih•DAH•suh) *c. 400s* An author during India's golden age, he is considered to be among India's greatest writers. p. 222

Kashta (KASH•tuh) *700s B.C.* King of ancient Kush, father of Piye. p. 172

Kennedy, John F. *1917–1963* Thirty-fifth President of the United States. p. 504

Khomeini, Ayatollah (koh•MAY•nee, eye•uh•TOH•luh) *1900–1989.* Leader of Shiite Muslims in Iran; supported the taking of American hostages. p. 504

Khrushchev, Nikita (KRUSH•chawf, nuh•KEE•tuh) *1894–1971* Soviet politician and premier. p. 505

Khufu *c. 2500s B.C.* Egyptian king who built the Great Pyramid at Giza, the most famous of Egypt's pyramids. p. 146

Klerk, Frederik Willem de *1936–* Former president of South Africa. Although an Afrikaner, he lifted the bans on the African National Congress and freed Nelson Mandela and other political prisoners. p. 491

L

Leakey, Louis *1903–1972*, **Mary** *1913–1996*, and **Richard** *1940–* Scientists well known for their discoveries relating to human ancestors. p. 52

Li Si (LEE SUH) *c. 260 B.C.* Adviser to Emperor Shi Huangdi of the ancient Qin dynasty in China. p. 252

Lincoln, Abraham *1809–1865* Sixteenth U.S. President, leader of the Union in the Civil War, and signer of the Emancipation Proclamation. p. 501

Louis XVI *1754–1793* King of France. His efforts to raise taxes led to the French Revolution. p. 483

M

Manco Capac (MAHNG•koh KAH•pahk) *c. 2000s B.C.* According to legend, the founder of the Inca city of Cuzco. p. 418

Mandela, Nelson *1918–* South African leader of the African National Congress. He was imprisoned for 25 years for conspiracy to overthrow the South African government. In 1994 he became president of South Africa. p. 491

Mark Antony *c. 82 B.C.–30 B.C.* Roman orator and general. He lost control of Roman lands when he was defeated by Octavian in 31 B.C. p. 340

Marie Antoinette (an•twuh•NET) *1755–1793* Wife of Louis XVI. Disliked for her many extravagances and her influence on the king, she was tried for treason and executed. p. 483

Menes (MEE•neez) *c. 3000s B.C.* According to legend, the king who united ancient Egypt. p. 140

Minos (MY•nuhs) *c. 2000s B.C.* According to legend, the ruler of ancient Crete during the years of its greatest success. p. 291

Moses *c. 1200s B.C.* Prophet and lawgiver who, according to the Bible, led the Israelites out of Egyptian captivity and received the Ten Commandments. p. 106

Motecuhzoma (maw•tay•kwah•SOH•mah) *1466–1520* Ruler of the Aztecs when they were conquered by the Spanish; also known as Montezuma. p. 411

Muhammad (moh•HA•muhd) *c. 570–632* Prophet who brought the message of Islam to the world. p. 458

N

Narmer *c. 2900s B.C.* Ruler who may have united the Two Lands of ancient Egypt. p. 140

Nefertiti (nef•er•TEET•ee) *c. 1300s B.C.* Wife of Akhenaton. p. 153

Netanyahu, Benjamin (neh•tahn•YAH•hoo) *1949–* Israeli prime minister elected after the assassination of Yitzhak Rabin. p. 497

O

Octavian (ahk•TAY•vee•uhn) *63 B.C.–A.D. 14* Julius Caesar's grandnephew, later known as Augustus. By defeating Mark Antony, he gained rule of all Roman lands. He was Rome's first true emperor. p. 340

Odoacer (OH•duh•way•ser) *433–493* Germanic chief who overthrew the Roman emperor in the west. p. 364

P

Pachacuti (pah•chah•KOO•tee) *?–1471* Inca ruler whose empire extended from Peru to Ecuador. p. 418

Paul *c. 5 B.C.–c. A.D.62* A Jew who converted to Christianity and became an apostle. He founded new churches and wrote many epistles, or letters, about Jesus to church members. p. 357

Pericles (PAIR•uh•kleez) *c. 495 B.C.–429 B.C.* Leader who ruled Athens during its Golden Age. p. 309

Peter *?–A.D. 64* One of the apostles, the group of men who were Jesus' closest followers. p. 357

Philip II *382 B.C.–336 B.C.* King of Macedonia and father of Alexander the Great. A military genius, he controlled most of the Greek peninsula by 338 B.C. p. 317

Pilate, Pontius *?B.C.–c. A.D. 36* Roman governor of Judaea. He was the judge at Jesus' trial and condemned him to death by crucifixion. p. 356

Piye (PEE•yeh) *c. 751 B.C.–716 B.C.* King of Kush and son of Kashta. He conquered Lower Egypt. Also known as Piankhi. p. 172

Pizarro, Francisco (pee•ZAR•oh) *c. 1475–1541* Spanish conquistador who conquered the Inca Empire. p. 422

Plato *c. 428 B.C.–c. 348 B.C.* Greek philosopher, student of Socrates, and teacher of Aristotle. p. 312

Pliny the Younger (PLIH•nee) *c. 61–c. 113* Roman government official in Asia Minor. He is perhaps best remembered for his account of the volcanic eruption of Vesuvius. p. 358

Pol Pot *1924–1998* Cambodian dictator. p. 504

Polo, Marco *1254–1324* Venetian traveler who was among the first European traders to visit China and record his experiences. p. 479

Polycarp *A.D. 69 –A.D. 155* Bishop who was killed for refusing to give up his belief in Christianity. p. 358

Porus *c. 300s B.C.* Indian king who fought against and lost to Alexander the Great. p. 321

Ptolemy (TAHL•luh•may) *300s B.C.* Military general under Alexander the Great. p. 155

R

Rabin, Yitzhak (rah•BEEN) *1922–1995* Prime minister of Israel who was assassinated. He signed a peace agreement with Palestinian leader Yasir Arafat. p. 496

Ramses II (RAM•seez) *1304–1237 B.C.* Egyptian pharaoh perhaps best known for the temples he had built. p. 173

Reagan, Ronald *1911–* Governor of California from 1967 to 1975 and President of the United States from 1981 to 1989. p. 444

S

Samudra Gupta (suh•MUH•druh) *c. 300* Son of Chandragupta I of India's Maurya dynasty. He extended the empire. p. 221

Sargon *c. 2334 B.C.–2279 B.C.* Warrior who founded the Akkadian Empire and so became first ruler of an empire in the Fertile Crescent. p. 97

Saul *c. 1000s B.C.* First king of Israel. p. 107

Schliemann, Heinrich *1822–1890* Archaeologist who discovered the remains of the ancient Mycenaean civilization. p. 295

Scipio (SIH•pee•oh) *c. 237 B.C.–183 B.C.* Roman general who defeated Hannibal. p. 335

Sesostris III (suh•SAHS•truhs) *c. 1800s B.C.* Middle Kingdom pharaoh of Egypt who reorganized Egypt's bureaucracy. p. 152

Shabaka (SHA•buh•kuh) *?–695 B.C.* Pharaoh who established the Kushite dynasty. p. 172

Shi Huangdi (SHIR HWAHNG•DEE) *c. 259 B.C.– 210 B.C.* Ruler of the Qin dynasty and unifier of China. p. 252

Sima Qian (SOO•MAH CHIH•YIHN) *c. 100s B.C.* Scholar who recorded China's history during the Han dynasty. p. 264

Socrates (SAH•kruh•teez) *c. 470 B.C.–c. 399 B.C.* Greek philosopher who taught by asking questions. p. 312

Solomon *c. 900s B.C.* David's son and king of Israel under whose rule Israel rose to the height of its greatness. p. 107

Solon *c. 630 B.C.–c. 560 B.C.* Poet and states-person who helped bring democracy to ancient Athens. p. 304

Sophocles (SAHF•uh•kleez) *c. 496 B.C.–c. 406 B.C.* Ancient Greek writer of tragedies, or serious plays. p. 310

Sesostris III (suh•SAHS•truhs) *c. 1800s B.C.* Pharaoh who changed ancient Egypt's government. p. 152

Strabo *?64 B.C.–?A.D. 23* Greek geographer. p. 109

Sulla, Lucius *138 B.C.–78 B.C.* Roman general, politician, and dictator of Rome. p. 335

Taharka (tuh•HAR•kuh) *c. 600s B.C.* Kushite pharaoh remembered for the many temples and pyramids he ordered built. p. 172

Theodosius (thee•uh•DOH•shuhs) *c. 347–395* Roman emperor who in 392 made Christianity the official religion of the Roman Empire. p. 359

Thucydides (thoo•SIH•duh•deez) *471 B.C.–c. 400 B.C.* Greek teacher who is considered the greatest historian of ancient times. p. 304

Thutmose I *c. 1500s B.C.* Pharaoh who expanded Egypt's rule far into Nubia. p. 152

Thutmose II *c. 1500s B.C.* Son of Thutmose I. He continued to expand Egypt's land. p. 153

Thutmose III *c. 1500s B.C.* Son of Thutmose II. He continued Egypt's conquests after Pharaoh Hatshepsut. During his rule the Egyptian Empire grew to its largest size and was at its wealthiest. p. 153

Tomyris (tuh•MY•ruhs) *c. 600s B.C.* Queen whose land was invaded by Cyrus the Great of Persia. Cyrus was killed during the battle with her armies. p. 224

Tutankhamen (too•tahng•KAHM•uhn) *c. 1370 B.C.–1352 B.C.* During his brief reign as pharaoh, his ministers restored the old religion of Egypt. He was buried in a solid-gold coffin. p. 154

Virgil (VER•juhl) *70 B.C.–19 B.C.* Roman poet who wrote the epic *Aeneid*, which is about the founding of Rome. p. 346

![W]

Washington, George *1732–1799* Commander in chief of the Continental Army during the Revolutionary War and first President of the United States. p. 483

Wilson, Woodrow *1856–1924* Twenty-eighth President of the United States. p. 478

Wu *c. 1100s B.C.* Founder of the Zhou dynasty in China. p. 244

Wu Di (WOO DEE) *c. 200s B.C.* Han ruler who established a civil administration to run the daily business of government in China. p. 263

![X]

Xerxes (ZERK•seez) *c. 519 B.C.–c. 465 B.C.* King of Persia and son of Darius I. p. 307

Xilingshi (SEE•LING•SHIR) *c. 2700s B.C.* Chinese ruler's wife who, according to a legend, discovered silk in 2700 B.C. p. 239

![Y]

Yeltsin, Boris (YELT•suhn) *1931–* Russian political leader and first popularly elected president in Russia. p. 493

You (YOO) *c. 1100s B.C.* Zhou dynasty king who reigned during the Warring States Period. p. 246

![Z]

Zarathustra (zar•uh•THOOS•trah) *c. 628 B.C.–c. 551 B.C.* Persian religious leader who founded a religion now known as Zoroastrianism. Its basic belief is that there are two gods—one good and one evil. p. 227

Zhang Qian (JAHNG CHIH•yihn) *c. 100s B.C.* Ancient Chinese ambassador who introduced the outside world to the resources of China. p. 265

Zoser *c. 2600s B.C.* King of Egypt in the twenty-seventh century B.C. p. 144

Biographical Dictionary

Gazetteer

The Gazetteer is a geographical dictionary that can help you locate places discussed in this book. The page number tells where each place appears on a map.

A

Abu Simbel (AH•boo SIM•buhl) Site of early Egyptian temples. (24°N, 33°E) p. 126

Abydos (uh•BY•duhs) An ancient Egyptian city. (25°N, 33°E) p. 126

Aconcagua (ah•kohn•KAH•gwah) A mountain in western Argentina. (31°S, 70°W) p. 420

Acre (AH•kruh) A city located on the west coast of Israel. (33°N, 35°E) p. 497

Actium (AK•shee•uhm) An ancient town in western central Greece, remembered as the site of a battle in which Octavius fought against Marc Antony and Cleopatra. (39°N, 21°E) p. 342

Addis Ababa (AH•dis AH•bah•bah) The capital of Ethiopia. (9°N, 39°E) p. 437

Adriatic Sea An extension of the Mediterranean Sea; located east of Italy and west of the Balkan Peninsula. p. 280

Aegean Sea (ih•JEE•uhn) An arm of the Mediterranean Sea between Asia Minor and Greece. p. 288

Aegina (ih•JY•nuh) An ancient Greek city-state; a Greek island in the southwestern Aegean Sea. p. 302

Afghanistan A country in central Asia; located between Pakistan and Iran. p. 200

Africa One of the world's seven continents. p. 44

Agra A city in northern central India on the Yamuna River. (27°N, 78°E) p. 452

Ajodha (uh•YOHD•yuh) An ancient city in India. (26°N, 82°E) p. 193

Akhetaton [el-Amarna] The ancient Egyptian capital built by Akhenaton; located on the Nile River in central Egypt. (28°N, 31°E) p. 126

Akkad (AH•kahd) An ancient kingdom in Mesopotamia. p. 106

Alaska The northernmost of the 50 states of the United States. p. 436

Albania A European country located on the Balkan Peninsula, on the Adriatic Sea. p. 298

Aleppo (uh•LEH•poh) An ancient city-state; a present-day city in northwestern Syria. (36°N, 37°E) p. 90

Alexandria (a•lig•ZAN•dree•uh) A port on the Mediterranean Sea; located on the northern coast of Egypt on the Nile delta; also the name of many other cities founded by Alexander the Great. (31°N, 30°E) p. 126

Algeria A country in northern Africa; located on the coast of the Mediterranean Sea. p. 437

Algiers The capital of Algeria; located in northern central Algeria on the Bay of Algiers. (37°N, 3°E) p. 437

Ali-Kosh An ancient settlement; located in present-day southeastern Iraq. (31°N, 46°E) p. 68

Alps The largest group of mountains in Europe; located in France, Switzerland, Italy, Austria, Slovenia, Bosnia and Herzegovina, Yugoslavia, Croatia, and Albania. p. 288

Altai Mountains (al•TY) A mountain system in Asia, where Russia, China, and Mongolia meet. p. 233

Al-Ubaid (oo•BAYD) An ancient settlement; located in present-day southeastern Iraq. (31°N, 46°E) p. 68

Amazon Basin All the land drained by the Amazon River, in northern Brazil, South America. p. 376

Amazon River The largest river in the world; flows across northern Brazil in South America and into the Atlantic Ocean. p. 376

Amman (ah•MAHN) The capital of Jordan; located northeast of the Dead Sea. (32°N, 36°E) p. 497

Amu Darya (AH•moo DAR•yuh) A river in central Asia. p. 493

Amur River A river in northeastern Asia; forms part of the border between Russia and China. p. 45

Anchorage A coastal city in southern Alaska. (61°N, 150°W) p. 463

Andaman Islands Islands in the Bay of Bengal, west of Burma (Myanmar). p. 200

Andes Mountains A mountain system in South America, extending along the western coast from Panama to Tierra del Fuego. p. 376

Angola A country in Africa; located on the Atlantic coast of southwestern Africa. p. 437

Gazetteer

Ankara (AN•kuh•ruh) The capital of Turkey. (40°N, 33°E) p. 448

Antarctica One of the world's seven continents. p. 58

Antioch (AN•tee•ahk) A center of early Christianity; located in western Asia Minor near Yalvac, Turkey. (36°N, 36°E) p. 336

Anyang (AHN•YAHNG) The last capital of the Shang dynasty of ancient China; located in present-day east central China. (36°N, 114°E) p. 236

Apennines (AP•uh•nynz) A mountain range; runs north and south through the center of Italy. p. 328

Appalachian Mountains (a•puh•LAY•chee•uhn) A large chain of mountains in the United States that extends from Maine to northern Georgia and central Alabama. p. 384

Arabia The historic name for the lands now known as the Arabian Peninsula, the Sinai Peninsula, Syria, and Mesopotamia. p. 153

Arabian Peninsula A peninsula bordered by the Red Sea, the Persian Gulf, and the Arabian Sea in southwestern Asia; location of the countries of Saudi Arabia, Yemen, Oman, the United Arab Emirates, Qatar, and Kuwait. p. 281

Arabian Sea The sea located west of India and east of the Arabian Peninsula; forms the southern border of southwestern Asia. p. 86

Aral Sea (AIR•uhl) A large inland body of water that flows through the countries of Kazakhstan and Uzbekistan in central Asia. p. 348

Arctic Ocean One of the four oceans of the world. p. 63

Argentina A South American country on the Atlantic coast. p. 419

Argos (AR•gohs) An ancient Greek city-state; a present-day town in the northeastern Peloponnesus. (38°N, 23°E) p. 302

Armenia A country in western Asia. p. 437

Asia One of the world's seven continents. p. 45

Asia Minor A peninsula at the western end of Asia; located between the Mediterranean and Black seas; occupied by Turkey. p. 86

Asini (AH•sih•nee) An ancient Greek city-state. (38°N, 23°E) p. 302

Assur (AH•sur) [also called Assyria] An ancient Mesopotamian city on the Tigris River; included lands from the Mediterranean coast to Iraq. (36°N, 43°E) p. 90

Assyria (uh•SIR•ee•uh) An ancient empire in southwestern Asia. p. 100

Aswan An ancient trade center; a present-day city; located in southeastern Egypt on the Nile River, near Lake Nasser and the Aswan Dam. (24°N, 33°E) p. 126

Atacama Desert (ah•tah•KAH•mah) A desert in the northern part of central Chile in South America. p. 376

Atbara River (AHT•buh•ruh) A river in northeastern Africa that flows into the Nile. p. 126

Athens An ancient Greek city-state; the capital of Greece; located near the southeastern coast of Greece. (38°N, 24°E) p. 302

Atlantic Ocean One of the world's four oceans. p. 44

Atlas Mountains A mountain system in northern Africa. p. 44

Australia One of the world's seven continents; a present-day country filling the continent of Australia. p. 104

Austria A country in central Europe. p. 437

Azerbaijan (a•zer•by•JAHN) A country in southeastern Europe; located west of the Caspian Sea; formerly part of the Soviet Union. p. 437

B

Babylon The capital of ancient Babylonia; located on the Euphrates River in central Iraq. (33°N, 44°E) p. 100

Babylonia (ba•buh•LOH•nyah) An ancient kingdom in the lower Tigris-Euphrates river valley in southwestern Asia. p. 100

Bactria (BAK•tree•uh) An ancient country of southwestern Asia. p. 225

Bahamas A country of islands, cays, and reefs; located southeast of Florida and north of Cuba. p. 436

Balearic Islands (ba•lee•AIR•ik) An island group in the western Mediterranean Sea; forms the Spanish province of Baleares; located off the eastern coast of Spain. p. 339

Balkan Peninsula A peninsula extending from mainland Europe into the Mediterranean Sea; occupied by Greece, Albania, Slovenia, Croatia, Bosnia and Herzegovina, Yugoslavia, Macedonia, Romania, Bulgaria, and Turkey. p. 288

Balsas River A river in central Mexico. p. 377

Bangalore (BANG•uh•lohr) A city in southern India. (13°N, 78°E) p. 453

Bangkok The capital of Thailand. (14°N, 100°E) p. 437

Bangladesh (bahn•gluh•DESH) A country in southern Asia on the coast of the Bay of Bengal. p. 200

Bay of Bengal An inlet of the Indian Ocean that runs alongside eastern India. p. 45

Beersheba (bir•SHEE•buh) A city in southern Israel; a part of the Negev region; the ancient town in which Abraham settled. (31°N, 35°E) p. 106

Beijing (BAY•JING) The capital of China; located in northeastern China. (40°N, 116°E) p. 255

Belarus (byeh•luh•ROOS) A country in Asia; located north of Ukraine, west of Russia, and east of Poland; formerly part of the Soviet Union. p. 437

Belgium A country in Europe; located on the coast of the North Sea. p. 437

Belize (buh•LEEZ) A country in Central America. p. 398

Bethel (BETH•uhl) An ancient town in southwestern Asia. (32°N, 35°E) p. 108

Bethlehem An ancient and present-day city in southwestern Asia; birthplace of Jesus, according to the Bible. (32°N, 35°E) p. 497

Bhutan (boo•TAN) A country in Asia; located south of China and north of India. p. 200

Black Sea A sea between Europe and Asia; surrounded by Bulgaria, Romania, Moldova, Ukraine, Russia, Georgia, and Turkey. p. 44

Blue Nile River Part of the Nile River. p. 132

Bogotá (boh•goh•TAH) The capital of Colombia, in South America; located on a plateau of the Andes. (5°N, 74°W) p. 436

Bolan Pass A mountain pass located in Pakistan. (30°N, 67°E) p. 211

Bolivia A country in South America. p. 419

Bonampak An ancient Mayan city. (16°N, 91°W) p. 398

Border Cave A site of early art finds; located in southern Africa. (28°S, 32°E) p. 63

Bosnia and Herzegovina (BAHZ•nee•uh and hairt•suh•goh•VEE•nuh) A country in Europe; part of the former Yugoslavia. p. 495

Botswana A country in southern Africa. p. 437

Brasília The capital of Brazil, in South America. (16°S, 47°W) p. 436

Brazil A country in eastern South America. p. 419

Brunei (broo•NY) A country in southeastern Asia. p. 437

Buenos Aires (BWAY•nohs EYE•rays) A port city and the capital of Argentina, in South America. (34°S, 58°W) p. 436

Bulgaria A country in southeastern Europe; located on the Balkan Peninsula. p. 298

Burkina Faso A country in western Africa. p. 437

Burma [Myanmar] A country in southeastern Asia; on the Indochina peninsula. p. 200

Burundi A country in central Africa. p. 437

Byblos An ancient town, located in what is now Lebanon. (34°N, 35°E) p. 112

Byzantium (buh•ZAN•tee•uhm) An ancient city that became Constantinople and then Istanbul. (41°N, 29°E) p. 336

C

Cairo The capital of Egypt; located in northeastern Egypt on the Nile River. (30°N, 31°E) p. 145

Calcutta A port in northeastern India, near the Bay of Bengal. (23°N, 88°E) p. 437

Cambodia A country in southeastern Asia; located on the Indochina Peninsula. p. 243

Cameroon (ka•muh•ROON) A country in western Africa. p. 437

Canaan (KAY•nuhn) An ancient region in southwestern Asia; located between the Jordan River and the Mediterranean Sea. p. 106

Canada A country in the northern part of North America. p. 436

Canary Islands An island group in the Atlantic Ocean; located off the northwestern coast of Africa. p. 450

Cape Verde (VERD) An island country in the Atlantic Ocean; located off the coast of West Africa. p. 450

Caracas (kah•RAH•kahs) The capital of Venezuela, in South America; located near the coast of the Caribbean Sea. (11°N, 67°W) p. 463

Caribbean Sea (kar•uh•BEE•uhn) The sea bordered by Central America, South America, and the West Indies. p. 376

Cartagena (kar•tah•HAY•nah) An ancient city and port in southeastern Spain; also called New Carthage (38°N, 1°W) p. 339

Carthage (KAR•thij) An ancient Phoenician city-state; located on the northern coast of present-day Tunisia. (37°N, 10°E) p. 336

Casablanca The largest city in Morocco. (34°N, 8°W) p. 437

Caspian Sea A salt lake between Europe and Asia, east of the Black Sea. p. 44

Çatal Hüyük (chat•AHL hoo•YOOK) One of the earliest human agricultural settlements discovered; dating from c. 7000 B.C. to 5600 B.C.; located in central Turkey. (38°N, 33°E) p. 68

Caucasus Mountains (KAW•kuh•suhs) A mountain range between the Black and Caspian seas. p. 44

Central African Republic A country in central Africa. p. 437

Central America The southernmost part of the continent of North America. p. 384

Chad A country in northern Africa. p. 437

Chan Chan (CHAHN CHAHN) An ancient city in present-day Peru, in South America; conquered by the Incas. (8°S, 79°W) p. 420

Chang Jiang (CHAHNG JYAHNG) A river in eastern China; flows from the Plateau of Tibet to the East China Sea. p. 45

Chang'an (CHAHNG•AHN) An ancient capital of the Han dynasty of China; now known as Xian, or Sian; located in central China on the Wei River. (34°N, 109°E) p. 193

Changchun (CHAHNG•CHUHN) A city in northeastern China. (44°N, 125°E) p. 255

Changsha (CHAHNG•SHAH) An ancient and present-day city in eastern China. (28°N, 113°E) p. 193

Chao Phraya (CHOW PRY•uh) A river in Thailand. p. 243

Chennai (CHIH•ny) A city in southern India; formerly Madras. (13°N, 80°E) p. 452

Chicago A city in Illinois; the third-largest city in the United States. (42°N, 88°W) p. 463

Chichén Itzá (chee•CHAYN it•SAH) An ancient Mayan city in what is now Mexico. (21°N, 88°W) p. 377

Chile (CHEE•lay) A country on the southwestern coast of South America. p. 419

Chimborazo (cheem•boh•RAH•soh) A mountain in central Ecuador. (2°S, 78°W) p. 420

China An ancient empire and present-day country in eastern Asia; currently the world's most heavily populated country. p. 193

Coco River (KOH•koh) A river in northern Nicaragua, Central America, that forms part of the border between Nicaragua and Honduras. p. 401

Colombia (kuh•LUHM•bee•uh) A country in northwestern South America. p. 419

Comoros (KAH•muh•rohz) An island group in the Indian Ocean; located off the southeastern coast of Africa. p. 450

Congo, Democratic Republic of the A country in central Africa; formerly Zaire. p. 437

Congo, Republic of the A country in central Africa. p. 437

Congo River A river located in southern Africa; begins in the central part of the Democratic Republic of the Congo and flows into the Atlantic Ocean. p. 44

Constantinople (kahn•stan•tuh•NOH•puhl) Formerly the ancient city of Byzantium; rebuilt, renamed, and made the capital of the Byzantine Empire by Constantine I in 330; present-day Istanbul, Turkey. (41°N, 29°E) p. 358

Cook Islands A group of islands in the south Pacific Ocean. p. 463

Copán (koh•PAHN) An ancient Mayan city. (14°N, 89°W) p. 398

Corfu A Greek island in the Ionian Sea. p. 298

Corinth An ancient city-state and a present-day city; located on the isthmus between the Peloponnesus and the Greek mainland. (38°N, 23°E) p. 292

Corsica A French island in the Mediterranean Sea; located east of Italy. p. 328

Costa Rica A country in Central America; located west of Panama; bordered by the Caribbean Sea and Pacific Ocean. p. 398

Côte d'Ivoire (koht dee•VWAR) A country in western Africa; the Ivory Coast. p. 437

Crete A large Greek island; located southeast of the Balkan Peninsula; separates the Mediterranean and Aegean seas. p. 294

Croatia (kroh•AY•shuh) A country in southeastern Europe; part of the former Yugoslavia. p. 495

Cro-Magnon A site of early fossil finds; located in France. (45°N, 1°E) p. 44

Cuba An island country; located south of the United States in the Greater Antilles of the West Indies. (22°N, 79°W) p. 436

Cuzco (KOO•skoh) The capital of the ancient Inca Empire and a present-day city in southern Peru. (14°S, 72°W) p. 419

Cydonia (sy•DOH•nee•uh) An ancient Greek city-state. (36°N, 24°E) p. 302

Cyprus (SY•pruhs) An island country in the eastern Mediterranean Sea. p. 281

Cyrene (sy•REE•nee) An ancient city in northern Africa; located in Libya near the Mediterranean Sea. (33°N, 22°E) p. 348

Czech Republic (CHEK) A country in central Europe; once part of Czechoslovakia. p. 437

Czechoslovakia (chek•uh•sloh•VAH•kee•uh) A former country in central Europe; located where the Czech Republic and Slovakia are today. p. 447

D

Damascus (duh•MAS•kuhs) The capital of Syria, in southwestern Asia. (33°N, 36°E) p. 90

Danube River (DAN•yoob) A river in central Europe; flows from southwestern Germany to the Black Sea. p. 336

Dead Sea A salt lake in Israel and Jordan; the world's lowest place at 1,302 feet (397 m) below sea level. p. 106

Deccan Plateau (DEH•kuhn) A triangle-shaped plateau in central India, between the Western and Eastern Ghats. p. 211

Delhi (DEH•lee) A city in northern India. (29°N, 77°E) p. 193

Delphi (DEL•fy) A sacred place to the ancient Greeks; located in central Greece, near the Gulf of Corinth. (38°N, 22°E) p. 292

Denmark A country in central Europe; occupies the northern part of the Jutland Peninsula. p. 437

Dhaka (DA•kuh) The capital of Bangladesh; located on the Indian Peninsula. (24°N, 91°E) p. 216

Djibouti (juh•BOO•tee) A country in eastern Africa. p. 450

Dniester River (NEES•ter) A river in the southern part of central Europe. p. 342

Don River (DAWN) A river in the western part of Russia. p. 493

E

East China Sea The part of the China Sea north of Taiwan. p. 45

East Germany Formerly a country in Europe, now part of Germany. p. 447

Eastern Ghats (GAWTS) A chain of mountains in southeastern India. p. 211

Ebro (AY•broh) A river in northeastern Spain that empties into the Mediterranean Sea. p. 280

Ecuador (EH•kwah•dohr) A country in north-western South America; located on the Pacific coast. p. 419

Edessa (ih•DES•uh) An ancient city and trading center located in present-day Turkey. (41°N, 22°E) p. 358

Egypt An ancient land and a present-day country in northern Africa; located on the coast of the Mediterranean and Red seas. p. 136

El Salvador A Central American republic; located southeast of Guatemala, on the Pacific Ocean. p. 398

Elephantine (eh•luh•fan•TY•nee) Island in the Nile River in Egypt where many ancient artifacts and structures have been found. p. 136

Ephesus (EF•uh•suhs) An ancient city on the coast of western Asia Minor; located between the Mediterranean Sea and the Dardanelles. (38°N, 28°E) p. 308

Equatorial Guinea A country in West Africa. p. 437

Eridu (AIR•uh•doo) The earliest known Sumerian city; located in Mesopotamia on the Euphrates River in present-day Iraq. (31°N, 46°E) p. 68

Eritrea (air•ih•TREE•uh) A country on the Red Sea in northern Africa; located north of Ethiopia. p. 437

Estonia A country in northeastern Europe; formerly part of the Soviet Union. p. 437

Ethiopia A country in northern Africa. p. 437

Euphrates River (yoo•FRAY•teez) A river that begins in Turkey, flows through Syria and Iraq, and empties into the Persian Gulf. p. 44

Europe One of the world's seven continents. p. 44

Ezion-geber (ee•zee•uhn•GEE•ber) An ancient town and present-day archaeological site; located near Aqaba, in southwestern Jordan. (29°N, 35°E) p. 106

F

Finland A country in northern Europe; located south of Norway and east of the Gulf of Bothnia and Sweden. p. 437

France A country in western Europe. p. 74

French Guiana An overseas department of France; located on the northern Atlantic coast of South America. (4°N, 53°W) p. 436

G

Gabon A country in western Africa. p. 437

Ganges River (GAN•jeez) A holy river in India; flows from the Himalaya Mountains into the Bay of Bengal. p. 45

Gaul An ancient land that included most of the present-day countries of France and Belgium; once part of the Roman Empire. p. 280

Gaza (GAH•zuh) A city in southwestern Asia; located near the Mediterranean Sea. (32°N, 34°E) p. 497

Gaza Strip A small piece of land northeast of Egypt, now under Palestinian control. p. 497

Gedrosia (juh•DROH•zhuh) An ancient land in southern Asia. p. 320

Georgetown The capital of Guyana, in South America. (7°N, 58°W) p. 470

Georgia A country on the Black Sea in southeastern Europe; formerly part of the Soviet Union. p. 437

Germany A European country; located in northern central Europe. p. 437

Ghana (GAH•nuh) A country on the western coast of Africa. p. 437

Giza (GEE•zuh) An ancient and present-day city in Egypt; located on the Nile River, across from Cairo. (30°N, 31°E) p. 126

Gobi (Desert) A desert in eastern Asia; located in Mongolia and China. p. 193

Godavari River (goh•DAHV•uh•ree) A river in central India. p. 200

Golan Heights A region of southwestern Asia under the control of Israel. (33°N, 36°E) p. 497

Gordium An ancient city; located in present-day Turkey. Alexander the Great was said to have cut the Gordian knot there. (40°N, 32°E) p. 320

Great Britain A western European kingdom; includes England, Scotland, and Wales. p. 486

Great Plains The western part of the Interior Plains in North America. p. 384

Greece An ancient land and present-day country in Europe; located on the southern end of the Balkan Peninsula. p. 281

Greenland The largest island in the world; located off northeastern North America; a territory of Denmark. p. 103

Greenwich (GREH•nich) Part of the city of London, England; the meridian it lies on serves as the center for time zones around the world. (52°N, 0°) p. 463

Grijalva River (gree•HAH•VAH) A river located in southeastern Mexico. p. 377

Guangzhou (GWAHNG•JOH) A Chinese port city; located on the Zhu River in southeastern China; formerly Canton. (23°N, 113°E) p. 193

Guatemala A country in Central America; former part of the region controlled by the Mayas and later a colony of Spain. p. 398

Guinea (GIH•nee) A country in western Africa. p. 437

Guinea-Bissau (GIH•nee bih•sow) A country in western Africa. p. 450

Gulf of Aqaba (AH•kah•buh) An inlet of the Red Sea; located between Saudi Arabia and the Sinai Peninsula. p. 106

Gulf of Mexico A gulf located south of the United States, east of Mexico, and west of Cuba. p. 377

Gulf of Thailand An inlet of the South China Sea; located between Malaysia and Thailand. p. 243

Gulf of Tonkin An inlet of the South China Sea; located between Vietnam and China. p. 243

Guyana (gee•AH•nuh) A country in the northern part of South America. p. 419

H

Hadar Site of an early fossil find; located in present-day Ethiopia. (10°N, 40°E) p. 44

Haifa (HY•fuh) A district and city located in northwestern Israel. (33°N, 35°E) p. 497

Haiti A country in the Caribbean, southeast of Cuba. p. 436

Hangzhou (HAHNG•JOH) An ancient and present-day city located on the eastern coast of central China. (30°N, 121°E) p. 193

Hanoi (ha•NOY) The capital of Vietnam; located on the northern Red River. (21°N, 106°E) p. 243

Hao (HOW) The ancient Zhou dynasty capital city; located in present-day China. p. 246

Haran (huh•RAHN) A place that Abraham traveled to on his way to Canaan, according to the Bible. (37°N, 39°E) p. 106

Harappa (huh•RA•puh) An ancient center of Indus civilization; located in the Indus Valley, in present-day Pakistan. (32°N, 73°E) p. 205

Harbin The capital of Heilungkiang province; located in northeastern China. (46°N, 127°E) p. 276

Hebron (HEE•bruhn) An ancient city of Judaea and a present-day city; located southwest of Jerusalem on the West Bank. (32°N, 35°E) p. 106

Helsinki A port city and the capital of Finland, in Europe. (60°N, 25°E) p. 463

Hermopolis (er•MOO•poh•lees) An ancient Egyptian city. (27°N, 31°E) p. 126

Himalayas (hih•muh•LAY•uhz) A mountain system on the northern edge of southern Asia; runs through Nepal, Bhutan, southern Tibet, and northern India. p. 45

Hindu Kush A mountain system that extends southwest from the Pamirs in eastern Tajikistan, through northwestern Afghanistan. p. 193

Honduras (hahn•DUR•uhs) A country in Central America; located between the Caribbean Sea and Guatemala. p. 398

Hong Kong A large city in southeastern China; formerly a British colony. (22°N, 114°E) p. 437

Honolulu (hah•nuh•LOO•loo) Hawaii's capital and largest city. (21°N, 158°W) p. 463

Huang He (HWAHNG HUH) A river that flows east from the Plateau of Tibet in China. p. 45

Huascarán (wahs•kah•RAHN) Peru's highest mountain. (90°S, 78°W) p. 420

Hungary A country in central Europe. p. 437

Hyderabad (HY•duh•ruh•bad) A city in central India. (17°N, 78°E) p. 448

Hyphasis River (HIF•uh•suhs) The ancient name for the Beas River; located in northern India. p. 320

I

Iberian Peninsula A peninsula that forms southwestern Europe; extends into the Atlantic Ocean and the Mediterranean Sea; occupied by the countries of Portugal and Spain. p. 288

Iceland A European island country in the northern Atlantic Ocean; located southeast of Greenland. p. 437

India A country in southern Asia; occupies much of a large peninsula extending from central Asia into the Indian Ocean; the name given to the ancient land that is present-day Pakistan and India. p. 193

Indian Ocean One of the world's oceans. p. 45

Indonesia A country of islands in southeastern Asia. p. 437

Indus River A river in southern Asia; flows from Tibet, through northern India and Pakistan, and into the Arabian Sea. p. 45

Ionian Sea The sea located east of Italy and west of Greece. p. 298

Iran A country in southwestern Asia; formerly known as Persia; located on the Persian Gulf. p. 86

Iraq A country in southwestern Asia; includes former lands of the Mesopotamians, Babylonians, Sumerians, and Assyrians. p. 86

Ireland A country of Europe; located in the British Isles. p. 437

Irrawaddy River (ir•ah•WAH•dee) A river in southern central Burma (Myanmar). p. 243

Irtysh River (ir•TUSH) A river in northwestern Asia. p. 493

Islamabad (is•LAH•muh•bahd) The capital of Pakistan. (34°N, 73°E) p. 216

Israel An ancient kingdom and present-day country; a holy land for Jews, Christians, and Muslims; located on the eastern coast of the Mediterranean Sea. p. 497

Isthmus of Tehuantepec (tay•WAHN•teh•pek) A narrow strip of land in southern Mexico. p. 409

Italian peninsula A boot-shaped peninsula extending from southern central Europe into the Mediterranean Sea. p. 328

Italy An ancient land and a present-day European country; located on the Italian Peninsula. p. 342

Ithaca (IH•thi•kuh) An ancient Greek village; a present-day island. (38°N, 21°W) p. 292

J

Jakarta (juh•KAR•tuh) The capital of Indonesia. (6°S, 107°E) p. 437

Jamaica An island country in the Greater Antilles of the West Indies. p. 436

Japan An island country in eastern Asia, located off the Pacific coasts of China and Russia. p. 437

Jarmo The site of the ancient village of Qallat Jarmo; located in the northern part of present-day Iraq. (36°N, 45°E) p. 68

Jericho The oldest known city in the world; located north of the Dead Sea, in present-day Jordan. (32°N, 35°E) p. 68

Jerusalem The capital of Israel; a holy city for Jews, Christians, and Muslims. (32°N, 35°E) p. 100

Johannesburg A city located in the country of South Africa. (26°S, 28°E) p. 463

Jordan A country in southwestern Asia. p. 497

Jordan River A river that flows from the mountains of Syria in southwestern Asia into the Dead Sea. p. 497

K

Kama River A river in eastern Russia. p. 44

Kanpur A city in northern India; located on the Ganges River, southeast of Delhi. (26°N, 80°E) p. 453

Karnak Site of ancient Egyptian temples. p. 126

Kathmandu (kat•man•DOO) The capital of Nepal, on the Indian subcontinent; located in the valley of the Himalayas. (28°N, 85°E) p. 216

Kazakhstan (ka•zak•STAHN) A country in central Asia; formerly part of the Soviet Union. p. 437

Kenya A country in eastern Africa. p. 437

Kerma A capital of the ancient kingdom of Kush; located on the Nile River in Sudan. (20°N, 31°E) p. 136

Khartoum (kar•TOOM) The capital of Sudan, Africa, located near the junction of the White Nile and the Blue Nile rivers. (15°N, 33°E) p. 181

Khyber Pass A narrow pass through the Hindu Kush Mountains on the border between Afghanistan and Pakistan in Asia. p. 211

Kinshasa The capital of the Democratic Republic of the Congo. (4°S, 15°E) p. 437

Kish An ancient Sumerian city-state on the Euphrates River, located in present-day Iraq. (32°N, 45°E) p. 90

Knossos (NAHS•uhs) The capital of the ancient Minoan civilization; located on the island of Crete off the coast of present-day Greece. (35°N, 25°E) p. 292

Kobe (KOH•bee) A Japanese seaport and commercial city; located on the southern coast of western Honshu. (35°N, 137°E) p. 460

Korea A peninsula off the coast of China, now divided between two countries—North Korea and South Korea. p. 233

Krishna River A river on the Indian subcontinent; flows through the Deccan Plateau and into the Bay of Bengal. p. 200

Kush An ancient Nubian kingdom; located in the Nile Valley in the northern part of present-day Sudan. p. 171

Kuwait (ku•WAYT) An independent state on the northwestern Persian Gulf; located between Iraq and Saudi Arabia. p. 437

Kyrgyzstan (kir•gih•STAN) A country in central Asia; formerly part of the Soviet Union. p. 437

L

La Venta An ancient Olmec city in what is now Mexico. (18°N, 94°W) p. 390

Lagash (LAY•gash) A city of ancient Sumer and a city-state in ancient Babylonia; located near the coast of the Persian Gulf, in southeastern Iraq. (31°N, 46°E) p. 90

Lake Chapala (chah•PAH•lah) Mexico's largest lake. p. 408

Lake Nasser An artificial lake in Egypt and Sudan; formed by the building of the Aswan High Dam. p. 181

Lake Texcoco (tays•KOH•koh) A dry lake near Mexico City; an island in the lake was the site of the Aztec capital Tenochtitlán. p. 377

Lake Tiberias A freshwater lake in northern Israel, also known as the Sea of Galilee. p. 497

Lake Titicaca (tee•tee•KAH•kah) A lake located between the borders of Peru and Bolivia in South America. p. 377

Lake Victoria A lake in Tanzania, Kenya, and Uganda in southeastern Africa. p. 44

Laos (LOWS) A country on the Indochina Peninsula in southeastern Asia; once part of former French Indochina. p. 243

Larsa A city in ancient Babylonia; located near the Euphrates River, in the southeastern part of present-day Iraq. (31°N, 46°E) p. 90

Lascaux (lah•SKOH) The site of early cave paintings, in what is now France. (45°N, 1°E) p. 63

Latvia A country in eastern Europe; formerly part of the Soviet Union. p. 437

Lebanon The land of the ancient Phoenicians and a present-day country on the eastern shore of the Mediterranean Sea in southwestern Asia. p. 437

Lerma River (LAIR•mah) A river in southwestern Mexico. p. 408

Lesotho An independent country located within the borders of the country of South Africa in Africa. p. 437

Liberia A country in western Africa; originally a republic for freed slaves from the United States; located on the Atlantic coast of West Africa. p. 437

Libya A country in northern Africa; located on the Mediterranean Sea. p. 437

Lima (LEE•mah) The capital of Peru, South America; an ancient Inca city. (12°S, 77°W) p. 419

Lithuania A country in eastern Europe; formerly part of the Soviet Union. p. 437

Loire River (luh•WAR) The longest river in France; located in southeastern France. p. 280

London The capital of the United Kingdom; located on the Thames River, in southeastern England. (52°N, 0°) p. 437

Los Angeles The largest city in California and the second-largest in the United States. (34°N, 118°W) p. 436

Lothal An ancient settlement in northern India. (22°N, 72°E) p. 205

Luoyang (luh•WOH•yahng) The former capital of the Zhou dynasty in ancient China; located in what is now central China, on the Huang He River. (35°N, 113°E) p. 256

Luxembourg A country in western Europe. p. 437

Luxor The site of ancient Egyptian tombs and temples. (25°N, 31°E) p. 126

Lydia (LIH•dee•uh) A region and an ancient kingdom in Asia Minor, on the Aegean Sea. p. 112

M

Macedonia A present-day country in Europe; an ancient kingdom near the Aegean Sea located on lands that are part of present-day Greece and Turkey. p. 288

Machu Picchu (mah•choo PEEK•choo) The ruins of an ancient Inca city; located in the Andes mountains in what is now central Peru in South America. (13°S, 72°W) p. 419

Madagascar An island country located in the Indian Ocean, off the eastern coast of southern Africa. p. 437

Madeira Islands An island group in the Atlantic Ocean, located off the northwestern coast of Africa; under the control of Portugal. p. 450

Magadan (mah•gah•DAN) A port city in eastern Russia. (60°N, 151°E) p. 463

Malawi (muh•LAH•wee) A country in southeastern Africa. p. 437

Malaysia (muh•LAY•zhuh) An independent federation; located in southeastern Asia. p. 437

Mali A former West African empire and a present-day country. p. 437

Manila (muh•NIH•luh) The capital of the Philippines. (15°N, 121°E) p. 437

Marathon (MAR•uh•thahn) An ancient Greek town in eastern Attica; the site of an ancient Greek victory during the Persian Wars. (38°N, 24°E) p. 308

Mari An ancient city-state near the Euphrates River; its ruins are called Tell Hariri; located near present-day Abu Kemal, Syria. (34°N, 41°E) p. 90

Mariana Islands An island group in Micronesia, Oceania; includes the unincorporated United States territory of Guam. p. A3

Marquesas Islands (mar•KAY•suhz) A group of ten islands of French Polynesia; located in the southern Pacific Ocean. p. 463

Mauritania (maw•ruh•TAY•nee•uh) A country in western Africa. p. 436

Mauritius (maw•RIH•shuhs) An island of the Mascarene Islands; located in the Indian Ocean. p. 437

Mayapán (my•ah•PAHN) An ancient Mayan city located in what is now Mexico. (20°N, 89°W) p. 377

Media (MEE•dee•uh) The ancient country of the Medes; located in present-day northwestern Iran. p. 225

Mediterranean Sea (med•duh•tuh•RAY•nee•uhn) The sea south of Europe, north of Africa, and west of Asia; connects to the Atlantic Ocean, the Red Sea, and the Black Sea. p. 44

Megalopolis (meh•gah•LAH•pah•lees) An ancient Greek city-state. (37°N, 22°E) p. 302

Mekong River A river in southeastern Asia; flows from the mountains of Tibet into the South China Sea. p. 45

Memphis An ancient Egyptian capital; located along the Nile River in northern Egypt. (30°N, 31°E) p. 132

Meroë (MAIR•oh•wee) A capital of the ancient kingdom of Kush; located on the eastern bank of the Nile River in northern Sudan. (17°N, 34°E) p. 136

Mesoamerica A world region; includes Mexico, the countries of Central America, and sometimes the islands of the Caribbean Sea. p. 390

Mesopotamia (meh•suh•puh•TAY•mee•uh) An ancient land in southwestern Asia; located between the Tigris and Euphrates rivers. p. 90

Mexico A country in southern North America; located between the United States and Central America. p. 376

Mexico City The capital of Mexico; located in central Mexico. (19°N, 99°W) p. 463

Mississippi River The largest river in the United States; flows from Minnesota to the Gulf of Mexico. p. 384

Missouri River A tributary of the Mississippi River; flows from Montana to St. Louis, Missouri. p. 386

Mohenjo-Daro (moh•HEN•joh dar•oh) An important center of ancient Indus civilization, on the western bank of the Indus River; located in present-day Pakistan. (27°N, 68°E) p. 205

Moldova (mahl•DOH•vah) A country in eastern Europe; formerly part of the Soviet Union. p. 437

Mongolia A country in eastern Asia. p. 233

Montenegro (mon•tay•NAY•groh) A part of Yugoslavia. p. 495

Montevideo (mon•tay•vee•DAY•oh) The capital of Uruguay. (35°S, 56°W) p. 470

Montreal (mahn•tree•AWL) Canada's largest city and chief port of entry. (45°N, 74°W) p. 463

Gazetteer

Monument Valley A site of early art finds, located in the western United States. (37°N, 110°W) p. 63

Morocco (muh•RAH•koh) A country in northern Africa; bordered by the Mediterranean Sea and the Atlantic Ocean. p. 437

Moscow The capital of Russia; located on the Moscow River. (56°N, 38°E) p. 437

Mount Olympus A mountain believed to be the home of the Greek gods of ancient Greek mythology; located on the eastern coast of Greece. (40°N, 29°E) p. 302

Mount Sinai (SY•ny) A mountain peak located on the Sinai Peninsula. (26°N, 34°E) p. 106

Mount Vesuvius (vuh•SOO•vee•uhs) A volcano near Naples, Italy; known for its famed eruption in A.D. 79, which caused the destruction of Pompeii. (41°N, 14°E) p. 342

Mozambique (moh•zuhm•BEEK) A country in southern Africa; formerly Portuguese East Africa. p. 437

Mumbai [Bombay] A city on the western coast of central India. (19°N, 73°E) p. 452

Mureybit A village in ancient Mesopotamia; located in present-day Turkey. (37°N, 38°E) p. 68

Mycenae (my•SEE•nee) An ancient city-state and empire in ancient Greece; located on the eastern side of the Peloponnesus. (38°N, 23°E) p. 288

Mytilene (mit•uhl•EE•nee) An ancient Greek city-state. (39°N, 26°E) p. 302

N

Nairobi (ny•ROH•bee) The capital of Kenya, Africa. (2°S, 37°E) p. 437

Namibia (nuh•MIB•ee•uh) A country in southwestern Africa. p. 437

Napata (NA•puh•tuh) A capital of the ancient kingdom of Kush; located on the east bank of the Nile River, in northern Sudan. (19°N, 32°E) p. 136

Naples (NAY•puhlz) An Italian port on the Tyrrhenian Sea; located on the western coast of southern Italy; an ancient city. (41°N, 14°E) p. 332

Narmada River (ner•MUH•duh) A sacred Hindu river; begins in eastern India and empties into the Gulf of Cambay. p. 205

Natal (nuh•TAL) A colony in South America begun by the Portuguese in 1597 and claimed by the Dutch in the mid-1600s. p. 455

Nazareth (NA•zuh•ruhth) A city in northern Israel. (33°N, 35°E) p. 108

Neander Valley (nee•AN•der) The site of an early fossil find; located in Germany. (51°N, 7°E) p. 44

Negev (NEH•gev) A desert located in southern Israel. p. 497

Nepal (nuh•PAWL) A country located in southern Asia, north of India. p. 200

Netherlands A country on the northern coast of central Europe, on the North Sea. p. 437

New Carthage *See* Cartagena.

New Delhi (DEH•lee) The capital of India; located in northern India. (29°N, 77°E) p. 216

New York City The largest city in the United States; located in New York at the mouth of the Hudson River. (41°N, 74°W) p. 436

New Zealand An island-group country; located in the southwestern Pacific Ocean, southeast of Australia. p. 436

Nicaragua (nih•kuh•RAH•gwah) A country in Central America. p. 398

Nicobar Islands (NIH•kuh•bar) Islands in the Bay of Bengal, southeast of the Andaman Islands. p. 200

Niger (NY•jer) A country in West Africa. p. 437

Nigeria (ny•JIR•ee•uh) A country on the Gulf of Guinea, in western Africa. p. 437

Nile River A river in northeastern Africa; flows north from Lake Victoria through Sudan and Egypt to the Mediterranean Sea. p. 44

Nineveh (NIN•uh•vuh) The capital of the ancient Assyrian Empire; located on the Tigris River, in what is now northern Iraq. (36°N, 43°E) p. 68

Nippur (ni•PUR) An ancient Sumerian and Babylonian city; located in what is now called Southwest Asia, in present-day central Iraq. (32°N, 45°E) p. 90

Norfolk Island An island in the south Pacific Ocean, belonging to Australia. p. 463

North America One of the world's seven continents. p. 58

North Korea The country that occupies the northern part of the peninsula of Korea. p. 233

North Sea The sea east of Great Britain and west of Denmark. p. 74

Norway A European country; located on the northwestern Scandinavian Peninsula. p. 437

Nubia (NOO•bee•uh) An ancient land in Africa that extended along the Nile River from Egypt's southern border to close to present-day Khartoum, Sudan. p. 136

Nubian Desert A desert region in Sudan, Africa; east of the Nile River. p. 126

O

Ob River A river in northwestern Asia. p. 45

Olduvai Gorge (OHL•duh•vy) The site of an early fossil find; located in present-day Tanzania, Africa. (3°S, 35°E) p. 44

Olympia A plain in the northwestern Peloponnesus; an ancient Greek religious center and site of the early Olympic Games. (38°N, 22°E) p. 302

Oman (oh•MAHN) A country in southwestern Asia; located on the Arabian Peninsula. p. 200

Omsk A city in southwestern Russia, in Asia. (55°N, 73°E) p. 448

Orkney Islands A Scottish archipelago; located off the northeastern coast of Scotland. p. 74

Osaka (oh•SAH•kuh) A Japanese port in southern Honshu where the Yodo River meets Osaka Bay. (35°N, 137°E) p. 460

Ottawa (AH•tuh•wuh) The capital of Canada; located in the province of Ontario. (45°N, 76°W) p. 436

P

Pacific Ocean The largest of the world's four oceans. p. 45

Pakistan A country in southern Asia. p. 211

Palenque (pah•LENG•kay) An ancient Mayan city. (17°N, 91°W) p. 398

Panama A country in Central America. p. 437

Papua New Guinea A country that occupies the eastern part of the island of New Guinea. p. 437

Paraguay (pah•rah•GWY) A country in central South America. p. 419

Paramaribo (pah•rah•MAH•ree•boh) The capital of Suriname. (2°N, 55°W) p. 470

Paris The capital of France; located on the Seine River. (49°N, 2°E) p. 437

Parthia (PAR•thee•uh) A land that was part of the ancient Assyrian and Persian empires; located in what is now Iran. p. 225

Patuca River (pah•TOO•kah) A river in Honduras, Central America. p. 401

Pella An ancient Macedonian city-state. (41°N, 23°E) p. 320

Peloponnesus (peh•luh•puh•NEE•suhs) A wide peninsula on the southern end of Greece; home of the ancient city-states of Sparta and Corinth. p. 292

Perito Moreno (pay•REE•toh moh•RAY•noh) The site of early art finds; located in Argentina, South America. (18°S, 69°W) p. 63

Persepolis (per•SEH•puh•luhs) The capital of the ancient Persian Empire; located near Shiraz in present-day Iran. (30°N, 53°E) p. 192

Persia An ancient empire that included the ancient lands of Persia, Egypt, Syria, Assyria, Mesopotamia, and Babylonia. p. 225

Persian Gulf A gulf in southwestern Asia; connected to the Gulf of Oman and the Arabian Sea. p. 86

Peru A country in South America; the former center of the Inca Empire. p. 419

Perugia (puy•ROO•jee•uh) An ancient city of the Etruscans and a present-day city. (43°N, 12°E) p. 332

Philistia (fuh•LIS•tee•uh) An ancient land in southwestern Asia. p. 108

Phnom Penh (NAHM PEN) The capital of Cambodia. (12°N, 105°E) p. 243

Phocaea (foh•SEE•uh) An ancient Greek city-state. (39°N, 27°E) p. 302

Phoenicia (fih•NIH•shuh) An ancient land; located in present-day Syria and Lebanon. p. 108

Pindus Mountains A mountain range in northwestern Greece. p. 288

Pisa (PEE•zuh) A city on the Arno River in northern Italy; an ancient Roman city. (44°N, 10°E) p. 339

Pitcairn Island An island in the south Pacific Ocean. p. 463

Plataea (pluh•TEE•uh) The site of an ancient Greek land victory that led to the end of the Persian Wars; located in what is now Greece, near Thívai. (38°N, 23°E) p. 308

Plateau of Iran A highland area in western Asia. p. 211

Plateau of Tibet A highland area in the southern part of central Asia. p. 211

Po River A river in northern Italy; flows from Mount Viso into the Adriatic Sea. p. 328

Poland A country in eastern Europe. p. 437

Pompeii (pom•PAY) An ancient city in what is now Italy, destroyed by an eruption of Mount Vesuvius in A.D. 79. (41°N, 14°E) p. 342

Popocatépetl (poh•puh•KAT•uh•peh•tuhl) An ancient Aztec city. (19°N, 99°W) p. 409

Portugal A country in Europe. p. 437

Pretoria The administrative capital of the Republic of South Africa. (26°S, 28°E) p. 437

Punt An ancient land probably located in Africa along the Red Sea; Queen Hatshepsut of Egypt sent an expedition there. p. 153

Pyrenees Mountains (PIR•uh•neez) The mountain range that separates the Iberian Peninsula from Europe; forms the border between Spain and France. p. 44

Q

Qatar (KAHT•er) A country in southwestern Asia. p. 437

Quito (KEE•toh) A present-day city in Ecuador; an ancient Inca city. (0°, 79°W) p. 419

R

Rangoon [Yangon] The capital of Burma (Myanmar). (17°N, 96°E) p. 243

Red Sea The sea between northeastern Africa and the Arabian Peninsula; connected to the Mediterranean Sea by the Suez Canal and to the Arabian Sea by the Gulf of Aden. p. 68

Reunion One of the Mascarene Islands; located in the Indian Ocean. p. 437

Rhine River A river in western Europe; flows across Switzerland, western Germany, and the Netherlands to the North Sea. p. 336

Rio de Janeiro (zhah•NAY•roo) A commercial seaport in southeastern Brazil, in South America. (23°S, 43°W) p. 436

Río Santiago (san•tee•AH•goh) A river in southwestern Mexico. p. 409

Riyadh (ree•YAHD) The capital of Saudi Arabia. (25°N, 47°E) p. 448

Rocky Mountains A range of mountains in North America that extend from Alaska to New Mexico; this range divides rivers that flow east from those that flow west. p. 384

Romania A country in southeastern Europe, bordering the Black Sea. p. 437

Rome The capital of the ancient Roman Empire and of present-day Italy; located on the Tiber River. (42°N, 12°E) p. 336

Rosetta The ancient site where the Rosetta stone was found, unlocking the secret of Egyptian hieroglyphics. (31°N, 30°E) p. 126

Russia A historic empire and the largest republic of the former Soviet Union; a present-day country in northeastern Europe and northern Asia. p. 437

Rwanda A country in eastern Africa. p. 437

S

Sahara A desert covering the northern third of Africa. p. 126

Salado River (sah•LAH•doh) A river in Argentina, South America. p. 376

Salamis (SAL•uh•muhs) A Greek island in the Aegean Sea; the site of an ancient Greek sea victory leading to the end of the Persian Wars. p. 308

Samaria An ancient area of southwestern Asia; located between Judaea and Galilee. p. 108

San Francisco The largest city in northern California; located on San Francisco Bay. (38°N, 122°W) p. 463

San Lorenzo (san luh•REN•zoh) An ancient Olmec city; located in what is now Mexico. (29°N, 113°W) p. 390

Santa Fe The capital of New Mexico. (36°N, 106°W) p. 463

Santiago (san•tee•AH•goh) The capital of Chile. (33°S, 70°W) p. 470

São Paulo (POW•loh) A city in southeastern Brazil. (23°S, 46°W) p. 436

São Tomé and Príncipe (SOW too•MAY and PREEN•see•puh) Equatorial islands; located off western Africa, in the Gulf of Guinea. p. 437

Sardinia An island in the Mediterranean Sea; located west of mainland Italy. p. 328

Sardis The capital of ancient Lydia; located in western central Turkey. (38°N, 28°E) p. 112

Saudi Arabia A country that occupies most of the Arabian Peninsula in southwestern Asia. p. 86

Sea of Galilee A freshwater lake in northern Israel, also known as Lake Tiberias. p. 497

Sea of Japan The sea located west of Japan and east of Russia, North Korea, and South Korea. p. 45

Sea of Marmara A small sea in northwestern Turkey; connects the Black and Aegean seas. p. 288

Sea of Okhotsk (oh•KAHTSK) A sea off the northeastern coast of Russia. p. 45

Senegal A country located in western Africa. p. 437

Seoul The capital of South Korea. (38°N, 127°E) p. 437

Serbia A part of the present-day country of Yugoslavia. p. 495

Shanghai (SHANG•HY) A port on the East China Sea; located near the mouth of the Chang Jiang. (31°N, 121°E) p. 255

Shechem (SHEH•kuhm) An ancient town located north of Jerusalem, Israel. (32°N, 35°E) p. 106

Shenyang (SHUHN•YAHNG) A city in northeastern China. (42°N, 123°E) p. 255

Siberia Region in north central Asia, mainly in Russia. p. 455

Sicily An Italian island off the southwestern tip of the Italian peninsula. (38°N, 14°E) p. 328

Sidon An ancient town; located in what is now southern Lebanon. (34°N, 35°E) p. 112

Sierra Leone A country on the Atlantic coast of West Africa; a former slave colony. p. 437

Sierra Madre del Sur A mountain range that runs along the Pacific coast in southern Mexico. p. 408

Sierra Madre Occidental A mountain range that runs along the Pacific coast in northwestern Mexico. p. 376

Sierra Madre Oriental A mountain range that runs along the coast of the Gulf of Mexico in eastern Mexico. p. 376

Sinai Peninsula The peninsula between northeastern Africa and southwestern Asia; part of the country of Egypt. p. 497

Singapore A small island country off the southern tip of the Malay Peninsula; located in southeastern Asia. p. 437

Skara Brae A Neolithic settlement located on the western coast of Mainland Island, Scotland. p. 74

Slovakia (sloh•VAK•ee•uh) A country in central Europe. p. 437

Slovenia (sloh•VEE•nee•uh) A country in southern Europe. p. 495

Somalia A country in eastern Africa. p. 437

South Africa A country located on the southern tip of Africa, between the Atlantic and Indian oceans. p. 437

South America One of the world's seven continents. p. 376

South China Sea The part of the China Sea south of Taiwan. p. 45

South Korea A country that occupies the southern part of the peninsula of Korea. p. 233

Soviet Union A former country in eastern Europe and western Asia. p. 486

Spain A country in southwestern Europe; located on the Iberian Peninsula. p. 280

Sparta An ancient Greek city-state and rival of Athens; located on the southern end of the Peloponnesus. (37°N, 22°E) p. 302

Sri Lanka An island country in southern Asia; formerly Ceylon; located off the west coast of India. p. 200

Sudan A country on the eastern coast of northern Africa. p. 437

Sumer (SOO•mer) An ancient region in southern Mesopotamia; located on the Persian Gulf, in what is now southeastern Iraq. p. 106

Suriname A country in northern South America. p. 436

Susa (SOO•suh) An ancient village in what is now southwestern Iran. (32°N, 48°E) p. 225

Sutlej River A river that runs through the Himalaya mountains into Pakistan and India. p. 45

Swaziland A country in southern Africa. p. 437

Sweden A European country on the southeastern part of the Scandinavian Peninsula. p. 437

Switzerland A country in central Europe. p. 437

Sydney A city in southeastern Australia. (33°S, 150°E) p. 463

Syracuse A present-day seaport in Sicily and an ancient Greek city; located on the Ionian Sea. (37°N, 15°E) p. 339

Syria A country located on the eastern coast of the Mediterranean Sea. p. 437

Syrian Desert A desert covering southeastern Syria, northeastern Jordan, western Iraq, and northern Saudi Arabia in southwestern Asia. p. 68

Tagus River (TAY•guhs) A river running through the center of the Iberian Peninsula; flows from Spain through Portugal. p. 336

Taiwan (TY•WAHN) An island country; located off the southeastern coast of China. p. 437

Tajikistan (tah•jih•kih•STAN) A country in western Asia; formerly part of the Soviet Union. p. 437

Takla Makan (tah•kluh muh•KAHN) A desert in northwestern China. p. 233

Tanis (TAY•nuhs) An ancient Egyptian city. (31°N, 32°E) p. 126

Tanzania (tan•zuh•NEE•uh) A country in eastern Africa. p. 437

Tarquinia (tar•KWEE•nyah) An ancient Etruscan city-state; located on the western coast of what is now central Italy. (42°N, 12°W) p. 332

Tashkent The capital of Uzbekistan; located in western Asia. (41°N, 69°E) p. 448

Taurus Mountains A mountain range in southern Turkey; runs parallel to the southern coast of the Mediterranean and the border between Turkey and Syria. p. 68

Gazetteer

Tehran (tay•uh•RAN) The capital of Iran. (36°N, 51°E) p. 448

Tel Aviv A city in Israel; former capital of Israel. (32°N, 35°E) p. 497

Tenochtitlán (tay•nohch•teet•LAHN) The capital of the ancient Aztec Empire; Mexico City has been built on the ruins of Tenochtitlán. (19°N, 99°W) p. 408

Teotihuacán (tay•oh•tee•wah•KAHN) A city and state in central Mexico. (20°N, 99°W) p. 409

Teotitlán (tay•oh•teet•LAHN) Independent city-state in the area of ancient Aztec control. (18°N, 97°W) p. 409

Texcoco (tes•KOH•koh) A city in central Mexico; located near Lake Texcoco. (20°N, 99°W) p. 409

Thailand A country formerly known as Siam; located in southeastern Asia on the Indochina and Malay peninsulas. p. 200

Thar Desert (THAR) Also called the Great Indian Desert; located in India and Pakistan. p. 205

Thebes The capital of ancient Egypt during the Middle Kingdom; located in southern Egypt. (26°N, 33°E) p. 132

Thermopylae (ther•MAHP•uh•lee) The site of an ancient Greek defeat during the Persian Wars; a mountain pass in southern Greece. (39°N, 23°E) p. 308

Thessaly (THES•uh•lee) An ancient and present-day region in Greece; located on the eastern Balkan Peninsula. p. 308

Thimphu (thim•POO) The capital of Bhutan; located north of western India. (28°N, 90°E) p. 216

Thinis An ancient Egyptian city. (26°N, 32°E) p. 163

Thrace An ancient land; located where the present-day countries of Turkey, Bulgaria, Macedonia, and much of northwestern Greece are today. p. 288

Tian Shan A mountain system in central Asia; extends northeast from the Pamirs into Xinjiang Uygur. p. 233

Tiber River A river in central Italy; flows from the Apennine Mountains, through Rome, and into the Tyrrhenian Sea. p. 328

Tigris River A river in southwestern Asia; begins in eastern Turkey and joins the Euphrates River. p. 44

Tikal (tih•KAHL) An ancient Mayan city in what is now Guatemala. (17°N, 89°W) p. 398

Tlacopán (tlah•koh•PAHN) An ancient Aztec city. (20°N, 100°W) p. 409

Tlaxcala (tlah•SKAH•lah) Ancient independent city-state; located in the ancient Aztec Empire. (18°N, 98°W) p. 409

Togo A country in western Africa. p. 437

Tokyo (TOH•kee•oh) The capital of Japan. (36°N, 140°E) p. 437

Tres Zapotes (TRAYS sah•POH•tays) A village located in eastern Mexico; an ancient Olmec site. (19°N, 95°W) p. 390

Trindade (treen•DAH•duh) An island in the south Atlantic Ocean under the control of Brazil. p. 463

Trinil The site of an early fossil find, in what is now Indonesia. (8°S, 111°E) p. 45

Troezen (TREE•zuhn) An ancient Greek city-state. (37°N, 23°E) p. 302

Troy An ancient city in northwestern Asia Minor. (40°N, 26°E) p. 288

Tula An ancient Aztec city. (20°N, 99°W) p. 409

Tunisia (too•NEE•zhuh) A country in northern Africa. p. 437

Turkey A country located in southeastern Europe and southwestern Asia. p. 86

Turkmenistan (terk•meh•nuh•STAN) A country in western Asia; formerly part of the Soviet Union. p. 437

Tuxtla Mountains (TOOST•lah) Mountains in southern Mexico. p. 409

Tyre (TYR) The capital of ancient Phoenicia; a present-day town; located in southern Lebanon. (33°N, 35°E) p. 112

Tyrrhenian Sea (tuh•REE•nee•uhn) The sea located west of the Italian peninsula, north of Sicily, and east of Sardinia and Corsica. p. 280

U

Uganda A country in eastern Africa. p. 437

Ujjain (OO•jyn) Ancient city in India. (23°N, 76°E) p. 193

Ulaanbator (oo•lahn•BAH•tor) The capital of Mongolia. (48°N, 107°E) p. 448

Union of Soviet Socialist Republics Another name for the Soviet Union, which ended in 1991. p. 493

United Arab Emirates (EM•uh•ruhts) A country on the eastern Arabian Peninsula. p. 437

United Kingdom A European country made up of four kingdoms in the British Isles: England, Scotland, Wales, and Northern Ireland. p. 74

United States A country in North America; a federal republic of 50 states. p. 436

Ur (UR) A city in ancient Sumer; located on the Euphrates River, near present-day Iraq. (31°N, 46°E) p. 90

Ural River (YUR•uhl) A river in Russia and Kazakhstan. p. 493

Uruguay (YUR•uh•gway) A country on South America's southern coast. p. 419

Uruk An ancient Sumerian city in southwestern Asia; located near the eastern bank of the Euphrates River, in present-day southeastern Iraq. (31°N, 46°E) p. 90

Usumacinta River (oo•soo•mah•SEEN•tah) A river that flows through southeastern Mexico and northern Guatemala. p. 377

Utica (YOO•tih•kuh) An ancient northern African city. (37°N, 10°E) p. 339

Uzbekistan (uz•beh•kih•STAN) A country in western Asia; formerly part of the Soviet Union. p. 437

V

Valley of the Kings The site of many ancient Egyptian tombs. (26°N, 33°E) p. 126

Valley of Mexico A large valley in central Mexico; site of the ancient Aztec Empire capital, Tenochtitlán; the location of present-day Mexico City. p. 377

Vancouver A city in southwestern Canada; located in British Columbia. (49°N, 123°W) p. 436

Venezuela (veh•neh•SWAY•luh) A country in northern South America. p. 419

Vientiane (vyen•TYAHN) An administrative capital of Laos. (18°N, 103°E) p. 243

Vietnam A country in southeastern Asia; located on the Indochina Peninsula. p. 437

Vindhya Range (VIN•dyuh) A mountain range in central India. p. 200

Volga River The longest river in Europe; runs from Russia to the Caspian Sea. p. 44

W

Washington, D. C. The capital of the United States; located on the Potomac River in a special district that is not part of any state. (39N, 77°W) p. 436

Wellington The capital of New Zealand. (42°S, 175°E). p. 463

West Bank An area of southwestern Asia long occupied by Israel and now partially under Palestinian control. p. 497

West Germany Formerly a country in Europe, now part of Germany. p. 447

Western Desert A large desert in northern Africa; part of the Libyan Desert. p. 126

Western Ghats (GAWTS) A chain of mountains in southwestern India. p. 211

White Mountains Mountains in western Crete. p. 294

White Nile River Part of the Nile River in Africa. p. 132

X

Xi Jiang (SHEE•JAHN) A river in southern China. p. 233

Xi'an (SHEE•AHN) A city in eastern China; also known as Sian; formerly Chang'an. (34°N, 109°E) p. 448

Xianyang (SHEE•AHN•YAHNG) The ancient Qin capital city; located in what is now China. (34°N, 109°E) p. 257

Y

Yellow Sea The sea west of the Korean Peninsula and east of China. p. 233

Yemen (YEH•muhn) A country on the Arabian Peninsula in southwestern Asia. p. 437

Yucatán Peninsula (yoo•kah•TAHN) A peninsula extending from the eastern coast of Central America; occupied by the countries of Mexico, Belize, and Guatemala. p. 390

Yugoslavia (yoo•goh•SLAH•vee•uh) The country in eastern Europe that broke up into several independent republics; today only Serbia and Montenegro remain part of Yugoslavia. p. 495

Z

Zagros Mountains (ZAH•gruhs) A mountain range located in western and southern Iran. p. 68

Zama (ZAH•muh) The site of Hannibal and Carthage's final defeat in the Second Punic War; located in northern Tunisia. (35°N, 9°E) p. 339

Zambia (ZAM•bee•ah) A country in southern Africa. p. 437

Zhoukoudian The site of an early fossil find; located in present-day China. (40°N, 116°E) p. 45

Zimbabwe (zim•BAHB•way) A country in southern Africa. p. 437

Gazetteer

Glossary

The Glossary contains important social studies terms and their definitions. Each word is respelled as it would be in a dictionary. When you see the stress mark (′) after a syllable, pronounce that syllable with more force than the other syllables. The page number at the end of the definition tells where to find the word in your book.

add, āce, câre, pälm; end, ēqual; it, īce; odd, ōpen, ôrder; tŏŏk, pōōl; up, bûrn; yōō as *u* in *fuse*; oil; pout; ə as *a* in *above*, *e* in *sicken*, *i* in *possible*, *o* in *melon*, *u* in *circus*; **ch**eck; ri**ng**; **th**in; **th**is; **zh** as in *vision*

A.D. (ā•dē) Stands for *anno Domini,* a Latin phrase meaning "in the year of the Lord." This abbreviation identifies approximately how many years have passed since the birth of Jesus Christ. p. 71

absolute location (ab′sə•lŏŏt lō•kā′shən) Exact location on Earth. p. 35

absolute monarchy (ab′sə•lŏŏt mon′ər•kē) A kind of monarchy in which a king or queen has absolute, or complete, authority. p. 503

acid rain (as′id rān) Rainwater mixed with gases from burning fossil fuels, such as coal and oil. p. 344

acropolis (ə•kro′pə•ləs) A walled fort built on a hill. p. 300

active volcano (ak′tiv väl•kā′nō) A volcano that may still erupt. p. 384

afterlife (af′tər•līf) Life after death. p. 139

agora (a′gə•rə) An open-air market and gathering place in many ancient Greek city-states. p. 301

agriculture (a′gri•kul•chər) The domestication of plants and animals. p. 66

alliance (ə•lī′əns) An agreement to cooperate. p. 317

alluvial plain (ə′•lŏŏvē•əl plān) Land formed from fine soils deposited by a river. p. 85

ally (a′lī) Supporter. p. 170

ambassador (am•ba′sə•dər) A representative of a government. p. 265

analyze (a′nəl•īz) To break something down into parts to see how those parts connect with each other. p. 29

ancestor (an′ses•tər) A deceased relative who lived longer ago than a grandparent. p. 237

annex (ə•neks′) To take over. p. 169

apartheid (ə•pär′tāt) The former government policy of South Africa that stressed the separation, or "apartness," of races. p. 491

apostle (ə•po′səl) A person sent on a mission; any one of Jesus' closest followers. p. 357

aqueduct (a′kwə•dəkt) A system of bridges and canals that carry water. p. 346

Arabic numerals (ar′ə•bik nŏŏm′rəlz) The base-ten number system: 1 through 9 and zero. p. 222

arable land (ar′ə•bəl land′) Land that can be used to grow crops. p. 328

archaeologist (är•kē•ä′lə•jist) A scientist who locates and studies the things left behind by people. p. 51

aristocracy (ar′ə•stä•krə•sē) A wealthy ruling class. p. 301

armistice (′är•mə•stəs) An agreement to stop fighting. p. 485

arms race (ärmz rās) A competition among countries to have the most weapons. p. 487

artifact (är′tə•fakt) A human-made object, especially from long ago. p. 55

Aryans (ar′ē•ənz) Warriors and herders from eastern Europe and western Asia who came to India beginning about 3,000 years ago. p. 210

assassination (ə•sas•ən•ā′shən) Murder for a political reason. p. 218

assembly (ə•sem′blē) A lawmaking group. p. 301

assimilate (ə•sim′ə•lāt) To accept into the general population of another culture. p. 209

authority (ə•thôr′ə•tē) The right to command or influence. p. 92

B

B.C. (bē•sē) Stands for "before Christ." p. 71

B.C.E. (bē•sē•ē) Stands for "before the Common Era." p. 71

band (band) A small group of people. p. 54

bar graph (bär graf) A graph that uses horizontal or vertical bars of different sizes to show and compare information. p. 114

barbarian (bär'ber•ē•ən) The name given to outsiders by the ancient Greeks; also used by the ancient Romans. p. 362

barter (bär'tər) The exchange of one good or service for another. p. 112

basilica (bə•si'li•kə) A huge marble government building in ancient Rome. p. 343

basin (bā'sən) A bowl-shaped area of land surrounded by higher land. p. 233

bias (bī'əs) A leaning toward or against someone or something. p. 425

bilingual (bī•ling'gwəl) Having two official languages, as Canada has. p. 446

bloc (blok) A group of countries with the same interests. p. 512

Buddhism (boo'diz•əm) An Asian religion based on the teachings of Siddhartha Gautama, who became the Buddha. p. 215

bureaucracy (byoo•rok'rə•sē) A network of appointed government officials. p. 152

C

C.E. (sē•ē) Stands for "Common Era." p. 71

caravan (kar'ə•van) A group of traders. p. 266

cardinal directions (kär'də•nəl də•rek'shənz) The main directions—north, south, east, and west. p. 39

cartogram (kär'tə•gram) A map that gives a certain kind of information about places by the size it shows each place. p. 488

caste (kast) A group in India's society. p. 213

cataract (ka'tə•rakt) A waterfall or a spot where water runs fast over rocks. p. 133

cause (kôz) Any action that makes something happen. p. 33

causeway (kôz•wā) A human-made land bridge. p. 409

cavalry (ka'vəl•rē) Soldiers who ride horses or other animals to make swift attacks. p. 224

cenote (si•nō'tē) A deep, natural well. p. 400

census (sen'səs) A count of people. p. 342

ceremonial center (ser•ə•mō'nē•əl sen'tər) An area used for religious ceremonies by the ancient people of the Americas. p. 389

character (kar'ik•tər) Symbol used in writing. p. 240

chinampa (chē•näm'pä) A human-made island built of natural materials. Aztec farmers grew vegetables on these "floating gardens." p. 408

Christianity (kris•chē•an'ə•tē) The religion based on the life and teachings of Jesus Christ. p. 357

chronology (krə•nä'lə•jē) A record of events in the order in which they happened. p. 33

circle graph (sûr'kəl graf) A graph that shows information in a circle divided into parts; also called a pie chart. p. 114

citizen (sit'ə•zən) A member of a town, state, or country. p. 23

city-state (sit'ē•stāt) A city and its surrounding farmlands, with its own leaders and government. p. 92

civil service (siv'əl sûr'vəs) The part of a bureaucracy that oversees the day-to-day business of running a government. p. 264

civil war (siv'əl wôr) A war in which groups of people from the same place or country fight one another. p. 150

civilization (siv•ə•lə•zā'shən) A centralized society with developed forms of religion, ways of governing, and learning. p. 89

climograph (klī'mə•graf) A graph that shows average monthly temperature and precipitation. p. 472

Code of Hammurabi (kōd uv ha•mə•rä'bē) The collection of laws organized by Hammurabi for the people of Babylon to follow. p. 99

cold war (kōld wôr) A conflict of words and ideas between countries rather than a conflict of armies. p. 487

colony (kol'ə•nē) A settlement separated from, but under the control of, a home country. p. 111

Columbian exchange (kə•lum′bē•ən iks•chānj′) The movement of people, animals, plants, and ideas between Europe and the Americas in the 1400s and 1500s. p. 481

comedy (kom′ə•dē) A humorous play. p. 310

command economy (kə•mand′ i•kon′ə•mē) An economy in which the government makes most economic decisions. p. 465

common market (kom′ən mär′kit) A group of countries that has free trade among its members and a single trade policy. p. 511

communism (kom′yə•niz•əm) A form of government in which a country owns all property and business. p. 447

compass rose (kum′pəs rōz) A direction marker on a map. p. 39

conformal projection (kən•fôr′məl prə•jek′shən) A map projection that shows directions correctly but distorts sizes, especially of places near the poles. p. 103

Confucianism (kən•fyōō′shə•ni•zəm) The ideas of the Chinese philosopher Confucius, which became a guide for the way people live. p. 248

conquer (kon′kər) To take over. p. 96

conquistador (kän•kēs′tə•dôr) Name given to Spanish explorers of the Americas during the early 1500s. p. 411

consequence (kän′sə•kwens) An effect. p. 56

constitutional democracy (kän(t)•stə•tōō′shə•nəl di•mok′rə•sē) A form of government in which the goals of the government and the way it will work to achieve them are laid out in a constitution. p. 502

constitutional monarchy (kän(t)′stə•tōō•shə•nəl mon′ər•kē) A kind of monarchy in which a king or queen is the ceremonial leader of government, while a prime minister and a cabinet run the government and a legislative body makes laws. p. 503

consul (kon′səl) One of two chief officials who held office in the ancient Roman Republic. p. 332

contour line (kon′tŏŏr līn) On an elevation map, a line that connects all points of equal elevation. p. 242

cordillera (kôr•dəl•yer′ə) A very long mountain range. p. 384

courier (kŏŏr′ē•ər) A person who delivers messages. p. 226

covenant (kuv′ə•nənt) An agreement. p. 106

crucifixion (krōō•sə•fik′shən) A type of execution in which a person is nailed to a cross and left to die. p. 356

crusades (krōō•sādz′) The battles that European Christians and Muslim Turks fought over the control of Jerusalem. p. 481

cultural borrowing (kulch′rəl bär′ə•wing) Adapting customs from one culture for use in another. p. 294

cultural diffusion (kulch′rəl di•fyōō′zhən) The spread of ideas from one place to others. p. 111

culture (kul′chər) A unique way of life that sets a group of people apart from others. p. 60

D

Daoism (dou′i•zəm) A religion and philosophy that teaches that the key to long life and happiness is to accept life as it is. p. 264

decree (di•krē′) Command. p. 141

deforestation (dē•fôr•ə•stā′shən) The widespread cutting down of trees. p. 203

delta (del′tə) Low land formed at the mouth of some rivers by the silt the river drops there; often in the shape of a triangle. p. 132

demagogue (de′mə•gog) A bad leader. p. 311

democracy (di•mok′rə•sē) Rule by the people. p. 304

developed country (di•ve′ləpd kun′trē) A country with a successful economy; it usually has enough food for its people, uses many resources, and has a high standard of living. p. 468

developing country (di•ve′lə•ping kun′trē) A country that must build a successful economy; it usually has a low food supply, uses few resources, and has a low standard of living. p. 467

dialect (dī′ə•lekt) A way of speaking. p. 233

Diaspora (dī•as′pə•rə) The settling of Jews outside of ancient Israel. p. 109

dictator (dik′tā•tər) A ruler with absolute authority. p. 332

disciple (di•sī′pəl) Follower. p. 356

dissident (di′sə•dənt) A person who speaks out against his or her government. p. 493

distortion (di•stôr′shən) An area that is not accurate on a map projection. p. 102

division of labor (də•vi′zhən uv lā′bər) A system in which the members of a group do different tasks according to their abilities and the group's needs. p. 67

domesticate (də•mes′tə•kāt) To tame plants and animals for people's use. p. 64

double-bar graph (də′bəl•bär graf) A bar graph that shows two sets of statistics, or facts shown with numbers. p. 402

drought (drout) A long time with little or no rain. p. 87

dynasty (dī′nəs•tē) A series of rulers from the same family. p. 141

E

economic system (ek•ə•nom′ik sis′təm) The way a country produces and uses goods and services. p. 464

economy (i•kon′ə•mē) The way people use resources to meet their needs. p. 65

effect (i′fekt) What happens because a certain action was taken. p. 33

elevation (el•ə•vā′shən) The height of land. p. 242

elite (ē•lēt′) Ruling class. p. 389

emperor (em′pər•ər) The ruler of an empire. p. 97

empire (em′pīr) A conquered land of many people governed by one ruler. p. 97

environment (en•vī′rən•mənt) Surroundings. p. 68

epic (e′pik) A long story-poem. p. 296

equal justice (ē′kwəl jus′təs) Fair treatment under the law. p. 100

equal-area projection (ē′kwəl•âr′ē•ə prə•jek′shən) A map projection that shows the sizes of regions in correct relation to one another but distorts shapes. p. 102

equidistant projection (ē•kwə•dis′tənt prə•jek′shən) A map projection that shows accurate distances from a central point. p. 104

ethnic cleansing (eth′nik klenz′ing) Using threats or violence to drive certain groups out of an area. p. 496

evaluate (i•val′yə•wāt) To decide whether information can be trusted. p. 424

evidence (e′və•dəns) Proof. p. 51

excavate (ek′skə•vāt) To uncover by digging. p. 53

exile (eg′zīl) The act of being forced to live in another place. p. 108

Exodus (ek′sə•dəs) The journey of Moses and the Israelites from Egypt, through the desert, and back toward Canaan, as described in the Bible. p. 106

export (ek•spōrt′) To send goods for sale to other places. p. 265

extinct (ik•stin(k)t′) No longer existing. p. 56

extinct volcano (ik•stin(k)t väl•kā′nō) A volcano that will never again erupt. p. 328

F

fact (fakt) A statement that can be proved to be true. p. 424

famine (fa′mən) Shortage of food. p. 454

filial piety (fi′lē•əl pī′ə•tē) Kind treatment of parents; translation of the Chinese word *xiao*. p. 248

fortress (fôr′trəs) A building designed to protect a city or army. p. 206

forum (fôr′əm) A public square in ancient Rome. p. 329

fossil (fos′əl) The remains of a once-living thing. p. 51

free enterprise (frē en′tər•prīz) A system in which people choose how they make and spend their money. p. 465

generalization (jen′rəl•lə•zā′shən) A summary statement made about a group of related ideas. p. 80

geographer (je•äh'grə•fər) A person whose work is to study geography. p. 35

geography (je•ä'grə•fē) The study of the Earth's surface. p. 35

glacier (glā'shər) A huge, slow-moving sheet of ice. p. 59

gladiator (glad'ē•ā•tər) In ancient Rome a slave or prisoner forced to fight. p. 344

glasnost (glaz'nōst) The "openness," or new freedom, that allowed Soviet citizens to speak out without fear of punishment. p. 493

glyph (glif') Picture-symbol that represents an object, idea, or sound. p. 399

Gospels (gos'pəlz) The first four books of the New Testament that describe Jesus Christ's life and actions. p. 360

government (guv'ərn•mənt) A system used to make laws and decisions. p. 92

graph (graf) A diagram that shows relations between numbers. p. 114

Great Depression (grāt di•pre'shən) The 1930s economic decline that was the worst in world history. p. 485

grid (grid) The north-south and east-west lines on a map that cross each other to form a pattern of squares. p. 40

gross domestic product (grōs də•mes'tik prä'dəkt) (GDP) The total value of goods and services produced in a country. p. 465

H

harbor (här'bər) Sheltered place with deep water close to shore. p. 289

Hellenistic (he•lə•nis'tik) Greeklike. p. 320

helot (he'lət) In ancient Sparta, a slave owned by the state. p. 302

heritage (her'ə•tij) A set of ideas that have been passed down from one generation to another. p. 244

hieroglyphics (hī•rə•gli'fiks) A writing system in which pictures or symbols stand for ideas, objects, or sounds. p. 142

Hinduism (hin'dōō•iz•əm) A religion native to India, featuring belief in many gods and reincarnation. p. 212

historical empathy (hi•stôr•i•kəl em'pə•thē) Understanding the actions and feelings of people from other times and other places. p. 32

historical map (hi•stôr•i•kəl map) A map that provides information about the past. Historical maps may show where events took place or how the world looked at a certain time in the past. p. 180

Holocaust (hō'lə•kôst) The mass killing of Jewish people during World War II. p. 486

human features (hyōō'mən fē'chərz) Buildings, bridges, farms, roads, and people themselves. p. 32

I

Ice Age (īs āj) A long cold-weather period when huge sheets of ice covered part of the Earth's surface. p. 58

imperialism (im•pir'ē•əl•iz•əm) The practice by a country of adding more lands, establishing colonies, and controlling the colonies. p. 484

import (im•pôrt') To bring in goods for sale from other places. p. 265

independence (in•di•pen'dəns) Complete freedom. p. 169

Industrial Revolution (in•dus'trē•əl rev•ə•lōō'shən) The period of technological advances, beginning in the 1700s, that forever changed the way people live and work. p. 483

innovation (i•nə•vā'shən) A new way of doing things. p. 95

inoculation (i•nä•kyə•lā'shən) Giving a person a mild form of a disease so that he or she will not get sick with a more serious form. p. 223

inscription (in•skrip'shən) A written message etched into a long-lasting surface. p. 208

inset map (in'set map) A small map within a larger map. p. 39

intercropping (in•tər•krä'ping) Planting different crops together. p. 388

intermediary (in•tər•mē'dē•er•ē) A go-between. p. 150

Glossary

intermediate direction (in•tər•mē′dē•it də•rek′shən) A direction between cardinal directions. p. 39

Internet (in′tər•net) A large computer network made up of thousands of smaller networks that are all linked with each other. p. 508

intifada (in•tē•fä′də) The Palestinian uprising against Israeli occupation of the West Bank and the Gaza Strip. p. 496

inundation (i′nən•dā•shən) The yearly time of flooding in ancient Egypt. p. 137

irrigation (ir′ə•gā•shən) The use of connected ditches, canals, dams, and dikes to move water to dry areas. p. 87

Islam (is•läm′) The religion of Muslims, based on belief in one God, or Allah. p. 458

isthmus (is′məs) A small strip of land, with water on both sides, that connects two larger areas of land. p. 287

J

Judaism (jōō′dē•iz•əm) The religion of the Jewish people. p. 106

L

league (lēg) A group of allies. p. 308

Legalism (lē′gə•li•zəm) Chinese teachings that express a belief in the strict following of laws and in the use of bureaucracy. p. 253

legend (le′jənd) A story handed down from earlier times to explain the past. p. 235

legion (lē′jən) A unit of soldiers in the ancient Roman army. p. 342

line graph (līn graf) A graph that shows change over time by using one or more lines. The lines connect dots that stand for specific information. p. 115

line of latitude (līn əv la′tə•tōōd) An imaginary line that runs east and west on a map or globe. p. 62

line of longitude (līn əv lon′jə•tōōd) An imaginary line that runs north and south on a map or globe. p. 62

livestock (līv′stok) Domesticated animals such as cattle, sheep, and pigs. p. 66

locator (lō′kāt•ər) A small map or picture that shows where the area shown on a main map is located in a state, in a country, on a continent, or in the world. p. 39

loess (lō′əs) Yellow silt. p. 231

logical conclusion (lä′ji•kəl kən•klōō′zhən) A decision or an idea formed as the result of a thoughtful study of the known facts. p. 507

M

Magna Carta (mag′nə kär′tə) The document that English nobles forced King John to sign in 1215, limiting the king's power and protecting the rights of the people. p. 482

maize (māz) Corn. p. 69

majority rule (mə•jôr′ə•tē rōōl) A system in which the ideas and decisions supported by the most people are followed. p. 304

Mandate of Heaven (man′dāt uv hev′ən) The right to rule; the ancient Chinese believed a god they called Heaven gave it to their emperors. When an emperor was weak or disasters occurred, the emperor was thought to have lost the Mandate of Heaven. p. 245

map key (map kē) The part of a map that explains what the symbols on the map stand for; sometimes called a map legend. p. 39

map scale (map skāl) The part of a map that gives a comparison of distance on the map itself with distance in the real world. p. 39

map title (map tī′təl) The words on a map that describe the subject of the map. p. 39

market economy (mär′kit i•kon′ə•mē) An economy in which individuals decide which goods and services they will buy. p. 465

martyr (mär′tər) A person who willingly suffers or dies for his or her beliefs. p. 358

megalopolis (meg•ə•lop′ə•lis) A large, heavily populated area where cities have blended together. p. 461

Glossary

merchant (mûr′chənt) A person who buys and sells goods to make a living. p. 93

meridian (mə•ri′dē•ən) Another name for a line of longitude, an imaginary line that runs north and south on a map or globe. p. 62

Mesoamerica (me′zō•ə•mer•ə•kə) The region that includes central and southern Mexico and Central America; also called Middle America. p. 388

messiah (mə•sī′ə) A wise leader who would establish the kingdom of God on Earth, according to Judaism. p. 356

metropolitan area (met•rə•pol′ə•tən ar′ē•ə) A city and its surrounding suburbs. p. 461

migration (mī•grā′shən) Movement of groups of people from one place to another. p. 57

missionary (mi′shə•ner•ē) A person sent out to teach about a religion. p. 220

mitima (mid′•ä•mä) The Inca practice of sending conquered people to different places. p. 420

monarchy (mon′ər•kē) The system of government in which a king or queen rules. p. 92

money economy (mu′nē i•kon′ə•mē) An economic system based on money rather than on barter. p. 113

monotheism (mä′nə•thē•i•zəm) A belief in one God. p. 105

monsoon (mon•soon′) The season when moist winds blowing from the Indian Ocean toward the Indian subcontinent bring heavy rains. p. 201

mosque (mosk) An Islamic house of worship. p. 459

multicultural (məl•tē•kulch′rəl) Relating to many cultures. p. 320

mummy (mum′ē) A preserved body. p. 143

Muslim (mus′ləm) A follower of Islam. p. 458

myth (mith) A story passed from generation to generation that usually tells about an ancient god or hero. p. 305

NAFTA (naf′tə) North American Free Trade Agreement; an agreement among the United States, Canada, and Mexico to trade freely with one another. p. 512

nationalism (nash′nə•li•zəm *or* na′shə•nəl•i•zəm) A strong feeling of loyalty to one's nation or country. p. 485

nation-state (nā′•shən stāt) A region with a single government and a united group of people. p. 135

New Testament (noo tes′tə•mənt) The second part of the Christian Bible; it tells about the life and teachings of Jesus Christ and his followers. p. 360

nomad (nō′mad) A person with no settled home. p. 66

nome (nōm) A city-state in ancient Egypt. p. 139

obsidian (əb•si′dē•ən) A volcanic glass often used for tools by ancient people. p. 389

Old Testament (ōld tes′tə•mənt) The Christian Bible's first part, containing the books of the Hebrew Bible. p. 360

oligarchy (ä′lə•gär•kē) A system in which a small group controls the government. p. 303

OPEC (ō′pek) Organization of Petroleum Exporting Countries; an organization formed by oil-producing countries that wanted to gain control of the price of their oil throughout the world. p. 511

opinion (ō•pin′yən) A statement of belief or judgment. p. 424

opportunity cost (ä•pər•tü′nə•tē kôst) The cost of giving up something when choosing something else instead. p. 474

oracle (ôr′ə•kəl) A person who gives wise advice. p. 239

oracle bone (ôr′ə•kəl bōn) A shell or bone that contains ancient Chinese writing. p. 239

paleoanthropologist (pā′lē•ō•an•thrō•pol•ə•jist) A scientist who studies the ancestors of modern people. p. 51

papyrus (pə•pī′rəs) A paperlike material used by ancient Egyptians; made from reeds that grow in the Nile River. p. 142

parable (par′ə•bəl) A story that teaches a religious idea. p. 355

parallel (par′ə•lel) Another name for a line of latitude, an imaginary line that runs east and west on a map or globe. p. 62

parallel time line (par′ə•lel tīm līn) A grouping of time lines that display different types of information for the same period of time. p. 70

patrician (pə•tri′shən) A descendant of Rome's earliest settlers. p. 332

perestroika (pâr•ə•stroi′kə) The rebuilding or "restructuring," of the Soviet political and economic systems. p. 493

persecute (pûr′si•kyo͞ot) To punish people for their religious beliefs. p. 357

perspective (pər•spek′tiv) Point of view. p. 32

pharaoh (fer′ō) A ruler of ancient Egypt. p. 141

philosopher (fi•los′ə•fər) A person who studies the meaning of life. p. 247

physical features (fiz′i•kəl fē′chərz) Landforms, bodies of water, climate, soil, plant and animal life, and other natural resources. p. 36

plague (plāg) A deadly sickness. p. 311

plateau (pla•tō) A high, flat area of land. p. 85

plebeian (pli•bē′ən) A citizen whose family came to ancient Rome after the patricians. p. 332

polar projection (pō′lər prə•jek′shən) An equidistant map projection that has one of the poles as its central point. p. 104

polis (pä′ləs) In ancient Greece, a city-state consisting of a city and the farms, towns, and villages around it. p. 300

pollution (pə•lo͞o′shən) Anything that makes a natural resource, such as air, soil, or water, dirty or unsafe to use. p. 469

pope (pōp) The leader of the Roman Catholic Church. p. 360

population density (pop•yə•lā′shən den′sə•tē) The average number of people living on a unit of land. p. 453

population distribution (pop•yə•lā′shən dis•trib•yo͞o′shən) The way a population is spread out over a certain area of land. p. 452

predict (pri•dikt′) To tell ahead of time what will happen. p. 137

prehistory (prē•his′tə•rē) Events that happened before the invention of writing. p. 51

primary source (prī′mer•ē sôrs) A firsthand account; a record made by a person who saw or took part in an event. p. 424

prime meridian (prīm mə•ri′dē•ən) The meridian, or imaginary line of longitude, that is marked 0° on a map or globe. p. 62

profit (prä′fət) Money gained in business. p. 266

projection (prə•jek′shən) A representation of Earth on a map; a view of the round Earth on a flat surface. p. 102

prophet (prä′fət) A person who others believe speaks or writes a divine message. p. 227

protectionism (prə•tek′shə•ni•zəm) A government policy that calls for some type of action, such as raising tariffs, to protect a market from imports. p. 509

province (prä′vins) A political region of a country. p. 256

pyramid (pir′ə•mid) A burial place for the dead, often for a dead ruler. p. 143

Q

Quechua (kech′ə•wə) The Inca language. p. 420

quinoa (kēn′wä) A high-protein grain grown by the ancient Incas. p. 418

quipu (kē′po͞o) Colored knotted strings used by the Incas for storing information. p. 421

Qur'an (kə•ran′ or kə•rän′) The holy book of Islam. p. 459

R

radiocarbon dating (rā•dē′ō•kär′bən dā′ting) A scientific process that tells the age of something once living by measuring the amount of radioactive carbon it contains. p. 56

rajah (rä′jə) An Indian prince. p. 218

refugee (re′fyŏŏ•jē) A person who leaves his or her home to escape from war or other danger. p. 454

regent (rē′jənt) Temporary ruler. p. 398

region (re′jən) An area on Earth whose features make it different from other areas. p. 37

reincarnation (rē•in•kär•nā′shən) The belief that the soul lives on after death and returns to life in a new body. p. 212

relative location (re′lə•tiv lō•kā′shən) What a place is near or what is around it. p. 32

representative democracy (rep′rə•zen′tə•tiv di•mok′rə•sē) A form of government in which citizens elect people to make laws and decisions for them. p. 501

republic (ri•pu′blik) A form of government in which the citizens elect representatives to make all government decisions. p. 331

ritual (rit′chŏŏ•əl) A set way of conducting a ceremony. p. 237

S

Sabbath (sab′əth) A day of rest. p. 107

Sanskrit (san′skrit) A language of India, first spoken by the ancient Aryans. p. 212

savanna (sə•va′nə) A grassy plain. p. 131

scribe (skrīb) A person who writes. p. 93

secondary source (sek′ən•dâr•ē sôrs) A secondhand record of an event. p. 424

senate (se′nət) A council of representatives. p. 332

Silk Road (silk rōd) A trade route that stretched from China to the Mediterranean Sea. p. 266

silt (silt) A mixture of bits of rock and soil carried or deposited by water. p. 87

slash-and-burn farming (slash and burn färm′ing) Cutting and burning forest lands to gain new farmland. p. 398

social class (sō′shəl klas) A group that has a particular amount of importance in a society. p. 93

society (sə•sī′ə•tē) An organized group of people living and working under a set of rules and traditions. p. 61

standard of living (stan′dərd uv liv′ing) A measure of how well people in a country live. p. 465

standardization (stan•dər•də•zā′shən) The practice of making all things of a certain type alike. p. 256

statistics (stə•tis′tiks) Facts shown with numbers. p. 402

subcontinent (sub•kon′tə•nənt) A large area of land that is part of a continent but separated in some way. p. 199

subsist (səb•sist′) To survive. p. 69

subsistence farming (səb•sis′təns färm′ing) Farming in which people raise only enough food to feed their families. p. 464

suburb (səb′ərb) Area around a large city. p. 461

surplus (sûr′plus) An extra supply. p. 93

synagogue (sin′ə•gôg) A Jewish house of worship. p. 109

T

taxation (tak•sā′shən) The practice of requiring people to pay taxes to support a government. p. 98

technology (tek•nol′ə•jē) The skills and knowledge to make products or meet goals. p. 89

telecommunications (tel•ə•kə•myŏŏ•nə•kā′shənz) All electronic ways of sending and receiving information. p. 508

telescoping time line (tel′ə•skōp•ing tīm līn) A time line that includes a second time line that gives a closer view of one time period. p. 361

temperate zones (tem′pər•it zōnz) The parts of the Earth north and south of the tropical zone; the climate there is cooler than in the tropical zone. p. 385

Ten Commandments (ten kə•mand′mənts) A set of laws for responsible behavior, which, according to the Bible, were given to Moses by God. p. 106

terrorism (ter′ər•i•zəm) The use of violent acts to further a cause. p. 494

Torah (tōr′ə) Jewish scriptures; the first five books of the Bible. p. 107

totalitarianism (tō•ta•lə•ter′ē•ə•ni•zəm) A kind of government in which the government has total authority over people's lives. p. 504

trade network (trād net′wərk) A group of buyers and sellers. p. 176

trade route (trād rŏot) A path that traders use as they exchange goods. p. 162

trade-off (trād•ôf) Giving up the use of resources in one way in order to use them in another way. p. 474

traditional economy (trə•dish′ən•əl i•kon′ə•mē) An economy that does not change much over time. p. 464

tragedy (traj′ə•dē) A serious play with an unhappy ending. p. 310

trend (trend) The way something changes over time. p. 115

triangle trade (trī′ang•əl trād) A system in which traders exchanged European goods for slaves in Africa, sold the slaves for products from plantations in the Americas, and then sold the products in Europe. p. 482

tribune (tri′byŏon) A plebeian official who could attend meetings of the assembly in ancient Rome. p. 332

tributary (tri′byə•ter•ē) A branch of a river. p. 87

tribute (tri′byŏot) Yearly payments. p. 225

trireme (trī′rēm) A large fighting ship, used by the ancient Greeks and others beginning in the late sixth century B.C. p. 289

tropical zone (trä′pi•kəl zōn) The part of Earth between the Tropic of Cancer and the Tropic of Capricorn, where the climate is warmest. p. 385

tumpline (tum′plīn) A kind of sling that makes it easier for a person to carry heavy loads. p. 393

tundra (tun′drə) A cold, treeless plain whose subsoil is permanently frozen. p. 59

turning point (tûrn′ing point) A time of important change. p. 220

tyrant (tī′rənt) In ancient Greece, someone who illegally took control of a government and ruled alone; a cruel ruler. p. 301

untouchables (un•tuch′ə•bəlz) In India, people below all castes. The name came from the idea that others would be made impure from their touch. p. 213

urban (ûr′bən) Relating to a city or cities. p. 85

urbanization (ûr′bə•nə•zā•shən) The changing of rural areas into cities. p. 456

vandal (van′dəl) Someone who purposely damages property; from the Germanic Vandal tribe, who attacked Rome and stole valuable items. p. 364

Vedas (vā′dəz) Ancient books of sacred Hindu writings. p. 212

veto (vē′tō) To stop passage of a law; from a Latin word meaning "I forbid." p. 333

virtue (vûr′chŏo) A good quality. p. 245

vizier (vī zir′) An adviser to a pharaoh of ancient Egypt. p. 141

ziggurat (zi′gə•rat) A huge mud-brick temple built by the ancient Sumerians. p. 91

Zoroastrianism (zōr•ə•was′trē•ə•ni•zəm) A religion started by Zarathustra that teaches belief in two gods—one good and one evil. p. 227

Index

Page references for illustrations are set in italic type. An italic *m* indicates a map. Page references set in boldface type indicate the pages on which vocabulary terms are defined.

Index

For permission to reprint copyrighted material, grateful acknowledgment is made to the following sources:

Atheneum Books for Young Readers, an imprint of Simon & Schuster Children's Publishing Division: From *The Avenger* by Margaret Hodges. Text copyright © 1982 by Margaret Hodges.

Cashmir, Inc.: Cover illustration from *Come With Me To India* by Sudha Koul. Copyright © 1997.

Cobblestone Publishing Company, 30 Grove Street, Suite C, Peterborough, NH 03458: "Discovery and Excavation of Shi-Huangdi's Tomb" by Helen Wieman Bledsoe from *Calliope* Magazine, October 1997. Text © 1997 by Cobblestone Publishing Company.

Grove/Atlantic, Inc.: From poem # 130 in *The Book of Songs*, translated from the Chinese by Arthur Waley. Text copyright 1937 by Arthur Waley.

HarperCollins Publishers: From *His Majesty, Queen Hatshepsut* by Dorothy Sharp Carter, cover illustration by Michele Chessare. Text copyright © 1987 by Dorothy Sharp Carter; cover illustration copyright © 1987 by Michele Chessare.

Heinemann Educational Publishers, a division of Reed Educational & Professional Publishing Ltd.: Cover illustration by Bill Le Fever from *Ancient Rome* by Simon James. Copyright © 1992 by Reed International Books Ltd.

Holiday House, Inc: From *Skara Brae: The Story of a Prehistoric Village* by Olivier Dunrea. Copyright © 1985 by Olivier Dunrea.

Houghton Mifflin Company: From "Friends and Neighbors" in *Jataka Tales*, edited by Nancy DeRoin. Text and cover illustration copyright © 1975 by Nancy DeRoin.

DK Publishing, Inc.: Cover from *A Visual Timeline of the 20th Century* by Simon Adams. Copyright © 1996 by Dorling Kindersley Limited, London.

Lothrop, Lee & Shepard Books, a division of William Morrow & Company, Inc.: Cover illustration by Fiona French from *Pepi and the Secret Names* by Jill Paton Walsh. Illustration copyright © 1994 by Fiona French.

The Millbrook Press, Inc.: Cover from *The Nubians: People of the Ancient Nile* by Robert Steven Bianchi. Copyright © 1994 by Robert Steven Bianchi. Cover illustration from *Around the World in 80 Pages* by Antony Mason. © 1995 by Aladdin Books Ltd.

W. W. Norton & Company: From "The Charms of Nian-nu" by Su Shi in *An Anthology of Chinese Literature*, edited and translated by Stephen Owen. Text copyright © 1996 by Stephen Owen and The Council for Cultural Planning and Development of the Executive Yuan of the Republic of China.

Oxford University Press: From *The Footsoldier* by Martin Windrow and Richard Hook. Text and cover illustration © by Oxford University Press.

Philomel Books, a division of Penguin Putnam Inc.: From *Boy of the Painted Cave* by Justin Denzel. Text copyright © 1988 by Justin Denzel.

Simon & Schuster Books for Young Readers, an imprint of Simon & Schuster Children's Publishing Division: Cover illustration by Michael Welply from *If You Were There: Aztec Times* by Antony Mason. Illustration copyright © 1997 by Marshall Editions Developments Ltd.

Steck-Vaughn Company: From *Egyptian Stories*, retold by Robert Hull. Text copyright © 1993 by Wayland (Publishers) Ltd.; U. S. version text copyright © 1994 by Thomson Learning. Originally published in the United States by Thomson Learning.

Tilbury House, Publishers, Gardiner, ME: From *Talking Walls: The Stories Continue* by Margy Burns Knight, illustrated by Anne Sibley O'Brien. Text copyright © 1996 by Margy Burns Knight; illustrations copyright © 1996 by Anne Sibley O'Brien.

Tundra Books: Cover illustration from *Gilgamesh the King*, retold and illustrated by Ludmila Zeman. © 1992 by Ludmila Zeman.

University of California Press, Berkeley: From *The Bhagavadgita: A New Translation* by Kees W. Bolle. Text copyright © 1979 by The Regents of the University of California.

Viking Penguin, a division of Penguin Putnam Inc.: Cover illustration by Bill Le Fever from *Ancient Rome* by Simon James. Copyright © 1992 by Reed International Books Ltd. Cover illustration by James Field from *Ancient China* by Brian Williams. Copyright © 1996 by Reed Educational and Professional Publishing, Ltd. From *The Aztecs* by Tim Wood, illustrated by Philip Hood, cover illustration by Bill Le Fever. Copyright © 1992 by Reed International Books Ltd.

Walker and Company, 435 Hudson Street, New York, NY 10014, 1-800-289-2553: From *Spirit of the Maya: A Boy Explores His People's Mysterious Past* by Guy Garcia, cover photograph by Ted Wood. Text copyright © 1995 by Guy Garcia; cover photograph copyright © 1995 by Ted Wood.

Franklin Watts: Cover illustration by Bob Masheris from *Tombs of the Ancient Americas* by Jeanne Bendick. Copyright © 1993 by Jeanne Bendick. Cover illustration by S. D. Schindler from *Digging Up the Past: The Story of An Archaeological Adventure* by Carollyn James. Illustration copyright © 1990 by S. D. Schindler.

Honi Werner: Cover illustration from *The Avenger* by Margaret Hodges. Published by Charles Scribner's Sons.

Zondervan Publishing House: Scripture from the *Holy Bible, New International Version*. Text copyright © 1973, 1978, 1984 by International Bible Society.

ILLUSTRATION CREDITS

Pages 56-57 Andrew Wheatcroft; page 81 Angus McBride; pages 90-91 Paolo Donati; page 140 Steven Adler; pages 144–145 Tony Smith; page 177 Stephen Snider; pages 186-187 Jeffrey Terreson; page 207 David Cook; page 245 Hrano Janto; page 258 Barbara Higgins; pages 266–267 Rodica Prato; pages 347, 349, 352–353 Angus McBride; page 418 David Cook; pages 378–379 Manuel Garcia; pages 396–397 Tony Smith; page 408 Rodica Prato; page 430–431 Dennis Lyall; pages 518–519 Jeffrey Terreson

All maps by GeoSystems

COVER CREDITS

Design Studio: Mariello Grafico, Inc.
Photography: Ken West Photography

PHOTO CREDITS

PAGE PLACEMENT KEY: (t)-top (c)-center (b)-bottom (l)-left (r)-right (fg)-foreground (bg)-background.

COVER

(By objects): columns, Egyptian painting, cave painting, Tony Stone Images; all others: Harcourt Brace & Company.

ENDPAPERS

(By object): Chinese soldier, Toni Stone Images; all others Harcourt Brace & Company.

HARCOURT BRACE & COMPANY PHOTOS

Page number iii, 24, 28, 33, 35, 428–429 (bg), R7 Weronica Ankarorn; 22 (fg), 25 (all), 31 (br), 34, 429 (inset), R4, R9 P&F Communications; 32 (bg), 516–517 (b) Victoria Bowen; 368–369 (c)(coins), 500 (t) Harcourt Brace & Company; 123, 189, 277, 373, 433, 521 Ron Kunzman; 350 (t) Julie Smith; 368 (t) Rodney Jones.

OTHER (STOCK PHOTOS)
CONTENTS

Page x Rob Crandall/Stock Boston; faces: Pages iv-ix (by chapter number) Chapter 1 Sisse Brimberg/National Geographic Society; 2 Ancient Art and Architecture Collection; 3 Erich Lessing/Art Resource, NY; 4 Museum Expedition, Nubian Gallery/Courtesy Museum of Fine Arts, Boston; 5 Burt Glinn/Magnum Photos; 6 Ancient Art and Architecture Collection; 7 Delphi Museum of Archaeology/Nimatallah/Art Resource, NY; 8 Napoli, Museo Nazionale/Scala/Art Resource, NY; 9 Boltin Picture Library; 10 Mereille Vautier/Woodfin Camp & Associates; 11 Jeremy Hartley/Panos Pictures; 12 Facelly/Sipa Press

ATLAS

A1 NASA.

INTRODUCTION

22 (bg) British Library, London/Bridgeman Art Library, London, Superstock; 23 The Granger Collection; 24 (insets left to right) Rijsmuseum van Oudheden-Egyptian Collection, Leiden, Netherlands/Erich Lessing/Art Resource, NY; 30 (t) Maritime Museum/Michael Holford Photographs; 30 (c) Erich Lessing/Art Resource, NY; 30 (b) Borromeo/Art Resource, NY; 31 (t) Kenneth Garrett/Woodfin Camp & Associates; 31 (bl) National Museum of American Art/Art Resource, NY; 32 (l)(inset) Bibliotheque Nationale, Paris, France/Giraudon/Art Resource, NY; 32 (cl)(inset) Rijsmuseum van Oudheden-Egyptian Collection, Leiden, Netherlands/Erich Lessing/Art Resource, NY; 32 (c)(inset) John Neubauer/Museo de Antropologia, Mexico City; 32 (cr)(inset) Museo Archeologico Nazionale, Naples; 32 (r)inset Michael Holford; 36 (t) Joachim Messerschmidt/The Stock Market; 36 (c) Nacchietto Della Rossa/Gamma Liaison; 36 (b) Joe Sohm/ChromoSohm/The Stock Market; 41 (t) Epix/Sygma Photo News; 41 (c) Jean Pragen/Tony Stone Images; 41 (b) Cheryl Sheridan/Odyssey Productions.

UNIT 1

42–43 Jack Unruh/© National Geographic Society; 46 (b) F. Gohier/Photo Researchers; 47 Sisse Brimberg/National Geographic Society;